THE LAW AND ECONOMICS OF
COMPETITION POLICY

Offering a unique cross-disciplinary approach to scholarship in law and economics, this much-needed work explores and critically evaluates all of the major doctrines of Canadian competition policy. The topics addressed include Canadian competition policy in a historical context, basic economic concepts, multi-firm conduct, horizontal agreements, the merger review process, predatory pricing and price discrimination, vertical restraints, intrabrand competition, interbrand competition, abuse of dominance, competition policy and intellectual property rights, competition policy and trade policy, competition policy and regulated industries, and enforcement.

The treatment of each topic is organized around a discussion of the relevant economic theory and legal doctrine, including case law. Each chapter contains a critique of existing law in light of contemporary economic theory. This is the only book available that offers an up-to-date, integrated analysis of economic theory and legal doctrine in the context of Canadian competition policy.

MICHAEL J. TREBILCOCK is Professor of Law and Economics at the University of Toronto.

RALPH A. WINTER is Professor of Economics at the University of Toronto.

PAUL COLLINS is a partner with the law firm of Stikeman Elliott in Toronto.

EDWARD M. IACOBUCCI is Assistant Professor of Law at the University of Toronto.

The Law and Economics of Canadian Competition Policy

Michael Trebilcock

Ralph A. Winter

Paul Collins

Edward M. Iacobucci

UNIVERSITY OF TORONTO PRESS
Toronto Buffalo London

© University of Toronto Press 2002
Toronto Buffalo London
Printed in the U.S.A.

Reprinted in paperback 2003, 2013

ISBN 0-8020-3557-4 (cloth)
ISBN 0-8020-8612-8 (paper)

Printed on acid-free paper

National Library of Canada Cataloguing in Publication Data

Main entry under title:
The law and economics of Canadian competition policy

Includes bibliographical references and index.
ISBN 0-8020-3557-4 (bound)
ISBN 0-8020-8612-8 (paperback)

1. Competition, Unfair – Canada.   2. Competition –
Government policy – Canada.   I. Trebilcock, Michael J., 1941–

KE1639.L39 2002   343.71'0721   C2001-902647-1

University of Toronto Press acknowledges the financial assistance to its publishing program of the Canada Council for the Arts and the Ontario Arts Council.

University of Toronto Press acknowledges the financial support for its publishing activities of the Government of Canada through the Book Publishing Industry Development Program (BPIDP).

Contents

Acknowledgments   vii

1. Canadian Competition Policy in Historical Perspective   3
2. Basic Economic Concepts in Competition Policy   37
3. Multi-Firm Conduct: Horizontal Agreements   86
4. The Merger Review Process   131
5. Predatory Pricing and Price Discrimination   288
6. Vertical Restraints: Intrabrand Competition   373
7. Vertical Restraints: Interbrand Competition   439
8. Abuse of Dominance   504
9. Competition Policy and Intellectual Property Rights   573
10. Competition Policy and Trade Policy   640
11. Competition Policy and Regulated Industries   690
12. Enforcement   736

Subject Index   783
Table of Cases   793

Acknowledgments

We owe a number of debts of gratitude for assistance in writing this book: to Pei-Ching Huang for invaluable research assistance; to Jason Rootenberg for preparing the case law and general indices; to Nancy Gallini (University of Toronto Department of Economics) and Jeffrey Brown (Stikernan Elliott) for assistance with the chapter on Competition Policy and Intellectual Property; to Quentin Markin and Rob Mason of Stikeman Elliott for their research assistance; to Bev Albert (assistant to Paul Collins) and Kristin DeMuth (assistant to Michael Trebilcock) for their invaluable assistance; to the editors at the University of Toronto Press for meticulous attention to the manuscript; and to two anonymous reviewers for the Press for helpful comments on an earlier draft of the manuscript.

We are also indebted to three institutions with which the authors are affiliated for financial assistance with the publication of this book: Charles River Associates Canada Inc. (Michael Trebilcock and Ralph Winter), Stikeman Elliott (Paul Collins); and the University of Toronto Faculty of Law (Michael Trebilcock, Ralph Winter, and Edward Iacobucci).

The text is current as of December 2001.

THE LAW AND ECONOMICS OF CANADIAN
COMPETITION POLICY

ONE

Canadian Competition Policy in Historical Perspective

I. The Preconditions to the Emergence of North American Competition/Antitrust Laws[1]

Competition or antitrust policy, at least in its broad strokes, has always been a matter of high politics, implicating both influential and often divergent economic interests and contested values, ideas, or ideologies relating to political economy that societal institutions – law making, law enforcement, and legal adjudication and interpretation – have been called upon to mediate. Modern competition or antitrust law belongs primarily to the family of legislative reactions to the upheavals of successive industrial revolutions, the first of which began in Britain in the eighteenth and early nineteenth centuries. Other members of the family include parliamentary reform, factory acts, child labour laws, legalization of trade unions, various schemes of railway regulation, the creation of civil police, municipal waterworks, and other institutional innovations designed to cope with the urbanization that powered industry brought. But we must explain why antitrust law was a relatively late arrival to this family and why it arrived first in North America.

A prior qualification is in order here, so that we may identify an important European precursor of the North American statutes – the British Statute of Monopolies (1623), a child not of the industrial but of

---

1 This section is drawn largely from Bruce Dunlop, David McQueen, and Michael Trebilcock, *Canadian Competition Policy: A Legal and Economic Analysis* (Toronto: Canada Law Book, 1987), chap. 1.

the earlier commercial revolution. The energetic bourgeoisie had grown increasingly restless at the practice of assigning private monopoly rights in certain domestic industries, such as salt and glass, to favourites of the reigning monarch. Some sought lower prices for these items but others were undoubtedly motivated by profit. By the time of James I, their combined influence in Parliament was sufficient to produce a statutory ban on such royal monopolies, although with two interesting and long-lived exemptions: patents of invention and globe-spanning export/import organizations such as the East India and Hudson's Bay Companies.

In England the common law of restraint of trade had since medieval times invalidated various restraints on trade, contractual or otherwise, if unreasonable. By the late nineteenth century, however, under the influence of laissez-faire philosophical precepts that privileged private property rights and freedom of contract, this body of law had largely fallen into desuetude, often condoning cartels and monopolization.[2] Not until after the Second World War would another British statute specifically address private monopoly and market power. By far the most important single reason for this hiatus was probably the pervasive procompetitive influence exerted on the British economy by the policy of free trade that prevailed for the better part of a century after the repeal of the Corn Laws in 1846.

Matters were to develop otherwise in North America. In the early nineteenth century the United States was an extremely vigorous entity expanding rapidly both seaward and landward. More than most nations, the United States had been founded on a base of ideas. Among those ideas was a strong revulsion against concentration of power, heavy-handed 'bigness,' and remote absentee control – epitomized notably by the late eighteenth-century British empire.

A geographic stage was being set for an economic drama. The Louisiana Purchase, the Oregon Boundary Settlement, the Mexican and Civil Wars, and the sometimes brutal westward advance of Manifest Destiny staked out the territory; steamboats and steam railways stitched it together. The result was, for many products, a single contiguous internal free trade area on a scale unprecedented in human history. Full exploi-

---

2 See Michael Trebilcock, *The Common Law of Restraint of Trade* (Toronto: Carswell, 1986), chap. 1.

tation of America's transcontinental market opportunities required the solution of technical and business-organizational problems, likewise on an unprecedented scale. As argued by Alfred Chandler,[3] the first American business to experience the modern type of 'business bigness' imperative was railroading. A huge congeries of geographic, technological, and other factors drove the railroad industry to institute organizational and other innovations that would not merely make corporate bigness possible but render it capable of capturing the full range of potential cost savings. First the railways were capital intensive. The railroads created Wall Street, and once created, Wall Street was available to help initiate other, non-rail bigness. On the physical side, the railroad's capital intensity placed a high premium on working plants and equipment as closely as possible to full capacity, and new and more sophisticated forms of internal coordination of continuous production processes were required to ensure that expensive rolling stock was at the right places at the right times – a task facilitated by the advent of the electric telegraph.

The knowledge of how to run a railroad big-business style, once created, became available for adaptation, extension, and use by other industries. Among the industries undergoing rapid transformation in the quarter-century following the Civil War, as they sought to meet the challenge of a continent-wide market, were steel-making, petroleum refining, farm machinery manufacturing, flour-milling, meat packing, sewing machinery manufacturing, and department store and mail-order retailing. Two significant common threads run through innovations in most of these industries: a high degree of relevance for the problems of exploiting a market that was rich and contiguous but also geographically extensive; and a recurrent displacement of former chains of market transacting (e.g., from manufacturer to wholesaler to small retailer) by bureaucratic organization within larger, more vertically integrated firms. Industrial innovation on the grand scale of the post–Civil War period created losers as well as winners. Travelling salesmen and other middle men were cut out. Numerous small manufacturers and retailers went out of business as railroads increasingly breached the transport cost barriers which had hitherto protected them, and as new, large-scale manufacturers and retailers found yet further

---

3 Alfred D. Chandler, *The Visible Hand: The Managerial Revolution in American Business* (Cambridge, Mass: Harvard University Press, 1977), at 89–92.

means to undersell them (Schumpeter's 'perennial gale of creative destruction').[4]

While technological and other considerations may have forced many railroads to be big, it did not necessarily require using that bigness, as some subsequently did, to corrupt legislatures and to help organize freight rate cartels. Also, the social imperative of organizing large and more vertically integrated firms in certain lines of manufacturing did not necessarily require linking such firms horizontally through the medium of trusts, combinations, or other devices to form more coordinated selling fronts against consumers – a phenomenon that emerged prominently in the United States in the latter years of the nineteenth century. Another visible hand at work in this phase of American economic development was a highly contentious political one: the tariff. The tariff sheltered domestic manufacturers but not farmers from foreign competition and pushed up input and final goods prices to farmers as well as to a growing body of urban consumers.

Recalling the philosophical hostility towards bigness and remote control strongly embedded in the American tradition, we may discern the outlines of a major political coalition against much that was happening in the economy. Drawn primarily from farmers, small businessmen, and urban employees and consumers, and cutting across normal party lines to a considerable degree, this coalition effectively brought to birth the first U.S. antitrust statute, the *Sherman Act*, in 1890. The essence of this Act was cryptically contained in two short sections – one dealing with anticompetitive agreements (s. 1) and another dealing with monopolization or attempted monopolization (s. 2). According to its principal sponsor, Republican Senator John Sherman, the Act was primarily intended to federalize the common law of restraint of trade, with the innovation of mechanisms for third-party enforcement. Senator Sherman was also a fierce protectionist who simultaneously promoted the McKinley Tariff, one of the largest and most anticonsumer tariffs in U.S. history, leading some commentators to view the *Sherman Act* as a political log-rolling exercise whereby higher tariffs were adopted to protect infant manufacturing industries while antitrust laws were adopted to placate farmers, small businesses, and consumers. Antitrust laws would provide some protection against abuses of eco-

---

4 See Joseph Schumpeter, *Capitalism, Socialism and Democracy* (Cambridge, Mass: Harvard University Press, 1975), at 87.

nomic power. However, this apparent congruence of interests masked important ambiguities as to the objectives of the Act. Was it intended to promote consumer welfare (preventing the elevation of prices above competitive levels) or total welfare (the sum of producer and consumer surplus, allowing efficiency gains to offset adverse price effects)? Was the purpose of the Act to provide legal protection to small businesses from competitive pressures from larger and more efficient rivals (maximizing the number of competitors – atomistic competition – rather than economic efficiency) or to curtail undue political and economic influence by corporate bigness, whether size was efficient or not?

In Canada similar developments were taking place. The central importance and manifold influence of the great railroad companies, the rise of department stores and mail order houses (e.g., the T. Eaton Company), and the appearance of unprecedented firm size in areas such as meat-packing, agricultural machinery, and flour-milling were very much present in Canada, as a national economy developed on an east-west basis with the advance of western settlement and the completion of the Canadian Pacific Railway in 1885. So, too, especially after the inception of the National Policy in 1879, was the protective tariff. But devotion to the philosophical ideal of competitive free enterprise or to the inherent virtues of small business enterprise as contrasted with large business seems to have been weaker in Canada than in the United States, among both businessmen and the public at large. Canadians seemed to have a more deferential attitude towards authority in general. This deference extended to the authority wielded by large business enterprises, authority frequently existing with the active aid and approval of governments. This attitude could probably be traced back, in part, to Canada's colonial past. But likely more important still was the defence of necessity: large organizations provided the sole means of capturing vital scale economies in a country so geographically huge yet peripheral in comparison to its southern neighbour, with a sparse population tenuously linked together.

Monopoly sanctioned (or owned) by government had always been a prominent feature of Canada's early economic development. Such monopolies included the Hudson's Bay Company and the Canadian Pacific Railway (and later the CBC, Air Canada, and provincially owned electricity and telephone utilities). Historically, it was sometimes easier to generate popular concern over whether an enterprise was foreign or Canadian than whether it was a monopoly. To the extent that monopolies raised concerns, Canadians were more inclined to resort to public ownership and/or detailed forms of public regulation than to invoke general framework competition laws. What Canadians primarily objected to was not the existence of monopolies, but what they saw as the unfair and unreasonable abuse of economic power by them. The proliferation of trade associations and various forms of business combinations in the latter years of the nineteenth century and a major consolidation movement through mergers in the first decade of the twentieth century heightened these concerns.

II. The History of Canadian Competition Policy[5]

Although there had been sporadic complaints about rings and trusts operating in Canada since at least the early 1870s, the combines question did not become a matter of government concern until February 1888, when a Select Committee of the House of Commons was appointed to examine the question under the chairmanship of N. Clarke Wallace, Conservative member of Parliament. In two months of sittings the committee heard from sixty-three witnesses and in an eight-page report it concluded that while the evils potentially produced by combinations had not by any means fully developed in Canada, sufficient evidence of their injurious tendencies and effects existed to justify legislative action. The combines investigated by the committee were for the most part loosely knit trade associations – small distributors or producers of groceries, watch cases, binder twine, coal, oatmeal, stoves, agricultural implements, and undertakers' supplies. The most egregious combine uncovered was the Coal Section of the Toronto Board of Trade, whose members fixed prices, engaged in collusive bidding, and tightly enforced their arrangements. In addition, the Wholesale Grocers' Guild was condemned as obnoxious to the public interest, particularly with respect to a combination that fixed the price of sugar.

---

5 For illuminating accounts of the early history of Canadian competition policy see Michael Bliss, 'Another Anti-Trust Tradition: Canadian Anti-Combines Policy 1889–1910,' (1973) 47 *Business History Review* 177; Carman Baggaley, 'Tariffs, Combines and Politics: The Beginning of Canadian Competition Policy 1888–1900,' in R.S. Khemani and W.T. Stanbury, eds., *Historical Perspectives on Canadian Competition Policy* (Halifax: Institute for Research on Public Policy, 1991); Jamie Benedickson, 'The Combines Problem in Canadian Legal Thought 1867–1920,' (1993) 43 *University of Toronto L.J.* 799; Paul Gorecki and W.T. Stanbury, 'The Administration and Enforcement of Competition Policy in Canada, 1889 to 1952,' in Khemani and Stanbury, eds., *Historical Perspectives.*

During the hearings, those who were involved in combines argued that they were necessary to avoid 'ruinous competition,' to ensure a 'living profit' or uniform quality standards, or to protect smaller businesses from being squeezed by larger enterprises. In some cases, the combinations had been formed in response to new entry and excess capacity induced by the high tariff policy enshrined in the government's National Policy. Professor W.J. Ashley, the country's leading political economist at the time, sympathized with a number of these concerns and stressed 'the laceration of spirit and vulgarization of business' involved in unregulated competition.[6] For Ashley and many of his fellow economists, combinations were not necessarily bad and competition was not necessarily good. Each case required review on its own facts.

Following the publication of the committee's report, Wallace, supported by the government, introduced a private member's bill into the House of Commons that prohibited combines that discriminated against third parties, restricted competition, enhanced prices, or restrained trade. After various amendments in the legislative process, which introduced modifiers such as 'unlawfully,' 'unduly,' and 'unreasonably,' the bill was enacted into law in 1889. The task of defining its realm of application was largely delegated (abdicated) to the courts. Section 1 of the statute read as follows:

1. Every person who conspires, combines, agrees or arranges with any other person or with any railway, steamship, steamboat or transportation company, unlawfully, –
   (a To unduly limit the facilities for transporting, producing, manufacturing, storing or dealing in any article or commodity which may be the subject of trade or commerce;
   (b To restrain or injure trade or commerce in relation to any such article or commodity;
   (c To unduly prevent, limit or lessen the manufacture or production of any such article or commodity, or to unreasonably enhance the price thereof; or
   (d To unduly prevent or lessen competition in the production, manufacture, purchase, barter, sale, transportation or supply of any such article or commodity, or in the price of insurance upon person or property

---

6 Bliss, 'Another Anti-Trust Tradition,' at 181.

is guilty of a misdemeanor and liable, on conviction, to a fine not exceeding four thousand dollars and not less than two hundred dollars, or to imprisonment for any term not exceeding two years; and if a corporation, is liable on conviction to a penalty not exceeding ten thousand dollars and not less than one thousand dollars.[7]

The inclusion of the world 'unlawfully' meant that in order to violate the *Wallace Act* an anticompetitive arrangement had to be unlawful at common law irrespective of the Act – yet the common law of restraint of trade condoned most combinations. The legislation was so benign that one member of the Opposition summed up the general feeling towards the bill during the House of Commons Debates: 'It need not be opposed; it will die of sheer inanition.' For the Liberal Opposition, the real evil was the protective tariff and the Anti-Combines Bill was a mere diversion. According to Bliss, 'The passing of the *Anti-Combines Act* of 1889 was no more than a political sham, the central figure in which was Canada's self-proclaimed trust-buster, N. Clarke Wallace. He deliberately watered-down his own Bill until it was ineffectual. He felt that the legislation would nonetheless be "a terror to evil-doers." This was fraudulent political posturing, designed partly to continue to enhance Wallace's popular reputation as the enemy of combines, almost certainly as part of a calculated Conservative manoeuver to deflect criticism from the combine-creating effects of the protective tariff. As expected, the legislation languished in desuetude.'[8] Parliament provided no federal official to enforce the Act. Enforcement was left to the attorneys general of the provinces, who had little interest in enforcing the federal legislation against often local interests. The prosecution of American Tobacco for exclusive dealing was the only prosecution undertaken between 1889 and 1900 and it proved unsuccessful.

In 1892 the 1889 Act was incorporated into the Criminal Code[9] and in 1900 the first major change occurred to the *Wallace Act*: elimination of the word 'unlawfully' and therefore reliance on the common law to

7 S.C. 1889, c. 41.

8 Bliss, 'Another Anti-Trust Tradition,' at 182.

9 W.T. Stanbury, 'The Legislative Development of Canadian Competition Policy, 1888–1981,' (1981) 2(2) *Canadian Competition Policy Record* 1 at 1.

find that an action in restraint of trade violated the *Act*.[10] In the subsequent decade nine prosecut.ons for conspiracies were undertaken and seven convictions obtained.[11]

Following the election of the Laurier Liberal government in 1906, the *Customs Tariff Act* was amended (1907) to provide that the Cabinet could appoint a judge to inquire into combines or conspiracies alleged to exist among manufacturers or dealers in any article of commerce to promote unduly the advantage of those manufacturers or dealers in articles protected by tariffs at the expense of consumers. The judge was to make his report to Cabinet, which could reduce the tariffs on such articles to give the public the benefit of reasonable competition.

In 1910 William Lyon Mackenzie King, Laurier's minister of labour, introduced the first *Combines Investigation Act*.[12] The factors immediately responsible for the 1910 legislation were a merger boom beginning in 1909 and the advent of sharply rising prices. According to King, anticombines prosecutions under the Criminal Code were subject to the constant complaint that proceedings were slow, uncertain, and expensive, which made it extremely difficult to secure convictions. The Code provisions were left in place, according to King, so that the penalties there provided might more easily be enforced should they be deemed to be, after investigation of conditions, the most suitable and effective form of punishment of the offenders. Under the 1910 Act any six or more British subjects resident in Canada and of full age could initiate the investigatory process. They were required to make an application to a judge for an order directing an investigation into an alleged combine. To convince a judge to order an inquiry, the six citizens had to establish a *prima facie* case that an offence had been committed. In those cases in which a judge ordered that an inquiry be initiated, the minister of labour was required to establish an *ad hoc* board of investigation consisting of three members: one nominated by the applicant; one nominated by the companies/ individuals accused of infringing the law; and one, the chairman, nominated jointly by the applicants and those to be investigated. The 1910 Act broadened the definition of combine to include monopolies

---

10 Gorecki and Stanbury, 'The Administration and Enforcement of Competition Policy in Canada,' at 62.

11 Ibid.

12 S.C. 1910, c. 9.

or mergers that operated or were likely to operate to the detriment of the public.

The boards of investigation possessed all the powers vested in any court of record in civil cases and were empowered to make recommendations for prosecutions. After a board held hearings it prepared a report which was published in the *Canada Gazette*, on the premise that publicity itself had a sanitizing effect.[13] If a board found a combine in violation of the Act, the combine had to cease and desist its unlawful activities within ten days of publication of the board's findings.[14] Failure to discontinue the combine resulted in a maximum fine of $1,000 per day.[15]

The 1910 Act was used only once: in the investigation of the United Shoe Machinery Corporation by a board in November 1910.[16] Despite the fact that the board found a combine, no prosecution was undertaken under the provisions of the Criminal Code, which remained in force.[17] The 1910 Act proved ineffective because of the requirement that the six citizens had to make out a *prima facie* case that an action in restraint of trade existed.[18] This burden could be heavy, thus discouraging use of the private enforcement mechanism which was the main thrust of the bill. In addition, the identity of the people launching the complaint was known.[19] Those hurt by a combination were often fearful of launching an inquiry, given the possibility of retaliation. And since the *ad hoc* boards ceased to exist with the issuance of their report,[20] there was no public official responsible for implementing the report. Even when combines were found to exist, they had little incentive to cease their unlawful activities.

The ineffective *Combines Investigation Act* was repealed in 1919 and

---

13 Gorecki and Stanbury, 'The Administration and Enforcement of Competition Policy in Canada,' at 68.
14 *Competition Policy in Canada: The First Hundred Years* (Ottawa: Bureau of Competition Policy, 1989) at 6.
15 Gorecki and Stanbury, 'The Administration and Enforcement of Competition Policy in Canada,' at 69.
16 Ibid.
17 *Competition Policy in Canada* at 9.
18 Gorecki and Stanbury, 'The Administration and Enforcement of Competition Policy in Canada,' at 71.
19 Ibid.
20 Ibid.

replaced with the *Board of Commerce Act* and the *Combines and Fair Prices Act*.[21] These statutes were a response to public concern about rising prices in the immediate post-war period.[22] Policy makers and legislators at the time argued that the problem with combines was not their existence, but rather their abusive behaviour.[23] If combines were to be allowed to exist, it was necessary to regulate them. The Board of Commerce was thus created to administer the *Combines and Fair Prices Act* and to undertake the necessary regulatory functions.[24] It had extensive powers to sanction or prevent the operation of a combine and to examine and regulate the production and price of goods.[25] The permanent three-member board was able to initiate investigations and to issue orders to desist from abusive practices.[26] The 1919 legislation initiated what were to become recurrent debates as to the appropriate roles of all-purpose courts and specialized administrative agencies in the administration and enforcement of Canadian competition policy.

The constitutional validity of the approach introduced by the 1919 Acts was challenged in the Supreme Court of Canada. The court was evenly split and thus unable to reach a decision. The matter was then referred to the Judicial Committee of the Privy Council and on 11 November 1921 the 1919 Acts were ruled *ultra vires* as infringing on the provinces' exclusive domain over property and civil rights.[27] Specifically, it was held that neither the residual powers granted to the federal government nor the federal government's power over the regulation of trade and commerce gave it sufficient power to enact the 1919 statutes.[28]

Once the 1919 Acts were found to be *ultra vires*, the criminal law again became the vehicle for the enforcement of competition policy and remained so until the passage of the Stage I amendments to the *Combines Investigation Act* in 1975. The second *Combines Investigation Act* came into force on 13 June 1923.[29] According to McKenzie King, now

21 Stanbury, 'The Legislative Development of Canadian Competition Policy,' at 1.
22 Dunlop, McQueen, and Trebilcock, 'Canadian Competition Policy,' at 46.
23 Ibid.
24 Ibid.
25 Ibid.
26 Gorecki and Stanbury 'The Administration and Enforcement of Competition Policy in Canada,' at 74.
27 *Re Board of Commerce Act and Combines and Fair Prices Act of 1919* (1920), 60 S.C.R. 456.
28 [1922] 1 A.C. 1919 (P.C.).
29 *Combines Investigation Act, 1923,* S.C. 1923, c. 9.

prime minister, the statute resembled its 1910 predecessor in purpose and function in that it was designed to detect and publicize undesirable combinations in restraint of trade. To facilitate this process the lodging of a complaint was made easier and less expensive. A permanent registrar was established to administer the Act under the minister of labour. Application for initiation of a combines inquiry could be made to the registrar by six persons, it could be initiated by the minister, or it could be initiated by the registrar himself. The results of the registrar's inquiry were reported to the minister who, in turn, decided whether a further, more formal investigation was justified. Formal investigations were conducted by the registrar or by a commissioner appointed by the minister on an *ad hoc* basis. Formal reports were transmitted to the minister and, in the case of a Commissioner's Report, were required to be published within fifteen days of the minister's receipt of the report. The separation of investigatory and judicial powers differed from the practice established by the earlier *Combines and Fair Prices Act.* Investigations were carried out by the registrar while adjudication rested with the courts. Like the 1910 Act, prosecutions under the 1923 Act were to be undertaken by a provincial attorney general to whom the report of the registrar or special commissioner had been referred by the federal government. The federal government would proceed with a prosecution only if the province did not and where an individual filed an information to this effect which was approved for prosecution by Cabinet. In addition, the central offence of conspiracy was altered. Under the 1910 Act, the crime consisted of a continuation of a combine judged to be a violation of the law; under the 1923 Act the offence lay in agreeing or assisting in the formation of a combine. Hence, prosecution could be undertaken even if the combine had ceased its unlawful activities in light of the investigation. From 1923 to 1935 between nineteen and forty-seven cases were opened each year under the *Combines Investigation Act.*[30]

In 1935 two changes to Canada's competition law were implemented. First, as a result of a report by the Royal Commission on Price Spreads, discriminatory discounts, territorial price discrimination, and predatory pricing were brought within the Act and made criminal offences, largely reflecting concerns of small businesses over the impact of

---

30 Gorecki and Stanbury, 'The Administration and Enforcement of Competition Policy in Canada,' at 132.

'destructive competition' from larger enterprises during the Depression years.[31] Second, the *Dominion Trade and Industry Act, 1935* established a commission to administer the *Combines Investigation Act* and to authorize combines prosecutions under the Criminal Code.[32] The commission was also given the authority to approve certain industrial agreements aimed at preventing wasteful or demoralizing competition. An approved agreement would not have been subject to prosecution even if it established a restraint on trade that lessened competition severely.[33] However, this power was declared *ultra vires* the federal government by the Supreme Court of Canada in 1937.[34] The Act was once again amended and the power to enforce it was returned to the hands of an individual, the commissioner.[35] Unlike the registrar's office created in the 1923 Act, the commissioner's office created in the 1935 Act did not have the power to initiate investigations on its own accord.[36] This power instead rested with the minister of labour, the attorney general of Canada, or six citizens of voting age.[37] The amendments also permitted the attorney general of Canada to bring prosecutions on his own accord under the Act or the Criminal Code. From 1935 to 1960 approximately 600 cases were opened under the *Combines Investigation Act*, the majority of which concerned conspiracies,[38] with the number of cases steadily increasing from 1945 onwards.[39] In 1945 the minister of justice was made responsible for the Combines Branch, rather than the minister of labour, who had held the responsibility since 1910.

The next major set of changes to the *Combines Investigation Act* were implemented in 1952. These changes were the result of the report of the MacQuarrie Committee[40] appointed following the resignation of the commissioner and widespread public criticism of the government's

31 Stanbury, 'The Legislation Development of Canadian Competition Policy,' at 4.
32 Roy M. Davidson, 'Independence Without Accountability Won't Last,' in R.S. Khemani and W.T. Stanbury, eds., *Canadian Competition Law and Policy at the Centenary* (Halifax: Institute for Research on Public Policy, 1972), at 564.
33 Dunlop, McQueen, and Trebilcock, *Canadian Competition Policy,* at 48.
34 *Reference re Dominion Trade and Industry Commission Act, 1935,* [1936] S.C.R. 379.
35 Davidson, 'Independence Without Accountability Won't Last,' at 564.
36 Ibid.
37 *Competition Policy in Canada,* at 5.
38 Gorecki and Stanbury, 'The Administration and Enforcement of Competition Policy in Canada,' at 95.
39 Ibid., at 132.
40 *Interim Report on Resale Price Maintenance* (Ottawa: Queen's Printer, 1952).

attempted suppression of his report on price fixing in the flour-milling industry. The Restrictive Trade Practices Commission and the Office of the Director of Investigation and Research were created at this time. Administration, investigation, and enforcement were vested in the latter while the former was assigned the functions of appraisal, report, and recommendations for enforcement action. Resale price maintenance was added as a new offence, reflecting concerns over price increases in the post-war inflationary environment.[41] In 1960, again reflecting recommendations of the MacQuarrie Committee Report, the provisions of the Criminal Code were repealed and prosecutions in respect of conspiracies, mergers, and monopolies were henceforth brought under the *Combines Investigation Act*.[42] From 1960 until the Stage I amendments in 1975 the *Combines Investigation Act* remained largely unchanged. However, a series of court decisions throughout the 1960s and 1970s severely limited the efficacy of the Act.

In the *BC Sugar* case, relating to the merger of the only two sugar refineries in western Canada, the court ruled that 'it is not an offence against the *Act* for one corporation to acquire the business of another merely because it wishes to extinguish a competitor.'[43] Detrimental effects were only found if there was a virtual elimination of competition.[44]

In the *Canadian Breweries* case[45] the views expressed in *BC Sugar* were reinforced and the *Combines Investigation Act* further weakened. The case concerned the mergers of several breweries in central Canada, which would have resulted in one firm having control of a large share of the market. The court ruled that the mergers that came under the scope of the Act had to operate to the detriment or harm of the public and that this harm had to arise from the merger directly and not from collateral acts. Even if the merger indirectly led to a substantial lessening of competition, this would not be enough to bring about a violation of the *Combines Investigation Act*, especially in an industry where prices were regulated. The so-called regulated industries defence was further broadened in *Jabour*,[46] where the Supreme Court of Canada held that a

41 Dunlop, McQueen, and Trebilcock, *Canadian Competition Policy*, at 49.
42 Ibid.
43 *R. v. British Columbia Sugar Refining Co.* (1960), 129 C.C.C. 7. (Man. Q.B.).
44 Ibid.
45 *R. v. Canadian Breweries Ltd.* (1960), 126 C.C.C. 133 (Ont. H.C.).
46 *Attorney-General of Canada et al. v. Law Society of British Columbia et al.: Jabour v. Law Society of British Columbia*, [1982] 2 S.C.R. 307.

rule of professional conduct banning lawyers' advertising, adopted by the Law Society of British Columbia pursuant to general delegated disciplinary powers, was immune from scrutiny under the *Combines Investigation Act*.

In *K.C. Irving*,[47] a case concerning the purchase and control of all English-language newspapers in New Brunswick, the Supreme Court of Canada further weakened the effectiveness of anticombines legislation by ruling that the fact that an entire industry was controlled by one firm did not imply that there was unlawful combine. The court found that it was essential for a conviction under the Act that a firm was acting or was likely to act to the detriment of the public. There was no presumption of detriment simply because one firm had gained complete control over an industry. For the Crown to be successful in a prosecution it needed to show that a complete elimination of competition was detrimental to the public interest.

In *Aetna Insurance Bill*,[48] a case relating to a price-fixing conspiracy in the Nova Scotia fire insurance industry, a majority decision of the Supreme Court of Canada found that even conspiracies could not be prevented unless they lessened competition severely. Evidence of a market operating outside the conspiracy would be sufficient to defeat the argument that competition was lessened unduly. Given that some firms operated outside the interfirm agreement to set prices within the fire insurance industry, and that the combination performed some socially useful activities in promoting fire prevention, no violation was found.

In *Atlantic Sugar*[49] an implicit agreement among the sugar refinery companies in eastern Canada (protected by trade restrictions from import competition) to maintain stable market shares over a twenty-five-year period (facilitated by practices such as advance public posting of prices) was held by a majority of the Supreme Court of Canada not to violate the conspiracy provisions of the Act.

By 1966 the Liberal government of Lester Pearson recognized that competition policy and its enforcement mechanisms needed to be reformed. Only one monopoly and no mergers had ever been found

---

47 *R. v. K.C. Irving*, [1978] S.C.R. 408.
48 *Aetna Insurance Co. v. R.* (1977), [1978] 1 S.C.R. 731.
49 *Atlantic Sugar Refineries Co. Ltd. v. A.G. Canada*, [1980] 2 S.C.R. 644.

detrimental to the public interest.[50] Business people also objected to the existing legislation on two counts. First, it violated a cardinal precept of criminal law in that it was unclear.[51] No one was certain what actions would be considered detrimental to the public, and thus what actions would result in prosecution and conviction. Second, the legislation was discriminatory in that it covered goods but excluded services, which were becoming an increasingly important feature of the economy.[52] Given that a series of court decisions had neutralized the legislation and that criminal law was not the appropriate regime under which combines and competition should be regulated, together with discontent among the business community, the government directed the newly formed Economic Council of Canada to study and recommend changes to the competition laws. In 1969 the council released a report recommending sweeping changes to the *Combines Investigation Act*.[53] These recommendations were the beginning of a long political saga that eventually culminated in the enactment of the *Competition Act* in 1986.[54]

The Economic Council's report argued that the objective of competition policy should be the efficient allocation of resources in the Canadian economy.[55] The council's report cited the lack of clarity and the discriminatory nature of the legislation as necessitating a new competition policy.[56] It recommended that collusive arrangements to fix prices, to allocate markets, or to prevent entry; resale price maintenance; and misleading advertising should be heavily penalized under the criminal law. However, with regard to the majority of competitive issues, the council recommended a regulatory regime. The council argued that the criminal law process was not an effective method of regulating eco-

---

50 W.T. Stanbury, 'The Record of Public Law Enforcement,' in J.R.S. Prichard, W.T. Stanbury, and W. Nielson, eds., *Canadian Competition Policy: Essays in Law and Economics* (Toronto: Butterworths, 1979), at 181.

51 Dunlop, McQueen, and Trebilcock, *Canadian Competition Policy*, at 50.

52 Ibid.

53 Economic Council of Canada, *Interim Report on Competition Policy* (Ottawa: Queen's Printer, 1969).

54 *Competition Act*, R.S.C. 1985, c. C-34, s. 1.

55 Ian Clark, 'Legislative Reform and the Policy Process: The Case of the Competition Act,' in Khemani and Stanbury, eds., *Historical Perspectives*, at 228.

56 C. Maule and T. Ross, 'Canada's New Competition Policy,' (1989) 23 *George Washington Journal of International Law* 59 at 67.

nomic activity. It also recommended that competition regulation be extended to the services sector.[57] The council thus advocated a hybrid approach that combined civil and criminal remedies as a way of enhancing economic efficiency. It recommended the creation of a board composed of non-judicial experts to review mergers and other anti-competitive practices, including monopolies and exclusive dealing.[58] It also contemplated a role for private enforcement of certain prohibitions in competition legislation, with double damages as a remedy.

The recommendations contained in the report of the Economic Council of Canada were introduced into the House of Commons as Bill C-256, in June 1971.[59] However, Canadian business interests strenuously opposed the enactment of the bill, which they believed would be harmful, cumbersome, and intrusive[60] and, in general, detrimental to their interests.[61] They believed the bill would create a bureaucratic regime with wide powers to interfere with business practices.[62] They argued that the extent of powers vested in the proposed administrative tribunal to determine the shape of the Canadian economy was excessive and that the private enforcement provisions would permit opportunistic harassment of firms by rivals or consumers. Bowing to pressures from the business community, the government withdrew Bill C-256.[63]

In light of the hostile reaction of the business community to the proposed *Competition Act*, the minority Liberal government announced in 1973 that it would split the proposed amendments into two stages, with the least controversial amendments being proposed as Stage I amendments to the *Combines Investigation Act*.[64] The government introduced the Stage I amendments twice more before they were finally passed and came into effect on 1 January 1976.[65] The Stage I amend-

---

57 Ibid.
58 Ibid.
59 Ibid., at 68.
60 W.T. Stanbury, *Business Interests and the Reform of Canadian Competition Law* (Agincourt, Ont.: Methuen Press, 1977), at 45.
61 Ibid.
62 Dunlop, McQueen, and Trebilcock, *Canadian Competition Policy*, at 253.
63 Gordon Kaiser and Ian Neilson-Jones, 'Recent Developments in Canadian Law: Competition Law,' (1986) 18 *Ottawa Law Review* 401 at 405.
64 David McQueen, 'Revising Competition Law: Overview by a Participant,' in Prichard, Stanbury, and Neilson, eds., *Canadian Competition Policy*, at 14.
65 Clark, 'Legislative Reform and the Policy Process,' at 230.

ments extended the *Combines Investigation Act* to cover services and made bid-rigging a *per se* offence, without a need to show a substantial lessening of competition.[66] However, the word 'unduly' was retained in the conspiracy section and the enforcement of competition policy remained a largely criminal matter. One notable change implemented with the Stage 1 amendments was the introduction of a private cause of action for single damages for anyone who suffered a loss as a result of conduct criminally prohibited by the Act.[67]

In two cases, the constitutional validity of the new provisions was challenged. In *City National Leasing*, the Supreme Court of Canada ruled that, as a remedial power, the civil right of action did not impinge on the rights of the province.[68] Given that the provision was part of an integrated scheme of economic regulation, the civil right of action was held *intra vires* under the general trade and commerce power allocated to the federal government under section 91(2) of the *Constitution Act, 1867*.[69] The *Rocois Construction*[70] decision confirmed the constitutionality of the new civil right of action and determined that the Federal Court was a court of competent jurisdiction for trying cases brought under this cause of action.

The amendments also created a number of reviewable practices, such as refusal to deal, consignment selling, tied selling, and exclusive dealing. The Restrictive Trade Practices Commission became the adjudicatory body which could make remedial orders in reviewable practices cases.[71] In relation to mergers and monopolies, enforcement remained a criminal matter. The burden of proof necessary for criminal convictions, as well as the decisions in *BC Sugar*,[72] *KC Irving*,[73] *Thompson Newspapers*,[74] and *Canadian Breweries*,[75] meant that these provisions remained largely unenforceable.

In May 1976 the Skeoch-McDonald report, *Dynamic Change and*

---

66 McQueen, 'Revising Competition Law,' at 15.
67 Kaiser and Neilson-Jones, 'Recent Development in Canadian Law,' at 408.
68 *General Motors of Canada v. City National Leasing et al.* (1989), 58 D.L.R. (4th) 255.
69 *Constitution Act, 1867* (U.K.), 30 & 31 Vict., c. 3, s. 91(2).
70 *Quebec Ready to Mix Inc. v. Rocois Construction* (1989), 60 D.L.R. (4th) 124.
71 *Competition Policy in Canada*, at 21.
72 *British Columbia Sugar Refining Co.*, *supra*, note 43.
73 *K.C. Irving*, *supra*, note 47.
74 *R. v. Thompson Newspaper* (28 October 1983) (unreported).
75 *Canadian Breweries Ltd.*, *supra*, note 45.

Accountability in a Canadian Market Economy,[76] was released. It called for amendments to the *Combines Investigation Act* that would facilitate long-run dynamic change within the Canadian economy and that would discourage restraints which were the result of market power rather than superior economic performance.[77] The report rejected extensive government intervention in the economy and excessive reliance on structural measures of market power and argued instead that a board made up of expert members should be created to oversee competition policy.[78]

Given the incomplete nature of the reforms achieved through the Stage I amendments – in particular their failure to address two key issues of contention, the regulation of monopolies and mergers – and the recommendations of the Skeoch-McDonald report, a first attempt at implementing more substantial changes to the *Combines Investigation Act* was undertaken in 1977.[79] These changes would have created a civil law standard for the review of mergers.[80] The legislation was reintroduced into the House after being referred to a standing committee. Due to the intensity of opposition from the business community, the minister of consumer and corporate affairs withdrew the proposed Stage II amendments on 4 April 1977 to await the recommendations of the standing committee.[81] From 1978 to 1986 repeated attempts were made to implement the Stage II amendments. However, each of these attempts met with significant opposition from the business community.[82]

In 1984 the first major progress towards enacting the State II amendments was made. Bill C-29 was the result of extensive consultation with business interests and signalled the end of a period of hostility between the federal government and the business community over competition policy reform.[83] While Bill C-29 was not passed (Parliament was dissolved and an election held, which was won by the Progressive Conservative Party), the groundwork undertaken for its

76 L.A. Skeoch and B.C. McDonald, *Dynamic Change and Accountability in a Canadian Market Economy* (Ottawa: Minister of Supply and Services Canada, 1976).
77 *Competition Policy in Canada*, at 21.
78 Ibid., at 22.
79 McQueen, 'Revising Competition Law,' at 16.
80 *Competition Policy in Canada*, at 22.
81 McQueen, 'Revising Competition Law,' at 18.
82 Clark, 'Legislative Reform and the Policy Process,' at 232.
83 Maule and Ross, 'Canada's New Competition Policy,' at 70.

introduction set the stage for the implementation of the *Competition Act*. After some minor changes, the Mulroney government introduced Bill C-91, which embodied many of the recommendations that the Economic Council of Canada had made in its report issued twenty years earlier.[84] The *Competition Act*[85] and the *Competition Tribunal Act*[86] finally came into effect in 1986.

The new Act contained many significant changes. It incorporated the criminal offences of the *Combines Investigation Act*, which are prosecuted in all-purpose courts. The prohibitions included agreements to limit competition unduly, resale price maintenance, bid-rigging, price discrimination, promotional allowances, and predatory pricing. As well, the new Act established a civil review procedure to deal with mergers and monopolies and other anticompetitive practices. The civil review procedures covered the following reviewable practices: abuse of dominant position, mergers that substantially lessen competition, registration of specialization agreements, refusal to deal, consignment selling, tied selling, exclusive dealing, exclusive territories, and delivered pricing. The Act established a quasi-judicial tribunal (the Competition Tribunal) to deal with mergers, abuse of dominant position, and reviewable practices. It also subjected Crown corporations to the new regulatory scheme.[87] The 1986 *Competition Act*, which was modestly amended in 1999, currently embodies competition policy in Canada.

III. An Overview of the Competition Act

A. *The Competition Tribunal and the Commissioner of Competition*

The Competition Tribunal is a hybrid tribunal composed of both judges and lay members who are 'knowledgeable in economics, industry, commerce or public affairs.'[88] The tribunal is responsible for hearing cases brought to it by the director (now commissioner of competition) under the reviewable practices provisions in Part VIII of the *Competition Act*.

---

84 Kaiser and Neilson-Jones, 'Recent Developments in Canadian Law,' at 468.

85 *Competition Act*, s. 1.

86 *Competition Tribunal Act*, S.C. 1986, c. 26, Pt 1.

87 *Competition Act*, s. 21.

88 *Competition Tribunal Act*, S.C. 1985, c. 19 (2nd Supp.), s. 3(3).

Under recent amendments to the Act, private parties can also initiate proceedings before the tribunal for certain reviewable practices. Throughout this book, we use the term 'director' for matters arising prior to the 1999 amendment to the Act, when the title was changed to 'commissioner,' and 'commissioner' for matters arising thereafter. Except in the case of the registration of specialization agreements, private parties do not have direct access to the tribunal.[89] They may apply for intervenor status once the commissioner has initiated a case, but they cannot initiate their own proceedings.[90] The tribunal is constituted as a court of record composed of four judges of the Federal Court – Trial Division and not more than eight lay members appointed by the governor-in-council on the recommendation of the minister of consumer and corporate affairs (now Industry Canada).[91]

Proceedings before the tribunal must be heard by panels of no less than three and no more than five members;[92] there must be at least one lay member and one federal judge on all panels;[93] and the presiding member must be a judge.[94] Only the judicial members may determine matters of law.[95] However, both the judicial and lay members may adjudicate issues of mixed law and fact or of fact alone.[96] In the event of an equally divided tribunal, the presiding member casts the deciding vote. Appeals from the tribunal lie to the Federal Court of Appeal.[97] On matters of law and mixed law and fact an appeal lies as of right. However, on findings of fact, leave to appeal by the court is required.[98] As well, orders of the tribunal can be rescinded on application by the commissioner.[99]

Unlike the Restrictive Trade Practices Commission, which it replaced, the Competition Tribunal exercises no investigative functions

---

89 Warren Grover and Robert Kwinter, 'The New Competition Act,' (1987) 66 *Can. Bar Rev.* 267 at 270.

90 Michael J. Trebilcock, 'The Evolution of Competition Policy: Lessons from Comparative Experience,' in Rong-I Wu and Yun-Peng Chu, *Business Markets and Government in the Asia Pacific* (Canberra: Pacific Trade and Development Conference, 1998), at 6.

91 *Competition Tribunal Act*, s. 3(2).

92 Ibid., ss. 12(1)(a) and (b).

93 Ibid.

94 W.T. Stanbury, 'The New Competition Act and Competition Tribunal Act: "Not With a Bang but a Whimper,"' (1986–87) 12(1) *Canadian Business Law Journal* 2 at 38.

95 *Competition Tribunal Act*, s. 12(1)(a) and (b).

96 Stanbury, 'The New Competition Act and Competition Tribunal Act.'

97 *Competition Tribunal Act*, ss. 12(1)(a) and (b).

98 Ibid., s. 13.

99 *Competition Act*, s. 106.

but is instead purely an adjudicative body empowered to make findings and issue remedial orders. The Competition Tribunal has a wide range of remedies available to it when it finds that the *Competition Act* has been violated. These remedies range from orders of divestiture of assets and shares to the dissolution of a proposed merger to requirements that a merger be restructured or conduct-oriented orders.[100] As well, the tribunal can approve terms agreed upon by the parties in the form of consent orders.[101]

B. *Reviewable Practices*

1. *Abuse of Dominant Position*
The 1986 Act replaced the criminal offence of monopoly with a civil review procedure that allows the tribunal to review the abusive practices of dominant firms and prohibit the continuation of these practices on application by the commissioner.[102] In order for the abuse provisions (s. 78 and 79) of the Act to be violated, the defendant must control wholly or substantially a class or species of business. The defendant must also be shown to have engaged in anticompetitive practices. Finally, the effect of these practices must be substantially to lessen competition in the market.[103] If these conditions are met, the tribunal can order remedial measures that are reasonable and necessary to overcome the effects of the practice. The Act outlines eight practices that are considered abuses of dominant position. However, this is not an exhaustive list and other practices not specified under the Act may fall under this provision. The practices outlined in the Act include squeezing by a vertically integrated supplier, vertical integration with the intent to eliminate competition, freight equalization for the purposes of preventing entry, use of 'fighting brands,' purchasing products to prevent price erosion, and selling articles at a price lower than acquisition cost for the purposes of disciplining or eliminating a competitor.

The abuse of dominant position section of the *Competition Act* has been invoked successfully on four occasions. The first of these cases was *NutraSweet*[104] in which the director brought an action under the

---

100 Ibid., s. 92.
101 Ibid., s. 105.
102 Ibid., s. 79.
103 Ibid., s. 78.
104 *Canada (Director of Investigation and Research) v. NutraSweet Co.* (1990), 32 C.P.R. (3d) 1 (Comp. Trib.).

abuse of dominant position, exclusive dealing, and tied selling provisions of the 1986 *Competition Act.* NutraSweet, whose process patent had expired shortly before the director's application, held 95 per cent of the artificial sweetener market in Canada. The tribunal granted the director's application and prohibited loyalty rebate and exclusivity provisions in contracts between NutraSweet and its customers.

The *Laidlaw*[105] case concerned waste disposal on Vancouver Island. The Laidlaw company had included rights of first refusal, rights to match competitors' prices, and rights to increase prices with a negative billing option in its standard form contracts with its customers. Attempts by customers to terminate had been met with threats of legal action and pressure had been placed on municipalities to grant Laidlaw a favourable position at tender. The tribunal found that these practices were anticompetitive and Laidlaw agreed to remove the offensive clauses from its standard form contracts.

In *Tele-Direct,*[106] it was found that Tele-Direct had substantial control over telephone directory (Yellow Pages) advertising, an advertising medium for which there were no close substitutes. Tele-Direct had tied its layout/consultant services to the acquisition of space in its directories. This practice was held to contravene the tied-selling provisions of the *Competition Act*; it was also viewed as an anticompetitive act by a dominant firm. The tribunal ordered Tele-Direct to cease their tying practices with respect to larger customers.

In the *Nielsen*[107] case in 1995, the tribunal found that Nielsen, a Dun & Bradstreet subsidiary, had engaged in anticompetitive practices in requiring suppliers of supermarket scanner data to sell to it exclusively.

2. Mergers

Anticompetitive mergers are now civilly reviewable by the tribunal under section 92 of the Act on application by the commissioner. If the tribunal finds that a proposed merger lessens or is likely to prevent or lessen competition substantially, it can prohibit the merger or order divestiture or dissolution. The tribunal can also approve a merger

---

105 *Canada (Director of Investigation and Research) v. Laidlaw Waste Systems* (1992), 40 C.P.R. (3d) 289 (Comp. Trib.).

106 *Canada (Director of Investigation and Research) v. Tele-Direct (Publications) Inc.* (1997), 73 C.P.R. (3d) 1 (Comp. Trib.).

107 *Canada (Director of Investigation and Research) v. D&B Companies of Canada Ltd.* (1996), 64 C.P.R. (3d) 216 (Comp. Trib.).

subject to certain conditions. Under section 95, certain joint ventures are not subject to merger provisions. As well, section 96 of the *Competition Act* allows for an efficiency defence. Thus, even when competition is substantially lessened, if the efficiencies likely to be realized by the merger more than offset the losses that would be brought about by the decreased competition, the tribunal may not prohibit the merger.

The *Competition Act* has also instituted pre-merger notification requirements aimed at improving compliance with the Act.[108] Notification is required if a transaction meets two thresholds: first, if the parties to the transaction and their respective affiliates collectively possess total assets in Canada in excess of Cdn $400 million or gross revenues in, from, or into Canada in excess of Cdn $400 million, and second, if the assets in Canada being acquired or the revenues derived from those assets have a value greater than Cdn $35 million.

The merger provisions of the *Competition Act* have not often led to litigation before the tribunal, despite large merger waves in the late 1980s and mid-1990s. Most cases have been resolved within the Competition Bureau. Between 1986 and 1999 the commissioner reviewed 3,328 mergers.[109]

In the first of four contested merger cases before the tribunal, *Hillsdown*,[110] a proposed merger of two meat-rendering plants in Ontario was challenged by the director. The tribunal found that there was excess capacity in the meat-rendering business in Ontario and that prices were disciplined by this excess capacity and by cross-border competition.

In *Southam*,[111] the acquisition of several community newspapers by the Southam group, which already controlled the two daily newspapers in the Vancouver area, was challenged by the director on the grounds that it substantially lessened competition in the retail print advertising market. The tribunal found that the daily and community newspapers did not compete in the same market as there was little evidence that advertisers were sensitive to the relative price of advertising in daily and community newspapers. On appeal to the Federal Court

---

108 *Competition Act*, s. 94.
109 Margaret Sanderson and Michael J. Trebilcock, 'Process and Politics in Canadian Merger Review,' University of Toronto Competition Policy Roundtable, 16 June 2000.
110 *Canada (Director of Investigation and Research) v. Hillsdown Holdings (Canada) Ltd.* (1992), 41 C.P.R. (3d) 289 (Comp. Trib.).
111 *Canada (Director of Investigation and Research) v. Southam Inc.* (1992), 4 C.P.R. (3d) 261 (Comp. Trib.).

of Appeal[112] this decision was reversed. The Federal Court of Appeal found that the Tribunal erred in discounting evidence of functional substitutability. On appeal to the Supreme Court[113] the decision of the tribunal was reinstated. The Supreme Court held that deference to the expertise of the tribunal was appropriate on matters of mixed law and fact and that market definition was such an issue.

In *Superior Propane*,[114] which involved a merger between the two largest propane distributors in Canada, the tribunal rejected the parties' contention that the relevant product market was all forms of fuel and held that the merger would substantively lessen competition in national account markets and in various local markets. However, adopting a total welfare or total surplus standard under section 96 of the Act, a majority of the tribunal found that efficiency gains outweighed or offset the effects of the substantial lessening of competition and approved the merger. The commissioner appealed the tribunal's decision to the Federal Court of Appeal which reversed the tribunal's interpretation of section 96, adopting a balancing or distributional weights interpretation of the section. Leave to appeal this decision to the Supreme Court of Canada was denied. In *Canadian Waste Services Inc.* (April, 2001), the tribunal held that a merger that entailed the acquisition of a land-fill site in southern Ontario substantially lessened competition in the waste disposal market and in a subsequent decision on remedies (October, 2001) ordered divestiture of the site.

3. Other Horizontal Practices

Specialization agreements are reviewable under section 86 of the *Competition Act*. They also represent the only context in which parties other than the commissioner can make a direct application to the tribunal. In these cases, firms may seek to have their specialization agreement registered. If the efficiency gains offset the lessening of competition, the agreement can be registered for a specified period, thus making it immune from prosecution under the Act. To date, no specialization agreements have been registered with the tribunal.

Section 95 of the *Competition Act* exempts certain joint ventures from the merger provisions. If two firms have agreed to undertake a specific

---

112 *Canada (Director of Investigation and Research) v. Southam Inc.* (1995), 127 D.L.R. (4th) 263.

113 *Canada (Director of Investigation and Research) v. Southam Inc.*, [1997] 1 S.C.R. 748.

114 *Canada (Commissioner of Competition) v. Superior Propane Inc.* (2000), 7 C.P.R. (4th) 385 (Comp. Trib.).

project or program which would not otherwise occur and if competition is not lessened to a greater degree than is necessitated by the joint venture, the venture is exempt from the merger provisions.

4. Vertical Practices

Practices between upstream buyers and downstream sellers or dealers are subject to review by the tribunal on application by the commissioner. These provisions include refusal to supply under section 75 of the *Competition Act*. If the tribunal finds that a person is substantially affected in his or her business due to an inability to obtain adequate supplies on usual trade terms, it may order that the supplier accept the downstream party as a customer. The tribunal has made orders of this nature on two occasions: in the *Chrysler*[115] and *Xerox*[116] cases. In *Chrysler*, the tribunal ordered Chrysler Canada to reinstate a dealer customer for the supply of automobile parts on the usual trade terms. In *Xerox*, the tribunal ordered Xerox to restore parts supply to independent service dealers, a practice which it had ceased in 1987.

Consignment selling is reviewable under section 76 of the Act. Where consignment selling is introduced to control the price at which a dealer in a product provides the product or to discriminate between consignees, the tribunal can order the supplier to cease the practice of consignment selling.

Another vertical practice reviewable by the tribunal is market restriction, under section 77 of the *Competition Act*. Arrangements between an upstream supplier and its downstream dealers that allocate customers by class or by geographic area may be subject to cease and desist orders if these practices are found to substantially lessen competition.

Exclusive dealing is reviewable under section 77 and remedial orders can be issued if an agreement to deal exclusively with one party is found to lessen competition significantly. This provision was first considered by the Restrictive Trade Practices Commission in *Bombardier*.[117] The Restrictive Trade Practices Commission ruled that a competitor must control a significant share of the market for a prosecution for exclusive dealing to succeed. Given that a significant portion of the

---

115 *Canada (Director of Investigation and Research) v. Chrysler Canada* (1992), 44 C.P.R. (3d) 430 (Comp. Trib.).
116 *Canada (Director of Investigation and Research) v. Xerox Canada Inc.* (1990), 33 C.P.R. (3d) 83 (Comp. Trib.).
117 *Canada (Director of Investigation and Research) v. Bombardier Ltd.* (1980), 53 C.P.R. (2d) 47.

market for snowmobiles was not controlled by Bombardier, its exclusive contracts with dealers did not violate the *Combines Investigation Act*.[118] This view was confirmed in *NutraSweet*[119] where it was found that, given NutraSweet's very high market share, the incentives provided to those buyers who agreed to use only NutraSweet products violated the exclusive dealing provisions of the *Competition Act*. In *Nielsen* (as noted above), exclusivity provisions in contracts with suppliers of scanner data and in contracts with product manufactures to whom Nielsen supplied information compiled from the data were also held to violate these provisions.

A final reviewable practice under section 77 is tied selling. Under such arrangements, a supplier only supplies a product, the 'tying good,' on condition that a buyer purchases a second product, the 'tied good,' or offers inducements for a buyer to buy two products from the same firm. The tribunal can order the supplier to cease this action if the action is found to have an exclusionary effect on the tied good market. In *Tele-Direct* (noted above), the tribunal ordered cessation of the tying of advertising space and advertising services in Yellow Pages directories for larger advertisers.

C. *Criminal Offences*

1. *Conspiracies*
Section 45 of the *Competition Act* makes it a criminal offence to conspire, agree, or arrange to prevent or lessen competition unduly in an industry[120] and such an offence is subject to a maximum fine of $10 million and five years' imprisonment. Between 1986 and 1997 forty-four conspiracy and bid-rigging cases were prosecuted. The average fine per firm has increased by eighteen times in real terms between the late 1960s and the early 1990s.[121] For example, in one recent (unreported) case, Archer Daniels Midland (ADM) was fined $16 million, over half of the profits earned by ADM Canada over the period when it was in

---

118 The exclusive dealing provisions of the *Combines Investigation Act* and the *Competition Act* are virtually identical.

119 *Supra*, note 104.

120 *R. v. Nova Scotia Pharmaceutical Society* (1993), 49 C.P.R. (3d) 289.

121 W.T. Stanbury, 'Expanding Responsibilities and Declining Resources: The Strategic Responses of the Competition Bureau, 1986–1996,' (1998) 13 *Review of Industrial Organization* 205 at 228.

violation of the *Competition Act*, as the result of a guilty plea for conspiring to price fix and allocate market share as a part of an international conspiracy to raise prices in the lysine and citric acid market. In another recent case involving an international price fixing conspiracy in the vitamin market, Hoffman LaRoche was fined $50 million following a guilty plea – the largest criminal fine in Canadian history.

Section 45 does not apply to collective bargaining agreements, underwriting agreements, amateur sports leagues, joint ventures, specialization agreements, export agreements, and product standards.

2. Other Criminal Offences

Bid rigging (s. 47) is a *per se* criminal offence unless the person calling for bids is notified of the agreement in advance. Interest-setting agreements between financial institutions are also subject to a *per se* prohibition (s. 49).

Under section 50(1)(a) of the *Competition Act*, it is a criminal offence for a supplier to grant discounts or rebates to a downstream buyer which are not also made available to competitors of that buyer in respect of a similar quality and quantity of articles. There have been three convictions for price discrimination, with fines ranging from $15,000 to $50,000.[122] Predatory pricing is also a criminal offence; under section 50(1)(c) of the Act it is an offence to sell products at prices that are unreasonably low and have the effect of substantially lessening competition or eliminating a competitor. Between 1980 and 1990 the director received 550 complaints alleging an offence under the predatory pricing provisions. Of these complaints, twenty-three resulted in formal inquiries under the Act, four were referred to the attorney general, and three resulted in the laying of charges.[123]

Finally, under section 61 of the *Competition Act* it is a criminal offence for a supplier to attempt to influence upward or discourage the reduction of the price at which another person sells or offers to sell a product (often referred to as resale price maintenance). It is also an offence to refuse to supply a product to a downstream party because of its low pricing policy. Between 1986 and 1997 fifty-seven prosecutions were

---

122 *Price Discrimination Enforcement Guidelines* (Ottawa: Consumer and Corporate Affairs Canada, 1992), at 1.
123 *Predatory Pricing Enforcement Guidelines* (Ottawa: Director of Investigation and Research 1992), at 1.

brought under this provision, although the number of prosecutions has fallen dramatically in recent years.[124]

IV. The Role of Economic Theory in the Evolution of Competition/Antitrust Policy[125]

The political history of the evolution of competition policy in Canada and the United States makes clear that economic theories were never the sole determinant of policies adopted in any given period. Nevertheless, prevailing economic theories have always been an important source of influence on the framing, enforcement, and adjudication of competition laws. Indeed, it is often claimed that Canada's *Competition Act*, 1986 is the most economically literate competition statute in force in any jurisdiction in the world. Even if this claim is broadly true, however, some of the residues of an ambivalent history are reflected in the purpose clause of this Act. Section 1.1 provides:

> 1.1 The purpose of this Act is to maintain and encourage competition in Canada in order to promote the efficiency and adaptability of the Canadian economy, in order to expand opportunities for Canadian participation in world markets while at the same time recognizing the role of foreign competition in Canada, in order to ensure that small and medium-sized enterprises have an equitable opportunity to participate in the Canadian economy, and in order to provide consumers with competitive prices and product choices.

When competition/antitrust laws were first introduced in the United States and Canada in the late nineteenth century, economists in general were sceptical of such laws. Much influenced by theories of social Darwinism, many economists viewed tendencies towards consolidation and combination as inevitable processes of economic evolution and believed that laws designed to impede such processes were at worst harmful and at best futile.[126] At the time of the enactment of

---

124 Stanbury, 'Expanding Responsibilities and Declining Resources,' at 230.
125 This section draws substantially from Herbert Hovenkamp, *Federal Antitrust Policy: The Law of Competition and Its Practice* (St Paul, Minn.: West Publishing, 1994), at 59–71.
126 William Letwin, *Law & Economic Policy in America: The Evolution of the Sherman Act* (Edinburgh: Edinburgh University Press, 1967), at 71–7.

these laws the marginalist revolution in economics was just emerging: Alfred Marshall's great treatise, *Principles of Economics*, which did much to formalize modern conceptions of price theory (marginal costs, marginal revenue, the demand curve, consumer surplus, and allocative efficiency), was published in the same year as the enactment of the *Sherman Act*. The new breed of economists, who were most heavily influenced by the neo-classical revolution, were more suspicious of big business than their classical predecessors and more inclined to see antitrust laws as serving a useful purpose.

During the 1930s, economic theories such as those developed by Edward Chamberlin emphasized the role of imperfections and product differentiation in American markets. Chamberlin stated that 'the explicit recognition that product is differentiated brings into the open the problem of variety and makes it clear that pure competition may no longer be regarded as in any sense an "ideal" for purposes of welfare economics'.[127] In a market with differentiated products and fixed costs, the perfect competition outcome, in which prices equal marginal costs – and in which prices therefore guide consumers to purchase products, or firms to purchase inputs, up to the socially optimal quantity where the marginal value of an additional unit equals the marginal social cost of producing the unit – is generally not feasible. Prices equal to marginal cost would leave firms without sufficient revenue to cover costs. Because consumers value product variety, the power of firms to set prices above marginal cost through the establishment of a brand name, or through intensive product promotion, generally should not be regarded as problematic. Nor is the price-setting power that results when only a limited number of firms are willing to incur the fixed cost of sustaining production necessarily inefficient. Price-marginal cost distortions' or deviations from the ideal competitive market are the cost that the economy bears in return for greater product variety.[128]

Chamberlin's message was lost on subsequent researchers in industrial organization who associated monopolistic competition with inefficient excess capacity, and the establishment of strong market brand

---

127 Edward H. Chamberlin, *The Theory of Monopolistic Competition*, 7th ed. (Cambridge, Mass.: Harvard University Press, 1962), 214.

128 As we will explain in Chapter 2, in the trade-off between lower prices and greater product variety a monopolistically competitive industry can in theory yield excessive variety. But this is not necessarily the case, nor is there any simple rule that would guide policy to identify exactly when variety is excessive.

names with the opportunity to exercise market power to the detriment of consumers. The competitive market structure, in which many firms with small market shares compete intensively on prices, remained the appropriate goal of antitrust policy in the view of many economists, especially those of the so-called Harvard school or structuralist school of industrial organization. Proponents of the structuralist school, such as Carl Kaysen, Donald Turner, and Joe Bain, argued first, that economies of scale were not substantial in most industries and dictated truly anticompetitive concentration levels in only a small number of industries; second, that barriers to entry faced by new firms were often very high and could easily be manipulated by dominant firms; and third, that non-competitive performance (monopoly pricing) associated with oligopolies began to occur at relatively low concentration levels. When the structuralist approach became prominent in the 1960s, 'those who believed in it were willing to go the next step. Not only were they willing to have merger guidelines based on the structuralist approach, but they also proposed deconcentration. If a four-firm concentration ratio is high enough to warrant enjoining a merger, then it is high enough to warrant deconcentration, because the same collusion theory results whether the concentration comes about because of a merger or because that is the way we find the industry.'[129] The structuralist theory emerged from a decade in which faith peaked in the ability of the government to intervene and fine tune the economy in areas ranging from antitrust to stabilizing the business cycle.[130]

The structuralist view was increasingly challenged by scholars associated with the so-called Chicago school of industrial organization theory, such as Aaron Director, Robert Bork, Frank Easterbrook, George Stigler, and Richard Posner. Proponents of this school tended to view firm size and dominance as a reflection of superior efficiencies and deconcentration policies as likely seriously to undermine the attainment of these efficiencies. These scholars argued that most markets are competitive even if they comprise relatively few sellers; that market

---

129 Ira Millstein, 'Are Economists Taking Over?' (a panel discussion), in E.M. Fox and J.T. Halverson, eds., *Antitrust Policy in Transition: The Convergence of Law and Economics* (Section of Antitrust Law of the American Bar Association, 1984), 30.

130 Macroeconomic theory had not yet seen the emergence of rational expectations models, which established that government's ability to smooth business cycles was very limited, and the success of the tax cuts of the early 1960s in stimulating economic growth was regarded as evidence that economic fine-tuning would work.

power, even when it exists, tends to be self-correcting by attracting new entry; that natural barriers to entry (in contrast to government barriers to entry) are typically no greater for new entrants than those previously faced by incumbents and hence should not be viewed as inefficient or anticompetitive; that economies of scale are more significant than often claimed once economies of distribution as well as intraplant or production economies are considered; and that economic efficiency should be the exclusive goal of antitrust policy.

According to Audretsch,[131] with respect to substantive areas of antitrust there was probably the strongest agreement between the two schools over the undesirability of bare horizontal agreements to restrict competition. With respect to monopolization, differences between the two schools were much stronger. As mentioned, the original structuralist position on monopoly favoured the deconcentration of industries through forced divestiture and dissolution of firms found to possess unreasonable market dominance. The Chicago school, on the other hand, viewed deconcentration as entailing significant productive inefficiencies and distorting incentives to achieve success in markets. With respect to merger policy, the Harvard school considered merger enforcement not only as desirable but as the most decisive component of antitrust policy, because of its pre-emptive quality, whereas the Chicago school considered scale economies resulting from mergers to be significant and a loss of such efficiencies to be especially deleterious. The Chicago school favoured a benign approach to vertical distribution restrictions such as tying arrangements, exclusive dealing, exclusive territories, and resale price maintenance, viewing them mostly as efficient mechanisms for internalizing various forms of externalities, while the Harvard school argued for more interventionist policies, tending to view such restraints as symptomatic of cartelization by either upstream manufacturers or downstream distributors or unilateral forms of market foreclosure mechanisms.

Chicago industrial organization theories were influential in antitrust policy circles in the United States and elsewhere throughout the late 1970s and 1980s. One aspect of this influence was the focus in merger policy enforcement on the risks of increased coordination of prices among firms – theories now labelled interdependence theories in

---

131 David Audretsch, 'Divergent Views in Antitrust Economics,' (1988) 33 *Antitrust Bulletin* 134.

merger enforcement guidelines as opposed to unilateral price effects of a merger. Chicago price theory before the 1980s relied almost exclusively on two basic models: perfect competition and monopoly. Oligopoly theory was a theory of the conditions under which firms could or could not collude. Market conditions that yielded outcomes between competitive prices and monopoly prices were not fully integrated into the analysis. The theory of monopolistic competition was explicitly rejected by the Chicago school, and theories of noncooperative equilibrium in oligopolies, in which firms exercised market power constrained only partly by competition did not receive much emphasis. Game theory, which provided a methodology for developing much more context-specific models of competitive interaction, was late to arrive at Chicago. Over the last few years, new thinking on industrial organization theory has emphasized the role of strategic behaviour in protecting the dominant positions of incumbents from competitive encroachment through strategic manipulation of various kinds of contractual foreclosure mechanisms and pricing strategies. In this literature, game theory tends to play a prominent role. As Hovenkamp notes, 'The Chicago school offers simplicity, elegance, and often relatively easy answers to antitrust questions. The alternatives are almost always messier, more expensive, and less determinate. But policy has to reflect the world we live in, and the world is a messy place.'[132] This observation also extends to some of the precepts of the original Harvard school of industrialization theory, which often advanced rather simplistic unidirectional models of market behaviour that revolved around a structure-conduct-performance paradigm. In the real world these variables often interact with each other in complex and context-specific ways, suggesting that less weight should be accorded to static and generalized measures of market structure as proxies for market power in competition/antitrust policy analysis, and more weight attached to competitive dynamics, including various conduct variables. In merger policy enforcement specifically, the emphasis has shifted from interdependence theories to unilateral theories. Theories are now presented in antitrust cases that are relatively sophisticated and strongly context-specific, and which allow the estimation of unilateral effects of a merger through the application of market-specific data. A modern antitrust case brings much more statistical evidence to bear

---

132 Hovenkamp, *Federal Antitrust Policy*, at 70-1.

than was available ten or twenty years ago, and there is somewhat more consensus in the methodology of economic analysis than there was then.[133]

In the next chapter, we set out in greater detail some of the key contemporary economic concepts relevant to competition/antitrust policy analysis and some of the common pitfalls often associated with these concepts. Differences between various economic schools of thought on competition/antitrust policy have narrowed significantly in recent years, yielding common ground on many economic issues while leaving unresolved divergences of views on others. The policy climate, as well as the intellectual climate, has also changed in important ways. The second-best world to which competition policy was often remitted historically, as a result of countervailing trade protectionist policies, has been substantially mitigated with extensive international trade and investment liberalization in the post-war decades. Similarly, recent trends towards privatization of state-owned enterprises and deregulation of potentially competitive industries have exposed new sectors to the application of competition policy. On the other hand, the increasing importance of innovation in knowledge-based industries has heightened the historical tension between competition policy and intellectual property rights. The relationships between competition policy and these cognate policy domains are also explored later in this book.

133 Not enough consensus, of course, to ensure that all economists and all lawyers agree on every issue.

TWO

Basic Economic Concepts in Competition Policy

I. Introduction

Competition policy addresses basic economic questions, such as whether a particular trade practice is designed to promote the efficient delivery of a product to customers or to exclude potential rivals from the market, or whether a prospective merger will enhance or diminish the economic performance of an industry. The language of the *Competition Act* reflects the underlying economic content of the law and application of the Act often revolves around the economic evidence and economic analysis necessary to address the questions at issue. In Canada as in the United States, economic theory and evidence play a much more central role in competition cases than they did twenty years ago. Economic evidence pertaining to the impact of a merger on prices and costs, for example, is at the core of a modern merger case from the outset. Theories and evidence on the exclusionary impact of a trade practice such as tying, exclusive dealing, or refusal to deal are pitted against evidence of the practice as efficiency enhancing or in the buyers' interest.

The rise in the role of economic evidence is explained in part by the general increase in the sophistication of courts, the Competition Tribunal, and the Competition Bureau, but owes more to developments in economic theory and the methods of econometrics (statistical methods applied to economics) and the greater availability of rich data sets. Twenty years ago the main economic theories underlying the application of competition policy were the theories of perfect competition and monopoly, the two extremes of market structure. While these theories remain the most important foundation for addressing the central question of competition policy – why is competition good and monopoly bad? – the economics of industrial organization has since developed a vast array of models and techniques for analysis of markets that are characterized by neither extreme. Modern economic theories of industrial organization can incorporate market features such as the dynamic interaction among a small number of firms, market frictions such as transportation costs or costs of searching for low prices, the inability of consumers to discern product quality prior to purchase, 'network externalities' in which the decisions of consumers to buy a product (e.g., fax machines or software) affect the value each consumer extracts from the product, and so on. A key feature of modern applications of economic analysis to competition policy is that the theories developed are *case specific*. Rather than applying a standard textbook model, such as perfect competition, the economist in the courtroom draws on the methods of economic analysis in a way that incorporates the key market conditions and strategic aspects of the interaction of firms. On the empirical side of the applications, the important developments are the availability of large databases, exemplified by transaction-by-transaction scanner data in retail markets, and the use of sophisticated econometric techniques. The substantial role of modern computer technology is obvious in both developments.

This chapter discusses the foundations of economics as applied to competition policy. The aim is to provide not an exposition of economic techniques but rather an outline of essential concepts.[1] We begin with a brief discussion of economic perspectives on the role of competition policy. This is not an abstract question to be set aside once one gets into the details of a case. Indeed, the objective of the *Competition Act* was the central issue in *Canada (Commissioner of Competition) v. Superior Propane Inc.*[2] The purpose clause of the Act was, in the context of mergers, translated by the tribunal in *Superior Propane* as a very specific economic criterion. Following this discussion, the chapter moves from normative economics (what should be) to positive economics (what is), with a discussion of basic market structures: perfect competition,

---

1 We minimize the amount of formal economics throughout the book. For example, while we discuss the strategic interaction among firms in cases involving mergers or practices such as exclusive dealing, tying, and resale price maintenance, we do not develop the formal tools of game theory or general theory.

2 (2000), 7 C.P.R. (4th) 385 (Comp. Trib.).

monopoly, oligopoly, and monopolistic competition. The chapter concludes with an outline of the economics of market definition in competition policy, including the pitfalls that await a less-than-careful application of economics to market definition and market power.

II. Economic Efficiency and the Purpose of Competition Policy

The goal of competition policy is often expressed simply as the protection of the competitive structure and competitive conduct of markets. Competition, however, is not an end in itself. Section 1.1 of the Canadian *Competition Act* states:

> The purpose of this Act is to maintain and encourage competition in Canada in order to promote the efficiency and adaptability of the Canadian economy, in order to expand world markets while at the same time recognizing the role of foreign competition in Canada, in order to ensure that small and medium-sized enterprises have an equitable opportunity to participate in the Canadian economy and in order to provide consumers with competitive prices and product choices.

The Act thus recognizes the encouragement of competition as a means of achieving more fundamental goals: efficiency, expansion of world markets, protection of the opportunity for small businesses to compete, and protection of competitive prices and product choices. Economists generally accept only one of these goals, efficiency, as the basic purpose of competition policy. The concept of efficiency encompasses technical efficiency, production of output at minimum cost; static allocative efficiency, the production of goods in socially optimal amounts and the allocation of those goods to the right consumers; and dynamic efficiency, the allocation of appropriate resources to research and development of new products and production processes.

In many cases, the fundamental goals described in section 1.1 of the Act are not in conflict. Promoting competition by preventing the monopolization of markets through inefficient exclusionary practices, for example, leads to both efficiency and competitive prices. But potential conflicts among the goals can arise. One potential conflict arises where small businesses would be harmed if a dominant firm were allowed to engage in efficiency-enhancing practices that disadvantage small firms, or if two large firms in a market were allowed to engage in a cost-saving merger that lowered prices, thus harming small firms competing in the same market. Policy analysts rarely argue that the efficiency goal of competition policy should be compromised so that small firms can survive. The interests of small firms, however, have historically affected competition policy (a U.S. example, *Brunswick Corp. v. Pueblo Bowl-O-Mat, Inc.*, is discussed later in this chapter).

A more contentious conflict arises between the fundamental goals of maximizing efficiency and achieving the most competitive prices for consumers. This conflict is most apparent in merger cases, where an acquisition may involve both significant gains in efficiency in the form of cost savings and an increase in prices because of a lessening of competition. As we shall discuss in detail in Chapter 4, this potential conflict in goals was resolved by the tribunal in favour of efficiency in *Superior Propane*.[3] The basis in economics for this resolution is sound. Competition policy is appropriately viewed as an instrument to maximize efficiency or the 'total surplus' gained by market participants. The use of competition policy to achieve not merely efficiency but an equitable distribution of wealth would result in an excessively complex and non-transparent set of legal rules that would be both uncertain and arbitrary – being determined by the opinions or values of whoever was sitting on the tribunal in a particular case. Government instruments such as taxes and social insurance are much better suited for the goal of distributing income equitably. Accordingly, we shall focus on the goal of economic efficiency in discussing the role of competition policy in this chapter.

Under ideal conditions, competitive markets promote economic efficiency. This is the most fundamental result of economics (the 'first theorem of welfare economics') and the basis for competition policy. Actual markets may depart from competitive or ideal conditions for many reasons. Externalities such as pollution may distort the market outcome. 'Common pool' effects may lead to the exploitation of resources at excessive rates. Economies of scale, which in the extreme are described as a 'natural monopoly,' may preclude a competitive market structure and require regulation of a market.[4] Competition pol-

---

3 Ibid. The Federal Court of Appeal, in an unreported decision, 1 April 2001, rejected the tribunal's adoption of the total surplus criterion (Chapter 4, below).
4 A natural monopoly describes a market in which any amount of output within a relevant range can be produced more cheaply by one firm than by two or more.

icy focuses on the departures from competitive markets that involve the exercise of market power, the ability profitably to raise prices above competitive levels.

The definition of efficiency in the allocation of resources in a society is more basic than the issue of *how* to allocate resources, that is, whether the resources are being allocated through a free-market economy or through central planning. An allocation of resources for society as a whole is said to be efficient, or *Pareto optimal*, if there is no other allocation that is superior for some individuals and not worse for any individuals. When we move to the context of a single market, a common context for competition policy, the efficiency criterion is expressed as the maximization of the total dollar benefits or 'surplus' value derived from the market.

The surplus that derives from the production of a commodity can be measured in dollars and is linked to the demand curve for the commodity. For example, suppose that the demand for tomatoes in a community is described by the following schedule: 100 kilograms (per day) are demanded at a price of 50 cents per kilogram or less; 75 kilograms are demanded at a price between 50 cents and $1.00; and 50 kilograms would be demanded at any price between $1.00 and $1.50. The demand schedule can be depicted with a demand curve, as in Figure 2.1. The demand curve provides, on the horizontal axis, the amount demanded in the community at the various prices presented on the vertical axis.

The demand curve can also be described as the marginal social value curve. The curve represents the relationship between the marginal social value of tomatoes and the total output of tomatoes: at each quantity on the x-axis, the demand curve provides the dollar value of an additional kilogram of tomatoes as measured by the maximum amount that some consumer would pay for the additional kilogram. For example, if 70 kilograms are currently being produced and allocated to those individuals who attach the highest value to the tomatoes, then the social value of an additional kilogram is one dollar. This is the amount that the 'marginal consumer' would willingly pay for the additional kilogram. Similarly, the total value to the community of any output of tomatoes can be read from the figure as the area under the demand curve. An output of 70 kilograms is worth a total of $95, because each of the first 50 kilograms is worth $1.50, and the next 20 kilograms are each worth $1.

To describe efficiency we must introduce the cost side of tomato production. Suppose that the marginal cost of tomatoes is 60 cents per

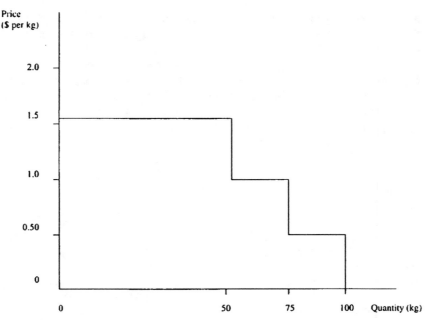

Figure 2.1
The demand for tomatoes

kilogram and that there are no fixed costs. This assumption can be represented as a cost curve, as in Figure 2.2. In this figure the cost curve represents both the marginal cost and the average cost at each level of output. The assumption of constant costs, or 'constant returns to scale,' means that as all inputs into production increase in the same proportion, the output increases by that proportion as well. Increasing returns to scale would lead to a declining average cost curve (as the result of fixed costs or declining marginal costs) and decreasing returns to scale would be represented by an increasing average cost curve.

The *net* social value of the production of any output of tomatoes is defined as the difference between the social value of output (which we have seen is the area under the demand curve) and total costs. The net social value can be represented graphically as the area between the demand curve and the constant marginal cost. For example, the net social value of the output of 70 kilograms is the $95 gross value minus the $42 cost of production, which equals $53. This is the shaded area in Figure 2.2.

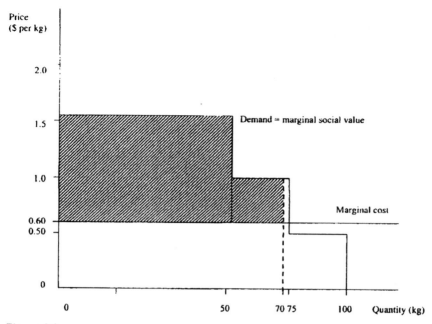

Figure 2.2
The net social value of output

The marginal cost curve for tomatoes is more realistically depicted as upward-sloping. The amount of land near any community that is particularly suitable for growing tomatoes is limited in supply. Only this land will be used for production at low output quantities. As quantity increases, however, less suitable land must be brought into production. Higher quantities therefore correspond to higher marginal cost. The marginal cost of tomatoes reflects the cost of inputs such as fertilizer, labour, and seeds needed in combination with the 'marginal land' or least suitable plot currently employed in the production of tomatoes. The marginal cost also includes the social opportunity cost of the marginal plot itself, that is, its value in the next best use, perhaps the production of corn.

The socially optimal amount of production, 75 kilograms in our example, is the quantity that maximizes the net social value of production. This is the quantity that equates the net social value of tomatoes, given by the demand curve, with the marginal cost of production. A lower quantity, such as 70 kilograms, leaves uncaptured social gains to additional production, since at 70 units of output the value to society of an additional unit of production exceeds the social cost of that unit.

The concept of efficiency in the output of a commodity as just described contains no reference to 'price' and does not depend upon whether a market system or a planning system is being used to determine the quantity. In the context of competition policy, however, the price mechanism is central. Given the price determined in the market for a commodity, the total social surplus or gains from trade in the market can be expressed as the sum of two components: producer surplus and consumer surplus. Producer surplus earned on a unit of production in a market is the difference between the price paid to sellers for the unit and the minimum price that would have sufficed to elicit the supply of that unit. For example, if an additional unit of a product would have been supplied at a price of $5, but a producer actually charges $8 for the unit, the producer's surplus for that unit is $3.

Producer surplus can be thought of as the sum of profits plus 'rents' accruing to the owners of inputs that are fixed in supply and specific to the market in question. For example, if the demand of an agricultural commodity rises, resulting in a higher market price, there may be some increase in the profits of suppliers (although not if the market is competitive) as well as an increase in the rent per acre charged by landowners for the use of land that is particularly well suited for growing the commodity. The increase in profits and in land rents represents the increase in the suppliers' share of gains from trade in the market. An economy-wide increase in the demand for computer programmers with a particular skill will lead to an increase in the rent charged by owners of that skill for their human capital. In applications to competition policy, the impact of a competition decision on rents is usually not significant, however, since inputs such as human capital are rarely *specific* to the markets affected by the decision.

The surplus earned by a consumer on the purchase of a particular unit of a good is the difference between the maximum value that the consumer would be willing to pay for the unit and the actual price paid. For example, a consumer valuing a unit at $12 and paying a price of $8 earns $4 in consumer surplus. Consumer surplus, the total gains from trade accruing to the consumers' side of a market, is the sum of the surplus earned on all units by all consumers in the market.

While Pareto optimality is non-controversial as an indicator of social welfare accruing to society from the allocation of goods across all markets, total surplus is highly controversial as a measure of the social welfare accruing from production in the context of a single market. There are two main potential problems in the inference of greater welfare from an increase in total surplus in a market. The first is a relatively technical problem: consumer surplus is in general not an exact measure of the net dollar value an individual consumer attaches to the gains from purchasing in a market, whenever the consumer's demand is sensitive to changes in the consumer's wealth.[5] The impact on a consumer of a price increase is generally not measured exactly by the loss in consumer surplus accruing to the consumer. Rather than describing the details of the problem, we note that applications of the total surplus criterion rely on an assumption that consumer surplus is a close approximation of the net dollar value accruing to consumers.[6] Robert Willig justifies this assumption in an article entitled 'Consumer Surplus Without Apology.'[7]

---

5 By 'net dollar value' we mean the amount that a consumer would have to be compensated, in order to leave him or her equally well off, if the right to purchase in the market were taken away from the consumer.

6 The difficulties introduced by income effects (dependence of demand upon wealth) into the measurement of consumer valuation via consumer surplus are suggested by the following example. Suppose that one estimates a consumer's demand curve and concludes that a price increase of 50 per cent would induce a loss of consumer surplus of $100. Does the transfer of $100 to the consumer, after the price increase, exactly compensate the consumer for the dollar loss in welfare incurred as a result of the price increase? If it did, it should be possible to compensate the consumer exactly with two bundles of $50 rather than one of $100. Suppose, however, that with the addition of the first bundle of $50, the consumer's demand for the product fell substantially because of the effect of the higher wealth (i.e., the product is a good for which demand is much lower at higher income levels). Then a new calculation of consumer surplus, under the revised demand curve, would be less than $100. In other words, the second $50 bundle would be more than necessary to compensate the consumer fully for the price increase – showing that the initial consumer surplus calculation of $100 exceeds the necessary compensation for the price increase. Consumer surplus is an exact and consistent measure of changes in consumer welfare only if demand for the product is independent of income.

7 (1976) 66 *American Economic Review* 589. Jerry Hausman, in 'Exact Consumer's Surplus and Deadweight Loss,' ([Sept. 1981] *American Economic Review* 662) shows that while consumer surplus may closely approximate a consumer's net value ('compensating variation'), the percentage error in dead-weight loss calculations induced by the use of consumer surplus may be substantial. Notwithstanding Hausman's conclusion, the approximation error in the use of consumer surplus is small relative to the range of estimation error involved in estimating demand and costs in typical

We have already alluded to the second and more important source of dispute in the use of total surplus as a measure of social welfare in our discussion of efficiency as a goal of competition policy. In using total surplus, one is aggregating welfare effects across individuals, without regard to who is gaining and who is losing from a particular decision or change in policy. For example, it is not uncommon for a prospective merger to involve a price increase as a result of reduced competition in a market. This price increase alone will result in a gain in producer surplus, a decrease in consumer surplus and a loss in the sum. If costs also fall as a result of the merger, however, then the total surplus may increase, as we shall explore in detail in Chapter 4. The merger then involves not just an increase in the total dollar surplus, but a redistribution of these gains from consumers to producers. The use of the total surplus measure treats the redistribution as neutral ('a dollar is a dollar') and under this standard a merger would not be prohibited under competition law even if it involved a substantial lessening of competition, provided the gains to suppliers from the merger exceeded the loss to consumers. Similarly, an exclusionary practice might result in higher prices to consumers if it prevented competitors from entering a market; but if the incumbent engaged in the practice had lower costs than the potential competitors, the practice may result in the industry output being produced at lower total cost. If the cost savings exceeded the loss in consumer surplus, then the practice would be allowed under the total surplus standard. The justification of total surplus as a criterion for competition policy has been debated mainly within the context of mergers and we defer a detailed discussion of the issue to Chapter 4 on merger review.

III. Competitive Markets

That competitive markets can, under ideal circumstances, assure an efficient allocation of resources is the most fundamental proposition of economics. Competition refers not to the intensity of rivalry in a market, but to a particular market structure and outcome. A competitive

---

competition law cases. Hausman demonstrates in any case, however, that the information used to estimate demand employing a common technique (the 'almost identified demand system') allows for the estimation of exact compensating variation rather than the consumer surplus approximation.

market structure requires the following conditions: a large number of suppliers, each with a small share of the market and each acting independently; the absence of any artificial barriers to entry, defined as expenditures required to enter the market that must be incurred by some firms but not by others; no significant economies of scale beyond a 'minimum efficient size' that is small relative to the total market; mobility of resources, including the absence of any restrictions on the movement of resources in and out of input markets; and a homogeneous product, with no differential transactions costs such as travel costs or search costs incurred by buyers.

A single firm in this ideal competitive market perceives that it can increase its output arbitrarily without any impact on the market price. In other words, the firm has no market power. While the *market demand curve* is downward sloping, as in Figure 2.1, the *individual firm demand curve* is perfectly flat. The distinction between market demand and individual firm demand is critical. It is a downward slope in the latter that defines market power. In a competitive market, no firm has market power. The competitive firm is a price-taker, not a price-setter. The elasticity of demand at any level of output, whether one is discussing market demand or firm demand, is defined as the percentage change in quantity that will be elicited by a 1 per cent change in price.[8] The price-taking assumption means an infinite elasticity of the firm demand curve in a competitive market: at a price even slightly above the competitive level, the quantity demanded of the firm drops to zero.

If the cost of production of each supplier in a competitive market is borne by the supplier itself, so that there are no external costs imposed on other suppliers or any individuals in the society, then the social marginal cost curve is also the private marginal cost curve, that is, the cost to suppliers of producing an extra unit of output. The private marginal cost curve measures not only the marginal cost of production at each quantity, but also a reverse relationship: the quantity that suppliers in aggregate would be willing and able to supply at each price. The amount that firms would be willing to supply at each price is called the *supply curve* of the competitive market.

---

8 Letting dQ/dP denote the change in quantity with respect to a change in price, the demand elasticity can be expressed as $dQ/dP \cdot (P/Q)$.

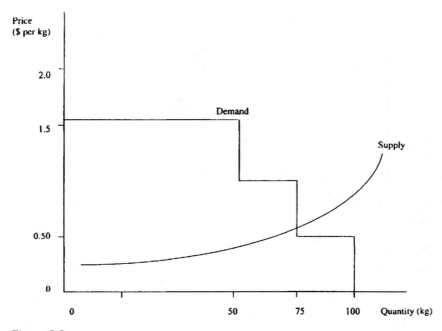

Figure 2.3
Competitive equilibrium in the market for tomatoes

The supply curve of the competitive market for tomatoes is upward-sloping, assuming as above a limited availability of land most suitable for growing tomatoes. The supply curve is identical to the social marginal cost curve.[9]

The competitive equilibrium price is the price that equates demand and supply. A higher price would elicit greater supply than demand. Suppliers would be stuck with non-revenue generating output, leading them to lower price until the competitive equilibrium was established. Price would be bid down until the market cleared. Similarly,

---

9 Each firm in the market is a price-taker not only with respect to tomatoes, the output, but also with respect to the prices of inputs such as land of a given quality. While the supply curve for tomatoes is upward-sloping due to limited availability of suitable land, an individual firm with constant returns to scale will perceive a flat marginal and average cost curve.

prices lower than market-clearing value cannot emerge as the competitive equilibrium price. The competitive equilibrium price and quantity, 60 cents per kg and 75 kg, are depicted in Figure 2.3.[10]

At the competitive equilibrium, the efficient quantity of output is traded: at the equilibrium the marginal social value of output and the marginal social cost of output are equated. Each economic agent, on either side of the market, reacts to the market price in determining its own demand or supply. The price translates the social marginal cost or benefit into a private cost or benefit for the agents, thus ensuring that each agent takes as his or her own interest the socially optimal decision 'as if guided by an invisible hand.'[11]

The benefits flowing from the market consist of consumer surplus and producer surplus. The former is the excess of each consumer's value for each unit purchased over the purchase price. For example, a consumer who would be willing to pay one dollar for a kilogram of tomatoes but pays only 60 cents is capturing 40 cents of surplus from the purchase of that kilogram. The producer surplus for each unit is the excess of price over the minimum price that would suffice to bring the unit to market. In our example of the tomato market, the producer surplus flows as income to the owners of inframarginal land – land more suitable to tomato growing than the marginal land. For example, if a particular plot of land can grow tomatoes at a cost of $5 per kilogram less than the marginal land from which supply is induced, then the surplus accruing to the owner of this land will be $5 per kilogram of tomatoes grown.

The competitive equilibrium maximizes the sum of consumer plus producer surplus, which is the area between the demand and supply curves (i.e., the marginal cost and marginal social value curves) in Figure 2.3.

The real world is not so ideal, of course. Features of real markets can prevent competitive markets and lead to differences between competi-

10 It is often useful to think of each competitive firm as having a single unit of a particular input, e.g. entrepreneurial talent. In this case, even if there are constant returns to scale at the industry level, the average cost curve at the individual firm level is U-shaped rather than flat. At the bottom of a U-shaped average cost curve, average cost is equal to marginal cost. This minimum average cost is the competitive price in such a market, since it is the only price consistent with zero economic profits. Thus even without constant returns to scale at the firm level, the competitive price equals marginal cost.

11 Adam Smith, *An Inquiry into the Nature and Causes of the Wealth of Nations* (Chicago: Encyclopaedia Britannica, Inc., 1952, vol. 39, Great Books of the Western World), 194.

tive prices and marginal social costs. The costs of information about product quality, the costs of searching for low prices, the costs of contracting to ensure delivery of the product are all costs no less real than the costs of production incorporated in the competitive model, but lead to market outcomes different from that described by the classical competitive market model. The economic foundations for competition policy are based on analysis of the consequences of a particular departure from competitive markets: the creation and exercise of market power.

IV. Monopoly

Consumers as a whole are willing to pay more for each unit of a product as the quantity available of the product declines. A firm that has control over the supply of a product therefore has the power to change the price of the product. Lowering the quantity will increase the price that can be charged. The control over the supply of a product, or a substantial portion of available quantity, is the essential requirement for market power over price. Market power is much more general than a pure monopoly, its extreme form. A restaurant or clothing retailer has some power over price because the demand for its product would not fall to zero if it were to raise price by 1 per cent and yet is not a monopolist. The consequences of market power, however, are illustrated most easily by considering the case of pure monopoly.

The monopolist is concerned with maximizing profits, the difference between revenues and costs. A firm that monopolized the tomato industry in our earlier example would inherit the marginal cost curve of the market, which is depicted in Figure 2.4. We must consider as well the marginal revenue the monopolist derives from selling additional output. The marginal revenue at any quantity is defined as the revenue that will be generated from the sale of one more unit of output. The marginal revenue at any quantity must lie below the price that clears demand at that quantity whenever demand is downward-sloping, that is whenever there is some market power. This follows from the fact that to sell an additional unit the monopolist must lower its price – not just on the additional unit but on all units.[12] The marginal revenue derived from selling an additional unit is the price at

---

12 The case where the monopolist can charge different prices for different units, price discrimination, is considered below.

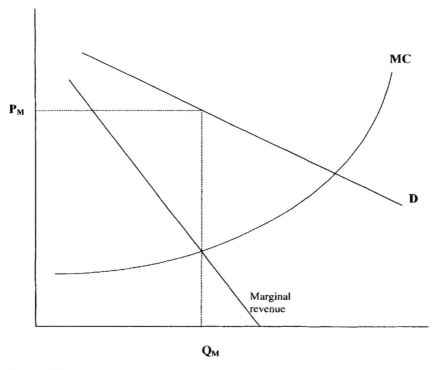

Figure 2.4
Monopoly price and output levels

which that unit can be sold minus the loss in revenue resulting from
the required reduction in price on the entire output.

Figure 2.4 depicts the marginal revenue curve of the monopolist as
well as the marginal cost curve and demand curve. The monopolist in
such a market maximizes profits by choosing the output at which marginal revenue equals marginal cost. This quantity is denoted as Q_M in
Figure 2.4. At any lower level of output, the monopolist could generate
additional profits by increasing its output by an additional unit, since
the marginal revenue generated by an additional unit exceeds marginal cost at lower levels of output. Similarly, producing a higher level
of output would involve sacrificing profits on marginal units because
the cost of those units would exceed the marginal revenue derived
from them.

Price

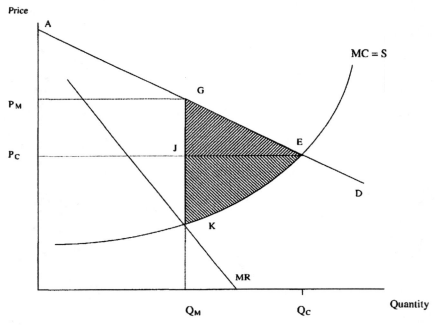

Figure 2.5
Welfare loss from monopoly

Figure 2.5 compares the competitive market solution and the monopoly solution. The monopolist, by setting quantity where marginal revenue equals marginal cost, instead of where price equals marginal cost, will supply less than the efficient, competitive outcome. The monopolist sets the price, P_M, at the level that allows the profit-maximizing quantity to be sold. At this price, consumer surplus is given by the area A P_M G. Consumer surplus is reduced relative to the competitive market by the area of the trapezoid $P_C P_M GE$. However, the major part of this trapezoid, the rectangle $P_C P_M GJ$, represents profit to the monopolist.[13] The attempt to capture as large a profit rectangle as pos-

---

13 The assumption here is that the monopolist is able to purchase or rent the tomato-growing land at rates reflecting the value of the land under competitive market conditions. If landowners are able to sell their land for a price greater than this, perhaps because two or more firms were competing for the 'right to be the monopolist,' then the landowners would capture some of the capitalized profit from monopoly. On the other hand, *monopsony* power by the single producer in the input market for land would translate into even greater profits than depicted in Figure 2.5.

sible is the entire goal of the monopolist. This profit is merely a transfer from consumers to the monopolist within this simple framework. A transfer among agents of the gains from exchange does not constitute a loss in economic efficiency in the market. The total efficiency loss from monopoly, commonly described as *dead-weight loss*, or 'the welfare loss triangle,' is GKE. The welfare loss triangle is the loss of surplus, consumer surplus plus producer surplus, on each unit of output between Q_M and Q_C.

An additional unit of production by the monopolist would entail both a change in profit and an increase in consumer surplus. The monopolist incorporates only the change in profit in its decision, ignoring the marginal gain to the consumer side of the market, and as a result produces less than the socially optimal quantity. The social cost of the monopoly distortion is entirely in the reduction of output in this framework, and the lost value of each unit of foregone output is the surplus that these units would have generated.[14]

It is useful to formulate the monopolist's problem algebraically, since this yields an important measure of the extent of market power. The monopolist's aim is to maximize profits. Profits can be expressed as $PQ - C(Q)$ where P and Q are price and quantity, and $C(Q)$ represents the total cost of producing Q units. Marginal revenue can be expressed as $d(PQ)/dQ = P + Q \cdot (dP/dQ)$, where dP/dQ represents the (negative) change in price that must be incurred to sell one more unit of quantity. Marginal revenue can also be expressed as $P \cdot (1 - 1/e)$ where e is the (positive) elasticity of demand.[15] Thus the marginal revenue is less than the current price to an extent that depends on the elasticity of demand. Setting marginal revenue equal to marginal cost,

---

14 It has been argued that the welfare triangle understates the problem of monopoly (Richard A. Posner, 'The Social Cost of Monopoly and Regulation,' (1975) 83 *Journal of Political Economy* 807). The existence of profits or rents anywhere in the economy will attract expenditure on the part of agents attempting to capture the rights to the rent. This is called rent-seeking. Posner argues that entry into the socially wasteful activity of rent-seeking will occur until the total expenditure equals the total amount of rents available. In the context of monopoly rents, this means that the entire rectangle of profits in Figure 2.5 must be added to the welfare triangle to arrive at a measure of the cost of monopoly. This is a useful point in the debate about the magnitude of monopoly distortions in the economy (relative to the resources spent on competition policy in reducing those distortions). For other competition policy questions, such as merger policy, however, the issue is somewhat less relevant.

15 This can be proved by evaluating dPQ/dp and using $e = |(P/Q) \cdot (dQ/dP)|$.

c, shows that at the monopolist's optimum,

$$\frac{p-c}{p} = \frac{1}{e} \qquad\qquad 2.1$$

That is, the percentage by which price exceeds marginal cost is equal to the inverse of demand elasticity.

The demand elasticity on the right-hand side of this equation is measured at the optimum price. This demand elasticity always exceeds 1.0; that is, a monopolist always sets price where the demand is elastic.[16] At a price where demand is inelastic, revenue, PQ, increases with price (because as price increases, quantity falls less than proportionately) so that the monopolist would increase revenue by raising price. Since costs fall with the increase in price, as a lower quantity is attracted, profits must rise.

For a competitive firm, this inverse is zero, since the competitive firm faces a flat or infinitely elastic demand curve. The extent to which the inverse exceeds zero, that is, the extent to which price exceeds marginal cost, is the 'Lerner measure of market power.'[17]

Note on 'Rents'

The terminology describing the benefits flowing to the suppliers in a market can be confusing. Six terms are used (and misused): Ricardian rents, quasi-rents, profits or 'pure' rents, accounting profits, and producer surplus. Ricardian rent refers to the income derived by owners of inframarginal factors of production available in limited amounts. Ricardian rent accrues to suppliers in most markets. In our earlier example of the tomato market, land that is particularly productive for growing tomatoes earns for its owner, whether the owner is the farmer or a landlord, a Ricardian rent above its value in the next best use. (We labelled these earnings producer surplus; in a competitive market these two concepts are identical.) In the market for legal services in competition cases, some lawyers are particularly well suited to the field relative to their next best alternatives because of inherent personal skills. A lawyer who bills $450 an hour doing competition law,

---

16 Demand is *elastic* if demand elasticity exceeds 1.0.
17 Abba Lerner, 'The Concept of Monopoly and the Measurement of Monopoly Power,' (1934) 1 *Review of Economic Studies* 157.

but could be induced to leave this fascinating field to practice, say, tax law if his or her rate were forced down to $350 per hour would be earning $100 per hour in Ricardian rents. Baseball players, to take another example, earn salaries that are in many cases almost entirely rent.[18] Nothing in the existence of Ricardian rents contradicts the competitiveness of a market. Ricardian rents reflect a return to inherent, market-specific attributes of factors of production.

If a competition lawyer's high hourly rate relative to the next best alternative, however, is the result entirely of specific investment in human capital in competition law (rather than a preference for or a genetic talent in competition law) then the extra $100 per hour is more properly viewed as a return on that investment. This type of return is referred to as a 'quasi-rent,' rather than a Ricardian rent.

Pure rents or profits refer to the excess of revenue over costs that is due to barriers to entry into a market. A firm that acquires and maintains a monopoly position in a market not through particular acumen in meeting the demands of consumers but through anticompetitive, exclusionary practices earns pure profits. Not surprisingly, the distinction among quasi-rents, Ricardian rents, and pure rents in practice is as controversial as competition policy itself. Does Microsoft earn pure rents, or does its income represent only the return to the brilliant investment decisions in meeting buyers' needs, combined with luck? The enormous size of the return relative to the initial investment does not prove that the return is pure monopoly rent. A firm that invests in research and development and acquires exclusive intellectual property rights to a brand name, process, or product may be rewarded with a realized return that is very high *ex post*. Competition in innovation and investment in becoming the dominant firm in a market, however, can lead to very small expected economic profits *ex ante*.

Rents refer in general to the return earned by a factor in excess of the minimum return necessary to attract the factor to a particular market or to induce the factor to remain in the market. Quasi-rents are not true rents, because the anticipation of quasi-rents *is* necessary to attract specific investment to a market. To express this differently, if pure rents or

---

18 An exception would be Deion Sanders, who played both baseball and football professionally and could have focused more intensively on football were it not for his baseball career. The opportunity cost of his baseball career may have been millions of dollars per year.

Ricardian rents on one side of a market are reduced through a distortion in the market, such as the exercise of market power on the other side of the market, the allocation of resources may be unaffected. For quasi-rents, however, this is true only *ex post*. If the extraction of quasi-rents is anticipated at the time of the investment, the incentives to invest will be compromised.

Economic profits must be further distinguished from accounting profits, such as are reported in financial statements. Economic profits refer to revenues minus *all* opportunity costs, including the opportunity cost of capital. The opportunity cost of capital is defined as the return that could be earned on investments of similar risk.[19] Accounting profits are gross of the cost of capital. This distinction is important because 'profits' to business persons refers to accounting profits, not economic profits.

As discussed earlier in this chapter, producer surplus is distinguished from economic profit by the inclusion of rents to owners of factors (inputs) that are fixed in supply. The producer surplus accruing to sellers in a typical agricultural market is comprised not of profits (these being close to zero in agricultural markets) but rather of rents to the owners of land that is particularly suitable for the commodity being marketed.

Finally, it is important to distinguish between *ex post* or realized profits and *ex ante* or expected profits. A pharmaceutical company may earn $100 million of net revenue per year on a drug that cost only $150 million to develop, but the expectation may have been that there was only a 10 per cent chance that the development of the drug would be successful. A very high measured profit for a firm, even when the cost of capital is properly accounted for, does not demonstrate the existence of excessive profits or rents. (These returns would, however, be quasi-rents.)

The empirical distinction among various kinds of rent in specific cases is contentious and almost impossible to determine precisely, and yet is often important in competition policy. Did the exclusionary practices allegedly used by Microsoft to suppress the market share of its

---

19 The opportunity cost of capital refers to the rate of return that could be earned on an amount of funds equal to the replacement cost of assets in place. Sometimes the opportunity cost of capital is mistakenly defined as the rate of return that could be earned on an amount of funds equal to the market value of the assets in place. In this case, 'economic profits' is defined away, since the market value incorporates the discounted value of future profits.

competitors in the browser and operating systems markets represent legitimate protection of the quasi-rents earned by Microsoft on its investment in the development of its operating system or simply the protection of pure monopoly rents in excess of what was necessary to justify this investment? To what extent will the decrease in the return earned by Microsoft as a result of the U.S. government's antitrust action against it inhibit the investment in similar software ventures in the future? These are not easy questions, although as a matter of law the protection of profits against competition is never in itself a sufficient justification for an exclusionary practice. In the simple models of economic textbooks economic profits or pure rents can be taxed, or decreased through competition policy, with no detrimental long-run effect on output. In reality, measured profits virtually always represent quasi-rents to some degree.

V. Perfectly Discriminating Monopolist and Contracting on Quantities

In the simple monopoly model presented above, it is assumed that the monopolist must set the same price for all consumers. In Chapter 5, we shall discuss cases where firms set different prices for different customers. This is referred to as price discrimination. A firm with market power has the incentive to engage in price discrimination providing it can distinguish among classes of buyers with different elasticities and these buyers cannot resell the product. The optimal price-discriminating monopoly price for each class of buyers is provided by equation 2.1, with the elasticities on the right-hand side varying across the classes.

Price discrimination does not generally carry the negative connotation that the word 'discrimination' would suggest. Most individuals would not find allowing senior citizens and children into movie theatres or onto ski slopes at lower prices objectionable on fairness grounds. The efficiency analysis of price discrimination is taken up in Chapter 5.

The extreme case of price discrimination is perfect price discrimination, the case in which a separate price can be charged for each unit. Assuming that the monopolist knows the value derived by consumers from each unit, that is, the demand price for each unit, charging this value extracts the entire surplus from the transaction. The surplus accruing to a perfect price-discriminating monopolist from selling a particular quantity is the total social surplus generated by that quantity, that is, the area between the marginal cost curve and the demand curve up to that quantity.

The profit-maximizing output under perfect price discrimination is identical to the competitive output, since this output maximizes the social surplus, which is the area between the demand or marginal social value curve and the marginal cost curve of Figure 2.1. There is no inefficiency in this case. The monopolist in capturing the entire social surplus will choose, efficiently, the quantity that maximizes the surplus. The problem of maximizing social efficiency becomes completely internalized in the maximization of profits.

Efficiency in a monopolized market does not *require*, however, that the monopolist be perfectly price discriminating. Suppose that the monopolist and each consumer can contract not just on price but on the quantity the consumer will purchase. That is, instead of assuming that the monopolist decides on a price with the consumer subsequently deciding on quantity, consider a market where the monopolist and each consumer sign a contract for the price-quantity pair. In this case, if the monopolist knows each consumer's value of the product, the monopolist and the consumer will agree to exchange the quantity that maximizes total surplus from the transaction – that is, the efficient quantity for the consumer. The parties will bargain or disagree only over the division of the surplus as determined by the price (i.e. on the total payment by the consumer to the monopolist). The total surplus from the transaction can be represented as the area between the individual consumer's demand curve and the monopolist's marginal cost curve. The negotiations between consumer and the monopolist may or may not leave all surplus with the monopolist.[20] Typically, however, the consumer will capture some of the surplus. In the case where the monopolist captures, say, two-thirds of the surplus, the price charged for each unit is described by a curve positioned between the marginal cost curve and the demand curve. This is depicted as the dotted line in Figure 2.6, for the case of a monopolist with a constant marginal cost curve. The total profits, given by the area between this pricing curve and the marginal cost curve, will be maximized at the efficient, competitive output. In markets where transactions are governed by contracts that include

20 The monopolist, engaging in many such transactions, typically has the higher incentive to invest in techniques that will allow it to commit to a take-it-or-leave-it offer. One such technique is to hire an agent with an incentive scheme that provides no reward unless the transaction price is 100 per cent of the maximum price that the buyer would willingly pay.

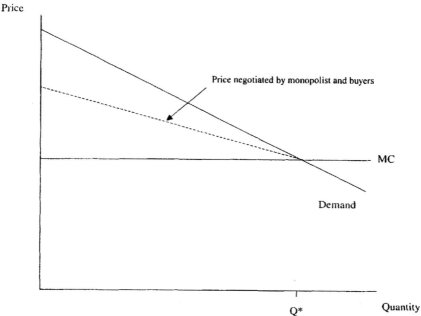

Figure 2.6
Negotiations on price and quantity lead to efficiency

price as well as quantity, there should be less of a presumption that market power leads to inefficiency.[21]

Both the perfect price discrimination model and its generalization, however, fail if buyers must invest in market-specific capital prior to entering the monopolist's market. This is generally the case in input markets; an example would be the investment spent on research and

---

21 The possibility that monopoly outputs can be efficient covers a third case, in addition to the two cases of perfect price discrimination and contracting on prices and quantities. If a contract with the monopolist establishes for each buyer a two-part price, whereby the consumer pays a fixed fee or lump sum for the right to buy the product and a variable price for each unit, then total surplus will be maximized. The two parties to the contract will establish a variable price equal to the monopolist's marginal cost (knowing that this will elicit the efficient quantity decision by the consumer under the contract) and bargain over the fixed fee. Any of the three mechanisms for an efficient monopoly – perfect price discrimination, contracting on prices and quantities, or two-part pricing – require both perfect knowledge about demand on the part of the monopolist and the absence of a resale market. With a perfect resale market, the only monopoly outcome is the standard uniform-pricing outcome depicted in Figure 2.4.

development of a product prior to buying an input into production from the monopolist. The monopolist will face a downward-sloping demand curve from buyers who are already in the market, having invested in specific capital. Extracting the entire surplus, or a large fraction of the surplus, from these buyers does not distort the quantity purchased from them. The buyers' surplus in this case, however, is merely a quasi-rent: the knowledge of buyers at the time of investment in capital that they will face a discriminating monopolist once in the market renders them reluctant to make the investment. The social cost of monopoly in this case is the distortion in buyers' investment prior to purchasing the monopolized product.

VI. Monopolistic Competition

Market power, defined as the ability to influence price by restricting output, is ubiquitous. A single restaurant will not lose all of its business by raising price by 1 per cent, for example. Yet there are hundreds of restaurants in a sizable city. The downward slope of the demand curve facing each restaurant derives not from its large size in the restaurant market, but from the differentiation between it and other restaurants. A small increase in price will leave the firm serving most of its clients because the customers prefer this restaurant, for at least some meals, to all other restaurants. Restaurants are differentiated by their locations as well as their decors, their menus, and the quality of food and service. On the cost side, entry barriers into the restaurant business are low, in the sense that there are only small or moderate costs to establishing a new restaurant. There are, however, substantial fixed costs incurred each month of maintaining a restaurant of given capacity, especially the rent of the restaurant location. The fixed costs, combined with a flat or upward-sloping marginal cost curve, give the restaurant an average-cost curve that is initially downward-sloping. Such an average cost curve is depicted in Figure 2.7.

A market with many small firms, fixed costs and low barriers to entry, and differentiated products is characterized by the economic model of monopolistic competition. In a monopolistically competitive market, as originally conceived by Edward Chamberlin,[22] entry occurs until the share of each firm in the market allows it to cover costs at its optimum

---

22 E.H. Chamberlin, *The Theory of Monopolistic Competition* (Cambridge, Mass.: Harvard University Press, 1933).

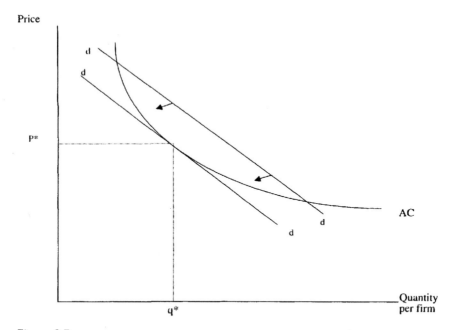

Figure 2.7
Equilibrium under monopolistic competition

quantity, but not to make economic profit. The monopolistically competitive equilibrium can be envisioned by starting with a monopoly diagram, as in Figure 2.7, with the demand curve d-d in the diagram representing the demand facing a single representative firm rather than the demand for the entire market. The profit earned by the representative firm attracts entry into the market. When entry occurs, the increase in the number of firms in the markets leaves each firm with a smaller demand. This is represented by a shift to the left of the individual firm demand curve in Figure 2.7. Entry occurs, and the representative firm's demand curve shifts left, until the maximum profits that can be achieved are zero. This occurs when the demand curve is tangent to the firm's average cost curve. The price at this tangency elicits a demand that allows the firm to cover costs (including, as always, a normal return to capital). No price allows positive profits for the firm represented in this diagram.

The description of a market, such as restaurants or retailing clothing stores, as involving market power on the part of every one of dozens of firms in the market, yet prices that just cover costs, may appear confusing to the antitrust practitioner. The source of the possible confusion lies in the fact that two definitions of market power are in common use. The first, which we have adopted here, refers to the power to raise price by restricting output, or equivalently the profitability of pricing above marginal cost. A second use of the term market power involves the ability to price above average cost, that is, to make a profit in an industry. Within the meaning of the second term, firms in a monopolistically competitive industry with no barriers to entry do not exercise market power.

As a matter of descriptive reality, all firms in a monopolistically competitive industry are not identical. Nor do all firms earn zero producer surplus (economic profits plus rent) as one might suppose. A restaurant that is particularly innovative, interesting, or of high quality may make positive measured (accounting) profit in excess of the normal rate of return to the physical capital invested. If the owner's time and entrepreneurial skill could be employed to earn the same measured 'profit' elsewhere, then their use involves an opportunity cost that reduces the economic profit to zero, and also leaves no rents with the owner. In this case, both the economic profit and the owner's surplus would be zero. To the extent, however, that the measured profits are attributable to a special talent of the owner specific to the restaurant business, then these measured profits do comprise positive producer surplus – but this entire surplus is properly defined as a (Ricardian) rent to the market-specific talent. Economic profits would be zero, but the rent would be positive.

VII. Oligopoly: Static Models

Oligopoly describes the industry structure that lies between the one-firm monopoly and the many-firm structures of competition or monopolistic competition. In an oligopoly, the number of firms is small enough that each firm, if it is to maximize profits rationally, must take into account the anticipated pricing behaviour of each of its rivals.

There is no single theory predicting the economic outcome of an oligopoly, as there is for the competitive or monopolistic market structures. Economists have a wide variety of oligopoly models. According to some models, the monopoly price may be sustained through a successful cartel among the oligopolists. The prediction of others is competitive prices, even with only two firms in the market. A prominent result of dynamic oligopoly theory is the 'folk theorem': in the case of a duopoly *any* profit levels between the competitive level of zero and the monopoly profit can be sustained as the outcome of rational decision making by both firms in an infinite-period model, with sufficiently low discount rates. The range of predictions is consistent with the observation that in reality 'anything can happen' in oligopoly. As Scherer and Ross point out, some oligopolistic industries succeed in maintaining prices well above production costs for years, while others engage in frequent periods of intense price competition.[23] In the summer of 1988, Coca Cola and Pepsi controlled over 65 per cent of the market for cola in Phoenix, Arizona, yet the prices for a six-pack of cola fell to 59 cents, barely covering the cost of the aluminum cans.[24]

The economic analysis of oligopolies fall into two broad classes: those that analyse oligopolistic markets in which firms do not cooperate, that is, thus do not establish explicit or tacit agreements; and those that study the ability of oligopolists to sustain such agreements. We sketch a version of the noncooperative oligopoly theory here, and in Chapter 3 discuss the conditions that facilitate coordination by oligopolists on prices. Noncooperative theory is applicable to the analysis of the 'unilateral effects' of a merger; the cooperative theory is applicable to merger analysis under the 'increased interdependence' theory.

A common noncooperative oligopoly model starts with an assumption that firms compete on the basis of prices.[25] We develop this model in the simple case of two firms – a duopoly – allowing the products to be differentiated. The specification of the demand side of such a market starts with the observation that the demand for either firm's product depends on the prices charged by both firms. An equilibrium or predicted outcome for the duopoly is taken to be a pair of prices charged by the respective firms, such that given the price set by the rival, either firm's price maximizes its own profits.

To describe this outcome, we need the concept of a 'best response' on the part of a firm to the price set by its rival. If we fix the price of its rival at some level, the demand curve for the duopolist is determined. The duopolist then faces demand and cost curves as depicted in the monopoly diagram, Figure 2.4. The optimal price in this diagram is the duopolist's best response to its rival's price. If its rival's price were to

---

23 F.M. Scherer and David Ross, *Industrial Market Structure and Economic Performance* (Boston: Houghton Mifflin, 1990), 199.

24 Ibid., n 1.

25 This is referred to in the economic literature at the *Bertrand* assumption. The *Cournot* model of oligopoly takes as the strategic instruments the quantities chosen by firms, assuming that once these quantities are chosen the market price that will prevail is the price at which the total quantity is demanded.

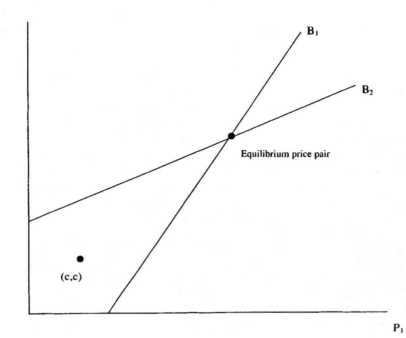

Figure 2.8
Static oligopoly equilibrium with price competition and differentiated products

increase, the demand facing the duopolist would increase, and typically become less elastic at any price. The optimal response by the
duopolist would therefore be to raise price in response to a price
increase by its rival.

If we label the two firms 1 and 2, then the best response of firm 1 to
any price set by firm 2 can be summarized by its 'best response curve,'
B_1, in Figure 2.8. This curve provides the relationship between the price
set by firm 2 and the profit-maximizing price set by firm 1. Firm 2's
best response curve can be described analogously, and is represented
by the curve B_2 in Figure 2.8. The equilibrium outcome in the duopoly
model is the pair of prices for which the price by each firm is the individually rational response to price set by the other firm – that is, the
intersection of the two best response curves.

Two properties of the resulting duopoly outcome are worth noting:
First, the pair of prices lies above the competitive levels of marginal

cost, indicated by the pair (c,c) in Figure 2.8. This is because the demand curve for each firm slopes downward, due to the product differentiation. As the products become more similar, however, the prices converge to the marginal cost levels: in a duopoly with identical products and competition on the basis of prices, 'two is enough' to generate the competitive outcome. Any price greater than marginal cost would not be sustained with identical products, because the rival would find it profitable to undercut this price by one cent. This would attract all demand in the market. The closer the products, the more intense the price competition.

Second, both prices are less than the monopoly price, provided that there is *some* substitutability (a non-zero cross-elasticity of demand) between the two products. Each firm sets its price below the monopoly price, to the detriment of its rival, because it does not incorporate into its own decision the loss in profit imposed on its rival when price is lowered below the monopoly level. As the products become more distant substitutes, this competitive externality becomes small, and the duopoly prices approach the monopoly prices.

VIII. Oligopoly: Dynamics

The static models of oligopoly, in considering only independent behaviour by firms, beg the key issue in actual oligopolistic markets: to what extent can firms collude on pricing and thus share monopoly profits rather than earn only noncooperative oligopoly profits? Dynamic models allow us to consider the stability of any cartel agreement by examining the costs and benefits to cheating on an agreement faced by a cartel member.

In the simplest dynamic model, a small number of identical firms can cooperate, setting the monopoly price, providing that it is in the individual interest of each firm to continue cooperating. If an individual firm finds it profitable to cheat on the agreement by undercutting the monopoly price then the agreement collapses and the firms compete, earning non-cooperative profits indefinitely. The incentives to cheat depend on the flow of profits a firm can make by undercutting its cartel partners and how long it takes for its partners to detect the cheating. Thus, if we accept that firms will collude when they can, the market outcome is either a shared monopoly, if the agreement is robust to the possibility of cheating, or noncooperative pricing from the outset, if firms know that an agreement could not be sustained.

The incentives to cheat on a cartel are illustrated in Figure 2.9. This

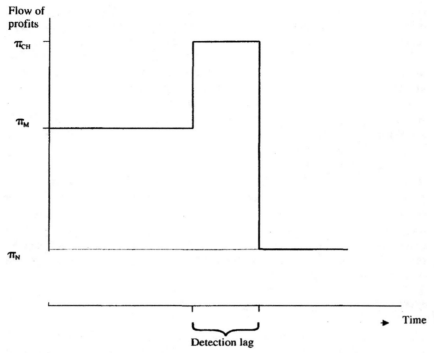

Figure 2.9
Incentive to cheat on a cartel

figure represents the flow of profits to an individual firm over time at the shared monopoly level (π_M), at a level that the firm would earn by cheating on the agreement (π_{CH}), and at the noncooperative level (π_N). The cheating profits represent the gains that an individual firm could capture by setting a price lower than the monopoly level. As long as the other cartel members do not detect the cheating, the deviant firm will gain. In Figure 2.9, the anticipated period to detection is indicated. Following detection of any cheating the cartel is assumed to break down, with the result that the individual firm's profits revert to the returns from the non-cooperative outcome reviewed in the previous section. These may be the profits resulting from price competition among producers of differentiated products, for example.

Cheating is profitable if the present value of the short-run gains from cheating to an individual firm exceed the long-run losses to the firm from the break-up of the cartel. Only two outcomes are possible in this simple model. If the detection period is short, the profits from cheating small, and the discount rate low, then cheating will not pay. Firms will share monopoly profits via an implicit or explicit cartel agreement.[26] Otherwise, firms would know that any pricing agreement would be rendered unstable by the incentives to cheat and an agreement would not be struck. The market price would be constant over time at the noncooperative level.

The simple model can be used to capture some elements of cartel stability, as we will discuss in Chapter 3, but represents only a glimpse into the economics of oligopoly dynamics. Two classes of extensions are particularly important. The first is an extension of the firms' strategy sets. The model assumes that firms have only two strategies: (1) price cooperatively unless cheating on the part of another firm is detected, then price non-cooperatively; (2) deviate from the cartel monopoly price by optimally undercutting the cartel price, then price non-cooperatively once other firms respond to the deviation. The theory of oligopoly pricing dynamics under certainty considers firms as competing in an infinite sequence of discrete time periods in which only one price level is set in each period. For example, firms may set a price at the beginning of each day. In this theory, a firm could set its price contingent on the entire history of past prices (assuming that all past prices are observable); the set of all such contingent plans is the full set of strategies available to firms. Examples of such strategies are the 'tit-for-tat' strategy in a duopoly, in which a firm matches its rival's strategy (cooperate or not) from the most recent period, and various punishment strategies. A dominant firm may choose to punish any deviant from an agreement by lowering price even below cost for a number of periods after the deviation is detected. An important possibility allowed in the richer model is that firms may attempt to re-establish a cartel agreement that has been dormant for some time.

The economic literature on dynamic oligopoly pricing under certainty yields some necessary conditions for cartel stability. For example, the discount rate must be sufficiently low that cheating on a monopoly agreement does not pay. If a firm values near-term profits highly relative to more distant future profits, it will always cheat on a

---

26 The model is too simple to distinguish between implicit and explicit cartel agreements.

cartel. The necessary conditions, however, are too weak to be practically useful in most cases. For example, if firms can set prices each day or each week, the day or week becomes a 'period' in the application of the model; the discount rate that corresponds to realistic interest rates is then extremely low. On the other hand, in markets where transactions are large and very infrequent – for example defence procurement – the length of a 'period' may be large enough that the necessary conditions have some bite in predicting where collusion is not possible.

Regarding sufficient conditions for cartel stability, the theory is empty. The most prominent result of the theory is the 'folk theorem,' according to which any outcome between competitive pricing and cartel pricing inclusive is consistent with rational behaviour on the part of firms.[27] The theorem means that economic theory has no predictions to offer on the fundamental question of whether repeated interaction among firms (or any entities involved in a situation of conflict of interest) will lead to greater cooperation. On the other hand, the result seems consistent with the wide range of outcomes observed in markets with few sellers, from stable cartels in some markets to intense competition in markets such as the market for cola soft drinks, in which there are only two important sellers.[28]

The second important extension of the simple model of oligopoly dynamics is the introduction of uncertainty in costs or demand. With fluctuations in these basic supply and demand conditions, the detection of cheating becomes more difficult. A firm may not be able to identify whether a sharp drop in its demand is due to cheating on an agreement by a rival firm or to a drop in demand. Jerry Green and

---

27 Formally, in the context of a duopoly, if discount rates are small enough then any pair of pay-offs (present value of profits) for the two firms between the noncooperative and cooperative pay-off levels can be supported as an equilibrium by some pair of strategies.

28 The theory of oligopoly dynamics in markets with finite time (a finite number of periods) predicts a single outcome with rational players: noncooperative pricing. Firms know that in the last period of interaction the outcome will be noncooperative, since there is no reason for an individual firm to refrain from pursuing only its individual short-run interest. In the second-to-last period, therefore, firms will again price noncooperatively, since they know that whatever the outcome in that period, the final period will involve noncooperative pricing. Application of this logic shows that in every period the pricing will be noncooperative – even if the number of periods is, say, 10 billion. Experimental evidence shows, however, that cooperation does emerge in the finitely repeated game, even with very sophisticated players (R. Axelrod, *The Evolution of Cooperation* [New York: Basic Books, 1984]).

Robert Porter have analysed the dynamics of cartel pricing under these conditions and Porter has applied the analysis to study an 1880s railroad cartel.[29] The outcome of interaction under these conditions involves periodic price wars, or fluctuations between periods of stable cartel pricing and noncooperative pricing.

IX. Monopsony

The exercise of market power on the buyers' side of a market – in the extreme case, a single buyer or monopsonist – leads to an inefficient outcome, just as market power does on the sellers' side of a market. The monopsony outcome is illustrated in Figure 2.10. As the monopsonist increases the amount purchased of a product, the total expenditure by the monopsonist on the product will, naturally, increase. The optimal purchase by the monopsonist maximizes the monopsonist's total value of the amount purchased (which may be the value of the product in consumption or, more commonly, the value of the product as an input into further production) minus the total expenditure. This optimum is determined by equating the marginal value of the product and the marginal expenditure of the product.

Whereas the monopsonist chooses quantity to equate its marginal value to marginal expenditure, the social optimum or surplus-maximizing quantity equates marginal value to marginal social cost (which is depicted by the supply curve, since the supply price measures the marginal social cost of production).[30] The monopsonist purchases a quantity that is too small to maximize total surplus. The distortion in the monopsony purchase arises because at any output, the marginal expenditure exceeds the supply price of the product. The marginal expenditure is higher than the supply price because to elicit an additional unit of supply the monopsonist must raise the price paid on all units, not just on the marginal unit.

The *socially* optimal transaction would involve equating the marginal value with the supply curve, or marginal social cost curve. As

29 E.J. Green and R.H. Porter, 'Noncooperative Collusion Under Imperfect Price Information,' (1984) 14 *Econometrica* 87, and R.H. Porter, 'A Study of Cartel Stability: The Joint Executive Committee, 1880–1886,' (1983) 14 *Bell Journal of Economics* 301.

30 This assumes that there are no distortions in the monoposonist's decisions other than monopsony power, e.g., that the monopsonist is not also a monopolist in an output market.

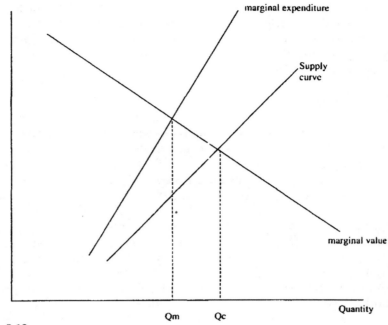

Figure 2.10
Monopsony

Figure 2.10 illustrates, the monopsonist's private optimum, equalizing marginal value with marginal expenditure, involves a quantity that is too low to maximize social welfare. Starting from zero, as the quantity purchased increases, the monopsonist gains some marginal surplus of value over expenditure and the suppliers gain some marginal surplus of expenditure (revenue) over cost. The monopsonist ignores the latter component of the marginal social value of production and as a result, like the monopolist discussed earlier in this chapter, chooses a quantity that is too small. The analysis of the monopsonist reminds us that inefficiencies associated with market power arise from insufficient quantities, not excessive prices. Low prices are not the ultimate goal of competition policy.

X. Market Definition

Market definition is key in both the law on mergers, sections 91 to 103 of the Canadian *Competition Act*, as well as in other sections of the Act, such as section 50 (price discrimination), section 77 (exclusive dealing, tied sales and market restrictions), and especially section 79 (abuse of dominance). The economics of market definition can be discussed most clearly with a focus on mergers, with extensions to other issues. Merger analysis is discussed extensively in Chapter 4.

Section 92 of the Act allows the Competition Tribunal to prohibit or dissolve a merger, or to require disposition of assets, where the merger or proposed merger is likely to lessen competition substantially. A merger is more likely to lessen competition, that is, to create or enhance market power, where it results in a concentrated market, a market in which a few firms sell most of the output. Merger analysis therefore starts with the identification of the relevant market in which the merging firms compete.

A market is defined in two dimensions, the set of products to be included in the relevant market and the geographic area served by the market. To define a product market in which a firm competes, we start with a product sold by the firm then add to the market all sufficiently close substitutes to the firm's product. Whether a product is a sufficiently close substitute to the merging firms' products is defined in terms of the product's potential to impose competitive discipline on the merged firm by attracting buyers away from the firm if it were to raise prices.

The hypothetical monopolist approach adopted in the *Merger Enforcement Guidelines* (MEGs)[31] is consistent with this approach. Under the hypothetical monopolist approach, we start with the product produced by the merging firm, then add products to the market, in order of closeness of substitution to the merged firm's product, until the point at which a (hypothetical) single supplier of all the products included so far could profit from a small but significant non-transitory increase in price. In both the Canadian and U.S. MEGs 'small but significant' is interpreted as 5 per cent; in the Canadian MEGs 'non-transitory' means for at least one year. The product is not expanded further than necessary to meet this condition. In particular, if a single supplier of the entire supply of the firm's product could profitably raise its price by a small but significant amount, the product market definition should not extend beyond that product. For example, if we are considering a merger between two producers of personal computers, we would not extend the product market definition beyond personal computers to

---

31 (Ottawa: Supply and Services Canada, 1991).

mainframe computers. A hypothetical supplier of all personal computers would be able to raise its price by a significant amount despite the
substitution (to a small degree) by consumers to mainframe computers

One class of evidence that can be used in merger cases to estimate the
substitutability of products is detailed price and quantity data from past
transactions for both the product at issue and the products hypothesized
to be in the same market. If these data are available, the cross-elasticity
of demand, the most direct measure of substitutability can be estimated
directly. The cross-elasticity of demand between two goods refers to the
percentage response in the demand for one of the goods when the other
good increases in price by 1 per cent. This elasticity is high for goods that
should be considered as competing in the same market.

Estimating cross-elasticities directly is uncommon because of the
general lack of adequate data. Methods of inferring cross-elasticity
indirectly are available, however. These include in particular evidence
on the functional substitutability of the products. For each important
use that the focal product has, can other products serve as cost-effective substitutes? Do buyers frequently switch between the products?
Do buyers tend to use one product or the other, or both simultaneously? We can also rely on evidence from business documents of the
transacting parties: whom do these documents recognize as the firms'
competitors in developing competitive business strategy? And we can
use evidence from buyers' testimony on whether they would have
strong competitive alternatives to a merged firm's products. These are
the questions that must be addressed with evidence on substitutability
of products. The underlying principle to which these pieces of evidence must be linked is that a product should be included in the market if it is a sufficiently close substitute to the focal product that a
hypothetical firm owning all closer substitutes could not increase its
price by a significant amount for a non-transitory period.

While cross-elasticities of demand provide evidence of whether two
items are close substitutes, it should be noted that it is ultimately the
own-price elasticity of demand of a hypothetical producer of a group
of products that determines whether that group of products constitutes
a market.[32] In particular, the relevant question is whether the own-
price demand elasticity of a group of products is sufficiently low that a

---

32 See G. Werden, 'Demand Elasticities in Antitrust Analysis,' (1998) 66 *Antitrust L.J.*
363.

small but significant non-transitory price increase would be profitable for a single firm monopolizing this market. (Recall that the Lerner expression for the optimal mark-up of price over cost involves the own-price demand elasticity of the seller.) The own-price elasticity conveys whether there are important competitive substitutes not included in a proposed product market: if there are such substitutes, demand is relatively elastic; if there are not, demand is relatively inelastic. Own-price elasticity of demand relates to key issues for competition policy: the existence of competition and the exercise or potential exercise of market power through higher prices. Therefore, as noted by the Competition Tribunal in *Superior Propane*,[33] own-price elasticity of demand is particularly helpful in defining the market.

Cross-price elasticity of demand, however, remains important to the inquiry for two reasons. First, if cross-elasticities between a group of products and producers outside the group are high, the own-price demand elasticity of a hypothetical seller of the group of products will also be high; quantitative or qualitative evidence on cross-elasticities is generally more readily available than evidence on the more directly relevant own-price elasticity. Second, cross-price elasticities of demand will suggest what products ought to be added to an insufficiently broad proposed market. That is, if a product market narrowly defined would face own-price demand so elastic that a non-transitory price increase would be unprofitable, it is necessary to include other goods in the market definition. Cross-price elasticities between the proposed market and other goods direct the analyst to the next closest substitute for inclusion in the defined market.

The geographic dimension of product market definition is also determined using a hypothetical monopolist test. A single firm may operate in a number of different geographical markets. Given the relevant product market, a geographic market in a merger case is defined as the minimum area within which a hypothetical, single producer of the relevant product could impose a small but significant, non-transitory increase in price. Again, the market definition is expanded as far as necessary to allow the hypothetical monopolist enough market power to raise the price by a significant amount but no further.

The first kind of evidence to be turned to in geographic market definition is transportation costs, relative to product prices. If the transpor-

---

33 *Superior Propane Inc., supra*, note 2, at paras. 61–3.

tation costs between two regions are a tiny fraction of price, the regions would be included in the same geographic market. Two additional types of tests are sometimes used for delineating geographic markets: shipments tests and price tests. Suppose that there are only two geographic regions at issue: region A and region B. Two firms in region A are merging, and the issue is whether firms producing in region B should be included in the relevant geographic market. In the context of Canadian cases, 'A' could be Canada, and 'B' could be the United States. The Elzinga-Hogarty test specifies two criteria, based on shipments data, that are *necessary* for delineation of a given area as a geographic market: 'little in from outside' (LIFO) and 'little out from inside' (LOFI).[34] If these criteria fail, in that there are substantial shipments between areas A and B, then A is not an geographic market. A number of authors have proposed tests based on the behaviour of prices in different geographic regions.[35] A necessary condition for two regions to fall in the same geographic area is that the prices move together, with the difference in the prices approximating the marginal transportation cost of shipment between the two regions. In terms of our example, a *sufficient* condition for region A to be a relevant market is evidence of substantial divergence (a lack of correlation) in price movements between regions A and B in the relevant product.

Regarding the use of these tests in cases, we naturally expect merging parties to argue for empirical failure of the necessary condition for the narrow market. Evidence in favour of the sufficient condition, divergent price dynamics, supports the challenge of the merger as substantially lessening competition. Of course, the evidence may show that the necessary condition holds (i.e., that there are few shipments between A and B) but the sufficient condition fails (i.e., that prices follow very similar patterns in regions A and B); in this case, the pair of tests is indeterminate. Scheffman and Spiller describe an alternative approach, the estimation of residual demands, that circumvents this difficulty.[36] Full estimation of demands allows direct implementation

---

34 Keneth Elzina and Thomas Hogarty, 'The Problem of Geographic Market Delineation in Antimerger Suits,' (1973) 18 *Antitrust Bulletin* 45.

35 These are discussed in David Scheffman and Pablo Spiller, 'Geographic Market Definition Under the U.S. Department of Justice Merger Guidelines,' (1987) 30 *Journal of Law and Economics* 123.

36 Scheffman and Spiller, 'Geographic Market Definition Under the U.S. Department of Justice Merger Guidelines.'

of the hypothetical monopolist test for both the product market definition and the geographic ma. ket definition.

Once the market is defined, one must address the question of which firms to include as participants in the market. The answer to this question depends on supply responses. If particular firms not currently producing a close substitute for the focal product have the capability of switching at very low cost to the production of these substitutes, and would be induced to supply these substitutes if a merged firm were to raise its price by a small but significant amount, then these firms are included in the market. Firms capable of very quick supply responses such as this are called 'uncommitted entrants.' An uncommitted entrant in the market for automobile hubcaps, for example, could be a firm that is engaged in sheet metal stamping but is not currently producing hubcaps.

Pitfalls in Market Definition

A number of potential traps, or pitfalls, await a less-than-careful development of the market definition in a competition case. The first trap to be avoided in arriving at a market definition is the 'cellophane trap.'[37] In the *Cellophane* case, the U.S. Supreme Court defined the market as flexible wrapping materials on the basis of evidence of a high cross-elasticity of demand.[38] It seems likely that what the court meant by a high cross-elasticity of demand was that there was some substitution between cellophane and other flexible wrapping material at the current price of cellophane. If so, then the court's conclusion on market definition was in error. In evaluating whether a firm has monopoly power in a market it is not enough to examine whether buyers have close substitutes at the current prices charged by the firm. If the firm is already in a monopoly position, it will have priced products to the point where there are substitutes available: a firm can always increase price to this point without suffering loss in demand. The relevant question for market definition is the set of products that are close substitutes for the focal product at its competitive price.

The second common failing of market definition analysis is to argue

---

37 See William Landes and Richard Posner, 'Market Power in Antitrust Cases,' (1981) 94 *Harvard Law Review* 937.

38 See *United States v. E.I. du Pont de Nemours & Co.*, 351 U.S. 377 at 399–400 (1956).

simply that 'there are substitutes for X, therefore the producer of X does not have market power.' One might conclude that there are many avenues for reaching consumers with advertising messages, therefore yellow pages directories do not constitute a separate market. Or, in analysing mergers of radio stations (which produce the delivery of radio advertisements) one might conclude that radio advertising is not a separate market, because televisions and newspapers are available as alternatives and account for much more advertising revenue than radio. In the *Nielsen* case,[39] the director of investigation and research argued that a relevant market consisted of marketing information derived from the data recorded from scanners at grocery store checkouts; Nielsen's response was in part that there are many sources of information about market demand.

Market power is not determined simply by the number of substitutes, and a market cannot be considered too small simply because many substitutes are available. The existence of *close* substitutes is the key to expanding the appropriate market definition. (Of course, many moderately close substitutes may provide as much disciplining power on a hypothetical monopolist as a few close substitutes.) Examination of product use can yield differences that render the products more distinct than might appear. Yellow-page advertising is unique in reaching the consumer just as he or she is determining which stores supply the good or service desired (although the internet may soon be a close substitute in this regard). This difference may well mean that firms would generally not shift substantially to other means of advertising in the event of a 5 per cent increase in the price of yellow-page advertising. Radio advertising has unique attributes in reaching consumers; for example, it is essentially the only means of reaching them during commuting hours and is much less expensive than other electronic media. Given these factors, a substantial number of advertisers might not switch media with a 5 per cent increase. Simply listing a large number of alternatives for achieving the same general purpose does not preclude a narrow product market definition.

On the other hand, of course, to draw the conclusion of a narrow product market it is not enough to identify a small number of minor functional differences between products, or to establish that the product is unique for a specific, small group of buyers. The focus must be

---

39 *Canada (Director of Investigation and Research) v. D&B Companies of Canada Ltd.* (1996),
64 C.P.R. (3d) 216 (Comp. Trib.) [hereinafter *Nielsen*].

on whether the differences are substantial enough to allow a firm producing the set of ₁ roducts within the narrow product market definition to raise its price by a small but significant amount.

An additional pitfall is related to the phrase '*the* relevant market.' In merger cases or, for example, abuse-of-dominance cases, it is often misleading to think of the relevant market as being unique. The competition commissioner, in application to the Competition Tribunal, has discretion in selecting the market in which he or she alleges that there is harm to competition. In the *Nielsen* case, the relevant market argued for in the application was the grocery store scanner-based market information. Part of Nielsen's response was that this set of products was only a subset of the range of market information products supplied by Nielsen, and that the relevant market in this case should therefore be much broader. In fact, application of section 79 requires only that a practice 'have the effect of preventing or lessening competition substantially in *a* market.' The commissioner has the discretion to select the relevant market for application to the tribunal; the market must be well-defined in the sense of including all sufficiently close substitutes for the product in question, but it need not encompass all or most of the goods and services produced by the respondent.

The same principle can apply to geographical market definitions. After a prospective merger, for example, the merged firm might supply a particular geographical area but face competition in only, say, the southern half of its area served. If it is in the position to set different prices for the two halves of its market – that is, if the northern half is a well-defined geographical market – then a substantial lessening of competition in this smaller market would be sufficient reason to challenge the merger.

A final pitfall to be avoided in cases involving allegedly anticompetitive contracting practices is the assumption that the relevant market must be the market in which the contracts are employed. In the *Nielsen* case, the director alleged anticompetitive effects of exclusivity restrictions in contracts for the sale of raw scanner data by retailers to Nielsen. In the market in which the contracts were employed, the wholesale market for raw scanner data, rivalry was at times quite intense with both Nielsen and its rival, Information Resources Incorporated, offering contracts with generous terms but exclusivity restrictions. The result of a single firm winning the intensive, competitive battle for exclusivity rights to the data from all grocery store chains, however, was a monopoly in a 'downstream' market: the market for information produced from the scanner data. Having obtained the exclusive rights to all grocery store scanner data in Canada, Nielsen was in a unique position to offer the downstream product. The director adopted the downstream market as the relevant market in his application to the tribunal, and the tribunal accepted this as a well-defined market in their decision.

XI. Market Power

Market power refers to the ability of a firm (or a group of firms acting jointly) to profit from pricing above competitive levels. In merger policy, the central criterion for disallowing a merger is whether the merger would create or enhance market power. Competition is lessened through a merger if greater market power can be exercised as a consequence of the merger. In other sections of the *Competition Act*, as we will discuss below 'control of a business' is necessary to find a firm in violation of the Act, a condition which the tribunal has interpreted as the existence of market power, or substantial lessening of competition, which can be interpreted as an increase in market power.

In considering sources of market power, a simple economic formula (the Lerner index, defined above) is useful. The profit-maximizing price for any firm will be the price, p, that satisfies:

$$\frac{p-c}{p} = \frac{1}{\varepsilon}$$

where c is the firm's marginal cost at the optimum output and ε is the firm's elasticity of demand at the optimum price. (This formula was discussed above for a monopolist, but is valid for a firm in any market.) The lower the elasticity of demand, the greater the market power. Market power is precisely the inverse of demand elasticity facing a firm.

Market power is linked, in the standard approach, primarily to two conditions of industry structure: concentration of the market, with a focus on the market share of the firm or group of firms, and barriers to entry into the market. The higher the concentration level in a market, the easier it is for the largest firm or firms to exercise market power. It is common – probably too common – to summarize the potential for a merger to create or enhance market power by the market shares of the merging firms.

The MEGs provide safe harbours for mergers in terms of market shares: under 35 per cent for a merger to be challenged under the theory of unilateral exercise of market power and a four-firm concentration ratio under 65 per cent or a market share under 10 per cent for a merger to be challenged under the interdependent exercise of market power (section 4.2).

The U.S. Merger guidelines, in setting out market share criteria for challenging mergers, adopt an index of market power that is more comprehensive than the single-firm or four-firm concentration measure: the Herfindahl-Hirschman index (HHI). This index is calculated by summing the squares of the market shares of all of the firms in the industry. It varies from near zero for an industry with near-infinitesimal firms to 10,000 for a monopoly. The HHI is the simplest measure satisfying the criterion that any merger should have a positive impact on measured concentration. As a predictor of market power, it also has some basis in economic theory: in a very simple theory of oligopoly, the HHI equals the ratio of total industry profits to total industry costs.[40] The use of the HHI in merger guidelines, however, comes at the cost of a loss of some transparency. A post-merger HHI above 1800 is the criterion for a 'highly concentrated' industry under the U.S. guidelines. For these industries a merger that increased HHI by less than 50 would be unlikely to be regarded as anticompetitive under the U.S. MEGs. The U.S. agencies regard industries with post-merger HHIs below 1000 as unconcentrated; mergers in these industries are unlikely to be anticompetitive. For 'moderately concentrated industries' with HHIs between 1000 and 1800, mergers that increase the HHI by less than 100 are unlikely to be challenged.

The trend in antitrust analysis generally is away from nearly entire reliance on market shares to the additional consideration of other industry conditions, especially barriers to entry. An example of an entry barrier is a sunk (non-recoverable) cost that must be incurred to enter an industry. The *Competition Act* is unique among antitrust statutes in recognizing explicitly that market shares alone cannot determine whether a merger is likely to prevent or lessen competition. In considering the impact of entry barriers in a merger case, any factor that would allow sufficient and timely entry is incorporated. Sufficient and timely entry under the Merger Enforcement Guidelines is entry that would ensure that a price increase could not be sustained for more than two years. The likelihood of entry disciplining a merging firm

---

40 The oligopoly model is one in which firms vary only by cost differences, but each has a constant-returns-to-scale technology, and demand is linear.

against exercise of market power depends as well on the barriers to entry (and exit), because in the presence of such barriers the prospect of undercutting a firm exercising market power is unlikely to induce entry on the part of a firm not already in the market.

In addition to market shares and barriers to entry, a third industry variable that must be incorporated in predictions of the impact of a merger on market power is the supply response of other firms in the market to a price increase by the merged firm. Compare a merger between two bakeries, to a market share of 50 per cent, and a merger of two radio stations to a market share of 50 per cent. Buyers of bread, facing a potential price increase by the merging bakeries, could turn to the remaining bakeries in the industry and obtain output from them, produced through the input of additional labour at these bakeries. The merging firm, recognizing this response, is likely to be disciplined against increasing its price by 5 per cent. On the other hand, the supply response of radio stations outside the merging parties will not be so rapid. Stations outside the merging parties cannot immediately offer substantial additional advertising coverage because of the prospective loss in listeners. The need to invest in programming to increase the audience size to expand the quantity of advertising messages delivered limits the ability of stations to respond quickly and therefore to discipline merging stations against a price increase. Similar arguments could be made in the case of newspaper mergers.

William Landes and Richard Posner extend the Lerner index formula to capture the effect of competitors' supply response described in the previous paragraph.[41] Letting s be the market share of the firm, ε_m the market elasticity of demand,[42] and ε_s the supply elasticity of the non-merging firms, Landes and Posner show that at a firm's optimum price:

$$\frac{p-c}{p} = \frac{1}{\varepsilon} = \frac{s}{\varepsilon_m + \varepsilon_s(1-s)}$$

Thus, the market power of a firm is increasing in its market share, decreasing in the market elasticity of demand, and decreasing in the

---

41 Landes and Posner, 'Market Power in Antitrust Cases.'
42 The market elasticity of demand is the percentage change in total industry demand when all firms reduce their price by 1 per cent. This is smaller than the elasticity of demand facing an individual firm.

supply elasticity of non-merging firms. The positive effect of a larger market share comes into p.ay in two ways: the response of the market price to a given output reduction of the firm will be proportional to its market share (the numerator), and the larger its market share, the smaller the discipline imposed by the supply response of competing suppliers (the denominator).

The Landes-Posner argument is based on calculation of the elasticities of *residual demand curves*: the demand curves facing the particular firm (e.g., the merged firm) when all other suppliers are price-takers in the sense that they do not themselves exercise market power. An economic literature has developed that examines the impact of mergers in oligopolistic markets under the more general assumption that each firm exercises market power, to the extent that it has any.[43]

Pitfalls in the Analysis of Market Power

The main pitfall to avoid in assessing the market power of a firm is the mechanical application of market definition and concentration calculations. The precise delineation of the market is arguably unimportant, provided that if a 'reasonably close' substitute is excluded, its disciplining power on the post-merger market is recognized. In other words, defining a market narrowly and using a high standard of concentration as predicting substantial market power or defining a market broadly and using a lower benchmark for concentration ratios are equivalent alternatives.[44]

This pitfall is generally recognized, and as mentioned above is avoided explicitly in the *Competition Act*. But at a more general conceptual level, courts and analysts have sometimes assumed that if a firm captures a higher market share through some practice or a merger the competitiveness of the industry must fall. An unconcentrated, rivalrous market becomes the end instead of the means. This confuses the competitiveness of a market with the degree of rivalry or lack of concentration in the market. In the *Brunswick* case in the United States, the plaintiff was a bowling centre challenging Brunswick's acquisition of

---

43 See esp. J. Farrell and C. Shapiro, 'Horizontal Mergers: An Equilibrium Analysis,' (1990) 80(1) *American Economic Review* 107.

44 As Landes and Posner note, Judge Hand's decision in the *Alcoa* case is consistent with this principle.

other bowling centres.[45] Its complaint was that the acquisition allowed the survival in the market of centres that would otherwise have failed, thus lowering prices and diverting business from its centre to Brunswick's. The lower courts held the acquisitions unlawful because of Brunswick's increase in market share and awarded the plaintiff treble damages. The Supreme Court was more enlightened. It dismissed the suit, noting that the antitrust objection to mergers is higher prices, not lower ones.[46]

In the *Standard Fashion* case, Standard Fashion induced retail department stores to carry their product, dress patterns, exclusively in exchange for a 50 per cent reduction in the wholesale price of the product.[47] The U.S. Supreme Court, in finding this exclusivity restriction unlawful, expressed the concern that the contracts would create monopolies in the 'hundreds if not thousands of communities' where there was, in 1922, a single retailer for the product. This decision again treats a competitive market *structure*, or the existence of many firms in the market, as an end in itself. In fact the goal is the efficiencies gained through lower prices, and in the *Standard Fashion* case, the increase in market share was accompanied by a price decrease.[48]

Discipline on prices is provided by potential competition in a market, not just by actual competitors in the market. In market circumstances such as those in *Standard Fashion*, potential competition – the continued presence of other suppliers from whom retailers could purchase – would keep prices low.

The risk of decisions like the lower courts' decisions in *Brunswick* is small in Canada. The 'failing-firm' argument is a criterion in the MEGs for allowing, not prohibiting, mergers. While a full analysis of the

---

45 *Brunswick Corp. v. Pueblo Bowl-O-Mat, Inc.*, 429 U.S. 477 (1977).

46 Easterbrook notes that: '*Brunswick's* "antitrust injury doctrine" has been extended beyond mergers. It is usually put as a restriction on remedies, though, and this diverts attention from the real problem.' F. Easterbrook, 'The Limits of Antitrust,' (1984) 63(1) *Texas Law Review* 1.

47 *Standard Fashion v. Magrane-Houston Co.*, 258 U.S. 346 (1922).

48 Price dropped at the wholesale level. The more pertinent issue is whether the price drop was passed on to consumers at the retail level. This would seem very likely, with a 50 per cent drop in the price of dress patterns at the wholesale level and substitutes available at the retail level, but was not investigated. Note that evaluation of the practice on consumer welfare in this case would have to take into account the loss in product variety. See G.F. Mathewson and R.A. Winter, 'The Competitive Effects of Vertical Agreements: Comment,' (1987) 77 *American Economic Review* 1057.

NutraSweet decision[49] in Canada is beyond our scope here, it could be argued that in this decision the Competition Tribunal did not acknowledge potential competition as source of market discipline, considering instead the participation of a firm in a market as a necessary condition for the firm to be providing competitive discipline.

NutraSweet dealt with a number of exclusivity provisions related to intellectual property rights. NutraSweet had a Canadian patent on the artificial sweetener aspartame, which expired in 1987. The central allegation of the Director of Investigations and Research in this case, filed in 1989, was that the NutraSweet Company had extended its market power beyond the life of the patent through the use of anticompetitive, exclusionary practices. These practices included the combination of an allowance offered to buyers (primarily diet soft drink manufacturers) to encourage them to display the NutraSweet logo, combined with a requirement for customers displaying this logo that they use exclusively the Nutrasweet brand aspartame. This, the tribunal concluded, created an 'all or nothing' choice for buyers. The restraint appears to have been effectively an inducement to exclusive purchasing for buyers. NutraSweet was a U.S. company, whose patent did not expire in the United States until 1992. (NutraSweet's European patents had expired at the time of the case.) Canada accounted for about 5 per cent of worldwide sales of aspartame. The diet soft-drink manufacturers were the main buyers (85 per cent) of aspartame in Canada, with Coke and Pepsi by far the largest purchasers. The only rival of NutraSweet was Holland Sweetener Company, a joint venture between two large companies, including Tosoh of Japan. Marketing in Canada was conducted by Tosoh Canada.

NutraSweet was able to offer a package of exclusivity and a price to each buyer that was more attractive than the best package Tosoh could offer. When Coke and Pepsi approached Tosoh to solicit bids, Tosoh's response was that it was unprepared to supply the buyer's entire requirements, a response conditional, presumably, on the price that Coke and Pepsi were willing to offer.

The question then becomes whether Tosoh's position as potential entrant was strong enough to have a downward influence on prices in the market. The tribunal, in its decision, states 'We agree with Tosoh's

---

49 *Canada (Director of Investigation and Research) v. NutraSweet Co.* (1990), 32 C.P.R. (3d) 1 (Comp. Trib.).

view that it was being used by Coke and Pepsi to obtain a better price from NSC and that there was little chance that either of them was seriously considering giving all of its Canadian business to Tosoh.' This description of a potential entrant as being used by buyers to obtain a better price is precisely a picture of potential competition at work. Competitive discipline does not require presence in the market-place.

But how significant was the power of this potential competition in disciplining prices in the market? The answer is suggested by the fact that the second major allegation by the director (dismissed by the tribunal) was that NutraSweet's prices were *too* low to be competitive. Pricing below acquisition cost is a potentially anticompetitive practice under section 78 of the *Competition Act*.[50]

XII. Market Power in Input Markets

The case of market power in input markets merits special discussion. A measure of market power for an input supplier is the Lerner measure, the inverse of the elasticity of demand facing the supplier, just as in the case of the supplier of an output. The elasticity of demand facing a single supplier of an input depends upon four factors:[51] the substitutability of the input with other inputs (as measured by the 'elasticity of substitution'), the expenditure of the input in question as a fraction of total costs of output suppliers, the supply elasticity of substitute inputs, and the elasticity of demand of the final product. If there are very close substitutes for the particular input, the elasticity of demand will be high and a single supplier of the input will have little market power. Producers would simply substitute to another input if the input supplier attempted to raise price by a significant amount. Regarding the second factor, if an input accounts for only a small share of total producer costs, the elasticity of demand for that input will be low. This principle is sometimes referred to as 'the importance of being unimportant.' A doubling of the price of automobile windshield wipers would have little impact on demand. A monopolist supplier of windshield wipers would have substantial market power.

---

50 A predatory pricing theory of NutraSweet's pricing and contract practices would require that NutraSweet set prices below cost in 1989 in the expectation that the resulting exclusion from the Canadian market would so deter Tosoh from investment in world capacity that prices in the future would rise in Canada. Among other factors, Canada's 5 per cent share of the world market makes this difficult to accept.

51 Alfred Marshall, *Principles of Economics* (London: Macmillan, 1890), 381–93, 852–6.

A high elasticity of demand for the final output can lead to a high elasticity of demand for an input. Suppose that a particular input has no substitutes, being used in fixed proportions with other inputs, and that at current prices it accounts for half of the expenditure of final producers on inputs. If the final market, or downstream market, is competitive, any price increase by the input supplier will be passed on one-for-one to purchasers of the final product. A high elasticity of demand for the final product (because of the availability of close substitutes for the final product) will translate into a high elasticity of *derived* demand for the input, because an increase in the input price will elicit a high proportional drop in final demand and hence in input demand.[52]

A high elasticity of demand for the final output is not sufficient to eliminate market power in input markets, however. Consider the example of a monopolist owner of a crude oil pipeline providing transportation from a particular set of oil fields to refineries or to a shipping port. The market for crude oil at the delivered point may well be competitive, and the oil fields may have a small share of total world crude oil output. However, an increase in the price charged by the pipeline for transportation services may have little impact on the flow of crude. The impact of the price increase may be instead to lower the rents earned by the oil field owners, who would continue to ship. The rents may be quasi-rents (if they are due to previous investment by the oil field owners) or Ricardian rents (if they are attributable to particularly low extraction costs). The market value of the oil fields would fall as the oil became more costly to bring to market, without a significant effect on the final world price of oil. In this case, a perfectly competitive final market would not preclude the exercise of market power in the input market.[53] A similar example would be the monopolistic supplier of seed or fertilizer to farmers producing and selling an agricultural crop in a perfectly competitive world market. The impact of monopolistic power in the supply of an input to a final market in which Ricardian rents are being earned is to reduce the rents.

---

52 Under fixed proportions and the assumption that the input accounts for half the expenditure, the elasticity of demand for the input will be half the elasticity of demand for the final output.

53 The efficiency cost of this exercise of market power would be in the timing of extraction of oil from this field relative to other fields. The efficient pattern of resource extraction, guaranteed by perfect competition in input and output markets, is to extract first from the lowest-cost oil fields. The higher costs of extraction from other fields are deferred. The exercise of market power by a pipeline could disrupt the efficient order of extraction.

THREE

Multi-firm Conduct: Horizontal Agreements

I. Introduction

The prohibition against price fixing and other forms of anticompetitive horizontal arrangements lies at the core of competition policy in virtually all sophisticated competition law jurisdictions.[1] This apparent consensus in the treatment of such arrangements is largely motivated by the economic rationale, discussed below in this chapter, which underlies these laws. Specifically, such arrangements typically result in a misallocation of resources by consumers to the point at which at least some consumers are forced out from the market, resulting in a 'dead-weight' social loss.[2] For example, in the case of cartels, gains from economies of scale or scope are rarely produced to offset the loss in economic welfare.[3] The inherent challenge facing competition law regulators, therefore, is to enact legislation and administer their policies in a manner that distinguishes between those forms of horizontal arrangements that negatively affect economic welfare and those that are potentially welfare enhancing.

This chapter addresses the foregoing and related issues as follows.

---

1 P.L. Warner and M.J. Trebilcock, 'Rethinking Price-Fixing Law,' (1993) 38 *McGill Law Journal* 679 at 681.

2 A 'dead-weight' loss in this context refers to the loss in consumer surplus that is not transferred to producers, i.e., the net social loss. For a recent detailed consideration of the issue of dead-weight loss, please refer to the Competition Tribunal decision in *Canada (Commissioner of Competition) v. Superior Propane Inc. et al.* (2000), 7 C.P.R. 385.

3 This takes into account the 'loss' of consumer surplus.

Part II considers the economics of horizontal arrangements. Part III provides a brief overview of the *Competition Act* and discusses the range of provisions that are potentially applicable to horizontal arrangements. Part IV reviews the law and jurisprudence related to horizontal arrangements in Canada, based on a conceptual framework developed by Warner and Trebilcock, whereby such arrangements are categorized into one of four classes of scrutiny. Having assessed the *Competition Act* against this 'four-class' framework, Part V addresses the current policy of the Competition Bureau in connection with the treatment of strategic alliances, which may have characteristics that fall into any one of the four classes discussed earlier. Finally, Part VI examines the policy basis for reforms to the treatment of anticompetitive horizontal arrangements under the *Competition Act*.

II. The Economics of Horizontal Arrangements

A. *Types of Cartel Agreements*

A cartel is associated with an agreement on the prices, output levels, or products that a group of competing suppliers will sell. A cartel can be associated with an explicit agreement, in which a written or oral contract is established among cartel members, or an implicit agreement, which simply establishes a common understanding among suppliers as to the benefits of cooperative pricing or output decisions and the consequences of deviations from cooperation. Explicit agreements, in turn, include overt agreements, as exemplified by the OPEC cartel or various export cartels (the latter being exempt from the legal prohibition against horizontal price agreements), or covert agreements.

Prior to the first competition law enacted in 1889 in Canada,[4] explicit agreements were safe from legal prohibition and overt cartel agreements were common across the economy. As discussed in Chapter 1, the wording of this legislation ensured that it would have little or no effect on price agreements. Subsequent revisions to the legislation had little effect and collusive activity remained substantial in Canadian

---

4 *Act for the Prevention and Suppression of Combinations Formed in Restraint of Trade*, S.C. 1889, c. 41 (*Wallace Act*).

industry at least until the Second World War.[5] According to Professor Lloyd Reynolds, in the 1930s, formal price agreements, typically facilitated by trade associations, were observed in the markets for fertilizers, leather, rubber footwear, tobacco, paper products (except newsprint), most plumbing and heating equipment, and many hardware products.[6]

Explicit agreements have naturally become more covert with the passage of stricter price-fixing statutes and the development of stronger case law. Evidence of the existence of such agreements must be obtained in order to prosecute successfully under price-fixing legislation such as section 45 of the *Competition Act*. For example, in *R. v. Deschenes Construction Co.*,[7] which involved bids for a City of Hull project, the winner of the sealed bid auction inadvertently included in its submitted envelope the bids of all other bidders in the auction. Typically, evidence of anticompetitive horizontal agreements is more difficult to come by.

As a matter of economics, cartel pricing (i.e., monopoly pricing by a number of competing suppliers) may also be implemented by implicit, or tacit, agreements.[8] The concept of tacit agreement or tacit collusion covers a wide range of behaviour. At the one end of this range, the distinction between a tacit agreement and an explicit agreement can be as tenuous as the difference between a wink and a handshake. At the other end of the range of tacit collusion, the border between agreement and rational, independent behaviour by competing suppliers becomes murky. In many oligopolies, each firm in the market sets a price close to the monopoly level purely as a matter of individual interest, with no communication whatsoever with other firms. The recognition by each firm of responses by other firms to potential price cuts leads to nonaggressive pricing. This kind of oligopoly clearly includes tacit agreements to charge monopoly prices but is much broader. (Do firms in any oligopoly *not* consider their rivals' reactions to potential price

---

5   Christopher Green, *Canadian Industrial Organization and Policy*, 2nd ed. (Toronto: McGraw-Hill Ryerson, 1985), 158–66; Tom Naylor, *The History of Canadian Business 1867–1914*, vol. 2 (Toronto: James Lorimer, 1975); Lloyd Reynolds, *The Control of Competition in Canada* (Cambridge, Mass.: Harvard University Press, 1940).

6   Reynolds, *Control of Competition*, 8–12; Green, *Canadian Industrial Organization and Policy*, 160.

7   (1967), 51 C.P.R. 255 (Que. Q.B., Crown Side).

8   Please refer to Figure 2.4 in Chapter 2 for a depiction of monopoly price and output levels.

changes?) Markets such as those for retail gasoline may go through periods of 'price wars' and periods of 'disciplined' or more cooperative pricing without any coordination strong enough to be considered an agreement. By way of example, please refer to Figure 2.8 in Chapter 2 for a depiction of a static oligopoly equilibrium with price competition and differentiated products.

Considerable debate has arisen on the issue of whether the domain of competition policy can sensibly include tacit collusion. As we shall discuss, contemporary Canadian competition law, like U.S. antitrust law, focuses on explicit attempts to fix prices; the actual effect of agreements is almost a secondary matter. Tacit collusion is therefore outside the scope of the law. In his 1976 text, Richard Posner is critical of this aspect of antitrust law:

> Once the conspiracy approach to explicit collusion became firmly ensconced in the minds of bench and bar, it was perhaps inevitable that tacit collusion would be considered beyond the reach of the antitrust laws ...

> As a consequence of these developments in legal policy and economic thought, the law relating to collusive pricing became empty of economic thought.[9]

Explicit collusion and tacit collusion are identical in their effects. The categorical difference in their legal status is, in Posner's view, *ad hoc* and a serious weakness in antitrust law.

The problem with Posner's position lies in the design of a remedy for tacit collusion. Posner argues that 'economic data could be used to identify serious limitations of output due to either explicit or tacit collusion ... by identifying those markets whose characteristics predispose them toward price fixing ... and by applying certain tests in the suspect markets to determine whether the market price is substantially above the competitive level.'[10] Imposing a legal standard for price fixing that depends on the difference between actual prices and competitive prices – where the latter are presumably to be determined by measuring costs of production, including a fair, risk-adjusted rate of return to

---

9 Richard A. Posner, *Antitrust Law: An Economic Perspective* (Chicago: University of Chicago Press, 1976), 40.

10 Ibid., 42.

capital – would be tantamount to imposing rate-of-return regulation on potentially any oligopolistic market in the economy and would be administered by the courts – institutions ill-equipped for the task.

The effects of tacit collusion are also relevant for merger analysis, as we shall discuss in another chapter, since mergers affect the structural conditions that favour collusion, but the problem of tacit collusion *per se* appears to be outside the scope of competition policy.[11] Pricing strategies that recognize rivals' reactions cannot be legally prohibited. Competition policy is not a powerful instrument in encouraging competition in many markets where firms are inclined to nonaggressive pricing. Generally speaking, in Canada, as in the United States, conscious parallelism without explicit agreement is not illegal, subject to the presence of sufficient facilitating practices that would lead to the overwhelming inference of an agreement.

B. *The Impact of Cartel Agreements*

Collusion among competing suppliers in a market has the effect of moving the market from a competitive outcome towards a monopoly outcome. The impact of a cartel, however, can be significantly more harmful than the high prices and inefficiencies associated with monopoly. A cartel that succeeds in setting collusive prices is less likely to succeed in coordinating non-price competitive instruments such as advertising, the number of distribution outlets, or product quality. High cartel prices encourage individual cartel members to try to capture larger market shares through non-price instruments, with the result of excessive non-price competition. This excess is both a private and social cost. A cartel also leads to inefficiencies in the allocation of output across suppliers. A cartel agreement on prices or output levels will often award or tolerate a relatively high output level for smaller firms, since these firms have the greatest incentive to cheat on an agreement – their deviations from the cartel agreement being less likely to destroy the agreement. The smaller firms generally have higher costs. Thus a cartel can lead not only to an inefficient total output in the market, but to excessive costs in the production of the output. Market separation agreements prevent unconstrained, efficient

---

11 Paul Collins, 'The Efficacy of Merger Policy as a Response to Tacit Collusion,' (unpublished, 1992).

matches between buyers and preferred sellers in the market. Finally, any resources spent by the cartel on monitoring or enforcing the agreement are a social dead-weight loss.

In contrast, agreements between suppliers of complementary products have the effect of decreasing prices, as the agreement internalizes the *positive* impact on each firm's profit of a decrease in the price charged by the other product. Vertical agreements are examples of such agreements and in this sense should be generally regarded favourably in competition policy.

C. Conditions Favouring Cartel Agreements

Understanding the economic conditions under which a cartel will or will not be successful is often critical to the development of a case for or against a cartel. A firm facing a charge of cartel pricing in an industry where there are dozens of firms producing under conditions of severe fluctuations in supply costs and demand, with little transparency of pricing, for example, would do well to bring these conditions to bear in arguing that a cartel is unsustainable in the market. Market conditions that favour cartels are analysed below.

The success of a cartel depends on its ability to *reach an agreement* on prices, output, or other decisions such as market division; its ability to *detect any cheating* on the agreement; and its ability to *punish any deviation* from the agreement. The cartel's success depends as well on any factors affecting the *incentive to cheat* apart from detection and punishment.[12] The incentive to establish a cartel agreement, and risk the associated legal penalties, depends on the elasticity of demand for the product being sold by the cartel (since this determines how high the cartel will raise the price above competitive levels) as well as the probability of detection *of* the cartel. Each of the conditions for cartel success depends on particular market conditions.

The conditions that facilitate or hinder collusion were first set out by George Stigler, then developed further in the industrial organization literature.[13] The following discussion draws heavily from this literature.

---

12 Please refer to Figure 2.9 in Chapter 2 for a depiction of incentives to cheat on a cartel.
13 George Stigler, 'A Theory of Oligopoly,' (1964) 762 *Journal of Political Economy* 44; F.M. Scherer, *Industrial Market Structure and Economic Performance* (Chicago: Rand McNally,

1. The Incentives for Cartelization

The incentives for a group of competing suppliers to establish an agreement on prices, output levels, or other market factors depends upon both the benefits of the agreement in terms of the increase in profits, the feasibility of enforcing the agreement in terms of monitoring and punishing deviations or 'cheating,' and the potential legal penalties.

The benefits of a cartel depend upon the market power that the cartel members can exercise collectively but not individually. The greater the price increase that can be achieved through cartelization, in other words, the greater the profits from cartelization. The extent of market power depends, in turn, on five market variables: (i) the elasticity of demand in the overall market; (ii) the market share of the colluding parties; (iii) the cross-elasticity of demand between the product sold by the cartel and the products sold by competing firms; (iv) the elasticity of supply of the competing firms; and (v) the speed of entry into the market. (The Landes-Posner expression for market power offered in Chapter 2 captures these effects algebraically.)

A cartel in a market for a vital product with inelastic demand, such as a unique drug treatment, is profitable because it can raise price substantially above the competitive level without suffering much loss in the quantity demanded. If a cartel has a large share of the market, and if the firms outside the cartel are constrained in their supply response to the price increase imposed by the cartel, the cartel is protected against substitution by buyers to suppliers outside the cartel. This protection is enhanced by a low substitutability (cross-elasticity of demand) between the cartelized products and the products offered by other suppliers.[14]

1980); T. Cooper, 'Most Favored Customer Pricing and Tacit Collusion,' (1986) 17 *Rand Journal of Economics* 377; Steven Salop, 'Practices that Credibly Facilitate Oligopoly Coordination,' in J.F. Stiglitz and G.F. Mathewson, eds., *New Developments in the Analysis of Market Structure* (Cambridge, Mass.: M.I.T. Press, 1986). A. Jacquemin and M.E. Slade, 'Cartels, Collusion and Horizontal Merger,' in R. Schmalensee and R. Willing, eds., *Handbook of Industrial Organization*, vol. 1 (New York: North Holland, 1989).

14 In this discussion, we have in mind cartelization to fix the price of outputs. A similar analysis would describe monopsonistic cartels, which set ceilings on the price of inputs. For example, in a 1960 decision, seventeen paper companies were convicted of conspiring to fix the maximum price they would pay for pulpwood supplies (*R. v. Abitibi Power and Paper Co. Ltd. et al.* (1960), 131 C.C.C. 201). Figure 2.10 in Chapter 2 illustrates a monopsony situation.

2. Reaching an Agreement

Reaching a cartel agreement in a market is facilitated where:

- the number of firms in the market is small;
- the sizes (capacities) of the firms are similar;
- the costs of the firms are similar;
- the products offered are similar;
- the products are standard rather than customized to each buyer; and
- costs (input prices) and demand conditions are stable.

With many firms in a market, a cartel agreement is generally difficult to reach, let alone maintain. Similarity across firms of costs, sizes, and products is in general necessary. Attempts to accommodate wide diversity in these variables leads to complexity. If firms attempted to agree on a single set of prices for the products in the market, low-cost firms would favour lower prices than high-cost firms, making an agreement difficult to reach. In addition, diversity would be associated with private information on the part of firms as to costs, capacities, and so forth, which would further complicate the task of reaching an agreement. Demand and cost stability is required so that the agreement need not change frequently or include complex automatic adjustments to changing market conditions.

3. Detection and Incentives to Cheat

The incentives to cheat are diminished, and the chance of detecting cheating on a cartel agreement is enhanced, under the following conditions:

- the number of firms is small;
- no firms are very small compared to the others;
- pricing is transparent;
- non-price competition, such as quality, is transparent or limited in scope;
- transactions are not highly idiosyncratic;
- transactions are frequent and each transaction is small relative to the capacity of the firm;
- the number of buyers in the market is large;
- costs and demand are stable; and
- marginal cost rises rapidly with output and capacity is slow to adjust.

Monitoring adherence to a cartel agreement is like a problem in statistical inference, in which the effects of shocks to demand and costs must be distinguished from cheating. Are sales to a cartel member low because demand has dropped or because another firm in the cartel is cheating on the price agreement? Did a particular buyer switch because of a change in its preferences or because another supplier's offer was more attractive than the cartel standard? A firm may suddenly lose substantial demand or particular buyers, and must decide whether this loss is due to a drop in demand for the product or to the attraction of its customers to a rival with lower prices. With instability in costs and demand, this inference is more difficult and firms are likely to try to exploit the situation by cheating on an agreement.[15]

If some of the firms are small, this incentive is magnified; a proportionate increase in output by each firm has a smaller impact on the market overall. Firms will cheat to the degree that balances the benefits of increasing demand against the probability of being caught and punished by the cartel or (in the absence of any specific punishment mechanism) the probability of the cartel breaking down. In making this decision, each firm ignores the cost to other members of the cartel of increased instability associated with lower prices. A concentrated market can support a more stable cartel because this externality is smaller. If prices are not transparent, or if transactions are highly idiosyncratic (e.g., the bundle purchased in each transaction is different), it is difficult to know when a rival has cheated. A combination of heterogeneity in buyer-seller relationships – for example, buyer-specific costs, multiplicity of products, and low transparency of some prices – makes collusion difficult or impossible. Suppliers can cheat on the least observable price in the bundle offered to buyers. If non-price elements of the transaction are variable, non-transparent or difficult to agree upon, cheating may take the form of offering excessive service. All of these factors limit the potential success of a cartel.

Where transactions are large and infrequent, such as in the procurement by the Department of Defence of weapons systems, or the sale of subway cars, the incentive to cheat on a single transaction is large: the immediate benefits of cheating are substantial and certain relative to the future costs of reduced market discipline. If buyers in a market are

---

15 The classic reference on this topic is E. Green and R. Porter, 'Non-cooperative Collusion Under Imperfect Price Information,' (1984) 52 *Econometrica* 87.

very large, the switch of a single buyer representing a large share of demand from one seller to another may represent either cheating by the more attractive seller or simply a change in the buyer's needs. Where there are many small buyers, this inference problem is mitigated.

Finally, if production technology is inflexible in the sense that marginal cost rises quickly with output (firms are near their capacity limits) and capacity is slow to adjust, detection of cheating may be easy, since cheating in these circumstances takes the form of expansion of capacity over a period of months or years. This final condition may even lead firms to agree collectively to refrain from the adoption of a new, low-cost, and flexible technology. The international quinidine cartel achieved stability when certain cartel members agreed not to switch to a new, synthetic means of producing the drug.[16] A related strategy is the cross-licensing between firms of low-cost/high-capacity technologies that are subsequently not used. These 'sleeping' licences serve as a threat that if the cartel were to break down, prices and profits would fall severely.[17]

4. Punishment

To the extent that any deviant from a cartel agreement can be punished effectively, cheating is deterred. The presence of a dominant firm is helpful to a cartel in this regard, as are market conditions that lead to some product differentiation, especially geographical specialization by firms, so that the cheater may be targeted specifically. Enforcing a cartel by lowering the marketwide price to punish one of, say, six firms would be costly and difficult. Targeting price retaliation to the customers of the firm caught cheating is less so.

In most cartels, 'punishment' takes the form of a switch to competitive market conditions. In this case, the greater the profit from forming the cartel in the first instance (i.e., the greater the price increase achievable by the cartel), the more stable the cartel may be: a return to competitive conditions imposes a larger penalty. But a higher cartel price leads to both a higher short-run benefit from cheating and a higher long-run cost in the form of the loss of cartel pricing. Either effect may dominate.

---

16 See *ACF Chmiefarma v. Commission* (Quinidine) Case 41/69, [1970] ECR 661.
17 See Mukesh Eswaren, 'Cross-licensing of Competing Patents as a Facilitating Device,' (1994) 27(3) *Canadian Journal of Economics* 689 for an exploration of this strategy.

D. *Potential Facilitating Devices*

Various devices in the form of contractual restrictions may be used by a cartel to facilitate cartel pricing. Each of these restrictions generally has other, more benign, uses as well. The role of these restrictions has been explored extensively in the economics literature.[18]

A *meeting-the-competition* policy is an announcement by a supplier or a provision in contracts with buyers that the supplier will meet any price reduction offered by a competing seller. Such a policy may be benign, in that it can guarantee to a buyer that it will obtain the lowest prices available in the market and encourage the investment by the buyer in assets specific to its relationship with a supplier.[19] A meeting-the-competition policy by a dominant firm or a group of firms in a cartel, however, provides a commitment that the firm will respond quickly and automatically to any cheating on a cartel price. The incentives to cheat are diminished by the policy and the stability of the cartel is strengthened.

A *meet-or-release* clause on the part of supplier provides a similar but weaker form of commitment to respond to lower prices. A dominant firm can use a meet-or-release clause to obtain immediate information on which of its rivals are cheating on a cartel price. The meet-or-release clause thus lowers monitoring costs in a cartel.

Most-favoured-nation clauses in a contract with a buyer confers on the buyer the right to the lowest price that the seller is offering to any of its customers. In some forms of this contract, a buyer has the right to retroactive price benefits (a refund) on any units purchased in a previous time period. A most-favoured-nation clause can play many different roles in a market and, in particular, can protect a firm against being in a position of paying more for an input than its rivals are paying. (Profits in competitive markets are very sensitive to differences in input costs across firms.) In the context of a cartel, any cartel member that offers a most-favoured-nation clause in its contract commits itself not to cheat

---

18 See Cooper, 'Most Favored Customer Pricing and Tacit Collusion'; Salop, 'Practices that Credibly Facilitate Oligopoly Coordination'; and Jacquemin and Slade, 'Cartels, Collusion and Horizontal Merger.'

19 For example, a pharmacist may be encouraged to carry one brand of a drug if it is guaranteed that the supplier will match future prices by suppliers of substitute drugs.

(rather than making a commitment to respond to cheating by others): decreasing its price to new customers would require that the cartel member pay a penalty in the form of a refund on past units sold. A most-favoured-nation contract would not likely be chosen individually by a cartel member – it could prevent that member from responding to price cuts on the part of its rivals – but the collective choice by the entire cartel to offer such contracts can enhance cartel stability.

A Canadian case, *NutraSweet*, provides an interesting illustration of the possible role of the combination of meet-or-release clauses and most-favoured-nation clauses.[20] NutraSweet had established contracts with both clauses. The combination meant that an entrant seeking its first buyer or buyers in the market would potentially be pre-empted from selling to all buyers, in that a better offer to one buyer could automatically result in the lowering of prices to *all* the incumbent's clients. The attempt by the entrant to secure a single 'toe-hold' in the market could mean that all toe-holds disappeared.

More common facilitating devices involve the periodic exchange of pricing information or the public posting of prices, such as through a trade association. The exchange of information greatly reduces the costs of detecting cheating on a cartel, thus enhancing cartel stability, especially when the range of products and product variations is large.

E. Canadian Case Law

We conclude this summary of the economics of horizontal agreements with a discussion of several economic case studies, to illustrate the variety of means by which cartels are organized and their impact.[21]

A cartel in the shipping container industry, operating under the name Container Materials Limited, whose sixteen members had been convicted of price conspiracy in 1940, re-established cartel pricing in the immediate post-war period. The government Wartime Prices and Trade Board, in establishing price controls during the Second World War, had set the prices of shipping containers at the levels set in 1940 by the cartel. The price-fixing manual, condemned as an instrument of price fix-

---

20 *Canada (Director of Investigation and Research) v. NutraSweet Co.* (1990), 32 C.P.R. (3d) 1 (Comp. Trib.).

21 More detail on these and other case studies of collusive behaviour is available in Green, *Canadian Industrial Organization and Policy,* 168–84.

ing before the war, was adopted by the government price controls board during the war. When the government-imposed price controls ended in 1947, the pricing manual became the basis for a new industry-wide cartel. New 'costing' manuals, developed by a single industry official, were, in effect, pricing manuals.[22] In its 1962 report on the industry, the Restrictive Trade Practices Commission recommended the removal of the 20 and 22.5 per cent protective tariffs on shipping containers and that the container board open the industry to foreign competition. This remedy was not adopted. The court again found the members guilty of a price-fixing conspiracy.[23]

The *Atlantic Sugar* case also involved maintenance over time of market variables that had been set by the Wartime Prices and Trade Board.[24] In this case, the variables were the relative market shares of the three largest sugar producers, which had been fixed by the government during the Second World War. The case also involved a range of other types of cartel-facilitating behaviour, including the posting of its prices in the lobby at the headquarters of Redpath Sugar, the largest firm. The relative market shares of the three firms were maintained at almost exactly the wartime levels – 43 per cent for Redpath, 35.5 per cent for Atlantic Sugar, and 21.5 per cent for St Lawrence Sugar – into at least the mid-1970s, with the exception of a short period in 1958, when Redpath departed from the scheme. This departure resulted in lower prices and profits in the industry. Internal memos showed clearly that Redpath re-established its strategy of maintaining its traditional share among the three major firms with the expectation that the rivals would follow suit.

Strategies by the three major firms of pricing so as to maintain constant *relative* market shares do not in themselves describe inherently stable market pricing where costs and demand fluctuate. The strategies involve 'multiple equilibria': one equilibrium in which each firm adopts this strategy with the firms' collective market share being 60 per cent, another in which the same strategies result in a collective market share of 90 per cent, and so on. This type of indeterminacy (and the associated risk of market instability) can be resolved with price

---

22 Ibid., 170.
23 *R. v. St. Lawrence Corporation* (1966), 51 C.P.R. 170.
24 *R. v. Atlantic Sugar Refineries Ltd.* (1976), 26 C.P.R. (2d) (Que. Sup. Crt.) 14.

leadership. Redpath, with the largest assigned market share, took on this role. Collectively, the market share of the firms dropped from over 95 per cent at the close of the war to 74 per cent in 1973.

There was no dispute in the case that the firms' strategies revealed conscious parallelism. The extraordinary stability in relative market shares was not coincidental, nor could it be attributed, as a lower court claimed, to geographical market division.[25] A majority of the Supreme Court agreed with the trial court that the uniformity of prices was the result of 'conscious parallelism,' which is not illegal. The key distinction drawn by the court between conscious parallelism and an agreement is communication among the companies. 'In order to make an agreement by tacit acceptance of an offer there must not only be a course of conduct from which acceptance may be inferred, there must also be communication of this offer. In the case of the list price, this was apparent and did cast a burden on the defence. But there was no such communication *of the marketing policy.*'[26] As a matter of economics, the outcome of a tacit agreement and an explicit agreement can be identical. Yet only the latter can sensibly be proscribed, as we have discussed, and the treatment of collusion under Canadian competition law is consistent with this.

Our treatment of horizontal price agreements in this section has considered only minimum price agreements. The next two cases illustrate that horizontal agreements may also establish maximum prices. In the first case, *Abitibi* (1960), seventeen paper companies were convicted of conspiring to fix the maximum price they would pay pulpwood suppliers.[27] Many of the suppliers were farmers and small firms. The defendants accounted for 55 to 65 per cent of total pulpwood purchases, including exports, in Canada during the period of the agreement, 1947–54. The decision in this case emphasized the unequal

---

25 In the decision of the Quebec Court of Appeal, Mayrand, J.A. stated: 'A la suite de cette coûteuse équipée commerciale, les trois raffineries renoncèrent à la guerre des prix et s'en tinrent au partage du marché tel qu'il existait alors. Ce partage correspond à peu près à la division territoriale suivante: Atlantic a pour domaine les trois provinces maritimes, Redpath a seule le contrôle du marché ontarien et partage le marché québécois avec St. Lawrence ...' (41 C.P.R. (2d) 5 at 17). In the Supreme Court hearing, the counsel for the Crown admitted that there was no evidence of a territorial market division (1980), 53 C.P.R. (2d) 1 at 7.

26 Ibid., at 10 (emphasis added).

27 *R. v. Abitibi Power and Paper Co. Ltd., supra,* note 14.

bargaining power between the large pulp and paper companies and the small pulpwood suppliers, as well as the fact that an undue lessening of competition does not mean the elimination of competition. *Abitibi* illustrates the context in which one would expect to see a horizontal agreement to implement maximum prices: the case of a cartel exercising *monopsony* power to achieve a lower buying price.

The second maximum price-fixing case, *R. v. Nova Scotia Pharmaceutical Society et al.* (the 'PANS' case) is more unusual.[28] As a matter of law, the *PANS* decision and its appeal to the Supreme Court are very important and discussed further in this chapter; for now we focus on the economic aspects of the case. The defendants in *PANS*, the pharmaceutical association, agreed to *maximum* allowed dispensing fees on behalf of its members in negotiations with insurance firms that covered the costs of prescription drugs of insured parties.

The Crown argued in this case that the maximum prices negotiated acted as a benefit to pharmacists, since prices tended to follow negotiated maximums. Boudreau J., in the decision the Nova Scotia Supreme Court, disagreed. He concluded that the maximum negotiated tariffs 'were clearly beneficial to the third party insurers' but that the clear indications of countervailing market power on the part of insurers 'does not, of itself, provide an excuse for unlawful collective action' on the part of the pharmacists.[29] Boudreau found that the arrangement amounted to an undue lessening of competition, in violation of section 45(1), but that the Crown had failed to establish criminal intent (*mens rea*) on the part of the defendants.[30]

The *PANS* decision incorporated relatively little economic analysis. Why would a group of sellers agree to a set of maximum prices? Was the agreement necessarily a manifestation of monopsony power on the part of insurance companies (and, if so, why were the pharmacists defendants in a criminal case)?

Mathewson and Winter suggest that contracts such as the *PANS*

---

28 *R. v. Nova Scotia Pharmaceutical Society* (1993), 49 C.P.R. (3d) 289 (N.S.S.C.). This decision followed the constitutional challenge related to section 45 of the Act considered later in this chapter. Please see footnote 55.

29 Ibid., at 325.

30 Note that the day after the *PANS* decision, all parties to the agreement at issue could reasonably be assumed to know of the effects of the arrangement (having been informed of the effects in the decision). The *mens rea* defence, successful in this case, would be ruled out in any subsequent case by the decision itself.

agreement can be explained as a consequence of the monopolistic competition market structure in the selling market.[31] Monopolistic competition, as discussed in Chapter 2, describes a market structure in which there are many sellers, low barriers to entry into the market, but some product differentiation. Despite having many possible competitors, each seller does not face a highly elastic demand curve because a substantial portion of its customers prefer its product or its location or are otherwise disinclined to shop for the lowest price (as are prescription drug consumers covered by insurers for the cost of their purchases). In monopolistically competitive markets, sellers have unexploited economies of scale. Many *potential* combinations of prices and densities (numbers) of sellers are consistent with zero economic profits, or free entry into the market. These combinations range from few sellers with very low prices to many sellers with prices high enough to cover their fixed costs. As a matter of economic theory, there is no reason to expect the market, unconstrained by any collective agreements, to yield the combination that is in the best interest of buyers; in fact, economic theory suggests that such markets often yield too many firms selling at excessive prices. Fewer sellers selling larger volumes at lower prices, but still covering costs, would make buyers better off on average. (The efficiency property of ideal competitive markets, which ensures that competitive market outcomes are Pareto optimal, does not extend to monopolistically competitive markets.)

As Mathewson and Winter demonstrate, this common property of monopolistically competitive markets is enough to generate the incentive for buyers collectively (or for a large subset of buyers) to offer a subset of sellers the right to their exclusive business in exchange for lower prices.[32] In Mathewson and Winter's terminology, this type of agreement represents 'a market solution to a market failure.' As a matter of economics, the efficiency implications of the theory are not so categorical as this language would suggest. As a matter of law, however, considerations of the impact of the *PANS* agreement on market participants did not appear to enter the *PANS* decision.

---

31 G.F. Mathewson and R.A. Winter, 'Buying Groups and Exclusivity: Towards a Theory of Managed Competition,' (1996) 15 *International Journal of Industrial Organization* 137. Please refer to Figure 2.7 in Chapter 2 for an illustration of equilibrium under monopolistic competition.

32 Ibid.

III. The *Competition Act* and Horizontal Arrangements: An Overview

The provisions of the *Competition Act* are, generally speaking, divided between those sanctioned criminally under Part VI and those practices that are subject to civil review by the Competition Tribunal under Part VIII.

In the case of the former, once the commissioner has commenced an inquiry, he or she may refer the matter to the attorney general at any time.[33] In the context of section 45 (the conspiracy provision), if convicted, defendants are liable to a maximum penalty of five years' imprisonment, a maximum fine of $10 million, or both.[34] The attorney general also has the ability to seek an interim injunction to restrain the offending conduct.[35] Furthermore, section 36 of the *Competition Act* confers a civil right of action on private parties for damages suffered as a result of a violation of either Part VI of the *Competition Act* or an order of the Competition Tribunal. Such actions typically arise following a Part VI conviction, since courts treat such a conviction as evidence of a breach of the applicable Part VI offence, in absence of any evidence to the contrary.[36]

With respect to the practices subject to civil review under Part VIII

---

33 An inquiry may be commenced by the commissioner under s. 10(1)(b); on the direction of the Minister of Industry under s. 10(1)(c); or on the basis of a 'six resident complaint' under s. 9.

34 S. 45(1).

35 Consistent with the common law, s. 33 of the *Competition Act* sets out the principles a court should consider when granting injunctions. Interestingly, in *Mead Johnson Canada v. Ross Pediatrics* (1997), 31 O.R. (3d) 237 (Gen. Div.), Justice Brennan held that interlocutory injunctive relief was available to Mead Johnson and granted an injunction restraining Ross Pediatrics from promoting the sale of its formula. Specifically, Ross Pediatrics had made representations that its infant formula was superior to that of others, that it was similar to breast milk, and that the formula strengthened infants' immune systems. This is a departure from previous cases where the court held that interlocutory injunctive relief was not available under s. 36: see, e.g., *ACA Joe International v. 147255 Canada Inc.* (1986), 10 C.P.R. (3d) 301 (F.C.T.D.). Please see N. Finkelstein and R. Kwinter, 'Section 36 and Claims to Injunctive Relief,' (1990) 69 *Can. Bus. Rev.* 298 which addresses the issue of equitable jurisdiction to grant injunctive relief and predates the *Mead Johnson* decision.

36 S. 36(2). Please note that this civil right of action exists with or without a prior criminal conviction.

of the *Competition Act* the commissioner has the exclusive discretion to bring such matters before the Competition Tribunal subject to proposed amendments to the Act before Parliament at the time of writing which are discussed in Chapter 12. In the context of horizontal arrangements, there are two relevant provisions under Part VIII of the *Competition Act*: the merger[37] and abuse of dominance[38] provisions. A critical advance in the evolution of Canadian competition policy occurred in 1986 when merger and monopolization law were decriminalized, reflecting a recognition that horizontal arrangements arising in these contexts *may* result in an enhancement to economic welfare. These provisions are discussed below in the context of horizontal arrangements that are subject to a rule-of-reason analysis.

IV. The Four Classes of Horizontal Arrangements Under the *Competition Act*

In their paper proposing reforms to the current price-fixing law, Warner and Trebilcock established a helpful framework for analysing horizontal arrangements. Specifically, they observed that the *Competition Act* effectively creates four categories of horizontal arrangements, which are subjected to different degrees of scrutiny by the courts and/ or the Competition Tribunal. Moving along a continuum from most offensive to non-offensive, these categories may be summarized as follows:

(i)   *per se* illegal horizontal arrangements;
(ii)   horizontal agreements that are subject to a partial rule-of-reason test, where an undue prevention or lessening of competition must be proven but where offsetting efficiency gains are not considered;
(iii) horizontal agreements that are subject to a full rule-of-reason review, that is, where offsetting efficiency gains are considered; and
(iv)   horizontal agreements that are *per se* legal.

Each of these types of horizontal agreements is discussed below, in turn.

---

37 Ss. 91 and 92.
38 Ss. 78 and 79.

A. Per Se *Illegal Horizontal Arrangements*

Two forms of horizontal arrangements are *per se* illegal in Canada: (i) bid-rigging;[39] and (ii) agreements or arrangements between federal financial institutions related to, among other things, the setting of interest rates on loans or deposits.[40]

1. Bid-Rigging

Under section 47 of the *Competition Act*,[41] it is a criminal offence to enter into an agreement not to bid or to bid at an agreed upon price, in response to a call or a request for bids or tenders. A party to bid-rigging is guilty of an indictable offence and liable on conviction to a fine in the discretion of the court or imprisonment for a term not exceeding five years, or to both. It is noteworthy that bid-rigging applies to bids related to both articles and services.

Essentially, bid-rigging involves an agreement or arrangement between or among two or more persons to manipulate bids in some manner. Unlike section 45, there is no requirement for the attorney general to prove that competition has been unduly restrained. Further-

---

39 S. 47.

40 S. 49.

41 S. 47 of the *Competition Act* states as follows:

   (1) In this section, 'bid-rigging' means

     (a) an agreement or arrangement between or among two or more persons whereby one or more of those persons agrees or undertakes not to submit a bid in response to a call or request for bids or tenders, or

     (b) the submission, in response to a call or request for bids or tenders, of bids or tenders that are arrived at by agreement or arrangement between or among two or more bidders or tenderers,

   where the agreement or arrangement is not made known to the person calling for or requesting the bids or tenders at or before the time when any bid or tender is made by any person who is a party to the agreement or arrangement.

   (2) Every one who is a party to bid-rigging is guilty of an indictable offence and liable on conviction to a fine in the discretion of the court or to imprisonment for a term not exceeding five years or to both.

   (3) This section does not apply in respect of an agreement or arrangement that is entered into or a submission that is arrived at only by companies each of which is, in respect of every one of the others, an affiliate.

more, the agreement or arrangement to rig bids need not be successful to be illegal.[42]

Two exemptions, however, apply to the application of the bid-rigging provision. First, an agreement or arrangement to rig bids is legal where such agreement or arrangement is made known to the person calling for bids *before* a time when the bid is tendered by any person who is a party to the agreement or arrangement.[43] This exemption was designed to enhance competition by allowing smaller firms to join forces in order to bid on larger or riskier undertakings (e.g., large construction jobs).[44] In order for an agreement or arrangement to have been made 'known,' the parties to it must affirmatively notify the person calling for tenders or bids. The second exemption allows for bid-rigging among affiliated corporations.[45]

(a) Forms of Bid-Rigging

Bid-rigging typically takes one of four forms. *Cover bidding* consists of bidders agreeing to submit token bids that are intentionally too high, in order to ensure that a pre-selected bidder is successful. *Bid suppression* refers to the scenario where a party agrees to refrain from bidding or withdraws its bid to allow a pre-selected bidder to win the bid. *Bid rotation* describes a scenario where a pre-selected bidder will submit the lowest bid on a systematic or rotating basis, thus ensuring the winning bid. Under a *market division* agreement, the suppliers agree not to bid in

---

42 For example, even if neither of two parties engaged in bid-rigging succeeds in ultimately winning the bid, the parties have offended s. 47.

43 S. 47(1).

44 An interesting scenario could arise if this exemption was purportedly used in the context where the supply of a given product is available from only few potential bidders. For example, assume there are only four potential suppliers of a service to a given factory or mill. Could two or more of these parties agree to make a 'joint bid' and avoid contravening s. 47(1) by ensuring compliance with the notice requirements stated therein? This would presumably offend the policy underlying the 'notice exemption.' Moreover, while compliance with the notice requirements of s. 47(1) might avoid the application of this section, s. 45(1) could still apply.

45 S. 47(3). This exemption, however, is poorly drafted in that it refers only to affiliated 'companies' and not other legal forms, such as partnerships. Interestingly, as a result of the amendments to the *Competition Act* arising from Bill C-20, implemented in March 1999, the definition of 'control' in s. 2(4) and thereby 'affiliate' in s. 2(2) have been expanded to include non-corporate forms. S. 47(3) should be amended to correspond with this expanded notion of affiliation.

designated geographic areas or for specific customers. Variations of these forms of bid-rigging would also offend section 47.

(b) What Constitutes a 'Bid'?

The terms 'bid' and 'tender' are not defined in the *Competition Act*. A bid is thus what participants in a given industry typically view as representing a bid. Traditionally, this would be defined as an offer that becomes binding upon acceptance. However, it would not usually extend to stages within a process of negotiation or, for that matter, a mere price quote. This definition has proven critically important where, for example, the party calling for bids subsequently returns to the initial bidders in order to solicit revised proposals for lower bids.

For example, in *R. v. York-Hanover Hotels Ltd.*,[46] the federal government undertook to publish rates in its directory in return for individual proposals from hotels with respect to maximum rates available to government employees. Only hotels below a certain rate would be listed in the most desirable section of the directory. On a frequent basis, the government actively solicited and encouraged a submission of revised proposals from hotels at a rate lower than stipulated in their initial proposals. The accused hotels were charged with bid-rigging as a result of their submission of identical rates and the existence of evidence that all proposals were submitted following a meeting of the accused. However, the Ontario Provincial Court held that the government, through its continued solicitation, had removed the characteristic of a 'bid' from the hotels' proposals as it had 'diluted the reward which the system held out to those who, in good faith, initially submitted their lowest rates.'[47] The accused were discharged in respect of the charge of bid-rigging but were ordered to stand trial under the conspiracy provisions of the Act. *York-Hanover* thus stands for the proposition that the bidding process must be *bona fide* in both form and substance in order for section 47 to apply.

(c) What Constitutes a 'Call or Request for Bids or Tenders'?

A call for bids contemplates a direct relationship, that is, a sufficient nexus, between the person calling for the bids and the person submitting a bid. This requirement was not fulfilled in *R. v. Coastal Glass &*

---

46 (1986), 9 C.P.R. (3d) 440 (Ont. Prov. Ct.).
47 Ibid., at 442.

Luminum Ltd.,[48] a case involving subcontractors submitting prices to general contractors, who were, in turn, interested in submitting bids to developers. The developers called for bids from the *general* contractors through newspaper advertisements, which did not mention subcontractors. Notice of the projects of the general contractors, who had picked up tender applications, were circulated in the industry, and, in accordance with industry practice, interested subcontractors then submitted their prices to the general contractors listed as having picked-up tender applications. The accused were subcontractors who had submitted prices to a general contractor in a form designed to ensure that a designated bidder submitted the lowest price. The court found that there was no individual or person who requested or called for the subcontractor bids – a fact which it viewed as essential to the operation of section 47. Despite the fact that the proposals had undoubtedly been agreed upon by the subcontractors, the agreement was found not to constitute bid-rigging as the invitation, if any, to tender arose generally from the practice of the industry and was not based on any specific request.

(d) Agreement or Arrangement to Rig Bids

Nothing in section 47 stipulates that an agreement or arrangement to rig bids needs to be expressed or made in writing. A tacit agreement or arrangement is sufficient to satisfy the provision. However, a 'meeting of the minds' between the prospective bidders must be found, as was held in *R. v. 215626 Alberta Ltd.*[49] In that case, one party was aware that the other party might be submitting a bid, but did not know it for certain, and only *understood* that if a bid were submitted by the other party it would be higher. This did not, in itself, assist the first party as the lowest tender was not necessarily the one that had to be accepted by the call for bids. The accused were therefore acquitted.

(e) Conclusions

It is clear from the foregoing cases that liability under section 47 is very much dependant on issues of process – for example, did the proposal constitute a 'bid'? In fact, the typical response from a party accused of bid-rigging is to take the position that its activity was not within a bidding context as is required by section 47. The immediate benefit of suc-

---

48 (1984), 8 C.P.R. (3d) 44 (B.C.S.C.), aff'd 11 C.P.R. (3d) 391 (C.A.).
49 (1986), 12 C.P.R. (3d) 53 (Q.B.).

ceeding with this argument is the avoidance of the *per se* illegal treatment under section 47 in favour of the partial rule-of-reason treatment under section 45 of the *Competition Act* (discussed below). It is submitted that there is no rational economic basis for distinguishing between the legal treatment of bid-rigging under section 47 and naked price fixing under section 45. The conduct of the parties and the anticompetitive impact is similar, if not identical, and this suggests that the legal treatment should therefore be consistent. Nevertheless, the legal distinction between bid-rigging and various forms of price fixing remains significant. This distinction is revisited in the discussion below related to section 45.

2. *Agreements or Arrangements between Federal Financial Institutions*

(a) Legislative Overview
Section 49(1) of the *Competition Act* proscribes certain agreements among federal financial institutions. As with bid-rigging, section 49(1) is a *per se* offence. That is, in order to support a conviction, it is not necessary to prove an anticompetitive effect. Rather, section 49(1) prohibits the specified conduct without regard to the presence of market power or the likelihood of injury to competition.[50] Specifically, subsection 49(1) of the *Competition Act* prohibits any federal financial institution from making an agreement or arrangement with another federal financial institution, subject to certain exceptions, with respect to any of the following:

(a) the rate of interest on a deposit;
(b) the rate of interest or the charges on a loan;
(c) the amount or kind of any charge for a service provided to a customer;
(d) the amount or kind of a loan to a customer;
(e) the kind of service to be provided to a customer; or
(f) the person or classes of persons to whom a loan or other service will be made or provided or from whom a loan or other service will be withheld.

---

50 Submission of the Director of Investigation and Research, Competition Bureau, to the Task Force on the Future of the Canadian Financial Services Sector, November 1997, at 21.

Pursuant to section 49(1), every federal financial institution that participates in such an impugned agreement, as well as every director, officer, or employee of a federal financial institution who knowingly makes such an agreement, may be found guilty of an indictable offence and liable to a fine not exceeding ten million dollars or to imprisonment for a term not exceeding five years, or to both.

The purpose of section 49(1) of the *Competition Act* is to protect the broad public interest in preserving a competitive environment for basic financial instruments and services. One author has described the 'thrust' of section 49(1) 'to be one of consumer protection within Canada.'[51] As well, the federal government observed in a discussion paper that the section 49(1) prohibitions serve the public interest by preventing 'anti-competitive agreements between or among banks' which, in turn, ensures that the 'interest rates and services charged [sic] by banks to borrowers and paid to depositors are determined by market forces.'[52]

Furthermore, as section 49(1) is a criminal offence, the Crown is required to prove the presence of the requisite *mens rea* and *actus reus* beyond a reasonable doubt. Given the absence of jurisprudence directly related to this provision, it is not possible to define all of its requisite elements conclusively. Nevertheless, it would be reasonable to be guided by the judicial decisions considering these elements in the context of section 45. That is, since section 49(1), like section 45(1), includes the concepts of 'agreements' and 'arrangements,' it is submitted that there is no basis for defining these terms differently under section 49 as opposed to section 45. In this regard, with respect to the *actus reus* component, the courts have held that each of the terms 'conspires, combines, agrees or arranges' in section 45(1) '... contemplate(s) a mutual arriving at an understanding or agreement between the accused and some other persons to do the [proscribed acts].'[53]

With respect to the *mens rea* component, it is reasonable to assume that, as with section 45, the necessary *mens rea* is established when the accused had an intention both to agree and to put the common design into effect. Thus, mere words purporting agreement without an assenting mind to the act proposed would not be sufficient.

---

51 M.H. Ogilvie, *Canadian Banking Law* (Scarborough, Ont.: Carswell, 1991), at 291.
52 Consumer and Corporate Affairs Canada, *Competition Law Amendments: A Guide* (Ottawa: Consumer and Corporate Affairs Canada, 1985), at 30.
53 *R. v. Armco Can. Ltd.* (1977), 13 O.R. (2d) (Ont. C.A.) 32 at 41.

Section 49(2) of the *Competition Act* sets out a variety of exceptions to the general prohibition, providing that section 49(1) does not apply in respect of an agreement or arrangement between federal financial institutions that relates to, among other things, i) a deposit or loan made or payable outside Canada; ii) a bid for, purchase, or sale of securities by federal financial institutions; iii) the exchange of statistics and credit information, the development and utilization of systems, forms, methods, procedures, and standards, and the utilization of common facilities and joint research; iv) reasonable terms and conditions of participation in certain guaranteed or insured loan programs; and v) persons or classes of persons to whom a loan or other service will be made or provided outside Canada.

In addition, section 49(2)(b) of the *Competition Act* sets out a relatively complex exception to section 49(1), consisting of three elements. The first of these applies in respect of dealings of or services rendered between federal financial institutions. This exception permits, for example, one bank to provide services to another bank as its agent in an area where the first bank does not have a branch. The second element of section 49(2)(b) applies to services rendered by two or more federal financial institutions 'as regards a customer of each of the institutions where the customer has knowledge of the agreement.' This exception permits, for example, syndications of large loans among financial institutions and pre-authorized transfers of money between the institutions. Finally, the third element provides an exception in respect of services rendered 'by a federal financial institution as regards a customer thereof, on behalf of that customer's customer.' This would, for instance, allow a business that deals with several banks and trust companies to permit each of them to accept bill payments by customers of the business.

(b) Conclusions

While it is not difficult to endorse the object and purpose of section 49, it is difficult to provide a rational justification for distinguishing the conduct of federal financial institutions from that of all other providers of products in the Canadian economy. For example, why should collusive behaviour among grocery store chains, gasoline retailers, or newsprint companies, to name a few, be treated any more leniently (i.e., under a partial rule-of-reason test as opposed to *per se* illegality) under the *Competition Act*? Certainly from an economic perspective, it is not obvious why collusive behaviour in one industry would necessarily have a greater anticompetitive impact than in any other industry. Attempts to distinguish industries in accordance with the 'potential anti-competitive harm' of collusive behaviour therein would, at best, be unreliable, and at worst, produce a flawed regime for addressing collusive behaviour. A regime that treats similar conduct similarly under the provisions of the *Competition Act* that deal with anticompetitive horizontal agreements would be preferable.[54] This premise is explored further in Part VI below, in discussing possible reforms to the *Competition Act* in the context of horizontal arrangements.

B. The Partial Rule-of-Reason Standard and the Legacy of PANS:[55] Section 45(1)

1. Overview

Section 45(1), which has remained largely intact since its inception in predecessor legislation beginning in 1889,[56] states as follows:

Every one who conspires, combines, agrees, or arranges with another person

(a) to limit unduly the facilities for transporting, producing, manufacturing, supplying, storing or dealing in any product,
(b) to prevent, limit or lessen, unduly, the manufacture or production of a product or to enhance unreasonably the price thereof,

---

54 Interestingly, the *Competition Act* and its accompanying Regulations were recently amended to address competitive issues specific to air carriage. Pursuant to Bill C-26, which received Royal Assent on 29 June 2000, the governor-in-council was empowered to make (i) regulations that specify the acts or conduct of a domestic air carrier which may be anticompetitive for the purposes of ss. 78(1)(j) and 79 of the *Competition Act* (which deal with abuse of dominance); and (ii) regulations specifying which facilities or services are essential to the operation of air services for the purposes of s. 78(1)(k) of the *Competition Act* (which provides for the refusal to supply certain facilities or services on reasonable terms and thereby constitute anti-competitive acts for purposes of s. 79). These regulations are in keeping with the additional enforcement granted to the commissioner to deal with the potential abuse by a dominant air carrier in response to the restructuring of the Canadian airline industry.

55 *R. v. Nova Scotia Pharmaceutical Society,* [1992] 2 S.C.R. 606.

56 *Act for the Prevention and Suppression of Combinations Formed in Restraint of Trade,* S.C. 1889, c. 41.

    (c) to prevent or lessen, unduly, competition in the production, manufacture, purchase, barter, sale, storage, rental, transportation or supply of a product, or in the price of insurance on persons or property,

    (d) to otherwise restrain or injure competition unduly,

is guilty of an indictable offence and liable to imprisonment for a term not exceeding five years or to a fine not exceeding ten million dollars or to both.

Section 45(1) consists of three principal elements: (i) an agreement; (ii) an 'undue' lessening of competition; and (iii) an anticompetitive purpose or intent.

2. *Agreement*

Although section 45 of the *Competition Act* refers to a person who 'conspires, combines, agrees or arranges,' courts have held each of these words to require 'agreement.'[57] An agreement, in turn, requires that there be a 'meeting of the minds' between two or more persons. As such, unless viewed as being part of a series of facilitating practices, culpability cannot be found on the basis of strictly unilateral action. The requirement that there be a meeting of the minds makes communication, in some form, an essential aspect of a conspiracy. Section 45(2.1), however, allows a court to infer the existence of an agreement from circumstantial evidence. In this regard, courts will consider whether conduct is explicable only through the existence of an agreement[58] and may draw adverse inferences from conduct suggesting an attempt to enforce or conceal an agreement or complaint about the conduct of competitors.

    Canadian courts tend to follow the U.S. approach of requiring 'plus factors,' such as enforcement activities, facilitating practices, and unexplained meetings, to transform questionable conduct into a conspiracy. Stated simply, the key factor for a court is whether each competitor makes its commercial decisions (principally those related to pricing) independently.[59] In *Atlantic Sugar Refineries Co. v. Attorney-General of*

---

57 *R. v. Gage* (1908), 18 Man. R. 175 at 220.
58 *R. v. Canadian Gen. Elec. Co.* (1976), 15 O.R. (2d) 360 at 395.
59 See *R. v. Dave Spear Ltd.* (1986), 11 C.P.R. (3d) 63.

Canada,[60] for example, the Supreme Court of Canada found only conscious parallelism and therefore acquitted the accused, despite conditions of less than vigorous competition on the part of the accused. In so finding, the court stated as follows: 'None of the refiners was obliged to compete more strongly than it felt desirable in its own interest. Each refiner was entitled to decide not to seek to increase its market share as long as this was not done by collusion.'[61]

Notwithstanding the decision in *Atlantic Sugar,* this is an area of uncertainty that presents significant risks for businesses, because courts potentially may seize on any evidence of there being more than conscious parallelism in order to find an agreement. Contrast, for example, the following cases. In *R. v. Armco Can. Ltd.,*[62] the accused were aware of the prohibition in section 45 and sought to avoid it by adopting an open pricing policy. Each accused published a price list that was distributed among them. With one exception, the only written evidence before the court suggested that the acceptance of prices on the lists was entirely voluntary. Nonetheless, the court found a violation of the *Competition Act* on the basis that there was an agreement and a conscious effort to stabilize prices. Conversely, in *R. v. Aluminum Co. of Can.,*[63] the court found no violation where industry participants obtained from their respective customers the price list of the industry leader. According to the court, such market surveillance was normal, and in any case, the price lists were used only as a starting point in determining prices.

3. 'Undue' Lessening of Competition

The term 'unduly' is not defined in the current statute, nor has it ever been defined in any preceding competition law legislation in Canada, dating back to the inception of such legislation in 1889.[64] The leading case related to the interpretation of the term 'unduly' and, for that matter, the balance of section 45, is the Supreme Court of Canada decision

---

60 (1980), 53 C.P.R. (2d) 1.
61 Ibid., at 382–3.
62 *Supra,* note 53.
63 (1977), 29 C.P.R. (2d) 183.
64 *Act for the Prevention and Suppression of Combinations Formed in the Restraint of Trade,*
    S.C. 1889, c. 41.

in *PANS*.[65] The appellants were indicted with conspiracy under section 32(1)(c) of the *Combines Investigation Act*,[66] the predecessor to the current section 45(1)(c). The defendants in *PANS*, the pharmaceutical association, as described in part II.E above, agreed to *maximum* dispensing fees on behalf of its members in negotiations with insurance firms that covered the costs of prescription drugs of insured parties.

Gonthier J., writing for the court, established a contextual framework for the 'unduly' inquiry based on the two forms of inquiry established under American antitrust jurisprudence: rule-of-reason review and *per se* illegal treatment. Gonthier J. observed that when applying a rule-of-reason review to an impugned arrangement, all surrounding circumstances of the arrangement are considered to determine whether it unreasonably restricts competition, including whether offsetting efficiency gains are generated. By contrast, a review conducted under a *per se* illegal framework condemns an arrangement on its face, without examining any surrounding circumstances related to the market. Gonthier J. situated the form of review required under section 45(1) along a spectrum between the rule-of-reason and *per se* illegality forms of review, in holding that the Canadian prohibition:

> ... lies somewhere on the continuum between a *per se* rule and a rule of reason. It does allow for discussion of the anti-competitive effects of the agreement, unlike a *per se* rule, which might dictate that all agreements that lessen competition attract liability. On the other hand, it does not permit a full-blown discussion of the economic advantages and disadvantages of the agreement, like a rule of reason would. Since 'unduly' in [section 45(1))(c)] leads to a discussion of the seriousness of the competitive effects, but not all relevant economic matters, one may say that this section creates a partial rule of reason.[67]

Based on this construct, the scope of the economic analysis under section 45(1) is typically limited to a consideration of whether the lessen-

65 *Supra*, note 55. Prior to *PANS*, the term 'unduly' had been interpreted in a number of cases including *Weidman v. Shargge* (1912), 46 S.C.R. 1; *Container Materials Ltd. v. The King*, [1942] S.C.R. 147; *Howard Smith Paper Mills v. The Queen*, [1957] S.C.R. 40. For a summary review of the interpretation of the term 'unduly' in jurisprudence preceding *PANS*, please refer to *Aetna Insurance Co. v. The Queen*, [1978] 1 S.C.R. 731.
66 R.S.C. 1970, c. C-23.
67 *PANS, supra* [1992] 2 S.C.R. at 650.

ing of competition arising from the impugned agreement is of a degree that would be considered 'undue.' Most horizontal agreements will inherently lessen competition by some margin and the fundamental issue under section 45(1) is determining the size of this margin. However, Gonthier J. was clear in excluding as part of this analysis efficiency or welfare gains, of any nature, from the list of legitimate economic considerations.[68] According to Gonthier J., the process whereby the 'undueness' of the horizontal agreement is assessed involves an inquiry into two major elements related to the parties to the agreement: (1) do these parties possess a sufficient degree of market power? and (2) is the behaviour of the parties likely to injure competition?[69] Gonthier J., however, acknowledged that the elements to this structure-behaviour framework were not mutually exclusive as the analysis involved '... an examination not only of market structure and firm behavior separately, but also of the relationship between them ...'[70]

Assessing these elements, first on an individual basis, with respect to market power, Gonthier J. defined it as the ability to behave independently of the market.[71] In terms of the level or market power necessary to trigger the application of section 45(1)(c), Gonthier J. recognized that it differed from other provisions of the *Competition Act*, such as the abuse of dominance provisions. Gonthier J. concluded, therefore, that a 'moderate amount' of market power would be sufficient to meet the requirements of section 45(1)(c)[72] and cited a non-exhaustive list of economic factors worthy of consideration, including the number of competitors and the concentration of competition; barriers to entry; geographic distribution of buyers and sellers; product differentiation; countervailing power; and cross-elasticity of demand.[73] These factors are very similar to the evaluative factors set out under section 93 of the *Competition Act*, which are applied in the context of assessing whether

---

68 Specifically, Gonthier J. stated that '[c]onsiderations such as private gains by the parties to the agreement or counterbalancing efficiency gains by the public lie therefore outside the inquiry under [45(1)(c)].' *PANS, supra* [1992] 2 S.C.R. at 649–50.

69 Ibid., at 651.

70 Ibid., at 652. In this regard, Gonthier J. was adopting the view of Gibson J. in *R. v. J.W. Mills & Son Ltd.*, [1968] Ex. C.R. 275 at 309.

71 Ibid., at 653.

72 Ibid., at 654. Gonthier J. accepts the analysis on this point from *Abitibi Power, supra* (1960), 131 C.C.C. at 249–52.

73 Ibid., at 653.

a merger will or will be likely to prevent or lessen competition substantially.[74]

In regard to the requisite behaviour of the parties to the horizontal arrangement, Gonthier J. stated that such behaviour '... must or must be likely to injure competition.'[75] In this regard, Gonthier J. concluded that, in addition to assessing which facets of competition (e.g., price, service, quality) were affected by the agreement, other factors, such as the manner in which the agreement has or will be carried out, will also be considered.[76]

However, when applying this structure-behaviour model, Gonthier J. established something of a 'moving target' approach that attempts to capture the overall effect on competition. As Gonthier J. stated,

> The agreement could either have an 'internal' effect, in consolidating the market power of the parties (as is the case with price-fixing) or have an 'external' effect, in weakening competition and thus increasing the market power of the parties (as is the case with market-sharing). Market power may also exist independently of the agreement, in which case any anti-competitive effect of the agreement will be suspicious. *A particularly injurious behaviour may also trigger liability even if market power is not so considerable. These are only examples of possible combinations of market power and behavior likely to injure competition that will be undue* ... (emphasis added).[77]

The threshold of 'undueness' is reached once the lessening of competition is 'serious.'[78]

Gonthier J. also addressed the process of adjudicating cases under section 45(1). Specifically, it was concluded that the process followed and the criteria used to arrive at a determination of 'undueness' are questions of law whereas the *application* of this process, including the

---

74 Evaluating horizontal arrangements among rivals under the same criteria as mergers is endorsed by Warner and Trebilcock and is consistent with the view espoused by the former head of the Antitrust Division of the U.S. Department of Justice, William Baxter in 'Substitutes and Complements, and the Contours of the Firm,' in F. Mathewson, M. Trebilcock, and M. Walker, eds., *The Law and Economics of Competition Policy* (Vancouver: Fraser Institute, 1990), at 27.
75 *PANS, supra* [1992] 2 S.C.R. at 656.
76 Ibid., at 655.
77 Ibid., at 657.
78 Ibid.

use of economic analyses, are questions of fact. The principal relevance of this distinction is for the purpose of establishing the scope of a party's right of appeal.[79]

The most significant decision since *PANS* under section 45 of the *Competition Act* was that rendered in November 1995 by the Ontario Court of Justice (General Division) in *R. v. Clarke Transport Canada Inc. et al.*,[80] which dealt with competition affecting the freight-forwarding industry, and, in particular, the business of pool car operators. The facts of this case may be summarized as follows. The 'modern era' of the pool car industry began in 1969 with the issuance of Tariff 505 (the 'Tariff'), which relaxed the commodity-mixing restrictions previously imposed by railway operators. The Tariff enabled pool car operators to be more competitive with long-distance trucking and provided incentives for heavier loading by allowing greater flexibility in terms of the mixing of commodities. In essence, the Tariff created an opportunity for the development of a niche player in the freight transportation business, that is, the pool car operator. As is discussed below, the critical issue in *Clarke Transport* was whether this niche business constituted a relevant market for competition law purposes.

The Tariff did, however, contain several restrictions. Only companies that met the definition of 'commercial pool car operator' had access to the Tariff rates. Another restriction was the so-called 50 per cent rule, which stated that, in applying the provisions of the Tariff, the weight of any commodity – as described in the Canadian Classification and loaded in a car for movement from consignor to consignee – must not exceed 50 per cent of the weight of all commodities in the car. The rule was intended to keep pool car operators in the 'mixed carload' rather than the 'carload' business. Having said that, evidence at trial confirmed that this rule was not rigidly enforced.

Turning to the specific facts, the corporate accused[81] were engaged in the pool car freight-forwarding business to western Canada over

---

79 This determination is also relevant in the context of Competition Tribunal hearings as s. 12 of the *Competition Tribunal Act*, R.S.C. 1985, c. 19 (2nd Supp.) stipulates that (i) questions of law shall be determined only by the judical members sitting in those proceedings; and (ii) questions of fact or mixed law and fact shall be determined by all the members sitting in those proceedings.

80 64 C.P.R. (3d) 289.

81 The following corporations were indicted under s. 45: Clarke Transport Canada Inc., Consolidated Fastfrate Transport Inc., Cottrell Transport Inc., Northern Pool Express Ltd., and TNT Canada Inc.

long-haul routes, generally distances of over 500 miles. Essentially, the business was comprised of assembling and consolidating less-than-carload shipments of freight into carload shipments, which were then transported by rail, typically in boxcars. The pool car operators paid the railways for their services in accordance with Tariffs fixed by the railways. The growth of the pool car operator business provided the railways with a critical backhaul business to complement their resource-based (e.g., forest products) head-haul business from western to eastern Canada.

The accused were charged with having conspired to unduly lessen competition in the transportation of carloads of mixed commodities from Toronto to various destinations in western Canada over an eleven-year period between 1976 and 1987. The key component of their alleged conspiracy was a 'customer protection scheme' (the 'CPS'), which operated in a manner that ensured parties to the agreement were protected from having their rates undercut by other parties to the agreement. Several means to this end were deployed, the most significant of which was the exchange of 'Special Rate Notices' ('SRNs'). The SRNs contained information from an individual member-operator regarding existing customers, the rates being charged, and the product to be shipped. It was understood that other members would not undercut those rates when quoting to such customers.

Having confirmed the existence of an agreement, Justice Moldaver addressed the issue of 'undueness.' In applying the structure-behaviour framework endorsed by Gonthier J. in *PANS*, Moldaver J. concluded that the absence of one of these features would be fatal to a section 45 prosecution,[82] but he also cited the dicta in *PANS* that '[a] particularly injurious behavior may also trigger liability even if market power is not so considerable.'[83]

Interestingly, the Crown in *Clarke Transport* relied, for its interpretation of the undueness requirement, on the decision in *R. v. Anthes Business Forms Ltd.*[84] where Houlden J. stated:

> If the Court could find on the evidence that the purpose or intention of the parties was to prevent or lessen competition unduly, undoubtedly this would be sufficient for a conviction. But the Crown was not required to

---

82 *Clarke Transport, supra* (1995), 64 C.P.R. (3d) at 302–3.
83 Ibid., at 304.
84 (1976), 26 C.C.C. (2d) 349 (Ont. C.A.).

prove such a purpose or intention. On the basis of the *Container Materials* judgment, it was only necessary for the Crown to prove that the effect of the agreement, if it was put into operation, would be to prevent or lessen competition unduly.[85]

Justice Moldaver distinguished *Anthes* on the grounds that it was an appeal case involving allegations that the trial judge had erred in imposing a burden on the Crown to prove an intention on the part of the accused to unduly lessen competition. Justice Moldaver concluded that Houlden J. was referring to the *mens rea* and not the *actus reus* component of the predecessor provision under the *Combines Investigation Act*. Moreover, Moldaver J. concluded that, while the *actus reus* requirements had not changed since *Anthes*, the *mens rea* components had been modified to require both a subjective and an objective fault component.

In defining the relevant market, Moldaver J. relied heavily on the decision of the Federal Court of Appeal in *Canada (Director of Investigation and Research) v. Southam Inc.*[86] Based on the analytical framework established in *Southam*, Moldaver J. concluded that the Crown failed to establish, as a fact, that pool car services constituted a relevant product market. Rather, he found that traditional truckers and intermodal operators were 'equally capable of moving and indeed did move the identical kinds of freight on behalf of shippers/customers from Ontario to parts west.'[87] While this conclusion cannot be said to be an unreasonable one, it leaves open the puzzling question of why the parties to the conspiracy maintained such an elaborate arrangement for such an extended period of time if it had no effect on the market. In other words, the conclusion regarding the relevant market implies that the conspiring parties misunderstood the market and pursued a fruitless strategy in an effort to achieve market stability. Needless to say, in light of the foregoing decision regarding the relevant market, the parties were ultimately acquitted under section 45(1).

4. Intent
As a criminal provision, section 45(1) has a *mens rea* component that Justice Gonthier divided into a subjective and an objective element. These elements were defined as follows:

85 Ibid., at 373–4.
86 (1996), 63 C.P.R. (3d) 1.
87 *Clarke Transport, supra* (1995), 64 C.P.R. (3d) at 315.

To satisfy the subjective element, the Crown must prove that the accused had the intention to enter into the agreement and had knowledge of the terms of that agreement. Once that is established, it would ordinarily be reasonable to draw the inference that the accused intended to carry out the terms in the agreement, unless there was evidence that the accused did not intend to carry out the terms of the agreement.

In order to satisfy the objective element of the offence, the Crown must establish that on an objective view of the evidence adduced, the accused intended to lessen competition unduly. This surely does not impose too high a burden on the Crown. [Section 45(1)(c)] requires that the Crown demonstrate that the effect of the agreement will be to prevent competition or to lessen it unduly. Once again, it would be a logical inference to draw that a reasonable business person who can be presumed to be familiar with the business in which he or she engages would or should have known that the likely effect of such an agreement would be to unduly lessen competition.[88]

The foregoing statement shed considerable light on the interpretation of section 45(2.2).[89] In *Clarke Transport*, Moldaver J. adopted this subjective/objective approach to interpreting the *mens rea* requirement of section 45(1).

C. Rule-of-Reason Horizontal Arrangements

Horizontal arrangements subject to a rule-of-reason analysis are addressed as both criminal offences and as practices subject to civil review under Parts VI and VIII of the *Competition Act*, respectively.

1. Criminal Offences
Section 45(3) of the *Competition Act* states that certain horizontal ar-

---

88 *PANS, supra,* [1992] 2 S.C.R. at 659–60.
89 S. 45(2.2) states as follows: 'For greater certainty, in establishing that a conspiracy, combination, agreement or arrangement is in contravention of subsection (1), it is necessary to prove that the parties thereto intended to and did enter into the conspiracy, combination, agreement or arrangement, but it is not necessary to prove that the parties intended that the conspiracy, combination, agreement or arrangement have an effect set out in subsection (1).'

rangements are exempt from the application of section 45(1). Their scope relates to one or more of the following parameters:

(a) the exchange of statistics;
(b) the defining of product standards;
(c) credit information exchange;
(d) defining terminology used in the trade, industry, or profession;
(e) cooperation with respect to research and development;
(f) restriction of advertising or promotion, other than a discriminatory restriction directed against a member of the mass media;
(g) sizes or shapes of containers in which an article is packaged;
(h) the adoption of the metric system of weights and measures; and
(i) measures directed to the protection of the environment.

Section 45(4), however, limits the application of the exemptions set out in section 45(3) where the arrangement has lessened, or is likely to lessen, competition unduly in connection with one of the following factors: prices; quantity or quality of information; markets or customers; or channels or methods of distribution.

In this regard, Warner and Trebilcock observed that arrangements that fall under the criteria set out in section 45(3) are subject to section 45(4), and not section 45(1). As Warner and Trebilcock stated: 'For subsection 45(4) to stand on its own, it must create a level of scrutiny which differs from the one mandated by subsection 45(1). Since Parliament has determined that arrangements which meet the subsection 45(3) criteria are likely to be in the public interest, it would seem sensible to infer that subsection 45(3)–type arrangements should be subject to a *full* rule-of-reason review before they are condemned' (emphasis added). Despite the soundness of the position advanced by Warner and Trebilcock in respect of the interpretation of section 45(4), Kennish and Ross point out correctly that the '[Competition] Bureau interprets these provisions differently, effectively considering them to be unavailable in any circumstance where s.45(1) would otherwise be contravened ...'[90]

---

90 T. Kennish and Thomas W. Ross, 'Toward a New Canadian Approach to Agreements Between Competitors,' (1997) 28 *Canadian Business Law Journal* 22 at 42–3.

2. Joint Dominance

While the concept of joint dominance is addressed in Chapter 8, which includes an analysis of the abuse of dominance provisions of the *Competition Act*, a brief discussion is also provided here, as it is a relevant civil provision to horizontal arrangements or agreements between competitors. That is, section 79 of the *Competition Act* may apply where 'one or more persons substantially or completely control, throughout Canada or any area thereof, a class or species of business.' As Kennish and Ross observe, the provision can apply where firms use market foreclosure techniques (e.g., exclusive dealing, tied selling) to act, effectively, as joint monopolists or where parallel behaviour by competing firms that has an anti-competitive effect is beyond the reach of section 45 (conspiracy provision) of the *Competition Act* due to the inability to meet the criminal burden of proof thereunder.[91]

D. Per Se Legal Arrangements

In a limited number of circumstances, both within and beyond the scope of the *Competition Act*, Parliament has concluded that certain horizontal arrangements are in the public interest and therefore should not be subjected to a sanction of any kind. Within the *Competition Act*, such arrangements include collective bargaining arrangements and fishing cooperatives;[92] underwriting agreements;[93] amateur sports leagues;[94] specialization agreements;[95] joint ventures;[96] and export agreements.[97] There is also industry specific legislation that exempts certain conduct from the application of the *Competition Act*.[98]

---

91 However, pursuant to s. 79(7) of the *Competition Act*, no application under s. 79 may be made by the commissioner against a person against whom proceedings have been commenced under s. 45.

92 S. 4.

93 Ibid., at s. 5.

94 Ibid., at s. 6.

95 Ibid., at ss. 85–90.

96 Ibid., at s. 95.

97 Ibid., at s. 45(6).

98 One example is the *Shipping Conferences Exemption Act, 1987*, R.S.C. 1985, c. 17 (3rd Supp.), at ss. 4–5.

V. Strategic Alliances

In their paper critiquing the existing law respecting horizontal agreements, Kennish and Ross[99] aptly select the treatment of strategic alliances as a form of 'case study' for illustrating the shortcomings of the current law. The selection is apt largely due to the way in which strategic alliances, in their numerous forms, are able to transcend the full scope of horizontal arrangements considered in this chapter.

Although definitive statistics regarding strategic alliances are unavailable, it is apparent that an increasing number of firms are participating in, or at least contemplating, some form of cooperative agreement. In an effort to clarify the enforcement policy of the Competition Bureau in respect of strategic alliances, the commissioner has issued an Information Bulletin on the subject of *Strategic Alliances* under the *Competition Act* (the 'Alliances Bulletin').[100]

In the preface to the bulletin, the commissioner has specifically cited a number of related factors contributing to the exponential growth in strategic alliances, including increasing competitive pressures, the globalization of markets, and generally decreasing trade barriers. A number of additional factors could also have been listed by the commissioner, particularly in the context of technological advances and research and development-based ventures. As noted in the Alliances Bulletin, the *Competition Act* contains no single provision that deals exclusively with strategic alliances. The absence of such a provision, however, is justified by the myriad legal forms a strategic alliance may take. An attempt to structure a statutory provision specific to strategic alliances would run squarely into an insoluable definitional problem. The Alliances Bulletin, therefore, attempts to provide guidance as to which provisions of the *Competition Act* will be triggered under various circumstances.

As observed by Kennish and Ross, the Alliances Bulletin provides a comprehensive discussion regarding the application of section 45 of the *Competition Act*, with a particular emphasis on issues surrounding the exchange of information. Unfortunately, due to the absence of an analytical framework for horizontal agreements under the *Competition Act* consistent with economic theory, the regime for the treatment of strategic alliances is marred by internal contradictions. Moreover, stra-

---

99 'Toward a New Canadian Approach to Agreements Between Competitors.'
100 (Industry Canada.) The final form was issued on 15 April 1996.

tegic alliances between competing firms that typically offer the greatest prospects for efficiency gains also raise the greatest prospect for intervention by the commissioner under criminal provisions of the *Competition Act*. As stated by Kennish and Ross, 'Notwithstanding the decidedly upbeat tone of the introductory concluding comments contained in the [Alliances] Bulletin, a careful reading of its full text suggests that their actual situation, in terms of possible enforcement action under the Act is considerably more ambiguous. However, that ambiguity, it is submitted, is merely reflective of the multi-various legal treatments to which such arrangements may be subject under the Act.'[101] Kennish and Ross conclude that the stated purpose of the commissioner in issuing the Alliances Bulletin – to resolve uncertainties for the business and legal community regarding the enforcement policy of the Competition Bureau – is 'largely impossible of achievement, given the nature of the legislation.'[102] Other commentators have also expressed their concerns regarding the inherent uncertainty plaguing strategic alliances.[103]

A paticularly interesting reference in the Alliances Bulletin is that related to specialization agreements. The *Competition Act* exempts from the application of the conspiracy provisions, specialization agreements among competing firms that satisfy the statutory criteria. The scope of this exemption is limited to the definition of a specialization agreement as:

an agreement under which each party thereto agrees to discontinue producing an article or service that he is engaged in producing at the time the agreement is entered into on the condition that each other party to the agreement agrees to discontinue producing an article or service that he is engaged in producing at the time the agreement is entered into, and includes any such agreement under which the parties also agree to buy exclusively from each other the articles or services that are the subject of the agreement.[104]

101 'Toward a New Canadian Approach to Agreements Between Competitors,' at 51–2.
102 Ibid., at 52.
103 C. Goldman and J. Bodrug, 'Antitrust Law and Innovation – Limits on Joint Research and Development and Company Communication in Canada' (paper delivered to the Canada/U.S. Law Institute of Case Western Reserve University School of Law, 21 April 1995).
104 See s. 85 of the *Competition Act*.

The Competition Tribunal may only register a specialization agreement where the gains in efficiencies will be greater than or offset any lessening of competition, where such gains in efficiency will not likely be attainable in absence of the specialization agreement and where there has been no attempt to coerce any person to become a party to the agreement.

There are a number of shortcomings to this provision. For example, as observed by Kennish and Ross, the exemption appears to be restricted to the rationalization of 'existing production' as opposed to extending to agreements that prohibit a party from undertaking certain types of manufacturing or service activity in the future.[105] Even the Alliances Bulletin recognizes that many strategic alliances contemplate something far more than a simple exchange of existing production, requiring cooperation across a broader range of both existing and future activities. The result is that the provision for specialization agreements under the *Competition Act* has been an unmitigated failure. To date, no such agreements have been registered or even presented for registration under this provision.

VI. Proposals for Reform

In recent years, there have been at least two detailed analyses undertaken with the objective of formulating proposed amendments to the current treatment of agreements between competitors under the *Competition Act*. As well, a now expired private member's bill had proposed to amend section 45. These proposals are considered and critiqued below in an effort to advance a further, largely hybrid, proposal.

A. *The Warner and Trebilcock Proposal*

The first of the two reforms was proposed by Warner and Trebilcock who, following a detailed comparative analysis of Canada and other jurisdictions, explored the prospects of drafting statutory language that could adequately distinguish between naked and other horizontal restraints.[106] Their solution to this dilemma was to draft a broad statu-

---

105 'Toward a New Canadian Approach to Agreements Between Competitors,' at 41.
106 P.L. Warner and M.J. Trebilcock 'Rethinking Price-Fixing Law,' (1993) 38 *McGill Law Journal* 679.

tory provision that would make any agreement or understanding among competitors *per se* illegal, but would also grant immunity from criminal prosecution to those parties who utilized a notification regime. Specifically, under their proposal the parties would have to notify the agreement to the Competition Bureau in advance of it taking effect or within thirty days of execution of the agreement, whichever was earlier. The Competition Bureau would then have the ability to decide whether or not to challenge the agreement before the Competition Tribunal. Warner and Trebilcock revised their initial proposal in recognition of its over-inclusiveness – that is, they allowed for a minimum market share threshold (20 per cent) below which parties would have no obligation to even notify, without risk of criminal prosecution.[107] Under the Warner and Trebilcock proposal, once having satisfied the notification requirements, the parties could proceed to implement their initiative subject only to a possible civil review by the Competition Tribunal. The review undertaken by the Competition Bureau and Competition Tribunal would be analogous to the current process used in the context of merger review.

B. *The Kennish and Ross Proposals*

In reviewing various proposals for reforming section 45 of the Act, including those of Warner and Trebilcock discussed above, Kennish and Ross presented a spectrum of options for restructuring the law of horizontal arrangements.[108] One, in particular, involved an the attempt to draft statutory language that would distinguish between naked and ancillary restraints of competition. Specifically, under this proposal a second, civil branch would be added to conspiracy law, governing agreements that did not have as their sole or predominant purpose an agreement not to compete. The principal difference between this proposal and that advanced by Warner and Trebilcock is that the distinction between naked and ancillary restraints is statutory as opposed to being assessed through the context of a notification regime.

Kennish and Ross identify specific concerns with the Warner and Trebilcock proposal. First, despite the adjustment made for minimum market share thresholds, the Warner and Trebilcock proposal is criticized for its overly broad application and the compliance costs to both

107 'Fixing Price-Fixing Laws,' (spring 1996) 17(1) *Canadian Competition Record* 48.
108 'Toward a New Canadian Approach to Agreements between Competitors' at 53–66.

the private and public sector. Second, from a practical perspective, Kennish and Ross express concern about the ability of the Competition Bureau and Competition Tribunal to deal with the administrative burden of the notifications which are likely to be voluminous. This burden, it is feared, will result in a certain number of agreements 'slipping by' without the appropriate level of scrutiny warranted. Third, Kennish and Ross point out that the secrecy of an initiative, prior to its introduction to the market, is critical to the parties and imply a 'chilling effect' arising from a notification obligation.

C. Bill C-472

Bill C-472[109] proposed to make certain far-reaching amendments to various provisions of the *Competition Act*.[110] In April 2000, the Competition Bureau issued a discussion paper (the 'Discussion Paper') in connection with a number of proposed amendments to the *Competition Act* (including Bill C-472).[111] As noted in the Discussion Paper, the stated objective for the amendments to section 45 is that criminal sanctions associated with section 45 'may unintentionally discourage some business people from entering into arrangements which cause no harm to consumers or which are, in fact, pro-competitive.'[112] In this regard, Bill

---

109 An act to amend the *Competition Act* (conspiracy agreements and right to make private applications), the *Competition Tribunal Act* (costs and summary dispositions) and the Criminal Code as a consequence. Bill C-472 died on the Order Paper with the dissolution of Parliament on 22 October 2000. In the context of a public consultation process related to possible amendments to s. 45, the bureau has commissioned three reports related to this issue, which have now been released: (1) R.S. Russell, Adam F. Funaki, and D.D. Akman, 'Legislative Framework for Amending section 45 of the *Competition Act*'; (2) A. Gourley with assistance from H. Do, P. Cho, and V. Hohots, 'A Report on Canada's Conspiracy Law: 1889–2001 and Beyond'; and (3) McCarthy Tetrault, 'Proposed Amendments to section 45 of the *Competition Act*.' Each of the foregoing is available under 'Publications–Reports' at the bureau website at (www.strategis.ic.gc.ca).
110 In addition to the proposed amendments to s. 45 of the *Competition Act* discussed in this chapter, Bill C-472 also proposed to amend the *Competition Act* related to (i) its scope for private actions: (ii) the broadening of powers of the Competition Tribunal to include cost awards and summary dispositions; and (iii) the introduction of cease-and-desist powers to allow the commissioner deal with abuse of dominance activities. The proposed amendments to s. 45, however, have been particularly controversial.
111 'Amending the *Competition Act*: A Discussion Paper on Meeting the Challenges of the Global Economy,' Industry Canada (17 April 2000).
112 Ibid., at 9.

C-472 purported to draw a 'clear line between egregious criminal behaviour to be caught by the conspiracy provisions and arrangements among competitors whose effects might be better assessed under civil law.'[113] The Discussion Paper noted the following three elements of Bill C-472 for achieving this objective:

- it created a *per se* prohibition against arrangements to fix prices, allocate markets, restrict production or supply, or engage in boycotts targeted at competitors;
- it introduced a companion civil provision to deal with arrangements substantially lessening competition but not amounting to price fixing, market allocation, output restrictions or boycotts; and
- it provided parties with the option of approaching the commissioner for clearance in respect of prospective strategic alliances, removing uncertainty about whether the parties would face prosecution or civil action if they were to proceed with the proposed arrangement. A clearance certificate issued by the commissioner was proposed to be valid for three years.

While it was difficult to take issue with the stated objectives of Bill C-472 in connection with its proposed amendments to section 45 of the *Competition Act*, the proposed statutory language raised a host of concerns. First, in attempting to define *per se* criminal forms of collusion, Bill C-472 was so overinclusive that it would have criminalized numerous arrangements which would not currently raise concerns with the Competition Bureau.[114] In this regard, it would operate in a manner directly contrary to its stated objective.

Second, the defences and exemptions to the application of criminal sanctions set out in Bill C-472 were fraught with shortcomings. As discussed in the CPG Submission, the elimination of the exemptions currently set out in section 45(3) was inappropriate, and the safe-harbour market share threshold of 25 per cent was inconsistent with the 35 per cent level applied by the Competition Bureau in the context of numerous other provisions of the *Competition Act*.[115]

---

113 Ibid.
114 For an extensive list of examples of such arrangements, please see 'Submission to the Public Policy Forum Regarding Proposals to Amend the Competition Act Contained in Bills C-471 and C-472' (submitted by McMillan Binch on behalf of the Competition Policy Group, (30 June 2000) (the 'CPG Submission').
115 For additional shortcomings with respect to the proposed amendments to section 45 contained in Bill C-472, please see ibid. at 26–8.

Finally, to have ensured its usefulness, the proposed notification/ clearance certificate process contemplated in Bill C-472 would have needed to address a number of issues, including the following: (i) the granting of complete immunity if notification by the parties was provided; (ii) a clearance certificate, if granted, should have also applied to protect parties from applications under the abuse of dominance provisions; (iii) section 29 should have been amended to include information provided in pursuit of a clearance certificate; (iv) the implementation of clear and tight deadlines for decision making by the Competition Bureau; and (v) the removal of any time limit on the validity of a clearance certificate.[116]

D. A Hybrid Proposal for Reform

At the core of the reform proposals discussed above appears to be the concern that the current provisions of the *Competition Act* related to horizontal arrangements are simultaneously overinclusive and underinclusive. They are overinclusive in that they fail to recognize the efficiency gains and other procompetitive features of some of these arrangements. At the same time, these provisions are underinclusive in that they allow naked price restraints the benefit of a partial rule-of-reason analysis. In this regard, there appears to be a consensus among the reform proposals to favour the objective of distinguishing naked restraints from non-naked restraints and to treat the former as *per se* illegal while the latter would have the benefit of a full rule-of-reason analysis. The crux of this reform objective is identifying a mechanism by which the distinction between these types of agreements can be made with a high degree of accuracy and efficiency.

Having considered the foregoing options, it would appear that the preferable mechanism for distinguishing between the various types of horizontal agreements is a notification regime. The survey of other jurisdictions undertaken by Warner and Trebilcock suggests that procompetitive arrangements will be vulnerable to challenge under any statutory language that attempts to distinguish between naked and other horizontal restraints. We conclude that the risk involved with this result outweighs that associated with a naked restraint being granted immunity inadvertently. In the latter situation, there is always the strong likelihood that market factors would cause the naked

---

116 Ibid., at 29.

restraint to unravel. Warner and Trebilcock address the contingency of this not occurring by allowing the commissioner to go to the tribunal, if necessary, to seek interim relief. Despite their laudable efforts, the statutory language proposed by Kennish and Ross is, on its face, susceptible to overinclusiveness in its application.

While supporting the notification concept proposed by Warner and Trebilcock, we also believe that it requires certain modifications. Our principal modification is to propose a two-tiered notification regime, which would address the concern expressed by Kennish and Ross in respect of confidentiality. Specifically, parties entering a horizontal arrangement should have the option of either notifying only the Competition Bureau, on a confidential basis, or notifying on a publicly accessible basis. In the former case, we would suggest that more information be required to forestall the real risk of administrative oversight identified by Kennish and Ross. Parties choosing a confidential filing should be required to discuss their 'business justification' for the initiative and to articulate its pro-competitive aspects. We would further suggest that, in the context of a confidential filing, immunity from criminal prosecution should not be automatic and that the parties be prohibited from implementing the agreement until a favourable ruling has been obtained from the Competition Bureau. If the parties selected the public filing route, the Warner and Trebilcock proposal would remain in tact – that is, automatic immunity from criminal prosecution would apply and the parties would have the right to implement the agreement at any time, subject to the commissioner's right to seek redress before the Competition Tribunal (including interim relief).

FOUR

The Merger Review Process

I. Merger Economics

Merger law differs from other areas of competition policy in that 'it is prophylactic in nature: rather than attempting to control the exercise or abuse of market power, it seeks to prevent its creation in the first place.'[1] Competition policy on horizontal mergers is based on the proposition that an increase in concentration in a market can lead to an increase in market power. The consequences of increased market power are higher prices, resulting in inefficiently low market output levels as well as wealth transfers from buyers to sellers. In this chapter, we first develop the economic foundation for this proposition and then discuss the economic analysis of mergers in practice, including the application of the *Merger Enforcement Guidelines* (MEGs) of the Competition Bureau.

A. *Economic Foundations*

1. *Introduction*
The link between increased market concentration and greater market power is obvious in the extreme case of a merger of two firms to monopoly in a market with strong barriers to entry. Monopoly prices exceed duopoly prices. The impact of mergers in more moderately con-

---

1 Thomas W. Ross and Andy Baziliauskas, 'Lessening of Competition in Mergers under the *Competition Act*: Unilateral and Interdependence Effects,' 2000 (33) *Canadian Business Law Journal* 373 at 374.

centrated markets with low barriers to entry is more difficult to assess, and depends upon market conditions. In a merger case, economic theory provides a framework for bringing evidence to bear on market conditions that affect the impact of the merger. The Competition Bureau adopts the MEGs as a framework for investigating mergers; however, as recognized in the guidelines themselves, the facts arising in each merger case are different and must be assessed on their own merits.

Two classes of theories underlie the link between market concentration and market power and are reflected in both the MEGs and the approach of competition authorities in Canada and the United States: interdependence theories and unilateral effects theories. Interdependence theories address the likelihood that a merger will result in greater collusion, especially tacit collusion, by eliminating a vigorous competitor or by rendering the market more susceptible to cooperative pricing. Until recently coordinated effects theories dominated merger policy enforcement in the United States. But unilateral effects theories are now far more the focus of antitrust enforcement agencies, especially agency economists, in their analyses of mergers.[2] Whether unilateral or interdependence competitive effects are of most concern for a particular merger is important, because different sets of evidence must be brought to bear under each theory.

The market structure that is broadly relevant for merger issues is oligopoly. One can choose from a wide, sometimes bewildering, array of economic theories of unilateral (noncooperative and static) price determination in oligopolistic markets. Three frameworks are prominent: (1) price competition with homogeneous products; (2) price competition with differentiated products; and (3) quantity competition with homogenous products. These theories of pricing were discussed in Chapter 2.

The static theory of price competition with perfectly homogeneous products would lead to the conclusion that two firms are sufficient for a perfectly competitive result. No price greater than marginal cost can survive in the market, since it will be undercut by a rival. In a market with homogeneous products cross-elasticities are infinite and even a slight undercutting of the price set by a seller will attract all of that seller's demand. Outside of the agricultural industry, however, mar-

---

2 Jonathon Baker, 'Unilateral Competitive Effects Theories in Merger Analysis,' (1997) 11 *Antitrust* 21–6.

kets with perfectly homogeneous products are rare. Differences in physical product characteristics, locations, or brand names lead to finite cross-elasticities.

Whether firms compete in setting prices or in setting quantities is an important distinction in merger analysis. As discussed in Chapter 2, prices are strategic complements, which implies that when firms compete in prices any price increases on the part of the merging firms will lead to price increases by rival firms. With a market-power enhancing merger the output of rival firms increases, as consumers gravitate towards the products sold by these rivals. The prices charged by the rivals do not increase by as much as the merging firms' prices, but the strategic variables – the prices – do increase.

Quantity competition refers to a market in which firms' strategic variables are quantities. Firms decide quantities, then the market price (which is a single price, given the homogeneous product) is determined as the price that equates demand to the total quantity offered by firms. An example of a market with quantity competition are some electricity markets, in which the output of each generation plant in a particular hour or day is committed to beforehand, with a price being determined in a 'power pool' market given the total quantities submitted. In a market with quantity competition, firms respond to an increase in market power on the part of a merged firm by becoming more competitive, not less – increasing their quantity decisions in response to a lower anticipated quantity from the merged firm.

2. Unilateral Theories of Competitive Harm

In terms of underlying economic models, unilateral and interdependence theories of competitive harm can be distinguished by static versus dynamic pricing behaviour in the post-merger market. Under unilateral theories of competitive harm, the price of a merged firm increases because the effect of the merger is to lower the elasticity of demand of the merged entity, as one competitive alternative to each of the merging units is eliminated by the merger. Within the static framework underlying these theories, prices are determined by the Lerner rule: the equality of price mark-ups over marginal cost to the firm's inverse demand elasticity. Prices are not established with an eye to the avoidance of retaliation or intense future price competition, as in the dynamic models of tacit collusion.

This is not to say, however, that unilateral price increases are restricted to the merging firm. (The term 'unilateral' in this sense is misleading.) When the merging firm increases its price, the effect is to decrease the elasticity of demand facing competing firms, since a competitive alternative to these rival firms has been rendered less attractive. This leads the rival firms to increase price in response to the (anticipated) higher price on the part of the merging firm. The increase in rival firms' prices has, of course, a feedback effect of decreasing the elasticity of demand facing the merging firm, and so on. In economic models of market equilibrium, the 'direct' effect of a price increase resulting directly from the merging firms' decrease in elasticity of demand and the 'equilibrium' effects on all prices in the market feedback effects work simultaneously and instantaneously, with each firm anticipating correctly the pricing of other firms.

Economic theory offers predictions as to when unilateral effects are likely to be strongest. In the pre-merger market, when one of the merging firms raises its price marginally, it loses some demand to its merging partner and some to other firms in the market (as well as some to other products). The demand to the merging partner is *internalized* with the merger. This is the source of the incentive to increase price. The direct effect of a merger on pricing incentives (i.e. on elasticity of demand) is larger, the larger the fraction of lost demand from a price increase that is diverted to the merging partner. Data on the proportion of consumers who would switch from one merging party to another in response to price increases can be used to estimate the competitive impact of mergers. The proportion of consumers dissuaded by a price increase by firm A who then purchase from firm B is referred to as the diversion ratio between firms A and B.[3]

Without these data or estimates of cross-elasticities of demand, we must rely on qualitative or cruder quantitative evidence. The fraction of customers who would switch between merging parties in response to price changes in the pre-merger market is greater:

(1)   the closer as substitutes are the two merging sets of products to each other, relative to available alternatives; and
(2)   the greater the market share of each merging firm in the market. (A large market share by either firm means that it is likely to capture diverted customers from any price increase in the market.)

---

3 Carl Shapiro, 'Mergers with Differentiated Products,' *Antitrust Magazine* (Spring 1996) 23–9, develops the diversion ratio approach to competitive impact analysis of mergers.

Thus, from consideration of the *direct* effect, the unilateral competitive impact is likely to be greater the higher the market share of the merging firms and the closer the merging products as substitutes relative to competing products.

Consideration of the *indirect*, or equilibrium effect leads to a third structural condition for unilateral effects. The greater the concentration in the rest of the market, the more pronounced is the reaction of the non-merging firms to a price increase by the merged firm. (At the limit, if the firms outside the merging parties are atomistic in size and therefore strongly competitive with each other, their prices will not adjust at all to the merged firm's price increase.) Thus, the market structure variables relevant for the unilateral effect include not only the market shares of the merging firms, but the overall concentration in the market.

Four additional factors affect the increase in market power of a merger under the unilateral theory:

- the ability of non-merging firms to increase their output rapidly;
- the ability of non-merging firms to expand any capacity limits through investment;
- the ability of new firms to enter the market to provide additional competition;
- the elasticity of *market* demand for the products (which reflects the willingness of buyers to substitute to expenditure on products outside the market as price rise).

These are discussed in turn below.

Non-merging firms with very little excess capacity (the ability to provide greater output without significant increases in marginal cost) provide little discipline against price increases by a merged firm. Buyers cannot substitute substantially towards these firms in response to a price increase post-merger because the firms' supply is constrained.[4]

---

4 The effect of constrained capacity or supply by non-merging firms is clearly expressed in Landes and Posner's formula for the model of a dominant firm with a competitive fringe (the limit of our price competition model as the non-merging firms become small in market share. This formula was discussed in Chapter 2. (William Landes and Richard Posner, 'Market Power in Antitrust Cases,' (1981) 94 *Harvard Law Review* 937. Letting s be the market share of the firm, ε_m be the market elasticity of demand, and e_s the supply elasticity of the non-merging firms, Landes and Posner show that at a firm's optimum price:

If capacity of non-merging firms is fixed and entry is blocked, even a relatively modest increase in concentration in the market as the result of a merger can have a substantial impact on market prices. Consider the following example, adapted from Jonathon Baker, 'Unilateral Competitive Effects Theories in Merger Analysis.'[5] Ten sellers in a market each produce one unit of a good to any buyer, and cannot increase their capacity. An individual buyer enters the market with an inelastic demand for exactly seven units of the product, and furthermore, sellers set prices that are specific to each buyer.[6] Suppose that sellers differ in their cost of providing the unit, with seller one having a cost of one dollar, seller two having a cost of two dollars, and so on. Firms compete by setting prices to the buyer. This is a market, in sum, with the following characteristics: capacity limits, each buyer purchases one unit, and buyer-specific prices. (Examples of such a market are discussed below.)

Consider a merger between two firms, say, firms one and two, in this market. Post-merger, the firm can offer the two units as a package to the buyer (or equivalently, offer a discount on the second unit purchased). This is a merger between two inframarginal firms in a market in which measured concentration rises by only a small amount.

Pre-merger, the buyer purchases from the seven lowest-cost sellers, at a price equal to (or just below) the cost of the eighth seller. This is a 'Nash equilibrium' in the price competition game in that no seller has an incentive to change its price, given the prices charged by other sellers. Each seller can raise price to the lowest price available from the buyer's best alternative, which is the eighth seller. Post-merger, however, the merged firm can sell its package of two units of the product at a higher price of $17 rather than $16: a buyer's alternative to purchasing from the merged firm is to buy from both firms eight and nine, and the seller can raise the price of its package to the lowest cost available from these alternative sellers. The impact of the merger on the price, in markets with capacity limits, depends not on the market concentration, but on the change in costs of the marginal seller, as the identity of this *marginal* seller is changed.

$$\frac{p-c}{p} \doteq \frac{1}{\varepsilon} = \frac{s}{\varepsilon_m + \varepsilon_s(1-s)}$$

Thus, the market power of a firm is increasing in its market share, decreasing in the market elasticity of demand, and decreasing in the supply elasticity of non-merging firms.

5 *Supra*, note 2.
6 Alternatively, all buyers are identical.

Baker's discussion of this type of model is motivated by the market for retail pharmacy services to managed care providers. A buyer such as Blue Cross negotiates a price with each of a number of individual pharmacy chains for prescription services to be provided to Blue Cross enrollees. Blue Cross needs to sign up a substantial portion of chains in a city, but not all of them. This market fits the assumptions: each seller has one unit of service to provide to Blue Cross, each has a limited capacity, and each negotiates a price with the buyer for its entire capacity before or after the merger. Pharmacy chains vary in convenience or suitability for Blue Cross enrollees, rather than in cost. Another market that would fit the general framework is the market for radio advertising: each buyer negotiates with a station group for the rights of access to the audience listening to stations owned by the group. Capacity (listening audience) is not easily increased in this market, as in the example, and prices are negotiated separately with each buyer. As a consequence, close attention must be paid not just to concentration but to the change in buyers' alternatives within the market in assessing the impact of a merger.

Entry of new firms is an alternative source of competitive discipline on a merged firm. Barriers to entry in the competition policy context refer to costs or constraints that must be borne by a new firm, but not by an existing firm.[7] The most prominent barriers to entry are market-specific investments by existing firms, also called sunk costs. Examples of market-specific investments are capital, including either physical capital or brand name capital, which has value only in a particular market, or government licensing requirements.

Substantial economies of scale can be a barrier to entry. They impose on the entrant the need to reach quickly a level of output that is a large portion of industry output in order to achieve economies. Entry requires a market-specific investment in the form of excessive costs incurred during the time that the output is growing to the point where economies are realized. Obviously, this entry cost is greater the higher

---

7 This definition suffices for competition policy but is not the most general definition of barriers to entry. For example, in a taxi market, our definition would exclude the limited number of taxi licences issued by the local government. The purchase of a taxi medallion is not a sunk cost, since it can be recovered at any time by reselling the medallion. The 'rental' cost of a medallion is a cost that must be borne by new firms or existing firms. The limitation on taxi medallions, however, is obviously a barrier to entry in the broadest sense.

the minimum efficient scale in the market and the longer the time that an entrant must take to win customers away from incumbents. The time to build the necessary clientele will be longer the more reluctant customers are to switch from the incumbent firms to an entrant. This time depends on factors such as buyer loyalty due to informational imperfections on product quality, the length of existing contracts buyers have with the incumbents, and any investments buyers themselves have made specific to their relationships with the incumbents.

At one extreme, if an entrant can attract customers instantaneously and incurs no sunk costs of entry, economies of scale are not a barrier to entry.[8] An incumbent firm charging even a dollar above its average cost would be undercut by an entrant selling only 50 cents above the same average cost. A market in which an entrant can perfectly discipline market pricing in this way, while having zero market share itself, is known as a *contestable* market.[9] A contestable market may consist of a single firm, like a monopoly, or many firms, like a competitive market. Whatever the market structure, the complete absence of any sunk costs of entry or exit allows the entrant to exploit any price in excess of average cost. In a contestable market, the prospect of being undercut leads incumbent firms, even a single incumbent firm, to price at average cost (and to produce the quantity at the output where the demand curve intersects the average cost curve).

The key characteristics of a contestable market are the absence of any sunk costs of entry or exit and the inability of an incumbent firm to respond instantaneously to an entrant's price or contract offer to buyers. In applying contestable markets theory to actual markets, neither assumption is likely to hold precisely. Even where sunk costs of entry are small, and the delay between the time when entry plans are announced or revealed is small, if the incumbent has an opportunity to pre-empt the entrant's plans of undercutting with low prices of its own, the market outcome may be very far from contestable. Airline routes are a market in which the specific investment by entrants is small (airplanes are not route-specific), but an incumbent could respond quickly

---

8 Most real-world examples of economies of scale involve sunk costs of one form or another. Economies of scale without sunk costs refer strictly to an average *flow* cost of production that is declining in the scale of production.
9 W. Baumol, J. Panzar, and R. Willig, *Contestable Markets and the Theory of Industry Structure* (New York: Harcourt, Brace, Jovanovich, 1982).

or pre-emptively to an entrant's plans to come into the market at low prices. Potential entry is unlikely to discipline prices as strongly through the mechanism of 'hit and run entry' in this market. Contestable markets are best illustrated by markets such as regional wholesale markets where bidding for contracts is essentially always open – not just to manufacturers currently supplying retailers or distributors in that region but to manufacturers whose current sales lie outside the region. If market shares were calculated on the basis of firms currently supplying retailers in the region, the measured concentration would understate the competitiveness of the market. The Canadian and U.S. guidelines on merger enforcement take this effect into account by measuring market shares on the basis of capacity to supply the defined market.

In assessing how close a real-world market comes to the theoretical ideal of contestability, even when there are economies of scale, both key market conditions must be considered: the sunk costs of entry and exit (including the time required to build a market share) and the likely lag in the response of incumbent firms to low prices by an entrant. Evidence of very low costs of entry is not sufficient in itself to render the market 'nearly contestable,' that is, to regard potential entry as essentially sufficient to remove any risk of substantial lessening of competition as a result of a merger. The ability of an incumbent to respond immediately to entry once the threat of entry or plans for entry materializes means that the incumbent's prices need not be maintained at low levels to avoid the risk of being undercut. Lags in the ability of incumbent firms to match entrants prices, or entrants' ability to contract very quickly with customers, are an important determinant of the power of potential competition to discipline pricing.[10]

Where product differentiation is low or moderate, the significance of economies of scale is measured by the minimum efficient scale of production relative to the total output in the market. A commonly used parameter in this respect is the output at which average cost falls to

---

10 Barriers to entry and barriers to writing 'complete' contracts with customers are two sides of the same coin. If a potential entrant into the automobile market could contract with 100,000 customers to provide their next automobiles prior to producing the automobiles or even investing in physical capital, then the required investment in physical capital would not be a sunk cost of entry. Of course, the detailed contracts that would be required for such a futures market are impossible to write; as a result the required physical capital is a sunk cost of entry.

within 5 per cent of the minimum average cost, as a ratio of total industry output. Where product differentiation is substantial, however, the measure of total market output is less meaningful. An additional issue arises here: the extent of product-specific, rather than market-specific, investment. If entry into the broad market is relatively easy but entry into the segment of the market where the merging firm is producing is not, then the scope of new entry to limit the exercise of market power is constrained. For example, the ease of entry into the low-quality and medium-quality sectors may not be enough to discipline a price increase following the merger of the two highest quality firms in a market.

The discipline imposed on a post-merger firm against price increases comes not only from within the market but from the ability of consumers to purchase products outside the market. This discipline in itself is not sufficient to prevent the exercise of market power. (If measured 'market' demand elasticity is so high as to prevent a substantial exercise of market power, then the market has been defined too narrowly.) The elasticity of market demand, however, does enter into the determination of a merged firm's own-demand elasticity, which is the 'bottom-line' measure of market power. For given values of cross-elasticities, the more elastic the market demand, the more elastic the demand facing any single firm.[11]

3. Interdependence Theories

Interdependence theories were until recently the focus of merger policy in the United States, if not in Canada. Interdependence includes the possibility that explicit agreements on prices will be facilitated by the merger. The focus, however, is on the impact of the merger on the likelihood of tacit agreements, or more generally on the reduction in the aggressiveness of competition in the market. Recall from Chapter 3 that the essence of tacit agreements or conscious parallelism is pricing 'cooperatively' because of the prospect of retaliation or the emergence of competitive pricing in response to any price cuts.

The focus within interdependence theories on tacit agreements is

---

11 For example, in a market with N products that are differentiated but enter demand symmetrically, at equal prices for all products, the elasticity of demand facing one firm is the sum of the market demand elasticity plus $(N-1)$ times the cross-elasticity between that product and any other.

sensible because tacit agreements are more common than explicit agreements. Furthermore, while competition policy offers at least the promise of constraining explicit agreements post-merger, it offers little in the way of effective remedies for tacit agreements. Where tacit agreements are a threat, they must be handled with structural remedies. Merger policy is the available structural remedy, setting aside the suggestions from some analysts in the 1960s that large firms in concentrated markets should be split up.

Interdependence theories of substantial lessening of competition from a merger are dynamic theories, in which the incentive for a firm to lower price is dampened by the prospect of punishment or aggressive competition from rivals for its failure to cooperate. Unilateral theories, in contrast, are based on static economic models.

The interdependence component of merger analysis proceeds by identifying market conditions in the relevant market that either favour collusion or render it difficult. In Chapter 3, we discussed the theory of collusion, and in particular, delineated the market factors that enabled oligopolists to solve the three cartel problems:

- reaching an agreement on a set of prices (or some other cartel strategy, such as market division);
- monitoring defections from the agreement; and
- punishing defectors.

The analysis of mergers under the interdependence theory is largely an analysis of how the merger is likely to affect each of these factors. Most prominent among these considerations is the possibility that the merger will eliminate an aggressive competitor – a firm that prior to the merger was preventing any tacit coordination of prices. The elimination of an aggressive competitor in research and development of new products is likewise harmful, as is the removal of a potential entrant that, without the merger, would likely disrupt collusive pricing behaviour. Beyond this, if the merger leads to a dominant firm in the market, cartel pricing may be easier because there is, post-merger, a natural price leader.

The analysis of mergers under the interdependence theory is in practice also an examination of whether the pre-merger market conditions are in general favourable or only marginally unfavourable to collusive pricing, rather than just the impact of the merger on these conditions. If conditions are very favourable to tacit collusion, the merger may have little marginal impact on market performance. The argument that 'we are colluding so successfully already that the merger will not create additional harm to consumers' is unlikely to win many cases, however. A successful defence of a merger against interdependence concerns requires the respondents to demonstrate both that the market conduct is competitive in the pre-merger market and that it is likely to stay that way with the merger.

The theory of interdependence rests on a simple economic principle: if a group of firms can raise price by successfully colluding, they will increase profits. Detailed analysis of conditions for interdependence is undertaken in the applications section below.

4. General Considerations

(a) Non-Price Competition

In addition to the impact of a merger on prices and output, we must consider the impact on non-price competition. In retail markets in particular, firms compete not only on price but on the quality of service. A monopoly does not necessarily produce lower quality service than a competitive market. If all consumers have similar preferences over the trade-off between higher quality and lower price, a monopolist will provide the socially optimal amount of quality, as discussed in Chapter 2.

It is reasonable to assume that for a typical product, however, those consumers who are inframarginal at the current market price (i.e., who would still demand the product at a higher price than the current price) would also willingly pay more for higher quality. In the automobile market, for example, customers who would have purchased a particular model even if the price were substantially higher are presumably wealthier on average than the marginal customers – those who would pay the current price but no more. Quality is a 'normal good,' that is, it is in greater demand by wealthier customers. It follows that for the typical product, willingness to pay for quality is greater among inframarginal customers than among marginal customers. Since a monopolist, in deciding the quality of a product, considers only the tastes of marginal customers (these being the only customers who would enter or leave the market in response to small changes in quality), quality is under-provided by a monopolist. The tastes of all customers should matter for a socially optimal choice of quality. The more 'quality' looks like a reduction in price (e.g., where quality is the number of years a consumer durable will last) the more likely it is that quality is underprovided in a monopolized or highly concentrated market. Concerns over reduction in quality or service are frequently expressed by buyers in merger cases, and the possibility of reduced non-price competition deserves consideration in merger analysis.

(b) Innovation

Innovation is another dimension of competition that may be affected by a merger. In an unconcentrated or an oligopolistic market, competition in innovation may be intense, as firms must continue to develop new product improvements or lower costs just to remain competitive in the market and to protect their market share. A firm in a consumer electronics market that cut back on research and development, for example, would not last long.

The impact of market structure on innovation incentives, and by extension the impact of mergers on innovation, is complex. Two arguments suggest that concentration decreases the incentives to innovate. First, in a competitive market, a single firm faces the potential gain of the entire market, or at least a substantial increase in market share, through a very substantial innovation in products or processes. The entire monopoly profits are 'up for grabs.' A monopolist, on the other hand, faces as a reward only the *difference* between monopoly profits under the new technology and monopoly profits under the old technology. Gains are less for a monopolist and the incentive to innovate is therefore lower.[12] By extension, a merger that substantially increases concentration in a market may reduce the incentives to innovate, to the detriment of customers. Second, a merger between two oligopolists engaged in research and development 'internalizes a negative innovation externality.' In a pre-merger market each of two rival firms invests in innovation to the extent that maximizes its own profits, without regard to the costs imposed on its rival from the risk of loss of market

---

12 There are offsetting advantages to monopoly in terms of innovation incentives, if intellectual property rights are not fully protected under the intellectual property law against free-riding by competitors. If competitors can easily imitate a new innovation, competition in the post-innovation market weakens the incentives to innovate. If engineering applications of fundamental research and development by one firm can be undertaken by any competitor, competitive spillovers again arise. These are internalized in a monopoly. These various effects, however, are unlikely to offset the positive impact of competition on innovation incentives.

share when the rival is left with out-dated technology or products. The merged firm, on the other hand, takes into account the loss in demand for each of its products and the impact on profits earned from all of its divisions when it decides on the level of investment for new products. The internalization of the negative externality in innovation tends to dampen incentives for innovation. This effect is analogous to the internalization of the negative competitive externality from increasing production quantity, which dampens competition in the product market.

On the other side of the ledger, an effect suggesting a positive impact of mergers on innovation is that firms tend to rely on internal capital, or accumulated earnings, as the lowest cost source of capital for financing investment. Accumulated earnings are greatest for monopolies. A second argument for a positive effect of increased innovation with higher concentration is that the fewer firms there are engaged in innovation, the lower is the chance that the marginal dollar spent by a firm on research will result in a discovery that is pre-empted by the establishment of intellectual property rights by another firm over a very similar discovery.

In balancing the various positive and negative effects of a particular merger on innovation, it is important to keep in mind that the relevant impact of the merger is on the 'market structure' or concentration levels of firms engaged in research and development, which is not necessarily the same as the structure of the product market. The consensus among most economists, and the position upon which competition policy is based, is that increases in concentration on balance have a negative impact on innovation. Empirical evidence, discussed by F.M. Scherer and David Ross, is found in 'the frequently observed tendency for market-dominating firms to be slow in developing important new products, but to razor back like tigers when smaller rivals – often new entrants with no historical market share at all – challenge their dominance. Examples include Gillette's lag behind Wilkinson on stainless steel razor blades in 1962–63; IBM's slow start in developing its first digital computers and their transistorized ... microcomputer descendants; ... AT&T's record in developing microwave radio relay systems and communications satellites; [etc.].'[13]

---

13 F.M. Scherer and David Ross, *Industrial Market Structure and Economic Performance*, 3rd ed. (Boston: Houghton-Mifflin, 1990), 635.

(c) Competitiveness of Pre-Merger Markets

An important but sometimes confusing consideration in the assessment of a merger is the competitiveness of the pre-merger market. It could be argued that if there is substantial market power in the pre-merger market then the potential increase in market power as a result of the merger is small. If pre-merger prices are close to monopoly levels, the merger will not substantially increase price.

This argument would be unlikely to carry much weight with either the Competition Bureau or the antitrust agencies in the United States, for several reasons. First, the pre-merger market, while currently lacking in competition, may have the potential for increased competition in the future. The merger may add to the stability of collusive pricing that while currently successful might not have remained so. Second, allowing firms to merge and thus solidify a collusive pricing arrangement *because* they were to some degree already colluding successfully injects into markets perverse incentives for collusion. Finally, the dead-weight loss in surplus resulting from a given price increase in a market is much greater if the pre-merger market already deviates substantially from the competitive ideal. This final point is explained below.

5. *Efficiencies*

If the only effect of mergers were sometimes to increase market power, merger policy would be easy: make mergers illegal. But the vast majority of mergers are not driven by the desire to increase profits through greater exercise of market power. Between 1986 and 1999, the Competition Bureau examined 3,328 mergers and found that 80 per cent posed no issue under the Competition Act.[14] Even if one believes that the Competition Bureau is very conservative in challenging mergers, the conclusion must be that mergers are almost always explained by the desire to increase profits by achieving efficiencies.

As discussed below, the main sources of efficiency in mergers are reductions in costs through the realization of economies of scale, such as the sharing of fixed costs or greater efficiency in the deployment of some types of capital; reduced transportation costs through rationalization of shipping and distribution networks; savings attributable to

---

14 Margaret Sanderson and Michael Trebilcock, 'Process and Politics in Canadian Merger Review,' University of Toronto Competition Policy Roundtable, 16 June 2000.

the transfer of superior production techniques, know-how, or intellectual property rights from one merging party to the other; and efficiencies accruing to buyers from the ability to choose from a wider variety of products or services.

(a) Balancing Efficiency Gains and Lessening of Competition in Merger Analysis

With respect to efficiencies, the central conceptual issue in merger policy and in defending a merger is how to assess a merger that presents both a lessening of competition and a gain in efficiencies. Section 96 of the *Competition Act* states that the tribunal shall allow a proposed merger to proceed even if the merger leads to a substantial lessening of competition providing the efficiency gains uniquely attributable to the merger offset and are greater than any lessening of competition. The Act, however, does not offer explicitly a criterion for balancing efficiencies against lessening of competition. The resolution of this issue turns on the choice of the underlying objective function in competition policy. As discussed in Chapter 2, there is consensus among economists that the appropriate measure should be the maximization of total welfare, measured by the sum of producer and consumer surplus.[15] An alternative is the consumer welfare standard: a merger should be permitted only if its impact on consumer welfare alone is positive. A third and closely related standard is the impact of a merger on market price. The decision in *Hillsdown*[16] can be interpreted as suggesting the possibility of a fourth standard for merger policy, in which the transfers from consumers to producers are added to the dead-weight loss in efficiency to yield the total social costs of a merger. The observations of Reed J. in *Hillsdown* were recently endorsed by the Federal Court of Appeal in *Superior Propane* (unreported, April 2001).

In spite of the treatment of efficiencies in merger cases before the tribunal, and publication of the MEGs by the Competition Bureau, the interpretation of section 96 and the general role of efficiencies in merger review in Canada were in an uncertain state prior to *Superior*

---

15 Michael Trebilcock and Ralph Winter, 'The State of Efficiencies in Canadian Merger Policy,' (1999–2000) 19 *Canadian Competition Record* 106.
16 *Canada (Director of Investigation and Research) v. Hillsdown Holings (Canada Ltd.)* (1992), 41 C.P.R. (3d) 289.

Propane.[17] The split decision of the tribunal in *Superior Propane* on this issue, and the rejection of the majority's interpretation of section 96 by the Federal Court of Appeal, perpetuate this state of uncertainty. The MEGs (section 5.5) state that in trading off efficiencies and lessening of competition the Bureau would follow a criterion of total surplus, that is, consumer surplus plus seller profits. The MEG's justification for the use of total surplus, without regard to distribution of gains between buyers and sellers, is that '[w]hen a dollar is transferred from a buyer to a seller, it cannot be determined *a priori* who is more deserving, or in whose hands it has a greater value.'[18] The tribunal's *obiter dictum* in *Hillsdown* questioned the neutrality of transfers between buyers and sellers and left the law uncertain as to the balancing test in the application of section 96. Howard Wetston, director of investigation and research at the time of *Hillsdown*, reassured the business community that in enforcing law the bureau would continue to apply the approach adopted in the MEGs.[19] Subsequently, however, the bureau proposed a two-stage test that departs from the simple total surplus standard and which is quite confusing.[20] A senior bureau official also stated that in cases where a merger creates a substantial lessening of competition but would pass under the total surplus standard, the bureau 'feels that it is more appropriate for the tribunal to determine whether the merger increases aggregate welfare of not.'[21]

In *Superior Propane*, a majority of the tribunal endorsed virtually without qualification the total surplus criterion. Issues of income redistribution do not matter in merger assessment under *Superior Propane*: a dollar received by individuals as shareholders counts as much as a dol-

---

17 *Canada (Director of Investigation and Research) v. Superior Propane* (2000), 7 C.P.R. (4th) 385.

18 (Ottawa: Supply and Services Canada, 1991), n 57.

19 Mr Wetston stated that he was 'of the view that, from an enforcement perspective, it is preferable not to depart at this time from the approach adopted in the Merger Enforcement Guidelines.' Howard Wetston, 'Developments and Emerging Challenges in Canadian Competition Law,' Speech at the Fordham Corporate Law Institute, New York, 22 October 1992, at 9.

20 Trebilcock and Winter, 'The State of Efficiencies in Canadian Merger Policy,' at 110–11).

21 Gwillym Allen, speech to conference attendees at 'Meet the Competition Bureau,' Toronto, 3 May 1999, published at *http://strategis.ic.gc.ca/SSG/ct01548e.html* (date accessed: 7 February 2000), 5.

lar received by individuals as consumers. The tribunal's endorsement of total surplus was made in spite of some evidence by an expert witness for the commissioner (Professor Peter Townley) that the redistribution of income resulting from the merger would likely be regressive, that is, from less wealthy individuals to more wealthy individuals. Professor Townley proposed a balancing approach in which the members of the tribunal were 'invited to use their individual judgment and discretion to evaluate whether the gains to shareholders are more or less important to society than the losses of surplus imposed on consumers by the exercise of market power' (*Superior Propane*, para. 431).[22] But the tribunal's endorsement of the total surplus standard and efficiency as an objective of merger policy is strongly phrased: '[E]fficiency was Parliament's paramount objective in passing the merger provisions of the Act and it intended the efficiency exception in subsection 96(1) to be given effect. Accordingly, the tribunal is not prepared to adopt a standard that frustrates the attainment of that objective' (437).

The endorsement of the total surplus standard, which stands in sharp contrast to the tribunal's *obiter dictum* in *Hillsdown*, is justified in *Superior Propane* on the following grounds. First, in the tribunal's reading of the *Competition Act*, 'distributional concerns do not fall within the ambit of the merger provisions of the Act' (432). Second, 'merger review must be predictable. Adopting Professor Townley's approach would result in decisions that vary from case to case depending on the views of the sitting members of the tribunal regarding the groups affected by the mergers' (433). Third, the evidence showed that the transfer from buyers to sellers resulting from the merger was much larger than the dead-weight loss.[23] As a consequence 'a standard that includes the transfer as an effect under subsection 96(1) would effectively result in the unavailability of the section 96 defence' (434). Fourth, government instruments such as specific tax and other social policy measures are more effective than merger policy as ways of

---

22 Subsequent references to *Superior Propane* refer to the paragraph numbers in the decision.

23 The 'dead-weight loss' associated with a price above marginal cost is the loss in total surplus in the market relative to the case where price equals marginal cost. In other words, the dead-weight loss associated with a price increase is that portion of the additional expenditure by buyers that does not represent simply a transfer to sellers. A merger that increases price will increase the dead-weight loss in a market to the extent that demand is elastic (responsive to price).

meeting distributional objectives (438). Finally, the tribunal cites the MEG's support of the total surplus standard. While noting that it is not bound by these guidelines, the tribunal 'recognizes that they contain a substantial degree of economic expertise' and agrees with the MEG's observation cited above that when a dollar is transferred from a buyer to a seller, it cannot be determined *a priori* who is more deserving, or in whose hands it has a greater value (439).

The purely legal arguments for total surplus as a criterion to be read directly in section 96 of the Competition Act are not persuasive. Just as the *Superior Propane* tribunal can state, 'If Parliament had intended that transfers from consumers to shareholders be considered, it would no doubt have clearly stated this intent in the Act' (432), the *Hillsdown* tribunal was able to state, 'If only allocative efficiency or the deadweight loss to the Canadian economy was intended by Parliament to be weighed in the balance then one would have thought that the section would have been drafted to specifically so provide.'[24] Section 96 of the Act is ambiguous.

It is obviously within the mandate of the tribunal to provide an interpretation of the statute, however, and the economic arguments that the tribunal draws upon to support its interpretation are persuasive. The alternative to the total surplus approach argued by the commissioner in *Superior Propane* invites the tribunal to apply welfare weights based largely or exclusively on the regressivity of the transfer from consumers to shareholders (a 'welfare-weights' approach). Are consumers of the products produced by the merging firms among the less wealthy members of society, and if so to what extent should the transfer be regarded as a negative outcome of the merger? In the commissioner's approach, the negative outcome would be incorporated in 'balancing weights' or welfare weights attached to surplus accruing to individuals of different wealth levels. The tribunal's decision to reject this approach has merit. If one were to incorporate redistributive effects in merger analysis, it would be necessary to consider not just the wealth of consumers but also the wealth of the shareholders of the merging firms. The income redistributive effect of a transfer from one group of individuals to another depends on the wealth levels of *both* groups. If redistributive effects were consistently accounted for, a merger that was unacceptable when wealthy Canadian families closely

---

24 *Hillsdown, supra* (1992), 41 C.P.R. (3d) at 337.

held the merging firms would suddenly become acceptable if a teachers' pension fund bought the shares.

Furthermore, carrying the welfare-weights approach to its full conclusion means that mergers such as the IntraWest acquisition of Whistler Mountain (which combined the adjacent Blackcomb and Whistler mountain ski areas) could be accepted in spite of *negative* cost efficiencies and a positive dead-weight loss because the merger produced a favourable redistribution of wealth from very wealthy consumers (on average) to less wealthy shareholders. A welfare-weights approach results in acceptance of some transactions with overall negative net efficiencies, including the dead-weight loss, if the distribution of wealth is improved with the transactions. The welfare- weights approach, in other words, would lead to the acceptance of mergers involving both a lessening of competition and negative cost efficiencies.

The dependence of merger decisions on the pattern of share ownership of the merging parties and the acceptance of cost-increasing, competition-lessening mergers, are arguably both absurd implications of the proposed use of competition policy not just to maximize the total wealth (surplus) of individuals but to distribute wealth fairly. At the very least, these examples suggest that the use of competition policy to redistribute income – rather than leaving income redistribution to government instruments such as taxation and social insurance, which are explicitly designed for this purpose – would be extremely complex.

Notwithstanding the attractions of the interpretation of section 96 adopted by the majority of the tribunal in *Superior Propane*, the Federal Court of Appeal, in a recent April 2001 decision on an appeal by the commissioner from the tribunal's decision rejected this interpretation. Relying principally on canons of statutory interpretation including the purpose provision in the *Competition Act* [s. 1.1], with its reference to providing 'consumers with competitive prices and product choices' and the legislative history of section 96, the Federal Court of Appeal held that the effects of a merger, for purposes of section 96, should not be confined to dead-weight losses but should properly take into account redistributive effects as between consumers and the merging parties, and endorsed Professor Townley's balancing weights approach. The Supreme Court of Canada declined to grant leave to appeal from this decision. The case has been remitted to the tribunal for redetermination.

The efficiencies/competition trade-off in the context of the total welfare standard are discussed below, following the classic treatment by Oliver Williamson.[25] For simpl.city, we consider efficiencies from a representative merger that take the form of reductions in per unit costs.

(b) Efficiency Trade-off with No Market Power in the Pre-Merger Market

The Williamson analysis shows that with even small efficiencies and an extreme lessening of competition – from perfect competition to monopoly – the net total welfare effect of a merger is likely to be positive. This analysis is outlined in Figure 4.1. This figure depicts the unit cost, Co, and the market demand curve for two firms that compete in a pre-merger market. Unit costs are assumed to be constant and price competition between these two firms is assumed to be so intense between these two firms that price equals the unit cost in the pre-merger market.

In the pre-merger market, the total surplus or gains to trade generated in the market is the area under the demand curve and above the cost curve. (This gain is entirely consumer surplus.)

The merger is assumed to result in a cost decrease from C_0 to C_1, as depicted in the figure. The post-merger monopoly price is equal to P_1 which, as drawn, would satisfy the Lerner condition for optimal monopoly price. At this monopoly price, a quantity Q^1 is demanded. In the post-merger market, the total surplus generated is again the difference between the social value (demand price) and cost (now C_1) for each unit generated – but this now represents the area between the demand curve and C_1 only to the left of the quantity Q_1.

The difference between the total surplus post-merger and the total surplus pre-merger is easily determined to be the area of the rectangle A minus the area of the triangle B. The triangle B represents the *dead-weight loss* in total surplus that is due to monopolization of the market. (More precisely, B represents the section of the dead-weight loss triangle above the pre-merger cost, C_0.) The rectangle A, on the other hand, represents the cost savings captured by the monopolist on each of the Q_1 units produced post-merger as a result of merger efficiencies.

For most realistic parameter values, the efficiency gains rectangle A

25 Oliver Williamson, 'Economics as an Antitrust Defence: The Welfare Trade-Offs,' (1968) 58 *American Economics Review* 18.

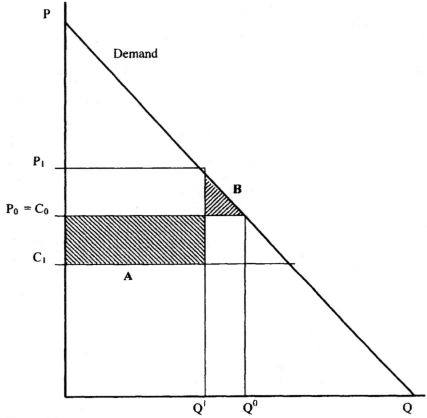

Figure 4.1
The Efficiency–Dead-weight Loss Tradeoff in Mergers

is larger than the dead-weight loss triangle B.[26] The dead-weight loss is
half the difference in quantity (between monopoly and competition at
the post-merger cost level) times the difference in price, or $.5\Delta Q\Delta P$.

---

26 The dead-weight loss triangle is what economists term a 'second-order' effect of
   monopoly power. That is, it depends upon the product of two differences: the difference between the monopoly price and the competitive price and the difference
   between the competitive quantity and the monopoly quantity. The efficiency gains
   rectangle, on the other hand, is a 'first-order' effect: it depends upon the *level* of post-
   merger output times the difference in costs.

TABLE 4.1
Cost efficiencies sufficient to offset various price
increases with a merger
(elasticity of demand = 1.0)

Price increase (%)	Cost savings required %
10	0.6
20	2.5
30	6.5

Using the approximate relationship that the elasticity of demand, e, can be expressed as

$$e = \Delta Q / \Delta P * (P/Q)$$

we can express the dead-weight loss as

$$L = (1/2) * PQ * e * (\Delta P / P)^2$$

The dead-weight loss depends only on the *square* of the proportionate change in price, reflecting the fact that the main effect of monopoly price increases is to transfer wealth from buyers to the monopolist, a transfer that does not enter into the total surplus criterion. The efficiency gains can be expressed as $Q * \Delta C$. In a market where the pre-merger elasticity of demand is 1, Table 4.1 provides the approximate cost savings that must be realized to offset various price increases as a result of a merger. Even for a substantial price increase, 20 per cent, only 2.5 per cent cost savings need be demonstrated to ensure that the merger is welfare increasing, under the total surplus standard.

As an aside, note that differences in elasticity of demand across markets have two opposing effects on the efficiency costs of monopoly: (1) the dead-weight loss expression provided above is increasing in the elasticity of demand, since a given price increase will have a greater distortionary effect the higher the responsiveness of quantity to changes in price; and (2) the greater the elasticity of demand, the lower will be the price mark-up over costs under monopoly. Using the now-familiar Lerner expression[27] for the price mark-up over costs and com-

---

27 In the notation of this section, the Lerner expression is $\Delta P/P = 1/e$.

bining this with the dead-weight loss expression leads to the following approximate expression for the dead-weight loss:

$$L = PQ/2e$$

This expression, which recognizes that price is endogenous, shows that of the two opposing effects discussed, the impact of elasticity on monopoly price is the stronger. Markets with less elastic demands have higher efficiency losses when they are monopolized.[28]

The fact that differences in elasticity of demand across markets have two opposing effects on the efficiency costs of monopoly has led to some confusion in competition policy analysis and even court decisions. In the 2001 Federal Court of Appeal decision in *Superior Propane*, Evans J.A. states at paragraph 103 that 'use of the total surplus standard for calculating the anti-competitive effects of a merger makes it easier to justify a merger between suppliers of goods for which demand is relatively inelastic than of goods for which demand is relatively elastic.' This effect the court views as paradoxical and this view is, in turn, part of the court's basis for rejecting the total surplus standard for assessing the net effect of mergers. The quoted statement, as Roger Ware notes in a critique of the appellant decision, is false.[29] As the equation in our previous paragraph shows, the dead-weight loss from a merger *increases*, not decreases, as demand becomes more inelastic. The court's statement that the total surplus standard makes it easier to justify mergers for suppliers whose demand is relatively inelastic considers only the first effect of elasticity differences across markets: that the dead-weight loss associated with a given price increase is smaller the more inelastic the market demand. The statement ignores the second more powerful effects: that the more inelastic the demand, the greater will be the price increase with a merger to monopoly. The correct view is that suppliers which would face rela-

---

28 We must qualify this proposition with the note that we are referring to demand elasticity at the post-merger price. For markets in which demand is relatively inelastic within the interval of prices between marginal cost (the competitive price) and the monopoly price – for example, a market with nearly rectangular demand – the efficiency costs of monopolization through a merger may be small. For practical purposes, however, markets with more inelastic demand at monopoly prices also tend to have more inelastic demand at lower prices. Our qualification is therefore minor

29 Roger Ware, 'Is Competition Economics "beyond the ken of judges"?,' forthcoming *Canadian Competition Record*, 2001.

TABLE 4.2
Cost efficiencies sufficient to offset various price
increases with a merger when the pre-merger price
exceeds marginal Cost
(elasticity of demand = 1.0; pre-merger price =
1.2* [marginal cost])

Price increase (%)	Cost savings required (%)
10	2.9
20	8.0
30	16.3

tively inelastic demand if combined in a merger sell to consumers who have relatively few attractive alternatives to the firms' products and that it is mergers between precisely these types of suppliers that present competition problems.

(c) Efficiency Trade-off with Market Power in the Pre-Merger Market[30] The welfare tradeoff between efficiencies and lessening of competition changes significantly when the pre-merger market is significantly non-competitive. Figure 4.2 illustrates a market in which the pre-merger price, denoted P_0, is significantly above marginal cost. In this market, the difference between total surplus post-merger (at a quantity Q^1) and total surplus pre-merger (at a quantity Q^0) is given by the area A, representing the efficiency gains, and the area B, representing the *increase* in dead-weight loss that would result from the merger if unit cost remained at C_0.

Note that B represents only part of the losses from distortion that would be incurred with the merger if it moved the market from intense competition to monopoly. The efficiency costs of the merger are smaller, and the net benefit of the merger therefore greater, than in the case of the identical merger starting from a situation of intense competition. However, if one charts the cost efficiency gains necessary to offset the dead-weight loss associated *with a given merger-induced change in price*, the results are much less favourable to an efficiency defence: In this case, a 20 per cent increase in price requires an 8 per cent savings

---

30 Frank Mathewson and Ralph Winter. 'The Analysis of Efficiencies in *Superior Propane*: Correct Criterior incorrectly Applied,' (2000) 20 *Canadian Competition Record* 88.

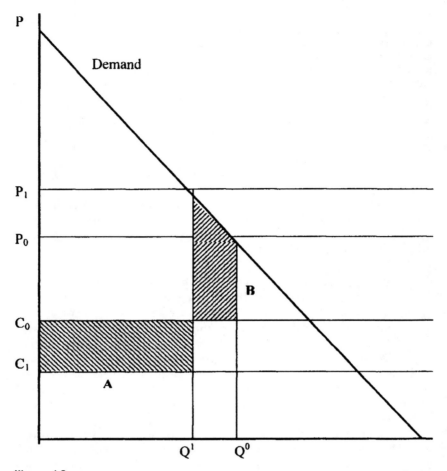

Figure 4.2
Efficiency–Deadweight Loss Tradeoff with Pre-Merger Market Power

in cost for total surplus to increase – approximately triple the cost savings required to offset a 20 per cent price increase starting from a position of competitive pricing.

As the tribunal noted in *Superior Propane* (para. 434), estimates of 'dead-weight loss triangles' tend to be small relative to even modest efficiency gains. Dead-weight loss triangles measure the surplus loss of a given price increase when one starts from a price equal to marginal cost. We have just demonstrated, however, that the dead-weight loss from a given price increase when one starts from a pre-merger price exceeding marginal cost can be very large. It may be helpful to elaborate on the simple economics of why pre-merger market power makes such a difference, without reference to triangles, rectangles, or trapezoids.[31] Consider, for example, a market in which a hundred consumers each purchase one unit of the product in the pre-merger market. Suppose that price is initially equal to a marginal cost of $10, then increases by 10 per cent to $11. A loss in total surplus, or dead-weight loss, arises with the departure from the market of consumers whose willingness to pay is between $10 and $11. Suppose that the size of this departing group is ten, or 10 per cent of initial purchasers.[32] The loss in total surplus associated with each of these consumers is equal to the difference between the consumer's willingness to pay and the marginal cost. This loss is on average only 50 cents for each departing consumer, for a total loss in surplus of about $5 or only 0.5 per cent of initial revenue. The key to the small size of the dead-weight loss is that the consumers lost in the market are those whose value for the product was only slightly above the cost of the producing the product. Total gains from trade in a market (total surplus) are the difference between the social value of the product (the aggregate of consumers' value for the product) and the social cost of producing the product. *Where the consumers discouraged by a price increase are those whose value is only slightly above cost, the loss in total surplus associated with the price increase will be small.*

Now consider a second example. Marginal cost is still $10; however, the initial price is $20. The percentage price increase is still 10 per cent now from $20 to $22; continue to assume that there are initially a hundred consumers and that ten of these are discouraged from buying by the price increase. In this second example, the average departing consumer will value the product at $21. The loss in total surplus represented by the average departing consumer is the difference in this value and marginal cost of $10, which is $11. This is a large number. As a consequence of the initial gap between price and marginal cost, *the departing consumers are no longer consumers whose value for the product is only marginally above the cost of production.* As a result, each of the departing consumers represents the loss of substantial gains to trade. The total

---

31 The following draws on G.F. Mathewson and R.A. Winter, 'The Analysis of Efficiencies in *Superior Propane*: Correct Criterion Incorrectly Applied,' (Fall 2000) *Canadian Competition Record* 88–97.
32 Equivalently, suppose that the elasticity of demand is –1.0.

loss of surplus in this second example is \$100 or 5.0 per cent of initial revenue, ten times the percentage loss found in the first example.

It is useful as well to address a question that may be raised by this discussion. Are we suggesting that a merger to a given post-merger price, or a merger of a given market to monopoly, involves a small dead-weight loss when the market is initially competitive but a large dead-weight loss when market power is exercised pre-merger? We may appear to be suggesting that 'pre-merger market power raises the dead-weight loss associated with a merger to monopoly in a given market.' Yet this could not be true, since the monopolization of a market that is already part way along the path towards monopoly pricing clearly cannot involve greater social loss that the monopolization of a market with competitive pricing.

The resolution to the apparent paradox lies in the phrasing of the question. Monopolization of a market – with *given demand* and costs – always involves greater dead-weight loss if the market is initially competitive than if market power is already being exercised. However, the dead-weight loss associated with *a given price increase* will tend to be larger when there is pre-merger market power than when there is not. The effect on dead-weight loss of pre-merger market power, in other words, depends on what is being held constant.

The existence of market power and consequent 'dead-weight loss' in the pre-merger market should not be interpreted as indicating a failure in that market. In many competitively structured markets, precisely measured marginal costs fall below prices. That is, market power is exercised in the sense (captured by the Lerner index) that prices are marked up above marginal cost. The resulting 'dead-weight loss,' however, may simply be the price society pays for greater product diversity or greater availability given a monopolistically competitive market structure, especially in markets where transportation costs are significant and geographical distribution systems are therefore important.[33] The pre-merger market in this case does not fit the mythical ideal of a textbook, perfectly competitive market but may be well functioning in the 'second-best' world in which frictions such as transportation costs are unavoidable.[34]

---

33 The market structure of monopolistic competition is discussed in Chapter 2.
34 In a pre-merger market such as discussed here, the market structure is described by monopolistic competition, as outlined in Chapter 2. Many economists would adopt a

The presence of market power, whether due to monopolistic competition, to dominance, or to (partially) successful collusion, must be incorporated into any calculation of dead-weight loss. Otherwise, the estimated dead-weight loss is understated. An example of this error is found in the expert evidence presented on behalf of the commissioner in *Commissioner of Competition v. Superior Propane Inc. and ICG Propane Inc.* (Aug. 30, 2000). In the expert report of Professor Michael Ward, the dead-weight loss is calculated in a merger simulation as the area of the triangle depicted in Figure 4.3, where the pre-merger equilibrium is (P_0, Q_0) and the post-merger equilibrium is (P_1, Q_1).[35] This analysis assumes that the pre-merger price is equal to marginal cost, whereas the estimates underlying the merger simulation show that there is significant market power in the pre-merger market. The estimated individual firm demand elasticities for the merging parties in the pre-merger market are –1.9 to –3.9 and Ward concludes as well that interdependence in pricing between the two parties leads them to price above marginal cost. From the individual firm demand elasticity estimates of approximately 3, and the Lerner expression equating the mark-up of price over marginal cost to the inverse demand elasticity, one can infer that according to Professor Ward's evidence, the pre-merger price is approximately 50 per cent above marginal cost. As illustrated in Figure 4.2, the correct estimate of the dead-weight loss resulting from the merger should include not just the triangle in Figure 4.3, but the rectangle between marginal cost and P_0, underneath the triangle. This increases the estimated dead-weight loss substantially.[36] Evidence on the correctly calculated dead-weight loss was not properly presented to the tribunal in the *Superior Propane* case.[37]

The dead-weight loss was seriously underestimated by Professor Ward, given his estimate of the merger-related price increase.[38] Under

broader concept of competition (or a narrower concept of market power) than that reflected in the Lerner index of market power, and state that no market power is exercised in a monopolistically competitive market with many small firms. We retain the simple Lerner index of market power, but recognize that market power is not in and of itself pernicious in a second-best world.

35 This figure appears as Figure 1 on p. 33 of Professor Ward's report.

36 Mathewson and Winter, 'The Analysis of Efficiencies in *Superior Propane.*'

37 At para. 451 of the decision, the tribunal refers to estimates of dead-weight loss that were 'based on information provided in final argument that was excluded.'

38 Mathewson and Winter, 'The Analysis of Efficiencies in *Superior Propane.*'

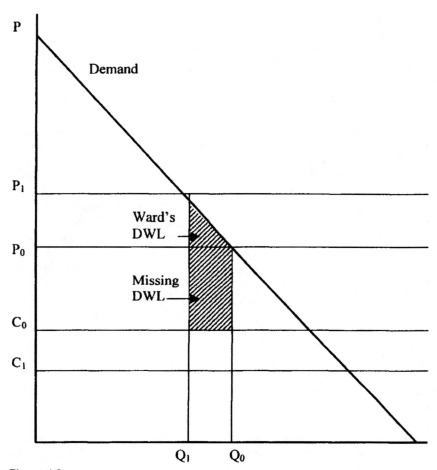

Figure 4.3
Incorrect Estimation of dead-weight loss in *Superior Propane*

the pure cost-benefit analysis approach followed in the *Superior Propane* decision, however, there will be cases in which the estimated premerger market power is so high that the merger will have little additional impact on prices and very modest efficiencies will be enough to offset the dead-weight loss. In cases like these, incorporating premerger market power into both the estimation of price impact (via merger simulation) and calculation of dead-weight loss can lead to a conclusion much more favourable to the merger. This would run against the traditional rejection by antitrust authorities of the argument that 'we are colluding so successfully already that the merger will have little additional impact on competition.' The resolution in future cases of the tension between this traditional position of the authorities and the cost-benefit analysis under *Superior Propane* is an interesting and open issue.

B. Application

1. Introduction
We turn next to the application of the economic principles of merger analysis, to analyse the kinds of evidence one must bring to assess the competitive effects of a merger. Our discussion of evidentiary requirements is informed by the MEGs, tribunal and court decisions, and our own experience. Among the published works this section draws upon, two are particularly valuable: Steven C. Salop and Joseph J. Simons, 'A Practical Guide to Merger Analysis'[39] and Malcolm B. Coate and A.E. Rodriguez, *The Economic Analysis of Mergers.*[40]

The natural starting point for assessing a particular merger is to investigate the impact of similar mergers in the past. We discuss this and related evidence, then turn to evidentiary requirements within the now-standard framework outlined in the merger guidelines of Canada and the United States. This framework starts by defining a market or markets within which the merging firms compete. The market must be defined in two dimensions: the relevant product market and the geographic market. The second step in the framework is to set out the competitive impact of the merger. This consists of determining the increase in concentration in the relevant market (for which safe harbour benchmarks are established in the guidelines) and analysing market conditions that would lead one to conclude that the calculated increases in concentration understate or overstate the anticompetitive impact of the merger under each of the unilateral and interdependence theories. These factors would include the ability of buying firms to provide the product internally through vertical integration as well as

---

39 (1984) 29 *Antitrust Bulletin* 663.
40 Center for Trade and Commercial Diplomacy, Monterey Institute of International Studies, March 1997.

the extent of competitive discipline provided by alternatives not strong enough to be included in the relevant market. Evidence on barriers to entry is then evaluated to determine if any potential anticompetitive impact of the merger would be eliminated or strongly mitigated by the prospect of entry into the market. Finally, evidence is brought to bear on efficiencies that could be expected from the merger.

2. *Direct Evidence of the Competitive Impact of a Merger*

(a) The Impact of Historical Mergers
Even before considering the issue of a relevant market for a merger, one should analyse evidence on the impact of mergers similar to the merger under consideration. The impact of these mergers on the prices of the merging firms' products and the products of their closest substitutes, when available, is more fundamental than market definition. If mergers of the type under consideration have not increased prices substantially in the past in other (geographic) markets where the impact on concentration has been similar, there is generally no basis for assuming that the current merger will – whatever the relevant market. This type of analysis has been used in analysing mergers of banks and of radio stations in the United States. Both industries have experienced more than a thousand mergers in recent times, providing a large potential data set. The results of historical merger analysis such as this can be 'imported' to Canadian markets, with careful consideration of potential differences between the industries in the United States. and Canada.

(b) Analysis of the Impact of Local Market Structure, or Structural   Changes
In the analysis of the proposed Canadian bank mergers in 1998, evidence on the price impact of the numbers of local branches and the concentration of local markets was considered by economic experts on both sides of the merger cases. This evidence is useful, of course, only for products that are priced locally. The evidence can be used to estimate directly the impact of a proposed merger (prior to consideration of the relevant market). For example, the empirical results of such analysis may show that a merger of the type being considered has no effect on pricing, whatever the conditions of the local 'market.' More frequently, the results are useful for both direct evidence on competitive effects as well as the product market definition. For example, in an

analysis of the impact of bank mergers, empirical results might demonstrate that the number of financial institutions broadly defined made a difference to local prices charged by banks, but that the number of banks *per se* did not – once the former variable was controlled for. This type of evidence would support a market definition broader than the services offered at banks alone.

The analysis of both historical data on similar mergers as well as cross-sectional data is essentially a 'reduced form' model. Reduced form econometric or statistical models estimate directly the relationship between fundamental conditions (market conditions) and the variables of interest (prices). Both reduced form and structural models side-step the issue of market definition that is so central to the standard methodology.

In reduced form or direct estimation of the impact of mergers or local concentration on prices, a host of econometric issues arise that require careful treatment. We mention here the most common problem: the assumption in these models that the market conditions – or the mergers – are 'exogenous' variables, not causally determined in any way by variables that also influence prices. If costs and demand vary across markets in a such a way that markets with high prices tend also to be markets with high concentration (because these markets cannot support many firms), then statistical estimation of the relationship between concentration and prices could appear to show that increases in concentration *cause* higher prices. This causal interpretation would be wrong. Equally, if mergers tend to take place as a defensive measure in markets where costs threaten to increase, then statistics could show that mergers are followed by increasing prices. Again, the correlation would be spurious, not causal. The problem of spurious correlation can possibly be resolved by controlling for appropriate variables in the statistical reduced form estimation, or by developing fuller, 'structural' models of the relationships to be estimated. In the 1997 *Staples* case in the United States, in which econometric evidence was prominent, the argument of the respondents that the correlation between costs and prices was spurious did not succeed.[41] Evidence on the immediate effects of entry into concentrated geographic markets helped to resolve the identification problem in this case; this evidence showed that entry had a significant impact in lowering prices.

---

41 *Staples, Inc. v. Federal Trade Commission*, 970 F. S. 1066 (D.D.C., 1997).

3. Evidence on Market Definition

The most important proposition underlying competitive impact analysis, developed earlier in this chapter, is that high levels of concentration in a market may lead to supra-competitive prices. The now-standard approach to the competitive impact analysis of mergers, which is followed by both the Canadian and United States MEGs, starts with the determination of a relevant market. There may be many potential relevant markets; an anticompetitive effect in any one relevant or well-defined antitrust market is generally enough to find a merger anticompetitive.

Market definition is an input into analysis in almost all areas of antitrust. The hypothetical monopolist test at the heart of market definition was developed in Chapter 2; the case law basis for various criteria (such as functional substituability) is developed in the merger law section of the present chapter. Here we outline the classes of evidence that should be developed in determining whether product B is in the same market as product A.

(a) Evidence on Product Market Definition

(i) *Estimation of Cross-Elasticities of Demand*: Estimates of the cross-elasticities of demand between products A and B can be used to provide an estimate of the elasticity that counts: the own-price elasticity of demand for the hypothetical monopolist. With sufficient data the latter demand elasticity can be estimated directly and can then be used, through the Lerner condition, to determine whether the hypothetical monopolist test requires the inclusion of product B in the relevant market or whether the iterative determination of the market stops short of including that product.

Evidence sufficient to estimate cross-elasticities or own demand elasticities is rarely available in adequate quality and quantity. Inevitably, analysts turn to other indicators of substitutability.

(ii) *Evidence that Buyers Have Frequently Switched Between the Products in the Past in Response to Price Changes*: Evidence that buyers switch between A and B in response to relative price changes indicates a positive cross-elasticity between the products. Sometimes switching evidence is presented without corresponding price data. The danger in this approach is that buyers often 'switch' between products that are complements. For example, in the media industry buyers may advertise more intensively on television in one quarter and more intensively on radio in another. This evidence, however, does not deny a complementary relationship between the inputs of television and radio advertising, where the former is used periodically (and intensively) to establish brand recognition and provide product information and the latter is used to provide information on pricing specials. To take a second example, if consumers' clothing budgets were aggregated each quarter, one might find that consumers switched between high expenditures on shirts and high expenditures on socks. This would not make the two products substitutes. Price data are necessary to show that switches are price sensitive. Evidence that consumers switch between products in response to quality fluctuations, however, could substitute for price information.

As discussed in Chapter 2, one must be aware of the 'Cellophane fallacy' in assessing evidence that buyers are willing to switch between products. If a product market is monopolized, consumers will show willingness to substitute with marginal changes in price. This is because a monopolist will always raise price to the point where there is some substitution – not because the market is too small to be considered an antitrust market. The market definition issue is whether buyers would willingly switch in response to small price changes starting from competitive prices, not monopoly prices. Thus evidence that prices are close to costs, that profit rates are not excessive, or that the current structure and conduct suggest a competitive market is valuable in conjunction with switching evidence to establish a product market definition.

(iii) *Evidence on Functional Substitutability of Products*
This evidence includes:
- evidence that the sets of buyers for the two products are the same or very similar;
- evidence from interviews with buyers that the two products can be used to achieve the same purposes;
- detailed cost estimates of using product B to serve the purpose of product A. Examples include cost analysis of fuel subsitutability for various end-uses; cost analysis of media substitutability for reaching similar numbers of individuals; and cost comparisons among different methods of shipping; and
- econometric estimates of production functions or cost functions, which are complete mathematical descriptions of production technologies. These can be used to determine the cross-elasticity of

demand between two inputs (or a closely related parameter called the elasticity of substitution).

(iv) *Evidence Pertaining to the Elasticity of Demand in the case of an Input*: The key piece of evidence of this type is often the fraction of total costs that an input accounts for. This evidence pertains directly to a hypothetical monopolist's own-price elasticity of demand, rather than cross-elasticities. If a particular product accounts for a very small fraction of total expenditures of buyers, then the demand for the product will be inelastic. The hypothetical monopolist test will define the market narrowly even if there are moderately close substitutes. High-quality windshield wipers could conceivably be an antitrust market, in spite of the close functional substitutability of low-end windshield wipers, because some automobile manufacturers are unlikely to compromise the quality of their final product by scrimping on the quality of such a small-cost item. (Even in final good markets, the same principle is relevant: toothpicks could be a relevant antitrust market for a merger, in spite of the close substitutability of toothbrushes with toothpicks, because toothpick prices are so low.)

More generally, Alfred Marshall posited four determinants of the elasticity of demand of any input: the expenditure on the input as a fraction of total costs; the elasticity of substitution between the input and other inputs; the elasticity of final demand, from which the input demand is derived; and the elasticity of supply of complementary factors. The last two factors deserve elaboration. If the final demand for a product is highly elastic because of close substitutes, the demand for an important input will likely be elastic even if the input itself has no substitutes. Any increase in input price cannot be passed on to buyers of the final goods. Thus, evidence on substitutability of a downstream product can be useful in market definition analysis. To illustrate Marshall's final determinant of input demand elasticity, consider a merger that results in a monopoly in the market for the sale of corn-specific fertilizer (or seeds) to all corn producers in a given geographical area. Is the sale of fertilizer in this area a well-defined antitrust market? The competitiveness of the final market would suggest a highly elastic demand for the input, fertilizer. However, if fertilizer is used in fixed proportions with land and if the supply of land for corn production is inelastic, then the impact of higher fertilizer prices will be simply a reduction in the rental value and price of land particularly suitable for growing corn. Higher fertilizer prices would not have a large impact on the quantity demanded of fertilizer. That is, the demand for fertilizer would be inelastic. Key evidence in the market definition in a corn fertilizer merger would be the substitutability in supply of a complementary input, land, between various crop outputs (corn versus soybeans, for example).

Sales forces and intermediaries are an important class of inputs for which merger analysis would rely on evidence regarding the ratio of input costs to total costs. Real estate commissions are only 5 to 6 per cent of the total cost of purchasing a home on average. A hypothetical monopolist could easily raise the price of the commission by 5 per cent (or 25 to 30 basis points) of this amount. In the case of intermediaries, which purchase products for resale, the 5 per cent standard for substantial lessening of competition on the selling price is sometimes considered too lax by U.S. antitrust agencies. The agencies are likely to use 10 to 20 per cent of *value added* of the intermediary as a standard, or even a price percentage standard as low as 1 to 2 per cent of the final price in merger assessment.

(v) *Sellers' Strategy Documents*: Evidence on whom the merging parties consider their competitors to be is often available in internal strategy documents of the parties. Communications by the parties to buyers or general advertisements describing the advantages of product A over product B are also suggestive of a broader product market.

Evidence is sometimes brought in merger cases regarding the use of customer lists from one product class (B) by sellers in another (A). The suggestion is that this is evidence that producers of A compete for the buyers of product B and therefore that the products are in the same market. However, product complementarity or 'preference correlation' must be ruled out as alternative explanations: a seller of expensive clothing may value the customer list of Mercedes Benz but this does not mean that a suit and a car are substitutes.

(iv) *Impact of Specific Structural and Innovation Shocks in Market B on Prices in Market A*: If a dramatic shock to the supply in one market has little impact on prices or availability in another, the products are likely in separate markets. If the periodic updates of one class of software have little effect on the sales of another, the two are likely in separate markets.

(vii) *Correlation of Prices*: For two products to be in the same market, prices must vary closely. While this test is more useful in geographic market definition, it has some relevance to product market definition as well. But the tight correlation of prices of two products is not sufficient to place them in the same market unless all possible extraneous sources of correlation (such as common inputs or common shocks to demand) are controlled for.

(viii) *Brand Loyalty, Information Costs and Reputation; Switching Costs Generally*: In markets where consumers have imperfect information about the quality of a product, they may be reluctant to switch from one supplier to another. The individual-specific information held by each consumer on the products that she has purchased in the past may tie her to existing suppliers. The reluctance of customers to switch to other suppliers may leave a hypothetical single supplier of a group of products in a position where it could exercise market power, in which it would otherwise be disciplined by the threat of consumers leaving.[42]

Buyers may face switching costs of other kinds in moving from one product to another. Investment in complementary assets, such as other inputs that are compatible only with a specific brand, is one example, as is knowledge of how best to use a product ('product-specific human capital'). These also reduce cross-elasticity of demand with other products. For example, the Windows operating system for personal computers is an antitrust market because of the investment by consumers in compatible software and in familiarity with the product.

(b) Evidence on Geographic Market Definition

The geographic market issue is how broad the geographic areas are from which producers in the relevant product market can have significant disciplining force on the prices of the products sold by merging parties. The geographic market is defined using the same hypothetical monopolist test that underlies the definition of the relevant product market. In markets such as those for books, diamonds, and internet consulting, where transportation costs are low relative to the value of the product, geographic markets are broad. Geographic markets may be bound only by trade barriers. In Canadian cases, a central aspect of the geographic market definition is often whether or not to include imports. For markets such as cement, producer transportation costs are high enough to limit the geographic market to a narrow region. In

---

42 A related phenomenon is the specific capital that successful incumbent firms have in their reputations. Reputation is discussed as a barrier to entry below.

retail markets, store locations are fixed and the geographic market depends on the ability of consumers, rather than the product, to travel cost effectively.

The following types of evidence are helpful in establishing a geographic market.

(i) *Direct Evidence on Transportation or Shipping Costs, Relative to the Value of the Product*: If transportation costs from a given region to a proposed geographical market are less than 5 per cent of the price of the product in the candidate market, a single seller in the proposed market would not be able to achieve a substantial, nontransitory increase in price (under the Competition Bureau's standard of 5 per cent for 'substantial'). Customers would switch to producers in the region. The proposed geographical market would fail the hypothetical monopolist test.

In assessing transportation costs, it is important to consider the typical size of the purchase, so that fixed transportation costs can be averaged over the appropriate quantity. One could also bring evidence on the potential ability of consumers to purchase larger quantities in response to a significant price increase by a hypothetical monopolist, bringing into consideration the costs of storage.

(ii) *Information on Shipping Patterns*: The Elzinga-Hogarty test for geographic market specifies two criteria, based on shipments data, relevant to the delineation of a given area as a geographic market: 'little in from outside' (LIFO) and 'little out from inside' (LOFI).[43] If these criteria both fail, in that there are substantial shipments between areas A and B, then A is not a geographic market. That is, shipments data provide a test on which the hypothesis of a narrow geographic market can be rejected.

(iii) *Price Co-movements*: A number of authors have proposed tests based on the behaviour of prices in different geographic regions.[44] For

---

43 Kenneth Elzina and Thomas Hogarty, 'The Problem of Geographic Market Delineation in Antimerger Suits,' (1973) 18 *Antitrust Bulletin* 45.

44 These are discussed in David Scheffman and Pablo Spiller, 'Geographic Market Definition under the U.S. Department of Justice Merger Guidelines,' (1987) 30 *Journal of Law and Economics*, 123–47.

two regions to fall in the same geographic area the prices must move together, with the difference between them approximating the marginal transportation cost of shipment between the two regions. In terms of our example of regions A and B, evidence for rejection of the *broad* market definition (A plus B) would be a substantial divergence (a lack of correlation) in movements between prices in region A and prices in region B of products in the relevant product market.

Regarding the use of these tests in cases, we naturally expect merging parties to argue for rejection of the narrow market. Evidence in favour of the narrow market, divergent price dynamics, supports the challenge of the merger as substantially lessening competition. Of course, the evidence may show neither that the narrow market definition (i.e., that there are few shipments between A and B) nor the broad market definition (i.e., that prices follow very similar patterns in regions A and B) can be rejected. In this case, the pair of tests is indeterminate. Scheffman and Spiller describe an alternative approach, the estimation of residual demands, that circumvents this difficulty.[45] Full estimation of demands allows direct implementation of the hypothetical monopolist test for both the product market definition and the geographic market definition.

(iv) *Foreign Competition*: In many Canadian competition cases, a significant share of the demand for the relevant product is supplied through imports from the United States. An issue that must be addressed is how the competitive discipline provided by imports fits into the market definition stage of the conventional approach to merger analysis.

In some cases, foreign competition fits smoothly into the conventional framework for assessing mergers. In the *Hillsdown* case, the *supra*, tribunal included nearby suppliers located across the U.S.-Canadian border on the basis that those suppliers represented competitive alternatives for buyers in the market. In other cases, however, physical transportation costs may be low and one could reasonably argue that the geographic market is at least national. If one then interpreted significant imports to mean that the entire capacity of U.S. firms were available for supply to Canada and should be included in the geographic market, the impact of a Canadian merger on concentration

---

45 Scheffman and Spiller, 'Geographic Market Definition under the U.S. Department of Justice Merger Guidelines.'

would typically be negligible. This could represent an extremely optimistic view of the power of foreign competition to discipline domestic price increases. On the other hand, some recognition of imports as a competitive discipline is necessary.

William Landes and Richard Posner take an optimistic position: 'We argue that if a distant seller has some sales in a local market, *all* its sales, wherever made, should be considered a part of that local market for purposes of computing the market share of a local seller. This is because the distant seller has proved its ability to sell in the market and could increase its sales there, should the local price rise, simply by diverting sales from other markets.'[46]

Landes and Posner explain that if a domestic producer has a net cost advantage over foreign producers, its best strategy is to set a price just below the cost of those foreign producers in its market and thereby keep them out entirely. 'If those firms can sell one unit of the product in the domestic market, they ought to be able to sell many units there at no appreciably higher cost, since they have only to divert output from other markets.'[47]

Implicit in the Landes-Posner view is an assumption that the elasticity of supply of imports is infinite, or at least extremely high. If one believed this, however, one would assess as benign any merger in a market where there was at least a trickle of imports: any attempt by a merged firm to raise price above the pre-merger level would result in a flood of entry into the market. If the import market shares were this responsive to changes in domestic price, they would be equally responsive to changes in exchange rates.[48] Available evidence, while crude, does not support this extreme sensitivity of imports to exchange rate changes.[49]

A more moderate view is that imports provide a discipline on the exercise of market power by domestic firms that depends on the elasticity of import supply, and that evidence on this elasticity must be brought to bear on the issue of how much discipline is provided. A

---

46 William M. Landes and Richard A. Posner, 'Market Power in Antitrust Cases,' (1981) 94 *Harvard Law Review* 964.

47 Ibid., 965.

48 From the perspective of a foreign supplier, an increase in domestic price is equivalent to an increase in the exchange rate.

49 Morris Goldstein and Mohsin S. Khan, 'Income and Price Effects in Foreign Trade,' *Handbook of International Trade*, vol. 2, ed. R.W. Jones and P.B. Kenen (Amsterdam: North Holland, 1984), Table 4.3.

merger case involving a product with low transportation costs can easily lead to analysis in which the national Canadian market is too small to pass the hypothetical monopolist test for market definition, indicating that under the test the market should be expanded further to include the output or capacity of firms selling in the United States. The next iteration in the test to include the United States, however, could well lead to measures of concentration changes that greatly understate the potential impact of the merger on market power. In such a case, foreign competition is best assessed as a disciplining factor on price increases in the domestic market. Concentration increases in the domestic market then have to be interpreted in this light.

(c) Market Definition and Price Discrimination
In some markets, prices are determined specifically for each buyer through negotiations or separate prices established for different classes of buyers. In a market with buyer-specific prices, or price discrimination, the competitive impact analysis of a merger must start with the designation of a 'target group' of concern: a group of buyers, identifiable by the merged firm, who are potentially harmed by the merger. Only after the group is identified can relevant product and geographic markets be determined. These are established through the consideration of purchase alternatives for the target group, not for other consumers. The issue of market definition in this case is not whom the merging firms compete against, but whether the merged firm could successfully exercise market power against the target group.

Evidence that price discrimination exists in the pre-merger market is sufficient, but not necessary, to conclude that it will exist in the post-merger market. Competition between the merging firms may be the only deterrent of price discrimination pre-merger. The necessary and sufficient conditions for price discrimination are (1) differences among buyers in their elasticities of demand (in particular, in their competitive alternatives); (2) some means for the post-merger firm of identifying, even imperfectly, buyers of different elasticities; and (3) the absence of a perfect re-sale market. Evidence on these three conditions, along with the identification of a target group, is essential to assess a merger under the condition of price discrimination.

(d) Identifying the Sellers in the Relevant Market
Identification of the relevant sellers is undertaken after establishing the market definition. In the U.S. merger guidelines, but not the Canadian

guidelines, the distinction between market definition and seller identification is explicit; the market definition depends only on demand-side factors. In the majority of cases the relevant sellers are those firms currently supplying the product. In some cases, however, sellers of other products could easily use their production facilities to produce the relevant product. Sheet metal producers could easily switch to the production of hubcaps; textbook publishers could switch to the production of novels. In these cases, the suppliers with the capability of switching rapidly to the production of the products in question are counted as suppliers in the relevant market (and labelled 'uncommitted entrants' in the U.S. guidelines). Their presence would not affect the calculation of market shares of *output* among existing sellers (the relevant market is not extended to include product currently being produced by the other suppliers), but market shares are more appropriately calculated on the basis of *capacity* when such suppliers are present.

4. Competitive Impact Analysis
Given the relevant market, the first step in predicting the competitive impact of a merger is to determine the level of concentration in the pre-merger market and the change in concentration with the merger. Market shares of existing suppliers may be calculated on the basis of unit sales, in the case of a homogeneous product market, or revenue. The choice between these two measures is often made on the basis of availability of data. Where there are firms currently supplying a technologically similar product that could enter the market without significant investment, market shares are calculated on the basis of capacity rather than sales. Substantial excess capacity among some firms in the market, or the presence of firms with capacity to produce and sell in the market which are not currently producing, points to capacity as the basis for share calculations.

The MEGs state that the director will generally not challenge a merger under the theory of unilateral exercise of market power if the post-merger market share of the merged entity would be less than 35 per cent. Similarly, the director will generally not challenge a merger under the interdependence theory if the post-merger market share of the largest four firms is less than 65 per cent or if the post-merger share of the merging entities is less than 10 per cent.

Similar safe-harbour levels are provided in the U.S. guidelines. Unlike the Canadian guidelines, however, the U.S. guidelines also contain benchmarks for concentration and changes in concentration above which the merger will be treated by the agencies as presumptively anti-competitive.[50] With concentration parameters in this range, the burden of proof, in negotiations with the agencies, falls on the parties to demonstrate that the merger will not create or enhance market power. In Canada, by contrast, section 92(2) of the *Competition Act* states explicitly that the tribunal shall not find that a merger is likely to lessen competition solely on the basis of evidence of concentration or market shares.

Where the Canadian MEGs use only the share of the largest four firms as a measure of concentration, the U.S. guidelines adopt the more elaborate Herfindahl-Hirschman index (HHI). This index is calculated by summing the squares of the market shares of all of the firms in the industry. It varies from near zero for an industry with near-infinitesimal firms, to 10,000 for a monopoly. The HHI is the simplest measure of market concentration satisfying the criterion that any merger should have a positive impact on measured concentration. As a predictor of market power, it also has some basis in economic theory: in a very simple theory of oligopoly, the HHI equals the ratio of total industry profits to total industry costs.[51]

A post-merger HHI above 1,800 is the criterion for a 'highly concentrated' industry under the U.S. guidelines. For these industries a merger that increased HHI by less than 50 would be unlikely to be regarded as anticompetitive. The U.S. agencies regard industries with post-merger HHIs below 1000 as unconcentrated; mergers in these industries are unlikely to be anticompetitive. For 'moderately concentrated industries' with HHIs between 1,000 and 1,800, mergers that increase the HHI by less than 100 are unlikely to be challenged.

(a) Evidence on the Potential for Unilateral Effects

The first piece of evidence that is likely to be used to summarize the impact of a merger is the combined market share of the merging firms.

---

50 'Where the post-merger HHI exceeds 1800, it will be presumed that mergers producing an increase in the HHI of more than 100 points are likely to create or enhance market power or facilitate its exercise. The presumption may be overcome by a showing that factors set forth in Sections 2–5 of the Guidelines make it unlikely that the merger will create or enhance market power or facilitate its exercise, in light of market concentration and market shares.' U.S. Horizontal Merger Guidelines, section 1.5.
51 The oligopoly model is one in which firms vary only by cost differences, but each has a constant-returns-to-scale technology, and demand is linear.

The commissioner will generally not challenge a merger under the theory of unilateral exercise of market power if the post-merger market share of the merged entity would be less than 35 per cent. In an assessment of the potential for unilateral effects, evidence must be brought on additional evaluative criteria. These criteria include:

- excess capacity available on the part of rival firms;
- the ability of rival firms to expand their output quickly;
- evidence on the degree of product differentiation in the industry generally;
- the closeness of products of the two merging parties, as indicated by evidence on diversion ratios, which measure the extent to which consumers switching away from the products of one party switch to the products of the merging party, or cross-elasticities of demand;
- closeness of the products of the two merging parties to the products of other firms in the market, as indicated by the extent of consumer switching and other types of evidence analysed under market definition;
- other qualitative evidence, such as similarity in functional use or physical characteristics of the merging products relative to the products of rival firms;
- the presence of foreign competitors in the market, and the extent to which tariff or non-tariff barriers constrain the participation of foreign competitors;[52] and
- the extent to which one of the merging parties is likely to fail in the absence of the merger.

Two of the evaluative criteria deserve elaboration. First, in a market with product differentiation, evidence that two firms produce each other's closest substitutes and that products elsewhere in the market are only moderate substitutes for the combined firm's products would suggest a greater risk of substantial lessening of competition with the merger. Conceptually, a critical parameter is the ratio of the cross-elas-

---

52 The MEGs (p. 25) provide long list of factors affecting the extent to which the effectiveness of foreign competition is hindered. These include regulations on product quality or labelling, shipping costs or delays, exchange rate fluctuations, and the uncertainties associated with selling in a foreign market.

ticity of demand between the merging firms' products and the cross-elasticity of demand between those products collectively and other products in the market. In the U.S. guidelines and practice, the issue is addressed in part by considering the number of customers for whom the two preferred product brands or varieties are provided by the merging parties. If this number is substantial, then the merger is problematic under the unilateral effects theory.

Second, if one firm is likely to fail, the structure of the pre-merger market may no longer be an option. If an alternative buyer is unavailable for the failing firm's assets, the failing-firm defence of a merger is likely to succeed. An acquisition of a failing firm does not lessen competition if in the absence of the merger the assets of the firm would be removed from the market.

The failing-firm defence is well-founded if the assets of the failing firm, once it fails, would have little value in the market or if these assets would be removed from the market. If, however, the assets are so specific to the market (having little value outside it), they will most likely remain in the market through reorganization of the security claims to the assets. In this case, the failing-firm defence is not well-founded. Not all markets are like the market for air travel, where the main assets (planes) can be transferred with essentially no loss in value to other geographic markets.

In this respect, it should be noted that evidence of very low returns to capital in a market is not in itself supportive of mergers. Increasing prices to levels that would cover returns investors originally expected in a market is not in any sense a valid objective of competition policy. The original cost of market-specific assets is a sunk cost and irrelevant for any sensible social objective.[53] Competition in a market will ensure that prices are in line with marginal social *opportunity cost*, which includes the cost of allocating assets elsewhere in the economy. The original dollar investment in the assets does not enter into the determination of opportunity cost.

---

53 It is true that restrictive merger policy at the declining stage of industry life cycle has a detrimental impact on *ex ante* incentives to invest, assuming that the policy is foreseen by investors in general. The attraction of capital could even have a beneficial effect of lowering costs and prices in the early part of an industry life cycle. This does not justify a permissive policy towards substantial lessening of competition in declining industries, however. Competitive prices provide the optimal incentives or signals for investment over the life cycle of an industry.

(b) Evidence on the Potential for Interdependence

(i) *Incentive to Collude*: A merger can lead to a substantial lessening of competition if it enhances firms' ability to collude, explicitly or tacitly, or if it reduces the intensity of competition among firms in a market. The first set of evidence to be examined in analysing interdependence is the *incentive* for firms to collude. If the pre-merger market is characterized by a small number of competitive firms, and the merger would remove a 'maverick' from the market or eliminate a potential maverick, then a substantial lessening of competition is likely. In some markets – for example, the market for cola soft-drinks – concentration is high but rivalry is intense. The elimination of rivalry in such markets can make collusion much easier among remaining firms, or competition among these firms less intense.

The private benefits of a cartel depend more generally on the market power the cartel can exercise collectively but not individually. The greater the price increase that can be achieved through cartelization, in other words, the greater the profits from cartelization. The extent of market power depends, in turn, on four market variables: the elasticity of demand in the overall market, the market share of the colluding firms, the cross-elasticity of demand between the products sold by these firms and non-members of the cartel (such as a competitive fringe), and the speed of entry into the market.

These conditions might appear to present the respondents in a merger case with a dilemma. An argument that the pre-merger market is intensely competitive will lead to the conclusion that the incentives for cartelization are strong; an argument that the pre-merger market is not competitive will surely lead to the conclusion that the lack of competition will be exacerbated by an increase in concentration. In practice, a high intensity of competition will favour respondents (unless it is due to a rivalry that will be eliminated by the merger). While incentives for cartelization are high with intense rivalry, it is unlikely that a cartel can be successful in such a market.

We turn now to a discussion of evidence on conditions that allow successful collusion in a post-merger market. These conditions must facilitate one or more of the three tasks of cartel members: reaching an agreement, detecting departures from the agreement, and punishing defectors.

(ii) *Ability to Collude: Conditions Facilitating Agreement*: Reaching a cartel agreement on the prices in the post-merger market or on allocation of sales among firms is easy if:

- the number of firms in the market is small;
- industry communication – for example, through trade associations – is clear and frequent;
- the sizes (capacities) of the firms are similar, or if there is a single dominant firm that can act as a price leader, effectively re-establishing the 'agreed-upon' prices as market conditions change;
- the costs of the firms are similar;
- the products offered are similar;
- the products are standard rather than customized to each buyer; and
- costs (input prices) and demand conditions are stable.

In markets where products or costs differ among firms, reaching an agreement on what prices should be is difficult because the preferred prices will vary across firms. Low-cost firms prefer lower prices, and where products vary each firm would want its products to be priced at the lowest levels. Agreement would therefore be difficult with substantial variation in costs or product types. Similarly, if markets required agreement on prices specific to each buyer, cartel pricing could well be impossible. Market division, in which each firm agreed not to solicit the business of its rivals' customers, may be sustainable, however. Finally, highly variable cost and demand conditions would mean that agreements had to be renegotiated (at least implicitly) with high frequency. Reaching an agreement every month is more difficult than reaching an agreement every year. The presence in the market of a natural price leader is likely to be a necessary condition for cartel agreement when markets are unstable.

(iii) *Conditions Facilitating Cartel Monitoring*: The incentives to cheat in a post-merger cartel are diminished, and the chance of detecting cheating on a cartel agreement is enhanced, under the following conditions:

- the number of firms is small, and no firms are very small compared to the others except for reasons of high cost;
- pricing is transparent;
- non-price competition, such as quality, is transparent or limited in scope;
- transactions are not highly idiosyncratic;
- transactions are frequent and each transaction is small relative to the capacity of the firm;

- the number of buyers in the market is large;
- costs and demand are stable; and
- marginal cost rises rapidly with output, and capacity is slow to adjust.

These cartel factors are discussed in detail in Chapter 3. To summarize the discussion in the context of mergers, if costs or demand are unstable then monitoring is problematic, because of the difficulty of distinguishing the effects of cartel cheating from the effects of shocks to the market. Non-price competition is difficult to monitor, as it is to agree upon, because of the typical non-observability of competitors' advertising expenditures and other non-price dimensions of competition. If some firms are small, but able to expand capacity, their incentive to chisel on the cartel is especially high: the disruption they are likely to cause in the market by (say) doubling their market share is relatively small. A merger that eliminates a small firm with the potential to expand by undercutting any potential cartel prices would lessen competition.

If prices are not transparent, or transactions are highly idiosyncratic (e.g., the bundle purchased in each transaction is different), then it is difficult to know when a rival has cheated. With the combination of heterogeneity in buyer-seller relationships – for example, buyer-specific costs, multiplicity of products, and low transparency of some prices – collusion is difficult or impossible. Suppliers can cheat on the least observable price in the bundle offered to buyers. If non-price elements of the transaction are variable, non-transparent, or difficult to agree upon, cheating may take the form of offering excessive service. All of these factors limit the success of a cartel and are often prominent in the defence of mergers against interdependence concerns.

If transactions are large and infrequent, such as in the procurement by the government of some services, the incentive to cheat on a single transaction is large; the immediate benefits of cheating are substantial and certain relative to the future costs of reduced market discipline. If buyers in a market are very large, the switch of a single buyer representing a large share of demand from one seller to another may represent either cheating by the more attractive seller or simply a change in the buyer's needs. Large buyers can thus mitigate potential competitive problems with a merger not just because of the counterveiling power that they represent in the market but because of the difficulty large buyers present for the maintenance of a stable cartel on the sellers' side of the market.

(iv) *Conditions Facilitating Punishment*: To the extent that any deviant from a cartel agreement can be punished effectively, cheating is deterred. The presence of a dominant firm is helpful to a cartel in this regard, as are market conditions that lead to some product differentiation, especially geographical specialization by firms, so that the cheater may be targeted specifically. Merger to a dominant market position may thus present competitive problems not just through unilateral dominance but through interdependence of prices.

5. Evidence on Barriers to Entry

If the impact assessment leads to the conclusion that a merger would result in a substantial lessening of competition, given the competitive alternatives currently in the market, then the question arises as to whether entry can be relied upon to eliminate the concerns. While it is common to analyse barriers to entry after the assessment of the impact of the merger on competition among current suppliers, entry or potential entry is of course integral to the defence of many mergers and the pre-eminent argument in defence of some.

Barriers to entry consist of the sunk investment that must be undertaken by an entrant to reach the minimum efficient scale in the market, as well as any impediments to entry into a market such as regulatory limitations, and any factors likely to delay entry. Sunk investment is investment that cannot be recovered in the event of failure or withdrawal. The cost of entry is not the entire investment in capital needed by an entrant; it is the portion of the investment that cannot be sold for use in other markets. The costs of entry into airline routes, for example, are low not because airplanes are cheap but because they are easily transported to other geographic markets.

It is helpful, for understanding the role of entry in competition policy and the evidentiary requirements for entry, to start with the extreme case of zero entry barriers. The absence of barriers to entry is associated with the economic theory of contestable markets discussed above. Recall that a contestable market is one in which the power of potential entrants to enter quickly and undercut any price increase is so strong that incumbents are forced to maintain prices that just cover average cost. Even a single firm supplying a contestable market is disciplined to price at average cost because of the threat that an entrant, facing the identical cost structure, would undercut any price greater than average cost, thus attracting all of the incumbent's demand.

The equilibrium price in a contestable market with a single firm is

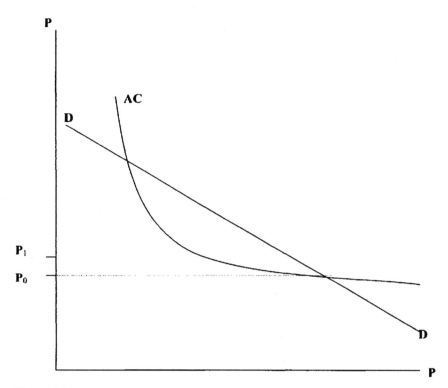

Figure 4.4
Equilibrium in a Contestable Market

depicted in Figure 4.4. In this figure the price, P_0, at which the demand curve intersects the average cost curve, AC, is the price at which average costs are covered. If the incumbent attempted to increase profits by raising price to, say, P_1, an entrant would immediately step in with a price between P_0 and P_1, capturing the entire market and earning positive profits. The entrant faces no risk of incurring losses with such entry, even if the incumbent subsequently responds, because the entrant can leave the industry without having incurred any sunk costs. The absence of sunk costs is a key to contestability.

Contestable markets are exemplified by a geographic retail market supplied at the wholesale level by a single firm. While Standard Fashion, discussed in Chapter 2, supplied the entire market for dress patterns in many cities, others stood ready to enter if prices were increased. To describe a market as contestable, one must visualize a line-up of potential suppliers bidding for the right to provide the demand in a market. The observed market structure reflects just the set of firms that won the bids and these firms (or firm) must continually win the right to supply the market against competition from potential entrants who can step in with no sunk entry costs whatsoever.

Reliance on contestability in merger cases, or complete reliance on entry, is sometimes invoked in industries where the concept is less realistic. Airline routes between cities are sometimes touted as a realistic example of contestable markets, since capital in this industry is 'on wheels' or wings: it is completely mobile. The absence of any market-specific investment is a key requirement for contestability. Airline routes, however, do not satisfy a second requirement of contestability. If the market is not one in which incumbents and entrants bid for the entire demand for the market, contestability requires that the prices of an incumbent be 'sticky' relative to the ability of an entrant to enter and leave. In the situation depicted in Figure 4.4, if the incumbent can quickly respond to proposed entry at a particular price (say, by finding out about the entrant's price at the same time as buyers are informed), that incumbent could respond to the entrant's price prior to any sales by the entrant. The strategy of entry in response to a high price would not be profitable.

In assessing barriers to entry, the bureau's assessment 'is directed toward determining whether entry by potential competitors would likely occur on a sufficient scale in response to a material price increase or other change in the relevant market brought about by the merger, to ensure that such a price increase could not be sustained for more than two years.'[54]

The role of barriers to entry interacts with the growth of demand, or the life cycle of the industry, in a way that is not widely appreciated. Consider, for example, an industry that is growing rapidly. Entry by new firms will take place in the future whether or not current prices increase. If a merger were to raise prices substantially, entry would simply take place at a faster rate. The rate of entry would remain higher than in the absence of the merger so long as prices remained above the level that would have prevailed in the absence of the merger. In a mar-

---

54 MEGs, 33.

ket with rapid growth and a high rate of entry, that is, the entry would soon re-establish the 'non-merger price path' over time. Entry would be very responsive to the exercise of market power because from the perspective of a potential entrant, the higher prices associated with the exercise of market power in a growing market do not have to justify *de novo* entry into the market; they need justify only *earlier* entry.

By way of contrast, consider a market on the downswing of its life cycle. Firms in this hypothetical market have invested substantially in market-specific assets in the past, have (possibly) earned a substantial return on those assets in previous years, and are now earning a very low rate of return on their original investment. A large increase in price would be insufficient to attract new capital to this market. The costs of entry in terms of specific investment required to reach minimum efficient scale, even if these costs are small, would be enough to deter entry even in response to a substantial exercise of market power.

Section 93(d) of the *Competition Act* highlights three types of barriers to entry: barriers to international trade, interprovincial barriers to trade, and regulatory barriers to entry. The following are additional market conditions related to barriers to entry for which evidence is needed in a merger case:

- past entry and turnover in the market;
- the time that it has taken new entrants to grow to a significant market share;
- evidence on scale economies using cost data at the plant or firm level, including estimation of the minimum efficient scale;[55]
- engineering studies on scale economies;
- evidence on the uncertainties faced by a new entrant;
- licensing restrictions and standard requirements;
- environmental laws that impose higher standards on new entrants than on incumbents;
- control over a limited stock of resource input;
- intellectual property rights such as patents or copyright;
- exclusive relationships (contractual or de facto) with downstream distributors or upstream suppliers;

---

55 Economists conventionally define the minimum efficient scale of a plant or firm to be the size necessary to achieve within 5 per cent of the minimum average cost attainable in a market.

- uncertainty on the part of buyers, leading to the need to establish a reputation; and
- firm-specific investment by buyers, or any commitment by buyers to existing sellers, including long-term contracts.

Analysis of barriers to entry and the evaluative criteria outlined above allow a conclusion as to the competitive impact of the merger. If the conclusion is that the merger will likely lead to substantial lessening of competition, evidence on efficiencies associated with the merger is critical.

6. Evidence on Efficiencies

Evidence of efficiency gains from a merger plays a role not just in demonstrating a possible trade-off between a lessening of competition and efficiency, but in the development of a business strategy explanation of why the parties are merging. Explanation of why the parties are merging – obviously one that does not involve increased ability to raise prices – is crucial to the respondents' side of a merger case. While the legal burden of proof rests with the commissioner, as a practical matter, without a well-developed alternative explanation of the benefits of a merger, the bureau or the tribunal is more likely to conclude that the merger is an attempt to increase market power. In practice, parties to a merger face a substantial evidentiary burden in demonstrating efficiencies. Potential cost-savings, or the ability to provide better service or products, must be supported with substantive and carefully documented evidence. Any efficiency claims that are merely asserted are unlikely to carry weight.

Canadian competition law on mergers differs from that of any other major economy in that the role for efficiency considerations is explicit. Section 96(1) of the *Competition Act* requires that efficiency gains be balanced against the effects of any prevention or lessening of competition that will result from the merger. The section explicitly constrains the tribunal from making an order against mergers that would involve a substantial lessening or prevention of competition if the gains from efficiency 'will be greater than, and will offset' the lessening of competition and if those gains would not likely be achieved through means other than the merger.

Evidence that is usefully brought on efficiencies includes the following:

- evidence that particular facilities could be shared by the merging parties;

- economic evidence of scale economies, using total cost data from firms in the industry or in similar industries;
- engineering estimates of scale economies;
- delineation of which job positions would be eliminated with the merger, with detailed explanations of why;
- evidence on the efficient design of joint shipping or distribution patterns for output that would rationalize the (overlapping) existing systems;
- gains from rationalizing the shipping of inputs to factories;
- gains from sharing of superior production techniques in one of the parties, as evidenced by lower average costs in achieving particular tasks in the pre-merger market;
- sharing of intellectual property;
- gains from superior inventory management, due to larger scale;
- gains from the ability of parties to specialize, post-merger, in different products or tasks within the combined firm;
- efficiencies in advertising or in raising capital.
- dynamic efficiencies in the more efficient development of future production techniques and products through more efficient innovation.

In delineating and quantifying the sources of efficiency gains, parties must be careful to avoid including efficiencies that are *private* gains but not *social* gains. These would include the ability to negotiate superior contracts with input suppliers – except to the extent that lower input prices are due to cost savings on the part of suppliers. Efficiencies that could be achieved without the merger, through internal growth or acquisition by a third party which presents no competition issues, are also properly excluded from efficiency calculations.

II. Premerger Notification: Information and Waiting Period Requirements

All mergers in Canada are subject to the substantive provisions of the *Competition Act*. The Competition Bureau is responsible for the review of mergers to determine whether a given transaction 'prevents or lessens, or is likely to prevent or lessen,'[56] competition substantially. While transactions exceeding certain size thresholds are subject to the prenotification requirements set out in Part IX of the Act before they can be

---

56 *Competition Act*, R.S.C. 1985, c. C-34, s. 92.

completed, the Bureau also becomes aware of transactions through voluntary disclosure by the parties; references from the Investment Review Division of Industry Canada; monitoring of transactions in newspapers, trade journals, and other publications; informal complaints from interested parties such as customers, suppliers, or competitors of the merging parties; and requests for formal inquiries by the minister of industry. In addition, under section 9(1) of the Act, any six Canadian residents who believe that (a) a person has contravened or failed to comply with an order made pursuant to section 32, 33, or 34 or Part VIII; (b) grounds exist for the making of an order under Part VIII; or (c) an offence under Part VI or VII has been or is about to be committed, may apply to the commissioner to conduct an inquiry into such matters.

The pre-merger notification provisions of Part IX of the Act apply if (1) the parties, together with their affiliates, have assets in Canada or annual gross revenues from sales in, from, or into Canada in excess of $400 million; (2) in the case of an asset acquisition, the value of the Canadian assets acquired or the annual gross revenues from sales in or from Canada generated by those assets exceed $35 million; (3) in the case of an acquisition of shares of a public company which owns assets in Canada (other than assets that are shares of the corporation or any corporations controlled by that public company) that exceed $35 million or whose gross revenues from sales in or from Canada would exceed $35 million, the acquisition results in the acquirer holding voting shares that carry more than 20 per cent of the outstanding votes (or more than 50 per cent if the acquirer already holds 20 per cent or more) attached to all the voting shares of the corporation, and in the case of an acquisition of shares of a private company, the acquisition results in the acquirer holding voting shares that carry more than 35 per cent of the outstanding votes (or more than 50% if the acquirer already holds 35% or more) attached to all the voting shares of the corporation; (4) in the case of an amalgamation, the corporation resulting from the amalgamation owns assets in excess of $70 million or has gross revenues from sales in or from Canada that would exceed $70 million and (5) in the case of a combination, the combination owns assets in Canada exceeding $35 million or has gross revenues from sales in or from Canada that would exceed $35 million.[57]

57 *Competition Act*, ss. 109–12. See A.N. Campbell and M.J. Trebilcock, 'Interjurisdictional Conflict in Merger Review,' chap. 5 in L. Waverman, W.S. Comanor, and A. Goto, eds., *Competition Policy in the Global Economy* (London: Routledge, 1997), 98–9

When a proposed merger is subject to the prenotification and waiting period requirements of Part IX of the Act, the merging parties can choose to submit either a short-form or a long-form filing to the bureau, along with the applicable fee of $25,000.[58] However, where the parties make a short-form filing, the commissioner may require them to submit a long-form filing within the fourteen-day waiting period applicable to a short-form filing.[59]

The 1999 amendments to the Act increased the information required for pre-merger notification from the requirements set out in the 1986 Competition Act. The short-form requires information including: (1) a description of the proposed transaction and the business objectives the acquirer intends to achieve through the transaction, (2) a list of foreign authorities which have been notified of the proposed transaction by the parties and date of the notification; (3) a description of the principal businesses of the merging parties; (4) the most recent annual report and, if the annual report is not available or if different than those contained in the report, audited financial statements relating to the parties' principal businesses for their most recently completed fiscal year, and financial statements for subsequent interim periods, plus the most recent drafts of legal documents pertaining to the transaction; (5) a summary description of the principal categories of the products of the merging parties; (6) statements identifying for each of those principal categories of products the twenty most important current suppliers and customers and the annual volume or dollar value of the transactions with such suppliers and customers; and (7) the geographic regions of sales for the principal businesses and the principal businesses of the affiliates of the parties.[60] The long-form has more onerous information requirements than the short form. It requires not only the information in the short-form filing but substantial additional information, such as all studies and reports prepared or received by a senior officer for the purpose of evaluating or analysing the proposed trans-

---

for a review of procedural issues in Canadian competition law. See generally C. Green, 'Mergers in Canada and Canada's New Merger Law,' (1987) 32 *Antitrust Bulletin* 253, R.S. Khemani, 'The Administration of Canadian Merger Policy 1986–1989,' (1994) 39 *Antitrust Bulletin* 771, and H.I. Wetston, 'Notifiable Transactions Under the Canadian Competition Act,' (1988) 57 *Antitrust L.J.* 907.

58 *Competition Act*, s. 120.

59 Ibid., s. 123.

60 See *Proposed Regulations Respecting Notifiable Transactions Pursuant to Part IX of the Competition Act*, s. 16, *Canada Gazette*, 15 May 1999.

action and all marketing, business, and strategic plans prepared or received by a senior officer that have been implemented in Canada over the last three years or are to be implemented in Canada for each of the principal categories of products produced, supplied, or distributed by each party and its affiliates.[61]

If parties opt to submit a short-form filing, the transaction is subject to a fourteen-day waiting period following the filing before closing of the transaction.[62] Parties who have submitted a long-form filing are subject to a forty-two-day waiting period, but where the proposed transaction is an acquisition of voting shares through a Canadian stock exchange, the waiting period is reduced to 'twenty-one trading days, or such longer period of time, not exceeding forty-two days, as may be allowed by the rules of the stock exchange before shares may be taken up.'[63]

III. The Compliance Approach to Enforcing the Competition Act: Possible Dispositions of the Commission with Regard to Merger Reviews

Recognizing that mergers are sensitive to delays and uncertainty, the bureau has adopted a 'compliance-oriented' approach that provides alternatives to fully contested proceedings, which can lead to long delays and higher costs for all parties. This approach provides businesses with a measure of certainty as to the likely view of the bureau regarding the competitive effects of the merger.[64]

A. Advance Ruling Certificates

Prior to a transaction, parties can apply to the bureau for an Advance Ruling Certificate (ARC), along with the applicable fee of $25,000.

---

61 See ibid. s. 17, for a list of the information required for a long-form filing.
62 *Competition Act*, s. 120.
63 Ibid., s. 123(c).
64 See G.N. Addy, 'The Bureau of Competition Policy's Compliance Approach,' (1993) 38 *McGill L.J.* 861, Director of Investigation and Research, *Information Bulletin No.3 – Program of Compliance* (Ottawa: Consumer and Corporate Affairs Canada, June 1989), and G.N. Addy, 'Private Rights and the Public Interest Under Canada's Competition Act: Procedural Guarantees and the Independence of the Director of Investigation and Research,' (1993) Antitrust in a Global Economy,' (New York, N.Y.: Fordham Corporate Law Institute, 21–2 Oct. 1993) Industry Canada (Speech).

Section 102 states of the *Competition Act*:

102. (1) Where the Commissioner is satisfied by a party or parties to a proposed transaction that he would not have sufficient grounds on which to apply to the tribunal under section 92, the Commissioner may issue a certificate to the effect that he is so satisfied.

(2) The Commissioner should consider any request for a certificate under this section as expeditiously as possible.

The bureau has provided case studies regarding the issuance of ARCs[65] and it has also provided some guidance as to the matters that will be considered by the commissioner on an ARC application.[66] However, cases in which an ARC has been issued are usually not reported, hence there is no publicly accessible body of precedents regarding the use of this disposition by the commissioner. In general, issuance of an ARC can be expected when no anticompetitive effects can be anticipated and/or when the commissioner concludes that a transaction is likely to be procompetitive.[67]

Parties who wish to have a high degree of comfort that the commissioner will not subsequently challenge the transaction find obtaining an ARC desirable, because under section 103 of the Act, the issuance of an ARC prevents the commissioner from applying to the tribunal under section 92 in respect of the transaction solely on the basis of information that is substantially the same as the information on the basis of which the ARC was issued, if the transaction is substantially completed within one year after the ARC is issued. It is important to note that the commissioner may revoke the ARC and challenge a merger if additional information that is not 'substantially the same' as that provided during an ARC application is revealed. Therefore, it is in the interest of merging parties to ensure that all information needed for an accurate assessment of the effects of the proposed transaction is provided from the outset.

---

65 Director of Investigation and Research, *Information Bulletin No. 2 – Advance Ruling Certificates* (Ottawa: Consumer and Corporate Affairs Canada, December 1988).

66 Ibid., 1999, Part III.

67 A.N. Campbell, *Merger Law and Practice: The Regulation of Mergers under the Competition Act* (Scarborough, Ont.: Carswell, 1997) at 252.

In addition, an ARC exempts parties from the pre-merger notification requirements of Part IX of the Act. In straightforward transactions that do not raise significant competition issues, the information required for an ARC could be more readily available and less costly to compile than the information required by Part IX of the Act.[68] A proposed Procedures Guide issued by the bureau states that the information provided should be similar to the short-form information requirements.[69] Information supplied to the Bureau in an ARC application is protected by section 29 of the Act, which provides that no information supplied in a request for an ARC may be disclosed by the bureau 'to any other person except to a Canadian law enforcement agency or for the purposes of the administration or enforcement of the Act.'[70]

The Act requires the commissioner to consider any request for an ARC as expeditiously as possible,[71] but does not set out a time limit in which the commissioner is required to decide whether to issue an ARC. In practice, the bureau usually requires approximately three to four weeks to consider ARC applications in straightforward transactions that do not raise significant issues.[72]

B. Advisory Opinions

To support the compliance approach, the bureau has developed a program of written and oral advisory opinions to assist businesses in complying with the Act, although there is no statutory provision for advisory opinions. Parties can request advisory opinions, on payment of specified application fees, before or after formal filing. However, advisory opinions do not exempt parties from the pre-merger notification requirements if the parties cross the threshold for prenotification. In practice, where the proposed merger is not subject to the pre-merger notifications of the Act, parties often request an advisory opinion in lieu of an ARC. Although, unlike ARCs, advisory opinions are not

---

68 C.S. Goldman and J.D. Bodrug, 'The Merger Review Process: The Canadian Experience,' (1997) 65 *Antitrust L.J.* 573 at 591. See also P.S. Crampton and R. Corley, 'Merger Review under the Competition Act: Reflections on the First Decade,' (1997) 65 *Antitrust L.J.* 535.
69 Proposed Procedures Guide, *Canada Gazette*, 15 May 1999, Pt III.
70 *Competition Act*, s. 29(1).
71 Ibid., s. 102(2).
72 MEGs, n7, s. 6.5.

binding on the commissioner, they do provide businesses with guidance as to whether the commissioner is likely to challenge the transaction. Further, the commissioner has a strong incentive to honour advisory opinions: the credibility of the compliance approach would be undermined by failure to do so. However, like ARCs, advisory opinions are issued on the basis of information provided to the bureau, and thus subject to reconsideration if the terms of the transaction change or if new information becomes available to the bureau. Merging parties recognize that advisory opinions are not legally binding but can be changed if the bureau receives new information. Therefore, they find it in their own interest to provide relevant information needed for the bureau's advisory opinion to ensure that they receive an accurate opinion. Moreover, the commissioner can initiate a formal inquiry under section 10(b) of the Act when he has 'reasonable grounds' to believe that the Act has been or is about to be contravened.[73] Pursuant to section 11 of the Act, the commissioner can compel disclosure by requiring parties to (i) attend one or more oral examinations under oath; (ii) produce 'a record, or any other thing' specified in the order; and (iii) deliver a written return. As well, if the commissioner has not made an application to contest a merger under section 92 of the Act but believes that parties intend to proceed with a merger that may be anticompetitive, the commissioner may apply to the tribunal under section 100 of the Act (amended in 1999 to relax the criteria) for an interim order preventing parties from proceeding with the merger, because the effects of the merger, if found to be anticompetitive, would be difficult to reverse.

Unlike requests for ARCs, information supplied to the bureau in requests for advisory opinions is not formally protected by the confidentiality provisions in section 29 of the Act, as it is considered information supplied voluntarily. However, the commissioner has confirmed in a 1995 statement that, given the generally sensitive nature of such information, it is his practice to treat all voluntarily supplied information as if it were protected by section 29.[74] Also, unlike requests for ARCs, the commissioner is not under any statutory obligation to respond expeditiously to advisory opinion requests. However, the bureau has generally been responsive to the time sensitivity of proposed mergers.[75]

---

73 *Competition Act*, s. 10(b).
74 Director of Investigation and Research, Communication of Confidential Information under the *Competition Act* (May 1995).
75 Campbell, *Merger Law and Practice*, at 263.

Advisory opinions are generally not reported. Thus cases in which advisory opinions have been sought provide little guidance to private parties as to whether such opinions may be issued. The principal types of advisory opinions include the following.[76]

(1) Clean 'no action' letter. Based on the information provided, the Commissioner is satisfied that grounds do not exist to bring an application under section 92 of the Act with regard to the proposed transaction. This favourable advisory opinion is similar to an ARC in that it allows merging parties to benefit from significantly reduced uncertainty. However, it preserves the commissioner's future enforcement options in situations where he is not sufficiently certain to issue an ARC.

(2) Qualified 'no action' letter – confidentiality limitation. In sensitive situations, parties may have provided confidential information and requested that the bureau not make any industry contacts until a later date. Hence, the bureau is unable to verify that information provided in an ARC application. Based on the information provided but without having verified the information, the commissioner has concluded that grounds do not exist to bring an application under section 92 of the Act, but that conclusion is qualified by the fact that the likely competitive effects of the proposed transaction could change once the bureau makes industry contacts.

(3) Qualified 'no action' letter – concerns raised and monitoring. This opinion is issued when, based on the information available, the commissioner is satisfied that grounds do not exist at that time to bring an application under section 92 of the Act, but there are concerns regarding the potential consequences of the transaction. The bureau will therefore monitor the effects of the merger for the three-year limitation period provided in section 97 of the Act. This opinion is typically given after a field investigation. The nature of the monitoring varies according to individual transactions, but in general, market conditions and the activities of the merging parties are monitored. Monitoring is only an interim disposition as, before the expiry of the three-year monitoring period, the commissioner may pursue other enforcement options, such as negotiating a

---

76 Discussion of the types of advisory opinions is drawn from Goldman and Bodrug, 'The Merger Review Process,' 594 and Campbell, *Merger Law and Practice*, chap. 10.

restructuring or launching a contested proceeding before the Competition tribunal.

(4) Proceed at your own risk. While the commissioner has not concluded the assessment of the proposed merger, he has identified serious potential concerns. The commissioner does not, however, intend to bring an application for an injunction provided by section 100 of the Act. If the parties wish to close regardless of the advisory opinion, they do so at their own risk. This opinion is generally given before a field investigation is completed and prior to the commissioner's decision whether to challenge the proposed merger. It thus involves a greater risk of a challenge after the transaction has closed.

(5) Serious concerns – request for delay of closing or a hold-separate arrangement. This opinion is issued when the commissioner has not concluded his assessment but has identified serious concerns. The commissioner may request that the parties (a) postpone the closing of the proposed merger pending the conclusion of his review, (b) provide an acceptable undertaking to hold separate the business to be acquired pending the conclusion of his review, (c) consent to an interim injunction under section 100 of the Act, failing which the commissioner will bring a contested application pursuant to section 92 of the Act, (d) give the commissioner notice as to the closing date.

(6) Serious concerns – advisory opinions based on pre-closing restructuring or post-closing undertakings. In some situations, serious concerns regarding the consequences of the proposed merger are raised, but the commissioner negotiates with the parties to reach an agreement to restructure the transaction so that anticompetitive effects are mitigated. Where restructuring will not be completed until after the merger, the commissioner may, in rare circumstances, be willing to accept post-closing undertakings from the parties. An undertaking is a written promise by one or more of the merging parties to take some action in the future, such as a partial divestiture.[77] After the pre-closing restructuring or post-closing undertaking, a favourable advisory opinion will normally be issued.

---

77 See, for example, the *Undertakings by the Great Atlantic and Pacific Company of Canada, Limited to the Director of Investigation and Research* (October 1990) in relation to the *A&P/Steinberg* merger.

Although there is no statutory provision for pre-closing restructuring or post-closing undertakings, and as noted previously advisory opinions are not legally binding, the credibility of the compliance approach would be seriously undermined if, after restructuring or negotiating an undertaking upon reliance on the commissioner's opinion, the transaction is subsequently contested before the tribunal. Thus, it can be expected that once the parties have restructured or the commissioner has accepted an undertaking, the transaction will not be challenged. Despite the lack of statutory authority for undertakings, the Competition tribunal in *Imperial Oil*[78] and the Federal Court of Appeal in *Ultramar*[79] have recognized the commissioner's ability to use undertakings to administer the Act.

In pre-closing restructuring settlements, the commissioner will sometimes include a monitoring clause to put the parties on notice that the transaction may be subject to future challenge despite the restructuring. For example, the commissioner approved of the Canada Safeway Limited/Woodward Stores Limited merger on condition that Canada Safeway undertake to divest twelve food stores in six urban markets and that it provide information that would enable the commissioner to monitor those six urban markets and three other markets for a three-year period.[80]
Parties typically prefer undertakings to consent order proceedings before the tribunal because undertakings are usually faster to implement than consent orders and entail less public visibility.[81] Common types of undertakings include partial divestitures and behavioural undertakings in which parties commit to engage or refrain from engaging in certain activities. Undertakings are normally monitored to ensure compliance, because if they are not honoured, the commissioner will not be able to contest the merger when the three-year limitation period for challenging a merger runs out. However, in *Ultramar*,

---

78 *Canada (Director of Investigation and Research) v. Imperial Oil Ltd.*, 26 January 1990, Doc. no. CT-89/3 (Comp. Trib.) (unreported).
79 *Nova Scotia (Attorney General) v. Ultramar Canada Inc.* (1995), 127 D.L.R. (4th) 517.
80 *Canada Safeway Limited/Woodward Stores Limited*, summarized in Director of Investigation and Research, *Press Release – D.I.R. Allows Safeway Acquisition* (Ottawa: Consumer and Corporate Affairs Canada, N–87–7, 20 May 1987).
81 The differences between consent order proceedings and undertakings are discussed in section III. C below.

the Federal Court stated that undertakings are 'deemed to be a contract governed and construed for all purposes under the laws of Ontario and Canada' and '[a]t the least those purposes include that of interpretation and that of enforcement,'[82] suggesting that undertakings may be enforceable through an action for breach of contract. As well, undertakings may be enforceable by way of conversion into a consent order, that is, the commissioner may accept an undertaking only if it is backed by a signed consent of the parties to a consent order on the same terms. This technique of an 'agreement to agree' to a consent order on the same terms as the undertaking was implemented in the *A&P/Steinberg* undertakings.[83]

However, despite the acknowledgment by the courts with respect to the enforceability of undertakings, in practice, where serious anticompetitive concerns are raised by a proposed merger, the commissioner is usually not disposed to accept post-merger undertakings for restructuring but would prefer instead a consent order, likely to provide for greater certainty of enforcement.[84] This reluctance to accept post-merger undertakings is borne out by the statistics, which show that for the 1,535 mergers assessed between 1986 and 1995, the commissioner has accepted post-closing undertakings in only 10 cases.[85]

In summary, advisory opinions seek to assist parties in complying with the Act and give some measure of guidance as to the likely actions of the commissioner. However, it is important to remember that advisory opinions are not legally binding and that the opinions are only as robust as the facts which have been provided to the bureau.

C. Consent Order Applications

After reviewing a proposed merger, the commissioner may also apply to the tribunal for a consent order under section 92 or section 105 of the

---

82 *Ultramar, supra* (1995), 127 D.L.R. (4th) at 544.

83 See *Undertakings by the Great Atlantic and Pacific Company of Canada, Limited, supra,* note 76, p. 4, cls.12 and 13.

84 For example, see *Canada (Director of Investigation and Research) v. ADM Agri-Industries, Ltd.,* [1997] C.C.T.D. No. 25 Trib. Dec. No. CT9702/13 (Q.L.) [hereinafter *Maple Leaf Mills*] where the director sought a consent order in which ADM agreed to the divestiture of certain assets. Instead of addressing anticompetitive concerns through a post-merger undertaking and arguably saving time, the director preferred a consent order.

85 Data from Campbell, *Merger Law and Practice,* 292 derived from *DIR (Annual Reports).*

Act.[86] Like undertakings, consent orders are negotiated between the commissioner and the parties.

Consent order applications differ from undertakings in that they are more formal and public, and hence more time-consuming and costly. In addition, consent orders endorsed by the tribunal become a judgment of the tribunal and are legally enforceable beyond the three- year limitation period in section 97 of the Act. Consent orders are sought in situations where a case has broad economic significance or public impact. A future variation of the obligations may be required beyond the three-year limitation period; or the case would otherwise be of unique and precedential value.[87] For example, Imperial Oil's acquisition of Texaco Canada was brought before the tribunal in a consent order proceeding because of the broad public interest in the impact of the merger on the petroleum industry.[88] Also, consent order applications are often the result of the settlement of contested proceedings prior to adjudication by the tribunal.[89] Consent order proceedings before the tribunal will be discussed in greater detail below. Under recent amendments to the Act (Bill C-23, 2001), the commissioner may register a consent order with the tribunal, and it becomes enforceable as if an order of the tribunal.

D. Contested Proceeding Applications

In situations where there are serious anticompetitive effects and no satisfactory restructuring can be negotiated, the commissioner will typically apply to challenge the merger before the tribunal.[90] Neither provincial authorities nor private parties can initiate a proceeding before the tribunal or a court to contest a merger. Only the commis-

---

86 The application for a consent order may or may not arise from an advisory opinion requested by merging parties. For a discussion on the differences in the scope of the tribunal's powers to issue consent orders under ss.92 and 105, see the discussion below in section IV.

87 C.S. Goldman, 'The Merger Resolution Process IV. under the Competition Act: A Critical Time in its Development,' (1990) 22 *Ottawa L.R.* 1 at 7.

88 Director of Investigation and Research, *Press Release – DIR Statement on Imperial Oil's Acquisition of Texaco Canada Shares* (Ottawa: Consumer and Corporate Affairs Canada, NR–89–11, 24 February 1989), 2.

89 For example, *Palm Dairies, Asea Brown Boveri, Gemini*, and *Seaspan*, started as contested proceedings and were converted into consent orders.

90 A contested proceeding application may or may not arise from an advisory opinion requested by parties.

sioner can initiate proceedings before the tribunal and apply to the tribunal for remedial orders, including orders to dissolve or enjoin a merger.

IV. Competition Tribunal Proceedings

The Competition Tribunal is empowered to issue consent orders under section 92 or section 105 of the Act. Section 105 allows the tribunal to issue a consent order without hearing such evidence as would ordinarily be placed before it had the application been contested. Thus the tribunal can issue orders under section 105 without making a finding as to whether the merger would have been anticompetitive. Under section 92 of the Act, the tribunal can issue remedial orders with respect to a merger only if it has been found anticompetitive, by requiring dissolution of the merger or divestiture of certain assets. It can also direct any other action to be taken provided that the commissioner and the person against whom the order is made both consent to that order.

In addition, the tribunal can make temporary orders before a contested merger proceeding or a consent order proceeding is formally launched. As noted above, the tribunal is empowered to grant interim orders and injunctions under section 100 of the Act to prevent parties from taking actions that could render the effects of a merger irreversible if the merger is found to be anticompetitive or if the tribunal finds that there has been a contravention of the pre-merger notification provisions in section 114.[91] Under section 100, an interim order of not more than thirty days is available where the commissioner has not yet filed an application challenging a merger under section 92 of the Act. The tribunal may also issue interim orders under section 104. The commissioner may apply for an interim order under section 104 of the Act after he has brought an application challenging the merger. Section 104 provides that the order may be on such terms and have effect for 'such period of time as the tribunal considers necessary and sufficient to meet the circumstances of the case'; such a provision thus allows the tribunal to issue interim orders that apply for a greater period of time than the thirty-day limit for interim orders in section 100. Because of the urgent nature of an application under section 100, where the commissioner may need to obtain an injunction to stop parties from taking action that would be difficult to reverse, although he has yet to bring

---

91 *Competition Act*, s. 100.

an application to challenge the merger, section 100(3) contains provisions for the tribunal to proceed with the application on an *ex parte* basis. Section 100(3) provides that the tribunal may proceed with the application *ex parte* if: (a) it is satisfied that the normal forty-eight hours' notice of an application for an interim order cannot reasonably be complied with; or (b) the urgency of the situation is such that service of notice would not be in the public interest. Where the interim order is issued on *ex parte* application because the merging parties have failed to comply with the pre-merger notification provisions contained in section 114 of the Act, the duration of the interim order is limited to ten days after the parties have complied with section 114; otherwise, the order is effective for thirty days after section 114 is complied with. In addition, under section 100(7) of the Act, the commissioner may apply to the tribunal for an extension of the duration of the interim order to a maximum of sixty days, if he provides forty-eight hours notice to the parties and is able to establish that he was unable to complete an inquiry within the period specified in the order because of circumstances beyond his control.

To date, *Superior Propane*[92] is the only application brought by the commissioner for an interim order under section 100 of the Act. Prior to the 1999 amendments to the Act, section 100 of Act provided that:

100.(1) Where, on application by the commissioner, the tribunal finds, in respect of a proposed merger of which an application has not been made under section 92 or previously under this section, that

(a) the proposed merger is reasonably likely to prevent or lessen competition substantially and, in the opinion of the tribunal, in the absence of an interim order a party to the proposed merger or any other person is likely to take an action that would substantially impair the ability of the tribunal to remedy the effect of the proposed merger on competition under section 92 because that action would be difficult to reverse, or

(b) there has been a failure to comply with section 114 in respect of the proposed merger,

the tribunal may issue an interim order forbidding any person named in

---

92 *Supra*, note 17.

the application from doing any act or thing that it appears to the tribunal may constitute or be directed toward the completion or implementation of the proposed merger.

The commissioner sought an interim order prohibiting the acquisition by Superior Propane Inc. of ICG Propane Inc. from a wholly owned subsidiary of Petro-Canada Inc. on the grounds that the proposed transaction was reasonably likely to substantially lessen or prevent competition in the propane industry. In rejecting the commissioner's application, the tribunal discussed the different standard of proof to be met on an application under section 100 of the Act compared to that under section 104. The tribunal observed that the jurisdiction vested in the it under section 100 of the Act was 'an extraordinary type of jurisdiction in that it grants the commissioner a form of relief, not only before trial, but before his pleadings have been filed' and that in such applications, public interest considerations would have to be given significant weight. The tribunal found that for an order to issue under section 100, the commissioner has to establish that: (i) the proposed transaction is reasonably likely, that is, on a balance of probabilities, to prevent or lessen competition substantially; and (ii) in the absence of an interim order, a party to the proposed merger, or any other person, is likely to take an action that would substantially impair the ability of the tribunal to remedy the effect of the proposed merger on competition under section 92 of the Act because the action would be difficult to reverse. On the other hand, the tribunal found that the standard of proof for an interim order under section 104 of the Act is lower: for an order to issue under section 104, the commissioner must establish that there is a serious issue to be tried or that the matter is not frivolous or vexatious. Ultimately, the tribunal found that the commissioner had failed to meet the burden of proof in section 100 because he did not establish that the proposed merger was reasonably likely to lessen competition substantially. In determining whether the proposed merger was reasonably likely to have that effect, the tribunal considered the criteria set out in section 93 of the Act.[93] In its decision the tribunal noted that the higher burden of proof for an interim order under section 100 was somewhat surprising, given the short notice on which the application is brought and the limited duration of the order. The

---

93 The criteria contained in s. 93 of the Act will be discussed in detail in section V.E.

amended Competition Act addresses the difficulty the commissioner faced in obtaining an interim order under the former section 100 and gives him greater scope to bring applications for interim relief before filing an application to challenge a merger. Under the amended section 100, the commissioner will only have to establish that an inquiry is being made under the Act; more time is required to complete the inquiry; and, in the absence of an interim order, a party to the proposed merger or any other person is likely to take an action that would substantially impair the ability of the tribunal to remedy the effect of the proposed merger. By removing the former requirement in section 100 of establishing that the proposed merger is 'reasonably likely to prevent or lessen competition substantially,' the amended section relieves the commissioner from bringing complex evidence regarding the effect on competition of the proposed merger and thus expands the scope for interim orders.

In *Palm Dairies*,[94] the tribunal discussed the difference in the scope of its powers of issuing consent orders under sections 92 and 105 of the Act. Section 92 states:

92(1) Where, on application by the commissioner, the tribunal finds that a merger or proposed merger prevents or lessens, or is likely to prevent or lessen, competition substantially ... the tribunal may ...

(f) in the case of a proposed merger, make an order directed against any party to the proposed merger or any other person
    (i)   ordering the person against whom the order is directed not to proceed with the merger,
    (ii) ordering the person against whom the order is directed not to proceed with a part of the merger, or
    (iii) in addition to or in lieu of the order referred to in subparagraph (ii) ...

(B) with the consent of the person against whom the order is directed and the commissioner, [order] the person to take any other action.

Although the tribunal ultimately declined to issue the consent order

94 *Canada (Director of Investigation and Research) v. Palm Dairies Ltd.* (1986), 12 C.P.R. (3d) 540.

requested, it was of the opinion that it had discretion to modify or amend an order submitted under section 92(1)(f) of the Act.[95] It stated that, had the order been sought under section 105, no such discretion existed. Section 105 states:

> 105. Where an application is made to the tribunal under this Part for an order and the commissioner and the person in respect of whom the order is sought agree on the terms of the order, the tribunal may make the order on those terms without hearing such evidence as would ordinarily be placed before the tribunal had the application been contested or further contested.

The tribunal interpreted section 105 to mean that while the tribunal could either issue the order in its entirety as submitted by the commissioner and the merging parties or reject the entire order, it could not modify the order. Subsequently, in the *Gemini I* proceedings, the tribunal followed its interpretation of section 105 in *Palm Dairies* and stated that 'when an application is brought pursuant to section 105 ... the tribunal's only mandate is to either accept the consent order or to reject it.'[96]

A. Consent Order Proceedings Before the Tribunal

1. Test for Issuance of a Consent Order

In general, a consent order will be issued if it is both effective and enforceable.[97] In *Palm Dairies*, the first consent order case under the Act, the application for a consent order was rejected because of effectiveness and enforceability concerns.[98] In that case, four major western dairy cooperatives proposed to jointly acquire their major competitor,

---

95 The tribunal expressed 'considerable doubt' as to whether the order sought should fall under s. 92(1)(f), but the director was of the opinion that it did. Ibid., at 554.

96 *Canada (Director of Investigation and Research) v. Air Canada* [hereinafter *Gemini I*] (1989), 27 C.P.R. (3d) 476 at 514.

97 See D.G. McFetridge, 'Merger Enforcement under the Competition Act aAfter Ten Years,' (1998) 13 *Review of Industrial Organization* 25 and C.S. Goldman and J.D. Bodrug, eds., *Competition Law of Canada* (Yonkers, N.Y.: Juris Publishing, 1997), chap. 10, for an overview of consent order cases adjudicated by the tribunal.

98 See A. McIver, 'The New Canadian Competition Law on Mergers and Consent Orders,' (1987) 19 *Ottawa L.R.* 363 (case note) for a discussion of the *Palm Dairies* case.

Palm Dairies. The terms of the settlement between the commissioner and the parties involved complex behavioural orders, such as requiring that Palm Dairies be operated independently of the acquirers with separate management in place and protective provisions against disclosure of confidential information. The tribunal objected to the draft consent order and expressed concern over enforcing the 'perpetual, mandatory' arrangement that would require permanent monitoring by the commissioner and probably frequent reassessments by the tribunal. Moreover, the tribunal found that some of the terms of the order were more vague and more imprecise than was usual in mandatory injunctions. As well, the tribunal was concerned about the complexity and effectiveness of some of the terms in maintaining Palm Dairies as a separate competitive force in the market, particularly as, in its view, 'a more simple, straightforward remedy' was available,[99] thus suggesting that a consent order might be refused because more effective alternatives were available. The tribunal stated that 'once the director has invoked the adjudicative powers of the tribunal, the tribunal has a duty to determine the nature of the anti-competitive conduct and to fashion an order which in its judgement serves the purposes of the Act.'[100] Thus, parties cannot always expect that the negotiated order will be issued. Rather, the tribunal will only issue the consent order sought if it is satisfied that the order meets a 'critical threshold of effectiveness,' that of 'eliminating the likely prevention or lessening substantially of competition that gave rise to the application for the order.'[101]

The second consent order proceeding before the tribunal was *Asea Brown Boveri*,[102] which involved the acquisition of assets of Westinghouse Canada's large power transformer business by its major competitor, Asea Brown Boveri. In this case, the tribunal approved the order sought by the parties despite the fact that included complex hold-separate arrangements with regard to Asea Brown Boveri's various operations that would apply until Asea Brown Boveri obtained specified

---

99 *Palm Dairies supra* (1986), 12 C.P.R. (3d) at 553.
100 Ibid., at 547.
101 Ibid., at 548.
102 *Canada (Director of Investigation and Research) v. Asea Brown Boveri Inc.* (1989), 27 C.P.R. (3d) 65 (Comp. Trib.) and *Canada (Director of Investigation and Research) v. Asea Brown Boveri Inc. (Reasons for Consent Order)* (CT-89/1, #1019a) (15 September 1989), [1989] (Q.L.) C.C.T.D. No. 35 Trib. Dec. No. CT8901/101 [hereinafter ABB].

tariff reductions and duty remissions for the importing of large power transformers into Canada As well, the test for granting a consent order was modified from that articulated in *Palm Dairies*. While noting that the tribunal would not 'rubber stamp' all consent orders, it 'must attach considerable weight to the fact that the parties ... have judged these measures to be reasonable,'[103] since such deference serves the public interest by facilitating the settlement of potential litigation. Accordingly, the tribunal noted that it was not its proper role to find the 'best possible remedies to solve the problem.'[104] Rather, its mandate was to 'ensure that the proposed order is within a range which may be reasonably expected to meet the objectives of the *Competition Act*,'[105] which included considerations of the effectiveness and enforceability of the proposed order. The 'elimination test' articulated in *Palm Dairies* was relaxed to establishing that 'the overall result will most probably be to prevent any substantial lessening of competition.'[106]

In *Gemini I*,[107] a consent order was sought to allow the merger of Air Canada's and Canadian Airline's computer reservation systems, with the merged entity known as Gemini. In that case, the tribunal approved the consent order negotiated between the commissioner and the parties, while again explicitly recognizing the responsibility of the commissioner to negotiate settlements in the public interest. Emphasizing that it was not to be a 'mere rubber stamp,' the tribunal accepted the commissioner's argument that the role of the tribunal is 'not to ask whether the consent order is the optimum solution to the anticompetitive effects which it is assumed would arise as a result of the merger ... its role is to determine whether the consent order meets a minimum test.'[108] In this case, the minimum test was a hybrid of the tests from *Palm Dairies* and *Asea Boveri Brown*: the test was 'whether the merger, as conditioned by the terms of the consent order, results in a situation where the substantial lessening of competition, which is presumed will arise from the merger, has, in all likelihood, been eliminated.'[109]

103 *ABB*, [1989] (Q.L.) C.C.T.D. No. 35 Trib. Dec. No. CT8901/101 at 23.
104 Ibid., at 31.
105 Ibid.
106 Ibid., at 24.
107 *Supra*, note 96.
108 Ibid., 197–8.
109 Ibid., 198.

In addition, the tribunal explicitly stated in *Gemini I* that the *Palm Dairies* outcome did not mean that the tribunal would not issue behavioural-type orders. Indeed, the consent order issued in *Gemini I* involved complex behavioural orders regarding the operation of the Gemini computer reservation system. Thus, behavioural-type orders would be issued when the remedy proposed was both effective and enforceable.

In *Imperial Oil*,[110] the parties encountered difficulties in obtaining a consent order. Imperial Oil had engaged in extensive discussions with the commissioner before entering into an agreement to acquire 78 per cent of Texaco Canada, and it had agreed to provide the commissioner with unconditional undertakings to divest any assets necessary to mitigate anticompetitive concerns. The initial draft consent order was rejected because the tribunal believed that the commissioner had not met the burden of proof of demonstrating that his proposal would be effective in preventing the substantial lessening of competition and because of enforceability concerns. The evidentiary burden was a new hurdle: the commissioner had not been required to meet such a burden in previous consent order cases.[111]

As well, in the subsequent proceeding to determine the issuance of the revised consent order, the tribunal provided some guidance with regard to the scope of the range of acceptable solutions.[112] It acknowledged that the remedy need not be optimal as long as it is within the range of reasonableness, and that settlements proposed by the commissioner are to be treated with deference, and went on to narrow the acceptable range of reasonableness where the pre-merger situation was 'highly uncompetitive.' The tribunal endorsed the *Gemini I* version of the consent order test, adding that 'where the pre-merger situation was highly uncompetitive, any solution, short of restoring to the fullest extent possible the pre-merger market situation, may have difficulty falling within the acceptable range.'[113]

The tribunal also endorsed the *Gemini I* test for issuing consent

---

110 *Supra*, note 78.
111 See Goldman, 'The Merger Resolution Process under the *Competition Act*,' 30–7.
112 *Imperial Oil, supra*, note 78, at 14.
113 Ibid.

orders in *Seaspan*[114] and *Waste Services.*[115] It issued the consent orders sought in *Seaspan,*[116] *Waste Services, Maple Leaf Mills,*[117] and *BAT/ Rothmans*[118] without any difficulty. However, in a decision of 26 April 2000 the Competition tribunal refused to approve the draft consent order proposed by the commissioner of competition relating to a proposed acquisition by Ultramar Ltd of the petroleum product terminal facility and wholesale supply business of Coastal Canadian Petroleum Inc. in the Ottawa area. Coastal was the only non-vertically integrated terminal operator and the largest wholesale supplier of gasoline and other petroleum products to independent marketers in that region; Ultramar is a vertically integrated refiner, wholesaler, and retailer of refined petroleum products in Canada and the United States, including the Ottawa region. Ultramar owned and operated a refinery near Quebec City; it also owned a mothballed petroleum products terminal in the Ottawa area adjacent to the Coastal facility. Ultramar shipped refined petroleum products into the Ottawa region principally through a terminal owned and operated by Imperial Oil. The commissioner was concerned that post-transaction all four terminal operators in the region would be integrated refiners and would have limited incentives to supply independent marketers. The draft consent order would have required Ultramar to offer to supply independent marketers a minimum volume of refined petroleum products for seven years at wholesale prices to be negotiated at no greater than a price determined from time to time pursuant to a formula based on posted Montreal rack prices; within two years to refurbish and reactivate its Ottawa terminal; and to continue to operate the Coastal facility to at least 40 per cent of its capacity for three years. The tribunal rejected the commissioner's application, principally on the grounds that the supply obligations in the draft consent order were unenforceable beyond establishing a max-

114 *Canada (Director of Investigation and Research) v. Washington* (Reasons for Consent Order Dated January 29, 1997), [1997] C.C.T.D. No. 4 Trib. Dec. No. CT9601/224 [hereinafter *Seaspan*].
115 *Canada (Competition Act, Director of Investigation and Research) v. Canadian Waste Services Inc.* (Reasons for Consent Order), [1997] C.C.T.D. No. 22 Trib. Dec. No. CT9701/12.
116 The consent order for *Seaspan* was issued after the transaction was closed.
117 *Supra,* note 83.
118 *Canada (Commissioner of Competition) v. British American Tobacco* No. 3 Trib. [1999] C.C.T.D No. 12 Trib. Dec. No CT9901/017 (consent order).

imum price. The tribunal referred to the prior case law and summarized the test for approving a draft consent order as follows: 'The tribunal must be satisfied that the measures proposed in the consent order are sufficiently well defined to be effective and to be enforceable ... and that the proposed remedy meets the objective of the Act. The tribunal is only determining if the measures proposed are adequate to eliminate the substantial lessening of competition that would arise from the merger. The tribunal is not determining whether other remedies might be more likely to achieve the elimination of a substantial lessening of competition.'[119]

2. Variation Proceedings

Under section 106 of the *Competition Act*, upon application by the commissioner or a person against whom an order has been made under Part VIII of the Act, the tribunal may rescind or vary its own order if it finds that in the current circumstances the original order either would not have been made or would not achieve its intended purpose, or if the commissioner and the person against whom an order has been made have consented to an alternative order. In *Gemini II*,[120] the commissioner applied to the tribunal under section 106 to vary the consent order in *Gemini I*. Canadian Airlines had incurred substantial losses and was facing severe financial difficulties and Air Canada had publicly announced that it was interested in merging with Canadian Airlines. The commissioner concluded that such a merger would result in a monopoly in most Canadian airline markets. However, Canadian Airlines had entered into a contractual agreement with Air Canada to use the Gemini computer reservation system and the commissioner asserted that the inability of Canadian Airlines to terminate the Gemini contract meant that the company could not pursue other, procompetitive solutions to its financial difficulties. At that time, Canadian Airlines was interested in entering into a transaction with American Airlines. The transaction involved a capital infusion by American Airlines which was conditional upon Canadian Airlines entering into

---

119 See John Bodrug, 'Competition Tribunal Dismisses Application for Consent Order for Ultramar/Coastal Canadian Petroleum Merger,' (2000) 20 *Canadian Competition Record* 87.

120 *Canada (Director of Investigation and Research) v. Air Canada* (1993), 49 C.P.R. (3d) 7 (Comp. Trib.) [hereinafter *Gemini II*].

long-term service agreements with American Airlines and using American Airlines' Sabre computer reservation system. Failing this transaction, Canadian Airlines would arguably not survive. In light of these new circumstances, the commissioner asked the tribunal to order the early termination of the Gemini hosting contract or to dissolve the Gemini partnership.

Initially, the tribunal refused to grant the variation order because it had interpreted section 106 narrowly: if the circumstances demonstrably taken into account by the tribunal in causing it to issue the consent order have not changed and the order was still effective in achieving its intended purpose, no variation could be granted. The majority of the tribunal reviewed the specific circumstances that caused it to issue the consent order in *Gemini I* and concluded that the operative circumstances leading to that order had not changed. The majority found that while the duopoly in the Canadian airline market and the hosting of the two major Canadian airlines on the Gemini computer reservation system had been noted in the documents forming the basis of the consent order, they were not identified to be the causes for making the order.[121] The majority of the tribunal panel noted that the principal matter focused on in the making of the *Gemini I* order had been concern over vertical integration by two dominant airlines with a single computer reservation system giving rise to potential anticompetitive results, but this aspect did not appear to have changed, nor had any obvious changes in the need to control vertical integration been demonstrated. Accordingly, the majority concluded that it did not have jurisdiction under section 106 to vary the original consent order. In anticipation of appeals, the majority went on to address the merits of the commissioner's assertions. It found that a substantial lessening of competition in most if not all airline passenger markets on southern routes in Canada would follow in the event of Canadian Airline's failure[122] and it agreed with the commissioner that the transaction with American Airlines was currently the only available choice to address Canadian Airlines' financial difficulties.[123] Furthermore, the majority stated that had the requirements of section 106 been met, it would have granted the commissioner's request for an amendment to the *Gemini I*

---

121 Ibid., at 25–6.
122 Ibid., at 49.
123 Ibid., at 39.

consent order and allowed Canadian to withdraw from the Gemini hosting contract on certain terms.[124]

On appeal to the Federal Court of Appeal,[125] the tribunal's interpretation of the section 106 causation threshold was unanimously overturned.[126] The court agreed that there must be a finding that there was a change in circumstances, but 'circumstances' should be interpreted broadly to include all facts and conditions relevant to the making of the order, including background facts,[127] not only 'those circumstances that demonstrably were taken into account by the tribunal at the time of, and directly caused, the making of the order.'[128] The court held that a variation may be granted if a 'simple causal relationship between the circumstances and the order' could be established. Neither a 'direct' nor 'demonstrable' relationship between the two need be established and it was not necessary to link the changed circumstances to the purposes sought to be achieved by the order.[129] Therefore, the existence of a duopoly in the airline industry was an important circumstance under which the *Gemini I* order had been made and the significant change in the financial position of Canadian Airlines (its imminent failure) constituted change in the circumstances that led to the making of that order, which, in the changed circumstances, would not have been made.

With regard to the variation, the court further held that as it related to a merger, the variation request was also governed by section 92 of the Act and the tribunal could only order a dissolution of the merger or the divestiture of assets or shares if it found that the merger, operating under the terms of the existing order, would lead to a prevention or substantial lessening of competition. Any other terms of variation could only be issued with the consent of the commissioner and the

---

124 Ibid., at 64–5.
125 *Canada (Director of Investigation and Research) v. Air Canada* (1993), 49 C.P.R. (3d) 417 (F.C.A.).
126 See C.L. Witterick and P.S. Crampton, 'Gemini II: The Saga Continues,' (1993) 14 *Canadian Competition Record* 77 for a discussion of the *Gemini II* decisions of the tribunal and the Federal Court of Appeal.
127 *Canada (Director of Investigation and Research) v. Air Canada, supra* (1993), 49 C.P.R. (3d) at 444, per MacGuigan J.A. (Heald and Hugessen JJ.A. concurring, 420 and 425–26).
128 *Gemini II, supra* (1993), 49 C.P.R. (3d) at 21–2.
129 *Canada (Director of Investigation and Research) v. Air Canada, supra* (1993), 49 C.P.R. (3d) at 426.

person against whom the original order was made. In its decision, the tribunal had stated that had the requirements of section 106 been satisfied, it would have varied the original order to allow the early release of Canadian Airlines from the Gemini hosting contract. However, the court stated that since there was no consent on the part of the private parties, as Air Canada did not agree to Canadian's early withdrawal, the tribunal could not make the variation order it had proposed. The court then remitted the case to the tribunal for determining the appropriate remedy. Subsequently, the tribunal varied the consent order by requiring the dissolution of the merger that had formed the Gemini computer reservation system.[130]

In its interpretation of the causation threshold necessary for a variation order, the Federal Court of Appeal allowed a potentially broad scope for variation of orders made under the merger provisions, raising concerns about the 'finality' of an order. For example, the tribunal pointed out in *Gemini II* that the commissioner had sought the variation over five years after the original merger, well after the three- year limitation period prescribed in section 97 of the Act, which is otherwise applicable to proceedings involving mergers. Parties to an order may well be apprehensive about variations and insist on the commissioner limiting and clearly identifying the 'circumstances' that could subsequently be presented to the tribunal.

3. Intervenors in Consent Order Proceedings
Under section 101 of the *Competition Act*, provincial attorneys general have the right to intervene in merger cases to make representations for the province. All other potential intervenors are governed by section 9(3) of the *Competition Tribunal Act*, which gives the tribunal broad discretion to grant leave to intervene 'to make representations relevant to those proceedings in respect of any matter that affects that person.' The threshold of 'affects that person' appears to be low: in the *Gemini I* proceedings, the tribunal observed that the statute 'imposes a very low threshold for the granting of such leave [to intervene]' and that interest groups need not show that they are affected as long as 'those they represent' are affected.[131] As well, in *Imperial Oil*, Reed J. noted that 'it is

---

130 *Canada (Director of Investigation and Research) v. Air Canada* (1993), 51 C.P.R. (3d) 143.
131 *Canada (Director of Investigation & Research) v. Air Canada (Requests for Leave to Intervene)* (1988), 23 C.P.R. (3d) 160 (Comp. Trib.)

very difficult to refuse leave to intervene to a person who will be directly and adversely affected without offending the rules of natural justice.'[132]

Leave to intervene has been denied on occasion. For example, in *Palm Dairies*, various parties in the dairy business were denied leave to intervene because it would have been prejudicial to the existing parties to have allowed argument by intervenors when no advance notice had been given to the parties. In addition, the tribunal considered that the appointment of independent counsel as *amicus curiae* would be adequate to represent the interests of the intervenors.[133]

In a decision regarding the rights of intervenors in the *Gemini I* case,[134] the tribunal granted certain parties the right to intervene for the purposes of attending and presenting argument on all motions and at all pre-hearing conferences and hearings on any matters affecting them. However, the tribunal noted that intervenors cannot be parties and thus they were not allowed to take part in the discovery process, call evidence at the hearing, or cross-examine witnesses. Strayer J. held that section 9(3) of the *Competition Tribunal Act* limited the role of intervenors to making 'representations,' and 'representations' meant 'arguments,' which did not encompass full participation as parties to a proceeding or the presentation of evidence.[135] Strayer J. noted that the expeditious determination of questions is 'particularly significant' for mergers. Therefore, if tribunal proceedings were prolonged through allowing the 'multiplication' of witnesses and the cross-examination of witnesses by intervenors, decision making by the tribunal would be delayed and parties would be discouraged from proceedings before the tribunal.[136] In addition, the tribunal commented that proposed intervention must relate to competition law issues rather than broader socio-political concerns.[137]

On appeal to the Federal Court of Appeal,[138] Iacobucci C.J. held that tribunals have inherent authority to control their procedures to ensure

---

132 *Supra*, note 78, at 100.
133 *Palm Dairies*, *supra* (1986), 12 C.P.R. (3d) at 555.
134 *Supra*, note 130.
135 Ibid., at 168–70.
136 Ibid., at 174.
137 Ibid. See the discussion below on the *Gemini I* case.
138 *American Airlines, Inc. v. Competition Trib.*, [1989] 2 F.C. 88; *Canada (Director of Investigation and Research) v. Air Canada* (1988), 33 Admin. L.R. 229.

the fulfilment of their statutory mandate. He further stated that this authority is so fundamental to their proper functioning that any limitation of such authority would require clearly expressed language. However, section 9(3) of the *Competition Tribunal Act* was not so clearly expressed as to restrict the tribunal's authority or discretion to permit extensive participation by intervenors. Furthermore, Iacobucci C.J. stated, 'I fail to see how allowing intervenors to have an effective and meaningful intervention to ensure they are able to show how they could be affected by an order, all subject to the discretion and supervision of the tribunal, cannot be reconciled with the adversarial or justiciable nature of proceedings before the tribunal. Moreover, such a role for intervenors will not necessarily displace the status of the parties before the tribunal, the carriage of the matter by the Director, or the *lis* nature of the proceedings.'[139] Although Iacobucci C.J.'s comments were made in the context of contested proceedings before the tribunal, because the *Gemini I* case had not yet been converted to a consent order proceeding, the court's decision makes it clear that the tribunal has jurisdiction to exercise its discretion regarding the role of intervenors in *any* proceedings brought before it, not only in contested proceedings. The court's decision was not meant to outline the role of intervenors in proceedings before the tribunal, but to make it clear that the tribunal has the jurisdiction to grant whatever rights to intervenors it deems necessary for them to demonstrate how they could be affected by the order being sought. Iacobucci C.J. also commented that if a wider role for intervenors did lead to longer and more complex proceedings before the tribunal, 'surely that [was] a necessary price to pay in the interests of fairness, which is expressly required under s.9(2)'of the *Competition Tribunal Act*.[140]

On further appeal, the Supreme Court of Canada upheld the decision of the Federal Court of Appeal.[141] Subsequently, the tribunal granted the intervenors the right to lead evidence and cross-examine witnesses in contested proceedings[142] but they were not allowed to

---

139 *Canada (Director of Investigation and Research) v. Air Canada, supra* (1988), 33 *Admin. L.R.* at 239.

140 Ibid., at 240.

141 *Air Canada v. American Airlines, Inc.*, [1989] 1 S.C.R. 236.

142 The *Gemini I* case started as a contested proceeding and was subsequently converted to a consent order proceeding.

participate in the examinations for discovery. Conversely, the parties were not permitted discovery of the intervenors.[143] The tribunal believed that such rights would give intervenors the opportunity to adduce evidence to support the arguments they wished to make and that they did not require involvement in the discovery process.

The *Gemini I* contested proceeding was subsequently converted to a consent order proceeding. Intervenors were allowed the rights granted at the time when the case was heard as a contested proceeding. In addition, the tribunal granted the Council of Canadian Airlines Employees leave to intervene on the grounds that 'not only will the employees be directly affected by the outcome, facing unemployment if the airline does not survive, but they are also parties to current negotiations for restoring financial stability to Canadian [Airlines] involving a potential equity investment in Canadian [Airlines] by its employees of approximately $185 million.'[144]

In *Imperial Oil*, which was not a consent proceeding converted from a contested proceeding, fifteen intervenors who sought to lead evidence and cross-examine in addition to making argument as in an adversarial proceeding were granted the right to do so. This unprecedented grant of rights to intervenors remains the high water mark for intervention. For the first time, the tribunal discussed the status of intervenors in consent proceedings. The parties had argued that intervenors should not be accorded the same rights in consent proceedings as in contested proceedings because as they applied at the time of the proceeding section 35 of the Competition Tribunal Rules[145] provided intervenors with the opportunity to file comments on the proposed order.[146] Those comments would be reviewed and responded to by the

143 *Canada (Director of Investigation and Research) v. Air Canada* (12 January 1989), CT-88/ 1 (Comp. Trib.).

144 *Canada (Director of Investigation and Research) v. Air Canada (Reasons for Consent Order)* (1989), 27 C.P.R. (3d) 476 (Comp. Trib.).

145 At the time of the Imperial Oil proceedings, the Competition Tribunal Rules SOR/ 87–373 applied. The Competition Tribunal Rules SOR/87–373 were revoked in 1994 by the Competition Tribunal Rules SOR/94/290. The 1994 Competition Tribunal Rules were amended in 1996 to create a special procedural code for consent orders. Sections 86–91 of the Competition Tribunal Rules SOR/94–290, Am. SOR/96–307 contain procedures for and the timing of requests for leave to intervene.

146 Section 35 of the Competition Tribunal Rules SOR/87–373 states that parties shall state a deadline for representations or comments on their proposed consent order to

commissioner and the respondent. Thus intervenor concerns would have been considered and no further right of involvement would be necessary. However, the tribunal rejected this argument and stated that '[t]he rationale for according an intervenor status in consent proceedings, when the order sought directly affects his or her interests, is even stronger than that ... in contested proceedings ... because in contested proceedings, it is not known, at the time intervenor status is requested, whether the would-be intervenor will be adversely affected by the order eventually given.'[147] On the other hand, in consent proceedings, a potential intervenor knows 'with certainty' whether his interests would be adversely affected if the order sought were granted. Thus, in the opinion of the tribunal, it would be very difficult to refuse leave to intervene without offending the rules of natural justice. The tribunal cited Iacobucci C.J.'s decision in *Gemini I* to support its decision that intervenors should be given a wider role in order to provide insights concerning how they would be affected by the order.[148] The tribunal acknowledged that the involvement of intervenors added substantially to the length of time of consent proceedings but nonetheless allowed intervenors an expanded role.[149]

In 1994, the Competition Tribunal Rules were amended to create a new procedural code and timing schedule for consent order proceedings.[150] Under the new Rules, anyone who wishes to participate in a consent order proceeding can do so either by filing comments with the tribunal or by filing a request for leave to intervene; where a request for leave to intervene is refused by the tribunal, the request remains on the record and is considered by the tribunal as if it were comments.[151] After the comments are filed, the commissioner is required to serve a reply on the person who filed comments within a seven-day period, thus ensuring that the comments have been reviewed by the commis-

---

be made, and that such a deadline cannot be earlier than twenty-one days after the date of publication of notice of the consent order proceedings in the *Canada Gazette*. Further, copies of representations on a consent order application would be sent to the director, the merging parties, and the intervenors. All parties would then have seven days to file replies to such representations.

147 *Imperial Oil, supra*, note 78, at 48–9.
148 Ibid., at 49–50.
149 Ibid.
150 Competition Tribunal Rules SOR/94–290, am. SOR/96–307.
151 Ibid., s. 82.

sioner.[152] Under the new Rules, persons wishing to intervene may file affidavit evidence together with their request for leave to intervene.[153] Moreover, section 86(1)(f) of the Rules expressly provides that persons can request leave to present evidence to the tribunal. Section 87(1) requires the commissioner to serve a response to a person who makes a request for leave to intervene within the seven-day period following the expiration of the period for filing requests for leave to intervene.

In addition to granting intervenors a wider role in the *Imperial Oil* proceedings, the tribunal also appeared to have formulated a broad test for intervenors to challenge the proposed consent order success-fully. As discussed above, the general test for issuing a consent order is whether the order falls within a range of solutions that would in all likelihood eliminate the substantial lessening or prevention of compe-tition arising from the merger. The commissioner argued that to chal-lenge the proposed order successfully, intervenors would have to prove that even as conditioned by the proposed consent order, there would still exist a substantial lessening or prevention of competition. However, the tribunal found that this was too stringent a burden on the intervenors. It stated that:

'A consent application proceeds on the basis of an evidentiary vacuum – an evidentiary vacuum with respect to the degree, nature and extent of the substantial lessening of competition which will occur as a result of the merger. While the intervenors may elect to challenge the order by filling the vacuum, they also may elect to challenge the order without doing so and by relying instead on the presumption which the parties have accepted as the base of their case. It is sufficient, then, if it can be shown that the DCO [Draft Consent Order] is not likely to accomplish the objec-tives which the Director claims for it because, for example, the terms of the order are contradictory or inconsistent or the terms of the order are not likely to be effective because they lack enforceability, either as being imprecise, impossible to monitor or because a breach, as a practical mat-ter, would not be susceptible of proof.'[154]

Thus, if intervenors can demonstrate that the draft consent order is

---

152 Ibid.
153 Ibid., s. 86(1)(b).
154 *Imperial Oil, supra*, note 78, at 15.

not likely to accomplish the objectives which the commissioner claims it will achieve, the order will not be issued.[155] This standard is questionable, because the merger provisions of the Act employ a test of whether a merger would result in the prevention or substantial lessening of competition, not whether the objectives which the commissioner claims will be achieved by the order will in fact be accomplished.[156] This standard also makes it possible that intervenors can displace a proposed order by focusing on detailed aspects of the order, thus forcing parties to undergo more delays to revise the proposed order.

In sum, although the full participation of intervenors may ensure that all competitive effects are canvassed, potentially extensive delays can also arise from such intervention. Such delays are in tension with section 9(2) of the *Competition Tribunal Act*, which provides that 'all proceedings before the tribunal shall be dealt with as informally and expeditiously as the circumstances and considerations of fairness permit.'

B. Contested Proceedings Before the Tribunal

Only the commissioner may commence contested proceedings before the tribunal. Contested proceedings are adversarial in nature in that many of the rules of procedure adopted by the tribunal are similar to traditional court procedures rather than reflecting section 9(2) of the *Competition Tribunal Act*, which provides for informal and expeditious proceedings. Thus, contested proceedings resemble court proceedings, consisting of pleadings, discovery, and oral examinations. If the tribunal finds a prevention or substantial lessening of competition, it may issue remedial orders, including prohibition orders, divestiture orders, dissolution orders, or conditional orders under section 92(1) of the Act unless the merging parties are able to meet the requirements of the 'efficiency exception' provided for in section 96. As of late 2001, the tribunal had adjudicated four contested proceedings, the *Hillsdown*,[157] *Southam*,[158] *Superior Propane*,[159] and *Canadian Waste Services Inc*[160] cases.

---

155 Ibid., at 16–17.
156 Goldman, 'The Merger Resolution Process under the *Competition Act*,' at 35.
157 *Supra*, note 16.
158 *Canada (Director of Investigation and Research) v. Southam Inc.* (1992), 43 C.P.R. (3d) 161 (Comp. Trib.).
159 *Supra*, note 17.
160 *Commissioner of Competition v. Canadian Waste Services Holdings Inc.* 2001 Comp. Trib. 3, 28 March 2001.

In *Hillsdown*, the commissioner challenged the acquisition of a majority of the shares of Canada Packers Inc. by Hillsdown Holdings (Canada) Limited in July 1990, which would give Hillsdown control of Orenco, a subsidiary of Canada Packers.[161] Hillsdown already operated a meat rendering operation through its subsidiary Rothsay, and the acquisition of Orenco would mean that Hillsdown would control the two largest meat rendering companies in southern Ontario. Rothsay operated rendering facilities in Toronto and Moorefield, Ontario and Orenco had facilities in Dundas, Ontario. However, Rothsay's Toronto location was expropriated by the City of Toronto in July 1988, prior to the merger. Rothsay vacated its Toronto property in November 1990, by which time the Dundas and Moorefield facilities had reorganized their operations to deal with the materials formerly processed by the Toronto plant. In what it characterized as a 'borderline decision,' the tribunal declined to issue a remedial order with regard to the merger because a lessening of competition was occurring as a result of 'dynamic changes' in the market independent of the merger, such as the closing of an aggressive competitor's Toronto plant, the expropriation of Rothsay's Toronto facility, and the decline in the red meat rendering industry in Ontario.[162]

In *Southam*, the commissioner applied to the tribunal for orders requiring Southam Inc. and various related companies to divest themselves of two community newspapers (the *North Shore News* and the *Vancouver Courier*) and one real estate publication (the *Real Estate Weekly*) in the Lower Mainland region of British Columbia.[163] The commissioner alleged that because Southam already owned the two daily newspapers in the Vancouver area, the above acquisitions, which were part of a larger acquisition of eleven community newspapers, three distribution businesses, and two printing businesses in the Vancouver area, would lessen competition substantially in the retail newsprint advertising market. A freelance journalist requested and was refused leave to intervene. The journalist had raised concerns about the

161 The facts of *Hillsdown* are drawn from C.S. Goldman and J.D. Bodrug, 'The *Hillsdown* and *Southam* Decisions: The First Round of Contested Mergers Under the *Competition Act*,' (1993) 38 *McGill L.J.* 724 and G.N. Addy and W.L. Vanveen, eds., *Competition Law Service* (Aurora, Ont.: Canada Law Book, 1997).
162 *Hillsdown, supra* (1992), 41 C.P.R. (3d) at 328–31.
163 The facts of *Southam* are drawn from Goldman and Bodrug, 'The *Hillsdown* and *Southam* Decisions' and Addy and Vanveen, eds., *Competition Law Service*.

monopolization of the dissemination of information to citizens and reduced opportunities to sell freelance newspaper stories; leave to intervene was apparently refused because those were concerns about different product markets and anticompetitive effects than had been alleged by the commissioner. The tribunal criticized the commissioner for not taking a position with respect to the leave request, and went on to deny leave on the ground that members of the public had no right of direct access to the tribunal to raise competition concerns that the commissioner had decided not to pursue.[164] It thus appears that if proposed submissions from potential intervenors do not join issue with the dispute as framed in the pleadings of the parties, leave to intervene will be refused.[165]

After reviewing the vast amount of information presented in evidence, the tribunal concluded that daily newspapers and community newspapers were not in the same product market:[166] community papers were a superior product for local advertisers, who did not find daily newspapers an effective substitute. Consequently, the tribunal found that Southam's acquisitions of the community newspapers were not anticompetitive. However, the tribunal did find that Southam's acquisition of the *Real Estate Weekly* lessened competition substantially in the real estate newspaper market in the North Shore of British Columbia and it issued a remedial order requiring the company to divest either the *North Shore News* or the *Real Estate Weekly*.[167] In its order, the tribunal stated that '[i]n contested proceedings, the appropriate test is whether the proposed remedy will restore the pre-merger competitive situation in the market in question.'[168] This was unlike the test for issuing a consent order articulated in the *Gemini I*[169] case and endorsed in subsequent consent order proceedings: 'whether the

---

164 *Canada (Director of Investigation and Research) v. Southam Inc.* (Order of August 9, 1991 Denying Request for Leave to Intervene) (1991), 37 C.P.R. (3d) 478 at 479 (Comp. Trib.).
165 Campbell, *Merger Law and Practice*, at 377.
166 The definition of product markets will be discussed below in section V.D.1. 'The Relevant Product Market.'
167 *Canada (Director of Investigation and Research) v. Southam Inc.* (1992), 47 C.P.R. (3d) 240 (Comp. Trib.) [hereinafter *Southam (Remedy)*]. The actual order was issued on 8 March 1993; see *Canada (Director of Investigation and Research) v. Southam Inc.* (1993), 48 C.P.R. (3d) 224 (Comp. Trib.).
168 *Southam (Remedy), supra* (1992), 47 C.P.R. (3d) at 245.
169 *Gemini I, supra* (1989), 27 C.P.R. (3d) at 514.

merger, as conditioned by the terms of the consent order, results in a situation where the substantial lessening of competition, which is presumed will arise from the merger, has, in all likelihood, been eliminated.' Rather, the *Southam* test is similar to the test for issuing consent orders articulated by the tribunal in *Imperial Oil*. The tribunal characterized the *Gemini I* consent order test as a test that set out a minimum standard; thus, if the remedy issued met the higher standard formulated in contested proceedings, it would clearly meet the minimum standard. The tribunal also emphasized that its 'paramount goal when fashioning remedies in contested proceedings under section 92 is to restore the pre-merger competitive situation in the affected market.'[170] Southam had argued that the appropriate remedy would be an order requiring divestiture of only the real estate insert of the *North Shore News* (known as 'HOMES'), which would limit the scope of the order to the real estate newspaper advertising market, but the tribunal found that as long as the remedy '[did] not seek to go beyond the pre-merger situation, it cannot be considered punitive ... even when parts of the merged businesses outside the market are affected.'[171]

Southam appealed the remedy proposed by the tribunal to the Federal Court of Appeal, but the appeal was dismissed.[172] Southam further appealed to the Supreme Court of Canada,[173] which held that the appropriate test for a remedy as formulated by the tribunal was incorrect. Iacobucci J. accepted Southam's contention that the test for issuing remedies should be the same as that for issuing consent orders, that is, whether the remedy eliminates any substantial lessening of competition arising from the merger.[174] Iacobucci J. observed that the tribunal's test for a remedy sought to restore the market to the pre-merger situation, but such a remedy had not been contemplated by Parliament when it enacted the Act.[175] Mergers themselves are not considered to be objectionable except when they result in a *substantial*

---

170 *Southam (Remedy), supra* (1992), 47 C.P.R. (3d) at 246.
171 Ibid.
172 *Canada (Director of Investigation and Research) v. Southam Inc.* (1995), 63 C.P.R. (3d) 1 (F.C.A.) The director also appealed the tribunal's decision in respect of Southam's community newspaper acquisitions; this decision involved product market definition and will be discussed in section V.D.1.
173 *Canada (Director of Investigation and Research) v. Southam Inc.*, [1997] 1 S.C.R. 748.
174 Ibid., at 789.
175 Ibid.

lessening or prevention of competition. Therefore, in Iacobucci J.'s opinion, some lessening of competition following a merger is tolerated; a remedy need not achieve restoration to the pre-merger situation, it has only to eliminate the substantial lessening of competition. However, because the remedy proposed by Southam would not be effective in eliminating the substantial lessening of competition, the tribunal's remedy should not be displaced.[176] Furthermore, the tribunal's remedy was not held to be punitive as it was the only effective remedy.[177]

It is noteworthy, nonetheless, that Iacobucci J. accepted Southam's contention that a remedy need only eliminate any substantial lessening of competition caused by the merger and that, moreover, this was the standard applied in cases under section 92(1)(e)(iii) of the Act, in which the parties have consented to the remedy for curing anticompetitive effects of a merger. This was the standard, for example, applied in the *Gemini I* consent order.[178] Iacobucci J. also noted that, in its decision in *Southam*, the tribunal had attempted to distinguish the test for a remedy from that of a consent order on the grounds that *Southam* was a contested merger and thus the commissioner did not consent to the appellant's proposed remedy. In his opinion, such a distinction was not 'sensible.'[179] By analogizing remedies to consent orders, the Supreme Court's decision could mean that the tribunal had also erred in formulating the test for issuing a consent order in *Imperial Oil*. As discussed above, in *Imperial Oil*, the tribunal had endorsed the *Gemini I* test for issuing a consent order, but added that if the pre-merger situation were highly anticompetitive, the consent order would have to operate to restore the market to the pre-merger situation or it may not be approved. This test tolerates no lessening of competition at all if the pre-merger situation were highly anticompetitive, whereas in *Southam*, Iacobucci J. found that the appropriate remedy is merely to 'restore competition to the point at which it can no longer be said to be substantially less than it was before the merger.'[180]

Subsequently, Southam applied for a variation of the tribunal's rem-

---

176 Ibid. at 790.
177 Ibid., at 791.
178 Ibid., at 789.
179 Ibid., at 790.
180 Ibid., at 789–90.

edy under section 106 of the Act.[181] The test for variation of a remedy is the same as that for variation of consent orders under section 106, as discussed above. In this case, the tribunal found that while the circumstances under which the remedy was made had changed, Southam's proposed remedy would still not meet the test of eliminating the substantial lessening of competition. The request for variation was denied.

In *Hillsdown*, although the tribunal concluded that there was no substantial lessening of competition, it went on to state that events subsequent to the merger, such as the expropriation of one party's facilities and the reorganization of its processes, had left the tribunal with no effective remedy.[182] This may result in the greater use of interim injunctions by the commissioner to prevent parties from taking irreversible actions that prevent the formulation of an appropriate remedy, particularly in light of the recent amendments to section 100 of the Act.

In *Superior Propane*, Superior Propane sought to acquire ICG Propane. The two companies were the principal distributors of propane and propane-related equipment throughout Canada, accounting for 40 per cent and 30 per cent market shares, respectively, nationally. The tribunal rejected the merging parties' argument that the relevant market was all forms of fuel and concluded that the relevant markets were local propane supply and national account coordination services, and that the merging parties would have a post-merger market share of 100 per cent in the national account coordination services market, a post-merger market share in excess of 95 per cent in sixteen local markets, and a sufficiently high market share in an additional forty-nine local markets that competition would likely be reduced substantially by the merger. The tribunal found that there were significant barriers to entry into propane distribution, including long-term contracts with exclusivity, automatic renewal, and right of first refusal provisions, as well as retention of tank ownership by the merging parties, which increased switching costs for customers. New entrants would face substantial sunk costs associated with entry, and the evidence of new entry over the prior decades suggested that the two merging parties had maintained high and relatively constant market shares. The tribunal further found that the acquisition of ICG would entail the removal of a vigorous and effective competitor; that foreign competition from U.S. pro-

---

181   *Canada (Director of Investigation and Research) v. Southam Inc.*, [1998] C.C.T.D. No.1 (QL) (Comp. Trib.).
182   *Hillsdown, supra* (1992), 41 C.P.R. (3d) at 343–5.

pane distributors located in border states had not materialized to date and was unlikely to do so; and that there would be no effective remaining competition post-merger: independent propane retailers were largely price followers and tended to avoid competing directly against the merging parties, competing instead primarily amongst themselves. The tribunal also concluded that the merger would substantially prevent competition in the Atlantic provinces, where ICG had previously maintained a marginal presence but had developed business plans for a substantial expansion.

The tribunal found that the only appropriate remedy for the substantial lessening and prevention of competition was total divestiture of ICG by Superior Propane and would have so ordered but for offsetting efficiencies claimed on behalf of the merger under section 96 of the *Competition Act*. The tribunal found that the merger was likely to result in some $29.2 million in efficiencies per year and the dead-weight loss caused to the Canadian economy by the lessening competition amounted to $3 million per year. Adopting a total welfare or total surplus interpretation of section 96, the majority of the tribunal held that this welfare trade-off saved the merger, and accordingly approved it. A dissenting member expressed scepticism about the scale of the efficiencies claimed, noting that they did not account for offsetting business costs in realizing the efficiencies; that they were merely theoretically possible and were not demonstrated to be realistically achievable through a well-developed business plan or by less anticompetitive means. She also rejected the majority's view that wealth transfers occasioned by an anticompetitive merger should be ignored in the efficiencies trade-off analysis, and considered that they should be given qualitative weight by the tribunal. The tribunal's decision was appealed by the commissioner to the Federal Court of Appeal and in a recent unreported decision (as noted above), the court rejected the majority's interpretation of section 96, and held that anticompetitive effects under section 96 could include a transfer of consumer surplus (through higher post-merger prices) to the merged entity.

In a recent (unreported, April 2001) decision of the Competition Tribunal in *Canadian Waste Services Inc.*, the tribunal granted the commissioner's application under section 92 with respect to the acquisition by the respondent of a waste disposal landfill site in southern Ontario. The respondent already owned a number of sites in the region and the acquisition of the additional site would have raised its market share from 48 per cent to 70 per cent of landfill capacity for ICI waste from the Greater Toronto Area and to almost 100 per cent of capacity in the Chatham-

Kent area. Excluded from the market in the tribunal's view were Michigan landfills, in spite of their substantial participation in the pre-merger market for disposing of Toronto's waste. This contrasts with the market definition in Hillsdown, where U.S. meat-rendering plants were included in the geographical market on the basis of only potential participation in the post-merger market in the event of an attempt by the merged firm to exercise market power. In a subsequent decision on remedies (October, 2001), the tribunal ordered divestiture of the landfill site.

C. Appeal of Tribunal Decisions

Section 13 of the *Competition Tribunal Act* provides a right of appeal of tribunal decisions to the Federal Court of Appeal on questions of law and questions of mixed law and fact:[183] questions of fact alone can only be appealed with leave of the court. In *Southam*,[184] the commissioner appealed the tribunal's decision on the basis that the tribunal had erred in concluding that daily and community newspapers were not in the same product market in the Lower Mainland of British Columbia.[185] The commissioner alleged that the tribunal had failed properly to apply its own stated approach to product market definition (which involved examining indirect evidence of substitutability such as buyer behaviour and the views of industry participants regarding which products are substitutes) and instead required 'direct' (i.e., statistical or anecdotal) evidence of high price sensitivity (cross-elasticity of demand) to find that two products were in the same relevant market.[186] In its decision, the Federal Court of Appeal first addressed the issue of whether it had jurisdiction to consider the appeal. Pursuant to section 13(2) of the *Competition Tribunal Act*, appeal on a question of fact requires leave

---

183 *Competition Tribunal Act*, R.S.C. 1985, c. 19 (2nd Supp.), s. 13(1).

184 *Canada (Director of Investigation and Research) v. Southam Inc., supra*, note 172.

185 See the section entitled 'Market Definition: The Relevant Product Market' for a further discussion of product market definition by the tribunal, the Federal Court of Appeal, and the Supreme Court of Canada. See also D.G. McFetridge, 'Merger Enforcement Under the *Competition Act* After Ten Years,' (1998) 13 *Review of Industrial Organization Review* 25 at 36 for a discussion of the implications of the tribunal's approach to product market definition.

186 See Paul Collins, 'Stop the Presses!!!!: *Southam* Reversed on Appeal,' (1995) 16(3) *Canadian Competition Policy Record* 21 and C.J.M. Flavell and C.J. Kent, '*Director of Investigation and Research v. Southam*: Where Do We Go From Here?' (1995) 16(3) *Canadian Competition Policy Record* 64 for a discussion of the decision of the Federal Court of Appeal.

from the court. Since the commissioner had not sought leave, the court would not have jurisdiction to consider his appeal if the issue of market definition was a question of fact. The court, however, concluded that the adoption of the appropriate framework for defining the relevant product market is a question of law,[187] while the issue of whether the facts in a particular case satisfy the requirements of the framework is a question of mixed law and fact.[188] As a result, leave was not required and thus the Federal Court of Appeal had the requisite jurisdiction to consider the commissioner's appeal.

As *Southam* was the first contested merger case under section 92 of the Act to reach the Court of Appeal, it was necessary to determine the appropriate standard of appellate review from a decision of the tribunal. Robertson J.A., writing for the court, relied on the Supreme Court of Canada's 'pragmatic or functional approach' in *Pezim*[189] in order to determine that standard. According to Robertson J.A., this approach required analysis of (1) the purpose of the *Competition Tribunal Act* and the reasons for the tribunal's existence; (2) the statutory provisions conferring jurisdiction on the tribunal and, in particular, the composition of the tribunal and the decision-making power of its constituent members; and (3) the nature of the problem before the tribunal.[190] With respect to the first criterion, Robertson J.A. found that '[t]he broad powers of the tribunal to act in the public interest suggest that curial deference is owed those decisions squarely within its expertise.'[191] However, turning to the second criterion, Robertson J.A. observed that the tribunal was the only federal tribunal composed of both judicial and lay members, and inferred from this 'a clear intent on the part of Parliament to divest the tribunal's lay members of the jurisdiction to decide questions of law.'[192] Moreover, section 12(1) of the *Competition Tribunal Act* specifically provides that:

187 See P.S. Crampton, 'Relevant Market Analysis in Recent Merger Branch Decisions,' in R.S. Khemani and W.T. Stanbury, eds., *Canadian Competition Law and Policy at the Centenary* (Halifax: Institute for Research on Public Policy, 1991), 243 for a discussion on approaches to relevant market analysis.

188 *Southam, supra* (1995), 63 C.P.R. (3d) at 29.

189 *Pezim v. British Columbia Superintendent of Brokers*, [1994] 2 S.C.R. 557.

190 *Southam, supra* (1995), 63 C.P.R. (3d) at 35.

191 Ibid., at 36.

192 Ibid., at 37–8. In A.N. Campbell, H.N. Janisch, and M.J. Trebilcock, 'Rethinking the Role of the Competition tribunal,' (1997) 76 *Can. Bar. Rev.* 297, the authors note that this observation is not strictly accurate as the Copyright Appeal Board includes judicial as well as non-judicial members.

In any proceedings before the tribunal,

(a) questions of law shall be determined only by the judicial members sitting in those proceedings, and

(b) questions of fact and mixed law and fact shall be determined by all members sitting in those proceedings.

Given the court's determination that product market definition is a question of law and the statutory provision that questions of law are to be determined only by the judges sitting on the tribunal, Robertson J.A. concluded that the issue of market definition did not fall squarely within the expertise of the tribunal. Curial deference was thus not owed to this determination by the tribunal and the appropriate standard of appellate review was one of correctness.

With respect to the third criterion (i.e., the nature of the problem), the court held that market definition is a legal construct, not an economic one. According to Robertson J.A., the absence of a definition for the term 'relevant market' in the Act was not 'an oversight on the part of Parliament but an implied recognition of the fact that the term is and always has been a judicial construct informed by economic principles and now guided by the practical experience of those familiar with the operation of markets – lay members of the tribunal.'[193] Therefore, it appears that although market definition is a legal construct, lay members still played an important role in it. Ultimately, the court overturned the tribunal's finding on the definition of the product market and remitted the case for rehearing by a new panel of the tribunal.

Southam further appealed the decision of the Federal Court of Appeal to the Supreme Court of Canada.[194] In a unanimous judgment delivered by Iacobucci J., the Supreme Court concluded that curial deference was owed to the tribunal's decision and reversed the decision of the lower court.[195] As had the Court of Appeal, Iacobucci J. referred to the Supreme Court of Canada's approach in *Pezim* and examined three relevant criteria in determining the appropriate standard of appellate

---

193 *Southam, supra* (1995), 63 C.P.R. (3d) at 39.

194 *Southam,* [1997] 1 S.C.R. 748. Southam Inc. also appealed the remedy requiring the divestiture of the *Real Estate Weekly* or the *North Shore News* to the Supreme Court of Canada.

195 See Campbell, Janisch, and Trebilcock, 'Rethinking the Role of the Competition tribunal,' for a discussion of the Supreme Court's decision in *Southam*.

review: (1) the nature of the problem before the tribunal; (2) the tribunal's constating statute; and (3) the purpose of the statute that the tribunal administers. He first acknowledged that the distinction between questions of law and questions of mixed law and fact may sometimes be difficult to draw, and then applied a sliding scale of generality or particularity to assist in this determination. That is to say, law should be seen as laying down propositions of wide application, while questions of mixed law and fact are more context specific. Iacobucci J. found that because the tribunal's decision depended heavily on the facts, it was too particular to have any great value as a general precedent. He concluded that the tribunal had forged no new legal principle, and if it had committed an error, the error was one of mixed law and fact.

In determining the standard of review to apply, Iacobucci J. noted that several factors counselled deference: the dispute was related to a question of mixed law and fact; the purpose of the Act is broadly economic and thus is better served by the exercise of economic judgment; and the application of the principles of competition law falls squarely within the tribunal's expertise. However, other factors counselled a more exacting form of review, including the existence of an unfettered statutory right of appeal from decisions of the tribunal and the presence of judges on the tribunal.[196] In Iacobucci J.'s opinion, 'because there are indications both ways, the proper standard of review falls somewhere between the spectrum [of "correctness" and "patently unreasonable"]. Because the expertise of the tribunal, which is the most important consideration, suggests deference, a posture more deferential than exacting is warranted.'[197] Consequently, Iacobucci J. held that the appropriate standard of review was one of reasonableness *simpliciter*, which is closely akin to the 'clearly wrong' standard and '[i]n the final result, simply instructs reviewing courts to accord considerable weight to the views of tribunals about matters with respect to which they have significant expertise.'[198]

In the recent (April 2001) decision of the Federal Court of Appeal in *Superior Propane*, the Court held that the interpretation of section 96 was a matter of law and no deference was required to judicial members of the tribunal in whom are vested decisions as matters of law,

---

196 *Southam, supra*, [1997] 1 S.C.R. at 775.
197 Ibid., at 775–6.
198 Ibid., at 779.

and that a standard of 'correctness' was appropriate. The Supreme Court of Canada denied leave to appeal from this decision.

V. Application of the Merger Provisions in the Competition Act

A. *Scope of Merger Provisions*

Section 91 of the *Competition Act* defines the term 'merger' to mean: '[T]he acquisition or establishment, direct or indirect, by one or more persons, whether by purchase or lease of shares or assets, by amalgamation or by combination or otherwise, of control over or significant interest in the whole or a part of a business of a competitor, supplier, customer or other person.' Section 91 broadly covers all horizontal, vertical, and conglomerate mergers.[199] The *Merger Enforcement Guidelines*[200] issued by the Competition Bureau in 1991 state that with respect to corporations, 'control' is defined pursuant to section 2(4) of the Act to mean *de jure* control, that is, a direct or indirect holding of more than 50 per cent of the votes that may be cast to elect directors of the corporation, and which are sufficient to elect a majority of such directors. While the Act does not define 'significant interest,' the MEGs indicate that the commissioner will consider that a 'significant interest' is held when one or more persons have the ability to materially influence the economic behaviour of a business, including the ability to make decisions relating to pricing, purchasing, distribution, marketing, or investment. Recognizing that a wide range of possible management and ownership structures exists, the MEGs state that a determination of whether a 'significant interest' is likely to be acquired or established can only be made on a case-by-case basis. For example, a 'significant interest' could be acquired through shareholder agreements or management contracts. As well, loan, supply, and distribution arrangements that are not ordinary course transactions and that confer the ability to influence management

---

199   The *Merger Enforcement Guidelines* issued by the bureau indicate that there are two limited situations in which a vertical merger may raise anticompetitive concerns and one situation in which a conglomerate merger may do so. These situations are discussed below.

200   While the MEGs are not legally binding, the commissioner notes in the preface that they are intended to provide a guide to the general approach taken to merger review by the bureau.

decisions of another business may be deemed a merger within the meaning of section 91.

The MEGs also provide for 'safe harbours,' stating that direct or indirect ownership of less than 10 per cent of the voting shares of a corporation has *generally* been found not to constitute ownership of a 'significant interest' in a corporation. Hence, it can usually be expected that the acquisition of less than 10 per cent of the voting shares of a corporation would not be subjected to merger review by the bureau. However, there is no rule of thumb governing ownership greater than 10 per cent but less than 50 per cent of the voting shares of a corporation. The MEGs state that 'inferences are difficult to make about situations which result in a direct or indirect holding of between 10 percent and 50 per cent of the voting shares of a corporation.' They also recognize that a greater level of voting interest is ordinarily required to materially influence a private company than a widely held public company.

The MEGs indicate that transactions that result in one company having acquired the ability to elect a sufficient number of directors to the boards of directors of two competitors to materially influence those boards, or representatives of two competitors having the ability to materially influence the board of directors of a third company, will be considered transactions in which a 'significant interest' has been acquired. However, the MEGs also note that anticompetitive concerns 'will not be presented if the board representation pertaining to one of the competitors is solely through "independent" directors, that is, 'persons who are not employees, executives or members of the board of directors of the company being represented, and who do not have any other interest in that company.'[201]

B. Exemptions from the Merger Provisions

Part VIII of the *Competition Act* provides a limited exemption from the merger provisions of the Act for certain financial institution mergers which have been approved by the minister of finance (s. 94) and for joint ventures formed for the purpose of undertaking a specific project or program of research and development (s. 95). One example of the minister of finance's involvement in the mergers of financial institutions is the unsuccessful bank mergers of 1998. In 1998, the Bank of

---

201 MEGs, 2.

Montreal and the Royal Bank of Canada, and the Canadian Imperial Bank of Commerce and The Toronto-Dominion Bank, proposed to merge. However, due to the important nature of the mergers in question, concurrent with the Competition Bureau's review of the proposed mergers, the minister of finance undertook a review of the possible effects of the proposed mergers under jurisdiction conferred on him under the *Bank Act*. He ultimately disapproved the proposed mergers, in part relying on concerns as to the anticompetitive effects of the mergers conveyed to the bank chairmen by the commissioner of competition following an extensive review.[202] The commissioner had previously issued a set of specific Merger Enforcement Guidelines for bank mergers.[203]

An additional exemption has recently been enacted with respect to mergers and acquisitions within the Canadian airline industry. Under Bill C-26, which came into force on 5 July 2000, the governor-in-council is required to approve such mergers and acquisitions, following review by the minister of transport, the commissioner of competition, and the Canadian Transportation Agency.

C. Theories of Anticompetitive Effects

The anticompetitive threshold for mergers stated in section 92(1) of the *Competition Act* provides that the tribunal may make an order in respect of a merger or a proposed merger where that transaction 'prevents or lessens, or is likely to prevent or lessen, competition substantially.' The MEGs describe two ways in which a merger can lessen competition:[204] (a) where it is likely to enable the merged entity to unilaterally raise price in any part of the relevant market; and (b) where it is likely to bring about a price increase as a result of increased scope for interdependent behaviour in the market.[205] Interdependent behav-

---

202 Letters by the director of the Competition Bureau to the bank chairman, 11 December 1998.

203 See *Bank Merger Enforcement Guidelines* (Ottawa: Competition Bureau, 1999).

204 Although the MEGs discuss anticompetitive effects from the seller's point of view, they also note that the analysis applies in mergers that raise concerns about market power on the buying side, that is, in monopsonistic situations.

205 MEGs, s. 2.2, p. 4; see Thomas W. Ross and Andy Baziliauskas, 'Lessening of Competition under the Competition Act: Unilateral and Interdepedence Effects,' (2000) 33 *Canadian Business Law Journal* 373.

iour includes 'an explicit agreement or arrangement with respect to one or more dimensions of competition, as well as other forms of behaviour that permit firms to implicitly coordinate their conduct, *e.g.* through facilitating practices, the interplay of market signals or conscious parallelism.'[206] While the MEGs state that most mergers that have raised concerns with the Competition Bureau have entailed unilateral market power, the commissioner identified interdependence concerns as central to his objections to recently proposed bank mergers[207] and in his draft consent order application in the proposed acquisition by Ultramar of terminal facilities from Coastal Canada Petroleum Inc.[208]

In addition to being recognized in the MEGs, both the unilateral effects theory and the interdependence theory have been endorsed by the tribunal. In *Imperial Oil*, the tribunal observed that the two issues that should be 'the focus of attention in any merger case (are): possible emergence of a dominant firm; [and] enhanced ability for tacit collusion.'[209] As well, in *Gemini I*, the tribunal noted that '[i]t is generally accepted that where there are only two major competitors in a market there is increased opportunity to engage in collusive behaviour.'[210] In two of the contested mergers adjudicated by the tribunal (*Hillsdown*[211] and *Southam*),[212] the focus has been on the anticompetitive effects of a dominant firm unilaterally exercising market power. In the third (*Superior Propane*),[213] the primary focus was on unilateral effects, although the tribunal also expressed concerns that the merger might facilitate interdependent behaviour in some local markets (without elaborating thereon) (para. 309).

---

206 MEGs, s. 2.2, p. 4.
207 Letter from commissioner to bank chairmen, 11 December 11 1998; see also Jay Holsten, ' Acquisition of Canada trust by T.D. Bank,' (2000) 20 *Canadian Competition Record* 106.
208 *Commissioner of Competition v. Ultramar Ltd.*, CT-2000-2001.
209 *Imperial Oil, supra*, note 78, at 54.
210 *Gemini I, supra* (1989), 27 C.P.R. (3d) at 498. Footnote 8 of the MEGs cites the above passages in *Imperial Oil* and *Gemini I* in recognition of the interdependence theory of anticompetitive effects.
211 *Supra*, note 16.
212 *Supra*, note 158.
213 *Supra*, note 17.

D. Market Definition

The first step in merger review is to identify the relevant market or markets in which the merging parties operate.[214] Although the *Competition Act* does not make any reference to or provide for the definition of relevant markets, they have to be identified for the purpose of assessing the competitive effects of a merger, including the calculation of the market shares of the merging parties. In *Southam*, the Federal Court of Appeal noted that 'market definition is vital to merger analysis and Parliament's concern over the exercise of market power.'[215]

The Competition Bureau employs the 'hypothetical monopolist' approach to identifying the relevant market. That is, a relevant market for merger analysis is defined in terms of 'the smallest group of products and smallest geographic area in relation to which sellers, if acting as a single firm (a "hypothetical monopolist") that was the only seller of those products in that area, could profitably impose and sustain a significant and nontransitory price increase above levels that would likely exist in the absence of the merger.'[216] This method of market definition, described in the MEGs, is utilized for virtually every provision of the Act.

The MEGs also note that in most contexts a 5 per cent price increase based on the price that would likely prevail in the absence of the merger[217] is considered to be significant, and a one-year period is considered to be nontransitory. However, the bureau also states that a different price increase or time period 'may be employed where the commissioner is satisfied that the application of the 5 percent or one year thresholds would not reflect market realities.'[218] As well, the MEGs state that assessing whether a significant and nontransitory price increase would be profitable involves examining likely responses from sources of product and geographic competition on both the demand and supply sides of the market.

It is important to note that markets are defined in terms of the smallest group of products and geographic area in relation to which a signif-

---

214 *Hillsdown, supra* (1992), 41 C.P.R. (3d) at 297.
215 *Southam, supra* (1995), 63 C.P.R. (3d) at 40.
216 MEGs, at 7.
217 Ibid., at 8.
218 Ibid.

icant and nontransitory price increase can be profitably imposed, because this is generally where a merger is most likely to adversely affect competition.[219] The base price used for calculating the 5 per cent price increase is usually the cumulative price, that is, it is the 'cumulative value of the product, inclusive of the value added (mark-up) at the industry level in question.'[220]

The identification of the relevant market involves identifying both the relevant product market and the relevant geographic market. Consistent with the MEGs, in *Hillsdown* the tribunal observed that 'the identification of the relevant market in which it is alleged a substantial lessening of competition is likely to occur is normally assessed from two perspectives: the product or products with respect to which a merged firm acting alone or in concert with others is likely to be able to exercise market power and the geographic area within which such power is likely to be exercised.'[221]

While the bureau employs the 'hypothetical monopolist' approach, the tribunal has not, until recently, explicitly followed the bureau's framework, preferring the more flexible approach articulated in *Hillsdown*. Indeed, in *Hillsdown*, the tribunal observed that it did not 'find it useful to apply rigid numerical criteria' such as 'a likely 5 per cent price rise sustainable for one year; a 5 per cent price rise sustainable over two years; a small but significant and non-transitory price rise' in determining what would amount to a 'substantial' lessening of competition.[222] However, in *Superior Propane*, the tribunal explicitly endorsed and applied the hypothetical monopolist test for determining relevant competition markets set out in the MEGs. The various factors that the tribunal has examined in defining the relevant market are reviewed below.

1. The Relevant Product Market

The MEGs state that the general approach to analysing the product dimension of a relevant market commences by 'focussing upon what would happen if one of the merging parties attempted to impose a sig-

219 Ibid.
220 Ibid., at 9. The MEGs also note that in some situations other prices, e.g., the mark-up price, could be used to calculate the postulated price increase in lieu of the cumulative price.
221 *Hillsdown, supra* (1992), 41 C.P.R. (3d) at 298.
222 Ibid., 329.

nificant and nontransitory price increase in relation to the product.'[223] If the price increase would likely cause buyers to switch their purchases to other products in a quantity sufficient to cause the increase to be unprofitable, the 'next best substitute' will be added to the relevant market. The 'next best substitute' is taken to be the product that would gain the largest percentage of the volume that would be lost by the hypothetical monopolist. The next step is to ask whether the seller of the 'next best substitute' and the merged entity in question, acting as a hypothetical monopolist, could profitably impose a significant and nontransitory price increase on their products. Again, if the significant and nontransitory price increase is not sustainable, the product that gains the largest percentage of the volume that would be lost owing to the price increase is added to the relevant product market. This process is continued until it would be possible for the sellers of the products, acting as a hypothetical monopolist, to profitably impose and sustain a significant price increase for a nontransitory period of time. The products of the hypothetical monopolist would then constitute the relevant product market.

In effect, the hypothetical monopolist approach identifies the smallest group of products within which market power is exercisable. The bureau recognizes that direct evidence in the form of statistical measures of cross-elasticities of demand and supply that would capture the degree of substitutability between products is rarely available. Thus, the MEGs list factors which would provide indirect evidence of substitutability, including the following: the views, strategies, behaviour, and identity of buyers; trade views, strategies, and behaviour; the degree to which two products are functionally interchangeable in end use;[224] the physical and technical characteristics of products; the costs incurred by buyers in switching between products; the price relationships and relative price levels between two products;[225] the cost that would be incurred by potential sellers to modify existing facilities to

---

223 MEGs, at 10.
224 The MEGs note that functional interchangeability is *generally* a necessary, but not a sufficient, condition that must be met for two products to be included in the same relevant market.
225 Although a high price correlation between two products suggests that there is significant competition between them, the MEGs also recognize that high correlation is not conclusive of substitutability, since high correlation could be attributed to other factors such as price changes in common inputs and inflation.

produce the relevant product;[226] and the existence of second-hand or leased products that could render the postulated significant and non-transitory price increase unprofitable.

While the tribunal has not until recently adopted the hypothetical monopolist paradigm, it has employed the same general approach of examining whether there are any close substitutes for the product(s) of the merging parties, but without specifying how 'close' substitutes have to be in order to be included in the same product market. This can be observed in the *Imperial Oil* decision, in which the tribunal briefly stated that the identification of the product market 'requires an assessment of whether or not there are close substitutes for the product in issue,'[227] but did not indicate the degree of 'closeness' required.

In *Hillsdown*, the tribunal recognized the necessity of determining the boundaries of the relevant market, but instead of referring to the hypothetical monopolist approach outlined in the MEGs, stated that 'in determining the product dimensions of the market, the first step is to identify the product or products with respect to which, prior to the merger, the two firms were competitors. The second step is to ask whether there are any close substitutes to that product to which consumers could easily switch if prices were raised (an indication of demand elasticity).'[228] The tribunal's analysis of the relevant product market in *Hillsdown* differs from that adopted in the MEGs in that the tribunal decided to examine supply-side substitution not in the market definition stage, but in the later stage of analysis regarding whether a 'substantial lessening of competition' arose or would likely arise from the merger.[229] Notwithstanding that the tribunal acknowledged that 'conceptually it would seem that supply elasticity with respect to the product dimensions of the market should also be

226 However, according to the MEGs, a potential seller will not be included in the relevant market despite possible adaptation of existing facilities to produce the relevant product if (i) the potential seller would likely encounter significant difficulty distributing or marketing the relevant product; or (ii) new production or distribution facilities would be required to produce and sell on a significant scale. Potential sellers that fall within either of these two classes are not included in the relevant market but will be assessed as potential entrants in the subsequent analysis regarding 'barriers to entry' (MEGs, at 13).

227 *Imperial Oil, supra,* note 78, at 15.

228 *Hillsdown, supra* (1992), 41 C.P.R. (3d) at 299.

229 Crampton and Corley, 'Merger Review under the Competition Act,' at 557.

included in defining the market,'[230] it chose to consider supply elasticity in the 'likely to lessen competition substantially' stage without any apparent reason.

Despite the different approaches to market definition used by the bureau and the tribunal in *Hillsdown*, their respective methods of the 'hypothetical monopolist' and 'close substitutability' ultimately rely on similar types of evidence as the bases for judgments about product substitution possibilities.[231] Furthermore, in *Hillsdown*, although the tribunal employed the broader approach of examining substitutability without specifying the degree to which two products have to be substitutable to be considered to be in the relevant market, it ultimately reached the same market definition as the bureau[232] because it accepted the commissioner's delineation of the relevant product as the provision of rendering services for noncaptive red meat renderable material.[233] The tribunal considered trade views and behaviour in the rendering industry in deciding to exclude captive rendering material from the market because such material is typically processed by 'integrated renderers' who process material produced in the slaughtering, packing, or processing activities of affiliates in a vertically integrated operation.[234] The tribunal also took into account the behaviour of buyers of rendering services by noting that, for example, when Orenco (the rendering facility acquired by Hillsdown) began charging seven cents a pound for the collection of blood rather than collecting it at no charge, a meat packing company started routing blood into a holding tank to be pumped out as sewage.[235] The tribunal found that consumers of rendering services had few product substitutes because there were few viable options: landfill-site regulations often prohibit the disposal of renderable material and renderable materials need to be removed on a daily basis.[236] It then concluded that the relevant product market was the provision of rendering services for noncaptive red meat renderable material.

---

230 *Hillsdown, supra* (1992), 41 C.P.R. (3d) at 300.
231 Campbell, *Merger Law and Practice*, at 66.
232 See Randal T. Hughes, 'The Canadian Merger Enforcement Guidelines: Lessons from Recent Litigation,' (1992) 13 *Canadian Competition Policy Record* 42.
233 *Hillsdown, supra* (1992), 41 C.P.R. (3d) at 301.
234 Ibid., at 293.
235 Ibid., at 300.
236 Ibid.

In *Southam*, the tribunal stated that the 'relevant market for purposes of merger analysis is one in which the merging parties acting alone or in concert with other firms could exercise market power.'[237] As in *Hillsdown*, the tribunal again employed a broad approach of examining product substitutability, asserting that it was necessary to assess the extent to which there are any 'close substitutes' for the merging parties' products, but again not providing any guidance as to how 'close' substitutes had to be to be included in the same relevant product market. However, in *Southam*, the tribunal modified its approach to defining product markets from that articulated in *Hillsdown*. In *Hillsdown*, as noted above, the tribunal had declined to examine supply elasticity when defining the relevant product market, postponing such considerations to the analysis in the 'likely to lessen competition substantially' stage. In contrast, in *Southam*, the tribunal examined supply elasticity when defining the market and noted that firms whose capacity is convertible 'quickly and with small investments'[238] could be included in the relevant product market. The tribunal did not explain its divergence from *Hillsdown*.

Notwithstanding the broader approach of 'close substitutability' used by the tribunal in comparison to the more focused 'hypothetical monopolist' approach, employed by the bureau, both methods ultimately entail examining similar types of evidence to evaluate product substitution possibilities.[239] In *Southam*, as we have seen,[240] the commissioner sought a divestiture order against two of the community newspapers (the *Vancouver Courier* and the *North Shore News*) acquired by Southam alleging that those acquisitions would result in a prevention or substantial lessening of competition in the market for newspaper *retail* advertising services in the Lower Mainland of British Columbia.[241] In response, Southam argued that dailies and community

---

237 *Southam, supra* (1992), 43 C.P.R. (3d) at 177.

238 Ibid., at 178.

239 Campbell, *Merger Law and Practice*, at 66. Despite the method of market definition set out in the Guidelines, the bureau has on occasion varied from the 5 per cent price rise rule in market definition.

240 See above, 216–20. See also Goldman and Bodrug, 'The *Hillsdown* and *Southam* Decisions,' for a detailed discussion of the tribunal's decision in *Southam*.

241 The relevant geographic market was identified to as the Lower Mainland of British Columbia and was not in dispute. The identification of the geographic market is addressed in section V.D.2 below.

newspapers were not in the same market, but if the market was defined to include both dailies and community newspapers, it should also include other forms of advertising (e.g., radio and television).

The central issue in *Southam* thus revolved around the definition of the relevant product market.[242] Like the MEGs, the tribunal recognized that direct evidence of substitutability in the form of cross-elasticities of demand is rarely available. Consequently it '[is] usually necessary to draw on more indirect evidence such as the physical characteristics of the products, the uses to which the products are put, and whatever evidence there is about the behaviour of buyers that casts light on their willingness to switch from one product to another in response to changes in relative prices.'[243] The tribunal went on to list several factors that would inform its evaluation of product substitutability, including the views of industry participants regarding what products and which firms are considered to be actual and prospective competitors; the views of experts concerning the extent to which two products are substitutes; and the views of the merging parties regarding the competition they face.[244]

The commissioner presented evidence regarding buyer behaviour that demonstrated that advertisers regarded dailies and community newspapers as effective substitutes, particularly because community newspapers in different areas had formed groups that offered to sell advertising in some or all of their papers in a single 'group buy' transaction, thereby offering an option that would provide coverage comparable to that of dailies. Despite this evidence, and additional evidence establishing that a number of corporate advertisers in the Vancouver area had switched their advertising from dailies to community newspapers, the tribunal found that '[t]he changes in newspaper use were not prompted by any discernible change in prices'[245] and concluded that '[t]here is no evidence before the tribunal that advertisers are highly sensitive to the relative prices of the dailies and the community newspapers.'[246] Instead, the tribunal found that retail advertisers had

---

242 See McFetridge, 'Merger Enforcement under the *Competition Act* After Ten Years,' at 38–48 for a discussion of product market analysis in *Southam*.
243 *Southam, supra* (1992), 43 C.P.R. (3d) at 179.
244 Ibid.
245 Ibid., at 238.
246 Ibid., at 277.

switched from dailies to community newspapers because community newspapers (which were distributed free to all households within a given community) offered better targeted advertising, as they had greater penetration in the areas from which retailers drew their customers.

However, the tribunal did find that Southam believed it was competing with the community newspapers for advertising dollars, as evidenced by the company's implementation of product modifications to make its products mc   lvertisers. In 1986 Southam had consulted Dr Urban, an American expert, about the problems its Vancouver dailies were facing. Dr Urban had identified Vancouver's strong community newspapers as the cause of the dailies' lost advertising revenue. Therefore, in September 1986, Southam introduced a flyer delivery service in the Lower Mainland of British Columbia. Known as 'Flyer Force,' this new service attempted to increase penetration by offering delivery to even the households that did not subscribe to the dailies. However, at the time of the contested proceedings, the 'Flyer Force' had been terminated because it was not financially viable.

Despite finding that Southam competed with the community newspapers for advertising dollars, the tribunal was not convinced that they were in the same market. The tribunal concluded that: 'the community newspapers and the dailies are very weak substitutes: small changes in relative prices are not likely to induce a significant shift by advertisers from one type of newspaper to the other. Although community newspapers have over time succeeded in attracting business from the dailies, this has been caused more by changes in the conditions facing advertisers than by their responses to changes in price.'[247] Accordingly, the tribunal concluded that 'the dailies and the community newspapers are too weak substitutes to be considered part of the same market'[248] and therefore Southam's acquisitions of community newspapers did not substantially lessen competition in the market for retail print advertising in the Lower Mainland. In spite of its earlier observation that it would be necessary to examine indirect evidence such as the views of the merging parties regarding the competition they face, the tribunal appeared to have placed insignificant weight on 'indirect' evi-

---

247   Ibid., at 278.
248   Ibid.

dence of substitutability and reached its conclusion largely because there was little buyer price sensitivity.[249]

In *Southam*, the commissioner also sought the divestiture of the *Real Estate Weekly*, alleging that this acquisition by Southam would prevent or lessen competition substantially in the supply of print real estate advertising services in the Lower Mainland of British Columbia. The tribunal reviewed evidence regarding trade views and buyer behaviour and strategies and found that for resale home advertising, the dailies were not close substitutes for the *Real Estate Weekly* with respect to print real estate advertising services. On the other hand, the tribunal found that one of Southam's dailies, the *Vancouver Sun*, and the zoned editions of the *Real Estate Weekly* were the closest available substitutes for the advertising of new homes in the Lower Mainland.[250] The tribunal ultimately ordered a divestiture of either the *Real Estate Weekly* or the *North Shore News* at Southam's choice.[251]

As noted previously, the commissioner appealed the tribunal's decision to the Federal Court of Appeal[252] on the basis that the tribunal had erred in concluding that the dailies and community newspapers were not in the same product market. The commissioner alleged that the tribunal had erred on two grounds: (1) it had failed to properly apply its own stated approach and instead required 'direct' (i.e., statistical or anecdotal) evidence of high price sensitivity; and (2) it had ignored indirect evidence of substitutability.[253] After resolving the jurisdictional question and establishing that the standard of appellate review was one of correctness,[254] the Court of Appeal went on to determine whether the tribunal had correctly defined the relevant product market on a substantive basis. The Court of Appeal attempted to clarify the product market definition analysis by noting that while the MEGs were not legally binding, they were instructive in identifying the rele-

---

249 Ibid., at 179.

250 Ibid., at 299.

251 *Southam (Remedy), supra* (1992), 47 C.P.R. (3d) 240.

252 *Supra*, at note 172.

253 See Collins, 'Stop the Presses!!!!' and Flavell and Kent, '*Director of Investigation and Research v. Southam*: Where Do We Go From Here?' for a discussion of the decision of the Federal Court of Appeal.

254 See above, section IV.C, for a discussion on the jurisdictional question and the appropriate standard of appellate review of tribunal decisions.

vant product market.[255] After reviewing U.S. jurisprudence regarding the importance of functional interchangeability in market definition, the Court of Appeal laid out the relevant sections in the MEGs pertaining to product market definition and went on to adopt the MEGs' principle of functional interchangeability being a necessary, but not sufficient, condition to be met before products are placed in the same market. The Court did not specify that the hypothetical monopolist approach or any other analytical framework should always be applied as a matter of law. Rather, the it merely described its approach to product market definition, an approach that is very similar to the 'close substitutability' test espoused by the tribunal. The court stated:

> Products [are] in the same market if they are close substitutes. In turn, products are close substitutes if buyers are willing to switch from one product to another in response to a relative change in price ... Direct evidence of substitutability includes both statistical evidence of buyer price sensitivity and anecdotal evidence, such as the testimony of buyers on past or hypothetical responses to price changes. However, since direct evidence may be difficult to obtain, it is also possible to measure substitutability and thereby infer price sensitivity through indirect means. Such indirect evidence focuses on certain practical *indicia*, such as functional interchangeability and industry views/behaviour, to show that products are close substitutes.[256]

Like the tribunal and the MEGs, the Court of Appeal also recognized that direct evidence of substitutability in the form of cross-elasticities is rarely available. Unfortunately, like the tribunal, it also failed to address the question of how 'closely' substitutable two products had to be in order to be included in the same market. Unlike the MEGs, the Court of Appeal did not address the magnitude of the 'relative change in price' to be postulated when identifying buyer price sensitivity, nor did it address the magnitude of lost sales of one product to another that would signify substitutability between two products. It would have been helpful if the Court of Appeal had identified the degree of price change to be used for finding price sensitivity, thereby providing businesses with a standard to apply when attempting to determine

---

255 *Southam, supra* (1995), 63 C.P.R. (3d) at 58.
256 Ibid., at 60.

whether two products are likely to be included in the same relevant market.[257]

In sum, although the Federal Court of Appeal did not clarify the identification of 'close substitutes,' it found that the tribunal had misapplied its stated approach to product definition, and that this error should be assessed on a standard of correctness. Invoking its power of substituting its own findings for those of a tribunal, the Court of Appeal held that the evidence of the functional interchangeability of daily and community newspapers and of interindustry competition was more than sufficient to show that the two types of newspapers are in the same market. Accordingly, the Court of Appeal remitted the matter to a differently constituted panel of the tribunal with instructions that it should inquire whether Southam's acquisitions of the community newspapers resulted in a substantial lessening of competition in the market for retail print advertising in the Lower Mainland.

As noted above, Southam appealed the Federal Court of Appeal's decision regarding the definition of the product market to the Supreme Court of Canada, which overruled the decision of the lower court.[258] Iacobucci J., writing for the court, concluded that curial deference was owed to the tribunal's decision and thus the appropriate standard of review was one of reasonableness *simpliciter*, not that of 'correctness' as the Federal Court of Appeal had determined.[259]

In applying the 'reasonableness' standard to the tribunal's decision, Iacobucci J. noted that the parties did not dispute that the tribunal had informed itself correctly on the law with respect to market definition. Rather, the commissioner was alleging that despite having stated the correct approach to market definition, the tribunal nevertheless did not apply that approach, as it had ignored indirect evidence such as functional interchangeability and the interindustry competition between the dailies and the community newspapers. In Iacobucci J.'s opinion, the tribunal had not ignored such relevant evidence. Rather, Iacobucci J. found that the tribunal had devoted a great part of its decision to examining such indirect evidence but had found such evidence inconclusive. Furthermore, Iacobucci J. dismissed the suggestion that the tri-

257 Crampton and Corley, 'Merger Review under the Competition Act: Reflections on the First Decade.'
258 *Supra*, note 173. Southam Inc. also appealed the remedy requiring the divestiture of the *Real Estate Weekly* or the *North Shore News* to the Supreme Court of Canada.
259 See Campbell, Janisch, and Trebilcock, 'Rethinking the Role of the Competition tribunal,' for a discussion of the Supreme Court's decision in *Southam*.

bunal had erred by failing to accord adequate weight to certain factors. According to Iacobucci J., assigning particular weights to certain kinds of evidence would be inimical to the balancing test the tribunal has to apply in market definition. If the tribunal were required to accord evidence such as functional interchangeability or interindustry competition decisive weight, such a balancing test would be stilted and impossible to apply. Thus, although the tribunal should be required to consider relevant indirect evidence, the allocation of weight to those factors should be left to the tribunal.

In sum, Iacobucci J. found that the tribunal had reviewed relevant indirect evidence and had not been unreasonable in finding that community newspapers and dailies were weak substitutes. However, Iacobucci J. clearly had some reservations regarding the tribunal's decision, for he observed as follows:

> It is possible that if I were deciding this case *de novo*, I might not dismiss so readily as the tribunal did what is admittedly weighty evidence of inter-industry competition. In my view, it is very revealing that Southam's own expert, an American newspaper consultant, identified the community newspapers as the source of Southam's difficulties in the Lower Mainland. To find, in the face of such evidence, that the daily newspapers and the community newspapers are not competitors is perhaps unusual. In that sense, the tribunal's finding is difficult to accept. However, it is not unreasonable. The tribunal explained that, in its view, Southam was mistaken about who its competitors were; and though I may not consider that reason compelling, I cannot say that it is not a reason for which there is a logical and evidentiary underpinning.[260]

In *Superior Propane*, the tribunal in finding that propane, and not all fuels, was the relevant product market, noted that there are two cross-price elasticities for any given pair of products A and B. The tribunal concluded that for A and B to be considered to be in the same product market, *both* cross-price elasticities of demand must be sufficiently high. The tribunal stated that to conclude that natural gas and propane are in the same competition market would require evidence that natural gas users would switch to propane when the price of natural gas increases, as well as evidence that propane users would switch to natural gas when the price of propane increases. In other words, reciprocal

---

260 *Southam, supra* [1997] 1 S.C.R. at 787–8.

substitutability must be demonstrated. This view needs clarification or response on two points. First, as a matter of economics, the number of units of demand that would switch from product A to product B in response to a 5 per cent increase in the price of product A is approximately *the same as the number of units of demand that would switch from product B to product A in response to a 5 per cent increase in the price of product B.*[261] Reciprocal substitutability, as measured by absolute numbers of switchers, is therefore automatic. It is true, however, that in response to each of the price increases respectively, the customers who switch from product A, as a *percentage* of the current demand for product A, will differ from the switch from product B as a percentage of the current demand for product B. These percentages, not the absolute numbers of switchers, enter into the calculation of the cross-elasticities of demands and, importantly, are the relevant measure of discipline imposed on a firm contemplating the exercise of market power in markets A or B respectively. In this respect, the tribunal is correct in noting that cross-elasticities may differ (in spite of the symmetry of the absolute numbers of switchers). Second, however, a more fundamental level the tribunal is incorrect in suggesting that evidence on both cross-elasticities is needed to determine the 'competition market' for a merger in market A. When examining a merger of two A suppliers, the purpose of market definition is to determine what sources of competitive discipline exist for the merging parties. It is therefore relevant whether an increase in the price of A would cause customers to switch to B. Such behaviour indicates that B suppliers discipline A suppliers. On the other hand, where the customers of product B will switch to A in response to the price of B does not indicate whether there is discipline of A suppliers; it only relates to competition facing B suppliers. Bearing in mind the purpose of market definition when considering a merger of A suppliers – to determine what constraints competition imposes on the merging parties – it is not paradoxical to conclude that, for the purpose of evaluating a merger of A suppliers, B

---

261 The economic principle underlying this proposition is called 'symmetry of the Slutsky matrix' (Hal Varian, *Microeconomic Analysis*, 3rd ed. [Norton, 1992], 123). For small price changes, demand switches between two goods in response only to a change in the relative price of the two goods, that is, the ratio of the prices of the two goods. The impact on this relative price of a 5 per cent increase in the price of good A is of the same magnitude but opposite in sign as the impact of a 5 per cent increase in the price of good B, and therefore the numbers of consumers switching in response to either price change is approximately the same.

is in the relevant product market, while for a merger of B suppliers, A is not in the relevant product market. In assessing a merger of A suppliers, the tendency of A customers to switch to B is relevant while the tendency of B customers to switch to A is not.

Notwithstanding this qualification, the tribunal was clearly correct in stating that a cross-elasticity estimate may identify substitutes and can be helpful in delineating a market, but it does not directly measure the ability of a firm to raise price. Thus, in the tribunal's view, the own-price elasticity of demand is the correct elasticity for defining competition markets and should generally be preferred over cross-price elasticity of demand. In *Superior Propane* the tribunal found that the own-price elasticity of demand was quite low, given the significant costs faced by most users of propane in switching to alternative fuels.

2. The Relevant Geographic Market

In determining the geographic dimension of the relevant market, the MEGs apply the same conceptual approach of the 'hypothetical monopolist' as that used for product market definition. Each location at which the merging parties sell the relevant product(s) is examined separately. The process begins by asking what would happen if one of the merging parties attempted to impose a significant and nontransitory price increase at the location where it sells the relevant product. If this price increase is unprofitable because buyers would switch a sufficient quantity of their purchases to the relevant product sold at other locations, then the location at which the sale of the relevant product is the 'next best substitute' is added to the relevant geographic market. The 'next best substitute' is defined as the location which attracts the largest percentage of the volume of lost sales of the relevant product. The next step is to ask what the result would be if the seller at the second location and the merging party in question, acting as a hypothetical monopolist, attempted to impose a significant and nontransitory price increase at the two locations. The process of adding the location at which the sale of the relevant product is the next best substitute for sales continues until it would be possible for a seller located within the relevant market, acting as a hypothetical monopolist, to profitably impose and sustain a significant and nontransitory price increase.[262]

The MEGs also list several additional factors relevant to geographic market definition, including the views, strategies, behaviour, and iden-

---

262 MEGs, at 14.

tity of buyers; trade views, strategies, and behaviour; switching costs incurred by buyers; transportation costs; local set-up costs; particular characteristics of the product, because suppliers may not be able to divert fragile or perishable products from one area to another; price relationships and relative price levels in two distinct geographic markets; historic shipment patterns; and foreign competition. With regard to foreign competition, the MEGs indicate that the relevant market may be expanded beyond Canada to include the sales location of the foreign seller. In *Hillsdown, supra*, the tribunal extended the boundaries of the geographic market beyond Canada to include competitors in the United States, thus confirming that supranational relevant markets may be used where appropriate.

In *Hillsdown*, the tribunal briefly outlined its method of identifying the relevant geographic market, which resembles its 'close substitutes' method for product market definition. It stated that '[a]n assessment of geographic boundaries requires an assessment as to whether a significant number of consumers within the alleged area are willing to turn to suppliers outside of that area to obtain [the relevant product] and whether there are suppliers outside the proposed boundary who could supply consumers within that area with [the relevant product] (indicators of demand elasticity and supply elasticity respectively).'[263] Although the tribunal did not consider supply elasticity in the definition of the product market, it considered supply elasticity in the definition of the geographic market, acknowledging that firms which could begin supplying customers in a particular area in response to increased prices should be considered in delineating the relevant geographic market.[264] This inconsistency has not been explained in other tribunal or court decisions.

Although the tribunal had not used the hypothetical monopolist approach to defining geographic markets (prior to *Superior Propane*), the effect of its approach of examining substitute locations was similar to that of the hypothetical monopolist approach. The hypothetical monopolist approach examines the degree to which, faced with the postulated significant and nontransitory price increase, buyers would likely switch to the same products (the relevant products identified in product market definition) sold in other areas, and the degree to which sellers

263 *Hillsdown, supra* (1992), 41 C.P.R. (3d) at 301.
264 Ibid.

located in distant areas would divert the sale of their products within the relevant nontransitory period. The locations to which buyers are willing to turn and at which sellers are willing to supply would therefore constitute the relevant geographic market. The tribunal's approach is less focused and does not specify the scope of the price increase or the period of time to be considered when examining locations at which buyers and sellers are willing to substitute purchases and supplying of the relevant product. However, the tribunal relies on similar kinds of evidence to those described in the MEGs to assess substitution possibilities.[265] For example, in *Hillsdown*, the tribunal observed that a useful starting point for geographic market definition is the pattern of competition which existed prior to the merger.[266] Hence, it looked at the history of shipment patterns of various renderers in the alleged relevant market with regard to the distances that renderers travelled to collect renderable material and it recognized that transportation costs and the perishable nature of the raw material were significant factors in the rendering industry. These factors are listed in the MEGs as criteria that would be informative in identifying the relevant geographic market. Taking into account such factors, the tribunal accepted the commissioner's distance limitation of a 200-mile radius around the Orenco and Rothsay plants (the two facilities owned by Hillsdown), observing that there '[had] not been and there [was] not much vigorous and effective competition' to Orenco and Rothsay from renderers located more than 200 miles away.[267]

The tribunal then examined whether regulatory constraints on shipments of renderable material across the Canada–United States border would further constrain the geographic market. The commissioner had alleged that provincial and international borders created boundaries to the geographic dimensions of the relevant market: U.S. restrictions regarding the importation of renderable material and Canadian federal and provincial legislation regarding the handling and disposition of renderable material posed significant impediments to the movement of such material across the Canada-U.S. border. The merging parties adduced evidence that such regulatory constraints did not hinder the cross-border movement of renderable materials. The tribunal also

---

265 Campbell, *Merger Law and Practice*, at 79.
266 *Hillsdown, supra* (1992), 41 C.P.R. (3d) at 302.
267 Ibid., at 304.

examined the history of shipment patterns across the Canada-U.S. border. It noted that there had been some cross-border transportation of renderable materials, but the small volume of cross-border activity was likely attributable to market configuration rather than to regulatory constraints arising from the existence of the border.[268]

In addition, the tribunal inquired whether possible buyer preferences should play a role in defining the market area, because it had been suggested that consumers were unwilling to turn to a renderer whose plant was more than 200–250 miles away, or whose rendering plant was located in the United States.[269] The tribunal found that consumers generally did not utilize rendering services more than 200–250 miles away largely because of the lack of supplier recognition and not because of distance or border constraints; hence it concluded that consumer preferences did not play a significant role in market definition. Ultimately, the tribunal determined that the relevant market was the area within a 200-mile radius of the Orenco and Rothsay plants, and that the market included renderers located within the United States.[270]

As well, the tribunal noted in *Hillsdown* that geographic boundaries of adjacent markets could overlap and that they are 'neither static nor precise.'[271] The issue of overlapping markets had been raised in *Imperial Oil, supra*, in which the tribunal recognized the difficulty of defining the relevant geographic market, particularly in the case of overlapping markets in the retail sector, where consumers are mobile and can travel at relatively low cost to other markets to purchase the relevant product. With respect to retail gasoline, the tribunal accepted the parties' delineation of the various retail markets, with urban areas chosen as separate markets, but it also stated that there was only a 'limited economic rationale'[272] for drawing those boundaries. The tribunal first observed that '[the] identification of the geographic market usually proceeds by reference to the homogeneity of the price of the product over the relevant geographic area.'[273] Thus, in defining an 'ideal' geographic market, it should be possible to find that 'all transactions, at

---

268 Ibid., at 309.
269 Ibid., at 310.
270 Ibid., at 311.
271 Ibid., at 301.
272 *Imperial Oil, supra*, note 78, 16.
273 Ibid., at 15.

a point in time within the defined market, could be at the same price,' but this ideal is 'rarely met.'[274]

According to the tribunal, the question therefore becomes one of assessing the extent to which departures from price homogeneity could be considered to be sufficiently unimportant so that transactions at different prices were still part of the same market. The tribunal reviewed evidence of retail gasoline prices in urban areas such as the greater Toronto area and noted that there was a high degree of uniformity across the areas assessed. In the opinion of the tribunal, this was not surprising since 'consumers of gasoline are inherently mobile and the search for a better price is relatively cost-free – it can be undertaken while travelling for some other reason.'[275] As well, the tribunal noted that switches in consumer demand can be easily accommodated on the supply side since retail gasoline outlets have the capacity to sell more gasoline and the incentive to maximize volume to reduce their fixed costs. The tribunal stated that because consumers are exposed to a fairly large number of retail outlets during the period of time when they are considering a purchase, any price change in one part of a city would be transmitted rapidly throughout the urban area via a 'domino effect.'

The tribunal accepted expert evidence that industry data suggest that up to 70 per cent of consumers tend to buy most of their gasoline within two miles of their homes, but owing to the overlapping of each consumer's two-mile radius with the next consumer's, such that a net of interlocking submarkets spans the city, a price change in any area is transmitted rapidly through the interlocking submarkets.[276] The tribunal noted that since the market structure of the retail gasoline market is one of interlocking submarkets, it was evident that the parties' choice of urban boundaries was necessarily arbitrary. The interlocking submarkets do not stop at urban boundaries but interlock with adjacent nonurban areas. For example, the tribunal recognized that in the case of medium-sized and small communities, using the municipal boundaries of those communities to define the geographic market would understate the true size of the relevant market as purchasers are mobile and clearly purchased outside the artificially delineated markets.[277] The

---

274 Ibid., at 16.
275 Ibid.
276 Ibid., at 16–17.
277 Ibid., at 17.

boundaries were chosen in the interest of administrative convenience, as there was no practical means of identifying the relevant geographic markets.[278] Furthermore, no analysis was made of highway markets, as such analysis was 'virtually impossible' given both the potential overlap of trade areas between highway locations and communities close to highways and the transient nature of highway customers.[279]

In *Superior Propane*, the tribunal defined geographic markets by reference to the hypothetical monopolist test set out in the MECs. It identified two classes of geographic markets: first, a national account coordination services market comprising large national customers who derived significant advantages from securing propane supplies from a single supplier nationwide, and second, numerous local markets, which were largely defined by reference to the economically efficient size of a distribution network from given supply points. In a recent decision (28 March 2001) of the Competition Tribunal in a contested merger case, *Canadian Waste Services Inc.*, involving the acquisition by the respondent of a landfill site in southern Ontario, where it already owned a number of such sites, the tribunal excluded from the geographic market Michigan and New York State, despite the fact that some of the relevant categories of waste (industrial, commercial, and institutional waste) are shipped from southern Ontario to landfill sites in these two states. The tribunal found that these shipment patterns were in large part explained by the fact that tipping fees at landfill sites for ICI waste in southern Ontario pre-merger already significantly exceeded marginal costs and that to regard sites in Michigan and New York State as good substitutes on the basis of existing shipment patterns would entail the so-called cellophane fallacy whereby alternatives to a product are purchased in prevailing prices only because the price of that product has been raised to supracompetitive levels. Thus, according to the tribunal, observed shipment patterns at prevailing tipping fees do not establish that those alternatives would be good substitutes in a market characterized by competitive pricing.

E. Assessment of Anticompetitive Effects: Evaluative Criteria

After the relevant market has been defined, an assessment of the anti-

---

278 *Imperial Oil, supra*, note 78, at 16–17.
279 Ibid., at 18.

competitive effects of a merger will be made.[280] Under section 92(1) of the *Competition Act*, the tribunal may make a remedial order in respect of a merger if it finds that the merger 'prevents or lessens, or is likely to prevent or lessen, competition substantially.' As noted previously, the bureau and the tribunal will assess whether a merger is likely to prevent or lessen competition substantially through the unilateral exercise of market power or through interdependent behaviour flowing from the ability of a small number of firms to collude overtly or tacitly. The MEGs indicate that the bureau will evaluate whether competition is likely to be prevented or lessened substantially by examining the likely magnitude, scope, and duration of any price increase that is anticipated to arise from the merger. The bureau will consider that a merger is likely to prevent or lessen competition substantially if the merged entity would likely be able to exercise a materially greater degree of market power in a substantial part of the relevant market after the merger, and if this market power would not likely be eliminated within two years by competition from domestic or foreign sources. Market power refers to the ability of firms to influence price, quality, variety, service, advertising, innovation, or other dimensions of competition, but the bureau will normally focus on the price dimension of competition, that is, on whether the prices of products of the merged entity would likely be materially higher after the merger than they would have been had the merger not taken place.[281] Unlike the 5 per cent 'significant' price increase postulated at the market definition stage, the MEGs state that a 'materially greater' price is not taken to be a particular percentage price increase, but will vary from industry to industry.[282] However, in practice, the bureau considers a 5 per cent price increase to be a material increase in price.

Like the MEGs, the tribunal has not provided an express quantification of when a lessening of competition would be found to be 'substantial.' In *Hillsdown*, the tribunal noted that '[m]arket power ... is the ability to maintain prices above the competitive level for a considerable period of time without such action being unprofitable' and that in assessing the likely effects of a merger, an important consideration is 'whether the merged firm will be able to exercise market power addi-

---

280 In the following section, 'merger' also includes 'proposed merger.'
281 MEGs, s. 2.1 at 3.
282 Ibid., s. 2.4 at 5.

tional to that which could have been exercised had the merger not occurred.'[283] Consequently, a merger 'will lessen competition if it enhances the ability of the merging parties to exercise "market power" by either preserving, adding to or creating the power to raise prices above competitive levels for a significant period of time.'[284] Moreover, whether the degree of any likely price increase could be considered 'substantial' would depend on the facts of the case, since every merger of competitors will lessen competition to some degree. The tribunal concluded that a lessening of competition would clearly result from the merger of two meat rendering companies that each rendered approximately 30 per cent of the noncaptive red meat material available in southern Ontario. Observing that '[i]t is difficult to articulate criteria which might be applicable apart from the obvious ones of degree and duration,' the tribunal went on to state that it did not find it useful to apply 'rigid numerical criteria' to determine whether a lessening of competition is 'substantial.'[285]

In *Southam*, the tribunal further elaborated on the exercise of market power. Like the MEGs, it noted that there are other dimensions to competition than the price dimension, and that market power may allow firms not only to influence prices, but also to influence non-price dimensions of competition such as service, quality or product choice.[286] As well, the tribunal briefly considered what would constitute a substantial lessening of competition, questioning whether the acquisition of two major community newspapers by Southam, which already owned the two daily newspapers in the Lower Mainland of British Columbia, would translate into 'significantly higher prices or significantly less choice over a significant period of time' for advertisers.[287] However, the tribunal did not specify how 'significant' the effects have to be to constitute a substantial lessening of competition.

In *Superior Propane*, the tribunal in accepting and endorsing the framework of analysis set out in the MEGs, appeared, at least implicitly, to accept the price effects test adopted in the MEGs, that is, is the merger likely to lead to an increase in prices of 5 per cent or more that can be sustained profitably for at least two years without attracting

283 *Hillsdown, supra* (1992), 41 C.P.R. (3d) at 314.
284 Ibid.
285 Ibid., at 329.
286 *Southam, supra* (1992), 43 C.P.R. (3d) at 177.
287 Ibid., at 285.

entry? On the evidence from *Propane*, the tribunal accepted that the merging parties would have the ability to raise prices on average at least 8 per cent post-merger.

In the *Imperial Oil* consent order proceedings, a majority of the tribunal noted that where the pre-merger situation was 'highly uncompetitive', a consent order would only be issued if it 'restores to the fullest extent possible the pre-merger situation,'[288] rather than employing the test formulated in previous consent order cases, that of being 'likely to eliminate the substantial lessening of competition.'[289] This seems to imply that if the pre-merger market is highly uncompetitive, the threshold for establishing a substantial lessening of competition would be very low. However, it must be recalled that the tribunal was considering the issuance of a consent order modifying the terms of the merger in question, rather than addressing the meaning of 'substantial.' It should also be recalled that Iacobucci J. for the Supreme Court in *Southam* stated that a remedy need only eliminate any substantial lessening of competition caused by the merger, not any pre-merger market power.

1. Evaluative Criteria Used in Assessing Anticompetitive Effects
Several quantitative and qualitative factors are examined in assessing whether a merger will give rise to a prevention or a substantial lessening of competition. The quantitative factors examined include the market shares of the merging parties and the concentration in the relevant market. The qualitative factors are specified in section 93 of the *Competition Act* and are criteria to which the tribunal 'may have regard' in assessing the anticompetitive effects of a merger:

(a) the extent to which foreign products or foreign competitors provide or are likely to provide effective competition to the businesses of the parties to the merger or proposed merger;
(b) whether the business, or a part of the business, of a party to the merger or proposed merger has failed or is likely to fail;
(c) the extent to which acceptable substitutes for products supplied by the parties to the merger or proposed merger are likely to be available;
(d) any barriers to entry into a market, including
    (i)   tariff and non-tariff barriers to international trade,

---

288 *Imperial Oil, supra*, note 78, at 14.
289 See the part entitled 'Test for Issuing Consent Orders,' above.

(ii)   interprovincial barriers to trade, and

(iii) regulatory control over entry, and any effect of the merger or proposed merger on such barriers;

(e) the extent to which effective competition remains or would remain in a market that is or would be affected by the merger or proposed merger;

(f) any likelihood that the merger or proposed merger will or would result in the removal of a vigorous and effective competitor;

(g) the nature and extent of change and innovation in a relevant market; and

(h) any other factor that is relevant to competition in a market that is or would be affected by the merger or proposed merger.

The MEGs state that the relevance of each factor should be assessed in every case, but some factors may be determinative of the outcome of the assessment depending on the circumstances of the merger in question.

2. Quantitative Factors: Market Shares and Concentration

Section 92(2) of the *Competition Act* provides that for the purposes of merger regulation, the tribunal 'shall not find that a merger or proposed merger prevents or lessens, or is likely to prevent or lessen, competition substantially solely on the basis of evidence of concentration or market share.' Therefore, evidence of high market share or concentration alone cannot provide a sufficient basis for concluding that a likely prevention or substantial lessening of competition would result from the merger in question. However, the MEGs state that a high post-merger market share or concentration is a necessary condition that must exist before a merger can result in a prevention or substantial lessening of competition. Accordingly, the MEGs provide non-binding safe harbours below which enforcement action is unlikely. A merger generally will not be challenged on the basis that the merged entity will be able unilaterally to exercise market power if the post-merger market share of the merged entity would be less than 35 per cent, or on the basis that the interdependent exercise of market power will be enhanced where either the post-merger market share of the merged entity is less than 10 per cent or the four-firm concentration ratio is below 65 per cent. The MEGs also note that as its market share increases, and as the disparity between its market share and the market shares of its competitors increases, the likelihood of a single firm being able to raise prices increases. Similarly, as the level of market concentration increases, the likelihood of a number of firms being able to coordinate a price increase through interdependent behaviour increases.

In *Hillsdown*, the tribunal observed that 'market share data can give a prima facie indication' as to whether a merger is likely to lead to increased market power.[290] However, it stated that by *prima facie*, it meant 'at first sight' or 'on first impression,' and that it did not intend to signify that the commissioner had merely to prove high market share to have 'thereby proved his case subject to whatever rebuttal evidence the respondents might adduce.'[291] The tribunal emphasized that '[a] responsibility still remains with the Director despite the market share evidence to adduce some evidence regarding barriers to entry.'[292] Later in its decision, the tribunal reiterated that 'market share is not necessarily a reliable determinant of market power,'[293] thus confirming that while high market share is an important indicator of market power, it is not a sufficient basis on which to conclude that a prevention or substantial lessening of competition will result from the merger.

With regard to firm concentration, the tribunal in *Hillsdown* referred to the four-firm concentration ratio and the Herfindahl-Hirschman Index (HHI)[294] presented in evidence. The tribunal observed that the calculations of HHI indexes based on plant capacity under a number of different market assumptions did not 'add much' to the case.[295] The pre-merger four-firm concentration ratio for the noncaptive red meat renderable materials processed in Southern Ontario was 90.4 per cent; after the merger, it increased to 91.6 per cent. Although the ratios proved that the market was highly concentrated, the tribunal observed that these figures 'tell little about the effects of the merger' and 'demonstrate the

---

290 *Hillsdown, supra* (1992), 41 C.P.R. (3d) at 314.
291 Ibid.
292 Ibid.
293 Ibid., at 318.
294 As discussed above, the HHI is an index for measuring market concentration used in the horizontal merger guidelines of the United States Department of Justice. The HHI is calculated by summing the squares of the market shares of all the firms included in the relevant market. For example, a market consisting of two firms, each with a 50 per cent share, would have an HHI value of $(50)^2 + (50)^2 = 5000$. The U.S. Department of Justice generally will not challenge mergers in markets where the post-merger HHI is below 1000, regardless of the increase in the HHI from the merger. See S. Salop and J. Simons, 'A Practical Guide to Merger Analysis,' (Winter 1984) 29 *Antitrust Bulletin* 663 for a discussion of the U.S. Merger Guidelines. The MEGs do not use the HHI to measure concentration or changes in concentration. Instead, as noted above, they provide non-binding market share and concentration thresholds below which the commissioner will generally not challenge a merger.
295 *Hillsdown, supra* (1992), 41 C.P.R. (3d) at 318.

inadequacies of the four-firm concentration ratio as a measure of increased concentration, in a case ... where the changes resulting from the merger are primarily occurring among the top four firms.'[296] Unlike the MEGs, which specify market share and concentration thresholds below which a merger would not be challenged, the tribunal did not provide quantitative benchmarks. In this case, the post-merger market share of the merged entity was 60 per cent and the four-firm concentration ratio 91.6 per cent, far exceeding the thresholds provided for in the MEGs. The tribunal concluded that the various measurements indicated that the merger would increase Hillsdown's market share considerably in an already highly concentrated market, giving rise to an initial concern that the merger would likely lessen competition substantially.[297]

(a) Calculation of Market Shares and Concentration

The MEGs provide details for calculating market shares and state that the bureau usually calculates market shares on the basis of actual output, or, in markets where firms have excess capacity, on the basis of a firm's total capacity, to reflect the firm's market position and competitive influence on the market. Market shares are usually measured in terms of dollar sales, unit sales, and production capacity. Where products in the relevant market are largely undifferentiated, calculations based on dollar and unit sales should yield similar results. The MEGs state that when products in the relevant market are differentiated, dollar sales rather than unit sales would more accurately provide the market share of a firm. For sellers located outside the relevant market who ship products into the market, market shares are calculated on the basis of their actual dollar sales in the relevant market immediately prior to the merger, whether or not the products are differentiated. The MEGs recognize that this calculation may understate the market position of these sellers, but given the difficulty in estimating the amount of output that is likely to be diverted to the relevant market by these distant sellers in response to a price increase, such a calculation will nonetheless be used.

The MEGs measure market concentration by determining the four-firm concentration ratio. However, this ratio may be misleading if the fifth or subsequent firms also have significant market share.[298] More-

---

296 Ibid., at 316.
297 Ibid., at 318.
298 Campbell, *Merger Law and Practice*, at 108.

over, it does not reveal disparities in the market shares of the top four firms.[299] For example, the tribunal noted in *Hillsdown* that this figure may not provide much insight into the competitive effects of a merger when the changes resulting from a merger involve the top four firms.[300]

In proceedings before the tribunal various measures of market share have been used, depending on the context of the merger. In *Hillsdown*, market share was calculated based on the pre-merger volumes of red meat renderable material that the parties processed. That is, it was based on the actual output of the firms. In *Gemini I*,[301] which involved the merger of the computer reservation systems of Air Canada and Canadian Airlines, the tribunal characterized the relevant market as being measured by the number of computer reservation terminals used to access computer reservation systems in Canada and by the number of flight segments booked on each system. The tribunal stated that the number of travel agency locations using each computer reservation system was not indicative of market size because of the considerable disparity in the size of agencies.[302]

3. Qualitative Criteria of Section 93
After determining market share and concentration, the next step in merger review is to assess the barriers to entry into the market in question. The *Competition Act* provides for the assessment of barriers to entry under section 93(d), but in practice, barriers to entry are considered after market share and concentration calculation because they can be determinative of the outcome of the analysis.[303] As noted above, the focus of the assessment of the anticompetitive effects of a merger is to determine whether the merged entity would likely possess a degree of market power that will allow it to sustain a price increase.[304] If barriers to entry do not exist or if they can be overcome within two years, a

---

299 The HHI is a better indicator of market concentration as it is calculated by summing the squares of the market shares of all the firms included in the relevant market.

300 *Hillsdown, supra* (1992), 41 C.P.R. (3d) at 316.

301 *Gemini I, supra*, note 96.

302 Ibid., at 482.

303 See S.C. Salop, 'Measuring Ease of Entry,' (1986) 31 *Antitrust Bulletin* 551 for a discussion of entry barriers in general.

304 As noted above, the assessment of possible anticompetitive effects of a merger usually focuses on the exercise of market power in terms of the ability to influence prices, although market power also refers to the ability to influence non-price dimensions of competition such as the level of quality and service.

price rise will not be sustainable, and thus the merger will not be challenged by the commissioner.[305] The MEGs state that the commissioner
will conclude that a merger is not likely to prevent or lessen competition substantially where it can be established that, in response to the
merger, sufficient entry into the relevant market would occur to render
a material price increase unsustainable in a substantial part of the relevant market for more than two years.[306]

(a) Section 93(d): Barriers to Entry
The MEGs characterize the assessment of potential competition as a
'central and fundamental' aspect of merger review under the *Competition Act*.[307] Such an assessment requires determining whether entry by
a potential competitor would likely occur in response to a material
price increase so as to ensure that such an increase cannot be sustained
for more than two years. As noted above, in the absence of barriers to
entry, a merger cannot prevent or lessen competition substantially.
Thus, the existence of significant barriers to entry can be determinative
of the outcome of a merger review, as it is a necessary condition for
finding a merger anticompetitive. However, the MEGs also note that
evidence indicating that entry barriers are high cannot by itself provide a sufficient basis for concluding that a merger is likely to prevent
or lessen competition substantially.

The tribunal has also made it clear that the existence of significant
barriers to entry is a necessary condition for finding a merger anticompetitive. In *Hillsdown*, the tribunal observed that 'in the absence of significant entry barriers it is unlikely that a merged firm, regardless of
market share or concentration, could maintain supra-competitive pricing for any length of time.'[308] If the merged firm attempted to raise
prices, competitors would enter the market and 'the additional supplies created ... would drive prices back to the competitive level.'[309] In
Southam, the tribunal again emphasized the importance of barriers to

---

305 S. 4.1 of the MEGs also notes that subject to certain conditions, a failing firm (s.
     93(b)) and a merger which does not reduce effective remaining competition in the
     market (s. 93(e)) will normally not be challenged. These factors are examined in sub-
     sequent sections.
306 MEGs, s. 4.1 at 20.
307 Ibid., s. 4.6.1 at 33.
308 *Hillsdown, supra* (1992), 41 C.P.R. (3d) at 324.
309 Ibid.

entry, observing that '[i]n light of the fact that all the other relevant elements clearly point to a substantial lessening of competition, the question is whether entry barriers are sufficiently low that actual entry or the threat of entry can be relied on to conclude that the acquisitions' are not likely to lessen competition substantially. Thus, consistent with the MEGs, barriers to entry can be determinative of the outcome of contested proceedings before the tribunal.

In the *Imperial Oil* consent order proceedings, the existence of low barriers was given substantial weight by the tribunal. In considering the retail gasoline markets in its interim decision, the tribunal observed that 'undoubtedly, the most significant consideration with respect to the retail markets has to be that generally low barriers to entry exist.'[310]

In *Propane*, the tribunal concluded that there were significant barriers to entry into the propane distribution business, including long-term contracts with exclusivity, automatic renewal, and right of first refusal provisions, along with retention of ownership of propane tanks by the merging parties. Also, the tribunal was persuaded that a substantial fraction of initial investments that new entrants would need to make would constitute sunk costs.

(i) *Effective Entry: Time and Scale of Entry:* The MEGs consider that to counter the anticompetitive effects of a merger, entry must be 'effective.' That is, it must be likely to occur 'on a sufficient scale' to ensure that a material price increase is not sustainable for more than two years.[311] This involves an assessment of the time it would take for a potential competitor to respond to and constrain a material price increase resulting from the merger. The MEGs note that, in general, the longer the period of time required for potential competitors to become effective competitors, the less likely it is that incumbent firms will be deterred by the threat of future entry and the longer any market power exercised can be maintained.[312] In *Hillsdown*, the tribunal found that the time needed for *de novo* entry was eighteen months and characterized this lag as 'moderately high.'[313]

---

310 *Canada (Director of Investigation & Research) v. Imperial Oil Ltd.* (1989), 45 B.L.R. 1 at 5 (Comp. Trib.).
311 MEGs, s. 4.6.1 at 33.
312 Ibid.
313 *Hillsdown, supra* (1992), 41 C.P.R. (3d) at 327.

Determining whether entry will occur on a 'sufficient scale' entails an assessment of minimum efficient scale in light of total market demand: it is normally assumed that entry at less than minimum efficient scale will not be sufficient to constrain market power, as sub-optimal production puts entrants at a cost disadvantage.[314] The higher the ratio of minimum efficient scale is to total market demand, the less likely it is that entrants will believe they can attract the level of sales needed to be profitable.[315] In *Hillsdown*, the tribunal noted that the declining nature of the rendering industry could mean that obtaining sufficient supplies of rendering material would be an important factor in determining the size of a plant a potential entrant might wish to construct.[316] In *Southam*, the tribunal briefly commented on the nature of entry into the community newspaper business, noting that it was 'easy to get in but difficult to survive.'[317] The difficulty of surviving meant that entry may not be viable, and thus entry may be ineffective despite the low costs required for start up.

(ii) *Possible Entrants*: The MEGs indicate that the Bureau generally focuses on the likelihood of future entry by considering: (i) expansion of output by existing firms; (ii) new entry by firms that sell the relevant product in adjacent geographic markets; (iii) new entry by firms within the relevant geographic market that sell similar products or use similar machinery or technology, which could be adapted to produce the relevant product;[318] (iv) new entry by firms in related upstream or downstream markets that may vertically integrate; and (v) new entry by firms that sell through similar distribution channels or that employ similar marketing methods.

In *Hillsdown*, the tribunal disagreed with the MEGs in choosing not to classify the expansion of output by existing firms as a form of entry. Instead, entry was considered to be either 'the establishment of a new

---

314 See Salop, 'Measuring Ease of Entry.'
315 Campbell, *Merger Law and Practice*, at 123.
316 *Hillsdown, supra* (1992), 41 C.P.R. (3d) at 326.
317 *Southam, supra* (1992), 43 C.P.R. (3d) at 279.
318 Note that sellers who could produce the relevant product by adapting facilities that are producing another product are considered to be part of the relevant market unless they would likely encounter significant difficulty in distributing or marketing the relevant product or if new production or distribution facilities would be required to produce and sell on a significant scale (MEGs, s. 3.2.2.7 at 13).

firm in the market whether entirely new to the industry or new to the geographic area or local firms which previously did not offer the product in question commencing to do so.'[319] Thus, fringe firms that would likely expand capacity in response to a price increase would not be considered potential 'entrants,' as they had already been included in the relevant market. The tribunal's analysis is flawed because the market definition stage does not take into account potential expansion by fringe firms, but only looks at the existing capacities of firms producing substitutes. Expansion can be viewed as a form of entry, since the increase in capacity is equivalent to the situation where a firm entirely new to the industry or to the geographic market decides to commence production, thus increasing the total output in the relevant market.

(iii) *Types of Barriers*: Section 93(d) of the *Competition Act* lists three broad categories of cost disadvantages that can present potential entrants with considerable barriers to entry: international trade barriers, provincial trade barriers, and regulatory controls over entry. In *Hillsdown*, the tribunal considered the past experiences of firms which had entered the relevant market to determine whether environmental and regulatory constraints would present barriers to entry by potential competitors. The tribunal noted that those experiences demonstrated the difficulties an inexperienced entrant into the market could encounter and led it to conclude that *de novo* entry would likely take eighteen months.[320] In *Asea Brown Boveri*, the tribunal accepted that (i) a history of effective antidumping protection; (ii) the domestic purchasing preference policies on the part of many Canadian provincial electric utilities; (iii) a lack of benchmark sales and demonstrated service and quality history by certain offshore suppliers; (iv) shipping costs; and (v) exchange rate exposure constituted non-tariff trade barriers to entry into the market for large power transformers.[321]

Potential sources of cost disadvantages noted in the MEGs include transportation costs and control over access to scarce or nonduplicable resources (e.g., technology and natural resources). In addition to cost disadvantages, the MEGs also state that start-up sunk costs can be a relevant consideration confronting potential competitors. Sunk costs

---

319 *Hillsdown, supra* (1992), 41 C.P.R. (3d) at 325.
320 Ibid., at 326–7.
321 *Asea Brown Boveri* (6 September 1989) CT-89/1, #101(a) at 8.

may include typical start-up costs such as market research and product development; investments to acquire and learn to use market-specific assets; expenditures needed to overcome product differentiation–related advantages created by incumbent firms; and costs involved in overcoming disadvantages presented by the strategic behaviour of incumbent firms (e.g., long-term contracts, exclusivity, or tying arrangements).[322]

Sunk costs are investments committed to the market once made and which cannot be avoided by withdrawing from the market.[323] They are irrelevant to the pricing decisions of incumbent firms and can be ignored in setting prices, while new entrants must price to recoup them. The MEGs state that this asymmetry presents potential entrants 'with a recognition that they face greater risks and a lower expected return' than that faced by incumbent firms. In general, it can be expected that as the proportion of sunk costs in relation to entry costs increases, risk and uncertainty increase, and thus the likelihood of significant future entry decreases. In assessing sunk costs, the MEGs indicate that the bureau focuses on whether the likely rewards of entry, the likely time required to become an effective competitor, and the risk that entry will not ultimately be successful justify making the sunk investments required for entry.

In *Southam*, the tribunal stated that economies of scale alone cannot qualify as a barrier to entry.[324] The MEGs likewise recognize that economies of scale or scope alone do not constitute an entry barrier in the absence of sunk costs.[325] However, the tribunal also stated that sunk costs must be accompanied by 'something more,' such as economies of scale, to qualify as a barrier to entry. This ignores the practical reality that heavy sunk costs may deter potential entrants even if they are not facing cost disadvantages through not achieving minimum efficient scale.[326]

As well, in *Southam*, the tribunal considered that the premium prices paid by purchasers to acquire community newspapers in the past constituted evidence of significant barriers to entry. The tribunal also com-

---

322 Campbell, *Merger Law and Practice*, at 126.
323 See Thomas W. Ross, 'Sunk Costs as a Barrier to Entry in Merger Cases,' (1993) 27 U.B.C.L.R. 75 for a detailed discussion on the role of sunk costs in merger cases.
324 *Southam, supra* (1992), 43 C.P.R. (3d) at 282.
325 MEGs, Appx 1, I.
326 Campbell, *Merger Law and Practice*, at 127.

mented that the assets of community newspapers mostly consisted primarily of intangible assets and concluded that experienced community newspaper operators would not pay premium prices 'for goodwill that could, if entry were easy, quickly be eroded by the entry of others.'[327]

In *Superior Propane*, the tribunal did not accept that high capital costs are in themselves a barrier to entry (if these costs were not sunk), that new entrants or expanding firms faced significant barriers to obtaining propane supply.[328]

(iv) *The Likelihood of Entry*: In assessing the likelihood of entry, the MEGs indicate that the bureau will generally examine whether entry or expansion is likely to be delayed or impeded by either the presence of absolute differences between the costs of the merged entity and the costs that would be faced by possible entrants or by the need for potential entrants to incur significant sunk costs. The bureau will thus focus on three key issues: (i) the actions that must be taken and the commitments that must be made by potential competitors to enter on a sufficient scale to eliminate a material price increase in the relevant market; (ii) the factors which are likely to delay entry and whether they are likely to prevent entry on a sufficient scale from occurring within two years; and (iii) the risks and rewards involved given the commitments that must be made and the time required to become an effective competitor.

In *Hillsdown*, the tribunal stated that the 'test as to whether potential entry will discipline the market is whether such entry is likely to occur, not merely whether it could occur.'[329] It went on to assess barriers to entry in the rendering industry, taking into account delays from regulatory and environmental approvals, delays from constructing a plant, the potential difficulty in obtaining sufficient volumes of renderable material, and the sunk costs required. Faced with these barriers, the tribunal concluded that 'given the [contracting] state of this market one would not expect *de novo* entry.'[330]

It must be noted that significant barriers are often the cumulative result of a group of impediments.[331] For example, in *Imperial Oil*, slow

---

327 *Southam, supra* (1992), 43 C.P.R. (3d) at 280.
328 Note 17, *supra*.
329 *Hillsdown, supra* (1992), 41 C.P.R. (3d) at 327.
330 Ibid.
331 Campbell, *Merger Law and Practice*, 127–8.

growth in demand, large sunk costs, economies of scale, and increasingly stringent environmental regulations combined to make entry into petroleum refining or wholesaling in Atlantic Canada unlikely.[332]

In assessing entry in *Southam*, the tribunal placed considerable emphasis on the history of entry and exit in the community newspaper industry.[333] In practice, the history of entry and exit is often used as an indicator of the likelihood of entry, although the MEGs note that the fact that entry has or has not occurred in the past does not in and of itself indicate that additional new entry would likely take place in response to a material price increase resulting from the merger. Additional information about the stage of growth of the relevant market would be useful in evaluating the likelihood of entry, as new entry is generally more likely to occur when a market is expanding than when it is declining. In determining whether new entry was likely to occur, the tribunal in *Hillsdown* took into account the declining state of the red meat material market and concluded that new entrants might not be able to obtain sufficient supplies of renderable material.[334]

In *Propane*, the tribunal noted stable or modest growth in demand for propane, and evidence over a ten-year period of very modest new entry.

(v) *Effects of Mergers on Barriers*: In addition to assessing whether barriers to entry exist independent of the merger, the MEGs also note the importance of assessing the extent to which mergers are likely to heighten barriers to entry into a market through increasing the sunk costs faced by future entrants. The MEGs identify four situations in which mergers could elevate entry barriers through increasing sunk costs: (i) where the merger would remove one of the few remaining supply sources or distribution outlets, forcing prospective competitors to enter at two stages of the industry; (ii) where the merger would eliminate a firm that represented an attractive entry opportunity through purchase of that firm; (iii) where the merger would result in potential entrants having to enter the relevant market on a greater scale; and (iv) where the merger would increase the risks associated with entry. In addition, the MEGs indicate that the bureau will assess

332 *Imperial Oil, supra*, note 78, at 23.
333 *Southam, supra* (1992), 43 C.P.R. (3d) at 283–4 and 301–5.
334 *Hillsdown, supra* (1992), 41 C.P.R. (3d) at 326.

whether entry is likely to require more time as a result of a merger. The tribunal has not discussed whether barriers to entry would be heightened by the mergers it has examined.

After an assessment of the barriers to entry, the other qualitative criteria listed in section 93 of the *Competition Act* are considered if they are relevant to the merger in question.

(b) Section 93(a): Foreign Competition

The MEGs recognize that foreign competition is an increasingly relevant factor given the globalization of markets. In some circumstances, foreign competition can provide enough of a constraining influence so that even a merger of the last two Canadian firms in a relevant market would not necessarily prevent or lessen competition substantially. The MEGs take note of the impact of the Canada-United States Free Trade Agreement[335] and the General Agreement on Tariffs and Trade, which may increase foreign competition. Several factors are relevant in evaluating the extent to which foreign competition is likely to provide effective competition in the relevant market. In particular, the existence of tariffs is an important consideration. In *Asea Brown Boveri*,[336] the acquisition by Asea Brown Boveri (ABB) of certain electrical transmission and distribution businesses of Westinghouse Canada would have given the merged entity a Canadian monopoly in the high voltage power transformer market, but the tribunal granted a consent order subject to several conditions, including that ABB seek accelerated tariff reductions and duty remission on imports of certain high voltage power transformers to facilitate foreign competition. As well, an undertaking by ABB Canada to forego initiating any antidumping proceedings for five years was filed with the tribunal prior to the grant of the consent order. Apparently, this was a factor in the tribunal's decision to issue the order, as such an undertaking would facilitate foreign competition.[337]

The MEGs also distinguish between markets in which prices are constrained by tariffs and markets in which prices can be adjusted with

---

335 The tariff reductions under the Canada–United States Free Trade Agreement will continue as a result of the North American Free Trade Agreement.

336 *Canada (Director of Investigation and Research) v. Asea Brown Boveri* (Reasons for Consent Order) CT-89/ (6 September 1989) varied on reconsideration CT-89/1 (1 March 1990) (Comp. Trib.)

337 *Supra,* note 102, at 14.

more freedom, despite the existence of tariffs. In the first situation, tariffs are relatively low. Thus, to attract sales, domestic producers set prices just below the maximum level permitted by the tariff protection. Domestic producers are forced to maintain such prices because if they attempted to impose a price increase, their prices would be comparable to or even higher than those of foreign products, resulting in sales lost to foreign substitutes. In the second situation, tariffs are high enough to create a large 'gap' between prices set by domestic producers and the price ceiling imposed on domestic firms by the tariffs. Even a material price increase would not result in lost sales to foreign competition, because the price after an increase would still be lower than that charged by foreign competitors, who are subject to tariffs.[338] In between these two extremes, the tariffs in certain markets may be low enough to permit foreign products to occupy a particular niche. For example, foreign products may pursue and occupy a profitable premium niche.[339] Thus, it is necessary to assess whether the foreign firm in such a niche could constrain price increases by the merged entity by evaluating the extent to which buyers would switch to the foreign product(s) in response to a price increase and the extent to which the foreign suppliers of the products would likely expand their production of the niche product to meet the increased demand. As well, in evaluating the feasibility and likelihood of success of potential responses of foreign firms, such as commencing the production and sale of products outside of this niche, the factors considered under section 93(d) (barriers to entry into the market) are also relevant.

The MEGs also list a number of factors that may hinder the effectiveness of foreign competition, such as exchange rate fluctuations and domestic ownership restrictions.[340]

(c) Section 93(b): Business Failure and Exit
The MEGs state that the commissioner will not challenge a merger if one of the parties to the merger is likely to fail or exit the market if the proposed merger does not proceed and there are no alternatives to which the firm would likely turn that would likely result in a materi-

---

338   MEGs, s. 4.3 at 24.
339   Paul S. Crampton, 'Canada's Merger Guidelines: A "Nuts and Bolts" Review,' (1991)
       36 *Antitrust Bulletin* 883 at 933.
340   For a complete list of the factors listed in the MEGs, see s. 4.3, 25.

ally higher level of competition in the relevant market.[341] For the purposes of section 93(b), a firm is considered to be failing where it is insolvent or is likely to become insolvent; where it has initiated or is likely to initiate voluntary bankruptcy proceedings; or where it has been, or is likely to be, petitioned into bankruptcy or receivership.

It is important to assess the competitive effects of other choices open to the firm alleging failure or exit, because if there is no alternative that would result in a materially higher level of competition than that which would prevail if the merger proceeded, there can be no prevention of competition. Any lessening of competition that can be expected to arise in the market subsequent to the merger cannot be attributed to the merger, because it would have occurred in any event.[342] The MEGs indicate that the bureau will assess three scenarios to determine if a less anticompetitive outcome is possible: (1) acquisition by a 'competitively preferable purchaser,' which requires that a third party carry out an independent search for up to 60 days; (2) the failing firm remaining in the relevant market in a retrenched form; and (3) liquidation, with a focus on whether it would facilitate the expansion of current competitors or entry by new competitors.

In assessing the outcomes of these scenarios, the financial health of the failing firm is relevant for three reasons.[343] First, as a firm approaches failure, it becomes easier to establish that there are no competitively preferable alternative buyers willing to pay a price that is greater than the net proceeds from liquidation and that the failing firm is not likely to pursue a competitively preferable retrenchment option. Second, the degree to which the acquisition of a failing firm can increase the market power of the acquiring firm is often reduced as the financial health of the failing firm and its market position deteriorates. Third, where the firm would in any event have exited the market, the loss of its competitive influence cannot be attributed to the merger.

The tribunal has not yet had occasion to address the failing firm factor in its assessment of a prevention or substantial lessening of competition arising from a merger, but the commissioner has considered it. For example, as discussed above, in the proceedings to vary the con-

---

341 MEGs, s. 4.1, 20.
342 Crampton, 'Canada's Merger Guidelines,' at 934.
343 Ibid., at 935.

sent order issued in *Gemini I*,[344] the commissioner alleged that Canadian Airlines would not survive unless it terminated its hosting contract with the Gemini computer reservation system, and entered into a transaction with American Airlines whereby it would be obliged to use American Airlines' Sabre computer reservation system. The tribunal was receptive to these concerns.

(d) Section 93(c): The Availability of Acceptable Substitutes

The key issue in section 93(c) regarding the availability of acceptable substitutes is the extent to which sellers of products included within the relevant market are likely to make their products available in response to a price increase in the market.[345] To be 'acceptable' and 'available' necessarily implies that the substitutes will have been included in the relevant product and geographic market in the market definition stage.[346] The MEGs indicate that an important factor to be considered under subsection 93(c) is the extent to which sellers of existing substitutes have, or could easily add, sufficient additional capacity to ensure that a material price increase cannot be sustained for more than two years in a substantial part of the relevant market. As well, it is also important to assess the extent to which buyers are likely to switch a sufficient quantity of their purchases to acceptable substitutes to ensure that a material price increase cannot be profitably maintained. In this regard, the extent to which the products of the merging parties are significantly better substitutes for one another than are other products in the relevant market will also be evaluated.

In *Hillsdown*, the tribunal examined whether the ease of increasing capacity and the existing excess capacity in the industry could constrain the merged firm's ability to exercise market power, concluding that these factors would provide 'a degree of competitive pressure on the merged firm and restrain to a considerable extent its ability to raise prices.'[347]

(e) Section 93(e): Effective Remaining Competition

The MEGs note that effective remaining competition is a broad concept

---

344 *Gemini II, supra* (1993), 49 C.P.R. (3d) at 11.
345 Crampton, 'Canada's Merger Guidelines,' at 940.
346 Campbell, *Merger Law and Practice*, 120–1.
347 *Hillsdown, supra* (1992), 41 C.P.R. (3d) at 321.

that refers to the collective influence of all sources of competition in a market. For the most part, ..1ese sources have already been addressed in section 93(a) (foreign competition), section 93(c) (availability of acceptable substitutes), and section 93(d) (barriers to entry). The MEGs also state that where it is clear that the level of effective competition that would likely remain in the relevant market is unlikely to be reduced as a result of the merger, this *alone* will generally not justify challenging the merger, whether or not the absolute level of effective competition in the market is high or low.[348]

As well, the MEGs highlight the importance of assessing the extent to which the effectiveness of remaining competition is likely to be affected by the probable nature and forms of rivalry. In particular, the MEGs state that the bureau will consider such factors as a history of price stability or the presence of other characteristics of the market; for example, discounting from list price and aggressive service offerings. In addition, an assessment will be made of the extent to which competitors are likely to remain as vigorous and effective as prior to the merger. In *Superior Propane*, the tribunal found that the independent propane suppliers remaining post-merger were not an effective source of competition, being price followers and largely competing amongst themselves.

(f) Section 93(f): Removal of a Vigorous and Effective Competitor
Section 93(f) is related to section 93(e) in that it examines remaining effective competition and draws particular attention to the possible removal of a vigorous and effective competitor as a result of a merger, leading to a reduction in competition. The MEGs highlight attributes that may indicate that the firm in question is a vigorous effective competitor, including: (i) whether the firm has been innovative in terms of product offerings, distribution, marketing, and packaging; (ii) whether it engages in aggressive price and non-price competition; (iii) whether it has a history of not following price leadership; (iv) whether it is a disruptive force in a market that appears to be otherwise susceptible to interdependent behaviour; (v) whether it provides unique service/warranty benefits to the market, or helps to ensure that similar benefits offered by other competitors are not reduced; (vi) whether it has recently expanded capacity or has plans to do so; (vii) whether it has

---

348 MEGs, s. 4.7, 38.

recently made impressive gains in market share or is positioned to do so; and (viii) whether is has recently acquired patents or will soon do so. The MEGs also state that a firm does not have to be among the larger competitors in the market to be a vigorous and effective competitor; small firms which are aggressive and innovative can 'exercise an influence on competition that is disproportionate to their size.'[349]

In addition, the MEGs state that the removal of a vigorous and effective competitor as a result of a merger is 'generally not sufficient, in and of itself, to warrant enforcement action under the *Act*.'[350] It is also necessary to establish that the removal of a vigorous and effective competitor will result in the merged firm being able to maintain materially higher prices. In *Superior Propane*, the tribunal found that the acquisition by Superior Propane of ICG would entail the removal of a vigorous and effective competitor.

(g) Section 93(g): Change and Innovation

Section 93(g) states that the tribunal may have regard to the nature and extent of change and innovation in the relevant market in assessing the effects of a merger. As a practical matter, changes and innovations that have begun to have a significant effect in the market have usually been accounted for at one of the preceding stages of the bureau's analysis, such as during market definition or when assessing the availability of acceptable substitutes, future entry, or effective remaining competition.[351] The MEGs indicate that pressures imposed on remaining competitors in a market by the nature and extent of developments in relation to distribution, service, sales, marketing packaging, buyer tastes, purchase patterns, firm structure, the regulatory environment, and the economy as a whole may ensure that a material price increase is unlikely to occur or is unsustainable. The MEGs note that this may be true when a merger stimulates or accelerates change or innovation.

As well, the MEGs note that it may be more difficult to establish that a merger is likely to prevent or lessen competition in the start-up and growth stages of a market, when changes occur rapidly and affect the dynamics of competition, than in the mature stage of a market. The Bureau will also determine whether a merger is likely to eliminate an

---

349 Ibid., s. 4.8, at 39.
350 Ibid., s. 4.7 at 39.
351 Crampton, 'Canada's New Merger Enforcement Guidelines,' at 949.

innovative firm and thus impede change and innovation with regard to the introduction of new products, processes, marketing approaches, aggressive research and development initiatives or business methods.

(h) Section 93(h): Additional Evaluative Criteria

Section 93(h) of the *Competition Act* provides that evaluative criteria in addition to those listed in sections 93(a) to 93(g) may be relevant to assessing whether a merger is likely to prevent or lessen competition substantially. The MEGs list two additional criteria that the bureau will consider: market transparency and transaction value and frequency. Both are relevant in assessing whether interdependent behaviour will be facilitated as a result of the merger. Market transparency refers to the ability of competitors to obtain information about each other, such as through exchanging information or posting prices. In general, as the level of market transparency decreases, coordinated behaviour is increasingly difficult to maintain, because firms find it more difficult to detect and retaliate against secret discounts. As well, when the frequency of sales of the relevant product decreases, collusion becomes more difficult because deviators from collusion become harder to detect and retaliate against. Similarly, when the value of individual sales increases, the incentive to engage in secret discounting increases and coordinated behaviour becomes more difficult to maintain. In addition to market transparency and transaction value and frequency, the tribunal has also recognized in *Hillsdown* that product heterogeneity is another factor that tends to make collusion or tacit price following more difficult.[352]

Another relevant criterion used by the bureau in assessing possible anticompetitive effects of a merger is the history of anticompetitive conduct either by the parties to the merger or in the relevant industry in general. For example, in *Gemini I*, the commissioner implied that the exercise of market power in the past by one of the parties to the merger is evidence that the merged entity is likely to exercise market power.[353]

Other relevant factors considered by the bureau in merger review include countervailing buyer power, concentration trends, transaction size, market size; and regulated conduct.[354]

---

352 *Hillsdown, supra* (1992), 41 C.P.R. (3d) at 328.
353 *Gemini I* (March 3, 1988) CT-88/1, #1 at 13.
354 Campbell, *Merger Law and Practice*, 138–48.

F. *Vertical Mergers and Conglomerate Mergers*

The MEGs state that vertical mergers generally only raise anticompetitive concerns if (i) the merger increases barriers to entry by forcing new entrants to enter two markets rather than one, because the merger has eliminated an independent upstream source of supply or an independent downstream distribution outlet and left only a small amount of unintegrated capacity at either of the stages at which the acquiror or acquiree operates;[355] or (ii) if, following the merger, there would be a high degree of vertical integration between an upstream market and a downstream retail market such that interdependent behaviour by firms in the upstream market is facilitated by making it easier to monitor the prices charged by rivals at the upstream level.[356]

The MEGs indicate that conglomerate mergers only give rise to anticompetitive concerns if it can be demonstrated that, in absence of the merger, one of the merging parties would likely have entered the market *de novo*. Further, enforcement action will only be warranted if it can be established that prices would likely be materially higher in a substantial part of the market for more than two years than they would be if the merger did not proceed.

G. *The Efficiency Exception*

When a merger has been found to be likely to prevent or lessen competition substantially, merging parties can nonetheless proceed with the merger by meeting the requirements of the 'efficiency exception' set out in section 96 of the *Competition Act*. Section 96 is reproduced below:

> 96.(1) The tribunal shall not make an order under section 92 if it finds that the merger or proposed merger in respect of which the application is made has brought about or is likely to bring about gains in efficiency that will be greater than, and will offset, the effects of any prevention or lessening of competition that will result or is likely to result from the merger or proposed merger and that the gains in efficiency would not likely be attained if the order were made.

---

355 The assessment of whether barriers to entry would likely be elevated as a result of a merger in s. 93(d) is pertinent in the analysis regarding a likely prevention or substantial lessening of competition in vertical mergers.

356 MEGs, ss. 4.11.1 and 4.11.2, at 41–2.

(2) In considering whether a merger or proposed merger is likely to bring about gains in efficiency described in subsection (1), the tribunal shall consider whether such gains will result in
(a) a significant increase in the real value of exports; or
(b) a significant substitution of domestic products for imported products.

(3) For the purpose of this section, the tribunal shall not find that a merger or proposed merger has brought about or is likely to bring about gains in efficiency by reason only of a redistribution of income between two or more persons.

Section 96 creates a trade-off framework balancing expected efficiency gains from a merger against the expected anticompetitive effects.[357] The tribunal is enjoined from issuing a remedial order when the efficiency gains expected to result from a merger outweigh the expected anticompetitive effects: thus merging parties have a 'defence' even if the bureau finds that substantial lessening of competition will result from the merger. In practice, merging parties often make efficiency arguments, not as a defence *per se*, but as further evidence of the benefits of the proposed merger to convince the bureau to allow it. Since the enactment of section 96 in 1986, only one reported merger (*Superior Propane*) has been permitted to proceed by virtue of having met the conditions of the efficiency exception.

Although not a factor in its decision not to issue a remedial order in *Hillsdown* because of its conclusion that there was no substantial lessening of competition, the tribunal discussed the efficiency defence at length in that case and suggested an interpretation of section 96 which is at variance with that outlined by the bureau in the MEGs. In contrast, a majority of the tribunal in *Superior Propane* endorsed the total surplus or welfare standard adopted in the MEGs.

1. The Nature of Efficiencies
Section 96(1) requires a finding that claimed efficiency gains 'would not likely be attained if the order were made.' 'The order' refers to the order sought by the commissioner or such order that may be made by

---

357 The balancing of efficiency gains against anticompetitive effects will be discussed in greater detail below.

the tribunal under section 92(1) of the Act. Therefore, the analysis within section 96(1) necessitates an assessment of whether the expected gains to be realized by the merger would likely be attained by other means if the order sought were made. Merging parties need to know the nature of the order that would likely be sought in order to assess whether the efficiencies they claim would likely be achieved if the order were made. The MEGs indicate that parties can generally obtain a description of the order likely to be sought by the commissioner. In general, the bureau considers other means of attaining efficiency gains such as internal growth; a merger with a third party; a joint venture; a specialization agreement or a licensing, lease, or other contractual arrangement. Given that, for each gain being claimed, the merging parties must demonstrate that it would not likely be obtained from such other means, the MEGs recognize that the commercial realities of the relevant market are relevant in assessing whether the merged firm is likely to pursue those efficiencies through other means if they cannot be realized through the merger. The MEGs indicate that efficiencies will generally not be excluded from consideration merely on the basis that they could theoretically be attained through alternative means. As long as parties can provide a 'reasonable and objectively verifiable explanation'[358] as to why efficiencies that are available would not likely be sought through other means if the order were made, even though they may theoretically be achieved through alternative means, the efficiencies claimed will be included in the section 96 analysis.

Consistent with section 96(3), which provides that gains through a redistribution of income are not acceptable efficiency gains, the MEGs also note that the following types of cost savings are not efficiency gains: (1) tax related gains; (2) reductions in output, quality, service, or variety; (3) revenues from anticipated price increases; and (4) wage concessions or discounts from suppliers obtained through increased bargaining leverage (unless discounts are cost justified).[359]

The MEGs state that the bureau will consider productive efficiency gains that allow firms to produce more output or better quality output from the same amount of inputs. Efficiencies that are acceptable include savings in production costs through economies of scale and

---

358 MEGs, s. 5.2 at 47.
359 MEGs, s. 5.3 at 48.

scope; savings from the rationalization of various administrative, distribution, and research fun_tions; and savings from superior management through the transfer of superior production techniques and know-how from one of the merging parties to the other. In addition to the general class of productive efficiencies, dynamic efficiencies, which include gains attained through the optimal introduction of new products, the development of more efficient productive processes, and the improvement of product quality and service, are also acceptable efficiency gains. In *Hillsdown*, the tribunal recognized that scale and scope economies as well as dynamic efficiencies are relevant considerations in the balancing of efficiencies against anticompetitive effects.[360] It examined, in detail, administrative cost savings, transportation cost savings, and manufacturing cost savings claimed by the parties to the merger. Also, in *Imperial Oil*, the tribunal was ostensibly prepared to accept that savings from lower inventories, advertising and marketing expenses, general overhead expenses, and output gains from specialization of production were potential sources of productive efficiency gains, although it suggested that the claims had been overstated due to quantification errors.[361] In *Superior Propane*, various efficiency savings from the merger, including corporate centre, customer support, and field operations, were recognized by the tribunal.

Section 96(2) of the *Competition Act* provides that:

In considering whether a merger or proposed merger is likely to bring about [efficiency gains], the tribunal shall consider whether such gains will result in

(a) a significant increase in the real value of exports; or
(b) a significant substitution of domestic products for imported products.

The MEGs note that this provision does not create a new class of efficiencies but 'is simply considered to draw attention to the fact that, in calculating the merged entity's total output for the purpose of arriving at the sum of unit and other savings brought about by the merger, the output that will likely displace imports, and any increased output that

---

360 *Hillsdown, supra* (1992), 41 C.P.R. (3d) at 331.
361 *Imperial Oil, supra*, note 78, 40–1.

is sold abroad, must be taken into account.' In *Imperial Oil*, the dissenting opinion of Dr Roseman stated that '[u]nder paragraph 96(2)(b) of the Act, the replacement of imports by domestic production is classified as an efficiency. The reverse should accordingly be considered an inefficiency where the result flows from the merger.'[362] Since this was stated in a dissenting opinion, it is not clear whether efficiencies that result in increased export or import substitution are a separate class of efficiencies or whether such efficiencies would be assigned greater weight in a section 96 assessment.

In sum, the MEGs indicate that generally, only efficiency gains that would likely be attained in a market where the merger is likely to result in a substantial prevention or lessening of competition will be considered. In *Hillsdown*, the tribunal questioned whether efficiency gains which Hillsdown had claimed with respect to products, such as renderable grease, that had not been included in the relevant product market should be considered to be part of the efficiency gains arising from the merger.[363] In practice, parties may be constrained from a full disclosure to each other of information pertaining to the efficiencies that can be achieved by the proposed merger, since full information exchange can potentially give rise to an investigation for conspiracy under the Act. Moreover, the MEGs specify that 'objective verification of particular sources of efficiency gains may be provided by plant and firm-level accounting statements, internal studies, strategic plans, capital appropriation requests, management consultant studies (where available) or other available data ... that describe the precise nature and magnitude of each type of efficiency gain expected.'[364] In practice, these documentation requirements may restrict the type of efficiency gains that can successfully be claimed.

2. Burden of Proof

In *Hillsdown*, the tribunal made it clear that the parties claiming the efficiencies have the onus of proving the existence of those efficiencies, or the likelihood of their existence when the merger has not been completed, on the balance of probabilities.[365] The tribunal concluded that

---

362 Ibid., at 61.
363 *Hillsdown, supra* (1992), 41 C.P.R. (3d) at 332.
364 MEGs, at 51.
365 *Hillsdown, supra* (1992), 41 C.P.R. (3d) at 335.

Hillsdown had not met this burden of proof as the efficiencies claimed had not been proven to arise out of the merger. Rather, they were the result of the restructuring caused by the expropriation of the acquiror's Toronto rendering facilities. The tribunal also rejected the commissioner's position that cost savings not arising uniquely out of the merger are not to be considered efficiency gains, and stated that the test to be applied is whether the efficiency gains would likely have been realized in the absence of the merger.[366] Thus, it would be sufficient to demonstrate that the efficiencies are likely to occur as a consequence of the merger. A similar position was taken by the tribunal in *Superior Propane* in holding that the merging parties bear the burden of proving all the elements of section 96 on a balance of probabilities except for the effects of any prevention or lessening of competition, which must be demonstrated by the commissioner.

3. Trade-off Analysis: Balancing Efficiency Gains against Anticompetitive Effects

To succeed in the efficiency defence, merging parties have to demonstrate that gains in efficiency will be greater than and will offset anticompetitive effects arising from the merger.[367] The MEGs indicate that, if all of the efficiency gains and anticompetitive effects can be measured in similar terms, such as in dollars, and the amount of efficiency gains is greater than the total of the anticompetitive effects, the efficiency gains will be considered to 'offset' the anticompetitive effects. However, certain efficiency gains – such as dynamic efficiencies and efficiencies realized through superior management – are difficult to measure and such difficulty is recognized by the MEGs. The MEGs acknowledge that the quantification of efficiency gains to determine whether they are greater than and will offset anticompetitive effects can be 'subjective in nature and will ordinarily require the exercise of the commissioner's discretion.' However, the qualitative criteria on which the commissioner will base this discretion are unclear. In addition, identifying efficiencies with precision is very difficult in the absence of detailed discussions between the parties – a practice the commissioner does not encourage pre-merger.

---

366 Ibid., at 332.
367 See McFetridge, 'Merger Enforcement Under the *Competition Act* after Ten Years,' at 49 for a discussion of the efficiency gains issue.

In balancing anticompetitive effects against efficiency gains, the MEGs indicate that the 'effects' to be considered consist of the reduction in producer and consumer surplus (total welfare) brought about by a price increase through the merger, that is, the dead-weight loss to the Canadian economy. According to the MEGs, the redistribution of surplus from consumers to producers is a neutral effect, since it cannot be determined *a priori* who is the more deserving or in whose hands the dollars to be transferred have more value, but the reduction in total surplus is a negative resource allocation effect, because the surplus lost is gained neither by producers nor consumers.[368] The MEGs indicate that the measurement of losses manifested through non-price dimensions, such as a reduction in service and quality, will receive a qualitative weighting. Also, in view of the difficulties in determining demand elasticity and quantifying the magnitude of anticompetitive effects, several trade-off assessments are generally performed over a range of price increases and demand elasticities. In calculating the magnitude of likely efficiency gains, the bureau will generally measure cost savings across the reduced level of output that will be required to bring about the anticipated material price increase. As well, timing differences between the future anticipated efficiency gains and anticompetitive effects are adjusted through discounting back to present constant dollar values by removing the effects of future anticipated inflation and applying a standard real discount rate to allow for the comparison of efficiency gains and anticompetitve effects which are likely to occur at different points in time.[369]

In *obiter dicta* in the *Hillsdown* decision, Reed J. expressly disagreed with the bureau's interpretation of section 96.[370] The key point of disagreement was which anticompetitive 'effects' should be considered in the section 96 balancing process.[371] Instead of taking into account only the reduction in total welfare from the price increase, the tribunal sug-

---

368 See also the *Bank Merger Enforcement Guidelines* (Ottawa: Competition Bureau, 1999).

369 The MEGs also state that the discount rate to be used to calculate prevent values should be consistent with the discount rates used to evaluate investment projects funded in whole or in part by the federal government.

370 *Hillsdown, supra* (1992), 41 C.P.R. (3d) at 336. See generally D.F. McFetridge, 'The Prospects for the Efficiency Defense,' (1996) 26 *Canadian Business Law Journal* 321.

371 Paul S. Crampton, 'The Efficiency Exception for Mergers: An Assessment of Early Signals from the Competition tribunal,' (1993) 21 *Canadian Business Law Journal* 371 at 375.

gested that a broader range of effects, such as the wealth transfer from consumers to producers, should be considered.[372]

The tribunal 'raised as a question' as to whether the wealth transfer between consumers and producers was always a neutral effect, posing two hypothetical situations: (i) a merger of two drug companies where the relevant product is a life-saving drug; and (ii) a merger resulting in a dominant firm which is foreign-owned and charges supracompetitive prices so that all the wealth transfer leaves Canada. However, while the tribunal in *Hillsdown* questioned the neutrality of wealth transfers, which is the basis of the total surplus standard, the majority of the tribunal in *Superior Propane* unqualifiedly endorsed this standard. In *Superior Propane*, the majority of the tribunal stated that they did not regard the redistributive effects of a merger as anticompetitive and that the only effects that can be considered under section 96 are the effects on resource allocation as measured in principle by the dead-weight loss, which takes both quantitative and qualitative effects into account. The tribunal offered five reasons for its view, related to (i) the absence of distributional concerns from the ambit of the merger provisions of the Act; (ii) the need for predictability of merger policy; (iii) the large size of the transfer from consumers to producers relative to the typical dead-weight loss, implying that a standard that included the transfer as an effect under section 96 would effectively eliminate section 96 as a defence; (iv) the availability of other government instruments that are superior for addressing distributional objectives; and (v) the endorsement by the bureau's own MEGs of the total surplus standard. These reasons are discussed above in section I A (subsection 5) of this chapter. The tribunal also rejected an argument by the commissioner that in the case of a merger to monopoly, these considerations should not apply. The tribunal pointed out that there was no such qualification in the text of section 96, and that in any event it would be arbitrary to apply one test for a merger to monopoly and a substantially different test for a merger to something just short of a monopoly.

We endorse the tribunal's decision to accept the total surplus standard for reasons discussed earlier in this chapter (where we also discussed the deficiencies in its application in the *Superior Propane* case).

---

372 *Hillsdown, supra* (1992), 41 C.P.R. (3d) at 336–42. See also L.P. Schartz, 'The "Price Standard" or the "Efficiency Standard"? Comments on the *Hillsdown* Decision,' (1992) *Canadian Competition Policy Record* 42.

We note, however, that on 1 April 2001 the Federal Court of Appeal rejected the tribunal's interpretation of section 96 involving a total surplus standard in favour of an approach that takes into account the redistributive effects between buyers and the merging parties. The Supreme Court of Canada declined to grant leave to appeal from this decision and the case has been remitted to the tribunal for redetermination. Readers should also note that in light of the decision of the Federal Court of Appeal in the *Commissioner of Competition v. Superior Propane Inc.*, the Efficiency Exception Part 5 of the guidelines no longer applies. In cases where efficiencies are claimed, the Competition Bureau will apply the principles set out in the *Commissioner of Competition v. Superior Propane Inc.* and *ICG Propane Inc.* 2001 F.C.A. 104.

VI. A Critique of the Merger Review Process

Since the enactment of the *Competition Act* in 1986, the tribunal has heard four contested merger cases (*Hillsdown, Southam, Propane,* and *Canadian Waste Services*) and two contested variations of consent orders (*Gemini II* and *Southam*), and dealt with about ten consent orders including (*Palm Dairies, Asea Brown Boveri, Gemini I, Imperial Oil, Seaspan, Canadian Waste Services, Maple Leaf Mills, BAT/Rothmans, Ultramar,* and *Indigo*).[373] However, merger review statistics demonstrate that the 1980s and the mid-1990s saw the largest merger waves in Canadian history,[374] indicating that despite the fact that the bureau has reviewed thousands of mergers, very few cases have proceeded before the tribunal. In most cases where anticompetitive concerns were raised, parties have either chosen to negotiate settlements with the commissioner or abandoned the transaction altogether.

As Grover and Quinn have observed, 'the existence of a tribunal does not ensure continued use if the tribunal does not respond effectively to the concerns of those who can initiate proceedings before it.'[375] The policy-making process that led to the enactment of the *Competition*

---

373 Many of these cases are discussed above.
374 Campbell, Janisch, and Trebilcock, 'Rethinking the Role of the Competition Tribunal,' at 299.
375 W. Grover and J. Quinn, 'Recent Developments in Canadian Merger Law,' in S. Khemani and W. Stanbury, eds., *Canadian Competition Law and Policy at the Centenary* (Halifax: Institute for Research on Public Policy, 1991), 230.

Act in 1986 contemplated that the tribunal would become the locus of authoritative expertise on the reviewable practices provisions of the Act, especially in more difficult cases. Such expectations have not materialized.[376] Faced with often unwanted publicity, huge costs, and long delays when involved in the proceedings before the tribunal, businesses prefer to deal with the bureau and to negotiate settlements if the bureau raises anticompetitive concerns during its review. For example, two of the contested merger cases heard before the tribunal since the enactment of the *Competition Act* (*Hillsdown* and *Southam*) took thirteen to twenty-five months from the time of the commissioner's application to the tribunal until the issuance of the tribunal's final decision, which followed a six- to ten-month period from the time the merger was announced or notified until the commissioner initiated formal proceedings, for a total of twenty-three to thirty-one months to dispose of the mergers (not including appeals). Oral discovery took 60–120 counsel days, interlocutory hearings and prehearing conferences took 10–26 counsel days, the hearings before the tribunal took 72–352 counsel days, and appeals occupied a further 4–6 counsel days, for a total of 146–524 counsel days from the time the commissioner initiated formal proceedings. An average of nine counsel were involved in each case, sixteen to forty-six witnesses testified at the hearings, seven to fifteen experts filed affidavits, and 448–520 documents were filed as exhibits with the tribunal.[377] In *Superior Propane*, the time elapsed from public announcement of the merger to the tribunal's decision was twenty-five months; the proceedings entailed forty-eight hearing days and involved ninety-one witnesses, including seventeen expert witnesses. The bureau called in excess of eighty of these witnesses. In *Canadian Waste Services Inc.*, despite an agreed statement-of-facts, elimination of oral and documentary discovery, and electronic document filing, the merger was under review in the bureau for twelve months and before the tribunal for seventeen months.

It is also difficult to predict the tribunal's treatment of proposed con-

---

376 Campbell, Janisch, and Trebilcock, 'Rethinking the Role of the Competition Tribunal,' at 299–300.

377 From ibid., at 301. These case studies are described in greater detail in M. Trebilcock and L. Austin, 'The Limits of the Full Court Press: Of Blood and Mergers,' (1997) 47 *U.T.L.J.* at 34–41.

sent orders with any certainty. For example, the tribunal's approach to issuing consent orders under section 105 of the Act has raised many concerns. Section 105 states that the tribunal 'may make the order ... without hearing such evidence as would ordinarily be placed before the tribunal had the application been contested,' but often the Competition tribunal has been inclined to analogize them to contested hearings, with the most notable example being the *Imperial Oil/Texaco* consent order proceedings. The proposed merger had been announced in January 1989. A five-month review by the commissioner resulted in a negotiated consent order, which was filed with the tribunal on 29 June 1989. Hearings began on 16 October 1989 and ended on 7 December 1989, after twenty-one days of hearings and arguments. Five experts and approximately fifteen other witnesses gave evidence before the tribunal; eight counsel were actively involved in the tribunal proceedings. After issuing interim judgments rejecting two versions of the proposed consent order, the tribunal finally approved a revised order on 6 February 1990.[378]

In contrast, three recent high-profile EU merger cases (*Aerospatiale-Alenia/de Havilland;*[379] *Procter & Gamble/VP Schickedanz;*[380] and *Nestlé/Perrier*)[381] each took five months from notification to final determination, four months of which related to the commission's decision to initiate formal proceedings (as prescribed by the EU Merger Regulation).[382] They involved no oral discovery, production of a relatively small number of documents, one or two days of hearings, between four and ten witnesses, and no cross-examination by opposing counsel. While the *P&G/VPS* and *Nestlé/Perrier* cases might be analogized to consent order proceedings before the Canadian Competition Tribunal, because of the negotiated settlements that occurred during the commission's review

---

378 See Campbell, Janisch, and Trebilcock, 'Rethinking the Role of the Competition Tribunal,' at 301.
379 *Re: The Concentration Between Aerospatiale and Alenia and de Havilland,* [1992] 4 C.M.L.R. 2. For commentary see M. Reynolds, 'The *de Havilland* Case: A Watershed for EC Merger Control,' (1991) *Int'l Financial L. Rev.* 21.
380 *Procter & Gamble/VO Schickedanz* (II), [1995] 1 CEC 2, 466 (Decision 94/893) at 2504 ff.
381 *Re: the Concentration between Nestlé SA and Source Perrier SA (Case IV/M190),* [1993] 4 C.M.L.R. M17.
382 *Council Regulation 4064/89 on the Control of Concentrations Between Undertakings,* O.J. 1990, L257/14, art. 10.

process, the *de Havilland* case was contested throughout. Nevertheless, the decision-making processes in all three cases were similar.[383]

The EU merger cases stand in stark contrast to the protracted proceedings before the Canadian Competition Tribunal. In addition to the delays and costs encountered in consent order proceedings before the tribunal, businesses are also reluctant to seek consent orders because of the uncertainty of their issuance. After the *Palm Dairies* proposed order was rejected by the tribunal in 1986, no applications were made for a consent order between November 1986 and early 1989,[384] parties preferring instead to negotiate a settlement with the commissioner, or even to abandon the proposed merger. Similar uncertainties are raised by the tribunal's recent rejection of the draft consent order in the *Ultramar* proceedings.

As a result of the uncertainty and costs of proceedings, the bureau has played a much larger role than the tribunal in enforcing the merger regulations of the *Competition Act*, thus diminishing process values such as transparency, accountability and reasoned public decision making.[385] Some institutional redesign options to mitigate the court-like orientation of the tribunal without an excessive risk of incorrect decisions are reviewed below.

A. *Analytical Framework*[386]

An ideal regime for adjudicating mergers would minimize the aggregate of three broad categories of 'costs':[387] (1) Type I Error Costs (i.e., costs of blocking procompetitive transactions); (2) Type II Error Costs (i.e., costs of allowing anticompetitive transactions); and (3) Transaction Costs (public and private costs, e.g., costs to the public of protracted proceedings and costs to private parties in assembling the vast

---

383 See Trebilcock and Austin, 'The Limits of the Full Court Press.'
384 From W.T. Stanbury, 'An Assessment of the Merger Review Process Under the Competition Act,' (1992) 20 *Canadian Business Law Journal* 422 at 433.
385 Campbell, Janisch, and Trebilcock, 'Rethinking the Role of the Competition tribunal,' at 300.
386 The following proposals are derived from ibid., at 303; see also M.J. Trebilcock and F. Iacobucci, 'Designing Competition Law Institutions,' September 2001.
387 See A.N. Campbell, 'The Review of Anti-Competitive Mergers' (PhD dissertation, University of Toronto, 1993), chaps. 3 and 9 and Stanbury, 'An Assessment of the Merger Review Process under the Competition Act,' at 451–4.

amounts of information requested in contested proceedings).[388] These costs are related in that focusing on reducing Type I errors tends to increase the risk of Type II errors and vice versa. Similarly, Types I and II error costs can often be reduced through more thorough adjudication processes, but at the expense of increased transaction costs. Over time, however, learning effects may improve the ability of adjudicators and enforcement agencies to discriminate between pro- and anticompetitive activities (thereby reducing Types I and II errors) and/or to operate decision-making processes more efficiently, thereby reducing transaction costs.

Parliament has expressly indicated that transaction costs should be a prominent consideration in the tribunal's adjudicative mandate by providing that '[a]ll proceedings before the tribunal shall be dealt with as informally and expeditiously as the circumstances and considerations of fairness permit'[389] in the *Competition Tribunal Act*. The tribunal has failed to effectuate Parliament's intention by adopting formalized courtlike procedures that 'give rise to extensive and time-consuming litigious steps comparable to those in any other contested commercial case.'[390]

Streamlining of proceedings is necessary to ensure that tribunal proceedings be dealt with informally and expeditiously. Streamlining is proposed in five major areas described below.

1. Time Limits
The tribunal has recognized the time sensitivity of mergers and attempted to expedite proceedings by treating time limits for pleadings as mandatory, issuing scheduling orders and refusing to grant extensions of time limits or adjournments of scheduled hearings unless persuasive reasons are offered.[391] However, these initiatives can be reinforced by requiring that the tribunal issue a mandatory deadline for its decision in a contested proceeding to ensure expedition and increase certainty. A four-month time limit from the date of the commissioner's application

---

388 In *Southam, supra* (1992), 43 C.P.R. (3d) 161, the tribunal frequently observed that more evidence with respect to certain aspects would have been helpful, despite its 266-page decision, which discussed the voluminous evidence presented. See Goldman and Bodrug, 'The *Hillsdown* and *Southam* Decisions,' at 739.

389 *Competition Tribunal Act*, Pt I, s. 9(2).

390 Goldman and Bodrug, 'The *Hillsdown* and *Southam* Decisions,' at 751.

391 See jurisprudence summarized in Campbell, *Merger Law and Practice*, chap. 13.

is worth considering, particularly as the European experience has demonstrated that that is an attainable standard. A shorter deadline (e.g., two months) would be appropriate for consent proceedings.[392]

2. Case Management
Active case management can be implemented during prehearing conferences. Each party could be required to state its position in its initial pleading. After the pleadings, a prehearing conference could be held to identify the specific points of disagreement between the parties and to narrow the issues. The tribunal could then set out specific questions it expects to be addressed and the documents it would want to review, or it could consider restricting the scope of proceedings to specific issues which are expected to be determinative of the outcome.[393] Such early delineation of key issues will assist parties in identifying the evidence required and the appropriate scope for expert opinion evidence.

3. Intervenors
As discussed above in *Imperial Oil*, the tribunal granted several intervenors the right to lead evidence and cross-examine witnesses in addition to making argument, notwithstanding that the commissioner had pointed out that intervenors have the opportunity, under section 35 of the Competition Tribunal Rules,[394] to raise their concerns and have them addressed by the commissioner and the merging parties. In 1996 the Tribunal Rules were amended to create a special procedural code for consent proceedings so that the tribunal can proceed more efficiently in considering consent orders by simplifying scheduling and prehearing management procedures, and by clarifying the procedures

---

392 The Competition Tribunal Rules, r. 65 currently requires that the commencement of a proceeding be published forthwith (which in practice usually means one to three weeks) in the *Canada Gazette*, and that at least twenty-one days be allowed for receipt of comments or requests to intervene in a consent proceeding. Thus it would be possible to target commencement of a hearing within forty days of the date of application and to expect the tribunal to render a decision within sixty days.

393 For example, in *Southam*, the decision turned on the identification of the relevant product market but the tribunal went on to assess barriers to entry at length.

394 Section 35 of the Competition Tribunal Rules SOR/87-373 had provided that intervenors be notified of the proposed consent order, be allowed at least twenty-one days to make comments or representations in respect of the proposed order, and that the parties reply to those comments or representations within seven days of the filing of those comments.

for and the timing of comments or requests for leave to intervene.[395] In addition, the following steps could assist in further delineating the role of intervenors: (i) the tribunal could make greater use of its discretion to impose strict terms and conditions on intervenors (e.g., regarding issues they may address); (ii) the presiding member must strike out arguments of intervenors whenever they are not relevant to the proceedings[396] or where they are repetitious; (iii) the tribunal must not continue to allow intervenors to play a greater role in consent proceedings than in contested proceedings on the questionable rationale that in consent proceedings, intervenors know, at the time intervenor status is requested, how they will be adversely affected by the order eventually given.[397]

4. Discoveries

The discovery process is the lengthiest of all prehearing procedures and tends to propagate interlocutory litigation. However, the two basic functions of discovery in civil litigation (information gathering and narrowing of issues to avoid surprises for parties) are not persuasive reasons for retaining discovery in contested reviewable practice proceedings. The *Competition Act* already provides the commissioner with extensive investigative powers that allow him to obtain relevant information possessed by respondents, including powers to compel disclosure.[398] As well, discovery of the commissioner is of limited value because various privileges severely limit the disclosure that can be obtained[399] and because respondents typically have much of the relevant information for a defence in their possession. Moreover, surprise can be avoided through case management techniques and prefiling of evidence. Eliminating documentary discovery and examinations for discovery would reduce the time taken for contested proceedings without materially impairing the ability of parties to obtain a fair hearing[400] or that of the tribunal to make informed decisions.

---

395 Goldman and Bodrug, 'The Merger Review Process,' at 611.
396 The tribunal heard submissions of this nature in both the *Gemini I* and the *Imperial Oil* consent proceedings.
397 *Imperial Oil*, *supra*, note 78, at 48–9.
398 See above, 191, for a discussion of the director's investigative powers.
399 See jurisprudence summarized in Campbell, *Merger Law and Practice*, chap. 13.
400 The chairman has suggested that the tribunal would be receptive to reducing discovery as long as trial by ambush is not the result and parties' rights to a fair hearing

5. Prefiling of Evidence

Expert evidence must currently be prefiled in affidavit form thirty days before commencement of the hearing; rebuttals are due fifteen days beforehand.[401] This assists in reducing the time taken for proceedings and could be extended to include prefiling of nonexpert evidence to further expedite tribunal proceedings.

B. Hybrid Membership

The inclusion of lay experts in the tribunal was an attempt to obtain the benefits of both judicial impartiality and economic and business expertise, but the influence of the judicial members has dominated tribunal decisions. In order for lay members to play a more meaningful role, the following measures may be considered: (i) questions of law should not be decided solely by judicial members, particularly as in this field they are likely to involve economic issues in which lay members could provide valuable input;[402] and (ii) panel composition should be modified to include two lay members on every three-member panel and a majority on any five-member panel, because it is the lay members who are expected to bring economic expertise to the tribunal.

C. Consent Orders

Instead of a highly interventionist approach in consent orders, the tribunal should restrain itself by adopting a deferential review of the proposed order as it did in *Asea Brown Boveri* and *Maple Leaf Mills*. The objective should not be to fine tune all aspects of a proposed order or expand its coverage to issues not raised by the commissioner,[403] but to

---

are preserved: see McKeown, 'Agenda for the Tribunal,' at 2. In *Canadian Waste Services*, oral and documentary discovery was dispensed with, electronic filing of documents was instituted, and the parties proceeded on the basis of an agreed statement-of-facts.

401 Competition Tribunal Rules, r. 47.

402 A notable example is Reed J.'s controversial interpretation of the s. 96 efficiency exception in *Hillsdown*, which the commissioner has subsequently indicated would not be followed by the bureau. See the section entitled 'The Efficiency Exception' for a discussion of this issue.

403 Such fine tuning arguably occurred in the *Imperial Oil* consent order proceedings.

identify proposed orders which are materially deficient in addressing the anticompetitive effects raised in a merger.

D. Development of Jurisprudence

Since the tribunal has adjudicated relatively few merger proceedings, there has been little progress made in developing merger jurisprudence. Jurisprudence is needed to flesh out the meaning of key elements and their application to diverse factual situations. To date, because of the marginal role played by the tribunal, the bureau has become the source of interpretations on key aspects of the *Competition Act*, such as what constitutes 'a substantial lessening of competition.' The foregoing proposals to streamline tribunal proceedings should result in a greater case flow, but attention must also be paid to the development of precedents, of appropriate use of *obiter dicta*, and to the credibility of and respect for tribunal decisions.

1. Precedents
The tribunal should pay more attention to its own past decisions when dealing with similar issues in subsequent cases, and it should refer move frequently to the Competition Bureau's guidelines. The tribunal has often ignored the bureau's MEGs in its decisions, although they were issued specifically to reduce uncertainty for businesses contemplating mergers. In contrast, U.S. courts and the Federal Trade Commission commonly refer to enforcement guidelines (either positively or critically) in the course of adjudicating cases.

2. Obiter dicta
The tribunal should address all issues which have arisen in the proceedings, even if they are not essential to the outcome of the case (as it did in *Hillsdown* with regard to the 'efficiency exception'), in order to accelerate the development of authoritative interpretation of the merger provisions to provide more certainty for Canadian businesses. *Obiter dicta* are not binding authority; rather, they are considered merely to be persuasive pronouncements by the tribunal in subsequent proceedings.

3. Credibility and Respect for Decisions
The Competition Tribunal's decision making has been unpredictable to date because of its case-by-case approach. The tribunal has tended to review the voluminous evidence presented at great length rather than

articulating general substantive principles. For example, it characterized its decision in *Hillsdown* as a 'borderline decision' that was
strongly influenced by the facts of the case such as the expropriation of
one party's Toronto rendering facility.[404] As a result, the tribunal's decisions have not been helpful in providing guidance in future cases.
Moreover, the commissioner has not appeared to give much weight to
tribunal pronouncements that diverged from the MEGs. Ignoring the
tribunal undermines its credibility and arrogates the law interpreter
function which Parliament had assigned to it.

In sum, it is important that the current regime for adjudicating mergers be modified to provide businesses with more certainty when proceeding before the tribunal and to give effect to the role of the tribunal
as envisioned in the enactment of the *Competition Act* in 1986.

---

404 *Hillsdown, supra* (1992), 41 C.P.R. (3d) at 328–31.

FIVE

Predatory Pricing and Price Discrimination

I. Predatory Pricing

While definitions of the practice vary, Joskow and Klevorick provide a useful working definition of predatory pricing: 'Predatory pricing behavior involves a reduction of price in the short run so as to drive competing firms out of the market or to discourage entry of new firms in an effort to gain larger profits via higher prices in the long run than would have been earned if the price reduction had not occurred.'[1]

Predatory pricing has given rise to considerable controversy. Despite its intuitive appeal as a profitable strategy for a firm seeking market power, a significant amount of commentary suggests that it is an implausible anticompetitive strategy.[2] In this chapter, we review scep-

---

1 P.J.. Joskow and A.K. Klevorick, 'A Framework for Analyzing Predatory Pricing Policy,' (1979) 89 *Yale L.J.* 213 at 219–20. Other definitions include Bork's, who states that predatory pricing occurs where a firm deliberately pursues business practices that would not be profit-maximizing except for the expectation that (1) rivals will be driven from the market, leaving the predator with sufficient market share to command monopoly profits, or (2) rivals will be chastened sufficiently to abandon competitive behaviour the predator finds inconvenient or threatening: R.H. Bork, *The Antitrust Paradox: A Policy at War with Itself* (Toronto: Free Press, 1993), at 144. Posner defines predatory pricing as pricing at a level designed to exclude from the market an equally or more efficient competitor: R.A. Posner, *Antitrust Law: An Economic Perspective* (Chicago: University of Chicago Press, 1976), at 188.

2 See, e.g., J. McGee, 'Predatory Price Cutting: The Standard Oil (N.J.) Case,' (1958) 1 *J. of Law. & Econ.* 137; L.G. Telser, 'Cutthroat Competition and the Long Purse,' (1966) 9 *J. of Law & Econ.* 259; J. McGee, 'Predatory Pricing Revisited,' (1980) 23 *J. of L. & Econ.* 289; Posner, *Antitrust Law;* Bork, *Antitrust Paradox;* F.H. Easterbrook, 'Predatory

tical economic approaches to predatory pricing, as well as theories more sympathetic to the view that predatory pricing is a plausible strategy. Following discussion of the theory, we assess the suggestions of various commentators as to appropriate legal responses to predatory pricing. Earlier efforts to provide guidance to courts focused on comparisons of price and cost to test for predatory pricing. Price-cost tests, however, cannot themselves be determinative. More recent suggestions have moved beyond price-cost comparisons and ask whether predatory pricing is a plausible strategy for the predator: is the predator likely to recoup losses suffered during the period of predatory pricing through the exit or deterred entry of competitors? We conclude by reviewing the law in Canada and its connection to the economics of predatory pricing.

A. Economic Theories of Predatory Pricing

1. The Long Purse
The simplest and most intuitively appealing theory of predatory pricing involves a firm with access to ample capital driving out a rival by setting prices below cost. Such prices impose costs on both the predator and victim firm, but the predator can survive the losses owing to its better access to capital. After the rival has departed the market as a result of these losses, the predator recoups profits lost during the low pricing period by raising prices above competitive levels. The absence of the failed firm from the market gives the predator sufficient market power to raise price. The long-purse version of predatory pricing clearly has negative welfare effects if there would have been successful entry in its absence. There is a social welfare loss from monopoly pricing following the victim firm's exit; moreover, there is a distortion if price is below marginal cost during the period of predatory pricing. If price is below marginal cost, consumers clearly benefit by realizing lower prices, but greater resources go into production of the goods than is socially optimal; the costs of production exceed the benefits to consumers, leading to a dead-weight loss.

Strategies and Counterstrategies,' (1981) 48 *U. Chi. L. Rev.* 263; D.G. McFetridge and S. Wong, 'Predatory Pricing in Canada: The Law and Economics,' (1985) 63 *Can. Bar Rev.* 685.

The long-purse version of predatory pricing has been the subject of much of the sceptical commentary on predatory pricing. McGee's pioneering work concerns the Standard Oil trust.[3] Contrary to the received wisdom, McGee contends that the Standard Oil trust was not built upon a foundation of predatory pricing, but rather upon merger. He provides a series of case studies to support his contention, as well as important theoretical insights into the likely profitability of predatory pricing. McGee points out that in a predatory pricing situation, the predator, not the prey, will suffer more losses. If the predator initiates lower prices, this must be through its own increased production, an increase the prey does not undertake. If each sale occurs at a loss, it is the predator, through its increase in market share, that will bear a disproportionate share of the industry losses. McGee also points out that since industry profits are dissipated by the period of predation, rational firms would not engage in such activity, but would prefer to merge instead. Merging allows firms to reap market power benefits similar to predation (merger, like successful predation, leads to one less firm in the market), yet the parties collectively avoid the losses of predation. Consequently, firms should rely on merger, not predation, to realize long-run market power.

Other commentators continue the assault on the 'long purse' theory of predation. Posner argues that successful predation requires that the predator rely on the ultimate victims of predation, the consumers, to act against self-interest by purchasing goods at prices that drive out competition and result in higher prices in the long run.[4] That is, predation requires consumers to accept a 'net loss' over time by purchasing from the predator. Posner acknowledges, however, that consumers may be ill-informed about the long-run effects of their purchasing decisions and that there may be a significant free-rider problem among consumers: while every consumer is better off if the predatory pricing campaign is unsuccessful, each is best off if others keep the victim firm afloat by continuing to purchase its goods at higher prices while the consumer purchases from the predator at very low prices. Since each consumer has an incentive to be the only consumer not buying from the victim firm, each may choose to free-ride on the other consumers'

---

3 McGee, 'Predatory Price Cutting.'
4 Posner, *Antitrust Law,* at 184–5.

efforts to keep the victim firm viable, and the victim firm may thus fail.[5]

In further opposition to the long-purse theory, Bork points out that in order for predation to be successful, exit barriers must be fairly low.[6] But if exit from the industry is easy, such as where the firm's equipment is useful for other industries and thus may be sold easily, entry is probably easy as well. And if entry is easy, Bork continues, predation is unlikely to be successful. When the predator attempts to raise price following the victim firm's exit, entry will prevent it from doing so.

Long-purse predatory pricing may also be unattractive, Bork suggests, in that while the costs of low prices are immediate, the benefits to the predator lie in the future and must be discounted accordingly because of the time-value of money.[7] Hovenkamp submits further that the future profits must also be discounted by the likelihood of failure, either through an unexpectedly resilient victim firm, unexpected entry, or an antitrust suit for predatory pricing.[8] The last factor is irrelevant to a policy discussion of predatory pricing law, at least insofar as the discussion concerns the plausibility of predatory pricing. One cannot say that predatory pricing never occurs and therefore there should be no law against it if one relies upon the law against it to support the conclusion that predatory pricing never occurs. We are also sceptical about the relevance of uncertainty. While the predator may discount its future profits from predation because of uncertainty, prior to a decision to prey, the firm will also be uncertain about the costs of such a strategy. The victim firm may prove unexpectedly vulnerable, for example. Uncertainty may work equally on the prediction of both the costs and benefits of predation, thus providing no *a priori* reason to suppose that it is more or less likely than without uncertainty.

---

5 Easterbrook, 'Predatory Strategies and Counterstrategies,' at 270–1 points out that there are techniques by which the victim firm can perhaps convince consumers to purchase from it. For example, it can offer long-term contracts to supply at the competitive price, perhaps making the contract contingent on obtaining enough commitments to ensure its survival into the future. Once it has succeeded in securing these commitments, the predator, realizing that it will not be possible to drive the victim firm out of the market, will cease its predatory pricing policy.

6 Bork, *Antitrust Paradox*, at 153.

7 Ibid., at 153–4.

8 H. Hovenkamp, *Federal Antitrust Policy: The Law of Competition and Its Practice* (St Paul: West Publishing, 1994), at 307.

The conventional long-purse story also relies on the questionable assumption that the victim has inadequate capital to last out the period of predatory pricing. Easterbrook suggests reasons to suppose that the victim firm will have ample access to capital.[9] First, during the period of predation the victim firm is actually more profitable (less unprofitable) than the predator, given that the predator's output must expand to meet demand at the low price, and thus the *victim* may be better able to withstand the price war and realize the monopoly profits if the *predator* is forced to exit. Investors will find the victim firm an attractive investment since it will be the more profitable survivor over the course of the predatory pricing and and subsequent monopoly pricing. Second, even if capital markets are for some reason blocked from backing the victim firm, the victim firm would be an attractive acquisition for a better-heeled existing firm for the same reasons that it would be an attractive investment in the capital markets.

Notwithstanding these many infirmities of the conventional long-purse story, there remains another problem: if all parties are equally informed, predatory pricing should never occur in equilibrium.[10] The conventional story envisages the predator and victim firm fighting to the bitter end. If, however, the victim firm is doomed to fail, it should exit immediately rather than incur the costs of a price war. Thus, if predatory pricing is a profitable strategy for the predator, the victim firm will not exist in the market; either it will not enter, or it will exit as soon as it is clear that predatory pricing is a profitable strat-

---

9 Easterbrook, 'Predatory Strategies and Counterstrategies,' at 269–70.
10 See Telser, 'Cutthroat Competition.' More recently, J.-P. Benoît, 'Financially Constrained Entry Into a Game With Incomplete Information,' (1984) 15 *Rand J. Econ.* 490 applies a more rigorous game-theoretic approach to demonstrate Telser's conclusion. Even if the predator is only willing to tolerate one period of unprofitable predatory pricing, this may be sufficient to deter entry or to induce exit. Consider the result when the prey has exhausted its resources to the point where it could only survive one more period of a price war. The predator will predate because it prefers one period of a price war followed by monopoly to competition. Consequently, the prey will exit the market prior to this period, anticipating the price war. But then, during the second-last period, the predator knows that the prey will exit if it preys for one period, since the prey will only have resources for one more period at the end of the second-last period and then will exit. Following this reasoning backwards ('backwards-induction'), the prey will not enter, or will exit immediately when it discovers that the predator would engage in a price war for even one period.

egy.[11] From a policy perspective, this criticism of the long-purse theory is less damning to a law against predatory pricing than some of the other criticisms. The *threat* of long-purse predation may result in exit, or lack of entry, and consequent social losses from market power. Reducing the credibility of this threat by outlawing predatory pricing may have socially beneficial effects; there may be less exit (or less non-entry) because of anticipated long-purse predation.

Despite a formidable list of arguments against the plausibility of predatory pricing, there are important responses that to some extent rehabilitate predatory pricing as a potentially viable strategy. With respect to the argument that merger is always a more attractive alternative to predation, there have been at least three cogent responses. First, mergers giving rise to substantial market power are illegal under many antitrust laws, including Canada's. As Posner points out, while both anticompetitive mergers and predatory pricing are illegal, predatory pricing may be more difficult to detect and may therefore provide a preferable means to eliminate a rival.[12] And as Ordover and Saloner argue, this may be particularly true since profitable predatory pricing requires the prospect of monopoly pricing, which generally implies a concentrated market – precisely when antimerger provisions are likely to prevent a merger.[13]

Second, the predator may 'soften up' the victim firm with a campaign of predatory pricing in order to obtain a favourable price when acquiring the firm. And third, a reputation for predatory pricing may be important in deterring future entry, while merging may in fact

---

11 However, the assumption of perfectly symmetric information and the foregoing logic would rule out many phenomena that are observed: protracted negotiations, labour strikes and lawsuits that are not settled prior to litigation. Some 'friction' such as asymmetric information, is necessary to explain predatory pricing and each of the phenomena mentioned.

12 Posner, *Antitrust Law*, at 185.

13 J.A. Ordover and G. Saloner, 'Predation, Monopolization and Antitrust,' in R. Schmalensee and R.D. Willig, eds., *Handbook of Industrial Organization*, vol. I (New York: North Holland, 1989), at 547. McGee 'Predatory Pricing Revisited,' responds that anti-merger provisions may make predation less attractive, since the predator may be legally incapable of purchasing the victim firm's assets following its failure, thereby inviting new entry. This assumes, however, that the assets are industry-specific. If the assets are industry-specific, why would the new entrant purchaser assume that it will fare any better than the previous firm against the predator? See Ordover and Saloner, 'Predation, Monopolization and Antitrust,' at 547, note 10.

encourage it. The second and third responses to the merger-as-profit-able-alternative argument will be discussed in greater detail below.[14]

Aside from the relative attractiveness of mergers, more recent theoretical work has focused on a key assumption of the conventional long-purse story and its critics: full information. If all parties are aware of all the relevant facts, the criticisms of the long-purse theory are formidable indeed. Relaxing the full information assumption, however, may give rise to plausible versions of the long-purse story. In particular, information asymmetries can explain the fact that internal financing is less costly than external financing. An incumbent firm will have a larger store of low cost capital (retained earnings) that will allow it to emerge as the sole survivor of a protracted price war.

Fudenberg and Tirole, for example, provide a version of long-purse predation that relies on imperfections in capital markets.[15] If creditors gave the victim firm an unlimited line of credit, there would be no long-purse predation: predators would know that the prey's resources would not dry up and thus would not prey. Fudenberg and Tirole offer a plausible reason why an unlimited line of credit will not be forthcoming: asymmetric information between the firm and its creditors implies that creditors will not extend unlimited credit. This asymmetric information may then give rise to predation. Suppose that the victim firm must finance its investment in capital markets, while the predator is able to self-finance. Suppose also that, given asymmetric information between the firm and the lender, external financing is limited. In two-period competition between the self-financing predator and the debtor victim firm, predatory pricing may be a profitable strategy in the first period, as it will lower the net asset value of the victim firm and thus impede the victim firm's access to capital in the second period, which may either induce the exit of the prey or at least constrain its expansion. This model can account both for profitable predatory pricing and why it would be observed in equilibrium: the victim firm may be profitable in the first period, but it will be unable to expand or will exit in the second period. Bolton and Scharfstein also provide a model in

---

14 Both of these responses were proposed initially by B. Yamey, 'Predatory Price-Cutting: Notes and Comments,' (1972) 15 *J. of Law & Econ.* 129.

15 D. Fudenberg and J. Tirole, 'A "Signal-Jamming" Theory of Predation,' (1986) 17 *Rand J. Econ.* 366.

which informational asymmetries lead to external financing constraints and a 'deep pockets' theory of predation.[16]

2. Reputation

If McGee is correct and predation is rarely a profitable strategy in a single market, incumbent firms facing potential entry are in the unhappy (for them) position of being unable to threaten credibly that they will prey on an entrant. The entrant knows that while the incumbent may threaten a price war, it will not carry out this threat when faced with actual entry, because it is more profitable not to price predatorily. As noted above, however, predation may be profitable, and therefore a credible threat, if the predator is concerned about the effect that not preying will have on the behaviour of future entrants.[17] One of the future effects of the decision to prey or not involves the predator's reputation. Even accepting McGee's analysis and assuming that predation is unprofitable with respect to the particular market in which it takes place, predation may nevertheless be a profitable strategy overall. Suppose the predator firm participates in several markets as a monopolist and faces an entrant in one of those markets. If preying in that market deters entry in the other markets by establishing a reputation for predation, predation may be profitable despite the loss the predator suffers.

Like the long-purse theory, the reputation version of predatory pricing has significant intuitive appeal, but some significant theoretical weaknesses as well. Foremost among these is the 'chain-store paradox.'[18] Suppose an incumbent firm faces entry in N markets in which it is presently a monopolist.[19] Suppose further that predatory pricing is unprofitable for the incumbent in the market in which it takes place and all parties know this. Selten demonstrates through 'backwards induction' that the potential predator will not prey, notwithstanding potential reputational effects. In the Nth market, the incumbent will not prey, given that predation in a single market is unprofitable and

16 Patrick Bolton and David Scharfstein, 'A Theory of Predation Based on Agency Problems in Financial Contracting,' (1990) 80(1) *American Economic Review* 93.
17 Yamey, 'Predatory Price-Cutting.'
18 R. Selten, 'The Chain-Store Paradox,' (1978) 9 *Theory & Decision* 127.
19 Or, alternatively, suppose there is a monopolist in a single market who will sequentially face N potential entrants over time. See B. Dunlop, D. McQueen, and M.J. Trebilcock, *Canadian Competition Policy: A Legal and Economic Analysis* (Toronto: Canada Law Book, 1987), at 223.

that there are no benefits from a reputation; there are no further markets in which the incumbent faces entry. Thus, there will be entry in the
Nth market by an entrant who is aware of the incumbent's incentives
not to prey. Now consider the second last period. The incumbent will
have no incentive to prey since, no matter what it does, the Nth market
entrant will enter. Thus, the potential entrant will enter the second last
market. Following this reasoning to its conclusion, the potential
entrant will enter the first market and the incumbent will never prey.

As indicated by Selten's reference to this reasoning as a 'paradox,' the
result he describes, while theoretically unassailable, is strongly coun-
terintuitive, especially where an incumbent faces potential competition
in many markets (say, a thousand). Two departures from Selten's
assumptions change the results. If there is an infinite number of potential entrants, it may be credible to threaten predation: at any time a reputation for predation may deter an infinite number of entrants.[20] But
Selten's assumption of a fixed number of markets/potential entrants is
more realistic.[21] To establish plausible predation in these circumstances,
some asymmetric information is required.

Kreps and Wilson[22] and Milgrom and Roberts[23] develop models in
which a very small change to the assumptions about the type of information available to the entrant and predator changes dramatically
Selten's chain-store paradox, even with a finite number of potential
entrants. Suppose that the potential entrants consider there to be a very
small probability that the incumbent firm is 'tough' and will prey in all
circumstances; that is, there is a small probability that the incumbent is
'irrational' and wants to prey even though it is unprofitable.[24] Kreps

20 P. Milgrom and J. Roberts, 'Predation, Reputation and Entry Deterrence,' (1982) 27 J.
   Econ. Theory 280.
21 In objecting to the infinite potential entrants model, Ordover and Saloner, 'Predation,
   Monopolization and Antitrust,' state at 533 that 'in many practical situations, such as
   rivalrous entry into distinct geographic markets, the number of potential entrants is
   finite' [emphasis in original].
22 D. Kreps and R. Wilson, 'Reputation and Imperfect Information,' (1982) 27 J. Econ.
   Theory 253.
23 Milgrom and Roberts, 'Predation, Reputation, and Entry Deterrence.'
24 'Irrationality' may result from the personal animus of the incumbent's owners or
   managers towards the entrant's owners or managers: see, e.g., H. Demsetz, 'Barriers
   to Entry,' (1982) 72 Am. Econ. Rev. 47. We would add that this may be particularly
   plausible if the incumbent's managers are not its owners and there are agency costs
   between owners and managers.

and Wilson and Milgrom and Roberts show that if there are a large enough number of potential entrants (i.e., N is large enough), it is rational for even a non-tough incumbent to act tough and set predatory prices in order to develop a reputation for predation.

Their reasoning is as follows. While the potential entrant starts with the belief that there is a very small possibility that the incumbent will be tough, as soon as the incumbent does not prey (acquiesces), it reveals that it is not tough and future potential entrants will enter knowing that the incumbent is not tough. It may be worthwhile, therefore, for a non-tough incumbent to keep alive the prospect of its toughness by preying upon the first entrant. If there are sufficient profits from deterring future entrants by developing a reputation for toughness, even a weak firm will imitate a tough firm and prey on early entrants. The benefits from deterring future entry exceed the costs of early predation. Kreps and Wilson and Milgrom and Roberts demonstrate that even a very small, exogenous probability that the incumbent is tough may be sufficient to give rise to profit-maximizing predatory pricing, even where the number of potential entrants is finite; this will be true so long as the number of remaining potential entrants is high, thus increasing the value of a reputation.

Not only does the multi-entrant reputational story give some plausibility to predatory pricing generally, it may also refute McGee's and others' argument that predatory pricing should never occur given that merger is a more profitable means of eliminating a competitor. In a situation with multiple potential entrants, acquiring early entrants rather than preying may create a reputation for acquiring, rather than preying, and thus may in fact encourage, not deter, future entry.[25] Predatory pricing may be more profitable in the longer run than merging, regardless of legal constraints on mergers.

Posner argues, however, that entry may occur notwithstanding the existence of incentives to establish a reputation.[26] Suppose there is an incumbent in several geographic markets facing potential entry. Rather than entering a single market at a time, the potential entrant may plan to enter a large number of different markets at once. If an entrant enters many markets at once, the number of remaining markets vulnerable to entry will be small, thus the value of a reputation for being

25 See Yamey, 'Predatory Price-Cutting.'
26 Posner, *Antitrust Law*, at 186-7.

tough will be small. Moreover, the costs of acting tough are large, given that the incumbent will have to prey in several markets at once. Consequently, the incumbent may not invest in reputation by preying on the multi-market entrant. The costs of predation exceed the benefits. As in the deep pockets theory of predation, an entrant with substantial financial capital (in this case, sufficient to enter many markets at once) is not an easy target for predation.

3. Limit Pricing and Signalling

Bain suggests that an incumbent firm may set low prices in order to discourage entry.[27] As Tirole notes, however, 'it [is] not clear how a low price could deter entry.'[28] One possibility is that price carries with it a commitment to price similarly in the future. A low price tells potential entrants that the future price will also be low. The problem with this theory is that prices should be easy to change. Low prices may result from the firm's production capacity, which may have some commitment value; it is then the capacity, not the price, that deters entrants.

The issue of whether low prices can in theory deter entry – and alternatively, whether high prices can attract entry – is critical in competition policy. In all areas of competition policy, especially mergers, entry is regarded as an important potential source of discipline on incumbent firms' pricing.

Milgrom and Roberts offer a theory of limit pricing based on asymmetric information.[29] Suppose that the potential entrant does not know the incumbent's costs, but if those costs proved to be low, the entrant would not find it profitable to enter the market. The incumbent's price may convey information to the potential entrant about the incumbent's cost structure that convinces the entrant that entry is not worthwhile. By setting a low price, the low-cost incumbent may signal to the entrant that its costs are indeed low. A high-cost incumbent may not price low in an attempt to imitate a low-cost firm, and thereby deter entry, because the costs from a low price exceed the benefits from deterring entry. Since the low-cost firm has a lower profit-maximizing price in any event than a high-cost firm, a low-cost incumbent may

27 J. Bain, 'A Note on Pricing in Monopoly and Oligopoly,' (1949) 39 *Am. Econ. Rev.* 448.
28 J. Tirole, *The Theory of Industrial Organization* (Cambridge, Mass.: MIT Press, 1988), at 368.
29 J. Milgrom and J. Roberts, 'Limit Pricing and Entry Under Incomplete Information: An Equilibrium Analysis,' (1980) 50 *Econometrica* 443.

price low and realize a net gain by deterring entry. Limit pricing may therefore be a profitable strategy.

Predatory pricing, in this instance, unlike in previously discussed contexts, may not be welfare-reducing relative to the symmetric information case. If the incumbent is low cost and the potential entrant knew this, it would not enter even if the incumbent initially set a monopoly price. With asymmetric information, on the other hand, the low-cost incumbent must set a low price initially to deter entry, thus resulting in a welfare gain relative to the full information case because of a less distortionary price in the initial period. However, the high-cost incumbent may in some circumstances find it profitable to imitate the low-cost incumbent with lower prices initially, in which case limit pricing may deter entry relative to the symmetric information case and thus may harm social welfare.[30]

Other commentators have used the Milgrom and Roberts limit-pricing model to suggest plausible reasons for predation in other contexts. Ordover and Saloner demonstrate that signalling may result in predation upon an existing competitor.[31] Their model is very similar to Milgrom and Roberts'. Suppose there are two firms: the potential predator and the potential victim. The potential victim does not know the potential predator's costs, but if the predator's costs are low, the victim would prefer to exit the market than to remain in it. Ordover and Saloner show that a low-cost firm may find it profitable to set a low price (expand output) initially in order to signal to the rival that it is low price and thereby induce exit. Thus, asymmetric information about costs may result in profitable predation upon an existing competitor.

Signalling may also provide an answer to those commentators who claim that predation would never take place because merger is always a preferable alternative. Signalling theory may imply that predatory pricing and mergers are not mutually exclusive strategies; rather, predatory pricing may precede an acquisition in order to 'soften up' the acquiree and reduce the purchase price.[32] Recall that McGee concludes that merger is preferable to predation, since the latter dissipates indus-

30 See discussion in Tirole, *Theory of Industrial Organization*, at 370–1.
31 Ordover and Saloner, 'Predation, Monopolization and Antitrust,' at 556–9.
32 G. Saloner, 'Predation, Merger and Incomplete Information,' (1987) 18 *Rand J. of Econ.* 165.

try profits. Rational actors should avoid this dissipation, he reasons, and merge rather than prey. The signalling models demonstrate a flaw in this argument: while the joint gains are higher if a merger occurs, this does not necessarily imply that each party's private gains are maximized by merger; a party may gain at the expense of the other through a strategy of predation followed by merger. Suppose there is a duopoly in which one firm, the acquiree, is unsure of the acquiror's cost structure. After one period of competition, the acquiror purchases the acquiree. The purchase price depends on the acquiree's assessment of its future profitability. A low-cost acquiror, but not a high-cost acquiror, may find it profitable to price low in the first period in order to convey to the acquiree that the acquiror is low cost, which in turn lowers the acquiree's assessment of its future profitability and therefore lowers the price of the merger. As Yamey states, 'A bout of price warfare initiated by the aggressor, or a threat of such activity, might serve to cause the rival to revise its expectations, and hence alter its terms of sale to an acceptable level.'[33]

The 'softening up' version of predatory pricing unambiguously improves welfare relative to the symmetric information case, but this improvement is sensitive to the assumption that the merger will occur no matter what after the first period of competition. Given the assumption of the merger's occurrence, the only question is the price at which the acquisition takes place, which has no implications for social welfare. The factor that improves social welfare is that the low-cost acquiror prices low in order to obtain a favourable acquisition price, and these low prices improve social welfare relative to the duopoly price that it would have charged in a full-information world.

B. Tests for Predation

Much of the discussion in the law and economics literature on predatory pricing concerns the appropriate legal rules to govern the practice. In the late 1970s and early 1980s, academic commentary provided a cornucopia of possibilities largely centred on price-cost comparisons. More recently, the focus has shifted to a broader strategic analysis of whether predatory pricing is plausibly a profitable strategy for the alleged predator. The focus on the plausibility of 'recoupment,' that is,

---

33 Yamey, 'Predatory Price-Cutting,' at 130.

whether the losses from predatory pricing can be recovered later through higher profits from a less competitive market, has had a strong influence on the legal treatment of predatory pricing in Canada. In this section we survey the suggested legal treatments and briefly discuss some of their relative merits.[34]

1. Per Se *Legality*

Discussion of the 'long purse' theories of predation sets out some fundamental objections to its plausibility. McGee, Telser, Bork, and others conclude that predatory pricing itself will rarely be profitable and that merger almost always appears to be more attractive than predation, given that merging preserves industry profits. Moreover, successful predatory pricing requires high barriers to entry, which according to commentators like those in the 'Chicago school' of antitrust, very rarely exist.[35]

Along with the probable scarcity, even non-existence, of predatory pricing in practice, sceptical commentators express concern about the costs of a rule against predatory pricing. Low prices, or at least marginal-cost prices, are one of the objectives of competition policy. Predatory pricing is extremely difficult to distinguish from competitive pricing both in theory and in practice. Any rule against predatory pricing risks 'chilling' procompetitive, aggressive pricing that is beneficial to consumers. The costs of identifying benign, though aggressive, pricing as predatory[36] may be substantial by deterring such procompetitive behaviour. Furthermore, there will be substantial administrative costs associated with a rule against predatory pricing.

In light of error and administrative costs, one option is simply to eliminate predatory pricing as an antitrust offence.[37] While this may allow occasional episodes of socially undesirable predatory pricing,

---

34 For excellent surveys of the suggested rules and the economic issues involved, see McFetridge and Wong, 'Predatory Pricing in Canada,' and J.F. Brodley and G.A. Hay, 'Predatory Pricing: Competing Economic Theories and the Evolution of Legal Standards,' (1981) 66 *Cornell L. Rev.* 738.

35 See R.A. Posner, 'The Chicago School of Antitrust Analysis,' (1979) 127 *U. Pa. L. Rev.* 925.

36 Joskow and Klevorick, 'A Framework for Analyzing Predatory Pricing Policy,' identify this error as a 'Type I' error.

37 See Bork, *The Antitrust Paradox*, Easterbrook, 'Predatory Strategies and Counterstrategies,' and McFetridge and Wong, 'Predatory Pricing in Canada.

proponents of this approach suggest that these will be rare. A rule of *per se* legality prevents the chilling effect on low prices of prohibiting predatory pricing as well as such a rule's attendant administrative costs.

Such a rule runs against the bulk of commentary on the subject. Most commentators acknowledge the dangers of an expansive predatory pricing rule, but would adjust the rule more precisely in order to avoid a chilling effect on low prices rather than abolish it altogether.

In the event that eliminating predatory pricing as an offence is unacceptable, Easterbrook offers a slightly less radical position.[38] He suggests that while predatory pricing may continue to be an offence, competitors should not be permitted to bring complaints. Since competition policy exists to protect consumers from high prices, and since the risk of an unwarranted chilling effect on competitive prices is greatest when a self-interested competitor is the complainant, Easterbrook suggests that complaints should be restricted to consumers. Such a rule would be acceptable in lieu of *per se* legality. Consumers who observe predatory pricing are the actors who will eventually be harmed by it during the period of higher prices, so they have the correct incentives to bring a complaint once the predator raises prices following the exit of a competitor. If the prices are merely aggressively competitive, consumers should have little incentive to complain.

As Hovenkamp points out, there are compelling reasons to reject Easterbrook's suggestion.[39] Consumers are unlikely to be sufficiently informed to be able to recognize predatory pricing; certainly they should not be expected to have detailed knowledge about costs, which a competitor, on the other hand, may have. Consumers are also likely to complain only after a rival has been eliminated (they would not bring suit during the period of low prices, since such prices are in their interests), so the information available to investigators and adjudicators may not be particularly fresh. Furthermore, competitors, with better information and the incentive to bring a timely suit, provide an 'early-warning signal' about a potentially undesirable practice when its social cost is still minimal. Finally, an individual consumer may not have sufficient financial incentives to undertake the time and expense involved in a predatory pricing allegation.

---

38 Easterbrook, 'Predatory Strategies and Counterstrategies.
39 Hovenkamp, *Federal Antitrust Policy,* at 313–14.

2. Price-Cost Rules

(a) Areeda and Turner

Areeda and Turner provide a rule that has been the focus of both academic and judicial analysis.[40] They share with Bork and Easterbrook significant scepticism about the plausibility of predatory pricing, but would stop short of *per se* legality with respect to low prices. They suggest that predatory pricing law be predicated on the relationship between a firm's costs and its prices. A firm that charges a price above marginal cost makes a profit on that sale, whereas a firm that charges a price below marginal cost would generally make more profit by not selling the additional unit. Areeda and Turner suggest that, since below-cost pricing will only occur, barring error on the part of the firm or on the part of the party measuring cost, if the firm is preying in order to make profits in the future, sales at a price below marginal cost should be illegal *per se*.

In recognition of the difficulties involved in attempting to measure 'marginal cost,' which is an economic concept, not an accounting concept, Areeda and Turner simplify the analysis by substituting average variable cost as a proxy for marginal cost. Prices below average variable cost are unlawful, while prices above average variable cost are lawful.

Several problems arise with reliance on average variable costs as a proxy for marginal cost.[41] First, distinguishing a firm's variable costs from its fixed costs is not an easy task. In the short run, it will be clear that some costs vary with production, while others do not, but virtually all costs are variable over time. For example, while the capital costs of a plant are fixed for a period once the plant is built, they are variable prior to the decision to build the plant. There is little theoretical guidance as to the proper time frame for determining fixed versus variable costs. Areeda and Turner propose a 'laundry list' of costs that should always be considered fixed, such as taxes that do not vary with output, interest on debt, and property taxes.[42] There is certainly an element of arbitrariness to such a list.

---

40 P. Areeda and D.F. Turner, 'Predatory Pricing and Related Practices Under Section 2 of the Sherman Act,' (1975) 88 *Harv. L. Rev.* 697.

41 See Dunlop et al., *Canadian Competition Policy*, at 224–6.

42 See P. Areeda and D. Turner, *Antitrust Law* (Boston: Little, Brown, 1978), para. 715c.

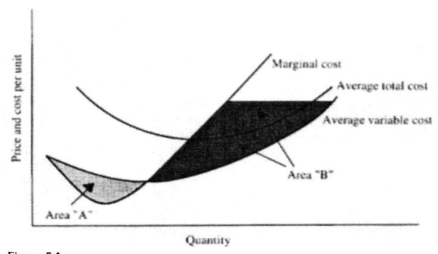

Figure 5.1
Firm cost curves in relation to predation
Source: B. Dunlop, D. McQueen, and M.J. Trebilcock, *Canadian Competition Policy: A Legal and Economic Analysis* (Toronto: Canada Law Book, 1987), 225.

A second problem with formulating a test relying on average variable cost is that it is not always a particularly good proxy for marginal cost. Figure 5.1 demonstrates the problem. Average variable cost may either overstate or understate marginal cost. If price and quantity lie in Area 'A,' marginal cost is below average variable cost. A firm may be convicted for predatory pricing under the Areeda-Turner rule even though it is pricing above marginal cost and thus making a profit on each additional sale. While a firm could not produce in Area 'A' indefinitely, given that it is not covering its total costs, it may be optimal in the short run in certain circumstances, as where there is significant excess capacity in the industry, to cover marginal costs and produce in Area 'A'.

On the other hand, if price-quantity lies in Area 'B,' prices may be below marginal cost, yet above average variable costs. A firm wishing to prey may set price in Area 'B' and avoid prosecution under the Areeda-Turner rule, even though it is taking a loss on each additional sale.[43]

---

43 F.M. Scherer, 'Predatory Pricing and the Sherman Act: A Comment,' (1976) 89 *Harv. L. Rev.* 869.

Areeda and Turner recognize the problem and suggest that any alleged predator attempting to defend itself on the basis of its price being higher than average variable cost must offer proof that marginal cost does not significantly exceed average variable cost.[44] As Hovenkamp points out, however, the purpose of relying on average variable cost in the first place is to avoid having to discover information about marginal cost, which, as noted above, is an economic rather than an accounting concept.[45]

Even if marginal cost were determinable, there would still be problems. First, there may be reasons for a firm to price below marginal cost that have little to do with predation. For example, McFetridge and Wong suggest that a razor blade manufacturer may find it profitable to sell razors below cost in order to make greater overall profits from its sale of razor blades.[46] We will discuss this and non-predatory explanations of below-cost pricing in more detail below. Williamson suggests in addition that it may be possible in certain circumstances for a firm to 'prey,' that is, to impose losses on its rivals, even though it is pricing above marginal cost.[47] Williamson argues that in an industry with scale economies, a dominant firm may carry excess capacity in order to impose losses on its competitors while not pricing below marginal cost or average variable cost. For example, suppose an industry faces a minimum efficient scale at a certain output. An incumbent monopolist may carry excess capacity well above minimum efficient scale such that when entry occurs, it could expand output considerably in order to prevent the entrant from achieving output at minimum efficient scale. The incumbent may be pricing above its own marginal and average variable costs, but in an industry with significant scale economies, other firms may suffer losses even though the predator is complying with the Areeda-Turner rule.[48] However, while anticompetitive excess

---

44 Areeda and Turner, *Antitrust Law*, at para. 715d.

45 Hovenkamp, *Federal Antitrust Policies*, at 302.

46 McFetridge and Wong, 'Predatory Pricing in Canada.'

47 O.E. Williamson, 'Predatory Pricing: A Strategic and Welfare Analysis,' (1977) 87 *Yale L.J.* 284.

48 It is a separate question, however, whether it would be a credible threat for the incumbent to expand output upon entry. Notwithstanding the fact that it may make a profit even on the expanded output, it may be more profitable for the firm to accommodate the entrant and reap duopoly profits, rather than pricing very low and making low profits in the short run.

capacity is a theoretical possibility, in our view it is as a matter of policy rarely or never possible to identify particular instances of excess capacity. To do so, a court would need to solve the market problem of socially optimal investment incorporating the full set of industry cost and demand data. Extending the concept of predation to include, as evidence of predation, *any* losses incurred by smaller rivals would be a mistake. Marginal-cost pricing may therefore be predatory in some sense, but it is as a practical matter foolish to attempt to identify such cases. Nevertheless, Williamson's observations further undermine a predatory pricing rule based solely on marginal cost.

(b) Posner

Posner defines predatory pricing as 'pricing at a level calculated to exclude from the market an equally or more efficient competitor.'[49] From this definition, Posner would add a long-term element to the law against predatory pricing: while Areeda and Turner provide a test based only on short-run marginal costs, Posner would also define as predatory prices below long-run marginal cost intended to eliminate a competitor. Prices below long-run marginal cost are only presumed predatory, however, since it may be profit-maximizing to price in such a range, such as where an industry has no future and the firm ignores the depreciation of a plant that will not be replaced when pricing, or simply where demand varies over time.[50] To establish long-run marginal cost, Posner suggests reliance on average balance sheet costs, defined as the company's total costs as stated on its books over the number of units produced. If the firm fails to cover these costs, in the long run it will not remain in the market.

Posner himself acknowledges two important weaknesses with his suggestion. First, it relies on balance sheet costs, which are backward-looking, as a proxy for marginal cost, which is forward looking. Since the problems of inaccurate proxies apply to his test, Posner would allow firms to rebut an allegation of predatory pricing even if prices are indeed below average balance sheet costs by, for example, showing that the low pricing arose because of changed conditions in demand or supply. Second, his reliance on intent is problematic. Posner himself provides a rather compelling critique of reliance on intent as a neces-

---

49 Posner, *Antitrust Law*, at 188.
50 Ibid., at 189.

sary condition to a finding of predatory pricing: 'What juries (and many judges) do not understand is that the availability of evidence of improper intent is often a function of luck and of the defendant's legal sophistication, not of the underlying reality. A firm with executives sensitized to antitrust problems will not leave any documentary trail of improper intent; one whose executives lack this sensitivity will often create rich evidence of intent simply by the clumsy choice of words to describe innocent behavior. Especially misleading here is the inveterate tendency of sales executives to brag to their superiors about their competitive prowess, often using metaphors of coercion that are compelling evidence of predatory intent to the naïve.'[51] We will return to these observations in the discussion below of *Hoffman LaRoche*.

3. Two-Stage Tests

The fundamental problem with price-cost tests is that accounting costs may overstate the true opportunity cost of a sale. Bolton, Brodley, and Riordan provide several examples of non-predatory, below-cost pricing.[52] It may be that a firm introducing a new product will efficiently promote the product through below-cost pricing; low prices attract first-time buyers who, discovering the high quality of the product, will be willing to buy even when price rises. It could also be that a firm in a network industry sells below price early in the life cycle of this industry in order to attract customers, which in turn, because of positive network externalities, serves to attract more customers. For example, a firm attempting to establish a telephone network may sell telephones at a price below cost in order to attract subscribers. The existence of subscribers will by itself serve to attract more subscribers since the value of having a telephone increases with the number of subscribers. (This dependence of value upon the number of existing subscribers is an illustration of 'network externalities.') Another possibility is pricing below cost in learning-by-doing industries as an investment in cost reduction. That is, a firm may price low in order to produce more, which brings costs down more quickly in a learning-by-doing industry.

In all these cases, comparing price with accounting cost is misleading. A benefit of each sale today is an increase in profit from a greater

---

51 Ibid. at 189–90.
52 P. Bolton, J.F. Brodley and M.H. Riordan, 'Predatory Pricing: Strategic Theory and Legal Policy,' (2000) 88 *Geo. I.J.* 2239 at 2274–82.

share of a much larger market or from lower costs tomorrow. If this benefit could be measured and subtracted from accounting costs to arrive at a net economic cost of sales today, properly measured costs would fall below prices. Price-accounting cost comparisons by themselves, therefore, cannot determine whether a price is predatory.

It might appear to a sceptical reader that we are redefining the economic concepts of price and cost so that the price-less-than-cost condition for predatory pricing *must* fail to hold. This is not so. What we are doing is insisting that all non-anticompetitive benefits from a sale today be included in a consideration of the cost of that sale. Any non-predatory benefits of a pricing strategy that involve measured accounting costs greater than price must be netted out from costs to arrive at a meaningful economic test. Of course, the price-cost test becomes difficult to implement if one attempts, as one must, to net out all possible benefits not due to predation-based exit. This difficulty reveals the fundamental flaw with price-cost tests: they have a veneer of simplicity that masks complex questions about the full opportunity cost of a particular sale. The underlying complexity of meaningful price-cost tests explains why the law and economics literature has shifted away from such tests to more contextual analyses. We survey some of the suggestions below.

(a) Joskow and Klevorick
Joskow and Klevorick were early advocates of moving beyond basic analyses of price-cost relationships.[53] They conclude that since predatory pricing will be profitable only if certain market conditions exist, in assessing whether predatory pricing has occurred the law should first look to determine whether there are suitable market conditions. The first stage of their test concerns factors that suggest the potential profitability of predatory pricing. Is there considerable market power in the industry? Is the alleged predator dominant? Are entry barriers (including scale economies) significant? Are exit barriers (specialized assets) significant? Is technological change insignificant to the market? Affirmative answers to these questions are more likely to result in a finding that the market is one in which predatory pricing may be a profitable strategy. If, and only if, there is a finding that the market is conducive to profitable predatory pricing does the Joskow-Klevorick inquiry move on to the next stage.

53 Joskow and Klevorick, 'A Framework for Analyzing Predatory Pricing Policy.'

Once satisfied that the market structure may give rise to profitable predatory pricing, Joskow and Klevorick would then examine specific conduct. In the spirit of Areeda and Turner, they propose various cost rules for this second stage. Prices below average variable cost would be considered predatory. Prices above average variable cost, but below average total cost, would be considered presumptively predatory; the firm may rebut the presumption by showing that the prices in question were profit-maximizing in the short run. Finally, a price decline followed within two years by a price increase would also be presumptively predatory.

The Joskow-Klevorick rule avoids penalizing a firm for low pricing where a predatory strategy would almost certainly be unprofitable. Where low prices are observed in such a situation, they must be explained by factors other than predation.

The second stage of Joskow and Klevorick's test raises some of the problems of the Areeda and Turner test, as well as novel ones. First, there is the familiar problem of reliance on average variable cost, rather than marginal cost. Second, by establishing rebuttable presumptions with respect to prices below average total costs but above average variable costs, and with respect to a price decrease followed by a price increase within two years, Joskow and Klevorick depart further from the (relatively) simple cost-based test of Areeda and Turner. As the test becomes more complicated, it is more expensive to administer, less predictable, and more difficult for non-economist adjudicators to perform. We will address particular difficulties with the price decrease/increase rule in discussing Baumol's suggestion below.

(b) Ordover and Willig

Ordover and Willig also propose a two-stage test.[54] In the first stage, the inquiry should determine whether the industry is concentrated and whether there are 'entry hurdles' and 're-entry barriers.' Entry hurdles exist when at least part of the costs of entering a market are irrecoverable. Re-entry barriers exist when a firm, having exited previously, must make additional, irrecoverable investments to re-enter. If these conditions exist, the inquiry proceeds to the second stage.

The second stage focuses on whether the alleged predator engaged

---

54 J. Ordover and R. Willig, 'An Economic Definition of Predation: Pricing and Product Innovation,' (1981) 91 *Yale L.J.* 8.

in behaviour that would be profitable if it causes exit, but not if it did not cause exit. Predatory pricing is established if it can be shown that an action that would have been more profitable, contingent upon no exit, could have been but was not undertaken by the alleged predator. For example, a price below marginal cost would be predatory since it would be more profitable absent exit to reduce output. On the other hand, with respect to multiproduct firms, Ordover and Willig suggest that where a firm produces complements, a price below average cost and marginal cost for one of the complements may not be predatory. This latter rule addresses one of the problems with strict cost-based rules: prices below cost for a good like a razor may be non-predatory but profit-maximizing to the firm that also sells razor blades.

The definition of predatory pricing involved in the Ordover-Willig test, while economically appealing, may suffer from imprecision in practice. Attempting to determine if a strategy may be more profitable only in the presence of exit rather than another strategy may be very difficult to determine in practice. As McFetridge and Wong indicate, Ordover and Willig are 'rather vague' as to the rigidity of their rule.[55] To the extent that it allows for a firm to plead that low prices were the most profitable strategy, the rule may entail a complicated investigation. To the extent that it rigidly finds predatory pricing whenever a dominant firm in a market characterized by entry hurdles and re-entry barriers sets prices below average cost, the test engages all the problems of the cost tests discussed in the previous sections.

4. Other Tes

(a) Williamson
Williamson was one of the first commentators to point out the scope for strategic behaviour by a dominant firm facing an Areeda-Turner test.[56] In an industry with scale economies, pricing that effectively drives out new entrants may occur even when prices are above marginal cost and average variable cost. Given this possibility, Williamson proposes a test that departs entirely from price-cost comparisons.

He suggests a rule that would prevent a dominant firm from increasing its output by over 10 per cent for a period of eighteen months fol-

55 McFetridge and Wong, 'Predatory Pricing in Canada,' at 719.
56 Williamson, 'Predatory Pricing'; see also Scherer, 'Predatory Pricing.'

lowing entry. However, where industry conditions are changing, this figure needs adjustment. For example, if sales are increasing prior to entry, the dominant firm would be allowed to increase output by more than 10 per cent to account for this trend. Following the period of non-increasing output, the firm would be required to set price at or above long-run average total cost and average variable cost.

As a general proposition, competition policy seeks to avoid price regulation, given the inordinate expense and expertise that would be required to regulate prices sensibly. Williamson's rule, however, would put competition authorities in the position of monitoring a dominant firm's output and prices, particularly during the eighteen-month period following entry. If conditions in the market were to change – for example, if demand were to grow considerably or if the cost of supply were to fall – there may be perfectly reasonable, non-predatory explanations for a firm's choice to raise output. Yet in order to account for such a possibility, authorities monitoring price increases would be required to examine carefully the industry to check for these shifts in conditions. This examination could amount to full-blown regulation if the firm alleged changes in industry conditions often enough. (Imagine trying to implement Williamson's rule in Internet commerce.)

Moreover, Williamson's theory is based on a notion of a predatory threat that may not be credible. Simply because a firm with excess capacity in an industry with scale economies could lower price to a level just above marginal cost and average variable cost and still make a profit does not mean that it will. The opportunity costs of the lost oligopoly profits during the period of low prices may imply that it is more profitable simply to accommodate entry, in which case the Williamsonian concern about strategic excess capacity is less compelling.

(b) Baumol

Baumol takes a position not far removed from Williamson's.[57] He proposes that any price cut made by an incumbent prior to an entrant being forced to leave the market must be maintained for five years, although it may be adjusted in response to exogenous demand or supply changes. This approach addresses the problem of a firm lowering price to prey and then raising it when there is exit/deterred entry, but it does not state

---

57 W.J. Baumol, 'Quasi-Permanence of Price Reductions: A Policy for the Prevention of Predatory Pricing,' (1979) 89 *Yale L. Rev.* 1.

that a certain price level is illegal *per se*. It discourages predatory pricing by helping ensure that the low profits during the period of low pricing are particularly unattractive to the would-be predator.

Like Williamson's suggestion, Baumol's rule would entail considerable practical problems. Authorities would have to determine whether industry conditions had changed sufficiently to permit a firm to adjust price during the five-year period following exit. The process would have to include full, quasi-regulatory hearings in which evidence on costs were brought before the courts, including cost-of-capital evidence and evidence on the amount of capital invested. Baumol's rule may also create a disincentive for a dominant firm to cut price in a non-predatory fashion, If a firm exits following the imposition of the low price, the dominant firm may face charging that price for five years.

(c) Scherer

Like Williamson's rule, Scherer's rule emerged in part as the result of dissatisfaction with the Areeda-Turner rule.[58] He points out that a price above average variable cost could drive out rivals, while a price below marginal cost may be socially beneficial if it drives out rivals and the dominant firm continues to produce the rivals' output at a lower marginal cost. Scherer proposes that predatory pricing be found only after a thorough examination of the particular circumstances in question. He would examine factors such as the relative cost positions of the dominant firm and rival firms, economies of scale, and whether the monopolist constricts output in the face of exit.

Scherer's test, while it has the virtue of flexibility, has the converse vices of unpredictability and complexity. A firm would face considerable uncertainty in determining whether a particular course of action might be deemed predatory in the future. Moreover, competition authorities would be called upon to engage in time-consuming and complex investigations of circumstances prior to deciding upon the validity of a predatory pricing claim. These costs would be considerable.

(d) Bolton, Brodley, and Riordan

Most recently, Bolton, Brodley, and Riordan[59] propose a contextual analysis for determining the existence of predatory pricing. Like

---

58 Scherer, 'Predatory Pricing.'
59 Bolton, Brodley, and Riordan, 'Predatory Pricing.'

Scherer, they would examine all the circumstances of a particular case to determine whether a pricing strategy was predatory. Bolton et al. discipline the process by setting out a specific list of questions that ought to be asked in any predatory pricing inquiry: 'Consistent with existing law, the proposed rule would require proof of the following elements: (1) a facilitating market structure; (2) a scheme of predation and supporting evidence; (3) probable recoupment; (4) price below cost; and (5) absence of a business justification or efficiencies defense.'[60]

The first element requires proof that a market structure exists that could make predation a profitable strategy. Some of the relevant factors are the market share of a dominant firm or jointly acting firms and entry barriers. If concentration and entry (and re-entry) barriers are high, predation is more likely to be plausible. The authors note that predation itself, through reputation effects, may create barriers to entry.

Bolton et al. would require any plaintiff in a predatory pricing case to furnish a theory of predation that is generally accepted as economically plausible, as well as supporting evidence. They would thus explicitly require reference to one of the theories of predation outlined above, such as financial market predation or signalling; otherwise, the plaintiff must furnish its own economically acceptable theory of predation. For supporting evidence, *ex ante*, plaintiffs could point to conditions consistent with the theory they rely upon, evidence, for instance, of external financing to support an allegation of financial market predation. *Ex post*, plaintiffs could point to the exclusion of rivals or other postpredation market developments that make recoupment plausible.

The third element, probable recoupment, depends on a showing of actual or probable exclusion of rivals as well as harm to competition and consumers. Harming competitors is, of course, not necessarily anticompetitive. The concept of the exclusion of rivals includes not only the elimination of a rival but also the disciplining of a particularly aggressive competitor that continues to exist, but is a less vigorous competitor.

The fourth element in establishing a *prima facie* case of predation is proof that price has fallen below cost. Bolton et al. would rely on a comparison of price with average avoidable cost, but they would also look to long-run average incremental cost. Average avoidable cost is the 'average per unit cost that the predator would have avoided during the

---

60 Ibid. at 2264.

period of below-cost pricing had it not produced the predatory increment of sales.'[61] Long-run average incremental cost is the 'per unit cost
of producing the predatory increment of output whenever such costs
were incurred.'[62] Bolton et al. would treat a price above long-run average incremental cost as conclusively lawful. A price below average
avoidable cost is presumptively unlawful, shifting the burden to the
defendant to offer an efficiency explanation for its pricing. At a price in
between long-run average incremental cost and average avoidable cost,
the defendant would have the burden of offering a legitimate business
explanation for its prices, which if met would shift the burden back to
the plaintiff to persuade the court of predatory pricing.

The fifth factor in the Bolton et al. approach is to examine whether a
legitimate business explanation or efficiencies defence exists, notwithstanding below-cost pricing by a firm with market power. They would
look to whether there was defensive price-cutting below long-run
average incremental costs to meet new competition. As set out above,
low prices may constitute investments in future market share (of a
larger market) in network industries and new products. They would
also ask whether low prices and high quantities were set in order to
take advantage of learning-by-doing.

In our view, the Bolton et al. approach is the most sensible of the proposed tests. It appears to be more complex than the simple price-cost
tests found in earlier literature, but, as noted above, for a price-cost test
to be economically meaningful, full account must be taken of any
future non-predatory benefits accruing to the alleged predator.
Accounting for these benefits requires sophisticated analysis of the
market. Simple price-cost tests merely mask a complex analysis that
must be undertaken in any event. It is better to acknowledge that
determining the existence of predatory pricing is an unavoidably complicated matter and to restrict attention to disciplining the inquiry, as
Bolton et al. do. For example, by requiring the plaintiff to offer an economically acceptable theory of predation in a particular case, the
inquiry can focus solely on evidence relevant to that specific theory.
This provides valuable guidance to the parties and considerably eases

---

61 Ibid., at 2271.
62 Ibid., at 2272.

the burden on adjudicators, who are required only to understand and evaluate the particular theory of predation presented by the plaintiff.

One criticism to be made of the Bolton et al. test, or at least of how the test is described, concerns its reference to an 'efficiencies defence.' While Bolton et al. in substance are referring only to the rebuttal of a *prima facie* case, the term 'defence' is potentially misleading. If low pricing has an efficiency explanation, it is not predatory and thus the firm does not require an 'efficiencies defence' against a predatory pricing allegation. It will be relevant throughout the analysis of market structure to consider whether market conditions are better suited to an anticompetitive or an efficiency explanation of predatory pricing.

C. The Law of Predatory Pricing

The law of predatory pricing in Canada emanates from three sources. First, the *Competition Act* contains a criminal provision, section 50(1)(c), that directly addresses the matter, while the abuse of dominance section, section 79, sets out predatory pricing as one of the anticompetitive acts in which a dominant firm may not engage. Second, there is case law, although sparse, which helps to establish the parameters of predatory pricing law in Canada. Third, the Bureau of Competition Policy has issued *Predatory Pricing Enforcement Guidelines*, which further delineate the law in Canada. These guidelines do not have legal authority *per se* but indicate the director's approach to predatory pricing complaints. Moreover, the tribunal and the courts may find the guidelines useful in interpreting the scope of the predatory pricing provisions. While on occasion the tribunal has challenged[63] or ignored[64] the bureau's guidelines, it has also adopted them explicitly in other cases.[65] We will discuss these sources of law in turn.

---

63 For example, in *Canada (Director of Investigation and Research) Hillsdown Holdings (Canada) Ltd.*, the tribunal in *obiter dicta* questioned the *Merger Enforcement Guidelines'* (Ottawa: Supply and Services Canada, 1991) (MEGs) approach to the efficiencies defence.

64 For example, *Southam* contained little discussion of the director's approach to market definition as set out in the MEGs.

65 In *Canada (Commissioner of Competition) v. Superior Propane* (2000), 7 C.P.R. (4th) 385, the tribunal accepted the MEGs' approach to market definition and to the efficiencies defence in s. 96.

1. Relevant Statutory Provisions

Section 50(1)(c) sets out the criminal provision on predatory pricing:

Everyone engaged in a business who ...

(c) engages in a policy of selling products at prices unreasonably low, having the effect or tendency of substantially lessening competition or eliminating a competitor, or designed to have such effect,

is guilty of an indictable offence and is liable to imprisonment for a term not exceeding two years.

Section 79 prohibits a dominant firm from engaging in anticompetitive acts, while section 78 provides a non-exhaustive list of such acts. Section 78(d) defines as an anticompetitive act the 'use of fighting brands introduced selectively on a temporary basis to discipline or eliminate a competitor.' Section 78(i) defines as anticompetitive 'selling articles at a price lower than the acquisition cost for the purpose of disciplining or eliminating a competitor.' Both of these definitions address specific types of predatory pricing; other types of predatory pricing could also be defined as anticompetitive acts for the purposes of section 79.

The Act itself provides no guidance as to when reliance on the criminal provision, section 50, or on the civil provision, section 79, is appropriate, but Part 1.2 of the *Predatory Pricing Guidelines* states that the director will choose the appropriate section according to the circumstances of the particular case. It further states that where the behaviour in question occurs in conjunction with other anticompetitive acts, or where the remedial flexibility offered by section 79 is particularly useful, the director will tend to rely on section 79 rather than section 50.

Recently, the Act has been amended to address predation in a particular sector, namely, the airline industry.[66] A regulation-making power has been granted to the governor-in-council (the federal Cabinet) to specify anticompetitive acts or conduct of a domestic air carrier on the recommendation of the ministers of industry and transport. Section 78

---

66 See generally, M. Sanderson and M.J. Trebilcock, 'Bad Policy, Bad Law: Bill C-26 Amendments to the *Competition Act* on Airline Predation,' (2000) 20 *Competition Policy Record* 32.

is enlarged to include such acts as are specified in the regulations. Moreover, the commissioner has the power (without consulting the tribunal) to make temporary orders prohibiting a person operating a domestic airline from doing anything that could, in the commissioner's opinion, harm competition. Such a temporary order may be made if the commissioner has commenced an inquiry pursuant to section 79, and, absent the order, injury to competition or a competitor that cannot be adequately remedied by the tribunal would result.

(a) Relevant Case Law

Predatory pricing cases in Canada are rare. The *Predatory Pricing Guidelines* report that in the period 1980 to 1990 the bureau received 550 complaints about predatory pricing, but only 23 resulted in formal inquiries and a mere 3 resulted in the laying of charges.[67] However, a few cases provide some guidance with respect to judicial approaches to the practice.

Two early cases both resulted in successful prosecutions for predatory pricing. *R. v. Eddy Match Co. Ltd.*[68] involved the use of 'fighting brands' of wooden matches by Eddy Match prior to the acquisition of its rivals. Eddy Match was convicted for unlawfully monopolizing the wooden match market. *R. v. Canada Safeway Ltd.*[69] involved selectively low prices by a food retailer, Safeway, which were allegedly designed to undercut local competition in Calgary and Edmonton for the purpose of limiting expansion by competitors and discouraging entry. Canada Safeway agreed not to pursue the impugned practices in the future and the court sanctioned this agreement with a prohibition order.

Interestingly, both these cases fit theoretical models of predatory pricing: *Eddy Match* may have involved predatory pricing for the purposes of encouraging the acquisition of its rivals at a price favourable to Eddy Match; *Canada Safeway* may have involved a dominant firm seeking to establish a reputation for predation.[70] There was, however,

---

67 *Predatory Pricing Guidelines* (Ottawa: Director of Investigation and Research, 1992), at 1.2.

68 (1951), 17 C.P.R. 17 (Que. K.B.), aff'd (1953) 20 C.P.R. 107 (Que. C.A.).

69 (1973), 14 C.C.C. (2d) 14 (Alta. T.D.).

70 D. West and B. Von Hohenbalken, 'Empirical Tests for Predatory Reputation,' (1986) 19 *Can. J. Econ.* 160, conclude that Safeway followed a successful strategy of predation for the purpose of establishing a reputation over the period 1959–73.

little analysis of cost-price relationships or other specific legal rules in the cases. Rather, the circumstances surrounding the low prices, such as the combination of price-cutting and merger in *Eddy Match* and the selectivity of the low prices in *Canada Safeway*, appeared sufficient for the court to find Eddy Match guilty and to prohibit Safeway from engaging in certain practices. The approach in these cases is perhaps closest to that of Scherer's rule of reason set out above in the survey of various suggested rules. Although Scherer would not ignore price-cost relationships, he would not rely exclusively on them.

Perhaps the most significant Canadian predatory pricing conviction resulted in *R. v. Hoffman-La Roche Ltd.*[71] In that case, a drug company was accused of predatory pricing with respect to its marketing of two of its tranquillizer drugs. Roche held the patents on chlordiazepoxide, marketed as Librium, and diazepam, marketed as Valium, and consequently had a monopoly over the sale of these drugs during most of the 1960s. In 1969, however, the laws concerning generic drugs were liberalized through the enactment of a compulsory licensing regime and other companies, including a firm called Frank Horner, threatened Roche's dominance. Roche responded aggressively by establishing various promotional programs. Specifically, it offered to give away capsules for every capsule purchased, it gave Valium free to hospitals for two six-month periods, and it tendered on government contracts at a price of one dollar each. The combination of the liberalized rules on generic drugs and the ensuing events resulted in dramatic drops in the price of the drugs. For example, in 1969, the price of a thousand 5 mg tablets of Valium to a hospital was $42.70; in 1972 it was $8.40.

Linden J. convicted Roche at trial. Both the verdict and his reasoning were undisturbed on appeal, thus Justice Linden's reasons provide the important precedent. A key issue in the case, and in any predatory pricing case under what is now section 50(1)(c), was whether the prices were 'unreasonably low.' Linden J. held that the test for unreasonableness is an objective one: it is irrelevant whether the accused intended to sell at an unreasonable price; rather, the question is whether the accused actually did so. The accused's state of mind may be relevant to *mens rea*, but that is distinct from the question of unreasonably low prices. He rejected the view that the relationship between price and cost is always determinative of reasonableness. Linden J. held   at

---

71 (1980), 28 O.R. (2d) 164 (H.C.J.), aff'd (1981), 33 O.R. (2d) 694 (C.A.).

while prices above cost are never unreasonable, prices below cost may or may not be unreasonable.[72] In setting out a test with which Scherer would be pleased, Linden J. stated that the court must examine all the circumstances of the case to determine reasonableness.

Justice Linden considered the following specific factors in finding the prices in the instant case to be 'unreasonably low.'[73] First, the magnitude of the difference between cost and price is important; the greater the difference, the more likely the prices are unreasonable. Second, a court should consider the length of time at which the goods are sold at 'questionable' prices. A transitory, promotional sale is unlikely to be predatory, but if sales below cost persist, they become more suspect. Third, the circumstances of the price reduction must be taken into account. Reducing price in reaction to a competitor's price reduction or anticipated reduction is different from initiating price cuts. Fourth, the court should consider any long-term benefits that may accrue to the seller by reducing price below cost. For example, a manufacturer may price below cost in the short run during lean times with the hope that economic conditions will improve and short-run losses will be recouped in the future.

Linden J. refused to convict for the policies of giving away capsules with the purchase of other capsules. The margins on the drugs were initially so high that what were effectively price reductions were not unreasonable, particularly since they were in response to price competition and were only in place for a finite time. The one dollar librium tenders to government were also not unreasonably low, given that there were only three sales of this type, that they occurred during a very competitive period, and that Roche expected benefits from testing demand and the reaction of its competitors. Similar $1 tenders on Valium government contracts were unreasonably low, according to Justice Linden, but defects in the indictment prevented a conviction on this front. The giveaway of Valium to hospitals, however, did amount to sales at unreasonably low prices and resulted in a conviction. While the giveaway responded to price cuts by Horner, cutting price to zero was 'overdoing it.'[74] Moreover, the projected losses from

---

72 Linden J. did not set out whether average total cost or average variable cost was appropriate, perhaps, as Dunlop et al., *Canadian Competition Policy*, point out at 236–7, because the issue was not important to the parties.

73 *Hoffman-La Roche, supra*, 28 O.R. (2d) at 200–1.

74 Ibid. at 204.

the giveaway, $1 million, were too large to suggest any 'legitimate' economic purpose.[75]

Separating 'intent' from an examination of the 'objective reasonableness' of prices is a difficult exercise, as the four factors set out by Linden J. demonstrate.[76] The first two factors, for example, the difference between price and cost and the duration of the low pricing, both go to the losses the alleged predator undertook. Why is this factor relevant? Is it because the greater the losses suffered, the more likely it is that the firm intended to prey? If so, Linden J. may be inconsistent in first stating that intent is not relevant and then considering factors that appear to go to intent. The third factor, the reactive or proactive nature of the price cuts, appears also to be relevant to intent, as does the question of whether long-term benefits accrue to the firm as the result of current low prices.[77]

Further confounding the import of intent is Linden J.'s analysis of the relevant substantial lessening of competition. Justice Linden held that while the policy may or may not have had the effect of lessening competition substantially, it was designed to do so and therefore caught by section 34 (now section 50). He pointed to various internal documents as demonstrating this design, but in discussing the objective nature of the reasonableness of prices, he had noted that aggressive, although legitimately competitive, statements may be misleading.

The confusion surrounding intent is difficult to avoid. Low, competitive prices are clearly one of the fundamental goals of competition policy. The central concern about predatory prices is their effect on future prices. That is, predatory prices result in higher prices in the future. The alleged predator's view of the future, then, is intrinsically linked with its motives for pricing in a certain way and therefore with the 'reasonableness' of current prices. The problem is, however, that intent may be misleading. As Posner points out, competitive hubris may inaccurately appear to reveal predatory intent.[78] All competition involves intent to do better than one's competitors and distinguishing legitimate aggression and illegitimate predation is not an easy task.

While these difficulties with intent have led some commentators to

---

75 Ibid.
76 See Dunlop et al., *Canadian Competition Policy*, at 236–8.
77 As an aside, one must presume that one of the future benefits of low prices in Linden J.'s test cannot be high prices, since that is precisely the mischief predatory pricing law addresses.
78 Posner, *Antitrust Law*.

call for its abolition as a factor in predatory pricing cases,[79] there may perhaps be a coherent way to incorporate intent into an objective test of the reasonableness of prices. Evidence of intent is not relevant for its own sake, but rather is potentially relevant as evidence that the current prices are likely to lead to the elimination of a competitor. On this basis, offhand statements of aggression are unlikely to reveal whether a rival will be eliminated and prices are going to increase in the future. On the other hand, calculated statements about the limited cash reserves of a rival, or about the need to maintain a reputation for starting price wars, may be relevant as revealing that the low prices would serve to harm future competition. After all, the firm in the market is likely to have a better idea about the competitive effects of its prices than the competition authorities and courts.

Intent under this approach would be relevant both to the reasonableness of prices and to the question of whether prices were designed to eliminate competition, but for different reasons. Intent does not make a price unreasonable; rather, it may reveal that the low prices are likely to harm competition. On the other hand, intent is directly relevant to the design requirement set out in the statute.

Another potentially problematic aspect of the decision in *Roche* concerns the treatment of the substantial lessening of competition.[80] Linden J. held that the Valium giveaway was illegal because it was designed to lessen competition. He noted as an aside, however, that Horner temporarily withdrew from the market as a result of the giveaway, but stated that this did not necessarily indicate a substantial lessening of competition. The withdrawing company accounted for a very small portion of the market and thus, Linden J. reasoned, its departure may not have lessened competition substantially. 'Eliminating a competitor' is explicitly prohibited by section 50(1)(c) (then s. 34(1)(c)), but it is troubling that Linden J. downplays the competitive impact of entry deterrence. As discussed, predatory pricing may be a profitable strategy if it deters potential competition.

Had Linden J. assessed carefully the entry conditions in the market, it is likely that his decision would have changed: soon after the alleged

---

79 See, e.g., L. Hunter and S. Hutton, 'Is the Price Right?: Comments on the *Predatory Pricing Enforcement Guidelines* and *Price Discrimination Enforcement Guidelines* of the Bureau of Competition Policy,' (1993) 38 *McGill L.J.* 830.
80 See Dunlop et al., *Canadian Competition Policy*, at 238.

predation in the *Roche* case, the market was flooded by more than a dozen suppliers of diazepam. This entry was predictable, showing that the prospect of recoupment of lost profits through price increases – a central condition for predation – was untenable.

In a market such as that for diazepam where demand is characterized by inertia, for example, where a strong brand name will attract market share even after entry of nearly identical products – an incumbent will respond to future entry by lowering prices in advance. Even prices less than cost can be a profitable means of purchasing future market share. Such a strategy is not predatory. It is a response, albeit an anticipatory response, to increased competition.

Shortly after the *Roche* case, *R. v. Consumers Glass Co. Ltd.* [81] was decided. The case involved the manufacture of plastic lids. Consumers Glass, through a subsidiary, Portion Packaging, was the only supplier of these lids in Canada, although certain potential customers went 'in-house' and produced them themselves. A group of Portion employees left Portion and established a competitor, Amhil Enterprises Ltd. Each firm had the capacity to satisfy market demand. Amhil initially undercut Portion's prices by 2-3 per cent, to which Portion responded by offering quantity discounts of up to 16 per cent. Amhil matched Portion's lowest price, but offered the price irrespective of quantity. Portion then matched this offer. Portion attempted later price cuts, but its market share declined considerably until it eventually left the market, leaving Amhil as the sole supplier. Portion (not Amhil) was eventually charged with predatory pricing.

O'Leary J., in acquitting Portion, examined the price-cost relationship carefully. He concluded that where the industry is in a situation of significant excess capacity, price may fall below average total cost as the result of competition. However, if price remains above average variable cost, the firm may simply be loss-minimizing. Each additional sale contributes to overhead, but competition prevents the firm from charging more than average total cost. In the present case, O'Leary J. found that the combination of Amhil's entry and excess capacity forced Portion to lower its price below average total cost, but that at all times the price was above average variable cost and therefore Portion was profit-maximizing/loss-minimizing. Given that Portion was profit-maximizing in the face of entry and excess capacity on the part of a rival, Portion's prices were not unreasonably low.

---

81 (1981), 33 O.R. (2d) 288 (H.C.J.).

McFetridge and Wong view *Consumers Glass* and *Roche* as inconsistent to some extent.[82] *Consumers Glass*, in their view, relied upon a 'modified Areeda-Turner' standard in holding that prices above variable cost are not predatory in times of excess capacity. On the other hand, *Roche* took a flexible approach that canvassed factors other than price-cost relationships.

Anderson and Khosla, on the other hand, view *Consumers Glass* as 'a special case of the flexible framework put forward in *Hoffman-La Roche*,' which holds that under conditions of excess capacity, a price above average variable costs is not unreasonable.[83] We tend to agree with this view. By examining industry conditions, O'Leary J. came to the conclusion that prices above average variable cost were loss-minimizing and not predatory. Not only did O'Leary J. examine a number of factors in reaching his conclusion, Linden J.'s approach in *Roche* does not preclude a finding that price-cost relationships can be exculpatory in particular circumstances. Indeed, Linden J. set out that prices above total cost are never predatory.

The role of intent is somewhat murky in *Consumers Glass*, as it is in *Roche*. O'Leary J. held that intent was irrelevant to the acquittal, given that there were circumstances of excess capacity and that prices were above average variable cost. However, at various points he noted that 'the evidence does not indicate that Portion lowered its prices for the purpose of hurting Amhil financially and so forcing it from the market;'[84] '[t]he various decisions to lower prices and to keep them low were taken to retain as much as possible of a small lid market that was rapidly being lost to Amhil, and to thereby make as large a contribution as possible to overhead;'[85] and 'Portion did not cut prices so as to drive Amhil from the market. It cut prices to retain as much of the market as it could so as to minimize the losses it realized it was going to suffer because of the entry of a competitor into the market.'[86] These comments all seem to go to intent to some degree.

As discussed with respect to the *Roche* case, the stated objectivity of the test of unreasonableness, can be reconciled with apparent canvassing of intent. If there was evidence that Portion was setting very low

---

82 McFetridge and Wong, 'Predatory Pricing in Canada,' at 699–701.
83 R.D. Anderson and S.D. Khosla, 'Review of McFetridge and Wong on Predatory Pricing in Canada,' (1986) 7 *Cdn. Comp. Pol. Rec.* 16.
84 *Consumers Glass, supra* (1981), 33 O.R. (2d) at 284.
85 Ibid., at 289.
86 Ibid., at 291.

prices as part of a calculated scheme to drive Amhil out of the market, this may be relevant evidence that the prices would have accompanied this goal. Given that Portion was hardly plotting to drive Amhil from the market, but rather was responding to excess capacity and strong competition, it was less likely that the prices would have driven Amhil out. That is, intent may provide evidence of the objective probability of the predatory effect of the prices. In *Consumers Glass*, Justice O'Leary seems to have been eminently justified in finding that the prices were not unreasonably low.

Another predatory pricing case *Canada (Director of Investigation and Research) v. NutraSweet*,[87] adressed the issue of abuse of dominance. NutraSweet was a near monopolist in aspartame, an artificial sweetener. NutraSweet was challenged by the director for the practice of 'selling below acquisition cost' for the purpose of eliminating or disciplining a competitor, one of the abuses of dominance listed in section 78 of the *Competition Act*. The tribunal held that selling below acquisition cost did not apply easily to a manufacturer, which NutraSweet largely was. With respect to NutraSweet's occasional purchases of aspartame from other producers, they were clearly resold at a price above acquisition cost (which does not include distribution costs) and thus did not constitute abuse of dominance.

The tribunal also briefly considered whether NutraSweet abused its dominance by engaging in predatory pricing defined more generally, which is an unenumerated anticompetitive act for the purposes of sections 78 and 79. The tribunal reviewed the Areeda-Turner analysis and concluded that the appropriate price-cost comparison for a firm operating at full capacity is between price and average total cost. Where a firm is operating below capacity, the comparison is between price and average variable cost. This is another way of stating that in periods of excess capacity, pricing above average variable cost may be a short-run profit-maximizing strategy, as discussed in *Consumers Glass*, but such pricing is suspicious in periods of full capacity. The tribunal's conclusions are consistent with observations in *Consumers* about price-cost comparisons.[88]

---

87 (1990), 32 C.P.R. (3d) 1 (Comp. Trib.).

88 Hunter and Hutton, 'Is the Price Right?', claim at 836 that the tribunal's observations about the appropriate measure of cost had 'not been considered in the predatory pricing cases.' We disagree; *Consumers Glass* clearly emphasized the relevance of excess capacity to the legal significance of pricing below average total cost, but above

The tribunal found that during periods of excess capacity NutraSweet priced above average variable cost, but the evidence could only sustain tentative conclusions about pricing above average total cost during periods of full capacity. However, the tribunal held that recoupment of lost profits from below-cost pricing was unlikely in Canada, although it acknowledged that NutraSweet may have wished to stifle competition in Canada and around the world in order to protect its monopoly in the United States, where the company was about to lose patent protection. In any event, the tribunal held that the director did not ask for a remedy concerning predatory pricing generally, but only one regarding sales below acquisition costs. Thus it did not come to any final conclusion on the subject.

Finally, the statutory prohibition of predatory pricing in section 50 condemns only a 'policy of selling' at unreasonably low prices. The question thus arises of what constitutes a 'policy of selling.' *R. v. Producers Dairy Ltd.*[89] provides some clarification of the term. In that case, there was a brief (forty-eight-hour) price war between dairy suppliers in Ottawa. Producers Dairy was accused of predatory pricing but acquitted on the basis that a forty-eight-hour price war did not constitute a 'policy of selling.'

While this survey covers the Canadian case law on the subject, it is worthwhile to review an important American case that reflects developments in the law and economic approaches to predatory pricing discussed above: *Brooke Group Ltd. v. Brown and Williamson Tobacco Corp.*[90] This case involved an allegation of predatory pricing in the cigarette market. The plaintiff introduced inexpensive, generic cigarettes that proved popular with customers. In response, the defendant Brown and Williamson introduced its own generic cigarettes and held prices below average variable cost for a period of eighteen months. At the end of this period of below-cost pricing, the plaintiff raised its prices. The defendant and other cigarette companies promptly followed suit.

The plaintiff argued that the defendant, which only had about a 12

---

average variable cost. It is functionally equivalent to state that the test will be a comparison of price and average total cost in circumstances where there is full capacity, or average variable costs where there is excess capacity, and to state that prices between average variable cost and average total cost may or may not be predatory depending on whether there is full capacity or not.

89 (1966), 50 C.P.R. (2d) (Ont. C.A.).

90 509 U.S. 209 (1993).

per cent market share, had engaged in predatory pricing designed to induce the plaintiff to cease its strategy of aggressive pricing. The Supreme Court upheld the lower court's dismissal of the case. Exhibiting a sceptical attitude towards the plausibility of predatory pricing, the court reiterated an earlier statement that 'predatory pricing schemes are rarely tried, and even more rarely successful.'[91] The court set out the following test for predatory pricing. First, the plaintiff must show that prices were below some measure of cost the (Court did not elaborate on the appropriate measure). Second, and more significantly, the plaintiff must show that there is a dangerous probability (under the *Sherman Act*) or a reasonable prospect (under the *Robinson-Patman Act*) of recoupment of any losses from predatory pricing. The court stated: 'For recoupment to occur, below-cost pricing must be capable, as a threshold matter, of producing the intended effects on the firm's rivals ... If circumstances indicate that below-cost pricing could likely produce its intended effect on the target, there is still the further question of whether it would likely injure competition in the relevant market. The plaintiff must demonstrate that there is a likelihood that the predatory scheme alleged would be sufficient to compensate for the amounts expended on predation, including the time value of money invested in it.'[92] On the facts of the case, the court found it to be implausible that Brown and Williamson could recoup the losses it incurred through oligopoly coordination and upheld the lower court's dismissal of the case.

The decision in *Brooke Group* follows developments in the law and economics literature on predatory pricing, in particular the realization that price-cost comparisons cannot themselves suffice to show predatory pricing. The analysis of recoupment follows more closely the suggestions of Joskow and Klevorick, and more recently Bolton et al. (who indeed argue that their test is consistent with *Brooke Group*), to account for a variety of market factors in evaluating predatory pricing. These factors will include questions about market power, like concentration and barriers to entry, as well as factors that suggest an efficiency explanation of below-cost pricing, such as a growing market. If, for example, promotional pricing explains low prices, the recoupment test in *Brooke Group* cannot be met, given that it requires demonstration of injury to competition in the relevant market.

---

91 Ibid., at 226.
92 Ibid., at 224.

Brooke Group provides a sensible standard for evaluating predatory pricing. While it is an American case, its approach is consistent with the Canadian Bureau's *Predatory Pricing Enforcement Guidelines*, as we discuss in the next section.

(b) Predatory Pricing Guidelines

Consistent with *Brooke Group*, the *Predatory Pricing Enforcement Guidelines* ('the guidelines' in this section) divide the inquiry about the reasonableness of prices into two parts. First, the director will examine the market in order to determine if there is market power or the potential for building market power. Second, if the first test indicates that there is potential for market power, the director will compare prices and costs.[93]

The director will begin by examining two fundamental questions market concentration and entry conditions. To determine whether the market is sufficiently concentrated such that market power may exist or potentially exist, the director will first define the market, following the procedure set out in the MEGs.[94] Then the director will calculate market shares in each of the markets concerned. If the market share of the alleged predator is less than 35 per cent, it is unlikely that it can unilaterally affect pricing, although the analysis will also depend on other factors, such as the difference between the size of the alleged predator and its rivals and the existence of a vigorous competitive fringe.

With respect to entry conditions, the inquiry attempts to determine whether the predator might have the power to recoup its losses by raising prices in the future. If entry conditions are easy, it is unlikely that the predator could sustain future supracompetitive prices for very

---

93 As Hunter and Hutton, 'Is the Price Right?', point out at 836–7, the director at one point appears to treat satisfaction of the first part of the test as a pre-requisite to further inquiry under the second part (see the guidelines, para. 2.2). Later, however, the director states that he will consider price-cost relationships under the second part, apparently regardless of the outcome of the first test (see the guidelines, para. 2.2.1.2). We agree with Hunter and Hutton that the director would have done better by clarifying the relationship between parts one and two of the test. Given part one's emphasis on potential recoupment of lost profits in the future as a necessary feature of predatory pricing, we agree with Hunter and Hutton that the director should have clearly stated that market power under part one is a prerequisite to price-cost investigations under part two.

94 See discussion in Chapter 4.

long. The director examines whether entry would occur within two years following price increases on a sufficient scale to constrain the price increase. In determining entry conditions, the director examines two factors in particular. First, if incumbent firms face cost advantages, such as tariff or non-tariff barriers to trade, this may constrain entry. Second, if an entrant must incur significant sunk costs, such as market specific assets, entry is less likely.

If a firm has market power under the first part of the test, the director determines whether the prices are 'unreasonably low' by making price-cost comparisons in the second part of the test. The director sets out the following rules. A price at or above average total cost can never be 'unreasonably low.' A price below average variable cost is likely to be considered 'unreasonably low' unless there is a justification, such as the need to sell perishable inventory.[95] The consideration of justification opens the door to inquiries into promotional pricing and other efficiency explanations of below-cost pricing. Prices between average variable and average total cost may or may not be considered 'unreasonably low,' depending on the circumstances. In circumstances of declining demand or excess capacity, prices in this 'grey range' may be reasonable. On the other hand, if prices in this range are intended to be predatory, they may be unreasonable.

Following *Producers Dairy*,[96] the guidelines also set out how the director will treat a 'policy of selling.' The director will look for evidence that the prices are 'not competitive expedients of brief duration, that they are not simply defensive reactions to the pricing initiatives or behaviour of other firms, or that they are not randomly occurring events attributable to specific business circumstances extant in the market at any given point in time.'[97] The prices need to be part of a deliberate pricing strategy applicable throughout the relevant market for a significant duration.

Having found that the alleged predator indeed engaged in a policy of selling at unreasonably low prices, the director will then turn to the question of the competitive impact of the policy. The guidelines acknowledge that evidence of competitive impact will often overlap with that going to the reasonableness of prices. The director will ask

---

95 Average variable cost is calculated by including all costs that vary with output.
96 *Supra*, note 89.
97 *Predatory Pricing Enforcement Guidelines*, at 2.3.

whether the pricing has had the effect of substantially lessening competition or has the tendency to do so, whether the pricing has eliminated a competitor or has the tendency to do so, or whether the pricing is or was designed to substantially lessen competition or to eliminate a competitor. The last requirement rests on intent, which may be inferred from the evidence, such as the magnitude of the losses incurred or the absence of any other rationale for the price cuts. The director states, however, that evidence of predatory intent without a reasonable likelihood of success is not likely to be pursued.

(c) Evidentiary Matters
In this section, building upon the economic theories of predation, we outline some of the evidentiary issues relevant to an investigation into predatory pricing. Key issues include the following:

* concentration in the selling and buying markets;
* price-cost relationships;
* excess capacity in the industry;
* the significance of sunk costs;
* whether the alleged predator competes in several markets;
* the vigour of the alleged victim firm; and
* history of entry, pricing, and exit in the market.

Concentration in the selling market (that is, the market in which the alleged predator participates) will be crucial to an assessment of the plausibility of predatory pricing. If the market is not concentrated, there would be little point to predatory pricing: the costs of below-cost pricing cannot be recouped in a competitive market. Even in a concentrated market, predatory pricing may not be profit-maximizing for the individual firm contemplating it, even where the conditions are perfect for predation. Suppose that predation against a new entrant would drive the entrant out and that further entry is unlikely – in other words, assume perfect conditions for profitable predation. Even in a market with a few firms, predation may not occur because of free-riding. Since all firms share the benefits of successful predation through less competition, each incumbent firm may attempt to let others bear the burdens of predation, while it later shares in the benefits equally. That is, while the incumbents may be better off if they collectively increase output, lower price below cost, and drive the entrant out, each individual incumbent may reason that it will let the others sell at a loss, while it cuts back on output in order to minimize its own losses. If each firm reasons this way, predation will not occur even in a market with only a few firms. Predation is therefore more likely where there is either a monopolist, or a dominant firm that knows that if it does not lower price, predation will not be successful.

Concentration in the buyer's market may also be relevant. Successful predatory pricing requires buyers to act against their long-term interests by purchasing products from the predator at very low prices, which will eventually (if successful) give rise to the prey's failure and higher prices. It is plausible to assume that buyers in markets with many buyers will act in this manner because of a collective action problem: purchasing from the prey in order to discourage its exit and enhance long-run competition is a public good among buyers. Each may attempt to let others shoulder the burden of higher prices, while it takes advantage of the predator's low prices. In markets with only one or two major buyers, on the other hand, since each buyer's decisions will have a significant impact on the health of the preyed-upon firm, it is more likely that buyers will resist predation (thus deterring predation) by spreading purchases among sellers, including the prey.

Price-cost relationships are also crucial, as noted. If price is above cost, it is less likely that the prices reflect predation and more likely that they reflect an efficient producer. While forms of predatory pricing, such as limit pricing, are possible with prices above cost, predatory pricing law avoids problematic attempts to distinguish predatory above-cost pricing from non-predatory pricing. The ideal theoretical comparison is between price and marginal cost, but marginal cost, as noted above, is an economic concept, not an accounting concept. The closest proxy for marginal cost is average variable cost or avoidable cost.

Relevant to the price-cost comparison is the existence of significant excess capacity in the industry. If there is significant excess capacity, firms may price below average total cost for reasons that have nothing to do with predation. Rather, such prices may be profit-maximizing in the short run. If, for example, demand unexpectedly drops, firms may be unable to sell at prices greater than average variable cost. Where there is no excess capacity industry, however, and firms set prices below average total cost, this may be more suspicious.

Sunk costs and other entry barriers are important to the analysis. For predatory pricing to be successful, the preying firm or firms must be able to raise price cost upon the exit of the preyed-upon firm. To be able to price above cost for an extended length of time, there must be barriers to entry, such as the requirement that any entrant must make sunk, industry-specific invest..ients that limit the disciplinary effects of potential entrants. Of course, the existence of sunk, industry-specific investment may make it difficult to drive a firm out of the market with low prices. If the assets of a firm are useful only in the industry in question, even the firm's insolvency is unlikely to result in the removal of those assets from the market. Rather, predation may result only in the reorganization of the distressed victim firm, and may not eliminate a competitor.

Predatory pricing itself may present a barrier to entry by creating a reputation for predation. One of the considerations relevant to reputational predatory pricing is the number of markets in which the alleged predator participates. If the preying firm operates in many similarly structured markets, preying on entry in one market may be rational in order to deter entry in other markets.

The status of the alleged victim firm may also be relevant to an investigation into the plausibility of predatory pricing. If the victim firm is an innovative, vigorous competitor, yet a relatively new entrant and thus vulnerable, as opposed to a price-taking, fringe player, predatory pricing may be more likely. Of course, the vigour of the victim firm in setting low prices itself may lead to the conclusion that the low pricing by the alleged predator was simply a short-run profit-maximizing response to vigorous competition.

Finally, the history of the industry may also indicate whether predatory pricing is plausible in a particular case. If there is abundant evidence of exit without consequent periods of high prices, then it is more likely that the market is simply competitive and low prices reflect this reality. If, however, low prices have in the past resulted in exit, high prices, and no entry for a considerable period, the market may be susceptible to predatory pricing.

As a cautionary note, it is worth emphasizing that while many of the issues identified here are sufficient to dismiss predatory pricing as implausible, none of them, either individually or collectively, are sufficient to conclude that predatory pricing is occurring. For example, if the market is competitive, this is sufficient to conclude that low prices do not reflect predatory behaviour, but if the market is not particularly competitive, it cannot be concluded that low prices reflect predatory pricing. A lack of competitive structure is necessary but not sufficient for predatory pricing. As reflected in the very low conviction rates in Canada, predatory pricing is not likely to be a common phenomenon.

A variety of factors may also be relevant to analysis of whether below-cost pricing can be explained by efficiency considerations. These include:

- a growing market and evidence of inertia in market shares;
- a network industry; and
- costs lowered by learning-by-doing.

If the industry is growing and there is evidence of inertia in market shares, below-cost pricing may simply reflect an efficient investment by a firm in future profits that do not depend on any harm to competitors or competition. Inertia in market shares may arise because of consumers' difficulty in determining the quality of alternative products. In such markets, customers may prefer to buy the brands they know. In this setting, offering low prices may be a means of inducing new customers to try a firm's product, which will lead to higher profits in the longer run. If a firm is in a network industry, it may be profit-maximizing, but not anticompetitive, to set low prices in order to attract customers, which will itself help attract future customers. Finally, in an industry characterized by learning-by-doing, setting low prices and high quantities may simply reflect an investment in cost reduction.

(d) Discussion

There are at least two ways in which to assess the guidelines, which have yet to receive the imprimatur of a court or tribunal decision. First, one could examine their consistency with the case law. Second, one could examine them in light of the economic theory of predatory pricing. We will conduct each type of examination in turn.

With respect to the case law, the guidelines in our view are largely consistent with the limited guidance courts have provided in Canada. While they expand on the courts' pronouncements to date, they are consistent with the approach in the case law.

The guidelines adopt a two-part test to reasonableness, which is not explicitly found in the Canadian cases.[98] However, the approach is consistent with *Roche* in the following way. *Roche* established that price-cost relationships are not determinative; even zero prices may not be 'unreasonably low.' Similarly, by not relying on price-cost relationships

---

98 It is found in *Brooke Group, supra,* note 90.

alone, but by first examining the market to determine whether a profitable predatory pricing scher.:e could occur, the guidelines take a variety of circumstances into account. While the two-part test limits the examination of the surrounding circumstances to market conditions and price-cost comparisons, which the test in *Roche* does not explicitly do, it would be difficult to identify relevant circumstances that are not captured by the two-part test. This is particularly true given the guidelines' statement that even if a firm with market power prices below average variable cost, it is open to the firm to justify the prices, for example, by pointing to the perishability of the goods.

The focus of the first step on the possibility of recouping lost profits is also consistent with the observations of the competition tribunal in *NutraSweet*. In dismissing the predatory pricing claim, the tribunal pointed out that even if NutraSweet were pricing below cost, it was unlikely to recoup from Canadian consumers the foregone profits from predation. The tribunal did not come to a definitive conclusion on the matter, but this comment clearly lends itself to an emphasis on recoupment.

We also view the price-cost aspect of the test set out by the director as consistent with the case law. As set out in *Roche*, prices above average total cost are not unreasonable. As set out in *Consumers Glass*, prices below average total cost, but above average variable cost, are not necessarily predatory, particularly in situations of excess capacity. Prices below average variable cost in a situation of market power or potential market are treated as predatory, unless justification for the low prices exists. This is consistent with the approach in *Roche*, which treated prices below average variable cost as requiring further examination, but held that all the circumstances must be examined before condemning the prices. The tests are also consistent with the tribunal's observation in *NutraSweet* that the appropriate price-cost comparison is with average total cost where there is full capacity, but with average variable cost where there is excess capacity. It is functionally equivalent to state that the comparison is with total cost where there is full capacity, or variable cost where there is excess capacity, and to state that prices below average total cost but above average variable cost may not be predatory if there is excess capacity, but may be predatory if there is full capacity.[99]

---

99 See note 93 referring to Hunter and Hutton, 'Is the Price Right?', at 836.

The treatment of intent is similar in the guidelines and the case law, although this similarity is not desirable given the confusion about intent in the case law. Intent in the guidelines is relevant both to the reasonableness of prices and to whether the prices were designed to harm competition. As discussed, the cases also appear to look to intent as a factor in determining the reasonableness of prices. What both the cases and the guidelines fail to do, however, is provide the principle that would explain why predatory intent is relevant in determining the objective reasonableness of prices. Why does the intention behind a price alter its characterization as reasonable or not? Moreover, distinguishing predatory intent from competitive intent is notoriously difficult.[100] Some commentators suggest abolition of intent as a factor going to reasonableness because of these infirmities.[101] As explained above, we would treat intent not as significant in itself with respect to reasonableness, as the cases and guidelines appear to do, but rather as potentially significant evidence that the prices in question are, as an objective matter, likely to harm competition.

The other factors set out in the guidelines, such as the treatment of a 'policy of selling' and the competitive harm of the prices, come either from the case law directly or from the *Competition Act*. They are consistent with the law in Canada.

Perhaps the more difficult question is whether the guidelines make sense as a matter of policy. Of the suggestions in the legal literature outlined above, the guidelines come closest to the two-step procedure outlined by Joskow and Klevorick and the multifactor test provided by Bolton et al. We will analyse the guidelines in light of the following considerations: their relationship to the economic theory of predatory pricing and the likelihood of error and administrative ease.

The first step in the guidelines is to evaluate market conditions essentially to determine whether recoupment of the forgone profits from predatory pricing in the future is plausible. If it is not, the inquiry ends. As we have noted, an emphasis on recoupment is appropriate. Price-accounting cost comparisons alone will ignore important benefits to the alleged predator from below-cost pricing, such as a nonpredatory investment in future market share. If the price-accounting cost comparison is abandoned for the economically sensible price-

---

100 See Posner, *Antitrust Law*.
101 See Hunter and Hutton, 'Is the Price Right?'.

opportunity cost comparison, then all the complexity of a full-blown efficiency analysis will take place in any event. Better to divide explicitly the analysis into a price-accounting cost comparison and an analysis of recoupment. The guidelines do just this.

Another strength is that the guidelines recognize in discussing barriers to entry that predation itself, if it helps establish a reputation, may create a barrier to entry by creating a plausible threat of predation. The guidelines set out that the director should consider whether firms have strategically attempted to raise entry barriers by adopting conduct that they would not have adopted but for its effects on rivals or potential entrants. For example, the director should consider whether an incumbent has 'signalled through responses to past entry initiatives that existing excess capacity will be employed to depress prices in response to an attempt to enter.'[102]

Two other factors, the risk of error and administrative costs, are also important. Predatory pricing, as has been alluded to several times, is unusual in competition policy as it condemns what is otherwise one of the law's objectives: low prices. The undesirable threat of 'chilling' low but non-predatory prices with an insufficiently cautious approach to predation law is a significant concern and test that relied on price-accounting cost relations alone would create a significant possibility of error. Accounting costs may not match true opportunity costs. Moreover, even if accounting costs did match opportunity costs in a particular case, marginal cost, an economic concept, does not fit comfortably into accounting cost figures, thus raising the possibility that the proxy for marginal cost will inaccurately reflect true marginal cost. The decision about which costs to characterize as 'variable' and which to characterize as 'fixed' is also theoretically problematic. All costs are variable over time; thus there will an arbitrary timing aspect to the distinction between fixed and variable. Finally, cost records will generally not be available publicly. A firm may therefore find itself subject to an undesirable allegation of predatory pricing even though it is pricing above cost.

While the risks of error in relying on a price-accounting cost relationship alone are significant, there is in addition the related point that such an investigation is administratively costly and unpredictable. Dis-

---

102 *Predatory Pricing Enforcement Guidelines* (Ottawa: Director of Investigation and Research, 1992), at s. 2.2.1.2.

covering price-cost relationships accurately would not be an easy task, particularly given the important judgment calls required in distinguishing variable from fixed costs. Consequently, if every complaint of predatory pricing required a price-cost comparison, the process would be expensive and it might also be unpredictable.

For these reasons, an initial recoupment test is sensible. In many markets, a quick examination of the market reveals the unprofitability of predatory pricing. While there may be reason to take an approach to recoupment that recognizes the possibility of strategic predatory pricing, as developed in recent economic literature, the first step of the guidelines is a pragmatic threshold test that should reduce the chilling effect of predatory pricing law on low prices and administrative costs.

The second aspect of the test, the price-cost relationship, also demonstrates some shaky theoretical foundations, but nevertheless constitutes sound policy. As the discussion of limit pricing demonstrates, prices above cost may be predatory in the sense of deterring entry, yet the guidelines hold that any price above average total cost will be considered reasonable. This is a potential theoretical infirmity, but since there is no way of practically identifying socially harmful, above-cost pricing, this is not a practical shortcoming.

On balance the guidelines' approach is sensible. Effective *per se* legality for above-cost prices reduces administrative and error costs; instances of anticompetitive prices above costs, if they exist in theory, are impossible to identify in practice. If the prices are above average total costs, the inquiry ends.

For similar reasons, treating with suspicion cases with prices below average variable costs also makes sense, despite the imperfections with reliance on price-cost relationships described above in discussing the first part of the test. Such an approach is predictable and more efficient to administer. Importantly, the potential errors entailed by reliance on a bright-line rule are reduced by the inquiry into market circumstances under the first part of the test, and by giving the alleged predator some chance to rebut the suspicion of illegality established by the guidelines for below-average variable cost pricing.

With respect to the 'grey area' between average variable cost and average total cost, while it increases administrative costs, we favour the contextual approach taken by the guidelines. There may be perfectly plausible, innocuous explanations for prices in this range, such as excess capacity, but where these explanations do not exist, the prices may be predatory. A bright-line rule with respect to this intermediate range would be either unacceptably underinclusive or overinclusive. Given the rarity of predatory p_icing, however, we consider the possibility of successful predatory pricing cases even more remote where prices lie in this grey area.

While the guidelines are largely consistent with the statute and case law, we would make some critical observations about the statute itself. Prices may be deemed predatory under section 50 where they are unreasonable and designed to eliminate a competitor. In our view, relying on 'design' to ground a predatory pricing offence is potentially problematic. Predatory intent or design is notoriously difficult to discern. After all, it is natural (and socially desirable) for a firm to seek to better its rivals. However, as we have noted, evidence of a calculated scheme of predation could be relevant evidence of the plausibility of predatory pricing; market participants presumably know their situation better than courts or other regulators. But this implies that reliance on 'design' itself does not advance the analysis: vague statements of predatory intent are notoriously unreliable, while more calculated statements of predatory intent are useful as evidence going to the issue of the likelihood of successful predation. This use of 'design' may be reconcilable with the Act, in that we would also view 'design' as relevant to a finding of predation because it is evidence that predation is plausible.[103] In our view, however, it would be preferable if 'design' as a separate basis for a finding of predation were eliminated from the statute. In the meantime, we agree with the approach in the guidelines, which, by relying on the recoupment test, tends to downplay the independent role of intent.

We also would prefer to eliminate from the statute the wording about possibly finding predation on the basis of the elimination of a competitor. Competition is designed to protect competition, not competitors. It is one of the central tenets of competition to seek to better, or even to eliminate, a rival, and in the vast majority of cases where a firm has been eliminated, it is likely the result of inferior performance, not predation. While eliminating a competitor *may* be anticompetitive, and thus the statute can be reconciled with an approach that focuses

---

103 The guidelines downplay the role of intent by focusing on the objective plausibility of predation. VanDuzer and Paquet, while sympathetic to the economic foundation for this approach, express concern that it is not consistent with the statute in this respect: A. VanDuzer and G. Paquet, *'Anticompetitive Pricing Practices and the Competition Act: Theory, Law and Practice'* (Ottawa: Competition Bureau, 1999), at 41.

only on harm to competition, it would be better if the statute focused solely on the ultimate concern: the lessening of competition.

Our final observation on the statute concerns the recent amendments regarding predation in the airline industry. As we have stressed, it is very difficult to distinguish vigorous competition from predation. The amendments, however, give the commissioner wide scope to make interim orders on the mere suspicion of predation. The fact that an incumbent airline matches or beats a recent entrant's prices may be consistent with predation, but it is also consistent with competition. Yet the amendments give the commissioner the unilateral power to make orders without a complete investigation. In our view, this power risks chilling procompetitive behaviour and could lead to higher prices in the airline industry.[104] For example, a high-cost entrant may price at a high level, anticipating that the incumbent will be reluctant to match prices, and face an interim order and investigation from the Competition Bureau. It would be better if these amendments were abolished.

To this point in the discussion, we have started from the implicit premise that some form of predatory pricing law is desirable. Some commentators, however, suggest the abolition of the law.[105] In our view, such an approach is misguided. Theory reveals that predatory pricing is not implausible, and empirical studies, while hardly indicating that predatory pricing is a rampant problem, do testify to the fact that it may take place.[106] A cautious approach to predatory pricing law, as we suggest has largely been taken in Canada, may serve to deter blatant predatory behaviour while failing to deter socially desirable

---

104 See Sanderson and Trebilcock, 'Bad Policy, Bad Law.'

105 See, in Canada, McFetridge and Wong, 'Predatory Pricing in Canada.'

106 The following is a sample of empirical studies. McGee, 'Predatory Price Cutting,' concludes that Standard Oil relied on merger, not predation, to realize its market power. On the other hand, Burns concludes that the American Tobacco Company trust during the period 1891–1906 may have successfully created a reputation for predation and thereby induced lower acquisition prices in its purchase of competitors: M. Burns, 'Predatory Pricing and the Acquisition Cost of Competitors,' (1986) 94 J. Pol. Econ. 266. (See D. McFetridge, 'Predatory and Discriminatory Pricing,' in F. Mathewson, M. Trebilcock, and M. Walker, The Law and Economics of Competition Policy [Vancouver: Fraser Institute, 1990], 71 at 84–5 for a critique of this study.) West and Van Hohenbalken, 'Empirical Tests for Predatory Reputation,' also find successful predatory behaviour on the part of Safeway, which opened stores in its rivals' market areas in order to deter the rival from opening new stores. (See McFetridge, 'Predatory and Discriminating Pricing,' at 85–6 for a critique of this study.)

price competition. Moreover, any claim that predatory pricing law (outside the airline industry) chills price competition falters on the evidence of prosecutions for the practice in Canada. VanDuzer and Paquet report that between 1994 and 1999, 382 complaints of predatory pricing were made to the Competition Bureau, but only 7 formal inquiries and no formal enforcement proceedings ensued, although 9 cases were categorized as Alternative Case Resolutions.[107] These statistics, plus the fact that predatory pricing law in Canada has resulted in only one conviction since 1980, suggest that the 'chilling' effect of predatory pricing law on price competition is unlikely to be significant.

II. Price Discrimination

Price discrimination occurs when a firm charges significantly different prices to two or more customers where the costs to the seller of supplying these customers do not differ significantly.[108] Price discrimination also occurs when the costs of supplying two customers differ significantly but the seller nonetheless charges both the same price. However, when the seller charges buyers prices that reflect the different costs of supplying the buyers, then there is no price discrimination. Put another way, two sales are discriminatory when they have different ratios of price to marginal cost; the firm realizes two different rates of return from the two sales.

Three conditions must exist for price discrimination to be viable. First, a firm must possess some market power. Second, it must have the ability to sort customers. Third, the firm must be able to prevent arbitrage; that is, it must be able to prevent customers who purchased at a lower price from selling to customers who paid a higher price.

With regard to the first condition, it is easy to see that the firm must possess some market power in order to price discriminate. If a firm is able to charge one buyer a higher price while charging another buyer the competitive price (i.e., at marginal cost), then the former buyer must be paying a price greater than marginal cost and providing the seller with supracompetitive profits. If the price-discriminating firm did not possess any market power, the buyer faced with a price greater than marginal cost would simply decline to pay such a price and find

---

107 VanDuzer and Paquet, *Anticompetitive Pricing Practices*, at 56.
108 Dunlop, McQueen, and Trebilcock, *Canadian Competition Policy*, at 208.

another seller willing to sell at the competitive price, with the result that the firm cannot charge buyers a price greater than marginal cost.

There is a qualification to the market power requirement. Unpredictable, changing market conditions imply that something that looks like price discrimination may occur even in competitive markets. For example, suppose a firm sells product x to Buyer A at price y in the morning. Later during the day, the market price of product x falls to z and the firm sells product x to Buyer B at price z. The firm has discriminated between two buyers in the same day, but this is not the result of market power, but rather the result of market price fluctuations. Short-run variations in prices may not reflect the short-run marginal costs of sellers and may appear to be discriminatory. Such transitory and sporadic price discrimination occurs even in competitive markets where buyers and sellers adjust to changing supply-demand conditions. In contrast, persistent price discrimination can only occur when a seller with market power systematically segregates customers into classes and charges them different prices to obtain different rates of return.[109]

Rather than stifling competition, and therefore raising competition concerns, price discrimination may reflect some competitive pressures on firms with market power. For example, in an oligopoly situation, the complete absence of sporadic price discrimination in a market may suggest that the sellers in the market are coordinating their prices. When sellers fix prices, they are concerned about granting concessions in price or other terms, which are the result of hard bargaining between individual buyers and sellers. When sellers form a cartel, they require that all sales within a certain category be made on the same terms, with the result that the market is characterized by a rigid price structure. Sporadic price discrimination may reflect competitive behaviour and can serve to upset cartels.

The central purpose of price discrimination is to realize greater profits by charging different customers different prices. In order to charge different prices, the firm must have a way to sort its customers. For example, a firm may wish to charge customers with inelastic demand higher prices than those charged to customers with elastic demand, since inelastic demanders are more likely to purchase products even in the face of higher prices. To price accordingly, the seller must be able to

---

109 Hovenkamp, *Federal Antitrust Policy,* at 517.

sort high- and low-elasticity types of customer. We will describe the different methods of sorting below.

Sorting is not sufficient for successful price discrimination. For a firm to charge different types of customers different prices, it must be able to prevent arbitrage; that is, it must be able to prevent low-price buyers from reselling to other customers. Without such a constraint, the firm's ability to segregate customers would be subverted, since low-price purchasers would resell to would-be high-price customers, and nobody actually buys at the higher price. There are two relevant types of arbitrage: one associated with the transferability of the commodity and one with the transferability of demand.[110] The first involves the basic case of a low-price customer reselling the particular good to a would-be high-price customer. The second involves a would-be high-price customer imitating a low-price customer and selecting a price-quantity-quality package that the seller intended for the low-price customers alone. For example, a high-demand airline passenger may purchase an economy class ticket even though the airline intended only low-demand users to fly economy.

Various techniques exist to minimize arbitrage. Several mechanisms can be used to prevent resale.[111] First, some products, such as medical services, haircuts, and electric power to a household, are intrinsically difficult to resell because of the nature of the goods. Second, a firm may legally prevent resale. For example, computer manufacturers often offer educational discounts with a contractual provision that restricts resale. Third, tariffs, taxes, transportation, and other transaction costs may prevent resale. In general, arbitrage will only work if there is a 'spread' between the prices that exceeds the costs of reselling the product. For instance, if one buyer pays x and another pays $(x+a)$, arbitrage will occur until the transaction cost of the arbitrage is equal to the price difference a. Once transaction costs exceed the price difference, a, arbitrage associated with the transferability of the commodity will not occur.

To prevent the type of arbitrage associated with the transferability of demand, a firm can modify its product so that the higher-priced group chooses not to purchase the lower-priced good. In economists' terms, it

---

110 Tirole, *The Theory of Industrial Organization*, at 134–5.
111 D.W. Carlton and J.M. Perloff, *Modern Industrial Organization* (New York: Harper-Collins, 1990).

is incentive-compatible for the higher-demand purchaser to pay the higher price for the modified package. Often this entails lowering the quality of the low-price good. For example, some firms sell student versions of software that do not have the complete set of features available in standard versions. Tirole cites the colourful example of third-class train travel in the nineteenth century, which involved roofless cars and hard wooden benches, not because of the expense of a roof or upholstery, but because the train company did not want those who could afford higher-class travel to purchase lower-class tickets.[112] Until recently, first-class and second-class subway cars in Paris were distinguished only by their colours. The higher price for first-class travel created less crowded cars, however. Consumers sorted by preference for lower prices versus lower congestion. The key demand condition that allows price discrimination through self-selection mechanisms is a negative correlation across consumers between taste for lower prices and a preference for higher quality or comfort.

A. *Types of Price Discrimination*

Price discrimination was classified by Pigou into the three categories of first-, second-, and third-degree discrimination.[113] First-degree price discrimination occurs when the seller charges a different price for each unit of good sold to each of its customers in such a way that the price charged for each unit is equal to the maximum price the customer is willing to pay. This maximum price is the customer's reservation price. First-degree price discrimination, or perfect price discrimination as it is also called, results in the same output as would occur in perfect competition, but with one important difference: with first-degree price discrimination, because each customer is charged the maximum amount she is willing to pay, all consumer surplus is captured by the seller. In practice, perfect price discrimination is almost never possible. First, it is usually impractical to discriminate so finely and charge each customer a different price without facing arbitrage problems (unless there are only a few customers). Second, a firm usually does not know the reservation price of each customer.

Second- and third-degree price discrimination involve sorting cus-

---

112 Tirole, *Theory of Industrial Organization*, at 150.
113 See ibid., at 134–5.

tomers more roughly into segments of demand types. While arbitrage may occur such that discriminatic.ı within a particular group is impossible (thus, both second- and third-degree discrimination is 'imperfect price discrimination'), it may be possible to limit arbitrage between groups, thereby allowing price discrimination across groups. The firm attempts to segment the market in order to charge higher prices to groups with higher demand. The difference between second- and third-degree price discrimination concerns the method of sorting the customers. Second-degree price discrimination involves various 'self-selection devices.'[114] The menu of available price-quantity-quality packages is chosen by the seller in order to induce customers to reveal their type by the package they choose. The price-quality package associated with first-class airline tickets, for example, may be designed to attract high-demand travellers, while the price-quality package of economy class is designed for lower-demand users. Alternatively, the price-quantity package may induce buyer self-selection. One of the methods of doing so is to offer two-part pricing comprised of fixed and variable prices, with the variable portion of the overall price designed to capture more surplus from higher-demand customers. Xerox's pricing policies in the 1960s may have reflected this type of secondary degree price discrimination.[115] Xerox's copying machines were leased for a low fee plus a charge per copy (which was higher than marginal cost). The number of copies made allowed Xerox to meter the intensity of use, with the intensity approximating the elasticity of each lessee's demand and willingness to pay. The use of leases rather than sales prevented arbitrage.

Third-degree price discrimination involves the sale of identical quantity-quality packages to different types of customer, but at different prices based on some observable signal of type. The seller categorizes buyers according to the signal, which has some relationship to the buyer's type of demand, and charges different prices accordingly. This is perhaps the most common type of price discrimination in practice, involving price menus based on factors such as age and occupation. For example, movie theatres may offer discounts for senior citizens

---

114 See ibid., at 135.
115 This example is drawn from Dunlop, McQueen, and Trebilcock, *Canadian Competition Policy,* at 210. See also E.A. Blackstone, 'The Copying Machine Industry: Innovations, Patents, and Pricing,' (1972) 6(1) *Antitrust Law & Econ. Rev.* 105 at 110 *et seq.*

and children, or for students regardless of age. The assumption under-lying these prices is that the elderly, the very young, and students are likely to have a higher elasticity of demand relative to others, and thus the price they face is lower than that charged to others.

B. Welfare Aspects of Price Discrimination

As discussed above, a condition of price discrimination is that the seller must possess some market power. However, market power with discrimination is not always more harmful to social welfare than the same initial amount of market power without discrimination.

As noted above, first-degree price discrimination increases output to the same level as in competitive markets, but results in the transfer of all consumer surplus to the seller. For ease of exposition, assume that the seller is a monopolist and that consumers have unit demand if price is below their reservation price. Without price discrimination, the one-price monopolist restricts output and sells the quantity where marginal cost equals marginal revenue. At this price, there will exist buyers with a demand for the good who would purchase if price equalled marginal cost, but whose reservation prices are lower than the price charged by the monopolist and thus are priced out of the market. The removal from the market of these low-reservation price buyers by monopoly pricing, rather than marginal cost pricing, results in a social dead-weight loss.

The perfectly price-discriminating monopolist, however, will charge each consumer her reservation price, so long as that price exceeds mar-ginal cost. Unlike a price-discriminating monopolist, the perfect price discriminator does not price low-demand customers out of the market. The discriminating monopolist maximizes profits by capturing *all* the consumer surplus of *all* potential customers, as opposed to only *some* consumer surplus from *some* potential customers, as a single-price monopolist does.

Perfect price discrimination is profit-maximizing relative to a single-price monopolist, and economists would also typically view perfect price discrimination as improving social welfare. A single-price monop-olist eliminates potential customers, thereby lowering social surplus, specifically consumer surplus. Perfect price discrimination leads to the same quantity purchased and the same number of customers as under perfect competition (the social optimum), thereby avoiding the dead-weight losses associated with single-price monopoly; perfect price discrimination is allocatively efficient. However, there is a significant distributive effect. Under perfect price discrimination, all social surplus is realized in the form of producer surplus: there is no consumer surplus. Under a single price, on the other hand, higher- demand customers will enjoy some consumer surplus. Thus, while the producer is clearly better off, some consumers are made worse off by a transition from a single price to perfect price discrimination, and none are made better off (all those who purchase under perfect price discrimination are indifferent between purchasing and not purchasing).

The welfare analysis of second- and third-degree price discrimination is ambiguous relative to the single-price case. The monopolist will always prefer price discrimination, because if it did not wish to differentiate customers, it would simply charge one price. Consumers, on the other hand, may or may not prefer price discrimination. Under imperfect price discrimination, customers are segmented according to demand characteristics. In general, imperfect price discrimination, by resulting in higher prices to buyers with a low elasticity of demand and lower prices to buyers with a high elasticity of demand, harms the former buyers and benefits the latter. Indeed, it may be that this segmentation results in some low-demand customers being served by the seller who would be priced out of the market if only a single price were available. In this case, price discrimination may be output increasing and welfare improving relative to the single price case: the monopolist is better off, since it realizes profits not only from high-demand buyers but from low-demand buyers as well; the high-demand buyers are no worse off, since they face the single price they would face in any event; and low-demand buyers are better off by realizing some consumer surplus.

On the other hand, price discrimination may be socially harmful in certain circumstances. For example, if there is only a small number of high-demand consumers, the single price in the absence of price discrimination may be relatively low, thereby providing significant consumer surplus to high demanders. If price discrimination were allowed, the resultant high price to high-demand buyers and the welfare losses resulting from some high-demand consumers dropping out of the market may reduce total output and lower social welfare relative to the uniform price case.

Another consideration in assessing the welfare effects of price discrimination is that the seller will often incur costs in segmenting the market. For example, if a theatre offers youth and senior citizen discounts, resources are devoted to enforcing this pricing scheme, such as the time to check patrons' identification to establish their age. The seller finds these expenditures worthwhile as they support a profit-maximizing pricing scheme, but from a social perspective, they are wasteful relative to the single-price scheme.

Posner points out another reason why examining the effects on output may not sufficiently capture the results of price discrimination.[116] Since price discrimination increases monopoly profits, firms will spend additional sums in an effort to gain a monopoly, and such expenditures of resources may be largely or entirely a social waste. As Bork observes, however, expenditures to obtain a monopoly are not generally socially wasteful.[117] For example, firms may expend more effort to gain patent monopolies if price discrimination were allowed, but it is impossible to determine that the innovative efforts of firms who fail to gain a patent, or who gain one only to discover that it does not confer market power, are socially wasteful.

In general, second- and third-degree price discrimination have ambiguous welfare effects relative to the single-price case. It can be shown that a necessary condition of welfare-improving price discrimination is that it increases output relative to the single-price case; the intuition is that an increase in output may recover some of the dead-weight losses associated with monopoly pricing.[118] As an aside, it is perhaps important to emphasize that the uniform price monopolist (or oligopolist), not the competitive firm, is the appropriate comparison when making welfare assessments of price discrimination. Price discrimination is symptomatic of market power, but it is quite another thing to suggest that it causes market power. Unless such a causal link exists, which it may or may not, the appropriate counterfactual is uniform pricing by a monopolist (or oligopolist), not competitive pricing.

C. Price Discrimination and Competition

If the welfare effects of price discrimination are uncertain, why is price discrimination prohibited? The public concerns that have motivated price discrimination legislation relate to fears of future price increases resulting from injury to competition, as well as a desire to preserve

---

116 R. Posner, *Economic Analysis of Law* (Boston: Little Brown, 1972), §7.8.
117 Bork, *The Antitrust Paradox*, at 396.
118 See Tirole, *Theory of Industrial Organization*, at 137–8.

small businesses, which are perceived to be socially valuable institutions. The feared injuries to competition are reasoned thus: persistent discriminatory pricing today might result in adverse effects on market structure, so that competition tomorrow will be harmed. An example is the situation in which big retailers drive out smaller retailers through discriminatory pricing practices by their suppliers.

The desire to preserve and promote small businesses can be observed from the inception of price discrimination legislation in Canada. The original price discrimination legislation introduced in 1935 arose out of the Royal Commission on Price Spreads and Trade Practices,[119] which had been established in response to concerns about small traders being unfairly injured by mass retailers. The expressed aim of the legislation was the protection of small retailers, whose numbers had decreased significantly during the 1920s as a result of the rapid growth of chain stores and mail order houses, which were able to exert their economic power to obtain larger discounts from upstream suppliers than small traders.[120]

In considering the injury to competition, it is customary to classify the injury the seller's discriminatory practices may bring about into primary, secondary, and tertiary lines. These 'lines' of injury reflect the injury that may occur at various stages of competition, that is, whether competition at the seller's level, or at some upstream or downstream stage, is harmed. Primary-line injury occurs when competition among sellers is harmed, secondary-line injury is inflicted when competition among the customers of the sellers is harmed, and tertiary-line injury occurs when competition among the customers of the sellers' customers is harmed. For example, in a three-stage productive process involving manufacturers, wholesalers, and retailers,[121] we can classify injury to competition resulting from seller price discrimination practised by one or more of the manufacturers as follows:

- Primary line – mostly injures competition among manufacturers;
- Secondary line – mostly injures competition among wholesalers; and
- Tertiary Line – mostly injures competition among retailers.

---

119 *Report of the Royal Commission on Price Spreads* (Ottawa: King's Printer, 1935).
120 Frank Zaid, *Price Discrimination and Promotional Allowances* (Canadian Bar Association, Ontario 1984 Annual Institute on Continuing Legal Education), at 2.
121 This example is drawn from Dunlop, McQueen, and Trebilcock, *Canadian Competition Policy*, at 215.

Situations of buyer discrimination where buyers with monopsony power coerce sellers into providing price reductions can also be categorized according to the same scheme. For example, if a large retailer compels its wholesale suppliers to provide price reductions, leading to injury to competition among retailers, this can be classified as 'secondary-line' injury, since the wholesalers can be considered to be buyer-coerced practitioners of seller discrimination, causing injury to competition one stage down the distribution chain. Historically, concerns about the possibility of this type of injury have motivated both Canadian and U.S. legislation on price discrimination. As noted above, the original price discrimination legislation introduced in Canada resulted from widespread concern regarding retail chains that were able to obtain reduced prices compared to independent small retailers. In the United States, concerns about the relationship between supermarkets and their food products suppliers also arose in the 1930s, where it was thought that some of these suppliers were coerced by supermarkets into practising seller price discrimination, to the injury of cornerstore and other competition at the retail level. In the major but subsequently much-disputed *A & P* decision, the U.S. Federal Court of Appeals found such injury.[122]

As indicated earlier, the fact that a seller must possess some market power in order to price discriminate does not necessarily imply that market power with price discrimination is always more injurious to social welfare than market power without discrimination. Only perfect price discrimination results in output which is the same as that in competitive markets. Under imperfect price discrimination, output is always lower. Therefore, with imperfect price discrimination (which is prevalent, since perfect price discrimination is difficult in practice), social dead-weight losses result. However, price discrimination in this case reflects monopoly power that already exists rather then causing such power.

There are theories, however, about the causal effect of price discrimination on future market power. Primary-line injury is said to increase market power precisely in the same manner as predatory pricing: low prices now drive competitors out of the market and allow the price discriminator to raise prices in the future because of the absence of these

---

122 See *United States v. New York Great Atlantic & Pacific Tea Co. Inc. Et al.*, 67 F. Suppl. 626 (Ill. Dist. Ct., 1946), aff'd 173 F. 2d 79 (7th Cir., 1949).

competitors. Moreover, the discriminating seller is thought to be able to finance his predatory price cuts by charging higher prices in other markets, so that once rivals are driven from the market, the seller can boost prices. These considerations are dealt with in Part 1 of this chapter. It suffices to say that predatory pricing is generally only rarely considered to be profitable. In any event, it is unclear why price discrimination law should address the problem, given the existence of better calibrated predatory pricing law.

Aside from the questionable plausibility of primary-line injury to competition, it may be that *preventing* price discrimination may harm competition between firms at a particular level of the distribution chain. As we observed earlier, price discrimination may benefit customers by facilitating the breakdown of cartels. In collusive arrangements, price fixers have strong incentives to cheat on the cartel by charging a lower price because this lower price will garner them a larger share of a profitable market. Most cartel cheating takes the form of discreet sales made at a price lower than the cartel price, rather than across-the-board price cuts; that is, price fixers discriminate among customers rather than offer uniform price cuts.[123] The more such discriminatory sales are made, the less will be the social harm done by the cartel, and the more likely that such cheating will result in the disintegration of the cartel.

Secondary-line injury, as noted above, occurs when competition among a seller's customers is harmed by price discrimination. The traditional social concern is that powerful buyers may coerce sellers to discriminate (this is often classified as 'buyer discrimination') to the disadvantage of smaller competitors who cannot exert similar coercive pressure. Buyer discrimination requires that there be some profit room on the part of sellers for coercion. Where sellers are competitive, there is no room for a large buyer to extract any discount that is not cost-justified. However, when sellers possess market power and are making supracompetitive profits, then there is room for a powerful buyer to negotiate a special discount.[124] This special discount may serve as a signal to other buyers that bargaining vigorously for lower prices can be to their advantage. If costs to all buyers decline, and some of this reduction in costs is passed on to consumers, the ultimate result may

---

123 Hovenkamp, *Federal Antitrust Policy*, at 521.
124 Bork, *The Antitrust Paradox*, at 359–60.

actually be more sales to final consumers at lower prices. Moreover, as mentioned already, if the sellers have organized themselves into a cartel and the powerful buyer has forced a concession from a cartelist, this may be the beginning of retaliatory discounts from the other members of the cartel, which will reduce the price for all buyers. In this case, consumers benefit if the buyers pass on their savings to consumers. Even if only one buyer is able to obtain discounts, consumers may benefit if the favoured buyer increases output and reduces prices.

Apart from the benefits that can accrue to consumers, the question still remains whether the powerful buyer may, by forcing big, non-cost-justified discounts upon its suppliers, harm its competitors and thereby gain market power. While such a result may be possible, there is reason to suppose that this will not occur. First, other large buying units, perceiving that price reductions are negotiable, will seek to gain the bargaining advantages enjoyed by the powerful buyer, or smaller buyers will band together to form a large buying group. Second, sellers who saw a monopoly developing, being desirous of avoiding a state of dependence on a monopsonistic buyer, may themselves offer the lower prices to other customers to prevent that outcome. A monopsonist would extract supracompetitive profit from cartelists by playing them off against each other and would also restrict output. Sellers would in their own interest seek to minimize their dependence on a looming monopsonist and preserve the economic health of other distribution channels.[125] Of course, sellers may face a free-rider problem, just as consumers do when facing predatory pricing.

With regard to tertiary-line injury, the main concern is that a manufacturer selling goods on discriminatory terms to different kinds of wholesalers and retailers – in particular, selling goods at significantly lower prices to captive distributors substantially controlled by itself – will eventually lead to the restriction of consumer choice brought about by the gradual wasting away of disfavoured, non-captive retailers.[126] This manner of price discrimination may not bring significant social benefits. However, in some cases, the manufacturer may be able to present a cost justification. It may argue that direct, manufacturer-controlled distribution is the most cost-effective method available; the

125 Ibid., at 390.
126 Dunlop, McQueen, and Trebilcock, *Canadian Competition Policy*, at 218.

differential prices offered through different distributive channels simply reflect those cost differences.

We have already referred to what is known as the 'cost-justification' defence to a charge of price discrimination. A seller, when charged with price discrimination as a result of offering different prices to buyers, may refute that charge by demonstrating that he is realizing the same rate of return because the costs of supplying buyers differ, thus justifying the different prices charged. The other classic defence is that the low, discriminatory price was made in good faith to meet an equally low price of a competitor. This 'meeting the competition' defence only permits a seller to meet the lower price of a competitor, not to 'beat the competition' by offering a lower price. It is important to note, however, that there is a distinction between price-lowering actions that can be destructive to competition and those whose main effect is to contribute to a general process of price lowering. As Dunlop et al. point out, *a priori*, the action of the first firm to move in a sequence of price lowering is as likely to fall into the second category as the first, and may be at least as socially beneficial as the conduct of the firms that subsequently follow its price downwards.[127] While 'good faith matching' may be a valid defence for price discrimination by the follower firms, it does not necessarily mean that the first firm intends to stifle competition. Rather, the first firm may have invigorated competition through lowering its price initially.

We see from the above discussion that the ambiguous welfare effects of price discrimination make it difficult for legislators to devise a detailed law that would only attack price discrimination that is injurious to competition and to consumer welfare. A few general principles may be laid down, such as the desirability of limiting consideration to relatively protracted and systematic discrimination, and of allowing full room for valid cost defences.[128] However, there are a host of other considerations. The many possible types of injury at all lines of potential injury to competition makes detailed legislation something which could, in actual courtroom practice, create huge demands for data and for accurate, microeconomic prediction. Among the empirical data required would be that concerning costs, demand, output, and profits. The difficulty of compiling these data is reflected in the difficulty in estimating the demand curve faced by a firm, for demand is constantly

---

127 Ibid., at 218–19.
128 Ibid., at 219.

changing and unpredictable. Moreover, price discrimination can be disguised in many ways. Variations in the quality of affected goods, or a discriminating buyer's purchase of large quantities of goods at low prices through long-term contracts, whose bona fides as cost-justified quantity discount arrangements may be suspect, may be difficult to disprove.[129] So difficult is it to identify the existence of price discrimination and to predict accurately the long-term effect on welfare and competition that some commentators believe that the costs of enforcing price discrimination laws may not justify the benefits derived and therefore argue for repeal.[130] We concur in this view, as explained below.

It is also important to recall that anticompetitive price discrimination, both real and alleged, is a major source of complaints from small businesses to competition policy authorities.[131] Consequently, competition authorities are kept under considerable pressure to have in place some credible means of investigating allegations of price discrimination and of providing remedies where appropriate. We turn now to a review of the law relating to price discrimination.

D. Price Discrimination: The Law

As noted earlier, the law prohibiting price discrimination was inserted into the Criminal Code in 1935 in response to the findings of the Royal Commission on Price Spreads. The commission stated that the discrimination which resulted from the economic pressure of large buyers was unfair because '... it operates inequitably as between competitors, because the burden of it is often pushed back to the wage-earner or primary producer without corresponding benefits to the consumer and because it deprives society of the benefit of fair and equal competition. Unfair price discrimination ... permits the survival of the powerful rather than the efficient.'[132]

---

129 Douglas F. Greer, *Industrial Organization and Public Policy* (New York: Macmillan, 1980), 359–60.
130 See for example, Bork, *The Antitrust Paradox*, chap. 20.
131 Dunlop, McQueen, and Trebilcock, *Canadian Competition Policy*, at 220. VanDuzer and Paquet, 'Anticompetitive Pricing Practices,' at 56 report that between 1994 and 1999 eighty-eight complaints about price discrimination to the Competition Bureau were dealt with; of these, only five involved full inquiries and none went to formal enforcement proceedings, although four were resolved in alternative ways.
132 *Report of the Royal Commission on Price Spreads*, at 270.

To address such concerns, the legislation sought to ensure that competition among purchasers of articles would not be distorted by discriminatory pricing practices on the part of suppliers. Since 1935, the text of the prohibition has remained largely unchanged. The current provisions in relation to price discrimination are contained in section 50 of the *Competition Act*,[133] which states:

(1) Every one engaged in a business who

    (a) is a party or privy to, or assists in, any sale that discriminates to his knowledge, directly or indirectly, against competitors of a purchaser of articles from him in that any discount, rebate, allowance, price concession or other advantage is granted to the purchaser over and above any discount, rebate, allowance, price concession or other advantage that, at the time the articles are sold to the purchaser, is available to the competitors in respect of a sale of articles of like quality and quantity,

... is guilty of an indictable offence and liable to imprisonment for a term not exceeding two years.

(2) It is not an offence under paragraph (1)(a) to be a party or privy to, or assist in, any sale mentioned therein unless the discount, rebate, allowance, price concession or other advantage was granted as part of a practice of discriminating as described in that paragraph.

(3) Paragraph (1)(a) shall not be construed to prohibit a cooperative association, credit union, caisse populaire or cooperative credit society from returning to its members, suppliers or customers the whole or any part of the net surplus made in its operations in proportion to the acquisition or supply of articles from or to its members, suppliers or customers.

In the entire history of the price discrimination provision, there have been only three convictions: *Commodore Business Machines Ltd. v. Canada (director of Investigation and Research)*, *R. v. Simmons Ltd.*, and *R. v. Neptune Meters Ltd.*[134] Moreover, these were not contested prosecu-

---

133 *Competition Act*, R.S.C. 1985, c. C-34.
134 *Commodore Business Machines Ltd. v. Canada (Director of Investigation and Research)* (1988), 27 O.A.C. 310, 63 O.R. (2d) 737, 50 D.L.R. (4th) 559, 41 C.C.C. (3d) 232, 21

tions, as the accused all pleaded guilty to price discrimination and were fined amounts ranging from $15,000 to $50,000. In addition, prohibition orders upon the accused's admission of price discrimination were issued in *R. v. Miss Mary Maxim Ltd.* and *R. v. Station Mont-Tremblant Lodge.*[135] While the case law thus provides little guidance, the Bureau of Competition Policy issued the *Price Discrimination Enforcement Guidelines*[136] in 1992 to provide some assistance to businesses on the application of the price discrimination provisions of the Act. Although not law, the guidelines set out the approach of the Director of Investigation and Research with respect to the enforcement of section 50 of the *Competition Act*. A review of the guidelines and the relevant case law examined pursuant to section 50 are provided below.

1. Price Discrimination Guidelines

(a) Introduction
The *Price Discrimination Guidelines* begin by offering a rationale for section 50(1)(a): 'competing purchasers who purchase articles of similar quality and quantity, should not have their ability to compete with one another negatively affected by unequal pricing treatment at the hands of the seller.'[137] Thus, the main concern of the guidelines, which reflects the statute, is secondary-line injury. The guidelines note that section 50(1) applies only to discrimination between competitors and is not meant to ban all forms of sales at different prices. Unlike most offences in the Act (e.g., conspiracy), the director need not demonstrate a lessening of competition to prove a violation of the criminal price discrimination provisions, although the abuse of dominance provisions, which may apply to price discrimination, require a substantial lessening of

C.P.R. (3d) 396, 36 C.R.R. 147; *R. v. Simmons Ltd.*, Ont. Prov. Ct. (Criminal Division), 15 October 1984, Richards P.C.J. (unreported); *R. v. Neptune Meters Ltd.*, Ont. Dist. Ct., 2 June 1986, Borins D.C.J. (unreported), reasons for committal are found in *R. v. Neptune Meters Ltd.*, Ont. Prov. Ct. (Criminal Division), 23 June 1983, Hashborn P.C.J. (unreported).
135 *R. v. Miss Mary Maxim Ltd.*, Ex Ct., 16 May 1968 (unreported); *R. v. Station Mont-Tremblant Lodge*, F.C.T.D., 6 April 1989 (unreported).
136 Director of Investigation and Research, *Price Discrimination Enforcement Guidelines* (Ottawa: Consumer and Corporate Affairs Canada, 1992).
137 Ibid., 2.

competition.[138] Thus, even a supplier with very little market power can violate s.50(1). Restricting the scope of the provision, however, is the fact that price discrimination under section 50 is a criminal offence, so every element of the offence must be proved beyond a reasonable doubt; this is likely one of the reasons why there have been few convictions for price discrimination.

(b) Parties to an Offence

Section 50(1)(a) applies to 'everyone engaged in a business who is a party or privy to or assists in' sales that discriminate. The guidelines state that this implies that persons, in addition to the actual seller of the articles, such as agents of the seller and brokers who assist in negotiating the sales transactions, may be liable. As well, the words 'discriminating against a purchaser of articles from him' lead to the conclusion that a purchaser cannot violate section 50(1)(a). Moreover, the guidelines set out that buyers should not be inhibited from bargaining vigorously to obtain lower prices that can be passed on to customers. If, however, the director finds that a buyer with significant purchasing power has coerced a seller to grant an illegal advantage over a competitor, the director will examine whether such behaviour might constitute the counselling of a price discrimination offence. In situations where competition is harmed as a result of the actions of purchasers with market power, the director may examine such actions under other provisions of the Act, such as the abuse of dominance provisions.

(c) Types of Transactions Covered

While most of the substantive provisions of the Act refer to 'supply' rather than sale, the guidelines state that the requirement of a 'sale' in section 50(1)(a) excludes other forms of supply such as renting, leasing, and licensing. The transfer of legal title will generally constitute a 'sale' for the purposes of the provision. The guidelines note that consignment arrangements, which are usually transactions in which the article remains the property of the original seller until the dealer sells it to the ultimate consumer, would not be a 'sale' and thus would not be subject

---

138 Appendix I of the guidelines discusses other provisions in the Act, including abuse of dominance, which could be relevant in fact situations raising issues of price discrimination.

to section 50(1)(a).[139] As well, the words 'any sale' and 'is available'
imply that only one sale need occur for an offence to be committed.
Competitors need not actually purchase articles at higher prices in
order to be considered victims of price discrimination because they
may have refrained from purchasing articles from the seller: without
the price concessions their competitor received, the seller's offer is not
attractive enough to induce them to make a purchase. However, while
only one sale need occur to satisfy the requirement of 'any sale,' it is
also necessary to satisfy the requirement in section 50(2) that the sale
be part of a 'practice' of discrimination. It is unlikely that one sale
would be considered a 'practice.'

The guidelines also note that section 50(1)(a) does not provide a specific affiliate exception; transactions between affiliates may therefore be
subject to section 50(1)(a). However, while recognizing this, the guidelines suggest that section 50(1)(a) may not apply to certain transactions
involving affiliates. First, the guidelines state that affiliates may coordinate their affairs as a single economic entity and thus transfer articles
at a price reflective of their common interest rather than negotiate
transactions only in their individual best interests. The guidelines
observe that in such transactions, affiliates may not be granting 'concessions in respect of a sale' as required by section 50(1)(a), presumably
because such concessions were granted as a result of their relationship.
Second, the guidelines also exempt situations in which a transaction
between affiliates involves price concessions given to a purchaser who
assisted the seller in entering the business of supplying an article. In
such situations, the director considers the price concessions as a form
of return to the purchaser on its investment in the seller's business and
thus the seller can grant price concessions over and above those attainable by competing purchasers.[140]

(d) Types of Products Covered
Unlike most other provisions in the Act, section 50(1)(a) applies only to

139 Note that the Competition Tribunal may order that a seller discontinue the practice
of consignment selling under s. 76 of the *Competition Act* where it finds that the practice has been introduced for the purpose of price discriminating.
140 Hunter and Hutton suggest that the director may be on shaky legal ground in creating this affiliate exception, given that there is no such exception in the Act: Hunter
and Hutton, 'Is the Price Right?' at 851. See also VanDuzer and Paquet, 'Anticompetitive Pricing Practices.'

the sale of 'articles.' The guidelines highlight that no distinction is made between articles purchased for resale and those purchased as business inputs. Notably, the section does not apply to services except for those specifically included in the definition of 'article' contained in section 2 of the Act. Section 2 of the *Competition Act* defines articles as follows:

> 'article' means real and personal property of every description including
> (a) money,
> (b) deeds and instruments relating to or evidencing the title or right to property or an interest, immediate, contingent or otherwise, in a corporation or in any assets of a corporation,
> (c) deeds and instruments giving a right to recover or receive property,
> (d) tickets or like evidence of right to be in attendance at a particular place at a particular time or times or of a right to transportation, and
> (e) energy, however generated.

In the director's view, section 2(d) applies to passenger transport but not to freight transport because the word 'tickets' is used in relation to passengers, not goods. As well, in transactions that involve the sale of an article and service, the guidelines state that section 50(1)(a) does not apply if the article is supplied only incidentally to the sale of the service.

(e) Discriminatory Sale

The guidelines specify that only sales that place a firm at a purchasing cost disadvantage vis-à-vis its competitors are considered discriminatory, and then only if they involve articles of like quality and quantity, in transactions taking place or being negotiated within the same time frame. Moreover, the relevant form of discrimination is the granting of a 'discount, rebate, allowance, price concession or other advantage' which is 'over and above' the concession or advantage 'available' to 'competitors' or a 'purchaser.'

(i) *'Discount, Rebate, Allowance, Price Concession or Other Advantage'*: The guidelines state that the terms 'discount,' 'rebate,' 'allowance,' and 'price concession' typically refer to monetary arrangements advanced by the seller that reduce the effective price paid by a purchaser to a level below that of the face or nominal transaction price. Furthermore, 'other advantage' is to be interpreted as any monetary arrangement by which the seller confers upon the buyer a lower net price per unit of article sold. Thus other types of 'advantages', such as the use of equipment and the provision of technical assistance, would not fall within the meaning of section 50(1)(a).

The guidelines provide that credit arrangements would normally fall within the concept of 'other advantage,' since they have the effect of lowering the net price paid. Therefore, the director may raise a question if discounts for prompt payment are not applied universally to all purchasers. However, the guidelines also state that s.50(1) does not restrict sellers from applying different credit terms to different purchasers; for example, new, unproven accounts or those with a poor credit history may be required to meet stricter terms. As long as the application of credit terms is 'reasonable (i.e. cause-related), having regard to all the circumstances,'[141] different credit terms need not be construed as discriminatory.

(ii) 'Available': The general principle is that as long as the same price concessions are 'available' to all competing purchasers, even if some purchasers in the end paid higher prices because they did not take advantage of the concession, the director will not raise any concerns under section 50(1)(a). In *Acier D'Armature Ro Inc. v. Stelco Inc.*,[142] the Quebec Court of Appeal referred to the guidelines in its decision and found that because all buyers knew about the discounts and thus had the discounts made available to them, the fact that the complainant did not take advantage of those discounts did not mean that the seller had violated the price discrimination provisions.

The guidelines indicate that whether the concession was 'available' depends on the nature of the disclosure by the seller. In contrast to section 51 of the Act, which requires those who grant promotional allowances to offer them on proportionate terms to competing purchasers, section 50(1)(a) does not require that the seller offer price concessions. The director is of the view that the obligation on the seller to disclose a price concession to competing purchasers depends on whether the concession is granted unilaterally by the seller or results from negotiations with a purchaser.

If a seller unilaterally grants a price concession, in the director's view the concessions must be disclosed to competing purchasers of

---

141 *Price Discrimination Enforcement Guidelines*, s. 2.5.1, 9.
142 (1996), 69 C.P.R. (3d) 204 (Que. C.A.).

like quality and quantity for it to be considered 'available' within the meaning of section 50(1)(a). As well, the method the seller chooses to communicate the availability of the concession has to be 'sufficiently timely and complete' so that the purchaser can make a sound business judgment as to the measures necessary to achieve the concession.

In contrast, the guidelines note that such broad disclosure is not required if the seller grants a price concession as a result of negotiations initiated by a purchaser who agrees to provide a service in exchange for the concession. In such situations, the director will be satisfied that the concession was 'available' as long as the seller responds to the initiatives of those competing purchasers who ask for similar concessions on similar terms as those granted to the favoured purchaser. The guidelines note that if sellers were required to offer concessions to all purchasers as a result of a successful negotiation by a particular purchaser, there would be little incentive for a purchaser to negotiate a deal, as the purchaser would know that it must share the advantage with other customers who benefit, at no cost to themselves, from that purchaser's innovation and negotiating skill. With regard to the amount of negotiation undertaken by a purchaser, the guidelines state that the seller is not obliged to communicate negotiated concessions to a purchaser who simply asks for the seller's 'best deal' as a matter of form. However, how much negotiation beyond asking for the 'best deal' would oblige the seller to offer the same concession is not clear.

The guidelines also set out the director's views with respect to different types of price concessions, such as conditional discounts, volume-based discounts, functional discounts, and exclusive dealing discounts. A key factor influencing the director's approach is the statutory restriction to sales involving 'like quality and quantity.' Such a limitation, which is not found in the United States,[143] avoids the difficulty of attempting to prove a cost justification for volume discounts.[144]

Like other price concessions, conditional discounts raise no question under the price discrimination provisions as long as they are 'available' to competing purchasers of like quality and quantity. The guidelines highlight two areas where the seller should take special care

---

143 See, e.g., *Federal Trade Commission v. Morton Salt Co.*, 334 U.S. 37 (1948).
144 See ibid.

when imposing conditions. First, the conditions to achieve the discount should not be contrived to unreasonably favour or deprive certain customers, such as when the seller imposes a condition knowing that certain purchasers do not possess the required facilities and cannot obtain them anywhere in the market on usual trade terms to satisfy that condition. Second, the condition should be verifiable when it has been satisfied and the seller should consistently grant the price concession when the condition is met.

With regard to volume-based discounts, the guidelines state that volume rebate plans are a well-established practice and do not ordinarily raise an issue under section 50(1)(a). However, sellers who provide volume rebates based on estimated purchases must make adjustments to the price paid by the purchaser if the actual volume purchased falls short of the quantity required to obtain the concessions. As well, price concessions related to increases in the volume purchased compared to a previous period (known as 'growth bonuses,' 'volume incentive allowances,' 'fidelity discounts,' or 'loyalty rebates') are not objectionable if the concession was made available to competing purchasers. The guidelines provide the following example of an acceptable growth bonus: '[T]he seller may grant a price concession to customers who increase their purchases by 10 percent over the previous year. Thus, one purchaser may qualify for this price concession buying only 400,000 units in Year 2 while a competing purchaser buys 500,000 units but does not qualify due to a failure to increase purchases by the required amount.'[145]

That the guidelines allow such growth bonuses is an important departure from previous enforcement of the price discrimination provisions by the director. In *R. v. Simmons*,[146] the director took the position that the accused's practice of offering discounts based on the percentage increase in purchases over the volume purchased in the previous year could result in price discrimination where different percentage sales increases result in purchasers paying different prices even though their total volume purchased in a given year is the same. The accused pleaded guilty to the charge of price discrimination and was fined $15,000. As well, the court issued a prohibition order requiring the company to submit any rebate plan to the director with a description and explanation for a period of three years. Under the new

---

145 *Price Discrimination Enforcement Guidelines*, s. 2.5.3.3, 12.
146 *R. v. Simmons Ltd., supra*, note 134.

enforcement approach outlined in the guidelines, such year-to-year growth bonuses are no longer objectionable. Moreover, it can be argued that as long as the growth condition was not contrived to deprive certain buyers of the discount, the fact that certain purchasers did not satisfy the growth condition should not be construed as price discrimination by the seller.

The guidelines also discuss the granting of functional discounts by sellers. Functional discounts are defined in the guidelines as 'concessions granted in return for the purchaser performing some service which the seller would otherwise have to perform at its own expense, such as the provision of warehouse facilities, transport of goods, or other services.' The guidelines recognize that buyer and sellers should be encouraged to seek the most efficient way of transacting business between them; if, for example, the purchaser were more efficient in transporting goods, the seller should not be prevented from offering inducements to purchasers willing to provide such services. As with other forms of discounts, the guidelines state that even if a buyer could only qualify for a discount by agreeing to perform services it does not presently offer but could offer in the future, as long as the seller's functional discount is available to competing purchasers with respect to purchases of like quality and quantity, such discounts are not objectionable. The guidelines note that if the seller and buyer arrange for the provision of the service through a separate contractual arrangement rather than through functional discounts, such arrangements raise no issue under section 50(1)(a). As a matter of statutory interpretation, section 50(1)(a) would not apply, since the arrangement would relate to the provision of a service rather than the sale of an article, and there would not be a lowering of the net price paid by a purchaser.

With respect to exclusive dealing discounts, the guidelines note that a seller is permitted to grant a price concession in return for the purchaser's agreement to deal exclusively in the seller's products as long as the concession is made available to competing purchasers of articles of like quality and quantity. This conforms with the general principle of the guidelines: that even if buyers choose not to take advantage of this concession because of other considerations, as long as the concession was available to them, there can be no complaint of price discrimination.

(f) Purchaser
The guidelines state generally that the 'true purchaser' in any transaction will normally be the firm that has made the necessary commit-

ment to acquire the goods sold. In addition, the guidelines discuss how the requirement for a 'purchaser' is applied in relation to buying groups, franchises, and international volume price concessions.

The guidelines define 'buying group' as 'any association of independent firms which combines the volumes of the members' purchases for the purpose of qualifying for or earning price concessions based on volume.' Buying groups are often formed to consolidate purchasing power and qualify for volume discounts or rebates based on the aggregate purchases of the group. Since section 50(1)(a) requires that all competing purchasers of goods of like quality and quantity be entitled to receive price concessions on the same basis, the buying group must qualify as a 'purchaser' in order to receive volume discounts based on the value of their aggregate purchases. A seller that knowingly grants volume discounts or other concessions to a buying group which is not a true purchaser can be guilty of a violation of section 50(1)(a). The guidelines identify three characteristics that the director considers to be important indicators in the seller's determination of whether the group is a true purchaser: (1) the group should be a legal entity capable of acquiring property in the articles purchased; (2) the group should in fact acquire title in the articles, although it need not take possession; and (3) the group should be liable and assume responsibility for payment of the goods purchased.

With regard to the first condition, the guidelines state that the group can adopt any legal form it wishes as long as the group can be held legally liable for its purchases. With respect to the second condition, the guidelines note that the group need not document a second transaction in which it conveys the articles to its members if this transaction can be 'deemed from the circumstances or by agreement with the members.'[147] With respect to the third condition, the guidelines state that if the seller requires other purchasers to meet certain financial requirements, the group should be in a position to satisfy the seller that it has the ability to meet those requirements. While the guidelines stress that the three conditions provided are indicia rather than rules that definitively establish that the buying group and not its individual members is the true purchaser, it would appear that a seller who fails to exercise any degree of diligence to ensure that the criteria in the

---

147 *Price Discrimination Enforcement Guidelines*, s. 2.5.4.2., 15.

guidelines are satisfied could be prosecuted. The *mens rea* element of section 50(1)(a) will be discussed below.

The guidelines treat franchise systems similarly to buying groups. The guidelines state that situations in which the franchisor is liable for payment of the articles and pays the seller directly for purchases of goods that its franchisees resell, or in which the franchisor takes delivery for the articles and distributes them to its franchisees, are unlikely to raise issues under the price discrimination provision. In the situation where the franchisee purchases articles for itself and is the only legal entity liable for payment for the articles purchased, the director will determine whether the seller has legitimately granted a concession based on the entire franchise system's purchase in light of the commitment made by the franschisor to the seller. If the franchisor commits, by contract, all of its franchisees to purchase from designated sellers, the director will likely find that the seller is justified in granting concessions based on the purchases by the entire franchise system.

As well, the guidelines indicate that the director will undertake a similar analysis as that used for franchises in respect of international volume price concessions. International volume price concessions are granted where the seller charges a price based on the total volume of all worldwide purchases by the buyer and its affiliates. The guidelines state that if the parent firm contracts to purchase the articles and commits its Canadian subsidiary and other affiliates to purchase from the seller, the purchases of the Canadian subsidiaries and other affiliates can be viewed collectively as that of a single purchaser.

(g) Competitors of a Purchaser
Section 50(1)(a) only prohibits a seller from knowingly discriminating against 'competitors' of a purchaser of articles from it. The guidelines make it clear that it is not 'competition in the purchase but competition in the downstream market of sale which is of relevance' in determining the identity of competitors of the purchasers. Therefore, the price discrimination provisions do not apply to sales to consumers; non-profit organizations such as educational and charitable institutions; and federal, provincial, and municipal governments as they normally do not compete in the business of reselling articles.

The guidelines state that whether two persons are competitors is a question of fact and determining whether the two are competitors involves an analysis of the relevant product and geographic markets. The guidelines indicate that the director will use the approach described in the *Merger Enforcement Guidelines* to define the relevant markets. Apart from applying the methodology of market definition in the MEGs, the director expects that sellers will normally be aware of customers' views, strategies, and behaviour with respect to the market in which they operate and who they consider to be their direct competitors. Furthermore, the guidelines observe that if the seller is not certain about the 'competitor' status of a customer, he can make inquiries of his customers. However, the guidelines also note that a seller who could not reasonably have been expected to know that particular customers were competitors and consequently failed to accord them the same concessions would not face review by the director because the 'knowledge' requirement of section 50(1)(a) would not have been met, although a seller's wilful blindness would not suffice to escape the 'knowledge' requirement.

(h) Relevant Time

A seller would only contravene the price discrimination provisions if the concession granted to a buyer was not made available to competitors 'at the time the articles are sold to the purchaser.' The guidelines recognize that while the issue of 'time' in straightforward, single-transaction sales is not complicated, it is difficult to resolve this issue with regard to complex purchases that provide for different prices over an extended period of time based on the application of an agreed-upon formula or schedule. The guidelines state that sellers should not be restricted from changing their prices over time and that section 50(1)(a) should not be used to extract from sellers prices that are no longer generally available because of changed market circumstances. The guidelines provide an example of a situation in which a purchaser enters into a two-year contract in year one with an option to purchase a minimum volume in year two at the year one price, and in year two the seller raises prices generally but sells to that purchaser at the lower price as stipulated. The guidelines state that in such cases, the director would consider that the relevant 'time' for purposes of comparison with the year two prices paid by the competitors was the 'time' at which the sale agreement had been entered into in year one. Therefore, provided that competing purchasers had available to them in year one the option of entering into similar contracts, the fact that some purchasers ended up paying higher prices because they had not taken advantage of such an option does not raise an issue under section 50(1)(a). This interpretation of the 'relevant time' of purchase is similar to that in *Hurtig Publishers*

Ltd. v. W.H. Smith Ltd.,[148] where the defendant, in a counterclaim pursuant to   section 36 of the Act,[149] sought to claim against its supplier, whom it alleged had granted a competing purchaser a lower, discriminatory price. The plaintiff supplier had entered into a contract to supply another buyer, Encyclopaedia Britannica, in 1983, and at that time, had given Encyclopaedia Britannica an option to purchase the articles at discounted prices in the future. Subsequently in 1987, Encyclopaedia Britannica exercised that option and received a lower price. In the same year, the plaintiff supplier sold the articles to the defendant at a higher price, resulting in the defendant's allegation of price discrimination. While the court found that there was no justiciable issue, it went on to consider whether or not there was any chance of success on a claim under section 50(1)(a). The court held that there would not be a violation of section 50(1)(a) because the purchases made by Encyclopaedia Britannica and the defendant were not made at the 'same time' within the meaning of section 50(1)(a). Although the articles were delivered at the same time, the purchase by Encyclopaedia Britannica was effectively made in 1983, when the plaintiff was contractually bound by the option. As well, the court stated: 'It would be an unreasonable interpretation of section 50(1) to say that if in 1983 a supplier offers a certain price for a product, which offer is accepted in 1987, the supplier must make the same offer in 1987 to all other prospective purchasers. It cannot be discrimination in pricing to not make the same offer in 1987 to other purchasers as was made to a purchaser in 1983.'[150]

(i) Directly or Indirectly
The guidelines highlight that sellers are not permitted to price discriminate among competitors by indirect means, such as incorporating a separate company whose sole purpose is to sell the article and grant concessions to a particular buyer, while continuing to supply other buyers of like quantity and volume at higher prices.

(j) Like Quality and Quantity
The guidelines state that the term 'like' in section 50(1)(a) means 'similar,' rather than 'identical.' In determining whether or not articles are

---

148 *Hurtig Publishers Ltd. v. W.H. Smith Ltd.* (1989), 99 A.R. 70 (Alta. Q.B.).
149 S. 36 of the *Competition Act* allows parties to sue for damages in respect of a contravention of the criminal provisions of the Act.
150 *Hurtig Publishers, supra* (1989), 99 A.R. 70 at 78.

of 'like quality,' the director may consider several attributes, including the physical or chemical composition of the articles; their functional or performance characteristics; their physical appearance; the fungibility of the articles; and the retail prices of two articles, because two articles sold at similar retail prices suggest a likeness, while dissimilar prices would suggest that buyers believe the products are not of 'like quality.' The guidelines also state that a trade mark or label alone may be suffi- cient to distinguish otherwise similar articles,[151] and that in general, a trade mark or label or other attribute that causes consumers to per- ceive a significant difference such that they are willing to pay a higher price for the article suggests to the director that the article differenti- ated through such means should not be considered to be of 'like qual- ity' when compared with physically identical articles without the trade mark or other differentiating features.

As with 'like quality,' the guidelines state that the director will gen- erally consider industry pricing practices in determining whether two quantities are 'like' one another. According to the guidelines, the chief area of concern regarding the determination of 'like quantity' is with respect to multiline sellers of articles who may wish to aggregate pur- chasers' volumes of different articles when calculating volume rebates. Conforming with the general principle of the guidelines, the director will not object to the seller aggregating different categories of articles as long as the products are related to one another (for example, where all products are consumer electronics) and the volume rebates are available to competing purchasers.

(k) Knowledge
According to the guidelines, the requirement in section 50(1)(a) that a person discriminate 'to his knowledge' means that the seller must have knowledge 'with respect to each and every one of the factors which, taken together, constitute a discriminatory sale.'[152] The guidelines state that knowledge may be determined through direct evidence or inferred from the circumstances surrounding the case and that wilful blindness will be treated in the same way as direct knowledge. The guidelines provide an example of wilful blindness in which the seller arbitrarily categorizes its purchasers into broad classifications and

151 *Price Discrimination Enforcement Guidelines*, s. 2.8.2, 22.
152 Ibid., s. 2.5.9, 23.

grants rebates based upon forecast purchase volumes without adjusting for the actual volumes purchased. The guidelines note that while negligence may be a mitigating factor, a question may nonetheless be raised where the seller is aware of the risk that its conduct could bring with respect to price discrimination, but still deliberately persists in omitting to make the necessary inquiries.

(l) Section 50(2): A Practice of Discriminating

Pursuant to section 50(2), there is no offence under section 50(1)(a) unless the discriminatory price concession was granted 'as part of a practice of discriminating.' The guidelines note that the word 'practice' is not defined in the Act although it is found in sections 45, 61, 76, 77, 79, and 81. For the purposes of section 50(2), it is the director's view that a 'practice' refers to 'a systematic pattern of behaviour as distinct from isolated acts or reactions to competitive market changes. "Practice" certainly contemplates more than the adoption of a temporary expedient designed to win a new account, enter a new market or match a competitor's pricing initiatives.'[153] The guidelines also state that in determining whether there is a practice, the director will consider factors including the frequency and duration of discrimination and the consistency and purposes of the pricing behaviour. As well, the guidelines note that price concessions granted on a temporary basis in order to meet prices granted or offered by a competitor or to attract a new account will not normally be considered to constitute a practice.

With respect to whether charging discriminatory prices constitutes a 'practice,' the court in *Hurtig Publishers Ltd. v. W.H. Smith Ltd.*[154] stated that words in a statute should be given their ordinary grammatical meaning unless indicated otherwise, and consequently, 'practice' meant 'habitual, customary, repeated, systematic.'[155] Thus, the court found that, *inter alia*, two sales of like quality and quantity at different prices did not constitute a practice of discrimination.

(m) Section 50(3): The Cooperative Exception

The guidelines state that the exception for the return of net surplus by a cooperative association, caisse populaire, cooperative credit society,

---

153 Ibid., s. 2.6, 24.
154 *Supra*, note 148.
155 Ibid., at 79.

or credit union contained in section 50(3) is restricted to those associations and does not exempt all conduct engaged in by those associations from the price discrimination provisions.

E. Analysis

Just as in the context of predatory pricing, the concerns of economists and those of lawyers differ on the issue of price discrimination. Economists offer a variety of explanations of why predatory pricing may or may not be rational, yet lawyers have tended to focus on proposing tests to catch predatory pricing that may or may not relate to the economists' various conceptions of it. With respect to price discrimination, economists tend to focus on the dead-weight losses associated with either price discrimination itself or its prohibition, while lawyers tend to focus on price discrimination's possible harms to competition. Indeed, a leading industrial organization economics textbook makes no reference to primary, secondary, or tertiary lines of injury in an extensive discussion of price discrimination,[156] although these concerns form the basis of price discrimination policy. The origins of this disjunction between the economic and legal perspectives are likely historical: price discrimination law initially responded to concerns about protecting small business, and thus had little basis in welfare analysis. The emphasis on harm to competition, which we will argue is essentially an emphasis on harm to competitors, is clearly reflected in both the *Competition Act* and the guidelines.

Various factors make it clear that secondary-line injury in the form of harm to competitors is the focus of the criminal prohibition. The statutory prohibition in section 50(1)(a) refers to discriminating 'against competitors.' The guidelines state that 'the theory behind section 50(1)(a) is that competing purchasers, when they purchase articles of similar quality and quantity, should not have their ability to compete with one another negatively affected by unequal pricing treatment at the hands of the seller.'[157] Moreover, unlike most offences under the Act, the provision does not require a substantial lessening of competition. The provision catches price discrimination whether or not it affects competition.

---

156 Tirole, *Theory of Industrial Organization*, chap. 3.
157 *Pricing Discrimination Enforcement Guidelines*, at 1.1.

Economic analysis of price discrimination does not turn on the harm to competitors, but rather on the output effects of price discrimination and the resultant effect on the sum of consumer and producer surplus. The presence of competitors is largely peripheral to this analysis; harm could occur even in the context of a monopolist with no potential competitors. If, on the other hand, an economist were to address the harm to competitors, such harm would only be relevant to a welfare analysis because of some harm to competition. It is far from clear what harm to competition may result from so-called secondary-line 'injury,' as we will discuss.

Suppose firms A and B both purchase widgets from firm C and resell them in the widget retailing market. To the extent that C has no significant market power, it will not have the discretion to price differently to A and B, except to reflect differences in costs. If C tries to charge significantly above costs to either customer, the customer will seek the products elsewhere. If differences in costs are difficult to verify, however, the price discrimination provision may protect high-cost purchasers and thereby create undesirable allocative distortions.

But even if C did have market power, it is unclear why C would have any incentive to advantage intentionally A or B in the downstream retailing market. Suppose that, over time, higher prices charged by C to B drove it out of the market, even though it was as efficient as A, thus increasing A's market power in retailing. A's increased market power in retailing suggests that it will increase the mark-up on C's products, which serves only to reduce the sales and profits C will realize. Moreover, A's increased market power in retailing may confer on it monopsonistic market power, lowering the price that C can charge. C would have to have good reason, therefore, to offer persistently a concession to A not offered to B.[158] For example, A may have a greater elasticity of demand, which makes a price cut to it more attractive, and a price increase less attractive, from C's perspective. While this difference in elasticity may affect competition between A and B, the question, is why does it exist? Is it, for example, because A is able to obtain supplies from alternative sources more easily than B? If so, why should A not be rewarded for this ability? Higher costs would also hurt B's ability to compete, but competition policy makes no effort to protect B in this

---

158 Note that s. 50 requires a 'practice' of price discrimination; sporadic price differences, which can result in competitive markets, are sensibly excluded.

instance. If the lower elasticity of demand for B reflects a competitive shortcoming, it is not clear why competition policy should intervene.

Another reason why C may price discriminate is that A may simply be a better bargainer. Again, it is unclear why bargaining ability is not viewed as part of the skills of doing business, and therefore why A's ability should not be rewarded rather than shackled by preventing C from offering idiosyncratic price cuts. Moreover, A's gains may eventually signal to B that it should bargain more vigorously, and prices in the industry would eventually fall – a desirable development given C's assumed market power. Lower prices to A may also result from lower costs of serving A that may not be verifiable. But if A is a lower-cost purchaser, why should it not benefit? Using competition policy to protect high-cost purchasers may create undesirable allocative distortions.

It is unclear what 'secondary-line injury' could mean, other than harm to less effective competitors. There is, however, no requirement of a substantial lessening of competition in the statute. Not only is secondary-line injury to competition, as opposed to competitors, theoretically questionable in the abstract, it is unnecessary to prove in the particular. Such a doctrine is outside the scope of Canadian competition policy's usual approach, which would normally seek to promote competition, but not at the expense of protecting ineffective competitors.

If, on the other hand, policy were in this instance directed at protecting competitors, particularly small competitors, it remains the case that the provision is ill-conceived. The provision allows for quantity discounts without any reference to costs. Thus, a large buyer of products may legitimately purchase at a lower price than a smaller buyer, regardless of whether there is any cost advantage to the large purchaser. Moreover, the guidelines allow volume discounts even where the volume is calculated across product lines, although the lines must be related to one another.[159] A smaller, niche purchaser may legally face higher prices even if it purchases the same amount of a particular product as a more broadly based purchaser that buys a number of products. As we will discuss, while we tend to agree with the approach of the provision and guidelines in these matters, this is because we do not view protecting competitors as sound policy. If that is indeed the purpose of price discrimination policy, the provision and guidelines come up short.

There is likely good reason why price discrimination law is rooted in a concern about primary-, secondary-, and tertiary-line injury, rather

159 *Pricing Discrimination Enforcement Guidelines*, at 2.5.8.

than in a concern about output effects and social welfare: price discrimination has ambiguous social welfare effects. As the discussion above shows, in some instances price discrimination may reduce output, but in many cases it may increase output and also increase social welfare. Framing the point in a different way, preventing firms from price discriminating may have harmful effects on social welfare. Moreover, the information required to assess the impact on welfare (e.g., demand and cost curves for all segments of the market, as well as the costs of limiting arbitrage) is extensive and extremely difficult to determine. Prohibiting price discrimination does not find solid footing in allocative efficiency grounds.

Our views of price discrimination policy in general can be summarized as follows. Given the existence of predatory pricing law, primary-line injury need not fall under the rubric of price discrimination law. Given the shaky theoretical foundation of 'secondary-line injury,' as well as 'tertiary-line injury,' for similar reasons, such injury fails to justify price discrimination law. The law should protect competition, not competitors. Moreover, even if the law were seeking to protect competitors, not competition, the law and guidelines fail to do so successfully by allowing terms like quantity discounts. Finally, the ambiguous efficiency effects of price discrimination eliminate it as a sensible basis for the cost and expense of a price discrimination regime. In short, we can see no compelling reason for the illegality of price discrimination.

Having said that, there are various aspects of the law in Canada which provide room for a considerable degree of price discrimination without legal concern. First section 50 only applies to a sale of articles; it does not apply to services.[160] This is a significant limitation. As set out above, arbitrage will undermine price discrimination in many con-

---

160 VanDuzer and Paquet, 'Anticompetitive Pricing Practices,' note the arbitrary nature of the exclusion of services from the price discrimination provision and suggest that the Act be amended to include services within the ambit of the price discrimination provision. They also suggest that price discrimination be treated as a possible abuse of dominance and thus require a lessening of competition test. As noted, we would also recommend eliminating the arbitrary distinction between the treatment of articles and services by s. 50, but we would do so by eliminating price discrimination as a competition offence. Given the difficulty in attempting to determine the welfare effects of price discrimination in any particular case, and given the dubious quality of secondary line injury as a basis for intervention, we would rather see the abolition of the price discrimination than its treatment as a species of abuse of dominance. VanDuzer and Paquet's suggestion that the law account for competitive effects, however, would lead to an improvement on the status quo.

texts, but the resale type of arbitrage is generally unavailable with respect to services. It is impossible to resell a haircut, for example. By restricting the provision's scope solely to articles, which are more likely to be subject to arbitrage and therefore less likely to be the subject of price discrimination, the Act significantly limits the scope of price discrimination laws in practice.

Another important limitation on the Act's reach is that it and the guidelines deal only with secondary-line injury. Price discrimination to consumers, which may have positive welfare effects, is legal.

An extremely significant consideration is that, unlike in the United States, price discrimination law allows for differing prices where quantity varies across customers. Thus, even if an order for a larger number of goods does not result in lower unit costs to the seller, the seller may set lower prices per unit without fear of prosecution, as long as these discounts are 'available' to other customers buying similar volumes. The guidelines expand such an important protection by permitting discounts based on the number of purchases across product lines. A purchaser of stoves may pay a lower price for those stoves by also purchasing refrigerators. As discussed, it is not entirely clear how such a permissive attitude towards volume discounts squares with the objective of addressing secondary-line injury to competitors. Both single-line and multi-line volume discounts may hurt smaller competitors in downstream competition, yet they are both treated by the guidelines as legal in Canada. While have some misgivings about the coherence of such an approach, we welcome these limitations since they undermine significantly what we view as a law without a principled basis.

Our overall conclusion about Canadian price discrimination law comes in 'good news, bad news' form. The bad news first. The law purports to address 'secondary line injury to competition,' yet offers no view of what the injury to competition, as opposed to competitors, is. Moreover, other considerations, such as primary-line injury, are either addressed by other provisions, such as predatory pricing law, or, like the immediate welfare effects of price discrimination, do not provide a basis for outlawing price discrimination. Given these observations, we would prefer the abolition of price discrimination law.

The law's considerable limitations, however, provide the good news. Various exceptions, such as where a sale involves services, end consumers or volume discounts, serve to limit considerably the instances of illegal price discrimination. Perhaps this explains why there have been only a very small number of convictions in Canada. If the law is to exist, we welcome these exceptions.

SIX

Vertical Restraints: Intrabrand Competition

I. Introduction

Vertical restraints represent an area of active research in economics and continuing controversy in competition law. This chapter reviews the law and economics of vertical restraints that tend not to exclude suppliers of rival product brands, but rather limit competition among downstream suppliers of a particular brand. We will review the law and economics of resale price maintenance, exclusive territories, and refusals to deal. Resale price maintenance (RPM) occurs where an upstream firm, often a manufacturer, sets a specific price (or price floors or ceilings) at which downstream firms, often retailers, are permitted to sell its products. Exclusive territories, or 'market restriction,' as set out in section 77 of the *Competition Act*,[1] occur where an upstream firm sells a product to a downstream firm on the understanding that the downstream firm will resell those products only within a specific geographic area, and that no other downstream firm will do so. The economic explanations for RPM and exclusive territories are similar and will be examined together. Refusals to deal may simply involve enforcement of other vertical restraints, such as RPM or tying. The section on refusals to deal in this chapter consequently focuses on the law and economics of refusals absent these other restraints.

In developing an economic framework for a synthesis of vertical restraints, a natural starting point is the benchmark of a simple, textbook contract for the transfer of a product. The simplest contract in a wholesale market would transfer to the retailer of a product a specific

---

1 R.S.C. 1985, c. C-34.

quantity of the product, which the retailer could then sell at any price and to any customer without limitations. The entire ownership of the product, that is, the bundle of property rights associated with the product, would be transferred. The contract would allow the retailer to purchase any quantity at the uniform price posted by the seller.

If the seller and the buyer are both firms in perfectly competitive and frictionless markets, then in fact this simple contract is optimal: the seller and retailer could not do better. At another extreme, if the buyer and the seller cannot monitor or enforce contractual restraints, and if the resale of the product cannot be prevented, then the simple contract is the only feasible one. A more complicated contract requires enforcement of some post-contractual right.

In reality, of course, observed contracts are more complex than the simplest contract. The seller may:

- set the price paid for the product as a function of the quantity paid (nonlinear pricing), including the possibility of minimum quantities (quantity forcing);
- impose floors or ceilings on the prices at which the reseller may transfer the product (resale price maintenance);
- insist that its products be purchased by the buyer in fixed proportions (bundling);
- require that the buyer purchase all of the buyer's requirements of a second good as a condition of purchasing any amount of a primary good (requirements tying);
- insist that the retailer carry all of its lines as a condition of carrying any of them (full-line forcing);
- restrict the geographical areas in which the buyer may sell the product, and in return guarantee the buyer exclusive rights to its own territory (exclusive territories);
- guarantee that the buyer will be the only retailer located in a specified area or country, but allow exports across areas (open territorial exclusivity);
- require that a retailer deal only with that seller (exclusive dealing); or
- agree to a buyer's requirement that the seller sell a particular product only to the buyer (an exclusive supply restriction).

Frequently these conditions appear in contracts between an upstream manufacturer and a downstream retailer and are known as vertical restraints.

In this chapter we first focus on RPM. This restraint describes any contract in which an upstream firm (e.g., a manufacturer) retains the right to control the price at which a product is sold downstream, usually in a retail market. Resale price maintenance often refers to the specific restraint of a minimum price at which a product can be resold, but it can refer to a price ceiling as well.[2] The context in which they are most often observed involves contracts between manufacturers and the distributors (resellers) of their products.

Historically, the attitude in the courts and general legal communities of most countries towards these organizational arrangements ranged from suspicion to outright condemnation. The intellectual basis for antagonism with respect to vertical restraints on competition appears to have two sources. The first is the legal principle of alienation, that once an individual transfers ownership of a good that individual has no further rights whatsoever to the good. If the ownership of the good, or any rights, is transferred, then all rights must be transferred according to this principle. The intellectual basis for the legal attitude towards restraints is distinctly non-economic. The second source of antagonism is the idea that the purpose of public policy in antitrust is to stimulate competition, for the benefit of increased economic efficiency or perhaps even as an end in itself. Since vertical restraints obviously reduce competition among retailers, even to the extent of creating monopolies, some critics argue is that they should be prohibited.

Support for the view that restrictions should be allowed comes from both law and economics. First, on legal grounds, the right to voluntary contracts for a manufacturer and retailers, or the right of an owner of a product to offer whatever contracts that owner wishes, supersedes the right of the possessor of a good to all decisions pertaining to the good. On economic grounds, various efficiency explanations consistent with a procompetitive role for the contracts have been offered. Observed contractual arrangements represent a choice of efficient distribution system by a manufacturer or upstream distributor, who is in the best position to determine such a system.

The economic reasons for RPM are reviewed below. We distinguish between private incentives that are in conflict with the social interest

---

2 Still more general are contracts, observed in the markets for gasoline and beer (U.S.) for example, which link the wholesale price charged to the retailer or the remuneration paid to the retailer to the price charged by the retailer.

and efficiency explanations of the contractual arrangements. We begin with a review of the empirical importance of RPM in the United States and in Canada, and then turn to a related matter: the economics of exclusive territories.

RPM is the most important vertical restraint in terms of both the frequency of use and the number of legal cases generated. It is currently illegal in most countries, but when the practice was permitted it was used in a wide variety of retail markets, including markets for many lines of clothing (jeans, shoes, socks, underwear, shirts), jewellery, sports equipment, candy, biscuits, automobiles, gasoline, and small and large appliances (stereos, shavers, and washing machines).[3] Estimates of the proportion of retail sales subject to RPM in the United States during the 1950s run from 4 per cent to 10 per cent.[4] In both the United Kingdom and Canada the practice was even more popular: in 1960, some 25 per cent of goods and services were subject to RPM in the United Kingdom, and in Canada, before the law prohibiting RPM was enacted in 1951, an estimated 20 per cent of goods sold through grocery stores and 60 per cent sold through drugstores were fair-traded.[5]

II. The Economics of Resale Price Maintenance

Any explanation of RPM (or any vertical restraint, for that matter) must begin from the observation that if both the upstream (manufac-

---

3 RPM has been observed to a lesser extent in contracts for the licensing of new technologies. See G. Priest, 'Cartels and Patent Licence Arrangements,' (1977) 20(2) *Journal of Law and Economics* 309.

4 See F.M. Scherer and D. Ross, *Industrial Market Structure and Economic Performance*, 3rd ed. (Chicago: Rand McNally, 1990), at 549; T. Overstreet, *Resale Price Maintenance: Economic Theories and Empirical Evidence* (Washington, D.C.: Federal Trade Commission, 1983), at 6.

5 See Overstreet, *Resale Price Maintenance* at 153–5. The issue of where RPM is most likely to be observed may provide information about which explanations of the practice are most important empirically. In particular, is RPM used more often in concentrated markets and is it invoked typically by well-established firms or by new entrants in a market? The relationship between market structure and the use of RPM in the United States was studied by the Federal Trade Commission. The findings (discussed in Overstreet, *Resale Price Maintenance*, at 71) were that the use of RPM was not correlated strongly with concentration.

turing) and downstream (retail) sectors were perfectly competitive, transacting in a frictionless wholesale market, RPM (or any other restraint) would never be observed. Manufacturers would sell at the market price to whomever chose to buy, without restraints on what the buyer could do with the product. This price would equal the marginal cost of production. No single manufacturer would have the incentive to restrain retailers in any way since to make such a contract acceptable to the retailers the price would have to be lowered below marginal cost. In an environment of perfect, frictionless competition, there are no incentives for complicated contracts.

On the other hand, market power on the part of a manufacturer is not sufficient to explain vertical restraints. Indeed, in a conventional market setting, once a manufacturer has set the wholesale price of the product, profit is maximized by ensuring the lowest possible retail price. A lower retail price means a higher quantity sold, since demand is downward sloping. Vertical floors on prices raise price and, other things equal, would harm the sales of a producer. Vertical price floors thus cannot be explained as an attempt by a firm to maintain a high monopoly price. Before competition policy towards resale price maintenance can be assessed, the puzzle of why manufacturers would impose this restriction must be answered. Three classes of theories have been advanced to explain resale price maintenance:

(a) resale price maintenance serves to support a cartel of manufacturers;
(b) the practice is a manifestation of retailers' monopsony power, supporting a cartel at the retail level; and
(c) the practice is implemented unilaterally by manufacturers as part of an efficient distribution system, necessary to elicit adequate service from retailers.

Each of these explanations is examined below.

A. Anticompetitive Explanations

1. Manufacturers' Cartel Hypothesis
Resale price maintenance has been explained in some cases as a device to facilitate cartel pricing at the manufacturers' level. Telser argued that General Electric and Westinghouse used RPM to aid in their cartel

pricing,[6] and McLaughlin found evidence that the Bakers of Washington Association was a manufacturer's cartel in the retail bakery market and had used RPM to maintain cartel prices.[7] The desire to fix prices is not in itself a reason for manufacturers' use of RPM. With a competitive retail market and stable retail cost conditions, manufacturers could assume agreed-upon retail prices by fixing their wholesale prices appropriately. In reality, however, variation over time in the costs of retailing would lead to fluctuating retail prices. If wholesale prices are not easily observed by each cartel member, cartel stability will suffer, because members will have difficulty distinguishing changes in retail prices caused by cost changes from cheating on the cartel. RPM can enhance cartel stability by eliminating the retail price variation. The facilitating power of RPM is in the increased cartel stability.

2. Retailer Cartel Hypothesis

The retailer cartel explanation of RPM is slightly more complicated. The cases to which this explanation has most often been applied are the retail drug stores in the United States and grocery outlets in Europe during the entry of large discount outlets. The conditions in these markets, necessary for this hypothesis, were that retailers had substantial assets invested in traditional, low-volume outlets. The quasi-rents earned by these outlets were threatened by the entry of discount chain stores.

According to this hypothesis, traditional retailers use manufacturers to coordinate cartel prices at the retail level.[8] The effect, if the cartelization is successful, is to delay or block the entry by discount stores. RPM thus serves the retailer cartel as an entry barrier against low-price, large-volume outlets.[9] It also allows coordinated pricing, even with

---

6 L. Telser, 'Why Should Manufacturers Want Fair Trade?' (1960) 3 *Journal of Law and Economics* 86 at 99–105.

7 A. McLaughlin, 'An Economic Analysis of Resale Price Maintenance' (Ph.D. dissertation, University of California at Los Angeles, 1979).

8 The cartel must involve a number of substitute products. With only one manufacturer, the interests of the retailers and the manufacturer are in setting the profit-maximizing price irrespective of how the profits are divided among them.

9 Contrary to most discussions on the retailer cartel hypothesis, barriers to entry are not necessary for the cartel. The protection of quasi-rents on specific assets in a declining industry in general provide the incentive for coordinated pricing, even with free entry.

free entry. The cartel prices allow a normal rate of return on the specific assets, if there is free entry into traditional outlets. The retailer cartel is enforced by boycotting any manufacturers who refuse to impose RPM.

While retailer cartel power may have had a modest, short-run effect of delaying the entry of discount drug stores in the United States, the effect could not have been large.[10] The possibility of successfully coordinating a cartel through retail druggists' associations is remote; cheating by a one of hundreds of retailer is easy. In addition, once the potential market share of discount houses grew, the gain to a manufacturer of maintaining resale prices would not have been worth the cost of foreclosing the discount sector of the market, even if traditional retailers had somehow prevented cheating on their agreement. The retailer cartel hypothesis for RPM is less relevant today than historically, since discount stores are well-established in most relevant retail markets. In addition, the hypothesis offers a clear, testable implication: the manufacturer of the fair-traded product would be worse off under the RPM agreement. In a study of a large sample of government and private resale price maintenance cases in the United States between 1976 and 1982, Ippolito found that cartel hypotheses were a possibility in less that 15 per cent of the cases.[11] By far, the typical resale price maintenance case involves a manufacturer acting unilaterally. Furthermore, as Easterbrook points out, a cartel could be prosecuted under existing horizontal price-fixing laws even if RPM were legal.[12] Ippolito found that most of the potential collusion-type cases involving vertical price control were pursued under price-fixing doctrines. Of course, proving collusion may be difficult, which may undermine this method of deterring anticompetitive uses of RPM.

A variant of the theme that retailers are the beneficiaries of RPM is found in the demonstration that RPM can be used in a world with

---

10 Nor does the traditional druggists' support of the fair trade laws imply that a retailer cartel was the driving force behind RPM in retail drug outlets. The value of specific assets in the traditional outlets was enhanced by RPM, even if the practice were invoked by manufacturers in the manufacturers' own interests.

11 P. Ippolito 'Resale Price Maintenance: Economic Evidence from Litigation,' (1988) 34(2) *Journal of Law and Economics* 263. Of course, since RPM is *per se* illegal in the United States, there was no need for those challenging RPM to bring forth any evidence of cartelization.

12 F. Easterbrook, 'Vertical Arrangements and the Rule of Reason,' mimeo, Law School, University of Chicago, 1984.

homogeneous manufacturers but differentiated retailers as a facilitating device to achieve non-competitive prices and to enhance firm profits. In this setting, manufacturers compete for scarce shelf space held by retailers. The manufacturers may use either a slotting allowance, where the manufacturers bid for shelf space, or price floors imposed upon concentrated retailers, or both. This model is developed in an article by Shaffer.[13] The role of RPM in this setting is to enhance retailer profits by committing the retailers to nonagressive pricing in the downstream market. Manufacturers are willing to consider this instrument as they compete for the scarce shelf space held by the retailers and the instrument enhances the profits of the retailers.

B. Efficiency Explanations

1. Price Floors and the Single Manufacturer
The majority of cases of resale price maintenance do not fit the cartel explanations, but instead appear to involve a manufacturer or manufacturers acting unilaterally. Why would a manufacturer, facing a downward sloping demand curve, impose a price floor on his retailers? A higher price, other things being equal, implies a smaller quantity sold of the product. The general explanation for RPM is that other things are not equal. The demand for a manufacturer's product may be increasing in the retail price, once the indirect effects of a retail price change are taken into account. In actual retail markets, demand depends on more than just price. Additional demand factors include the number of outlets or availability of the product, the convenience of the outlet's location, the information provided to customers at the point of sale, the sales effort and talent of dealers, the reputation of the product for quality, the prominence of the display of the product, and so on. The very existence of a retail distribution system for a product implies that retailers provide some value-added through provision of these demand factors – otherwise the product could be sold by mail order. An increase in the retail price through the imposition of a price floor will in general have the effect of increasing the demand determinants other than price. Protecting a higher retail margin increases the marginal benefit that each retailer gains from attracting an additional

---

13 G. Shaffer, 'Slotting Allowances and Resale Price Maintenance: A Comparison of Facilitating Practices,' (1991) 22(1) *Rand Journal of Economics* 120.

customer by providing service, and therefore increases the amount of service that each retailer will provide.[14] The general 'service hypothesis' is that the increase in demand resulting from enhanced service, elicited through a protected retail margin, will more than offset a negative impact on demand of a higher retail price.

Alternatively, under the 'outlets' or 'availability' hypothesis, a protected retail margin may expand the number of retail outlets willing to carry a product. The wider distribution of the product will increase demand. If the indirect effect on demand of an increase in the availability of the product more than offsets the negative direct impact of a price increase, a manufacturer will profit from establishing a price floor.

An examination of the service hypothesis requires explanation of why the unrestrained retail market does not produce exactly the combination of price and non-price or service competition that the manufacturer would want. The traditional response to this question is that the services offered by retailers are subject to free-riding: where services include the provision of information about the product being sold, some retailers may choose to discount on prices and attract consumers who have been informed at other outlets. If the search or shopping costs for most consumers are very low, then only a very few outlets will offer information and the sales of the product will suffer as a result. Complex products such as computers and audio equipment are candidates for this type of free-riding externality, with some outlets offering extensive advice, listening rooms, product demonstrations, and so forth and other outlets selling the product 'in the crate'. Resale price maintenance, however, has been used for a much wider variety of products than the standard free-riding theory would predict. Products such as candy, books, pet food, pharmaceuticals, and many lines of clothing were fair-traded when it was legal in the United States and Canada. In the case of clothing, for example, 'services' include fitting rooms, sales staff, and prominent or central displays in department stores. These services are not realistically subject to the free-rider problem.

Some authors have criticized the efficiency defence of vertical

---

14 The amount of service provided increases not because each retailer has 'more profit to spend on service' as is often argued, but because the marginal benefit of providing service has increased. Each retailer offers service to the point where the marginal benefit of offering service equals the marginal cost.

restraints as ensuring product services on the basis that the free-rider argument rarely applies.[15] The limited applicability of the service argument has motivated alternative theories of resale price maintenance, including free-riding on retailers' 'certification' of products as high quality,[16] free-riding on the provision of manufacturers' services,[17] protection of rents in the retail sector as part of a scheme to ensure adequate dealer services in the presence of costly monitoring,[18] and as part of contractible instruments set to control vertical externalities in non-price decisions made by both manufacturer and retailer subject to moral hazard.[19] The variety of explanations available for resale price maintenance leads to the issue of the necessary and sufficient conditions for resale price maintenance (as opposed to asking for yet another possible explanation or sufficient condition). The question can be addressed within a canonical model of a manufacturer selling to many (say, two) retailers.[20]

Suppose that a manufacturer sells a single product at constant cost to two retailers, who set prices along with some other variable that affects demand (effort, enthusiasm, number of sales staff, the comfort of the shopping environment, etc.). Each retailer faces a demand curve that

15 See, e.g., R. Pitofsky, 'Why Dr. Miles Was Right,' (1984) 8 *Regulation* 27; F.M. Scherer and D. Ross, *Industrial Market Structure and Economic Performance*, 3rd ed. (Chicago: Rand McNally, 1990), at 551–2.

16 See T. Greening, 'Analysis of the Impact of the Florsheim Shoe Case,' in R.N. Lafferty and R.H. Lande, eds., *Impact Evaluations of Federal Trade Commission Vertical Restraints Cases* (Washington, D.C.: Federal Trade Commission, 1984); H. Marvel and S. McCafferty, 'Resale Price Maintenance and Quality Certification,' (1984) 15(3) *Rand Journal of Economics* 340; and S. Oster, 'The FTC v. Levi Strauss: An Analysis of the Economic Issues,' in Lafferty and Lande, eds., *Impact Evaluations*. Greening argues, for example, that the use of vertical restraints to encourage greater dealer services in the sale of shoes was necessary because consumers interpret greater service as a signal of quality. Some stores could free-ride on this signal by offering the shoes with lower amounts of service but at a lower price. Marvel and McCafferty develop a model of free-riding on quality certification.

17 H. Marvel, 'Vertical Restraints in the Hearing Aid Industry,' in Lafferty and Lande, eds., *Impact Evaluations*.

18 B. Klein and K. Murphy, 'Vertical Restraints as Contract Enforcement Mechanisms,' (1988) 31(2) *Journal of Law and Economics* 265.

19 R. Romano, 'Double Moral Hazard and Resale Price Maintenance,' (1994) 25(3) *Rand Journal of Economics* 455.

20 This argument follows R.A. Winter, 'Vertical Restraints and Price versus Non-price Competition,' (1993) 108(1) *Quarterly Journal of Economics* 61.

depends on its own actions and the actions of the other retailer. Suppose that the manufacturer can contract over the wholesale price and the retail price (which will be binding as either a floor or ceiling), but that contracts specifying the non-price determinant of demand (enthusiasm, for example) cannot be enforced. We will refer to this non-verifiable, non-price determinant of demand generically as 'service.'

Finally, suppose that the contract offered by the manufacturer has the objective of maximizing total profits of all agents that result from symmetric retail competition under the contractual restraints. The manufacturer seeks to maximize the size of the pie to be divided among itself and the retailers. Under a 'complete contracting solution' in which any contracts were possible, the manufacturer would simply set price and service levels equal to the first-best, profit-maximizing values. However, this solution is unattainable. The question is whether setting a wholesale price is sufficient to elicit the optimal amount of service and price from the retailers.

The answer to this question depends on firm (i.e., retailer) and market elasticities of demand with respect to the two variables, price and service. Individual firm elasticities are always greater than market elasticities: it is more difficult for a single firm to raise price without losing many customers than it is for all firms acting collectively to raise price without losing many customers. *Individual retailer choices of service can be optimally elicited simply by setting the wholesale price if, and only if, the ratio of firm to market elasticities of demand with respect to both price and service are equal.* If these ratios are equal, each firm will, as a result of acting in its own self-interest in competing with other retailers, choose the optimal mix of price and service such that the aggregated result of independent retailer actions is collectively optimal.

The intuition behind the optimality of a simple wholesale price under certain conditions can also be developed by considering the case where the optimal conditions do not hold. It would be simply coincidence if the ratios of firm to market elasticities in price and service were equal. If, for example, the ratio of firm price elasticity to the market price elasticity were greater than the ratio of firm service elasticity to the market service elasticity, then the aggregate of retailers' individual choices is collectively sub-optimal: there is too much price competition. Since price competition has a greater proportionate effect on quantity sold by that individual retailer than service competition, price competition is more attractive to individual retailers. Consequently, price competition is more intense (prices are lower) among retailers

competing with one another than it would be if the retailers acted collectively. In these circumstances, a price floor may be optimal: suppressing price competition gives retailers incentives to compete on
service. By adjusting the margins available to retailers by setting both
wholesale and retailer prices, manufacturers can alter retailer incentives to provide service.

The advantages of specifying a retail price over directly contracting
for the service level lie in the monitoring and enforcement costs. Violations of price floor agreements are usually reported by competing dealers. (The typical resale price maintenance case involves termination of
a discounter after complaints by a higher-priced competitor.) Individual dealers may not know that competing retailers offer inadequate
service. Monitoring of price floors can itself be centralized, whereas the
contractual specification of service cannot. In addition, any departure
from list prices must be communicated to consumers if it is to be of any
value, and it is therefore easily detected by the manufacturer or other
dealers.[21] Enforcement costs are lowered because service may be non-
verifiable, that is, not susceptible of proof in the courts.

The condition for the optimality of price floors (that the ratio of firm
to market price elasticities exceeds the ratio of corresponding service
elasticities) is satisfied by many existing resale price maintenance
explanations, the free-riding explanation in particular, but because it is
the most general condition (within the modest constraints of the
model) for the profitability of RPM, it is a useful guide to understanding cases. Free-riding, for example, leads to the condition but is much
stronger than necessary. Too much of the literature on RPM tries to
force the RPM 'square cases' into the free-riding 'round holes.'

This reduced-form model captures the results of several other
authors. For example, Perry and Porter examine the mix of retailer service and optimal competition across retail outlets.[22] There is a monopoly manufacturer with monopolistic competition at the retail level. In
this model, any service externality across retail outlets is not necessar-

---

21 As Klein and Murphy, 'Vertical Restraints as Contract Enforcement Mechanisms,'
   point out, however, RPM cannot always be freely enforced. In this case, RPM plays
   the additional role of protecting rents to retailers. We discuss this further below.
22 M. Perry and M. Porter, 'Can Resale Price Maintenance and Franchise Fees Correct
   Sub-optimal Levels of Retail Service,' (1990) 8(1) International Journal of Industrial
   Organization 115.

ily corrected through RPM because the results depend on the level of the service externality. This corresponds to the reduced-form result above that outcomes depend on relative elasticities from the perspective of the downstream retailers and the upstream manufacturer.

Blair and Lewis augment the usual upstream/downstream tension in incentives by considering the impact of hidden action by the downstream firm.[23] The general finding is that the optimal contract involves some form of both retailer price and quantity control by the upstream manufacturer. The direction of the effects turns on the substitutability between a random factor that expands demand (which is privately observed only by the retailer) and retailer promotion.

In another paper, Bolton and Bonnano play on the theme of the manufacturer's having minimally sufficient instruments to achieve retailing objectives.[24] The economic point is related to the desire of a vertically integrated structure to price discriminate by offering different price and quality packages to different consumers. When consumers are heterogeneous and the manufacturer is limited to a single retail price instrument such as RPM or franchise fees, the efficient outcome will not be forthcoming. Franchise fees can redistribute rents as incentive devices but cannot remedy any deficiency from the retailers' incentive to compete in price. RPM fails to elicit the appropriate retailer incentives for product differentiation. While these contracts improve on the manufacturer contract with a single wholesale price, there exists another contract with a price-dependent franchise fee that is capable of achieving the efficient outcome.

Finally, in O'Brien and Shaffer, downstream competing retailers are assumed not to know the contracts negotiated between the upstream manufacturer and the other downstream rivals.[25] This permits the upstream firm to engage in *ex-post* secret bilateral deals with selected downstream firms to negotiate reductions in wholesale prices so as to shift customers and profits away from rival retailers to the negotiating parties, a form of opportunistic rent shifting. Searching for wholesale prices that are immune to renegotiation leads to wholesale prices equal

---

23 B. Blair and T. Lewis, 'Optimal Retail Contracts with Asymmetric Information and Moral Hazard,' (1994) 25(2) *Rand Journal of Economics* 284.

24 P. Bolton and G. Bonnano, 'Vertical Restraints in a Model of Vertical Differentiation,' (1988) 103(3) *Quarterly Journal of Economics* 555.

25 D. O'Brien and G. Shaffer, 'Vertical Control with Bilateral Contracts,' (1992) 23(3) *Rand Journal of Economics* 299.

to marginal production costs. The ensuing retail prices and profits may be below those set by a vertically integrated firm, leaving room for vertical constraints to improve joint profits. For example, exclusive territories would prevent customer stealing. Price ceilings with wholesale prices sufficient just to cover the marginal costs of the downstream retailers also work, as they eliminate retailer quasi-rents that are the subject of the ex-post secret deals. Price floors do not achieve the first best but to the extent that they are a commitment to an industry price, they eliminate the *ex-post* secret deals that permit a selected retailer to lower his prices to enhance the sum of that retailer's and the manufacturer's profits.

When will markets fulfil the 'reduced-form' condition for the profitability of resale price maintenance, that the ratio of *firm* price elasticity of demand to service elasticity of demand exceeds that of the *market*? In the remainder of this section, we identify several structural models or arguments that logically imply the condition.

2. Free-Riding
The traditional hypothesis of free-riding on point-of-sale service is a positive externality, which implies that increased service by one retailer enhances demand at other retailers. Under this assumption, any store violating an RPM agreement by cutting both price and service is free-riding or benefitting from the positive externality exerted by service provision at other stores. As a recent example, in *Applewood Stoves v. Vermont Castings, Inc.*, Judge Richard Posner writes:

> As a new company, selling a somewhat complex product [wood-burning stoves], Vermont Castings ... needs dealers who understand the product, can explain it to consumers and can persuade them to buy it in preference to substitute products ... These selling efforts, which benefit consumers as well as the supplier, cost money - money that a dealer can't recoup if another dealer 'free-rides' on the first dealer's efforts by offering a discount to consumers who have shopped at the first dealer ... As one of Vermont Casting's dealers explained in a letter to it, 'The worst disappointment is spending a great deal of time with a customer only to lose him to Applewood because of price ... This letter was precipitated by the loss of 3 sales of V.C. stoves today [to] people whom we educated and spent long hours with.'[26]

---

26 CCH *Trade Regulation Reports*, 58, 344 12.

Whether the retail market equilibrium is asymmetric, with some firms discounting, or symmetric with all firms setting similar prices and services, positive externalities in servicing or maintaining quality at the retail level can explain resale price maintenance.

But as we argued above, resale price maintenance is used in a much wider variety of products than the free-riding story would predict. Even in the recent *Sharp* case involving a relatively complex product (calculators), and the strongest endorsement of the efficiency arguments for RPM, the U.S. Supreme court was sceptical of the evidence on free-riding: '[M]uch of the evidence in this case was conflicting – in particular, concerning whether petitioner was "free-riding" on Hartwell's provision of presale educational and promotional services by providing inadequate services itself.'[27]

The use of resale price maintenance as a means of competing through enhanced service is much more general than free-riding. The free-riding story has been understood by the courts, and it is the most extreme basis for RPM. But evidence on free-riding should not be a necessary part of a defence or economic explanation of a resale price maintenance case.

3. Correlation of Product Information Costs and Price Information Costs
In general, retailers sell to a variety of consumers, some of whom are sensitive to price and some of whom are sensitive to service levels. Figure 6.1 depicts in abstract the set of potential customers of a product and the subsets of these consumers who purchase from each retailer. A marginal decrease in price or increase in service at either retailer will cause the set of its customers to expand, and the same action by both will cause the entire set of purchasers to expand. This figure reveals the incompatibility between the retailers' incentives and the manufacturer's interest in setting prices and service levels. In this figure, the potential consumers along the 'interretailer' margin are indifferent between buying at the two retailers, but inframarginal in their decision to buy the product. In general, demand of these consumers will be relatively price elastic, and service inelastic, compared to the consumers along the 'product' margin, who are indifferent between buying and not buying the product.

For example, in the market for complex products like personal com-

---

27 *Business Electronics Corp. v. Sharp Electronics Corp.*, 485 U.S. 717 at 718 (1988).

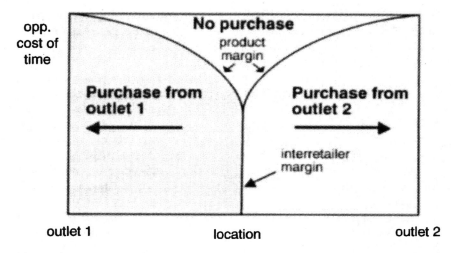

Figure 6.1
Partition of Consumers into Purchase Decision Sets

puters or business calculators, most consumers who shop among retailers do so mainly on the basis of price. (a recent Canadian case [sentencing hearing], *Epson*,[28] involved personal computers when they first began to appear in the market.) These intensive shoppers have relatively low information costs and are less concerned about advice. In the market for automobiles, the customers most likely to be influenced by a persuasive salesperson are in general those who have done the least amount of their own research and are the least aware of interretailer differences in price. Consumers at the inter-retailer margin, in contrast, are sensitive to price and insensitive to dealer persuasion. In both of these examples, the assumption is that information costs about prices or shopping costs are correlated across consumers with information costs about the product (and therefore with the value of services). A final example is the market for department store products such as clothes. The role of services for these products, such as adequate sales staff, short line-ups at cashiers, prominent store locations, and so on, is largely to reduce the time cost of shopping for consumers. Those consumers who are at the interretailer margin are those who have low

---

28 *R. v. Epson (Canada) Ltd.* (1987), 19 C.P.R. (3d) 195 (Ont. Dist. Ct.).

time costs of comparison shopping among retailers, therefore low time costs of shopping at any given store, and who therefore attach low value to retailer services. The upshot of these three examples, which together represent many of the types of products for which resale price maintenance has been used, is that the marginal consumers for the retailer (which include consumers on both the interretailer and the product margin in Figure 6.1) are relatively price-elastic on average compared to the marginal consumers of the product.

The incentive for vertical restraints on competition (that the ratio of firm to market price elasticity exceeds the ratio of firm to market service elasticity) follows from the correlation across consumers of product information costs and price information costs, not just from free-riding effects. The correlation leads to a bias in the preference of consumers on the interretailer margin – relative to consumers on the product margin – towards lower prices and away from greater service. Retailers accommodate the preferences of consumers on the wrong margin (the interretailer margin), from the perspective of collective profit maximization, leading to a bias towards too much price competition. Resale price maintenance corrects this bias.

Klein and Murphy[29] and Scherer and Ross[30] also offer RPM arguments based on the difference in tastes between infra-marginal and marginal consumers.

4. Monitoring Costs

The explanation of RPM provided above is based on the relative advantages of contracting on price instead of service directly. It is much easier to enforce a contract against cutting price than a contract against inadequate sales effort or service and, as we and others have argued, the former can have indirectly the same effect on service. For simplicity, we have taken the relative advantage of enforcing price restrictions to the extreme, assuming that they are freely enforced. As Klein and Murphy point out, however, resale price maintenance restrictions can sometimes be circumvented by providing the fair-traded product in combination with other goods.[31] When American Airlines tried to constrain travel agents against undercutting their

---

29 'Vertical Restraints as Contract Enforcement Mechanisms.'
30 *Industrial Market Structure.*
31 Klein and Murphy, 'Vertical Restraints as Contract Enforcement Mechanisms.'

price schedule, agents simply offered exceptionally low prices on hotel and car rental packages with the tickets.[32] Where monitoring of both resale price maintenance and service levels is costly, Klein and Murphy show that resale price maintenance plays the role of protecting rents to retailers. One means of achieving the optimal level of retailer servicing is through direct contractual specification of the servicing together with periodic monitoring of service levels and termination of those dealers who are found to be violating the contract by providing inadequate service. The potential problem with this method of ensuring service is that the act of termination must have some value as a penalty – otherwise dealers would have no incentive to honour the contract when monitoring is only periodic. The penalty value of contract termination must be in the form of the loss of quasi-rents accruing to the dealer under the contract. The role of resale price maintenance in the Klein-Murphy explanation is to protect retailer quasi-rents against erosion by retail price competition, to ensure that contract termination has sufficient value as a threat.[33] As in the basic service explanations, contracting on price is an indirect means of ensuring service.

A difficulty with the Klein-Murphy explanation of RPM, at least insofar as it is used as a policy justification, is that there are substitutes to RPM for ensuring that the service-providing retailer receives quasi-rents. For example, annual lump sum payments contingent on ade-

---

32 See discussion by Judge Frank Easterbrook in *Illinois Corporate Travel v. American Airlines Inc.* (CCH *Trade Regulation Reports*, 61,921)). See also *Robert's Waikiki U-Drive, Inc. v. Budget-Rent-A-Car Systems, Inc.*, 491 F. Supp. 1199 (D. Hawaii, 1980), aff'd 732 F. 2d 1403 (9th Cir., 1984).

33 The Klein and Murphy claim of quasi-rents as incentive devices is derivative from the argument of Klein and Leffler describing quasi-rents as contractual assurances of quality: B. Klein and K. Leffler, 'The Role of Market Forces in Assuring Contractual Performance,' (1981) 89 *Journal of Political Economy* 615. Telser 'Why Should Manufacturers Want Fair Trade?', has criticized as inefficient the use of quasi-rents as incentives where monitoring is still required to verify performance. It is known that the equilibrium of a simultaneous game where a manufacturer can monitor and a retailer can shirk on input is a mixed strategy. Telser shows that when the manufacturer must monitor the retailer to verify performance, the probability of the retailer shirking increases in the absence of the payment of a penalty by a shirking retailer to a manufacturer. Telser claims that offering a quasi-rent to the retailer in this setting is not an equilibrium as the manufacturer could do better without the quasi-rent and therefore the rationale for a quasi-rent in this setting must be found elsewhere, perhaps in a retailers' cartel.

quate service provision may also serve as a contract enforcement mechanism.[34]

5. Inventory Arguments

Deneckere, Marvel, and Peck offer explanations for RPM as supporting greater inventory among retailers, to the benefit of the manufacturer and in some cases to the benefit of consumers.[35] One of their articles, for example, begins with Prescott's 'hotels' model. This is a model of a single market, with a competitive structure, in which demand is uncertain and consumers arrive sequentially. The equilibrium involves a dispersion of prices charged by firms, from low prices to a highest price; consumers enter sequentially, going to the lowest price until the last consumer enters. Any firms that have not sold at that point are stuck without a sale. All firms earn zero expected profits.

Imagine that this is happening in a downstream retail market intermediating between a manufacturer and an uncertain number of consumers, all with the same reservation price. The manufacturer sees an equilibrium with a range of retail prices charged, and a amount of quantity offered at each price. The firm charging the highest price will sell only with some probability, but in the event that it does, the demand will (normally) exceed the quantities supplied at all prices. Suppose that the upstream manufacturer sets a price floor at the highest price charged in the previous equilibrium, and leaves its wholesale price unchanged. Then no firms will drop out, and firms will have the incentive to purchase additional quantity. The manufacturer's profit will therefore increase with the price floor. Total quantity actually transacted (and therefore total welfare) also increases.

C. Price Ceilings

As noted above, RPM may involve either price floors or price ceilings, although price floors are more commonly observed and arguably the more contentious. It is well known that price ceilings are a candidate to

---

34 E. Iacobucci, 'The Case for Prohibiting Resale Price Maintenance,' (1995) 19 *World Competition Law and Economics Review* 71.
35 R. Deneckere, H. Marvel, and J. Peck, 'Demand Uncertainty, Inventories, and Resale Price Maintenance,' (1996) 109(3) *Quarterly Journal of Economics* 885; R. Deneckere, H. Marvel, and J. Peck, 'Demand Uncertainty and Price Maintenance: Markdowns as Restrictive Competition,' (1997) 87 *American Economic Review* 619.

solve the 'double mark-up' problem. This problem involves sequential firms in the production process, each with price-setting power. In the simplest setting, consider a downstream firm that takes the product produced by an upstream firm and brings it to the market with no additional costs. The downstream firm takes any wholesale price given to it by the manufacturer as a given and marks-up its retail price according to the usual 'monopoly' price mark up. This generates a derived demand curve for the upstream manufacturer's product. Limited to a single wholesale price and facing this derived demand curve, the upstream firm in turn sets a wholesale price marked up on its marginal cost again by the 'monopoly' price mark-up. From the perspective of the two firms, this double mark-up is inefficient in the sense that it does not maximize their joint profits. The issue is whether there are other instruments that could avoid this double marginalization over the marginal cost of the good.

In theory, there are several options. The upstream firm could set a wholesale price equal to marginal cost (thus mimicking the efficient transfer price of a vertically integrated firm) and then set a fixed 'franchise' fee to the retailer that distributes the resulting monopoly profits between the two players according to their relative bargaining positions. Alternatively, the upstream firm could use RPM, imposing a price ceiling on the downstream firm at the price level that maximizes their joint monopoly profits, and then use the wholesale price as a 'lumpy' instrument to distribute the monopoly profits between the two.

Price ceilings, however, have arisen in another set of circumstances which are not explained by considerations of double marginalization. One set of such facts arose in a recent Canadian case, the *PANS* case,[36] which involved the use of negotiated price ceilings (pharmaceutical dispensing fees) between pharmaceutical insurers and the retail pharmacists of Nova Scotia. Although the case involved price ceilings, it was brought under the criminal price conspiracy section of the *Competition Act* (s. 45) and not under the RPM provisions of the Act. The product markets involved in this case were both the `direct-pay' market and the cash-paying market for prescription drugs. In the former, pharmacists, in dispensing drugs to a consumer, invoice and receive payment directly from the consumer's insurance company. Otherwise,

---

36 *R. v. Nova Scotia Pharmaceutical Society,* [1992] 2 S.C.R. 606.

the consumer pays the pharmacist cash for the dispensed drug. This is the cash-paying market. Consumers in this market may be covered by pharmaceutical insurance. The facts were that the two principal insurers in Nova Scotia had negotiated dispensing fee caps (price ceilings) with the professional trade association representing retail pharmacists in the province. Not all retail pharmacists charged the negotiated price ceiling. The Crown alleged that the price ceilings were simply negotiated price signals among retail pharmacists and alleged that these price signals spilled over into the cash-paying segment of the market to coordinate prices there as well. The Pharmacy Association of Nova Scotia was acquitted of the charges in this case.

One interpretation of the economics of this case and of the potential role of price ceilings under some circumstances comes from the excess capacity 'theorem' of monopolistic competition. According to this theorem, open entry in a two-stage game will under some circumstances lead to an excess number of firms.[37] If so, the open question is why the market would not respond to such an excess by reducing the number of competitors. The answer must be that if there is an excess number of firms and in the absence of any identified market failures, the market will respond when doing so is worthwhile, that is, when the costs of organizing the contracts that 'weed out' firms are below the realizable gains from this thinning-out of market participants.

In the context of the *PANS* case, the trade-off is between price (dispensing fees of pharmacists) and the number of retail pharmacies, where their density represents 'quality' to consumers: more retail outlets increase the ease of purchase for consumers but require enhanced revenues to sustain the enlarged retail network. The market under open entry into the retail pharmacy business will determine an equilibrium where the prices generated through competition are just sufficient to yield sustainable revenues (competitive profits) for market participants. The question is whether this leads to the trade-off between quality and price that is most preferred by consumers. The excess capacity theorem of monopolistic competition suggests that the answer is no.

The excess capacity theorem means that under certain circumstances

---

37 For the development of a model of monopolistic competition with this result, see J. Tirole, *The Theory of Industrial Organization* (Cambridge, Mass.: MIT Press, 1988), at 287.

consumers would be better off with negotiated price ceilings that cap revenues and lead to a thinner retail network: the market under open entry could lead to the incorrect quality-price equilibrium. According to the excess capacity conjecture, consumers would prefer lower prices and fewer retail pharmacies. In the case at hand, the agents that reorganize this equilibrium are the pharmaceutical insurers. On behalf of their clients, they negotiate price caps for direct-pay coverage which have a bite. Price caps that lower dispensing fees will yield fewer retail pharmacies under open entry into the retail pharmacy business. Lower dispensing fees, while reducing the number of retail pharmacies, save resources and this saving is passed along to consumers through lower insurance premiums for their 'direct-pay' coverage.

There is one further twist on the prices paid by cash-paying customers. As noted, not all consumers are covered by direct-pay insurance; some consumers pay cash. These cash-paying customers (independent of their ultimate insurance status) pay whatever fee the retail pharmacist can charge in a market where the location of the retail pharmacy differentiates the pharmacy's product. Lower dispensing fees to 'direct-pay' customers reduce revenues to retail pharmacies. The equilibrium with price caps will support fewer retail pharmacies. Fewer retail pharmacies reduce the vigour of competition, increasing the dispensing fees to cash-paying customers. Conditional on the application of the monopolistically competitive model, with its excess capacity conjecture to this particular market, the predictions are twofold: 'direct-pay' insurance consumers should realize lower dispensing fees (and thus lower insurance premiums) and over time the number of retail pharmacists should decline in those markets with these schemes. Simultaneously, however, the dispensing fees to cash-paying customers should rise, because fewer retail pharmacies diminish the vigour of competition, leading to higher prices in the cash-paying segment of the market. Cash-paying customers face both higher dispensing fees and reduced product choice, since there will be fewer retail pharmacies.[38]

These issues are not unique to the *PANS* case but have arisen in similar U.S. antitrust cases. Most notable is the *Maricopa* case[39] where the

---

38 These results are taken from G.F. Mathewson and R.A. Winter, 'Buyer Groups,' (1997) 15(1) *International Journal of Industrial Organization* 137.

39 *Arizona v. Maricopa County Medical Society,* 457 U.S. 332 (1982).

market in question was the market for physicians' services in Maricopa County, Arizona. Physicia_s in the plan agreed to cap their fees for certain services but they were free to continue to service non-plan members and to continue to charge to these customers whatever fees they had in the past. Unlike the *PANS* case, however, not all continuing physicians in Maricopa county were signatories to the participating physician contract: some physicians were sustainable operating independent of the plan(s). In contrast to *PANS*, where all of the relevant suppliers were included, the presence of outside non-signatory physicians serves to enhance the competitive vigour for cash-paying consumers, mitigating the welfare reduction accruing to these patients from potential price increases as suppliers are netted out of the system. Whatever the competitive merits of such a scheme, they never surfaced, for the scheme was judged to be a *per se* offence, a price agreement that violated section 1 of the *Sherman Act*. The case was appealed to the U.S. Supreme court, where a majority of the court upheld the applicability of the *per se* rule: The price ceilings were held to be *per se* illegal. In a remarkably similar set of facts in another case, *Kartell v. Blue Shield of Massachusetts Inc.* the appellate court found that the respective plans of Blue Shield, a medical insurer, were not only to be judged on their merits but that the contracts in force, with their price caps, were distinctly procompetitive.[40] More recently, the U.S. Supreme court has explicitly reversed itself, holding in *State Oil v. Khan*[41] that maximum RPM was to be judged under the rule of reason, not the *per se* rule.

D. RPM versus Territorial Restraints

Mathewson and Winter develop an integrated theory of the profitability of resale price maintenance, vertical territorial restrictions, quantity forcing (a minimum quantity restraint), and fixed franchise fees.[42] These restraints are explained as operating as substitutes in some cases and as complementary components of contracts in others, to correct retailer incentive distortions arising from the types of market imperfections or frictions that we have been discussing.

---

40 749 F. 3d 922 (1984).
41 118 S. Ct. 275 (1997).
42 G.F. Mathewson and R.A. Winter, 'An Economic Theory of Vertical Restraints,' (1984) 15(1) *Rand Journal of Economics*, 27.

We compare here the use of resale price maintenance versus territorial restrictions as instruments for correcting the incentive distortions leading towards too much price competition. Resale price maintenance involves setting a price floor at the profit-maximizing price, then lowering the wholesale price. Lowering the wholesale price leads to a higher retail margin, since the retail price is constrained, which increases the marginal profit from each consumer attracted through greater service. Service therefore increases, and the manufacturer can lower the wholesale price just enough to elicit the optimal level of service.

In the simplest use of territorial restraints, however, the manufacturer simply divides up the geographic market area (or divides up the set of customers in some other way) and 'sells' the right to each area, along with the right to a wholesale price equal to marginal cost, to an individual retailer. Providing there are no spillovers among the retailer's information or service provision, the incentive problem is internalized through this contract. The retailer captures the full costs and benefits of pricing and service decisions at the margin. A free-riding problem, in which there are spillovers, can in theory be neutralized with a territorial contract such as the one described if the wholesale price is actually below marginal cost, so that the purchase of the product is subsidized by the manufacturer, or with the addition of minimum quantity restrictions.[43] In the simpler explanations of bias arising from the difference between consumers on the product versus the interretailer margins, territorial restraints of this type work by eliminating the interretailer margin. This leaves the retailer focusing on the right margin: the product margin.

Territorial restraints can correct distortions in cases where RPM would not work. Specifically, if there are many dimensions of service, as is surely the case in reality, the use of RPM as a first-best instrument requires that the ratio of firm to market service elasticities be identical for each type of service. Once the optimal retail price is set, the single instrument of a wholesale price can elicit the first-best incentives across all types of service only if, by coincidence, this ratio is the same for all dimensions. Some cases in which RPM fails, such as *Illinois Corporate Travel v. American Airlines, Inc.*, can be interpreted as cases in which the ratio of service elasticities varies across dimensions of service. A territorial restraint is not compromised by multidimensionality of service

---

43 Ibid.

decisions, since the internalization of incentive effects through a residual claimancy contract does not depend on service being a single dimension.

Territorial restraints, however, suffer from many practical problems. It is simply impossible in many markets to divide the set of consumers, allocating them among retailers. The purchaser of a pair of skis does not have to submit her address to purchase at a particular retailer, nor would this be practical. Resale price maintenance would be feasible for this product; strict territorial division of the market would not.

Territorial restraints exist in many other forms, especially in the simple form of a guarantee that no other retailers will be allowed to locate within a specified distance, once a particular retailer is established. This form of restraint is explained in most cases as protection against the incentive of a manufacturer or franchiser to exploit the retailer's sunk investments in promoting the product (the 'hold-up' problem of extracting the returns from a retailer's sunk investment).

Mathewson and Winter criticize the asymmetric legal treatment of price and territorial restraints in the United States on the basis that the two contractual restraints can be substitute instruments to respond to the same set of incentive problems. But differential treatment is appropriate if RPM is more likely to have anticompetitive effects than exclusive territories. Whether this is so is open to debate. While RPM does have anticompetitive potential uses, so do exclusive territories. For example, the combination of RPM and exclusive territories reduces a manufacturer's incentive to cut wholesale price, since such a reduction will not result in a greater quantity sold, and thus may help support a cartel of manufacturers. On balance, however, it seems accepted that RPM is more likely to have anticompetitive effects than exclusive territories. Perhaps reflecting this, in Canada, as we discuss below, there are no important cases in which territorial restrictions have been struck down.

As we see, apart from the cartel candidate a class of principal-agent theories support the use of RPM. There is not a great deal of empirical evidence to differentiate across these explanations. Thomas Overstreet reviews empirical work during the fair trade era;[44] Thomas Gilligan

---

44 Overstreet, *Resale Price Maintenance.*

analyses a set of RPM cases from the 1960s, and 1970s;[45] Pauline Ippolito considers recent RPM litigation.[46] In another paper, Ippolito and Overstreet[47] examine the FTC's case against RPM by Corning Glass Works.[48] After a series of hearing and appeal decisions, Corning was prevented from using RPM. To understand this case, it is necessary to understand the categories of legal treatment of RPM. The American states were divided into three categories: (i) 'free-trade states,' where RPM was *per se* illegal, (ii) 'signer-only states,' where RPM was legal but only enforceable against dealers who had signed contracts with RPM provisions in them, and (iii) 'nonsigner states,' where all dealers were bound by RPM restrictions provided one dealer in the state had agreed to them. Corning used RPM essentially to prevent the sale of product from wholesalers in signer-only states to dealers who had not signed contracts with RPM provisions in them. Ippolito and Overstreet examine the *ex ante* and *ex post* evidence to see if this evidence can discriminate across the three competing hypotheses on RPM that we outline above: supplier cartel, dealer cartel, and agency motivations. The tests do not support the two cartel hypotheses but there is insufficient detail in the data to select from among the various agency candidates. Statements from company officials indicate that Corning relied on its dealers for non-price services associated with the sale of Corning's products. This suggests RPM played the role of altering the marketing mix to suppress price competition and promote non-price services.

The 1975 prohibition on Corning's use of RPM resulted in a decline in Corning's sales, but there was no significant decline in the sales of its rivals (and so no 'exogenous-to-the-industry' effect to account for Corning's declining sales). This result suggests an agency and not a cartel motivation for RPM. After 1975, the evidence is that Corning, denied the use of RPM to manage the price and non-price strategies of its dealers, increased its own advertising expenditures to promote non-price components of its marketing mix. The advertising expenditures of its rivals revealed no such adjustment. This observation is also

45 T. Gilligan, 'The Competitive Effects of Resale Price Maintenance,' (1986) 17(4) *Rand Journal of Economics* 544.
46 Ippolito, 'Resale Price Maintenance.'
47 P. Ippolito and T. Overstreet, 'Resale Price Maintenance: An Economic Assessment of the Federal Trade Commission's Case against the Corning Glass Works,' (1996) 39(1) *Journal of Law and Economics* 285.
48 FTC v. Corning Glass Works, 509 F. 2d 293 (7th Cir., 1975).

consistent with the use of RPM by Corning to manage its marketing instruments at the dealer level. It is inconsistent with a cartel explanation. Firms in a cartel freed from restricted price competition should reduce both their prices and advertising expenditures. Finally, stock market evidence reveals that the market 'expected Corning to lose value if required to drop its RPM policy ... This evidence is inconsistent with the anticompetitive dealer theories or the possibility that Corning made an error in continuing its RPM policy.'[49]

III. The Law of Resale Price Maintenance

As a legal matter, resale price maintenance involves the attempt by an upstream firm in a vertical distribution arrangement to affect the price at which a downstream firm resells its product.[50] In 1951, the Mac-Quarrie Committee recommended that resale price maintenance be prohibited in Canada.[51] The committee concluded that resale price maintenance, 'represents a real and undesirable restriction on competition by private agreement or "law" and its general tendency is to discourage economic efficiency.'[52] Following this recommendation, the *Combines Investigation Act* was amended to make resale price maintenance a criminal act.[53] The section provided that manufacturers should not 'directly or indirectly by agreement, threat, promise or any other means whatsoever' require or induce any other person to sell an article or commodity at a specified or minimum price or mark-up.[54] Refusals to deal as a consequence of a customer's refusal to engage in RPM were also made illegal.

As Skeoch observes, critics opposed to this development were of the view that banning resale price maintenance would lead to untrammelled 'loss-leading,' whereby products would be offered at prices below cost in order to attract customers to a store, where they will buy

---

49 Ippolito and Overstreet, 'Resale Price Maintenance,' at 332.
50 Note, however, that the definition of RPM is general enough to encompass non-vertical relationships, such as where a competitor attempts to influence the price at which another competitor has its downstream firms sell: see, for example, *R. v. Campbell* (1979), 51 C.P.R. (2d) 284.
51 *Report of the Committee to Study Combines Legislation* and *Interim Report on Resale Price Maintenance* (MacQuarrie Report) (Ottawa: Queen's Printer, 1951).
52 Ibid., at 71.
53 R.S.C. 1951, c. 314, s. 34(2).
54 Ibid.

other products as well.[55] When the Conservatives, who were initially opposed to criminalizing RPM,[56] took power, they amended the provision in 1960 to allow some defences against a charge of RPM. Specifically, the amendment permitted a refusal to deal where a customer was engaging in loss-leader selling, 'baiting and switching,' or misleading advertising, or where the downstream firm had provided inadequate services.[57]

Unlike many of the statutory provisions concerning competition policy at the time, the resale price maintenance provision had a significant impact on firms and markets. The Economic Council stated in 1969 that while the *Combines Investigation Act* had largely been ineffective, 'the banning of resale price maintenance has probably encouraged the entry into some sectors of price-cutting retailers.'[58] As Dunlop, McQueen, and Trebilcock point out, the comparative importance of RPM law was not particularly surprising, given the clarity of the provisions dealing with RPM and the absence of clarity concerning other practices such as mergers and monopolies.[59]

In 1975 the RPM section was amended to apply to those who grant credit through credit cards.[60] It also redefined the offence as 'attempt-[ing] to influence upward, or to discourage the reduction of, the price at which any other person engaged in business in Canada supplies or offers to supply or advertises a product within Canada.' A manufacturer's advertisement including price information was deemed to be an attempt to influence prices upward unless it was made clear that prices could differ from the advertised price.

However, the section also provided that the supplier could not enforce RPM through 'agreement, threat, promise, or any like means.' The Ontario court of Appeal held that 'any like means' implied that an advertisement by a manufacturer for a product at a specific, inflexible

---

55 See, L.A. Skeoch, ed., *Restrictive Trade Practices in Canada* (Toronto: McClelland and Stewart, 1966).

56 F. Mathewson and R. Winter, 'The Law and Economics of Vertical Restraints,' in F. Mathewson, M. Trebilcock, and M. Walker, eds., *The Law and Economics of Competition Policy* (Vancouver: Fraser Institute, 1990), 109 at 116.

57 S.C. 1960, c. 45, s. 14.

58 Economic Council of Canada, *Interim Report on Competition Policy* (Ottawa: Queen's Printer, 1969), at 64.

59 B. Dunlop, D. McQueen, and M. Trebilcock, *Canadian Competition Policy: A Legal and Economic Analysis* (Toronto: Canada Law Book, 1987), at 267.

60 S.C. 1974–75–76, c. 76, s. 18.

retail price was not illegal; this method of RPM did not rely on means like an 'agreement,' 'threat,' or 'promise.'[61]

The present prohibition of RPM is found in section 61 of the *Competition Act*. Its main charging section provides:

61(1) No person who is engaged in the business of producing or supplying a product, or who extends credit by way of credit cards or is otherwise engaged in a business that relates to credit cards, or who has the exclusive rights and privileges conferred by a patent, trademark, copyright or registered industrial design shall, directly or indirectly,

(a) by agreement, threat, promise or any like means, attempt to influence upward, or to discourage the reduction of, the price at which any other person engaged in business in Canada supplies or offers to supply or advertises a product within Canada; or

(b) refuse to supply a product to or otherwise discriminate against any other person engaged in business in Canada because of the low pricing policy of that person.

A refusal to deal related to RPM is excused in the following circumstances: where the customer has used the products as part of a 'bait and switch' scheme; where the customer has used the products in 'loss-leader' sales; where the customer has engaged in misleading advertising; and where the customer has provided inadequate services.[62]

Enforcement activity relating to RPM has been fairly vigorous. During the period 1994–9, VanDuzer and Paquet report that the bureau received 461 complaints relating to RPM. Of these, only 3 were resolved through formal enforcement proceedings, but another 77 were resolved through alternative means.[63]

A. To Whom Does Section 61 Apply?

Aside from its specific reference to credit card markets and patent and copyright holders, the provision applies to persons who are engaged in

---

61 *R. v. Moffat* (1980), 30 O.R. (2d) 129 (C.A.).

62 See s. 61(10).

63 A. VanDuzer and G. Paquet, *Anticompetitive Pricing Practices and the Competition Act: Theory, Law and Practice* (Ottawa: Competition Bureau, 1999), at 56.

the business of producing or supplying a product, which includes both goods and services.[64] The 'engaged in the business' restriction applies both to upstream firms attempting to set price and downstream firms facing resale price restrictions. This limitation may be important, as *R. v. Camrost Group Ltd.*[65] demonstrates. In that case, a condominium developer attempted to influence upward the resale price of condominiums it had earlier sold. The developer was convicted with respect to attempts to influence earlier purchasers who were known real estate developers but acquitted with respect to individual purchasers who were not normally engaged in the real estate business.

B. Attempts to Influence Prices Upward

The key action under section 61 is to attempt to influence prices upward by agreement, threat, promise, or any like means. Courts have taken varying approaches to this requirement, perhaps reflecting judicial attitudes about the wisdom of criminalizing RPM.[66]

Strict interpretations of 'attempt to influence [price] upward' are found in several cases. *R. v. Cluett, Peabody*[67] involved, *inter alia*, a supplier of shirts (Cluett, Peabody's Arrow division) asking retailers not to resell Arrow shirts to a fellow retailer who had been selling shirts below the supplier's suggested retail price. While the court convicted Cluett, Peabody on two other counts of RPM, it acquitted on the described count on two grounds. First, the court held that the essence of Arrow's action was not to influence prices, but rather to attempt to prevent retailers from reselling to another particular retailer at *any* price. Second, the court held that while the RPM provision could involve the 'attempt' provisions of the Criminal Code, the court could not accept that 'an attempt to agree to attempt to affect prices' was an offence known to law.[68]

Both of these grounds limit the importance of the RPM provision. The court took a narrow view of what influencing prices is, dismissing

---

64   See *Competition Act*, s. 2.
65   Ont. Dist. Ct., 10 May 1985 (unreported), as cited in Davies, Ward, and Beck, *Competition Law of Canada* (Toronto: Juris Publishing, 1998), at para. 4.06(2).
66   Davies, Ward, and Beck, *Competition Law*, at para. 4.06(2).
67   (1982), 64 C.P.R. (2d) 30 (Ont. Co. Ct.).
68   Ibid., at 36.

the plausible contention that attempting to cut off a discounter was in essence an attempt to influence prices. Moreover, it took a narrow view of what 'attempt' means in this context. It would have been reasonable to conclude that attempting to prevent a discounter from acquiring inventory was an attempt to influence prices upward, without breaking it down into an attempt to agree to attempt to influence prices. Of course, any supplier asking a retailer to stop reselling to a discounter risks the agreement of the retailer, perhaps giving rise to an unlawful attempt even under the court's definition in *Cluett, Peabody.*

Another narrow view of what is required to be convicted of improperly attempting to influence prices upward is found in *R. v. Philips Electronics.*[69] In that case, Philips had advertised its products at set retail prices. Pursuant to section 61(4),[70] the court found that Philips had indeed attempted to influence the retail price of its products upward. However, the court acquitted on the basis of the wording 'any like means' in section 61. The majority held that it was satisfied that 'the impugned advertisements standing by themselves are in no way similar to an agreement, threat or promise and accordingly are not included within the purview of the words "any like means."'[71] Section 61, however, is clearly aimed at preventing upstream firms from influencing downstream prices, which advertising at fixed prices does (indeed, s. 61(4) deems that it does). Excluding advertisements at fixed prices from its purview is empty formalism, likely reflecting judicial antipathy to the policy expressed in section 61.

Curiously, earlier versions of section 61 referred to any attempt to influence price upwards by 'agreement, threat or promise or any other means whatsoever,' thus avoiding the limitation found by the Ontario Court of Appeal because of the words 'any like means.' It is also interesting to note that previous versions of section 61 made no reference to advertising, although case law acknowledged that an attempt to influ-

---

69 (1980), 30 C.P.R. (2d) 129 (Ont. C.A.), aff'd [1981] 2 S.C.R. 264.

70 S. 61(4) provides: '(4) For the purposes of this section, the publication by a supplier of a product, other than a retailer, of an advertisement that mentions a resale price for the product is an attempt to influence upward the selling price of any person into whose hands the product comes for resale unless the price is so expressed as to make it clear to any person to whose attention the advertisement comes that the product may be sold at a lower price.'

71 *Philips Electronics, supra* (1980), 30 C.P.R. (2d) at 134.

ence the advertised price amounted to an attempt to influence price.[72] Thus, the decision in *Philips Electronics* brings about the peculiar result that the earlier provision, which did not define advertised prices as attempts to influence prices upward, *did* outlaw advertising such as that found in *Philips*, while the revised statute, which directly defines the advertisement of set prices as an attempt to influence prices upward, *fails* to outlaw such advertising.[73]

Other decisions reflect a more activist attitude with respect to finding an attempt to influence prices. In *R. v. Kito Canada Ltd.*,[74] Kito indicated to a retailer that it would cease supplying it with carpet sweepers unless the retailer raised the retail price from $15.99 to $19.99. The retailer refused to raise price, but Kito continued to supply it. The court held that the threat alone constituted the illegal attempt to influence price, even if it was never acted upon.

R. v. Shell Canada Products Ltd.[75] involved comments by the supplier to a retailer that the retailer's low prices were 'irresponsible' and that the retailer should 'get the price back up.' The court held that in a context where the retailer was dependent on the supplier in an easily terminable arrangement, such comments amounted to a threat. Shell was convicted accordingly.

As this sample of cases suggests, courts vary unpredictably in their approach to determining whether there has been an attempt to influence prices upward.

C. Refusal to Supply

Courts have also varied in setting out the required causal nexus between the termination of supply and the low pricing polices of a retailer. Some courts have taken the view that low pricing must be the *only* cause of the refusal to supply for there to be an offence under section 61(1)(b).[76] Others have held that low pricing must be a proximate cause of the refusal to supply, but it need not be the only proximate

---

72 *R. v. Moffats*, [1957] O.R. 93 (C.A.).
73 S. 61(4) explicitly permits advertising of 'suggested' prices, so long as it is made clear that the actual downstream prices may vary.
74 (1975), 22 C.P.R. (2d) 275 (Man. Q.B.).
75 (1989), 24 C.P.R. (3d) 501 (Man. Q.B.).
76 *R. v. Griffith Saddlery & Leather Ltd.* (1986), 14 C.P.R. (3d) 389 (Ont. Prov. Ct. (Crim. Div.)).

cause.[77] If a law against RPM is to have any teeth, for better or for worse, the former position is undesirable. It will often be easy for an accused to plausibly suggest a reason for termination other than low prices.

D. Defences

As mentioned, there are four defences to a refusal to supply on the basis of RPM set out in section 61(10): the 'bait-and-switch' defence; the misleading advertising defence; the loss-leader defence; and the inadequate services defence.

1. The Misleading Advertising and Bait-and-Switch Defences
The misleading advertising and bait-and-switch defences involve illegal practices found elsewhere in the *Competition Act*. These defences serve to supplement public enforcement of the illegal marketing rules. Private parties can sanction the practices by refusing to deal with a firm engaged in such activities.

2. The Loss-Leader Defence
It is puzzling why the law treats manufacturers' complaints about loss-leader selling differently from resale price maintenance in general. Whether it is preventing loss-leadering, or simply resale price maintenance, the upstream firm attempts to prevent lower prices even though, all things being equal, the lower the price at which the downstream firm sells, the greater the quantity sold by the upstream firm at a given wholesale price. Other than an implicit concern about inadequate service, it is difficult to see why loss-leadering is treated differently from RPM in general.

A leading case on the loss-leader defence is *R. v. Philips Appliances Ltd.*[78] That case involved the sale by a large retailer, Simpson-Sears, of Philips' electric shavers. Philips refused to deal to Simpson-Sears in response to the retailer's price cutting and was accused of illegal price maintenance. Philips claimed the loss-leader defence. The court held that only where prices fall below wholesale price, that is, below the

---

77 *R. v. Royal LePage Real Estate Services Ltd.*, 24 October 1994 (unpublished), cited in Davies, Ward, and Beck, *Competition Law of Canada*, para. 4.06(4).
78 [1969] 1 O.R. 386 (C.A.).

retailer's purchase price, may the accused invoke the loss-leader defence. Given that prices were above wholesale prices, the loss-leader defence failed. The case stands for the proposition that the loss-leader defence allows RPM at the level of wholesale prices.[79]

The loss-leader defence was successful in *R. v. William Coutts Co. Ltd.*[80] In that case, a manufacturer of greeting cards refused to sell to a store that was reselling greeting cards at low prices. Specifically, the store offered a second card at a price of one cent for each card bought. The store made losses on these sales and the court found that it had been loss-leadering such that the refusal to deal was lawful. The court held:

> I accept the testimony of William G. Kay, the vice-president of sales that it was the policy of the accused company to confine the sales of its cards as much as possible to outlets which provided a satisfactory display and sold other products of a class which would tend to maintain and present and atmosphere of quality to its cards. Stores which engaged extensively in discount sales would reduce the excellence of the company's product. He put it that the company was more concerned with quality presentation of the cards by its retailers than the price at which they were sold. It is clear that a dealer's business may be seriously affected by the retailers of its products using the name as a loss-leader. Such practice may have the effect of causing other retailers to withdraw from the sale of such product and if carried on extensively may tend to eliminate competition and thus defeat one of the principal purposes of such Act.[81]

3. The Inadequate Services Defence

The inadequate services defence potentially responds to efficiency theories of RPM. Some commentary suggests that RPM is designed to overcome excessive price competition among retailers in the provision of a product.[82] If the legal prohibition of RPM indeed gives rise to excessive price competition and implies that certain retailers offer inadequate services in their sales efforts, then the *Competition Act* gives some recourse to the upstream firm by permitting it to refuse to deal to

---

79 F. Mathewson and R. Winter, 'The Law and Economics of Resale Price Maintenance,' (1998) 13 *Rev. Ind. Org.* 57 at 61.

80 [1968] 1 O.R. 549 (C.A.).

81 Ibid., at 554–5.

82 Mathewson and Winter, 'Law and Economics of Resale Price Maintenance.'

the retailer providing services at a level below that which a reasonable buyer would expect.

Case law has provided some further clarification of the inadequate services defence. The defence was not given significant weight in *R. v. H.D. Lee of Canada.*[83] In that case, various retailers in Regina, Saskatchewan, and Winnipeg, Manitoba, complained about discounting retailers in each city.[84] Lee eventually induced the discounters in Winnipeg to sell at Lee's suggested prices and discontinued supply to the discounter in Regina that refused to comply. Lee was accused and subsequently convicted of illegal RPM.

Lee claimed in its defence that the discounting retailer to which it discontinued supply had been providing inadequate services in selling the jeans. Lee said that it would expect Lee jeans to have a 'special location in the store; special display with mannequins, individual hangers etc., whereas Army and Navy simply stacked up the jeans on the counter where the customer had to select his size and take it to the cashier.'[85] Such a complaint resonates with the efficiency theory of RPM: RPM was designed to limit price competition and provide incentives for service provision.

The court, however, rejected the inadequate services defence. First, it noted that the French-language version of the services defence referred to post-sales service, rather than the pre-sales service referred to in the case (and generally considered important for RPM). Second, it noted that there had been no complaints about inadequate services from customers. The test, it said, was whether *consumers* were satisfied with the amount of service provided, not whether the *supplier* was satisfied. The emphasis on consumers' views, which clearly finds a basis in the *Competition Act*, is misguided from an economic perspective. Expecting consumers to complain about inadequate services, such as the absence of mannequins, is ill-conceived. Even if consumers did care about the level of services, they would be unlikely to take the time to complain. Any benefits they would receive personally would almost certainly fail to compensate for the time and effort required to make a complaint.

---

83 (1980), 57 C.P.R. 186 (Que. Ct. Sessions of the Peace (Montreal District).

84 A colourful detail was that a non-discounting retailer, the main floor of a Hudson's Bay Company store in Winnipeg, complained to Lee about discounted prices at the Bay's own discount basement retailer.

85 *Lee, supra* (1980), 57 C.P.R. at 198. Army and Navy was the retailer in Regina refused supply because of its discounting.

This is particularly true given that those who would prefer the services that reduce the cost of shopping are likely to have a higher opportunity cost of time.[86] Moreover, if the economic theory about inadequate services is correct, retailers generally will offer inadequate services in the absence of RPM, thus consumers may not expect anything but inadequate services and hence would be even more unlikely to complain.

Third, in rejecting the services defence, the court also noted that Lee never complained to the discounting retailer in question about services. Evidence about the extensive contact between Lee and the retailer never referred to service, but rather focused exclusively on price.[87] If inadequate service provision was a concern of Lee, it is indeed peculiar that they never mentioned the problem in their conversations and correspondence with the retailer.

The implications of this case for the services defence are not entirely clear, although on balance it does not appear that it will be generously applied. The court generally took a sceptical attitude towards the defence, suggesting a more limited role for it. On the other hand, the failure of Lee to mention inadequate servicing to the retailer in question casts doubt on this explanation of RPM in the instant case. Perhaps the court's scepticism should be taken to be directed only at the defence on the present facts, rather than evincing a more general unwillingness to consider seriously the service defence.[88]

E. Case Law and the Theories of RPM

As exemplified by the *H.D. Lee* case, the case law in Canada generally fails to confirm any one theory of RPM. This is not too surprising,

---

86 See Mathewson and Winter, 'Law and Economics of Resale Price Maintenance.'

87 *Lee, supra* (1980), 57 C.P.R. at 198.

88 E. Iacobucci, 'The Case for Prohibiting Resale Price Maintenance,' (1995) 19 *World Competition* 71 at 100, notes that another jeans manufacturer, Levi Strauss, pleaded guilty to RPM during almost the same period as that involved in the *Lee* case, which the court in the Levi's case described as a period when jeans were in short supply, perhaps suggesting the existence of market power: *R. v. Levi Strauss of Canada* (1979), 45 C.P.R. 215 at 217. These facts are at least not inconsistent with the theory that RPM served as a facilitating device in a manufacturers' cartel. Moreover, Lee responded in enforcing RPM to complaints from other retailers about price-cutters, not inadequate service providers, which is at least not inconsistent with a retailers' cartel. Of course, observing low prices at rival retailers may be easier than proving inadequate service.

given that proving the motive or effect of RPM is unnecessary under section 61.

Many of the cases involve complaints by retailers about undercutting by other retailers.[89] In *Kralinator*, for example, Kralinator, a supplier of various automobile supplies, such as oil filters, entered into agreements with its customers concerning the price schedule for reselling the products. One dealer agreed to the price schedule, but then promptly ignored it. In response to complaints, Kralinator refused to continue supplying the dealer and a prosecution for RPM followed. As the court observed, Kralinator was 'plainly concerned with price stability.'[90] While this is indeed clear, it is more difficult to answer why the company was so concerned. There was no suggestion of inadequate servicing, nor is it apparent that cartelizing was the motive, although the record is not extensive on these matters.

Manufacturers have on occasion referred to concern about the prestige of their products. Low prices, they argue, reflect badly on the product, undermining its brand image. In *R. v. Moffats Ltd.*,[91] for example, a manufacturer of stoves, refrigerators, and televisions stated that it attempted to influence retail prices upward 'if for no other reason than prestige.'[92] Such an attitude is difficult to explain from a theoretical perspective. Price may have some relationship to quality in special circumstances, such as where some fraction of customers is aware of the product's quality, while the rest are not.[93] While there may be other circumstances in which price can act as a signal of quality,[94] theory suggests that such circumstances will be rare. Moreover, if protecting image through higher prices were important, why would the manufacturer not simply charge a higher wholesale price? However, there is no

---

89 See, e.g., *Lee, supra*, note 83; *R. v. Kralinator Filters Ltd.* (1962), 41 C.P.R. 201 (Man. Q.B.).

90 *Kralinator, supra* (1962), 41 C.P.R. at 269.

91 [1957] O.R. 93 (C.A.).

92 *Moffats, supra*, [1957] O.R. at 104.

93 If the margins on a higher quality product are sufficiently high, and the proportion of informed consumers is high enough, a monopolist may produce a high-quality product and set a high price for it. Because of the informed customers, it would not be profitable for a low-quality producer to set a high price, thus price acts as a signal of quality. See Tirole, *Theory of Industrial Organization*, at 107–8.

94 J. Stiglitz, 'The Causes and Consequences of the Dependence of Quality on Price,' (1987) 25 *Journal of Economic Literature* 1.

disputing that manufacturers do on occasion claim defence of a product's image as a motivation for RPM.[95]

William Coutts appeared to rely on a relationship between prestige, loss-leadering, and inadequate services. This case, as set out above, involved the loss-leader defence with respect to the sale of greeting cards. The court held that the refusal to deal was justified on the basis of the retailer's loss-leadering, which would 'reduce the excellence of the company's product.'[96] The case raises questions about why the loss-leader defence exists as an independent defence. First, why would a manufacturer object to a retailer setting very low prices for its product? For a given wholesale price, this will increase sales, thereby increasing profits for the manufacturer. Second, even if the manufacturer did object, why would antitrust law give weight to the objection?

One response is that if a retailer is loss-leadering, its service provision will be inadequate. As the passage cited from *William Coutts* demonstrates, a court may relate very low prices with inadequate services and conclude that the retailer is harming the product's image, and therefore that the manufacturer's refusal to deal was justified. There are two reasons why this justification of the loss-leader defence is unconvincing. First, the inadequate services defence should presumably serve to address inadequate services. Second, if the law accepts that there is a correlation between loss-leader pricing and inadequate services, why does it not accept that low prices, but prices above wholesale prices, are correlated with inadequate services? If the loss-leader defence is justified on the basis of a correlation between price and service, the RPM provision generally is undermined.

Another justification for the loss-leader defence is that it protects the manufacturer's concern about the prestige signalled by price. While in general an upstream firm can assure higher retail prices by setting higher wholesale prices, if the retailer engages in loss-leadering, the manufacturer may not be able to protect its prestige through high retail prices. As set out above, however, in only a subset of circumstances will price reflect quality.

In *William Coutts*, the court also expressed disapproval about loss-leadering because it may cause other retailers to withdraw from the provision of the product. Even if retailers did withdraw, however, pre-

---

95 See, e.g., *William Coutts, supra*, note 80.
96 Ibid., at 554–5.

suming a competitive retailing market, the manufacturer should sell more products, given the low price of the loss-leading retailer. To the extent that the loss-leading retailer's sales fail to compensate for the discontinued retailers' sales, this must be because there are customers who would not travel to the discounting retailer. But such a scenario suggests that other retailers would not discontinue supplying the product in the first place, notwithstanding the loss-leading retailer. In light of these deficiencies, the economic basis for the loss-leader defence to otherwise illegal RPM is not entirely clear. While cases such as *Coutts* seem to imply the correlation of low prices and inadequate service, accepting this argument suggests revisiting the illegal status of RPM generally.

RPM as a device facilitating cartelization appears at least possibly relevant to various cases, including two involving the sale of gasoline, which industry has been the subject of several competition investigations. In *R. v. Sunoco*,[97] Sunoco and a retailer entered into an agreement whereby the dealer would buy its gas requirements from Sunoco and Sunoco would supply the gasoline at a certain price. The evidence was that Sunoco also agreed to provide price support payments to the retailer, but only if the retailer did not initiate price cuts. If nearby gas stations, Esso and Petro-Canada outlets, lowered their prices, Sunoco would allow the retailer to lower its price to match them. If an 'unbranded' outlet, Pioneer, lowered prices, however, price support payments would be withheld if the Sunoco retailer lowered its prices to match. The evidence was that Sunoco did not believe Pioneer, as an unbranded station, to be in competition with Sunoco retailers. Sunoco was convicted for entering into an agreement in an attempt to influence prices upward.

While there is no evidence about the competitive situation among suppliers of gasoline, since the evidence was not relevant to the investigation under the RPM provision, it is clear that the arrangement in question could serve to preserve peace among upstream cartelists. The arrangement delegated to the dealer the power only to match lower prices, not to initiate price cuts, and further made it profitable for the dealer to lower price in response to others' price cuts, given that the profits it earned largely derived from the price support payments. If other upstream suppliers enforced such policies as well, the arrange-

---

97 (1986), 11 C.P.R. (3d) 557 (Ont. Dist. Ct.).

ments could serve to stabilize an upstream cartel. Downstream price cuts would be discouraged, given that retailers could not initiate price cuts, thus eroding the benefits of cheating by the upstream firm in the form of lowering price to the downstream retailer since final prices would not decrease and therefore quantity would not increase.[98] Moreover, allowing the retailer to match lower prices by its competitors without suffering a profit loss would diminish the incentive of other upstream firms to influence their retailers to lower prices. They would know that the Sunoco dealer would at least match the lower price, undermining the benefits of a price cut. As the court inferred, these provisions appeared to be designed to 'avoid a price war.'[99]

A similar approach was adopted by another upstream gasoline firm, Shell, in a different case.[100] Shell had been selling gasoline on consignment, which allowed it to set downstream prices. It then changed its consignment policy and allowed its retailers to set price. But when one retailer, which was located slightly off the well-travelled roads and typically attracted customers because of its car wash, began to set low prices in order to attract business on a rainy day, it was very shortly thereafter approached by Shell. Shell indicated that the retailer was pricing 'irresponsibly' and that it should raise its prices. Again, this situation is not inconsistent with a cartel member seeking to preserve peace among the upstream oligopolists. At the very least, it is difficult to tell what service explanations could apply in either gasoline case.

While there are hints with respect to motivation in some cases, in general it is unclear what motivates RPM in Canada. This is due in no small part to the virtually *per se* illegal status of RPM. Unless one of the defences is engaged, the authorities need only show the existence of RPM to support a conviction; its explanation is unnecessary.

1. Price Ceilings

While the discussion thus far, and much of the jurisprudence, has concerned upstream manufacturers setting minimum downstream prices, RPM may also involve the setting of maximum prices downstream.

---

98 The retail outlets had exclusive arrangements with the upstream suppliers, thus a price cut by upstream firms would not increase quantity by displacing their rivals' sales to the retailer in question. The only way to increase quantity sold would be to lower retail price.

99 *Sunoco, supra* (1986), 11 C.P.R. (3d) at 566.

100 *R. v. Shell, supra,* note 75.

Section 61 refers only to attempts to influence prices upward, not downward, so price ceilings are exempt unless they could be seen as attempting to influence price upward. If, for some reason, setting a maximum price effectively set a minimum price, section 61 would presumably apply.

A recent case involving maximum RPM, *R. v. Nova Scotia Pharmaceutical Society*,[101] was tried under the conspiracy provision, section 45. The case involved an agreement between the two principal health insurers in Nova Scotia and an association of pharmacists to set maximum dispensing fees with respect to customers on whose behalf the insurers paid the fees directly. In a curious chain of reasoning, the court found that the agreement did lessen competition substantially, but that the parties were not aware that it did, and thus did not have the requisite *mens rea* to support a conviction. In effect, the court's reasons indicated that it thought it knew more about market circumstances than did the parties.

On the contrary, it is unlikely that the insurers, who in effect were the customers' agents in this context, would have had any incentive to lessen competition, nor was the agreement likely to have done so. Mathewson and Winter[102] suggest that the maximum prices were imposed in order to keep prices low, thereby discouraging socially inefficient entry into the pharmaceutical market. On this view, the price ceilings were likely efficient.

Whatever the efficiency characteristics of the agreement, the case indicates that maximum RPM may raise concerns under competition law, perhaps pursuant to the conspiracy provision.

IV. Market Restriction

A type of vertical restraint with generally similar economic effects as resale price maintenance is market restriction. Practices that may be characterized as market restriction are regulated by section 77 of the *Competition Act*. Market restriction, or 'exclusive territories,' refers to the distribution practice whereby a supplier orders its dealers to sell only to certain customers or in a restricted geographic market. To enforce such restrictions, a supplier may impose penalties on those

---

101 (1993), 49 C.P.R. (3d) 289 (N.S.S.C.).
102 'Law and Economics of Resale Price Maintenance.'

dealers or distributors who violate this condition, or, equally, it may offer rewards to dealers who adhere to exclusivity. Market restriction arrangements are found in a variety of business undertakings in Canada, including franchising contracts, non-competition covenants, and distributorship and agency agreements. There have been no reported cases under the market restriction provisions; the statutory framework is reviewed below.

A. *Definition of Market Restriction Pursuant to section 77(1) of the Act*

Section 77(1) defines market restriction, a civilly reviewable practice, as '... any practice whereby a supplier of a product, as a condition of supplying the product to a customer, requires that customer to supply any product only in a defined market, or exacts a penalty of any kind from the customer if he supplies any product outside a defined market.'

It is clear from this definition that three elements must be satisfied in order for market restriction to occur. First of all, the arrangement must be part of a 'practice' of customer and market restrictions. Second, the definition contemplates a supplier imposing a requirement upon a customer. Third, either a supplier must require a customer to resell the product only in a defined market as a condition of supplying the product to the customer or the supplier must exact a penalty from a customer for supplying any product outside a defined market.

1. *Practice of Market Restriction*
The first step in the market restriction analysis is determining whether the supplier is engaged in a practice of customer and market restrictions. While there is no jurisprudence to give content to the meaning of the term 'practice' in relation to market restriction,[103] it seems likely that it would be found to have a similar meaning as the word is employed in the context of the Act's exclusive dealing and tied selling provisions.

---

103 The only reported inquiry under the market restriction provisions was commenced in August 1979 after the director received complaints alleging that a supplier of telephone answering systems was engaged in market restriction and exclusive dealing. However, the inquiry was discontinued because the evidence indicated that the incidents at issue were isolated occurrences and did not constitute a practice. See Director of Investigation and Research, *Annual Report* (Ottawa: Consumer and Corporate Affairs, 1980), at 31.

This said, it seems likely that 'practice' encompasses repetition of conduct or conduct that endures for a continuous period of time.[104] Isolated instances of market restriction would likely be excluded from successful attack before the Competition Tribunal. As well, different individual anticompetitive acts taken together may constitute a practice.[105]

It should also be noted that because 'practice' in the Act's definition of market restriction is expressed in terms of a supplier's dealings with a customer, it is not necessary that a supplier have a policy of imposing a market restriction upon all or most customers. Rather, a supplier's relations with a single customer may be sufficient to constitute a practice.[106]

2. Focus on Supplier Imposing Market Restriction

A second requirement of the market restriction definition set out in section 77(1) of the Act is that it must be the *supplier* who imposes the customer or market restriction on a distributor. This definition would likely exclude a commercial situation whereby a *customer* demands that a supplier enter into a market restriction arrangement. The tribunal should, therefore, when reviewing a supplier-customer agreement that may contain a market restriction clause, consider the source of the impetus for the requirement and not confine its attention to the mere fact that such a requirement exists.[107]

Consideration of their origins may allow efficiency considerations to influence the legal treatment of exclusive territories. Exclusive territories, as explained above, may respond to retailers competing on price, as opposed to service, excessively (as compared to the manufacturer's preferences, and as compared to the social optimum) in order to attract customers at the interretailer margin. That is, sales services, which tend to be more important to the inframarginal customers, are underprovided by retailers competing with one another. Such a bias to price competition may lead to complaints by a retailer about another price-cutting, service-cutting retailer selling the same brand, which may in turn lead to the imposition of an exclusive territory. Following such a sequence of events, it may be found that the requirement that the sup-

---

104 D.S. Affleck and K.W. McCracken, *Canadian Competition Law* (Scarborough, Ont.: Carswell, 1992) (looseleaf), at 17–2.
105 See *Canada (Director of Investigation and Research) v. NutraSweet Co.* (1990), 32 C.P.R. (3d) 1 at 35.
106 Affleck and McCracken, *Canadian Competition Law*, at 17-2.
107 Ibid.

plier must impose the market restriction is not met. If so, this would indirectly allow efficiency motivations to sanitize exclusive territories in some circumstances. As the cases on resale price maintenance discussed above indicate, it is often the case that manufacturers attempt to implement RPM in response to complaints by retailers about rival, discounting retailers.

3. The Form of Conduct that Qualifies as a Market Restriction

The third requirement of the market restriction definition pertains to the type of conduct that qualifies as a market restriction. Section 77(1) specifies that a market restriction must take one of two forms. In the first a supplier requires a customer to resell the product only in a defined market as a condition of supplying the product to the customer. It has been suggested that the tribunal's interpretation of section 77(1)(a) in the context of exclusive dealing (i.e., that a supplier must actually refuse or threaten to refuse to supply the product unless the buyer agrees to supply in a defined market) will apply here as well, given the similarity in wording of the two provisions.[108]

The second instance of market restriction defined in section 77(1) occurs when a supplier exacts a penalty from a customer for supplying any product outside a defined market. It is unclear whether this penalty requirement will be read more narrowly than the broadly interpreted inducement requirement of exclusive dealing set out in section 77(1)(b). As observed by one legal writer, '[i]t makes little sense to allow the tribunal to interfere with negative inducements to restrict a market, such as penalties, but to exclude positive market restriction inducements, such as bonuses, from the Tribunal's reach if the net effect of both is to cause an undesirable lessening of competition.'[109] Put another way, a contractual framework that involves a penalty for not adhering to an exclusive territory can, for all practical purposes, be characterized equally as a framework that involves a bonus for adhering to an exclusive territory.

B. Exclusionary Effects and Substantial Lessening of Competition

Where a practice of market restriction is established, the analysis proceeds to section 77(3) of the Act, which sets out the following test:

---

108 C.J.M. Flavell and C.J. Kent, *The Canadian Competition Law Handbook* (Scarborough, Ont.: Carswell, 1997), at 71.
109 Ibid.

Where, on application by the Commissioner, the Tribunal finds that market restriction, because it is engaged in by a major supplier of a product or because it is widespread in relation to a product, is likely to substantially lessen competition in relation to the product, the Tribunal may make an order directed to all or any of the suppliers against whom an order is sought prohibiting them from continuing to engage in market restriction and containing any other requirement that, in its opinion, is necessary to restore or stimulate competition in relation to the product.

Therefore, in order for the tribunal to issue a remedial order in respect of market restriction, it must find that because market restriction is engaged in by a major supplier of a product or is widespread in relation to a product, it is likely to lessen competition substantially in relation to the product.

1. Major Supplier
The tribunal has not considered the meaning of 'major supplier' or 'widespread' in the context of market restriction. Nevertheless, it is helpful to consider how these terms have been interpreted in respect of other vertical restraints pursuant to section 77(2). As noted in our analysis of the *Competition Act's* exclusive dealing and tied selling provisions,[110] the term major supplier has been interpreted as '... one whose actions are taken to have an appreciable or significant impact on the markets where it sells.'[111] Similarly, a finding of market power on the part of the supplier has been deemed sufficient by the tribunal for the supplier to be a 'major supplier.' Given that it is difficult to imagine anticompetitive effects from exclusive territories in the absence of market power, this definition of 'major supplier' is sensible. Furthermore, a practice engaged in with 'virtually all' customers has been considered widespread.[112]

While the section 77(2) jurisprudence provides some guidance as to how section 77(3) may be interpreted, it is important to recognize that there are slight differences between the wording of these sections. The tribunal must find that market restriction is engaged in by a major sup-

---

110 See Chapter 7 dealing with (exclusionary; interbrand) vertical restraints.
111 *Canada (Director of Investigation and Research) v. Bombardier Ltd.* (1980), 53 C.P.R. (2d) 47 at 55.
112 *Nutrasweet, supra* (1990), 32 C.P.R. (3d) at 56.

plier of a product or is widespread in relation to a *product*, whereas, for exclusive dealing or tied selling, the activity must be engaged in by a major supplier of a product or be widespread *in a market*. It is unclear whether this difference in wording will lead to material differences in the application of sections 77(2) and (3).[113] It could make a difference, for example, if market restrictions are not widespread in the particular geographic market, but are in other geographic markets for the product in question. The practice may be considered widespread with respect to the 'product,' but not in any 'market,' which would be defined along both product and geographic dimensions. Such a distinction would make little economic sense. A lessening of competition would only occur in a market, thus finding a practice widespread because of its occurrence in other geographic markets would not be related to the ultimate inquiry: whether competition in a market is threatened by market restriction. In our view, using the market as a reference point in determining whether a practice is 'widespread,' as does the law on tied selling and exclusive dealing, is appropriate with respect to market restriction as well.

It is not required that a supplier have individual market power in order to be caught by either section 77(2) or (3), as long as the conduct in question is widespread, either in relation to a product or in a market.[114] This is a questionable approach. As noted with respect to our consideration of 'major supplier,' it is unclear how any anticompetitive effect could result from market restriction in the absence of market power. If, for example, exclusive territories are used, perhaps in conjunction with other vertical restraints such as RPM, to facilitate cartels, it must be that there is a market structure that would allow cartelization. This implies a non-trivial degree of market power for the firms involved.[115] If the market restriction is widespread in a market with many competing firms, it is not clear how anticompetitive effects could result.

2. *Substantial Lessening of Competition*
The final element to be proven before the tribunal may issue an order in respect of a market restriction is that the practice engaged in is likely

---

113 Flavell and Kent, *Canadian Competition Law Handbook*, at 71.
114 Ibid., at 72.
115 See Chapter 3 on collusion.

substantially to lessen competition in relation to a product. The meaning of the phrase 'substantiall, lessen competition' is difficult to ascertain, since it has not been interpreted in relation to market restriction. In the context of exclusive dealing, the tribunal held that the test for 'substantially lessening competition' involves a determination of whether the practice in question enhances or preserves the supplier's market power and the degree to which such conduct creates barriers to entry in the market and industry.

One of the keys in determining whether such a practice warrants intervention by the tribunal is the market position of the supplier engaging in it. For example, if the supplier were a monopoly or a dominant firm, it is likely that a market restriction would exert a substantial impact on the market.[116] This is not to say that the market restriction is likely to lessen competition, given that monopoly power exists in the upstream market with or without market restriction, but some market power upstream is likely a *necessary but not sufficient* condition for a substantial lessening of competition. If the market restriction exists because of efficient distribution concerns, there should be no finding of a lessening of competition, notwithstanding the existence of upstream market power: the market restriction may have no effect on competition, except to ensure that there is more competition among retailers of different brands in providing sales service. Where a number of competing suppliers are present, on the other hand, it is difficult to conceive how a market restriction arrangement could substantially lessen competition. Widespread market restriction in these circumstances almost certainly reflects its efficiency as a means of distribution.

As long as there is a reasonable degree of competition between suppliers, even if all the suppliers are relatively large and employ market restriction as a distribution practice, the tribunal ought to hold that there is sufficient competition to protect consumers and thus not impose an order under section 77(3).[117]

---

116 Dunlop, McQueen, and Trebilcock, *Canadian Competition Policy*, at 277.

117 Ibid. The authors raise an interesting issue with respect to whether s. 77 could be used to promote intrabrand competition in cases where a firm, that holds a monopoly or a dominant position in a product through intellectual property rights uses a market restriction strategy to prevent the importation or reimportation into Canada of such rights at highly competitive prices. This practice is known as parallel importation or grey marketing and is discussed, for example, in J. Palmer, 'Polaroid Canada Inc. v. Continent-Wide Enterprises: A Case Comment,' (1995) 1 *Competition Law* 46.

3. Market Restriction Exemptions

A number of exemptions apply in the case of market restriction. As with exclusive dealing, for instance, the tribunal is prohibited by section 77(4)(a) of the Act from making an order in respect of market restriction where, in its opinion, the practice in question is to be engaged in for only a limited period of time, the period of time is reasonable, and the arrangement has the purpose of aiding entry into a market of a new supplier or new product. Such an exemption appears to recognize explicitly, although in a limited way, the potential efficiency explanations of market restrictions. As noted, these explanations may also be relevant to determining whether the supplier or customer sought the restriction and in inquiring whether the practice resulted in a substantial lessening of competition.

Market restriction is also protected by the section 77(4) exemption that applies where the practice is 'between or among companies, partnerships and sole proprietorships that are affiliated with one another.'[118]

V. Refusal to Deal

The law of refusal to deal in Canada empowers the Competition Tribunal to issue an order compelling a supplier to supply a purchaser with one or more of the supplier's products. It is a reviewable practice, and thus only the director may bring such a case forward and only the tribunal may issue an order concerning a refusal to deal.

The law originated in the Economic Council of Canada's 1969 Report on Competition Policy. The council reasoned that in markets with only a few suppliers, the refusal to supply by one or two major suppliers could have a significant negative effect on a downstream purchaser's business.[119] Since many markets in Canada had only a few suppliers,

---

118 This affiliation exemption is also made specifically applicable, pursuant to s. 77(6) of the Act, to market restriction arrangements involving certain food products. To explain, where two persons are in a relationship such that the first person supplies or causes to be supplied to the second person an ingredient or ingredients that the second person processes by the addition of labour and material into an article of food or drink that he or she sells in association with a trade mark that the first person owns, or in respect of which the first person is a registered user, s. 77(6) deems such persons to be affiliated in respect of that supply arrangement for the purposes of s. 77.

119 See Z. Chen, T. Ross, and W. Stanbury, 'Refusals to Deal and Aftermarkets,' (1998) 13 *Rev. Ind. Org.* 131 at 132.

the report recommended legal protection for purchasers. A predecessor version of the present section was passed in October 1975, and the current law was enacted as section 75 of the 1986 *Competition Act*. As the discussion here will demonstrate, the Economic Council's concern about protecting downstream business manifests itself clearly in the current law, even at the expense of economic efficiency.

Refusals to deal are addressed directly by section 75, but may also infringe other provisions related to other practices. Section 77 involves the practice of tied selling.[120] If a supplier refuses to deal in order to support a tie, this refusal may result in an order by the tribunal pursuant to section 77. Also, section 61(1)(b) sets out the criminal illegality of resale price maintenance.[121] If an upstream firm refuses to supply a downstream firm because of the latter's refusal to price according to the upstream firm's price policy, it may be guilty of illegal price maintenance. Since these practices are discussed elsewhere in this book, the remainder of this chapter will focus on the law and economics of refusals to deal *simpliciter*.

A. The Economics of Refusals to Deal

As noted, upstream firms may rely on refusals to deal in order to enforce other vertical restraints such as tying and resale price maintenance. The economics of these practices are discussed elsewhere in this chapter and in this book. Here, while the issues often overlap, we will focus on the economics of refusals to deal as an independent restraint. In particular, we focus on the issue of refusals to deal in aftermarkets, defined as markets for products used in conjunction with a product purchased earlier (the 'original equipment'). Such markets were implicated in the only two refusal to deal cases before the tribunal to this date.[122] There are, as Chen, Ross, and Stanbury point out, a variety of reasons for firms to refuse to deal with respect to aftermarkets, some efficient, some inefficient and others ambiguous.[123]

---

120 See Chapter 8 for a discussion of tied selling.
121 See above for a discussion of resale price maintenance.
122 See *Canada (Director of Investigation and Research) v. Chrysler Canada Ltd.* (1989), 27 C.P.R. (3d) 1 (Comp. Trib.), aff'd (1991), 38 C.P.R. (3d) 25 (F.C.A.), leave to appeal denied [1992] 1 S.C.R. vi; *Canada (Director of Investigation and Research) v. Xerox Canada Que.* (1990), 33 C.P.R. (3d) 83 (Comp. Trib.).
123 'Refusals to Deal and Aftermarkets,' on which much of this review draws.

1. *Opportunism*

One of the theories of aftermarket refusals to deal is premised on the upstream firm (the 'original equipment manufacturer' or 'OEM') initially keeping prices low by supplying independent downstream firms ('independent service organizations' or 'ISOs') with vital parts required to service the product, but eventually raising prices for aftermarket parts and services by, among other things, refusing to supply ISOs with parts. The reason for this is opportunism. Once a purchaser has bought the original equipment, she may be 'locked in' to the model in question. That is, because of the costs of switching original equipment, she will be compelled to purchase aftermarket parts and services even if they are sold at high prices. Consequently, the argument runs, the OEM may initially attract customers to buy its equipment by supplying independent ISOs and keeping aftermarket prices low, but then may exploit past customers (the 'installed base') by raising prices in parts and services, supporting higher prices with refusals to deal with ISOs.

There are problems with this argument. As Chen et al. point out, exploiting the installed base through higher prices will have harmful reputation effects for the OEM.[124] First, prospective customers who observe the change in policy and the higher aftermarket prices will be deterred to some extent (unless they are compensated with lower equipment prices) from making a purchase of the original equipment. This will make such opportunism unprofitable in a wide range of cases. Second, the OEM may earn a reputation for gouging, which hurts it in other product markets.

Another problem with the opportunism theory is that it is not clear why refusals to deal are necessary to accomplish the goal of higher aftermarket prices. If refusals to deal with ISOs are to have any impact, it must be because the parts in question are proprietary to the OEM. To raise prices in aftermarkets, therefore, why would the OEM not simply charge ISOs higher prices for parts?

Supposing opportunism to be plausible, there is the further objection that customers may anticipate such opportunism. Consequently, even if aftermarket prices are low at the time of purchase, the buyer may anticipate future opportunistic exploitation of the installed base through higher aftermarket prices. The buyer may demand compensation in the form of lower equipment prices, but this would create inefficiencies by changing the relative prices of equipment and aftermarket

---

124 Ibid., at 137–8.

parts and services: higher aftermarket prices will imply too little consumption of parts and services and too much consumption of original equipment. Hence, the both OEMs and buyers will have some incentive to find a way for the OEM to commit not to raise prices. Concern for prospective customers provides implicit commitment by the OEM, but explicit contractual strategies, long-term service contracts for example, may be another means of commitment.

2. Customer Myopia
Customers may fail, because gathering information is costly, to anticipate correctly the cost to them of purchasing in aftermarkets.[125] OEMs, therefore, may find it profitable to increase prices in aftermarkets because buyers improperly discount aftermarket expenses in deciding whether to buy original equipment.

As Shapiro points out, costly equipment and the consequent importance of accurate life-cycle pricing, repeat buyers, and intermediaries such as consultants, *inter alia*, may render the ignorant customer on whom this theory relies empirically implausible.[126] Moreover, there is no reason *a priori* to assume that customers, even those with bad information about the true cost of aftermarkets, will systematically discount them, as opposed to inflating them. Raising prices in aftermarkets could therefore have a disproportionate impact on customers' assessment of life-cycle prices.

3. Price Discrimination
The price discrimination theory of refusals to deal is clearly related to theories of tying discussed elsewhere in this book.[127] By refusing to deal to ISOs, the OEM can raise prices in aftermarkets above marginal cost, thereby earning more profits over the life cycle of the machine from those who use the machines more intensively and thus are willing to pay more over their life cycle. The refusal thus facilitates a 'metering' form of price discrimination. Of course, as noted elsewhere, price discrimination has ambiguous welfare effects.[128] A criticism of this explanation is that OEMs could simply raise prices on proprietary parts to facilitate price discrimination.

---

125 Ibid., at 138–9.
126 C. Shapiro, 'Aftermarkets and Consumer Welfare: Making Sense of *Kodak*,' (1995) 63 *Antitrust L.J.* 483 at 493.
127 See Chapter 7 on vertical restraints (interbrand competition.).
128 See Chapter 5 on price discrimination.

4. Efficiency

There may be efficiency explanations of refusals to deal in aftermarkets. The explanations Chen et al. describe are also related to tying in aftermarkets generally. Chen and Ross suggest that if an OEM in a competitive market that provides a warranty is unable to identify heavy users, the OEM may suffer losses from dealing with these users because of intensive demands during the warranty period.[129] By setting price above marginal cost in the aftermarkets, however, the OEM may be able to recover its costs by realizing disproportionate returns from intensive users in the post-warranty period. By using refusals to deal in this manner, an OEM in a competitive market can charge each customer, over time, the full costs of its service demands.

Another suggestion Chen et al. review is that of Schwartz and Werden,[130] who suggest that refusing to supply ISOs, or tying services to purchases of original equipment, can signal quality. A high quality OEM can signal quality by charging a low price for original equipment and high prices in aftermarkets. Only original equipment of high quality, that is, high durability, will find it profitable to do so because only high quality machines will last long enough to allow the OEM to recoup its losses on low prices for original equipment through higher prices on services. We suggest, however, that it is more plausible that *low* quality equipment needs more frequent servicing and parts than high quality equipment, and therefore that low quality OEMs would have the incentive to 'mimic' the signalling strategy of the high quality OEMs in the Schwartz-Werden theory.

B. The Law of Refusals to Deal

1. The Statutory Provision

The provision of central importance to refusal to deal law is section 75(1), which is reproduced below:

75(1). Where, on application by the Commissioner, the Tribunal finds that

(a) a person is substantially affected in his business or is precluded from

---

129 Z. Chen and T. Ross, 'Refusal to Deal and Orders to Supply in Competitive Markets' (1997) mimeo, University of British Columbia, cited in Chen et al. 'Refusals to Deal and Aftermarkets,' at 140.
130 M. Schwartz and G. Werden, 'A Quality-Signalling Rationale for Aftermarket Tying,' (1996) 64 *Antitrust L.J.* 387.

carrying on business due to his inability to obtain adequate suppliers of a product anywhere in a market on usual trade terms,

(b) the person referred to in paragraph (a) is unable to obtain adequate supplies of the product because of insufficient competition among suppliers of the product in the market,

(c) the person referred to in paragraph (a) is willing and able to meet the usual trade terms of the supplier or suppliers of the product, and

(d) the product is in ample supply,

the Tribunal may order that one or more suppliers of the product in the market accept the person as a customer within a specified time on usual trade terms unless, within the specified time, in the case of an article, any customs duties on the article are removed, reduced or remitted and the effect of the removal, reduction or remission is to place the person on an equal footing with other persons who are able to obtain adequate supplies of the article in Canada.

The requirements in section 75 must all be met for the Competition Tribunal to make an order. That is, the purchaser in question must be 'substantially affected in his business ... due to his inability to obtain' satisfactory alternative supply 'because of insufficient competition among suppliers of the product in the market,' even though the buyer is willing to meet the 'usual trade terms' and the product is 'in ample supply.' Notably, and we conclude regrettably, there is no 'substantial lessening of competition' test in section 75, unlike many other reviewable practice provisions, including tied selling in section 77. Rather, it simply must be shown that the business of the would-be purchaser has been 'substantially affected.'

2. Introduction to the Case Law

In discussing the case law on section 75, we begin by briefly setting out the facts of two cases to which we will refer repeatedly, given that they are the only two reported cases concerning section 75. *Canada (Director of Investigation and Research) v. Chrysler Canada Ltd.*[131] involved the refusal of Chrysler Canada to continue to supply Chrysler automotive parts to Richard Brunet. Brunet had a small business that exported Chrysler parts to buyers outside North America, in South America, the Middle East, Scandinavia and the United Kingdom. Chrysler Canada

---

131 *Supra*, note 122.

had at first encouraged Brunet, but in 1986 informed him that it would
no longer supply him. After 8 October 1986 Chrysler Canada accepted
no new orders from Brunet and directed him to Chrysler U.S. for parts
supply. Brunet was initially successful in obtaining Chrysler parts from
Canadian dealers, but Chrysler Canada then took steps to ensure that
Chrysler dealers in Canada ceased to supply him. As a result of this
refusal to supply by Chrysler Canada, Brunet's export business in
Chrysler parts declined significantly. Brunet informed the director, and
the Competition Tribunal eventually ordered Chrysler to supply.

The other reported section 75 case is *Canada (Director of Investigation
and Research) v. Xerox Canada Inc.*[132] Xerox refused to supply an 'ISO',
which sold second-hand photocopiers and photocopy repair services,
with Xerox parts. Analogously to the *Chrysler* case, Xerox had initially
encouraged the firm, Exdos; indeed, it assisted Exdos's principal, a
former Xerox employee, in establishing Exdos. Xerox sold parts to many
ISOs. In 1988, however, following a change in its American parent's policy, Xerox Canada refused to sell parts to anybody but the end-user of
the machine, which would effectively eliminate ISOs from the service
and put an end to second-hand markets. Exdos brought the matter to
the Competition Bureau's attention, and the Competition Tribunal
eventually ordered Xerox to continue to supply Exdos and other ISOs.

3. Market Definition

Section 75 applies to a refusal to sell a 'product' (which, according to
section 2, includes both articles and services) in a 'market.' *Chrysler*
indicated that the approach to product and geographic market definition pursuant to section 75 may not necessarily be identical to the
approach taken in other areas of the *Competition Act*, such as mergers.
The important difference is that while other areas of the Act often look
to the ultimate question of whether competition has been or is likely to
be lessened substantially, the refusal to deal provision looks to the ultimate question of whether the business of the purchaser has been substantially affected. The tribunal stated:

> Products and markets can only be meaningfully defined in a particular
> context and for a particular purpose. The approach in defining these
> terms may be entirely different where, as in the case of a merger, the ulti-
> mate test is whether the merger will substantially lessen competition and

the definition must be consistent with the attempt to determine whether the merger will result in an increase in prices or in other effects consistent with a lessening of competition. In the case of paragraph 75(1)(a), the ultimate test concerns the effect on the business of the person refused supplies. Where products are purchased for resale, the effect on the business of the person refused supply will depend on the demand of the person's customers and whether substitutes are acceptable to them. Therefore, the starting point for the definition of 'product' under section 75 is the buyer's customers.[133]

The tribunal concluded that since Brunet's customers demanded Chrysler-brand parts and there was no question of substitution, the correct product definition was Chrysler parts.

The tribunal's emphasis on the question of whether the purchaser's business has been affected limits the relevance of market power and competition to refusal to deal analysis. Competition remains relevant at some level, particularly where there are homogeneous goods. A refusal to supply by a firm in a very competitive homogeneous goods market, such as wheat farming, is unlikely to affect a buyer's business, given the abundance of alternative supply. The product would likely simply be 'wheat of a certain quality' and the refusal would not be found to 'substantially affect' the purchaser's business. But where there are heterogeneous goods markets, the tribunal's analysis significantly curtails the importance of market power. Even if a supplier of a differentiated product has no significant market power, the emphasis on the preferences of downstream customers could lead to the conclusion that the market should be defined as the particular product in issue. There may be a subset of customers with a strong preference for a particular product, and thus the business of the purchaser may be 'substantially affected' by its inability to supply such customers.

The reported aftermarkets cases demonstrate the relative insignificance of market power to the analysis in heterogeneous goods markets. In Chrysler, Chrysler's expert[134] argued that since Chrysler held little market power in the automotive market, any attempt to behave anticompetitively in the aftermarket for parts would adversely affect its auto sales such that it would not rationally pursue such a strategy. If Chrysler cut off Brunet in order to raise prices for parts, prospective

---

133 Chrysler, supra (1989), 27 C.R.R. (3d) at 11.
134 Ralph Winter, one of the authors of this book.

purchasers of Chrysler automobiles would anticipate higher prices in aftermarkets and, on the basis of the price over the life of the product, would shy away from Chrysler automobiles. Thus, the product market, the expert unsuccessfully asserted, was the worldwide sale of automobiles.

The tribunal's focus on the preferences of the purchaser's customers short-circuits such an argument. It was not relevant to the tribunal that Chrysler would not have the incentive to behave anticompetitively in the parts market, given the absence of market power in automobiles;[135] rather, what was relevant was that there was an installed base of Chrysler customers that demanded only Chrysler parts. Since the inquiry focused on whether Brunet's business was affected, rather than whether there was a substantial lessening of competition, the important fact was that Brunet's customers wanted only Chrysler parts. Since they did, the product market was Chrysler parts.

The tribunal confirmed such an approach in *Xerox*. In that case as well, an expert, Leonard Waverman, argued on behalf of Xerox that the relevant product market was the provision of a package of services that leads to the creation of an imaged piece of paper. Consumers, Waverman argued, would base their purchasing decision on the price of these services over the life of the machine, thus competition in the market for machines would discipline prices in the parts market; parts did not constitute a distinct market.

The tribunal rejected this submission. Aside from the issue of Xerox's possible market power in the original equipment market (Xerox had about 90 per cent of the high-volume copier market and about 50 per cent of the low-volume market), the tribunal observed that those customers who had already purchased the Xerox machines could not easily switch to another brand of copier, which would have given rise to market power over these 'locked-in' customers.

Perhaps more importantly, the tribunal emphasized that section 75 'is not limited to ensuring the availability of *final* products at competitive prices.'[136] Moreover, the tribunal pointed out that the purpose clause of the *Competition Act*, section 1.1, does not reflect such a limited purpose either. Section 1.1 states that one of the purposes of the Act is 'to ensure that small and medium-sized enterprises have an equitable opportunity to participate in the Canadian economy.' By emphasizing

---

135 They did qualify this, however, as we will discuss below in outlining how efficiency may enter into the tribunal's analysis.
136 *Xerox, supra* (1990), 33 C.R.R. (3d) at 108.

these objectives, and the absence of a substantial lessening of competition test in section 75, the tribunal supported its conclusion that Xerox parts was the relevant market. Exdos could only serve Xerox customers by obtaining Xerox parts; preserving enterprises like Exdos was the central objective of section 75; therefore, the market was Xerox parts.

The tribunal went on to note that both the European Union and the United States have defined aftermarkets as relevant product markets. *Hugin Kassaregister AB v. Commission of the European Communities*[137] and *Image Technical Service, Inc. v. Eastman Kodak Co.*[138] both resulted in the definition of aftermarket parts as the relevant product market. *Hugin* concerned proprietary parts for cash registers; like *Xerox*, *Kodak* involved the parts market for photocopiers. The tribunal pointed out that even in the context of jurisdictions where refusal to deal is not a stand-alone provision as it is in Canada, but rather is part of the law of abuse of dominance or illegal monopolization, aftermarkets have constituted the relevant product market.

Whether one agrees with the tribunal's narrow approach to market definition depends in part on whether one agrees with the objective of preserving small businesses, regardless of economic efficiency. As a matter of law, we cannot say that the tribunal was clearly wrong in pursuing this objective. Section 75 does not include a substantial lessening of competition test, but rather emphasizes the harmful effect on small businesses, and the purpose clause does mention the aim of preserving smaller businesses. However, we do not see the tribunal's approach to protecting small businesses as compelling in this context. First, as a fundamental matter of policy, its analysis implies that a practice that is efficient and does not lessen competition may nevertheless be subject to intervention. We cannot see why competition policy would outlaw such a practice. Second, even accepting that there are goals outside of efficiency and that protecting small businesses is a legitimate aim of competition policy, the tribunal's approach may in fact serve to harm smaller businesses.

If the goal were protecting smaller businesses, fledgling enterprises might be considered to be in particular need of protection. Yet the section appears to provide little protection for businesses attempting to obtain supply for the first time. Davies, Ward, and Beck conclude that,

---

137 [1979] C.M.L.R. 7439 (E.C.J.).

138 *Image Technical Services v. Eastman Kodak Co.*, 903 F. 2d 612 (1990, 9th Cir.), aff'd 112 S. Ct. 2072 (1992). The tribunal quoted extensively from the 9th Circuit decision; the Supreme court decision had not been issued at the time.

in light of the bureau's 1976 Background Papers, which suggested that protecting 'comparatively new entrants' should be within the ambit of the refusal to deal provision, a person attempting to enter a market may be considered substantially affected by a 'refusal if it causes him to lose the possibility of additional sales and profits ...'[139] As Davies, Ward, and Beck further point out, however, the tribunal in *Xerox* restricted its order to concern only those parts that Xerox had supplied previously; parts for new models and other models not previously supplied were not subject to the order.[140] While the tribunal did not give reasons on this matter, it is apparent that they viewed the mischief to be the discontinuation of parts already supplied, rather than parts yet to be supplied. Following this approach, refusal to supply is, in law, refusal to continue to supply.

In commenting directly on the question in the context of setting out their discretion to make an order in *Xerox*,[141] the tribunal stated '[I]t has been suggested that if an order can be given in the circumstances of this case one might also issue in a situation where a manufacturer/supplier of proprietary parts had never unbundled the sale of its parts from the sale of its machines. Whether such an order could properly be obtained under s. 75 is not in issue in this case, but one can ask whether the Director, in such circumstances, would be able to prove the existence of a market for the product in question; one can ask whether a complainant could say that his or her business was substantially affected by such a refusal to supply.'[142] At the least, as a practical matter, proving that a business that has never received a certain product has been 'substantially affected' by a refusal will be difficult, perhaps impossible.[143]

In our view, this apparent failure to protect new and fledgling businesses runs counter to the apparent objective of encouraging smaller enterprises. Not only does it make an arbitrary distinction between established businesses and fledgling enterprises, but the refusal to deal section, by addressing situations in which supply has occurred in the past, but ignoring situations in which supply has not taken place, raises the potential costs to the supplier of beginning to supply outsiders. Even if the firm decides that it is more efficient to discontinue sup-

---

139 Davies, Ward, and Beck, *Canadian Competition Policy*, at para. 5.02(2).
140 Ibid.
141 See discussion below under the heading '8, *Discretion.*'
142 *Xerox, supra* (1990), 33 C.P.R. (3d) at 118.
143 Davies, Ward, and Beck, *Canadian Competition Policy*, at para. 5.02(2).

ply in the future, it may be prevented from doing so after it has begun supplying the product. This will predictably make firms more reluctant to begin supplying. Hence, new entrants and smaller firms may suffer from section 75's creation of a disincentive to supply. The section's distinction between smaller firms that had been supplied and smaller firms that had not is not only arbitrary, but, by creating a disincentive to supply, may on balance hurt smaller firms.

In *Xerox*, the tribunal provided a possible way out of this policy quagmire. Xerox argued that in defining the market, the tribunal should have taken note of the fact that the industry norm was one of vertical integration. That is, since all firms in the industry refused to supply outside purchasers in aftermarkets, the product market should not be defined on the basis of aftermarkets. The tribunal rejected the submission given the absence of evidence on the matter, but conceded that in some cases such a factor may lead to the conclusion that a particular product market did not exist.[144]

This comment may allow certain efficiency arguments to have some influence. If it is typical for firms in the market to refuse to sell to outsiders, particularly where there is no possibility of market power, such a norm likely exists because it is efficient not to supply outsiders. The tribunal's comment may invite indirect efficiency arguments as explanations of vertical integration. Of course, efficiency arguments may only be made indirectly on this approach; moreover, the tribunal's scepticism in *Xerox* indicates that the onus of proving the industry norm is likely on the parties. However, there is at least some hope that the tribunal will take an approach to market definition in the future that is related to competition concerns, rather than self-defeating concerns about small business.

Section 75 refers to a refusal to sell a product 'in a market.' Both *Chrysler* and *Xerox* approached this as the geographic market. In *Chrysler*, Chrysler contended that the geographic market was North America. The tribunal, however, noted that there were different market conditions in the two countries, as evidenced by different prices and different trade terms, such as a 'price protection' clause, which was offered in Canada, but not the United States, between the time of order and delivery. It concluded on the basis of these differences that the market was Canada. In *Xerox*, the tribunal observed that all parties assumed the geographic market to be Canada.

---

144 *Xerox, supra* (1990), 33 C.P.R. (3d) at 113–14.

4. Business

A refusal to deal properly as the subject of an order by the tribunal must affect a person's 'business' substantially, or preclude that person from carrying on a 'business.' The tribunal in *Chrysler* adopted a wide definition of 'business,' finding that it includes not only the particular activity to which the refusal relates, but all activity in which the refused supplies play a part. Thus, in *Chrysler*, rather than finding that Brunet's business was exporting Chrysler Canada auto parts, as the director urged, the tribunal found the relevant business to be 'exporting automotive parts.' The tribunal stated that the narrow definition 'would be unnecessarily restrictive since this could preclude a proper understanding of the effects of the refusal to supply.'[145] While it is unclear what the tribunal meant by this statement, perhaps it relates to the notion that accepting the director's definition of business, which essentially maps 'business' onto the product market definition, would vitiate the effects test: if 'business' is defined to relate only to the products no longer supplied, then by definition the refusal to supply would substantially affect the business.

In *Xerox*, the tribunal found that Exdos's business had three aspects: the purchase and sale, refurbishing, and servicing of photocopiers. As all three aspects relied upon the supply of Xerox parts, the tribunal did not find whether each aspect was a business on its own pursuant to section 75.

5. The Effects Test

A refusal to deal may be the subject of an order if it 'substantially affects' a business or 'precludes' a person from carrying on a business. The tribunal in *Chrysler* set out four questions to assist in this determination:

(a) does the product in issue account for a large percentage of the overall business?
(b) is the product easily replaced by other products sold by the business?
(c) does the sale of the product use up capacity that could be devoted to other activities?
(d) is the product used or sold in conjunction with other products and services so that the effect on the overall results of the business may be

---

145 *Chrysler, supra* (1989), 27 C.P.R. (3d) at 18.

much greater than indicated by the volume of the product purchased?[146]

In *Chrysler*, the complainant enjoyed greater sales and profits overall
in the years after the refusal than before. The tribunal held that this did
not preclude a finding that Brunet had been substantially affected in his
business, given that the growth in sales elsewhere was unrelated
entirely to the products in question. The other sales did not take up the
slack caused by the refusal to deal, but rather would have happened
even if Chrysler had continued to supply. The tribunal also held that
while Brunet was able to obtain some supplies from Chrysler dealers in
the past, Chrysler had taken steps to ensure that dealers stopped this
practice, including a threat to discontinue supplying a dealer if it purchased products for export. The salient factor for the tribunal in determining whether there had been a 'substantial' or, equivalently
according to the tribunal, 'important' effect on Brunet's business was
the decline in sales of the relevant products of $200,000 and in gross
profits of $30,000 over the period 1986 to 1988. (In 1986, sales of these
products were over $360,00 and gross profits were $47,000.) These losses
constituted 'a substantial effect for a small business such as Brunet's.'[147]

In *Xerox*, the analysis was straightforward. The tribunal concluded
that the refusal to supply parts would substantially affect, if not
destroy, the complainant's business. As discussed above, however, the
tribunal's order concerned only the discontinuation of particular parts
previously supplied, thus casting doubt on whether the section could
apply where a firm had never supplied a product to the complainant.

6. 'Usual Trade Terms'

'Trade terms' is defined broadly in section 75(3) to mean 'terms in
respect of payment, units of purchase and reasonable and technical servicing requirements.' It is relevant to section 75 in three ways. First, the
director under section 75(1)(a) must show that the complainant cannot
obtain supplies on the usual trade terms. Second, the complainant must
be willing under section 75(1)(c) to meet those terms as a condition of
supply. Third, the tribunal must base any order on the usual trade
terms. In *Chrysler*, for example, the tribunal ordered Chrysler to supply

---

146 Ibid., at 23.
147 Ibid.

Brunet according to the terms 'usual and customary' prior to the refusal to deal. An alternative, more sensible definition of the terms 'usual and customary' would have been the terms paid to Chrysler Corporation by every one of Brunet's competitors: the U.S. dollar price paid to the Chrysler U.S. parent. Chrysler was simply attempting to level the playing field among its distributors by charging them all the same prices.

The reference to 'usual' terms both in the *Competition Act* and in *Chrysler* lends further support to the notion that it will be difficult for a firm that has never received supply to obtain an order. If no terms had ever existed, how could the tribunal base an order on the 'usual terms'? There will at least be considerable practical difficulties for a firm seeking such an order. Given this failure to protect new entrants and fledgling firms, we reiterate the harm the section may inflict on small business by raising the costs to a potential supplier of beginning to supply outsiders. If the supplier changes its mind about doing so in the future, the law may prevent it from stopping after it has started.

7. 'Insufficient Competition'

Pursuant to section 75(1)(b), the refusal to supply may be the subject of an order only if the purchaser is unable to obtain supplies owing to 'insufficient competition among suppliers of the product in the market.' Such a condition suggests that market power may be relevant to the analysis. However, the prospect for a rule based on market power diminishes considerably when one considers the way in which the tribunal defined the market in both *Chrysler* and *Xerox*. In both those cases, as discussed, the tribunal defined the market with an emphasis on whether the purchaser had its business substantially affected. This analysis led to extremely narrow definitions of product markets: Chrysler and Xerox brand parts. Once the market is defined so narrowly, it will be easy for the tribunal to find, as it did in *Chrysler* and *Xerox*, that insufficient competition resulted in the failure to obtain supply. In *Xerox*, the tribunal acknowledged that its characterization of the product market essentially answered the question of 'insufficient competition,' noting in finding insufficient competition that 'Xerox is, for all practical purposes, a monopolist in its own proprietary parts.'[148]

The tribunal has held, however, that insufficient competition must be the 'overriding reason' for the refusal.[149] While the tribunal did not

---

148 *Xerox, supra* (1990), 33 C.P.R. (3d) at 117.
149 Ibid., at 116.

accept on the facts that the refusal in *Xerox* was based on the improper conduct of Exdos, it did accept that such a reason may have justified the refusal. Such a factor, if proven, may lead the tribunal to the conclusion that 'the inability of the complainant to obtain adequate supplies did not arise "because of insufficient competition among suppliers of the product in the market" but rather for objectively justifiable business reasons.'[150]

While the tribunal's comments arose in the context of an allegation of improper conduct, similar reasoning may open the door to an efficiency argument. If a refusal to deal is based on an efficient vertical distribution scheme, such as Chen and Ross's description of an OEM differentiating between high- and low-cost users, a party may be able to argue that efficiency reasons caused the inability to obtain supplies, not insufficient competition. Indeed, the tribunal included the 'administrative burden and other costs' as factors that may be relevant to an assessment of 'objectively justifiable business reasons,' rather than insufficient competition, as the overriding explanation for the inability to obtain supply.[151] Moreover, the tribunal held in *Xerox* that an industry norm of vertical integration may suggest insufficient competition is not responsible for inadequate supply. Efficiency arguments may find their way in through the 'insufficient competition' test.

8. Discretion
If the requisite elements in section 75 are all present, the tribunal 'may' make an order to supply. Such an order is not mandatory. In discussing its discretion in *Chrysler*, the tribunal considered a number of factors, including the reasons behind the refusal, the market position of the supplier and the changes generally to its distribution system, the length of the association between the supplier and complainant, any previous encouragement of the association by the supplier, and the manner in which the cut-off was implemented.[152] These factors fall into two categories: efficiency and other business considerations and equitable considerations. The first two potentially fall into the first category. In considering the reasons behind the refusal in *Chrysler*, the tribunal rejected the contention that the refusal responded to Brunet's violation of a condition of supply, namely that he not supply dealers outside North America in competition with Chrysler U.S. The tribunal opened

---

150 Ibid., at 115.
151 Ibid., at 114–15.
152 *Chrysler, supra* (1989), 27 C.P.R. (3d) at 24.

the door to efficiency arguments at this stage of the inquiry by briefly considering the reasons why Chrysler may have wanted to change its distribution system and consolidate control of its parts exports. It concluded, however, that Chrysler had failed to provide evidence of any harm it would incur by the granting of an order. Nevertheless, by referring to business reasons and the market structure in the industry, the tribunal has signalled some willingness in future cases to entertain efficiency arguments at the stage of determining whether to issue an order.

The second category involving equitable factors reflects the concerns about protecting smaller businesses that motivate much of the tribunal's analysis of section 75. In considering the length of the relationship,[153] which in both *Chrysler* and *Xerox* was several years; the fact that the suppliers in both cases had initially encouraged the complainants; and the abrupt decisions to halt supply in both cases (the tribunal noted that there was no face-to-face meeting in the *Chrysler* case), the tribunal appears to be determining whether the refusal was somehow 'unfair.' We wonder how these considerations relate to competition policy. Would the competitive effects, or indeed the effects on the complainant's business, of the refusal been any different in *Chrysler* had the supplier been more courteous to Brunet in discontinuing supply? The already undesirable extension of section 75 beyond efficiency into the domain of protecting small business for its own sake should not continue, in our view, into an assessment of the parties' manners.

Despite these questionable equitable considerations, it is encouraging that the tribunal has shown some sympathy to efficiency arguments at the stage of considering whether to make an order.

9. Theories of Refusals to Deal and the Case Law

In our view, the refusal to deal section should take greater account of efficiency considerations. The tribunal has set out an approach that seeks as its primary objective to protect small businesses, whether or not the refusal reduces competition substantially or is based on efficiency grounds. While protecting small businesses may be attractive to some, we wonder whether the refusal to supply section, by seeming to exempt firms from supplying where they have not supplied in the past, may raise the costs of beginning to supply and thereby hurt small

---

153 We note that consideration of this factor lends further credence to our doubt that the section would apply to a new or fledgling firm seeking to obtain supply for the first time.

businesses attempting for the first time to obtain supply. As noted above, we cannot say that the tribunal's approach is wrong as a matter of law, given the absence of a substantial lessening of competition test, but we have significant doubts about it as a matter of policy. A legislative amendment adding a substantial lessening of competition test would both bring the provision in line with the approach to other reviewable practices found in the *Competition Act* and address the serious policy concerns that presently exist.

Tempering this negativity, however, is the observation that, as the law is presently set out, there is some scope for efficiency arguments. For example, parties may introduce efficiency considerations in claiming that the inability to obtain supply was not based on insufficient competition, but rather on 'objectively justifiable business reasons.' Moreover, the tribunal will entertain such arguments in deciding whether to issue an order.

Chrysler illustrates the perversity of competition law that does not turn on substantial lessening of competition as the pivotal criterion for whether a practice is prohibited. Brunet competed with distributors located in the United States for the business of overseas dealers in auto parts. Brunet had historically been located in the United States, sourcing from Chrysler U.S. along with other distributors to overseas dealers, but received permission from Chrysler to move to Canada and source from Chrysler Canada. This move occurred during a period of stable exchange rates, and did not result in an immediate and significant difference in the wholesale costs between Brunet (whose prices from Chrysler Canada were in Canadian dollars) and its competitors in distribution (whose prices were in U.S. dollars). But after the Canadian dollar began to fluctuate wildly against the U.S. dollar – falling by as much as 13 per cent in a single year in the late 1970s – Chrysler found itself in a peculiar position. Like any multinational firm, it did not as a matter of practice immediately adjust the prices of its auto parts in Canada and the United States to account for fluctuations in the exchange rate; retail buyers would not tolerate such fluctuations in prices. Chrysler was therefore selling to overseas dealers through two sets of intermediaries, the U.S. distributors ('set A') and Brunet ('set B'), with different prices to each set of intermediaries. The price difference fluctuated monthly, even daily, with changes in the value of the Canadian dollar. No manufacturer can tolerate a distribution system with two sets of distributors, A and B, facing random cost differences because of factors (in this case, the exchange rate) outside the control of the manufacturer. Such a system results, for example, in distributors in set A investing in relationships with final retailer clientele only to have its prices undercut by distributors in set B when the random factors changed to favour the B distributors. Chrysler quite naturally tried to 'level the playing field' between Brunet and U.S. distributors by insisting that they all source from Chrysler U.S. at the same prices. The restriction placed on Brunet that it could no longer source from Chrysler Canada was an efficient and indeed eminently sensible business practice. But because Chrysler Canada was an economic entity in itself, as a matter of law this restriction constituted a refusal to deal and not just an insistence by the parent, Chrysler Incorporated, that Brunet pay the same wholesale price for its auto parts as other distributors. The economic efficiency of the restriction and its failure to have any lessening of competition were irrelevant under Section 75.[154]

In *Xerox*, the scheme likely related to price discrimination. By controlling aftermarket prices, Xerox was able to capture more consumer surplus from end-users who used their machines more intensively, and therefore had a higher demand for the machines.[155] Klein concluded that a similar refusal by Kodak in the United States.[156] was motivated by price discrimination.[157] While simply increasing prices for parts might also have accomplished Xerox's goal, doing so would have created inefficiencies by altering the relative prices of parts and service, creating inefficiently high demand for service and inefficiently low demand for parts. On this account, the refusal should not have been subject to an order. Price discrimination itself is often socially desirable, but even if it were not in this particular case, ordering supply may simply have led to a less efficient form of price discrimination: higher relative prices for parts.

In neither Chrysler nor Xerox was a clear anticompetitive theory articulated by the director. We would recommend the addition of a legislative substantial lessening of competition test, or in its absence, that the tribunal in the future expand the role of efficiency in the current framework. This would not require a radical shift, given the scope for such considerations under the established test.

---

154 We should note that the economic efficiency explanation was advanced by Chrysler's expert, Ralph Winter, but, presumably because efficiency and competitive impact are not criteria under section 75, the efficiency explanation was not relied upon in argument.
155 See Chen et al., 'Refusals to Deal and Aftermarkets.'
156 *Kodak, supra*, note 138.
157 B. Klein, 'Market Power in Antitrust: Economic Analysis after *Kodak*,' (1993) 3 *Supreme Court Economic Review* 43.

SEVEN

Vertical Restraints: Interbrand Competition

I. Introduction

In the context of competition law, vertical restraints may be divided into two categories. One category, vertical restraints on *intrabrand* competition, refers to restraints imposed by an upstream supplier on downstream distributors or retailers of its products that affect competition among these distributors or retailers. Conduct of this kind includes resale price maintenance and territorial restraints. The second category, vertical restraints on *interbrand* competition, refers to restraints imposed by upstream suppliers on downstream firms that potentially affect the degree of competition among upstream suppliers and their rivals. Where Chapter 6 is dedicated to vertical restraints on intrabrand competition, this chapter will focus on vertical restraints on interbrand competition and the operation of the two principal related statutory provisions under the *Competition Act*[1] (Act) sections 77 (exclusive dealing/tied selling) and 79 (abuse of dominance).

II. The Key Statutory Provisions of the *Competition Act* Related to Vertical Restraints on Interbrand Competition

Section 77 of the Act specifically captures two forms of vertical restraints on interbrand competition: exclusive dealing and tied sell-

---

1 R.S.C. 1985, c. C-34.

ing.[2] Section 79 also encompasses exclusive dealing and tied selling, but does so under the broader concept of abuse of dominant position. The scope of section 79 includes, but far exceeds, vertical restraints on inter-brand competition.[3]

From an enforcement perspective, the practices addressed in sections 77 and 79 are subject to civil review by the Competition Tribunal. As discussed in Chapter 12, there is currently a Bill before Parliament that would allow for private access to the Competition Tribunal in respect of sections 75 and 77.[4] Until the Act is amended, intervention by the Commissioner of Competition (commissioner) is required. In its most extreme form, this involves the filing of an application with the tribunal for a remedial order. However, such action is relatively rare. Typically, where the commissioner chooses to intervene in a matter, such intervention is undertaken on an informal basis with an eye to resolving the differences between the parties on commercially reasonable terms.

A. Section 77

For the purposes of this chapter, the discussion related to section 77 will be confined to the two types of vertical restraints on interbrand competition contained therein: exclusive dealing and tied selling.[5]

Despite the significant amendments made to the Act over the past

---

2 S. 77 of the Act also addresses the concept of *market restrictions* such as territorial restraints. However, as such market restrictions represent forms of intrabrand competition, they are discussed in Chapter 6.

3 As discussed further below, s. 79 addresses conduct that is '... predatory, exclusionary, or disciplinary ...' where carried out by a party with a dominant market position (*Canada (Director of Investigation and Research) v. NutraSweet Co.* (1990), 32 C.P.R. (3d) 1 at 34).

4 See the discussion in Chapter 12 related to Bill C-23 which proposes to open up private access to the Competition Tribunal, subject to certain limitations, in connection with exclusive dealing, tied selling, market restriction and refusal to deal.

5 Ss. 77(1) and (2) (as they apply to exclusive dealing and tied selling) state as follows: '77(1) For the purposes of this section, 'exclusive dealing' means:
(a) any practice whereby a supplier of a product, as a condition of supplying the product to a customer, requires that customer to
   (i) deal only or primarily in products supplied by or designated by the supplier or the supplier's nominee, or
   (ii) refrain from dealing in a specified class or kind of product except as supplied by the supplier or the nominee, and
(b) any practice whereby a supplier of a product induces a customer to meet a condition set out in subparagraph (a)(i) or (ii) by offering to supply the product to the

twenty-five years, the current treatment of exclusive dealing and tied selling has remained largely intact since a series of amendments to its predecessor legislation – the *Combines Investigation Act*[6] in 1975. At that time, various classes of vertical restraints, including exclusive dealing and tied selling, which had previously not been specifically addressed by the legislation, were made civilly reviewable by the predecessor to the tribunal, the Restrictive Trade Practices Commission (RTPC).[7] However, while not explicitly addressed in the legislation until 1975, such conduct had always been subject to the scrutiny of the Competition Bureau, to the extent that it arose in the context of the general prohibitions against combinations and monopolization.

---

customer on more favourable terms or conditions if the customer agrees to meet the condition set out in either of those subparagraphs ...

... 'tied selling' means:

(a) any practice whereby a supplier of a product, as a condition of supplying the product (the 'tying' product) to a customer, requires that customer to
   (i) acquire any other product from the supplier or the supplier's nominee, or
   (ii) refrain from using or distributing, in conjunction with the tying product, another product that is not of a brand or manufacture designated by the supplier or the nominee, and
(b) any practice whereby a supplier of a product induces a customer to meet a condition set out in subparagraph(a)(i) or (ii) by offering to supply the tying product to the customer on more favourable terms or conditions if the customer agrees to meet the condition set out in either of those subparagraphs.

(2) Where, on application by the Commissioner, the Tribunal finds that exclusive dealing or tied selling, because it is engaged in by a major supplier of a product in a market or because it is widespread in a market, is likely to:
(a) impede entry into or expansion of a firm in a market,
(b) impede introduction of a product into or expansion of sales of a product in a market, or
(c) have any other exclusionary effect in a market,

with the result that competition is or is likely to be lessened substantially, the Tribunal may make an order directed to all or any of the suppliers against whom an order is sought prohibiting them from continuing to engage in that exclusive dealing or tied selling and containing any other requirement that, in its opinion, is necessary to overcome the effects thereof in the market or to restore or stimulate competition in the market.

6 S.C. 1974–75–76, c. 76.
7 Other vertical restraints included in the 1975 amendments were *refusal to deal* and *market restriction*.

1. *Exclusive Dealing*

A supplier engages in exclusive dealing under the Act if it requires a customer to deal exclusively or primarily with products supplied or chosen by the supplier. More particularly, exclusive dealing includes conduct whereby a supplier of a product:

- as a condition of supplying that product to a customer, requires that customer to either deal only or primarily in products selected by the supplier or to refrain from dealing in a specified class or kind of product except as supplied by the supplier or someone chosen by the supplier; or
- induces a customer to agree to these same conditions by offering to supply the product to the customer on more favourable terms or conditions than the supplier would in the absence of that agreement.

Engaging in exclusive dealing, however, will raise an issue under the Act only within relatively narrow circumstances. The tribunal may make an order prohibiting a supplier from engaging in exclusive dealing only where (i) it is engaged in as a 'practice' (ii) by a 'major supplier of a product[8] in a market' or 'is widespread in a market' and (iii) such practice is likely to impede entry into or expansion of a firm in the market, impede introduction of a product into or expansion of sales of a product in the market, or have any other exclusionary effect in the market, (iv) with the result that competition is or is likely to be lessened substantially. Section 77(4) explicitly provides that exclusive dealing is permissible if it is engaged in '... only for a reasonable period of time to facilitate entry of a new supplier of a product into a market or of a new product into a market.'

Turning to the principal elements of the exclusive dealing provision, one of the threshold considerations is whether the impugned conduct constitutes a *practice*. This term is not defined under the Act. The tribunal[9], however, provided considerable guidance regarding its

---

8 Pursuant to s. 2(1), the Act defines a product to include both an *article* and a *service*.

9 The tribunal largely accepted the submissions of the director in *NutraSweet* related to the interpretation of the term *practice*. The submissions of the director were, in turn, influenced significantly by the findings of the court in *R. v. William E. Coutts Co.* (1966), 52 C.P.R. 21; aff'd 54 C.P.R. 60. In *Coutts*, a resale price maintenance case, the trial judge found that conduct with respect to the sale of greeting cards over

interpretation in the *NutraSweet* decision: 'The interpretation of "practice" must be sufficiently broad so as to allow for a wide variety of anti-competitive acts. Accordingly, the tribunal is of the view that a practice may exist where there is more than an "isolated act or acts". For the same reasons, the tribunal is also of the view that different individual anti-competitive acts taken together may constitute a practice. It is important to stress, however, that this does not relieve the [commissioner] of the burden of establishing an anti-competitive purpose for each of the acts.'[10] Therefore, theoretically, exclusive dealing can exist in respect of a supplier's relationship with even a single customer, provided that the conduct with this customer is sufficiently repeated. That is, it may not be necessary for the commissioner to establish that the supplier carries on the same type of exclusive dealings with other customers in order to prove the existence of a practice. Presumably, however, the fewer the number of parties affected by such conduct, the more difficult it will be for the commissioner to prove that such conduct resulted in a substantial lessening of competition.[11]

Sections 77(1)(a) and (b) (under 'exclusive dealing') also focus on the actions of the supplier in regard to it either (i) requiring that the customer deal only or primarily in its products or refrain from dealing in a specified class or kind of product; or (ii) inducing a customer to meet one of the conditions set out in item (i) above. In both instances, it must be the *supplier* that drives the exclusive nature of the relationship for an issue to arise under the Act. The statutory definition of exclusive dealing would not appear to include an exclusive arrangement in which the *customer* requires that the entire output of the supplier be sold to it.[12]

---

a week constituted a *practice* and concluded that the word *practice* '... is used in the section in the sense that it denotes a distinction from an isolated act or acts.' Ibid. at 28.

10 *NutraSweet, supra* (1990), 32 C.P.R. (3d) at 35.

11 If the customer is relatively small, the market impact would be unlikely to meet the statutory test. By contrast, if the customer is very large, presumably, it would possess sufficient countervailing power to prevent a substantial lessening of competition.

12 As discussed in Part III of this chapter, there are instances where the customer will seek the exclusive arrangement (e.g. assurance of supply). Where this is the case, in order to avoid allegations of exclusive dealing, it would be advisable to document the commercial circumstances leading to the exclusive arrangement.

In order for a supplier's conduct to qualify as exclusive dealing pursuant to section 77(1)(a), the supplier must, in addition to satisfying the 'practice' and 'supplier' elements discussed above, require a customer to either (i) deal only or primarily in products supplied by or designated by the supplier or (ii) refrain from dealing in a specified class or kind of product except if supplied by the supplier or its nominee. The tribunal has interpreted this element as requiring the supplier to actually refuse or threaten to refuse to supply the product unless the buyer agrees to the terms described in sections 77(1)(a)(i) or (ii).[13] Therefore, it would appear that, at least under the first branch of the 'exclusive dealing' definition, there must exist, at minimum, an implicit threat by the supplier to refuse to supply the product in issue.

A further factor determining the scope and applicability of section 77(1)(a) is the interpretation of the word 'primarily.' The legislative background to section 77(1)(a) suggests that 'primarily' is intended to apply to those cases where '... the supplier permitted the customer to deal only in one or two insignificant articles obtained from sources other than the supplier.'[14] It has been suggested by some commentators that the reference to 'primarily' was included in the provision in order to prevent suppliers from evading the provision simply by specifying that some proportion less than 100 per cent of the customer's requirements must be taken from the supplier or other designated source.[15] Therefore, allowing a customer to deal in some other products, which do not represent a significant threat to the supplier's competitive position, will not preclude a supplier from having such conduct scrutinized under section 77 of the Act.

An interesting question relating to the scope of section 77(1)(a) is whether it applies to requirement contracts, that is, where a supplier requires a customer to use only or primarily its products as inputs in a production process. Unfortunately, the answer to this question remains unclear. Certain commentators have pointed out that requirement contracts will only be caught by section 77(1)(a) if the phrase 'deal ... in products supplied by ... the supplier' includes using the product as an

---

13 *NutraSweet, supra* (1990), 32 C.P.R. (3d) at 53.
14 *Minutes of Proceedings and Evidence of the Standing House of Commons Committee on Finance, Trade and Economic Affairs*, 3 Dec. 1974 at 50.
15 M.Q. Connelly, 'Exclusive Dealing and Tied Selling under the *Combines Investigation Act*,' (1976) 14 *Osgoode Hall L.J.* 521 at 534.

input in the production of another product.[16] Consistent with the analysis of MacCrimmon and Sadanand, we suggest that requirement contracts do not fall within the ambit of the current wording of section 77.

If a supplier's conduct does not constitute exclusive dealing pursuant to section 77(1)(a), it may nevertheless qualify under the second branch of this definition, as set out in section 77(1)(b). To constitute exclusive dealing pursuant to paragraph 77(1)(b), a supplier must, in addition to satisfying the 'practice' and 'supplier' requirements common to both parts of the definition, induce a customer to deal with it exclusively by offering to supply the product to the customer on more favourable terms or conditions if the customer agrees to an exclusive arrangement. The scope of this branch of the exclusive dealing definition is potentially much wider than that under section 77(1)(a).[17] In fact, some commentators have observed that '[o]ffering distributors any advantages in exchange for exclusivity will almost certainly bring a supplier within the definition in s.77(1)(b).'[18]

Based on section 77(2), before the tribunal can prohibit an exclusive

---

16 This question was considered by M. MacCrimmon and A. Sadanand, 'Models of Market Behaviour and Competition Law: Exclusive Dealing,' (1989) 27(4) *Osgoode Hall L.J.* 711 at 715. The authors reasoned as follows:

> 'The issue is whether "deal" is equivalent to the concept of purchasing a product, which connotes a single transaction, or whether "deal" requires a purchase and a subsequent resale by the customer ... If a purchase is sufficient, then the customer deals in the product when it acquires the product from the supplier. It is irrelevant whether the customer uses the product as an input, consumes it, or resells it. However, the ordinary meaning of "to deal" is to buy and sell a product. Thus it is natural to say that a firm which buys and sells radios, deals in radios. But, a firm which buys transistors and makes radios is not described as dealing in transistors. The ordinary meaning is reinforced by the wording of the section which states that the supplier must require the customer "to deal ... in products supplied ... by the supplier ..." To deal in a product is to buy and sell a product, not merely to buy the product. The phrase "dealing with a supplier" would be more consistent with an interpretation that "deal" refers to the transaction between the supplier and the customer and does not require a subsequent resale by the customer ...'

17 In *NutraSweet, supra,* note 3, for example, the tribunal concluded that the provision of rebates in the form of logo display allowances and cooperative marketing funds to customers using the NutraSweet logo fell within the boundaries of s. 77(1)(b) of the Act.

18 C.J.M. Flavell and C.J. Kent, *The Canadian Competition Law Handbook* (Scarborough, Ont: Carswell, 1997), at 67.

dealing situation, it must first conclude that the situation is engaged in by a 'major supplier of a product in a market or is widespread in the market.' The basis for this requirement is that, absent this fact, it is assumed that prospective suppliers could find alternate distribution outlets.[19] The term 'major' is not defined in the Act. Nevertheless, its meaning was discussed extensively in *Bombardier*,[20] which involved an application by the director to the RTPC for an order to prohibit Bombardier from participating in exclusive dealing in connection with the distribution of snowmobiles through dealers in Ontario, Quebec, and the Maritimes. In considering the appropriate interpretation of a 'major supplier,' the RTPC concluded that: 'A major or important supplier is one whose actions are taken to have an appreciable or significant impact on the markets where it sells. Where available, a firm's market share is a good indication of its importance since its ability to gain market share summarizes its capabilities in a number of dimensions. Other characteristics of a supplier which might also be used in assessing its importance in an industry are its financial strength and its record as an innovator. However, the characteristics which are most relevant will vary from industry to industry.'[21] The RTPC found that Bombardier's share of North American sales was in the order of 30 per cent and, while denying the director's application, did conclude ultimately that Bombardier was a major supplier of snowmobiles in the North American market and at the retail level in the local markets in question.[22]

In *NutraSweet*, the tribunal expressly adopted the definition of 'major supplier' set out by the RTPC in *Bombardier* and reiterated the RTPC's view in that case when stating that '... a firm's market share is a good indicator of [a supplier's] importance, along with characteristics

---

19 MacCrimmon and Sadanand, 'Models of Market Behaviour,' at 716. The authors also note that '[t]he widespread in a market rule does, however, have the strange effect of making guilt of a small or medium-sized supplier depend heavily on whether others are also guilty.'

20 *Canada (Director of Investigation and Research) v. Bombardier Ltd.* (1990), 53 C.P.R. (2d) 47.

21 Ibid., at 55.

22 Ibid. at 56. It should be noted that there can be more than one major supplier in a market for the purposes of s. 77. The RTPC noted that the relevant statutory provision refers to 'a major supplier' and not '*the* major supplier' of a product in a market. Therefore, the RTPC suggested that the scope of s. 77 was not intended to be limited to the most important supplier in a market.

such as its financial strength and record as an innovator, and possibly other factors depending on the industry.'[23] More recently, the tribunal concluded in *Tele-Direct* that a finding of market power on the part of the supplier satisfies the 'major supplier' criterion.[24]

Regardless of the exact definition of 'major supplier' adopted by the tribunal, it is likely, as a practical matter, that any supplier who can substantially lessen competition in a relevant market by implementing a practice of exclusive dealing will be held to possess sufficient market power and influence to be a 'major supplier.' The concept of a 'major supplier' is, therefore, from a practical perspective, not likely to represent a significant impediment to the application of section 77 of the Act where the other necessary elements are present.

Section 77(2) also permits the tribunal to prohibit exclusive dealing engaged in by a supplier that is not 'major,' where the practice is 'widespread in a market.' However, this phrase is not defined in the Act, nor is there sufficient guidance in the jurisprudence as to its definition. Having said that, in *NutraSweet*, the tribunal did note that where virtually all customers in a market were buying pursuant to contracts involving exclusive dealing provisions, the practice may be said to be 'widespread in the market.'[25] Therefore, a practice engaged in with respect to 'virtually all' customers is clearly widespread. Ultimately, each case must be examined separately in the context of the particular market in question.

Where it is found that exclusive dealing is engaged in by a major supplier or is widespread in the market, the tribunal must then determine whether the supplier's practice of exclusive dealing is likely to impede entry or expansion of a firm or product in a market or to have any other exclusionary effect. In *Bombardier*, the RTPC held that:

---

23 *NutraSweet, supra* (1990), 32 C.P.R. (3d) at 55. In this case, NutraSweet conceded that if 'major' denoted nothing more than the quantitative share of sales, it would be a major supplier. Since it did not present any counterbalancing factors, the tribunal concluded that NutraSweet was indeed a major supplier.

24 *Canada (Director of Investigation and Research) v. Tele-Direct (Publications) Inc.* (1997), 73 C.P.R. (3d) at 107. It should also be noted that the tribunal may be prepared to consider a wide range of factors in addition to market share in assessing whether a firm is a major supplier. For example, in *Canada (Director of Investigation and Research) v. Hillsdown Holdings (Canada) Limited* (1992), 41 C.P.R. (3d) 289, the tribunal, in the context of a merger, recognized that market power may be exercised in relation to non-price dimensions of competition, such as quality or service.

25 *NutraSweet, supra* (1990), 32 C.P.R. (3d) at 55.

'Whether exclusive dealing by a supplier impedes expansion or entry of competitors in the market is most easily and meaningfully considered as part of the determination of whether there is or is likely to be a substantial lessening of competition as a result of the practice.'[26]

In addition, in *NutraSweet*, the tribunal concluded that paragraphs (a), (b), and (c) of section 77(2) '... are most conveniently and logically, considered as part of the over-all question of whether the exclusive dealing results in a substantial lessening of competition in the market.'[27] In turn, whether competition is or is likely to be lessened substantially is a question of fact for the tribunal to determine.

In *Bombardier*, for example, the RTPC did not agree with the director that Bombardier's exclusive dealing policy resulted or was likely to result in a substantial lessening of competition. While finding that sales at the manufacturing level constituted about 20 per cent of North American manufacturers' total sales, and that Bombardier accounted for more than half of them, the RTPC concluded that the long-term viability of competing snowmobile manufacturers would not be threatened if they were denied access to such sales. As well, with respect to the rate of turnover and sales figures at the distributor and retail levels, the RTPC held as follows: 'Changes in sales shares may also be a helpful guide in determining whether an exclusive dealing arrangement is inhibiting the growth or expansion of competitors. The extent to which competitors are able to increase their shares is indirect evidence of the effectiveness of exclusive dealing as an entry barrier.'[28]

It is interesting to note that the same test for 'a substantial lessening of competition' under section 77 of the Act is applied by the tribunal in the context of both the Act's abuse of dominance and merger provisions. In cases under these provisions, the tribunal has equated the ability of the relevant entity to exercise market power with a 'substantial lessening of competition.' For instance, in *NutraSweet*, the tribunal observed that the fundamental test of substantially lessening competition was the same for both sections 77 and 79 of the Act and could be reformulated as '... whether the anticompetitive acts engaged in by [NutraSweet] preserve or add to [NutraSweet's] market power.'[29] The

26 *Bombardier, supra* (1980), 53 C.P.R. (2d) at 56.
27 *NutraSweet, supra* (1990), 32 C.P.R. (3d) at 56.
28 *Bombardier, supra* (1980), 53 C.P.R. (2d) at 59.
29 *NutraSweet, supra* (1990), 32 C.P.R. (3d) at 47.

tribunal will also consider whether the anti-competitive acts add to the entry barriers into the Canadian market and, additionally therefore, into the industry.[30] At least one commentator has interpreted the *NutraSweet* decision to mean that the determination of whether market power exists, in and of itself, will be sufficient to decide whether there is or is likely to be a substantial lessening of competition.[31]

Section 77 of the Act also includes certain exemptions that operate to prohibit the tribunal from making an order in respect of exclusive dealing. Section 77(4)(a), for example, provides that the tribunal may not issue an order under section 77 where, in its opinion, the exclusive dealing arrangement is (i) to be engaged in only for a limited period of time; (ii) the period of time is reasonable; and (iii) the arrangement has the purpose of aiding entry into a market of a new supplier or a new product. While the meaning of a 'reasonable period of time' is largely a question of fact, it should be assessed in relation to the time required to effect a successful entry.[32] Some commentators have held that if a supplier has already established itself as a 'major supplier' in the market, then it has likely surpassed the reasonable period contemplated by section 77(4)(a).[33] Therefore, this exemption may be most applicable in the

---

30 Ibid.

31 L.A.W. Hunter, 'Tribunal Releases *NutraSweet* Decision,' (1990) 11(4) *Can. Comp. Pol. Rec.* 74 at 78.

32 It has been suggested that a useful frame of reference for assessing a reasonable period of time is the two-year period utilized by the commissioner in merger cases to determine whether the future entry will likely discipline any exercise of significant market power. See A.N. Campbell and J.W. Rowley, 'Non-Price Vertical Restraints' (May 1993) *Insight* at 8. However, this approach has been criticized. For example, in Davies, Ward, and Beck, *Competition Law of Canada* (Yonkers, N.Y.: Juris Publishing, 1994), at 5-89, it was stated that: 'The analysis in the merger guidelines asks whether an exercise of market power would be alleviated by entry within two years for the purposes of assessing whether competition is otherwise likely to be prevented or lessened substantially. The Commissioner may be prepared to tolerate an exercise of market power for less than two years, on the basis that it would not be a substantial lessening of competition. Different considerations, however, arguably ought to apply in the context of Section 77, which seeks to promote new entry, rather than rely on new entry to rebut a finding that a merger or trade practice is otherwise likely to result in substantial lessening of competition. For purposes of Section 77, therefore, there would appear to be no reason to limit the "reasonable period" to two years if in any particular industry, effective entry would take longer.'

33 Davies, Ward, and Beck, *Competition Law of Canada*, at 5-88.

context of a new entrant in a market in which the practice of exclusive dealing is widespread.

Section 77(4) also provides an exemption for exclusive dealing that occurs among affiliated companies. Specifically, it provides that no order of the tribunal under section 77 in respect of exclusive dealing shall apply with respect to arrangements between or among companies, partnerships, and sole proprietorships that are affiliated with one another. The definition of 'affiliate' under the Act[34] is consistent with its definition under most corporate law statutes. Parties may also be deemed to be affiliated in certain circumstances relating to the licensing of trade marks.[35]

On finding that an exclusive dealing practice fits within the statutory definition and has the requisite degree of anticompetitive effect, the tribunal, in the absence of applicable exemptions, may make an order prohibiting one or more of the suppliers from continuing to engage in such practices and containing any further requirement necessary to overcome the effects thereof in the market or to restore or stimulate competition in the market.[36] However, the tribunal has held that in considering the appropriate remedy in any case, it is confined to those remedies sought by the commissioner in his original notice of application.[37]

2. Tied Selling

Tied selling occurs where a supplier, as a condition of supplying a product (the 'tying product'), requires or induces a customer to purchase another product (the 'tied product') or to refrain from using a

---

34 Please refer to ss. 2(2)–(4).
35 S. 77(5)(d) of the Act, for example, known as the 'franchise exemption,' sets out that where a company, partnership, or sole proprietorship has granted another company, partnership, or sole proprietorship the right to use a trade mark or trade name to identify the business of the grantee, and 1) the business of the grantee is related to the sale or distribution, pursuant to a marketing plan or system prescribed substantially by the grantor, of a multiplicity of products obtained from competing sources of supply and a multiplicity of suppliers, and 2) no one product dominates the business, the grantor and the grantee shall be considered affiliated with one another for the purposes of s. 77. This deeming provision exempts the distribution of a number of products pursuant to a distribution or franchise agreement on terms which, but for this exemption, could otherwise support an order under s. 77.
36 For instance, in *NutraSweet*, in addition to a general prohibition against continuing the impugned conduct, several provisions of the tribunal's order specifically sought to remedy the effects of NutraSweet's exclusive dealing in the market.
37 *NutraSweet, supra* (1990), 32 C.P.R. (3d) at 58.

particular brand of product in conjunction with the tying product. The tribunal may make an order (i) in respect of a supplier that engages in the practice of tied selling in a market if (ii) the supplier is a major supplier of the relevant product or the practice is widespread in a market, and (iii) if the practice is likely to have an exclusionary effect that results in a substantial lessening of competition in a market. The exclusionary effects, which are identical to those applicable to exclusive dealing, include impeding the entry or expansion of a competitor or product in the market. However, section 77(4)(b) permits tied selling if it '... is reasonable having regard to the technological relationship between or among the products to which it applies.'

The statutory treatment of tied selling under section 77 of the Act parallels very closely that of exclusive dealing under this provision. Many of the points of statutory interpretation discussed above related to exclusive dealing therefore apply equally in the context of tied selling. The discussion below will focus on those elements of the Act specific to tied selling. Most notable in this regard is the requirement for the existence of two separate product markets, that is, the tying and tied product markets. In discussing this analysis in its decision in *Tele-Direct*, the tribunal adopted the conceptual test established by the majority of the Supreme Court of the United States in *Jefferson Parish Hospital District No. 2 v. Hyde*,[38] which may be summarized as follows: '... in this case no tying arrangement can exist unless there is sufficient demand for the purchase of anesthesiological services separate from hospital services to identify a distinct product market in which it is efficient to offer anesthesiological services separately from hospital services.'[39]

In considering the question of separate product markets, the tribunal in *Tele-Direct* noted the importance of the demand characteristics. Having said that, the tribunal recognized that efficiency is also critical and that the requirement of demand for separate products should not govern if providing the products separately would result in higher costs that would outweigh the benefits to those who seek to purchase them separately.[40]

As a general premise, consumer demand for separate products will become stronger and the efficiency justification for tying arrangements

---

38 466 U.S. 2
39 *Tele-Direct, supra* (1997), 73 C.P.R. (3d) at 119.
40 Ibid.

will become weaker, the less the products in question complement one another. This does not imply, however, that the functional dependence of two products will necessarily preclude the existence of tied selling. For example, in *Tele-Direct*, the tribunal found tied selling to have occurred through Tele-Direct's tying of the provision of advertising space with advertising services, even though advertising space and services are arguably complementary products. In fact, in *Tele-Direct*, the tribunal expressly rejected the functional approach, applied by the minority in *Jefferson Parish*, whereby the existence of a tied selling relationship depended on whether one product was functionally useless in the absence of the other.[41]

It is evident from the jurisprudence that demand characteristics and efficiency considerations are important criteria for distinguishing competitively harmful tying arrangements from natural product combinations.[42] For example, when demand exists for separate products, efficiency becomes the criterion against which the tying arrangement is judged.[43] The tribunal indicated in *Tele-Direct* that it will not intervene solely on the basis of a finding of separate demand, if providing the products separately would result in higher costs that exceed the benefits to those who seek the products separately.[44] The supplier's motivation for tying products is also important when considering the separate products requirement of tied selling.

B. Section 79

The evolution of the abuse of dominance provision of the *Competition Act* is relatively recent. Specifically, it was part of a significant legislative amendment package in 1986 which led to the current Act.[45] The predecessor to the abuse of dominance provision was the criminal monopolization provision enacted in 1910. That provision's obvious

---

41 Ibid.

42 Paul Collins, D. Jeffrey Brown, and Sean Vanderpool, 'National Antitrust Laws in a Continental Economy Revisited: A Comparative Analysis of Marketing Practices and Antitrust in Canada and the United States,' Canadian Bar Association Competition Law Section, Annual Fall Conference on Competition Law (Ottawa: Juris Publishing, 1999).

43 Flavell and Kent, *Canadian Competition Law Handbook*, at 75.

44 *Tele-Direct, supra* (1997), 73 C.P.R. (3d) at 119–120.

45 S.C. 1986, c. 26.

ineffectiveness – a single contested conviction between 1910 and 1986[46] – led to its amendment.

The primary substantive abuse of dominance provision is section 79 of the Act, which provides, in part:

(1) Where, on application by the Commissioner, the Tribunal finds that
    (a) one or more persons substantially or completely control, through-out Canada or any area thereof, a class or species of business,
    (b) that person or those persons have engaged in or are engaging in a practice of anti-competitive acts,[47] and

---

46 *Eddy Match Co. Ltd. et al. v. R.* (1953), 20 C.P.R. 107 (Que. C.A.). In no case was the ineffectiveness of the prior criminal monopolization provision more evident than in *R. v. K.C. Irving Limited,* [1978] 1 S.C.R. 408, where, notwithstanding the fact that K.C. Irving Limited acquired all five English-language daily newspapers in New Brunswick, Laskin C.J.C. (as he then was), in writing for the court, held that the acquisition of entire control over a business in a given market was not an offence *per se,* unless the Crown could also prove (beyond reasonable doubt) that it would be detrimental to the public.

47 A non-exhaustive list of anticompetitive acts is set out in s. 78 of the Act, which states as follows:

For the purposes of section 79, 'anti-competitive act', without restricting the generality of the term, includes any of the following acts:

(a) squeezing, by a vertically integrated supplier, of the margin available to an unintegrated customer who competes with the supplier, for the purpose of impeding or preventing the customer's entry into, or expansion in, a market;
(b) acquisition by a supplier of a customer who would otherwise be available to a competitor of the supplier, or acquisition by a customer of a supplier who would otherwise be available to a competitor of the customer, for the purpose of impeding or preventing the competitor's entry into, or eliminating the competitor from, a market;
(c) freight equalization on the plant of a competitor for the purpose of impeding or preventing the competitor's entry into, or eliminating the competitor from, a market;
(d) use of fighting brands introduced selectively on a temporary basis to discipline or eliminate a competitor;
(e) pre-emption of scarce facilities or resources required by a competitor for the operation of a business, with the object of withholding the facilities or resources from a market;
(f) buying up of products to prevent the erosion of existing price levels;
(g) adoption of product specifications that are incompatible with products produced by any other person and are designed to prevent his entry into, or to eliminate him from, a market;

(c) the practice has had, is having or is likely to have the effect of pre-
    venting or lessening competition substantially in a market,
the Tribunal may make an order prohibiting all or any of those persons
from engaging in that practice.

In light of the substantial jurisprudence since 1986 under the abuse of
dominance provision, there is considerable guidance related to the
interpretation of the language in section 79(1). First, the notion of
'control' in section 79(1)(a) has been interpreted to be 'treated as synonymous with "market power."'[48] Second, the interpretation of the controversial phrase, 'class or species of business,' was finally settled in the
Nielsen[49] case, in which the tribunal concluded that the traditional
approach to market definition provided the objective basis upon which
the common characteristics of a 'class or species of business' should be
assessed. Therefore, this phrase is synonymous with the well-established concept of a 'relevant market' under the Act. The reference to a
practice in section 79(1)(b) was discussed above. Finally, the notion of
'preventing or lessening competition substantially' is identical to that
applied throughout numerous other provisions of the Act.
    Where the foregoing elements of section 79 are satisfied, the tribunal
may make an order, on application by the commissioner, prohibiting
the anticompetitive conduct. Indeed, the tribunal's powers are ex-

---

(h) requiring or inducing a supplier to sell only or primarily to certain customers, or
    to refrain from selling to a competitor, with the object of preventing a competi-
    tor's entry into, or expansion in, a market;
(i) selling articles at a price lower than the acquisition cost for the purpose of disci-
    plining or eliminating a competitor;
(j) acts or conduct of a person operating a domestic service, as defined in subsection
    55(1) of the Canada Transportation Act, that are specified under paragraph (2)(a);
    and
(k) the denial by a person operating a domestic service, as defined in subsection
    55(1) of the Canada Transportation Act, of access on reasonable commercial terms
    to facilities or services that are essential to the operation in a market of an air ser-
    vice, as defined in that subsection, or refusal by such a person to supply such
    facilities or services on such terms.

Please note that ss. 78(j) and (k) were recently added to s. 78 as a result of the enactment of the former Bill C-26, which received Royal Assent on 29 June 2000.
48 *NutraSweet, supra* (1990), 32 C.P.R. (3d) at 28.
49 *Canada (Director of Investigation and Research) v. D&B Companies of Canada Ltd.* (1996),
   64 C.P.R. (3d) 216 [hereinafter *Nielsen*].

tremely broad, including the power to 'make an order directing any or all the persons against whom an order is sought to take such actions, including the divestiture of assets or shares, as are reasonable and as are necessary to overcome the effects of the practice in that market.'[50] However, section 79(3) imposes a limitation on such orders of the tribunal to ensure that the interference of rights of any person to whom the order is directed, or any other person affected by it, is limited to that interference necessary to achieve the purpose of the order.

Section 79 contains further limitations regarding its application. First, section 79(4) provides for an efficiency-type defence where a prevention or substantial lessening of competition in the market is the result of 'superior competitive performance.' Furthermore, section 79(5) exempts conduct undertaken pursuant only to the exercise of rights under certain legislation pertaining to intellectual or industrial property rights.[51] Finally, section 79(6) provides that no application may be made under section 79 for anticompetitive acts that occurred more than three years after the practice in issue ceased.

III. The Economics of Vertical Restraints on Interbrand Competition

A. Introduction

The economic exchange of private goods involves inherent exclusivity. If I provide you with all your requirements of a product, other sellers are foreclosed from providing the same product to you at the same price. If I have a limited supply of a product for sale, your purchase of the product excludes other buyers from acquiring the same units. At the extreme, our relationship may even be one in which I supply only to you, and you purchase a product only from me.

Vertical restraints on interbrand competition, however, impose exclusivity, or financial inducements to exclusivity, that extend beyond the exclusivity inherent in exchange. In a contract between a buyer and a seller, these restrictions may be placed on either party. For example, a buyer may purchase for resale a product under the restriction that it

---

50 S. 79(2).
51 This legislation includes the *Copyright Act, Industrial Design Act, Integrated Circuit Topography Act, Patent Act, Trade-Marks Act,* and other related legislation.

cannot carry any competing brands. This is *exclusive dealing*. An *exclusive supply* contract prevents the seller in a contract from supplying a specified product to a competitor of the buyer.[52]

Exclusivity restrictions represent one end of a spectrum of restrictions that link the terms of one contract to the terms of other contracts entered into by one of the contractual parties. Exclusivity restrictions simply preclude entry into a specified class of other contracts. Other types of contracts are less categorical, but can in some market circumstances have the effect of exclusivity. An obvious example is a contract in which exclusivity is not a restriction but an option attached to more generous terms for a contractual party, such as a lower price for a buyer who purchases all requirements from a single seller. The following are among the most important and common exclusivity-type contractual restrictions or clauses:

- *Exclusive dealing.*
- *Exclusive selling.*
- *Requirements tying:* the restriction that ties the right to buy one good to the obligation to buy all requirements of a second good from the same buyer. That is, the seller in a tying contract gains the exclusive right to provide the second good.
- *Bundling (tying):* in which one product is available from a seller only in combination with another product. In a common variant, termed 'mixed bundling,' the product is available on its own at a moderate or high price and as part of a bundle at a very low marginal price. An offer by a seller to provide a second good at a very low price relative to the prices at which the product is available in the market (and relative to its own cost, if produced by the seller) is a financial inducement to purchase a bundle. This offer approximates bundling.[53]
- *Most-favoured-nation clause:* the guarantee that a buyer receive the lowest price of any offered by the seller over the period of the contract. In the most common version, the clause is retroactive in the

---

52 Vertical restrictions on intrabrand competition such as exclusive territories, under which each distributor has sole rights to a given territory, can also involve exclusivity restrictions.

53 Note that, in contrast, requirements tying is always associated with a high price for the tied product relative to prices charged by other firms.

sense that the buyer has the right to a refund of past payments in excess of the price charged subsequently to another buyer.

- *Meeting-the-competition clause:* the guarantee by a seller that it will meet any price offered to a buyer by competing sellers.
- *Meet-or-release clause:* the guarantee by a buyer that the seller have the right to meet any future price offer that the buyer may receive. A variation in this clause goes one step further in allowing the buyer to terminate a contract prior to its expiration in favour of a better offer unless the current seller meets the terms of this better offer.
- *Output royalty contract:* this type of arrangement specifies that the payment by the buyer for the use of an input be made on the basis of the number of units of an output produced, rather than the number that used the particular input. Sales of products with competing inputs are not prohibited as in the exclusive dealing contract, but the purchase of other inputs involves an implicit tax, relative to the zero marginal cost use of the input in question.
- *Non-linear pricing contract:* these types of contracts include two-part pricing and minimum quantities or discounts such as sliding royalties. Suppose that a seller were simply prohibited from writing contracts with explicit exclusionary or requirements restrictions. The seller could in some cases simply forecast the quantity demanded by each buyer, and require the purchase of this amount as a condition of the contract with the buyer.[54] A minimum quantity contract (e.g., a 'take or pay' contract) is a special case of non-linear pricing, where the marginal price for all units between the first unit and the minimum quantity is zero.

In exclusive dealing, exclusive selling, and tying contracts, exclusivity is explicit. A most-favoured-nations clause or a meeting-the-competition clause may deter potential competitors from entering the market, as is explained below, and in that sense can result in *de facto* exclusivity. An output royalty, once established, reduces to zero the cost to the downstream producer of substituting away from competitors' inputs. This reduces the incentive to purchase substitute inputs, possibly to

---

54 The exclusionary effect of a minimum quantity restriction was an issue in the 1994 *Microsoft* matter in the United States. Proposed Final Judgment and Competitive Impact Statement: *U.S. v. Microsoft*, 59 Federal Register 42845, 19 August 1994. Microsoft responded to a prohibition against exclusivity-inducing output royalties in a consent decree by requiring a minimum quantity in the contracts with buyers.

the extent of leaving the output-royalty setter as an exclusive supplier of the input. A similar effect can be induced by minimum quantities.

The various strategies that incumbent firms can undertake to deter entry into a market have been explored in detail in the economics literature. Entry deterrence strategies typically involve expenditure on capital as a means to lowering marginal cost and hence providing a commitment to low prices were a potential rival to enter the incumbent's market. The strategies outlined above all involve contracts with buyers in a market. Each of the strategies can be, and in fact usually is, explained as an efficient contractual response to market conditions. As in other areas of competition policy, distinguishing between the efficient use of exclusivity-type restrictions and their anticompetitive use is the central issue. The debate between the (procompetitive) efficiency explanations and the horizontal (anticompetitive) explanations, as well as the evidence necessary to distinguish the two, is discussed below.

B. *Efficiency Explanations of Exclusive Dealing and Exclusive Supply Restraints*

1. *Assurance of Supply or Demand*
Perhaps the most compelling explanation for contractual exclusivity restrictions is that they can provide, simultaneously, a secured market for a seller and a secured source of supply for a buyer.[55] In the *Tampa Electric*[56] case, Tampa Electric Company contracted with a group of coal mines to supply all of the coal it would need for a twenty-year period. While the contract did not explicitly prohibit Tampa Electric from purchasing coal from competing mines, the District Court and Court of Appeals reasoned that the 'total requirements' provision had the effect of exclusivity. The issue before the courts was whether the

---

55 A common scenario where 'assurance of supply or demand' would appear to explain an exclusive relationship arises where a party outsources a stage in its production process. In these circumstances, the party outsourcing this task will have a strong incentive to ensure that the supply of the product remains stable and uninterrupted. On the other hand, the party now providing this product seeks to ensure that a market for the product exists and, typically, will be willing to commit much, if not all, of its production to that relationship, at least for some initial 'transaction' period. Over time, it is also common to observe both parties loosening the grip of contract to enable them to explore other opportunities in the market. This is often achieved by reducing the proportion of production under contract over a period of time.

56 *Tampa Electric Co. v. Nashville Coal Co. et al.*, 365 U.S. 320 (1960).

contract violated section 3 of the *Clayton Act* as foreclosing competition in a substantial share of a line of commerce. The District Court concluded that the contract for a period of twenty years excluded competitors from a substantial volume of trade, and the Court of Appeals affirmed the decision. Upon a further appeal to the Supreme Court, the Supreme Court held that the exclusive contract would not violate section 3 of the *Clayton Act* unless it was believed that performance of the contract would be likely to foreclose competition in a substantial share of the line of commerce affected. In this regard, the Supreme Court noted that the volume of coal covered by the contract was less than a 1 per cent share of the relevant market (i.e., coal mines that could have supplied Tampa Electric) and cited *Standard Oil Co. v. United States*, 337 U.S. 293 (1949): '[W]e seem to have only that type of contract which "might well be of economic advantage to buyers as well as to sellers." ... In the case of the buyer "it may assure supply" ... while on the part of the seller it "may make possible the substantial reduction of selling expenses, give protection against price fluctuations, and ... offer the possibility of a predictable market."'[57]

The logic of the District Court in this case – that the contract signed by Tampa Electric and the coal mines excluded (coal mine) competitors from a substantial volume of trade – would appear to apply to a large transaction in *any* market. A purchase by *any* buyer of all of its requirements from a seller always precludes other sellers from supplying the same product to the same buyer. If buyers have unconstrained choices, a large transaction is the outcome of competition, not the foreclosure of competition. We would submit, therefore, that the Supreme Court's assessment of the contract is the correct one.[58]

---

57 Ibid., at 334.
58 Subsequent U.S. jurisprudence has developed the broad statement of law in *Tampa Electric* into a number of specific factors to be considered by courts when judging the reasonableness of exclusive dealing arrangements. These factors include:
   • percentage of the market foreclosed, with courts being reluctant to find liability where the foreclosure is less than 20 per cent of the market;
   • duration of the arrangement, with agreements for a relatively short term or specifying a short notice for termination being presumed to be reasonable;
   • accepted industry practices, with evidence that competing suppliers also employ exclusive dealing arrangements weighing against a finding that a contract is anti-competitive;
   • barriers to entry into the market and the availability of other distribution channels,

2. *Asset-Specificity and the Hold-Up Problem*

Exclusivity can protect the returns on relationship-specific investments and, thereby, protect against expropriation through opportunistic 'hold-up' behaviour. Specific investments refer to expenditures by a contractual party on assets that have value only in connection with the contract entered into. More precisely, the degree of specificity of the asset to a particular use or relationship is measured by the extent to which the asset value is greater in that use than in the next best use (i.e., the degree to which the expenditure is truly a sunk cost). Suppose, for example, that a buyer has invested in substantial specific assets, and enters into negotiations with the seller over future prices, sometime after their original contract is struck. The seller, knowing that the buyer's assets are committed to the relationship, has the power to bargain for a large price increase via the threat of moving its business to another buyer. The return that the buyer captures on its assets after the future negotiations may well be less than the buyer's opportunity cost of capital. The specificity of the assets makes it impossible for the buyer to move the assets profitably to another use. Anticipating this problem at the outset of the contract, the buyer will be reluctant to invest at all. The potential gains to both parties can disappear. Efficient investment by the buyer is deterred by the prospect of capturing only part of the collective returns to the investment.

If prices and all other rights and obligations of parties could be fully specified in contracts, indefinitely into the future and for all contingencies, asset-specificity would not be an issue. There would be no future negotiations in which the buyer's return would be vulnerable. Of course, such *complete contracting* is not feasible in reality, and protection of returns to relationship-specific investment is a critical part of contract design. Exclusivity is an instrument commonly used to provide such protection. Exclusivity prevents the hold-up problem by removing the opportunistic party's (in our example, the seller's) threat to do business elsewhere. The asymmetry in bargaining power in future renegotiations is removed or, at least, mitigated with exclusivity, with the result of increased efficiency in contracting.

---

with courts tending to uphold exclusive dealing arrangements where the defendant establishes that entry into the affected market is easy;
- nature of the purchaser, with anticompetitive effects tending to less where purchasers are distributors rather than end users; and
- the nature of the product or service involved.

Vertical territorial restraints, addressed in Chapter 6, also involve exclusivity that can be explained as protection against hold-up. As discussed in that chapter, these restrictions in many cases are a response to product-specific and location-specific investment by retailers or distributors of a product. The guarantee for a retailer that it will have exclusive rights to locate in an area can protect it against expropriation of the returns to its investment by the allocation of another retailer in the same area after it has invested to build up the local market for the product.

3. Free-Riding

Franchise contracts typically prevent a franchisee from selling the products offered by competitors of the franchisor. The role of this exclusivity restriction is clear: it prevents other sellers from free-riding on the sales expenditure and more general development expenditures of the franchisor in establishing each franchisee. There is nothing anti-competitive in the contractual restriction that prevents McDonalds restaurants from selling KFC chicken. Howard Marvel has applied this free-riding explanation for exclusivity in life insurance agencies.[59] Customers attracted to an independent agent by the advertising of one insurance company may end up purchasing the product offered by another insurance company at the same agency. Any expenditure by the seller in advertising or even improving the product offered by the agent would be subject to free-riding in the case of a common agent. The free-riding effect, which would lead to under-investment in the promotion and improvement of products, disappears when each agent represents only a single seller. Provided that there are enough providers of life insurance, an exclusive agency structure will enhance competition.

4. Exclusivity and Potential Competition

In the well-known *Standard Fashion* case, a manufacturer of dress patterns established exclusive dealing contracts with retail department stores.[60] The U.S. Supreme Court concluded that in each of the 'hundreds if not thousands of communities' in which there was a single retailer for the product, exclusive dealing would lead to a local monop-

---

59 Howard Marvel, 'Exclusive Dealing,' (1982) 25 *J. Law Econ.* 1.
60 *Standard Fashion Co. v. Magrane-Houston Co.*, 258 U.S. 346 (1922).

oly. Mathewson and Winter argue, however, that purely horizontal motives for exclusivity – the use of the restraint by a dominant firm in order to capture a larger market share or even the entire market – are not necessarily inconsistent with efficiency.[61] Standard Fashion did capture the entire market for dress patterns in many local communities via exclusive dealing, but in order to induce the local retailer to agree to exclusive dealing, the dominant firm had to lower the wholesale price of its product by as much as 50 per cent or more. The price that Standard Fashion was able to charge under exclusive dealing, in other words, was disciplined not by the *actual* competition that emerged in the market but by the *potential* competition provided by alternative suppliers of dress patterns.

By invoking an exclusive dealing strategy, Standard Fashion was making the decision to move away from a situation in which prices were disciplined by actual competition to a situation in which prices were disciplined entirely by potential competition. The greater power of potential competition relative to actual competition in disciplining prices was evident in the fact that the company had to lower its price by half to maintain retailers once it invoked exclusive dealing. Retailers had the option of forgoing Standard Fashion lines and carrying competitors' dress patterns. Therefore, a lower wholesale price for retailers was necessary to induce them to forgo this option. If Standard Fashion had had a more dominant position in the market, however, it could have both invoked exclusive dealing and *raised* price to the monopoly level; to the point where the profits that retailers would have gained facing the monopoly price would have exceeded the profits from purchasing only from other suppliers.

The trade-off faced by Standard Fashion was between (i) gaining a larger market share (up to the entire market) at lower prices with exclusive dealing and (ii) charging higher prices without exclusive dealing. Was exclusive dealing inefficient in this case, in the sense of reducing total surplus in the market? The social or efficiency effects of exclusive dealing would net out the benefits of lower prices with exclusive dealing, with the cost of reduced product variety in the market. Consumer preferences vary among brands; under exclusive dealing, consumers' choices are limited to products sold by the dominant

---

61 G. Frank Mathewson and Ralph A. Winter, 'The Competitive Effects of Vertical Agreements: Comment,' (1987) 77(5) *American Economic Review* 1057.

supplier. Mathewson and Winter find that the private interest of the dominant firm and the social efficiency effects of exclusive dealing can operate in the same direction. Total surplus can increase with exclusive dealing in cases like Standard Fashion. As is the case with price discrimination, the practice may or may not be in the social interest. However, a signal that exclusive dealing is not in the public interest when it is used as a purely horizontal instrument to gain market share is an increase in price when that practice is invoked. Where this occurs, both the price increase and the drop in product variety in the market act to decrease market efficiency.

An important implication of this analysis of exclusive dealing is that observed market shares are not necessarily a reliable proxy for the competitiveness of pricing in a market. Exclusive dealing forces the market into a contestability framework, where competition is *for* the market instead of *within* the market.

C. *Efficiency Explanations of Tying*

Many examples of tied sales represent obviously efficient means of economizing on transaction costs. These include tying shoelaces with shoes, stove elements with a stove, an automobile with an engine, and so on. Controversy and litigation arise only when there are truly separate markets for the tied goods. Examples include salt and salt tablets tied to the sale of industrial salt machines for use in canning or making brine solutions;[62] the sale of advertising space in one newspaper being tied to the sale of similar space in a companion paper or radio station co-owned with the newspaper;[63] anaesthesiology services sold by a hospital with its surgical services;[64] and television program ratings sold with radio station ratings.[65]

Requirements tying is observed frequently in 'after-markets,' markets for parts and services for durables such as photocopy machines and automobile parts. The purchase of a photocopy machine could be tied to the obligation to obtain all post-sales service from the manufacturer. The same constraint may be implemented by refusing to supply

---

62 *International Salt Co. v. U.S.*, 332 U.S. 392 (1947).
63 *Lorain Journal Co. v. U.S.*, 342 U.S. 143 (1951).
64 *Jefferson Parish, supra*, note 38; *Hospital Dist. No. 2 v. Hyde*, 466 U.S. 2 (1984).
65 DIR., *RTPC v. BBM Bureau of Management* (1981), 60 C.P.R. (2d) 26.

parts to independent service organizations. (Without parts, service cannot be provided by independent service operators.) In the photocopier market, the purchase of a copier may be tied to the purchase of all requirements of toner fluid. Similar restrictions are seen in aftermarkets for automobiles (with restrictions against the substitution of parts). Since the Supreme Court decision in *Kodak*, U.S. courts have seen dozens of after-market cases.[66]

1. Product Information Related Explanations

One argument heard in after-market cases concerns the assurance of high-quality service. If a machine receives poor-quality service, the argument goes, then the rate of breakdown for the machine will be higher. Since consumers cannot identify perfectly the source of the higher rate of breakdown (as between poor service or a poor machine), the reputation of the machine will suffer. Moreover, the incentives of the service provider are distorted by the sharing of any reputational damage from breakdowns with the machine provider. Tying, according to this argument, corrects the reputational externality between the independent service provider and the manufacturer and protects the manufacturer's reputation.

However, this argument must be qualified. Rational consumers should recognize the impact of the reputational distortion and market conditions on independent service providers' incentives to provide quality service, and should infer from the compromise in incentives that any damage to their durable product is highly likely to be caused by the service provider. The manufacturer's reputation does not necessarily suffer from independent, low-quality service. Consumers themselves are free to choose to avoid independent service providers by purchasing service from the manufacturer. Eliminating consumers' choice to purchase lower quality service from independent service providers is not obviously in the manufacturer's interest. The explanation of tying as protecting manufacturers' reputations is therefore suspect.[67]

A slightly different argument has more plausibility. While the buyer of the service anticipates limited incentives on the part of independents to provide high-quality service, some buyers may knowingly purchase

---

66 *Eastman Kodak Co. v. Image Technical Services*, 504 U.S. 451 (1992).
67 For development of these ideas see Edward Iacobucci, 'Tying as Quality Control: A Legal and Economic Analysis,' unpublished paper, University of Toronto, 2001.

low-quality service. Such purchases may (but may not) have negative implications for the machine's reputation. If the machine does not perform well, its reputation will suffer, even if low-quality service was knowingly purchased. On the other hand, if the machine does perform well even with low-quality service, the purchase of low-quality service will, in fact, have enhanced the machine's reputation: customers will, *ex post*, observe the machine performing well in spite of inexpensive, low-quality service and as a result these customers will infer that the machine's quality is likely to be high. For a machine of a given quality, either the negative reputational effect of low-quality service on machine reputation or the positive effect may dominate when one averages across consumers (and events of machine success or failure).[68]

Whatever the effects on reputation, buyers will not fully account for them in making purchase decisions. If the negative effects dominate, it may be rational to impose a tie to address the negative buyer-seller externality. The tie ensures that high-quality service is provided with the machine. Negative effects may dominate, for example, if outsiders observing performance of the machine-service package do not know the identity of the service provider and assume that it may be the manufacturer. In such a case, the purchase of poor-quality service would be expected to hurt the manufacturer's reputation for quality. The argument generalizes from consumer durables and maintenance to other pairs of complementary goods, such as cellular phones and service.

Another reason to impose a tie for quality-control reasons arises where the seller of the tying good shares the cost of performance with the buyer. For example, under a warranty of the performance of the tying good, a buyer may impose costs on the seller by purchasing inferior tied goods.[69] A tie may rationally respond to this distortion in incentives. Similarly, in a franchise context, a franchisee may impose costs on the franchisor's reputation for a higher quality franchise system.[70] A tie addresses such a concern. For example, automobile manufacturers, in order to protect the reputation of the automobile itself, may require dealers to sell only parts approved by the manufacturer.[71]

---

68 See Iacobucci, 'Tying as Quality Control.'
69 Such an explanation was discussed in *International Salt, supra*, 332 U.S. at 397.
70 B. Klein and L. Saft, 'The Law and Economics of Franchise Tying Contracts,' (1985) 38 *J.L. & Econ.* 345.
71 See, e.g., *Pick Mfg. Co. v. General Motors Corp.*, 80 F. 2d 641 (7th Cir., 1935); *Mozart Co. v. Mercedes-Benz of North America Inc.*, 833 F. 2d 1324 at 1348 (9th Cir., 1987).

466 The Law and Economics of Canadian Competition Policy

Another information-related explanation for tying has been offered by Yoram Barzel.[72] The monopolist in the wholesale diamond market, deBeers, sells diamonds in lots. A buyer has the choice of purchasing an entire bundle of diamonds or refusing the bundle. The buyer cannot sort through the bundle, choosing the diamonds that he or she has identified as having particularly high value. The alternative, determining the appropriate price of each diamond, would involve significant sorting expenditures by buyers to identify the highest value purchases and even larger expenditures by deBeers to ascertain the quality of each diamond. DeBeers would receive less total revenue from its sales because the 'cherry-picking' strategy by buyers would leave it with relatively over-priced diamonds, the prices of which would then have to be reduced. Analogous to this is fresh fruit, which is often sold in bags, arguably, to avoid the same wasteful expenditure on sorting. Compare the sale of fruit such as oranges, grapefruit, or apples prepackaged in bags of uniform price and their sale, loose in bins, at a uniform unit price. When the fruit is sold unbundled in a bin, each consumer has an incentive to search for the better products, leaving the inferior ones for others. This sorting has no productive pay-off but is merely a transfer from late customers to early ones. The unproductive sorting is eliminated if the products are prepackaged in bags of approximately equal quality. Barzel argues that bundling and vertical integration can often be explained as the avoidance of excessive expenditures on sorting or monitoring of quality.

2. Buyer Information Related Explanations

In certain instances, tying can serve as an instrument for price discrimination. The essential feature of any price discrimination instrument is that it enables a producer to charge a higher price to those buyers of its product who have a more inelastic demand or a higher willingness to pay. Where a producer cannot identify consumers of different demand elasticities and explicitly charges them different prices, the producer must rely on indirect means of monitoring demand elasticities. For example, when IBM sold adding machines that required punch cards, it required its customers to use IBM cards, which it supplied at a variable price in excess of marginal cost. The sale of cards was effectively a means of monitoring the intensity of a buyer's use. It is reasonable to

---

72 Yoram Barzel, 'Some Fallacies in the Interpretation of Information Costs,' (1997) 20 J. Law Econ. 291.

assume that the more intense users of the product had the highest willingness to pay for the product. Charging a price in excess of marginal cost on the variable input was a means of directing higher prices to those customers with the highest willingness to pay. A similar argument could explain why franchise contracts may constrain a franchisee to purchase inputs (e.g., milk for a convenience store) only from the franchisor, at prices above the franchisor's costs.

An important principle in the economics of durable good pricing is that in the absence of buyer heterogeneity, the optimal price for a monopolist to charge for a variable input is marginal cost. The monopolist does not exercise market power by charging both a high price for the durable input and a high price for a variable input. The monopolist's tasks can be viewed as (i) maximizing the total surplus gained in the market, and (ii) extracting as high a fraction of this surplus as possible. Generally there is some compromise between these two goals, and in meeting the second of its goals, the monopolist compromises on the first – which explains why monopoly pricing is inefficient. In charging a price in excess of marginal cost for the variable input (punch cards), for example, IBM was compromising the goal of maximizing total surplus in order to increase its share of the surplus.

A second price-discrimination use of requirements tying arises where there are two or more variable inputs related to the intensity of use of a product. Consider an after-market in which the manufacturer attempts to extract higher prices from more intensive users of a durable product through the use of tying. Two variable inputs related to intensity of use, service provision and parts, are candidates for use as monitoring devices. If there is any scope for substitution between the two variable products, the mechanics of optimal pricing dictate that *both* variable inputs be sold at prices above marginal cost. Pricing above marginal cost involves a distortion, which reduces total surplus in the market. Spreading out the distortion across as many variable inputs as possible reduces the loss in total surplus from the distortion; the monopolist captures some of the gain in surplus as profit. If the manufacturer is the sole supplier of parts, tying service to parts ensures that the manufacturer can charge positive mark-up on both variable inputs.[73]

---

73 This explanation of tying is developed in G.F. Mathewson and Ralph A. Winter, 'Tying as a Response to Demand Uncertainty,' (1997) 28 *Rand Journal of Economics* 566–583.

In *Standard Oil*,[74] Standard Oil of California imposed exclusive sup-ply contracts on its independent dealers, requiring them not only to buy their gasoline exclusively from Standard but also, in many con-tracts, tying the purchase of tires, batteries, and other automobile accessories to the sale of gasoline. In two other cases, the Federal Trade Commission challenged 'sponsorship' agreements in which major oil companies required dealers to purchase tires, batteries, and other auto-mobile accessories from leading producers. Under the agreements between the oil companies and these other producers, the oil compa-nies received a 10 per cent commission on the sales of the accessory products. Evidence reviewed by Mathewson and Winter shows that the sales of accessories are correlated with the sales of gasoline across stations. Such cases, therefore, fit the theory of tying related variable inputs together in order to spread out the distortion caused by the mark-up of price over marginal cost.

D. *Efficiency Explanations of Related Instruments*

The efficiency explanations of the other potentially exclusionary instruments delineated earlier in this chapter are numerous, and we simply sketch the more important aspects of these explanations here. Most-favoured nation clauses can serve simply to insure buyers that they are receiving the best price available from the seller of an input. Profits in competitive markets are very sensitive to relative input prices faced by competitors. A buyer may be reluctant to commit to carrying a particular brand or to using a particular input without the assurance that it will not be left in a disadvantageous position relative to a competitor dealing in the same brand or input.

Both a meeting-the-competition clause and a meet-or-release clause may enhance competition or the power of potential competition in a market, by causing the best offers available from potential competitors of incumbents to become immediately reflected in current transactions. If there are many firms, or if investment by potential competitors is unlikely to be influenced by meeting competition or related clauses, this theory is the most realistic explanation of the practices.

---

74 *Standard Oil Co. of California v. United States*, 337 U.S. 393 (1949). See also *Atlantic Refining Co. v. FTC*, 381 U.S. 357 (1965) and *FTC v. Texaco Inc.*, 393 U.S. 223 (1968).

An output royalty may be efficient because it avoids the distortion in the input mix caused by exercising market power through a high input price. When a downstream firm faces a monopoly price for one input and competitive prices for other inputs, its input mix (which reflects the minimum of private costs, not social costs) is inefficient. If an input supplier charges marginal cost per unit of input, collecting profits through a downstream output royalty, the distortion in input prices is removed. Output royalties have been used in cases where the product supplied by the upstream firm is an intellectual property right – for example, the right to sell computer software or the right to use a particular technology, which carries a zero marginal cost. The use of output royalties in place of any input price therefore eliminates the input mix distortion.

Competitors of the input supplier, however, may be constrained by market conditions and their lack of an established product to charge input prices.[75] In this case, the 'constrained optimal' price for the established input supplier would exceed marginal cost. In addition, offsetting any efficiency from the removal of a distortion in relative input prices is the fact that one source of market discipline on the upstream monopolist's exercise of market power has been dampened: the ability of the downstream buying firm to substitute on the margin between the monopolized input and other inputs.

Finally, non-linear pricing is ubiquitous and in most cases efficient. In the simple monopoly model, if buyers' demands are known and the monopoly is able to charge a non-linear price to each buyer, preventing resale among buyers, then first-best efficiency is achieved (albeit with all surplus in the market accruing to the monopolist). More generally, non-linear pricing allows firms with market power to set lower – and more efficient – marginal prices, without sacrificing profit.[76]

E. Horizontal Incentives for Exclusivity Restrictions

Both exclusivity and tying appear to some commentators to be anti-

---

75 An input supplier with little or no presence in the market could not demand a royalty on output as a condition of a contract. The output royalty would shift the risk of product failure from the input supplier to the downstream purchaser.

76 In the Microsoft matter in the United States, non-linear pricing could be interpreted as exclusionary, as will be discussed. This is a relatively rare example, however.

competitive at face value. Exclusivity restrictions might appear to prevent competition by definition, since buyers are prevented from purchasing from other suppliers. Tying imposes on buyers purchases that they may not necessarily want at prices that are higher than available elsewhere. In that sense, it is argued, tying is anticompetitive at face value.

Both of these horizontal incentive arguments are flawed. If an exclusivity restriction or tying restriction harms buyers, its removal from a contract should make the contract more valuable to buyers. The seller should recognize the higher willingness to pay on the part of buyers and raise the price to reflect the higher value after removal of the restriction. The net effect on buyers is, therefore, unclear.

What theory allows the prediction that buyers will necessarily be better off without the restraints? Assessing the efficiency of tying or exclusivity requires a positive theory of *why* the restraints are imposed. It is incorrect to say simply that tying is profitable because it enables a monopolist to charge a supracompetitive price on a second product (the tied good): the tying restraint imposes a cost on customers that will be reflected in a lower willingness to pay for the overall package, which must lower the price that the monopolist can charge on the tying good. In the typical context of a durable and a variable input, the theory of tying must start from the simple proposition that if consumer demands were identifiable, the optimal pricing for a monopolist would be marginal cost pricing for the variable input and a monopoly price for the durable. This scheme maximizes the total surplus generated by the contract or transaction, to the benefit of the monopolist that will collect the maximum that buyers are willing to pay.

In the previous section, we outlined explanations of tying and exclusivity that were consistent with efficiency. An explanation of either practice as exclusionary and inefficient must recognize that the exclusion of a competitor from the market through a contractual clause will harm buyers, and reduce the value that buyers attach to the contract. Why will the drop in the value of the contract to buyers not be fully reflected in a drop in the maximum price that a firm with market power could extract from buyers? Which market conditions negate the basic result that any seller, even a monopolist, wants to make a product or contract as valuable to buyers as is economically efficient, and will pay for any reduction in efficiency through a reduced willingness of buyers to pay for the product?

The issues in this debate can be illustrated with the well-known

United Shoe case.[77] The focus of this case was United Shoe Machinery's practice of leasing machines under long-term contracts that required customers to pay a penalty for switching to a competing supplier. The court ruled that these agreements violated the *Sherman Act*, describing them as an important instrument by which United Shoe Machinery had monopolized the shoe machinery manufacturing market for more than fifty years.

Until recently, the dominant view on exclusivity contracts such as United Shoe's leasing contracts was that advanced by the 'Chicago school' – that such contracts could not be imposed on consumers without efficiency benefit because customers will not accept constraints in contracts unless compensated for the cost of their loss in economic freedom.[78] The argument may seem to rely upon consumers wielding significant bargaining power against a monopolist, but it does not. Even where the monopolist captures almost all gains from trade, it will bear the cost to consumers of any loss in contract value attributable to the constraints. According to this view, restrictions such as exclusivity or tied sales must either increase total surplus available in a market or, as price discrimination devices, allow a manufacturer to capture a larger share of the gains to trade generated.

In an important article, Phillipe Aghion and Patrick Bolton provide two powerful counterarguments.[79] The dynamics of contracts and future entry are brought into play in these explanations of the exclusionary role of exclusivity and long-term contracts with liquidated damages. The more important of these is an explanation of the type that is sometimes labelled a 'reverse free-riding' argument. Consider the following example. A market has a hundred consumers entering contracts with an incumbent monopolist today, with the knowledge that a potential entrant may come into the market tomorrow. The entrant's costs of entering or producing in the market are uncertain. If the entrant successfully enters the market, the competition between the

---

77 *United States v. United Shoe Machinery Corporation*, 110 F. Supp. 295 (D. Mass., 1953), off'd *per curiam*, 347 U.S. 521 (1954).

78 See Richard A. Posner, *Antitrust Law: An Economic Perspective* (Chicago: University of Chicago Press, 1976), 203–4; Robert H. Bork, *The Antitrust Paradox: A Policy at War with Itself* (New York: Basic Books, 1978), 138, 304, 309.

79 Phillipe Aghion and Patrick Bolton, 'Contracts as a Barrier to Entry,' (1987) 77(3) *American Economic Review* 388.

incumbent and the entrant will yield $10 of additional surplus to each consumer, as compared to the continuation of the current monopoly in the market, because of the lower prices that the competition between the incumbent and entrant would produce.

In a market with some costs of entry or economies of scale, the entrant will require a minimum number of customers to be profitable. The precise minimum number will depend upon the realization of its costs. Suppose, however, that the incumbent induces consumers to sign long-term exclusive contracts that include a substantial liquidated damages clause – a penalty to the customer for leaving the contract. Then the entrant would be deterred from entering the market, unless its costs are so low as to enable it to charge a price that would compensate all consumers joining it for the liquidated damages that they must pay the incumbent to switch.

To induce customers to sign such an entry-deterring contract, the incumbent must offer each customer a 'bribe' in the form of a reduced price. This is the point made by the Chicago school: the imposition of a contractual constraint means a reduction in the buyer's willingness to pay. In the circumstance described, however, the bribe can be minimal: whether all other customers have signed exclusive dealing contracts or not, the probability that a particular customer is the 'marginal customer' in terms of deterring the entrant is very small. Each customer, in signing the contract, is imposing a negative externality on all other customers by increasing the chance of a detrimental market structure in the future. The incumbent can take advantage of this reverse free-riding problem to ensure that enough customers have signed the contract so as to deter the entrant, under a wide range of circumstances (realizations of future costs) where entry would be socially efficient. When the focus is shifted from asking why a seller might want to impose exclusivity to why *buyers* would sign exclusivity contracts that make them, collectively, worse off, it becomes clear that the exclusivity restrictions can block entry by competitors. The seller exploits the reverse free-riding problem among buyers.

In their other (in fact, more celebrated) explanation of the entry deterrence role of exclusivity, Aghion and Bolton consider a buyer and a seller entering a long-term contract that contains a liquidated damages clause. The buyer, who is to purchase only one unit of a product in the future, must pay the liquidated damages if she decides to purchase from a future entrant rather than from the seller of the current contract. Aghion and Bolton note that the role of the liquidated damages clause is to lower the price that the future entrant must offer to attract the buyer, since to switch suppliers, the buyer must be induced by a price difference at least as large as the liquidated damages amount. The commitment in the contract to a lower acceptable price from a future entrant thus results in a transfer from the future entrant to the current pair of contracting parties. This transfer will be shared between the two, depending on their relative bargaining power. Aghion and Bolton show that through the commitment effect of the current contract, the parties are able to extract the same rents from the future entrant as would a monopsonist. The effect of the high liquidated damages is to deter entry in situations where entry would otherwise be efficient. The anticompetitive effect of the contract arises not through an exploitation of a reverse free-riding effect, as in the first explanation, but through a joint commitment to exploit monopsony power against a future entrant – monopsony power acquired through the 'first-mover' advantage and commitment power of the contractual parties.[80]

F. Horizontal Explanations of Tying

Like exclusivity restrictions, the restraint of tying has a popular, anticompetitive explanation that has been criticized by the Chicago school. Tying has had a long history of negative treatment in U.S. antitrust law.[81] The basis for the harsh legal treatment lies in the adoption of the 'leverage theory' of tying by courts: that tying allows a firm with monopoly power in one market (the primary market, or tying good market) to leverage or extend its monopoly power to a second market (the secondary market, or tied goods market).

---

80 The assumption in the Aghion-Bolton analysis that the contract, once struck, is a commitment is questionable. If an entrant appears whose costs are lower than the incumbent seller's costs but not so low as to offset the liquidated damage, then within the Aghion-Bolton model there would be an incentive for the buyer and seller to renegotiate the contract to a lower liquidated damage. Allowing renegotiation freely, however, negates the commitment power of the contract and eliminates the anticompetitive, entry-deterrence effect in the Aghion-Bolton model. Katherine Spier and Michael Whinston extend the analysis to incorporate investment by the contractual parties in relationship-specific assets. 'On the Efficiency of Privately Stipulated Damages for Breach,' (1995) 26 Rand J. Econ. 180.

81 Tying doctrine originated in patent cases (Motion Pictures Patents Co. v. Universal Film Manufacturing Co., 2453 U.S. 502 (1917) and was developed in a long line of case law under both s. 1 of the Sherman Act and s. 3 of the Clayton Act.

Critics of the simple version of the leverage theory prefer an argument that originated with Aaron Director of the University of Chicago.[82] If a monopolist has extracted full monopoly profits from the sale of the primary good, then each consumer is paying the maximum she is willing to pay for the good. Forcing the consumer to pay one dollar more for the secondary good than she would have to pay in a competitive market lowers her willingness to pay for the primary good by one dollar. Each dollar extracted from the consumer through the tying constraint reduces the price that can be charged for the primary good. Why would a monopolist undertake such a strategy? The only explanation that the critics of the leverage theory entertain is one of price discrimination, arising from the fact that the monopolist has not extracted the full surplus from each consumer in setting the price of the primary good. Tying can be used as a price discrimination device, the purchases of the secondary good serve to monitor the intensity of demand for the primary good, with the result that a higher share of total surplus is extracted. The welfare effects of this use of tying, as explained earlier, are ambiguous and do not justify intervention.

In another paper, Michael Whinston has shown that if the secondary market is not competitive, as in the Chicago theory, but is rather characterized by scale economies, tying can serve to leverage monopoly power from the primary market to the secondary market.[83] Suppose that a monopolist in a primary market faces a single competitor or potential competitor in the secondary market. Suppose further that the monopolist can *commit* to tying through product design or the setting of production processes. It could be argued that Microsoft, for example, tied the provision of its Internet browser, Internet Explorer©, to its operating system through development of the products as a joint bundle. By tying, the monopolist can reduce the feasible scale of its rival in the secondary market to the point where its profits do not justify continued operation or, in the case of a potential entrant, entry into the market.

In the context of a contractual tying restraint, rather than a technological tying together of two products, the logic of Whinston's argu-

82 See Aaron Director and Edward Levi, 'Law and the Future: Trade Regulation,' (1956) 51 *Northwestern University Law Review* 281; Posner, *Antitrust Law*, and Bork, *Antitrust Paradox*.

83 M. Whinston, 'Tying, Foreclosure and Exclusion,' (1990) 80(4) *American Economic Review* 837.

ment follows, provided one is willing to accept that the monopolist can commit to the tying restriction and prices. Without the rival in the secondary market, a contractual tying restraint is – for each individual customer – costless. There is no alternative supplier of the tied good. The assumption that a firm can commit to a particular pricing strategy, whatever the reaction of its rival, however, is not generally acceptable. Whinston's argument, in short, is less than persuasive as a theory of how a contractual tying restraint, as opposed to technological tying, can leverage monopoly power from one market into another.

G. Horizontal Explanations of Related Instruments

The horizontal effects of the instruments listed in the introductory section of this chapter, other than tying, tend to be case-specific rather than having systematic effects that are widespread across various industries. These effects are discussed briefly below.

Consider the effect of a most-favoured-nation clause in a contract with the suppliers of essential inputs. This clause would require that each supplier, having been paid a very generous price by an incumbent firm, charge the same price to a new entrant (or refund the difference to the incumbent). A high price may not be feasible for a new entrant, since the profit it would derive from purchasing the essential input is the profit of a duopolist, rather than an incumbent monopolist. The combination of a most-favoured-nation clause and a *high* price can thus serve to deter entry. (Normally, we think of low prices by an incumbent as discouraging entry.) Most-favoured-nation restrictions might have had this effect in *Nielsen*,[84] discussed below.

Meeting-the-competition clauses commit an incumbent monopolist to an aggressive reaction to entry into its market by a lower-priced firm. The entrant knows that any attempt to gain market share as a new entrant through lower pricing will be automatically matched, at least among existing customers, by the incumbent firm. Without the 'meeting-the-competition' clause, it would generally pay the incumbent, once entry has taken place, to be more accommodating to the entrant in its pricing strategy. To express this differently, the entrant pays the incumbent to be more aggressive in pricing strategies it can commit to *ex ante* than in those established *ex post*. This contractual

---

84 *Supra*, note 49.

commitment to an aggressive reaction by the incumbent can have the effect of deterring entry that would otherwise be profitable.

A meet-or-release clause does not provide the incumbent with the same degree of commitment to aggressive pricing as a meeting-the-competition clause. But it does facilitate a price response by an incumbent to any attempt by an entrant to entice customers away from the incumbent through lower pricing. In markets where prices are negotiated individually rather than posted, the informational advantage to the incumbent of knowing where the entry threat is striking and how strong the threat is, can be significant.

Output royalties are similar to a simple exclusive dealing provision, except that the use of other brands' products is 'taxed' rather than prohibited. For example, if a supplier of operating systems is charging a hundred dollars per personal computer sold (an output royalty), rather than a hundred dollars per unit of its operating system employed, it is effectively selling its own product at a hundred dollars and taxing the purchase of competing systems at a hundred dollars per unit. The effect can be the same as that of exclusive dealing. In a consent decree with the U.S. Department of Justice in 1994, Microsoft agreed not to sell its operating system to original equipment manufacturers on the basis of output royalties.[85]

Following the consent decree, however, Microsoft allegedly offered OEMs price discounts for purchasing the quantities they would have purchased under the previous output-royalty scheme. The marginal cost to an OEM of using Microsoft Windows rather than a competing operating system, for the units of downstream output that were vulnerable to a competing product, was close to zero. As this case illustrates, quantity discounts or non-linear pricing generally can serve to deter entry by committing an incumbent to sell marginal units at a very low price.

IV. The Law of Vertical Restraints on Interbrand Competition

A. Overview

To date, there has been relatively little jurisprudence in Canada in the context of vertical restraints on interbrand competition, for several rea-

---

85 *Supra*, note 54.

sons. First, as discussed earlier in this chapter and again in Chapter 12, such restraints are enforced under the Act as practices subject to civil review, and, as at the time of writing, only the commissioner has the jurisdiction to commence a formal proceeding with the tribunal to enforce such provisions of the Act. Second, as discussed in Part III above, the competitive impact arising from such conduct is often ambiguous from a consumer welfare perspective, in that it is often explicable by either pro- or anticompetitive economic theories. Presumably, the commissioner would be reluctant to exercise his or her jurisdiction in the presence of ambiguity regarding the competitive impact of such conduct. Third, as such matters are frequently reduced to a commercial dispute between parties, they are often resolved outside of formal proceedings, with or without the commissioner facilitating the resolution.[86]

In the following sections we discuss jurisprudence related to exclusive dealing and other exclusionary arrangements adjudicated under both sections 77 and 79 of the Act; jurisprudence related to tied-selling, again whether formally adjudicated under section 77 or 79, and jurisprudence related to conduct that falls only within the abuse of dominance provisions of the Act.

B. Exclusive Dealing and Other Exclusive Arrangements

1. The Bombardier Case

In February 1979, the director applied to the RTPC for an order directed against Bombardier Limited, to prohibit it from continuing to engage in the practice of exclusive dealing in Ontario, Quebec, and the Maritimes (which does not include Newfoundland). Bombardier conceded that it entered into exclusive agreements with dealers of its products and that it enforced these exclusive covenants. This was evidenced by, among other things, Bombardier's termination of eight dealers, who were relied upon by the director in his submissions to the tribunal.

The salient facts in *Bombardier* may be summarized as follows. The RTPC identified three relevant product markets – the markets of manufacturing, distributing, and retailing snowmobiles – and assessed the effect on competition at each of these three levels of supply. The relevant

---

86 For example, the commissioner may conduct an investigation of the facts and determine that it merits a more thorough review. Once this is conveyed to the parties, it will often facilitate a private resolution.

geographic market at the manufacturing level was held to be North America. Bombardier accounted for approximately 30 per cent of North American sales. Bombardier's share of retail sales in Quebec and the Maritimes was about 60 per cent; its share in Ontario was about 40 per cent. The sales of snowmobiles in Ontario, Quebec, and the Maritimes accounted for approximately 20 per cent of North American snowmobile sales. Only about 4 per cent of dealers carried more than one brand of snowmobile in Ontario, Quebec, and the Maritimes.[87]

Based on the foregoing and other facts, the RTPC concluded that Bombardier was a major supplier who engaged in exclusive dealing; however, it also concluded that such conduct did not result in a substantial lessening of competition. The application of the director was dismissed.

The decision of the RTPC is important for two reasons. First, it established the current interpretation of the term 'major supplier' in section 77, which was subsequently adopted by the tribunal in *NutraSweet*.[88] Second, the RTPC undertook an analysis that was well-reasoned and consistent with economic theory. In this regard, it resisted the temptation to rely simply on the fact that Bombardier had between a 40 and 60 per cent share of sales in the geographic areas in question (i.e., Ontario, Quebec, and the Maritimes) in order to condemn Bomardier's conduct. Rather, the RTPC carefully assessed the key market factors in concluding that Bombardier's exclusive dealer arrangements did not lead to a substantial lessening of competition.

While acknowledging the advantage that incumbents have in their relationship with dealers,[89] the RTPC nevertheless concluded that there was sufficient remaining competition as a result of (i) the presence of at least several other large producers of snowmobiles such as Yamaha Motor Co. Ltd., Canadian Kawasaki Motors Limited, and Arctic Sports Products Ltd.; (ii) the low barriers to entry for new dealers; (iii) the common nature of exclusive dealership arrangements in the industry; and (iv) the economic viability of dealers selling even a very

---

87 This statistic confirmed that, whether induced contractually or not, the overwhelming majority of dealers carried a single line of snowmobile.

88 *Supra*, section II.A.1.

89 Having said that, the common duration of the dealer arrangements was only one year, which promoted contestability within the dealer market.

few units of a single brand of snowmobile.[90] The RTPC also undertook a micro-market analysis to confirm that there were very few communities in which Bombardier was the only dealer. It was consequently able to conclude that sufficient competition would remain at both the manufacturer and distribution/retail levels for the supply of snowmobiles.

Despite the overall sound economic basis for the decision in *Bombardier*, the RTPC did not articulate the specific economic theories it considered in its analysis. With the benefit of hindsight, we suggest that the facts in *Bombardier* most closely accord with the procompetitive explanation for exclusive arrangements described above in Part III (B)(4) of this chapter as 'exclusivity and potential competition.' As noted in that discussion, observed market shares are not necessarily a good guide to the competitiveness of pricing in a market. Exclusive dealing forces the market into a contestability framework, where competition is *for* the market instead of *within* the market.

Each dealer, even in towns in which Bombardier had an *apparent* monopoly, had an option of selling alternative brand(s). This competition *for* the market limited Bombardier's market power. Central to the procompetitive explanation is the supplier inducing its retailers to agree to an exclusive arrangement in exchange for more advantageous terms. It is not clear from the decision in *Bombardier* whether the RTPC considered this specific point. However, it did appear to conduct a sufficient analysis of the market to enable it to conclude implicitly that the fundamental aspect of the procompetitive economic theory was satisfied: the prices Bombardier would be able to charge under an exclusive dealing arrangement would be disciplined not only by the actual competition that emerged in the market but also by the *potential* competition provided by alternative suppliers of snowmobiles.

2. The NutraSweet Case

In *NutraSweet*,[91] the director made a series of allegations under two broad categories, the first of which is emphasized below. Specifically, this category involved exclusionary contractual arrangements between

---

90 Expert witnesses on behalf of both the director and Bombardier agreed that this was the result of (i) the broad variety of lines of retail products and services that a dealer would provide; and (ii) the dynamic characteristics of retailer recruitment by competing manufacturers.

91 *Supra*, note 3.

NutraSweet and its customers under both sections 77 and 79 of the Act. The basic premise underlying the director's submissions was that the contractual arrangements undertaken by NutraSweet had captured such a large percentage of the Canadian aspartame market that the company effectively prevented existing and potential competitors from achieving 'toe-hold' entry. As *prima facie* proof of this submission, the director offered NutraSweet's market share of 95 per cent.

The alleged anticompetitive contractual arrangements may be categorized as follows. First, it was alleged that NutraSweet used its U.S. position (i.e., an operating patent) to negotiate exclusive supply contracts with the parent companies of its largest customers – predominantly, large soft drink manufacturers. Second, NutraSweet was alleged to have negotiated long-term exclusive supply contracts just prior to the expiration of its Canadian patent, effectively extending the duration of this patent for practical purposes. Third, it was submitted that NutraSweet created 'market transparency' through its contractual arrangements in an effort to better monitor its competition. Such arrangements included the utilization of 'meet-or-release,'[92] 'extended release,'[93] and 'most-favoured-nation'[94] clauses. And fourth, the director contended that NutraSweet, through the structure of its supply contracts, induced its customers to purchase NutraSweet aspartame exclusively. The contractual provisions in question included explicit exclusive supply obligations as well as a variety of fidelity rebates for customers, the most contentious of which involved significant discounts (up to 40 per cent) for displaying the NutraSweet logo on their packages. The director submitted that these acts effectively foreclosed the aspartame market in Canada to existing and potential competitors and thus requested an order by the tribunal to find the challenged clauses to be of no force and effect.

NutraSweet's principal response to the allegations of the director was that the impugned contractual provisions merely represented the

92 This clause required that NutraSweet release a customer from its contractual obligation if the customer accepted a more favourable offer from a third party which NutraSweet refused to meet.
93 This clause allowed a customer of NutraSweet to source aspartame elsewhere in the event that another third-party customer of NutraSweet aspartame was released from its supply contract.
94 This clause guaranteed a given purchaser of NutraSweet aspartame the lowest price paid by any customer for an equivalent volume.

outcome of a negotiating environment characterized by a product whose domestic patent had only recently expired; that had a very large minimum efficient scale, and thereby high sunk costs; and that had few but large and sophisticated buyers (most notably Coke and Pepsi). Those buyers, due to the fiercely competitive nature of their market (i.e., the market for diet soft drinks), demanded the impugned provisions in order to secure their input supply, the quality of this supply, and common supply terms to ensure that neither gained a competitive advantage over the other arising from their sourcing of aspartame. In short, NutraSweet submitted that the impugned contractual provisions, rather than being symptomatic of a market characterized by a dominant and oppressive producer, were the inevitable result of freely negotiated contracts in a unique, though highly contestable, market.

The principal findings of the tribunal were as follows. First, the tribunal held that the meet-or-release clauses dissuaded entry in that they discouraged the submission of rival bids from competitors. Second, by inducing exclusive arrangements, the most-favoured-nation clauses were also held to be entry-deterring instruments. The rationale applied by the tribunal was that only a firm with a sufficiently large market share (making it likely that it also supplied its customers' competitors) could feasibly be expected to confer a most-favoured-nation clause on its customers. And third, the fidelity rebates associated with the use of the NutraSweet logo were held to impose upon customers an 'all-or-nothing' choice, and thereby prevent a potential supplier from achieving an output large enough to exploit the significant economies of scale. Therefore, the tribunal found that there would be a substantial lessening of competition under both sections 79 and 77(1)(b) ('exclusive dealing') of the Act.

The decision in *NutraSweet* is disappointing, not necessarily in terms of its result, but rather in terms of the analysis undertaken by the tribunal and the virtual absence of an economic framework therein. This was most evident in the context of two critical issues in the decision: (i) the contestability of the market; and (ii) the influence of customers in motivating the exclusionary practices.

With respect to the contestability of the market, several key facts merit further consideration. First, the importance of market share in *NutraSweet* was highly overstated, based on the fact that NutraSweet's Canadian use patent for aspartame had expired a mere eight months before the director filed his application with the tribunal. In considering the short timeframe that had elapsed, exceptionally high market shares should have been anticipated. Other characteristics suggesting the existence of market contestibility were trends in the market output and the price of aspartame. Specifically, in the short period of time between the expiration of the Canadian patent and the director's filing with the tribunal, market output of aspartame had increased and price had decreased steadily. While precise statistics were not provided in the tribunal's decision, it did concede that 'NutraSweet's prices were falling.' The tribunal further conceded that '[w]hat this evidence does show ... is that what, if any, market power [NutraSweet] currently possesses is much less than it held prior to the expiration of its Canadian use patent.'[95] The tribunal, unfortunately, failed to expand on this point, but one can only infer from its eventual findings that Nutra-Sweet's market power had not diminished sufficiently to create what in the tribunal's opinion would constitute a contestable market. Moreover, the impugned contracts in *NutraSweet* were generally of a short duration (one to three years). This being the case, market contestability should not have been a serious concern for the tribunal.

A curious aspect of the *NutraSweet* decision was its treatment of the relative bargaining power between, on the one hand, NutraSweet and, on the other hand, its principal customers, most notably Coke and Pepsi. As NutraSweet argued before the tribunal, by being the predominant buyers of asparatame, Coke and Pepsi had the resources at their disposal to ensure their interests were protected and to counteract any attempt by NutraSweet to exercise market power. The uncontraverted evidence before the tribunal supported this conclusion. However, the tribunal flatly rejected the claim that Coke and Pepsi could use their high-volume purchases to present a viable threat either to establish a rival producer (for example, through backward integration) or to enhance their bargaining power when it was combined with the high sunk costs associated with aspartame production. The tribunal held that rather than strengthening the respective bargaining positions of Coke and Pepsi, the combination of both extensive sunk costs and economies of scale 'exaggerated' their ability to enter the production market.

The tribunal's assessment of the potential influence of Coke and Pepsi seriously underestimates the power and sophistication of both companies. For these two firms, aspartame represented a single input

---

95 *NutraSweet, supra* (1990), 32 C.P.R. (3d) at 29.

in one facet (diet soft drinks) of their production, which, if deemed necessary, could be sourced elsewhere. By contrast, from the perspective of NutraSweet, Coke and Pepsi were by far their largest customers of its sole product. In a statement that is in conflict with its findings, even the tribunal could not avoid acknowledging that '... success or failure for an entrant into aspartame sales hinges on its ability to obtain business from Coke or Pepsi.'[96] It would appear naïve to suggest – after taking into consideration all surrounding factors – that the presence of such dominant buyers could not prevent the exploitation of NutraSweet's alleged market power. This conclusion is ironically strengthened by the tribunal's examination of a common clause in NutraSweet's contracts, wherein it states that 'in the view of the tribunal, the meet-or-release clause is there at the *behest* of the largest customers, Coke and Pepsi ... as a way of mitigating the effects of being locked in by an exclusive contract.'[97] Although not stated explicitly in relation to the most-favoured-nation clause, the implication is similar.

With respect to the meet-or-release clause, the tribunal held that there was no reason to conclude that it, in fact, did mitigate the entry-deterring effects of an exclusive rights contract, as it was held to dissuade competitors from submitting competing bids. This is an unsatisfactory explanation in light of the fact that both Cadbury-Schwepps and Stafford Foods had recently switched their purchases of aspartame from NutraSweet to Tosoh Canada Ltd. In regard to this clause, the tribunal held that it also failed to mitigate entry-deterring effects by reasoning that a large firm would be more inclined to apply pressure to NutraSweet where assured – unlike the case in *NutraSweet* – that it alone would benefit from its effort. However, the tribunal did not make it clear how the competitors of Coke and Pepsi would necessarily benefit from the pressure exerted by these two firms. Furthermore, this holding by the tribunal implies that, when applied, such pressure would be effective, which conflicts with its earlier assessment that Coke and Pepsi could not counteract the alleged market power of NutraSweet.

Finally, the tribunal's holding that the logo display allowance merited prohibition, on the basis that NutraSweet utilized this strategy for the purpose of excluding future or existing competition, appears ques-

---

96 Ibid., at 48.
97 Ibid., at 42 [emphasis added].

tionable. For example, the customer received a discount in the range of 40 per cent off the gross price of aspartame in exchange for displaying the logo. While admittedly the cost of removing the logo must be factored into any contemplation of sourcing aspartame elsewhere, the tribunal found no evidence that any customer considered the cost of removing the logo to be prohibitive. The switch away from Nutra-Sweet by Schwepps and Stafford Foods provided practical support for this factual determination.

3. The Nielsen Case

The facts in *Nielsen, supra,* are relatively straightforward. The application filed with the tribunal by the director was concerned with the field of marketing research relating to consumer packaged goods. The case addressed three channels of distribution of such goods: grocery stores, drug stores, and mass merchandisers, with the focus on grocery stores. Marketing research related to such products is commonly used by retailers and, more notably, manufacturers to assist them in decision making and planning towards an enhanced approach to the marketing and distribution of their products. The range of marketing research services available in Canada is broad and their specific scope is dictated by the particular requirements of customers. At the time the application was brought, Nielsen offered the widest range of marketing research services in Canada. The type relevant to the application by the director were: (i) market tracking services; (ii) household (or consumer) panels; and (iii) key accounts.

In his application to the tribunal, the director made the following allegations: (i) Nielsen substantially or completely controlled the supply of scanner-based market tracking services in Canada, which the director defined as being the relevant market; (ii) the supply of scanner-based market tracking services constituted a distinct class or species of business synonymous with the relevant product market; (iii) Nielsen had engaged in or was engaging in a practice of anticompetitive acts within the meaning of section 78 of the Act; and (iv) such anticompetitive acts had the effect of lessening competition substantially in the supply of scanner-based market tracking services in Canada.

With respect to item (iii) above, the director identified the following acts as being anticompetitive: (i) the signing of exclusive contracts with retailers, many of which contained staggered terms, for the acquisition of raw scanner data; (ii) the offering of significant financial inducements for exclusive contracts; and (iii) the entering into of long-term contracts with manufacturers of consumer packaged goods for the sale of its scanner-based market tracking services.

Nielsen disputed each of the foregoing grounds of the director's application. In particular, one of Nielsen's principal allegations was that the key intervenor, Information Resources, Inc. (IRI), was the first company to attempt to introduce, albeit unsuccessfully, exclusive contracts with retailers for scanner-based data in Canada. The argument made by Nielsen, in essence, was that it was simply 'meeting the competition.' Interestingly, unlike Nielsen, which had negotiated independent and sequential exclusive contracts with retailers, IRI had pursued an 'all or nothing' exclusive contract initiative.[98] In addition, the respondent disputed the director's definition of the relevant market, arguing that it should be defined as either decision support services or market tracking services in general.

The order issued by the tribunal focused on retailer contracts, manufacturer contracts, and historical scanner data and may be summarized as follows. First, with respect to the negotiation of future retailer contracts, Nielsen was ordered not to (i) enter into contracts that precluded or restricted a supplier of retailer scanner data from providing a supplier or potential supplier of a scanner-based market tracking service with access to scanner data necessary for the provision of that service; (ii) offer an inducement to a supplier of retailer scanner data to restrict access to its data necessary for the provision of a scanner-based market tracking service; and (iii) enter into contracts with suppliers of retailer scanner data containing 'most favoured nation' clauses.

Second, with respect to existing retailer contracts, Nielsen was ordered not to enforce the following provisions in such contracts: (i) exclusivity provisions; (ii) 'preferred supplier status' provisions; and (iii) most favoured nation clauses.

Third, in regard to existing manufacturer contracts, Nielsen was ordered not to enforce any provisions that, (i) prevented the customer from giving notice of termination during any 'minimum commitment period'; (ii) required the customer to give more than eight months' notice; and (iii) required the customer to pay a penalty or lose a discount for early termination of its contract with the respondent.

---

98 This was a strategy that appeared destined for failure due to what is known in economic parlance as the 'holdout' problem. Specifically, in 1985 IRI attempted to secure the exclusive supply of grocery scanner data from all the key grocery retailers. It signed ten of eleven retailers, but failed to secure a contract with Safeway, rendering the ten signed agreements effectively null and void.

C. *Tied Selling*

1. *The BBM Case*

An early tied selling case brought by the director involved the business of providing radio and television audience listening and viewing statistics.[99] The facts in *BBM* may be summarized as follows. BBM was organized in many respects like a professional or trade association in that it had 'members,' including advertisers, advertising agencies, and broadcasters. At the time, BBM had been the only full supplier of local and national radio audience data on a regular basis in all provinces of Canada. BBM also supplied television audience data in Canada on a regular basis in all provinces. The only other supplier in this regard was A.C. Nielsen Company of Canada Limited ('A.C. Nielsen'). In addition, A.C. Nielsen offered wide-ranging market assessment data for consumer products. The director alleged that BBM was engaging in a tied sale by offering to supply the radio data on a discounted basis if the customers also purchased the television data. It is noteworthy that the customers could purchase either products separately. The RTPC concluded that the tied sale constituted a barrier to entry for A.C. Nielsen, which had exited the radio data market, but wished to continue to supply television data.

Although not explicit in its decision, it would appear that the RTPC believed that BBM was using its 'radio monopoly' as a lever to achieve a television monopoly as well. We will never know whether such a strategy would have succeeded. While A.C. Nielsen had lost money for a number of years, it had not withdrawn from the television market. Nor will we ever know how long BBM could have sustained any monopoly position it would have achieved.

2. *The NutraSweet Case*

A minor aspect of the *NutraSweet* case, *supra*, involved the allegation by the director that NutraSweet had engaged in tied selling. Specifically, the director argued that NutraSweet's trade mark constituted a tying product. He argued that, as a condition of supplying the trade mark (i.e., the NutraSweet brand name and logo) to a customer, NutraSweet required that the customer purchase another of its prod-

---

99 *Canada (Director of Investigation and Research) v. BBM Bureau of Measurement* (1981), 60 C.P.R. (2d) 26 (R.T.P.C.), aff'd (1985), 82 C.P.R. (2d) 60.

ucts, namely aspartame, and refrain from using the aspartame of any other producer. The director further argued that the respondent also offered to supply the trade mark on more favourable terms, through the logo display allowance arrangement.

Due largely to the inconsistent manner in which the director advanced the tied-selling argument, the tribunal chose to make no finding with respect to tied selling. Nevertheless, the tribunal confirmed that in appropriate circumstances, a trade mark might be the subject of a tying arrangement. The difficulty for the tribunal in *NutraSweet* was that, in his submissions, the director oscillated between defining the tying product as the NutraSweet branded aspartame and the trade mark itself.

3. The Tele-Direct Case

The most significant Canadian tied-selling case to date is *Canada (Director of Investigation and Research) v. Tele-Direct (Publications) Inc.*[100] The *Tele-Direct* case concerned two aspects of telephone directory advertising (or, as the tribunal noted it is commonly called, 'Yellow Pages' advertising), which the tribunal described as follows:

> The first aspect is the provision of advertising space in a published directory or the publishing business. This aspect of the business encompasses activities such as the compilation, printing and distribution of the directory. The second aspect is the provision of the advertising services required to create a finished advertisement for publication in a directory. The services aspect of the business includes such elements as locating customers, selling advertising space, and providing advice and information to customers on the design, content and placement of directory advertising.'[101]

The director applied to the tribunal for an order against two affiliated

---

100 *Supra*, note 24. As noted above, tied selling was a minor issue in the *NutraSweet* case and the tribunal's predecessor, the RTPC, decided a tied-selling case in *BBM*. However, as the tribunal noted in *Tele-Direct*, *Tele-Direct* was 'the first case in which tying [was] raised as a "principal" or substantial allegation.' *Tele-Direct* (1997), 73 C.P.R. (3d) at 17. For a thoughtful review of *Tele-Direct*, please refer to J.B. Musgrove and D.G. Edmonstone, 'Abuse of Dominance and Tied Selling: Some Thoughts on the *Tele-Direct* Case, (Summer 1997) *Canadian Competition Record* at 29.

101 Ibid., at 12.

companies, Tele-Direct (Publications) Inc. and Tele-Direct (Services) Inc. (for ease of reference, all further references to these entities are in the singular form 'Tele-Direct') under the tied selling and abuse of dominance provisions of the Act.

With regard to tied selling, the director alleged that:

- as a condition of supplying advertising space in telephone directories, Tele-Direct had engaged in a practice of requiring or inducing customers seeking advertising space to acquire from it telephone directory advertising services;
- Tele-Direct was a major supplier of advertising space; and
- Tele-Direct's alleged practice of tied selling had impeded entry into or expansion of firms in the market such that competition had been, or was likely to be, lessened substantially.

The director's tied selling allegation stemmed from the manner in which Tele-Direct organized the sale of advertising space in its publications, which included the provision for advertising services. In addition to Tele-Direct's own sales force, which sold both advertising space and advertising services, advertisers could purchase advertising services from independent advertising agencies. Advertising agencies provided services similar to those provided by Tele-Direct, but they were not remunerated directly by advertisers. Instead, advertisers paid Tele-Direct a single fee for advertising space and services, a percentage of which Tele-Direct paid to advertising agencies as a commission. However, advertising agencies received commissions only for so-called national accounts, which were identified based on certain eligibility criteria established by Tele-Direct.[102] While the definition of a national account had changed over time, since 1 July 1993 an account had qualified as such if the advertiser advertised in a minimum of twenty directories, including directories in at least two provinces; each advertisement had at least the value of a trade mark; and 20 per cent of the total value of the advertising was placed in directories outside Tele-

---

102 Advertising agencies were eligible to receive commissions only if they were accredited by Tele-Direct. Advertisers could also purchase advertising services from 'advertising consultants,' which were not accredited and hence ineligible for commissions. Advertising consultants were paid directly by advertisers, presumably from savings that advertisers expected to gain as a result of adopting their advice.

Direct's territory (i.e., Ontario and Quebec).[103] Tele-Direct offered a commission on all national accounts so defined, reserving for itself the servicing of all remaining accounts, which accounted for over 90 per cent of Tele-Direct's revenue.[104]

The tribunal agreed with the director's allegations that Tele-Direct had engaged in a practice of tied selling contrary to section 77 of the Act. In reaching this conclusion, the tribunal provided considerable analysis of section 77 and its application to tied selling. Indeed, the tribunal was compelled to do so by the almost total lack of agreement among the parties about the issues to be determined, which 'often left [the tribunal] to identify and define, as well as resolve, the issues.'[105]

The tribunal defined tying as 'the supply of one product *on the condition that* the buyer takes a second product as well *or* on terms that *induce* the buyer to take the second product as well.'[106] Tying arrangements are, however, far from prohibited absolutely under the Act. A tying arrangement 'may only be prohibited by the Tribunal under section 77 if it meets all the other requirements of that section, namely that the tying is a practice engaged in by a major supplier and results in a substantial lessening of competition.'[107]

The tribunal confirmed that the first step of a tied selling (and an abuse of dominant position) analysis is to identify the relevant market. As the parties agreed that the relevant geographic market was local in nature (corresponding roughly to the scope of each Tele-Direct telephone directory), the tribunal focused on defining the relevant product market. In particular, it set about defining the market for telephone directory advertising by examining factors identified in the bureau's *Merger Enforcement Guidelines*.[108] The tribunal began by applying functional interchangeability as a preliminary filter to identify media containing 'directional' advertising (i.e., advertising that directs consumers to a product). The tribunal narrowed the relevant product market by

---

103 Prior to 1 July 1993, the criteria for national accounts were less restrictive. Advertisers who qualified under the former criteria were grandfathered so long as they did not discontinue advertising at any time after 1 July 1993, in which case, upon recommencing advertising the new eligibility criteria would apply.
104 *Tele-Direct, supra* (1997), 73 C.P.R. (3d) at 113. ·
105 Ibid., at 17.
106 Ibid., at 106–7 (emphasis in original).
107 Ibid., at 107.
108 (Ottawa: Supply and Services Canada, 1991).

examining such factors as permanence and comprehensiveness, which eliminated, for example, newspapers. Furthermore, the tribunal noted that the behaviour of advertisers supported a conclusion that telephone directory advertising constituted a separate market from other advertising in other media. For example, there was little switching by customers of Tele-Direct to other media, and competitive initiatives by Tele-Direct did not elicit a response by customers in other media. Finally, the tribunal noted the difficulty of making price comparisons between telephone directory and other advertising. For these reasons, the tribunal concluded that the relevant product market was limited to telephone directory advertising.

Having identified the relevant market, the tribunal turned to determining whether a tying arrangement existed at all. According to the director, tying occurred because Tele-Direct refused to sell either advertising space or advertising services in an unbundled fashion; one could only be bought with the other. Conversely, Tele-Direct argued that 'advertising services' were not a separate product from 'advertising space,' and therefore no tying could occur, given the precondition that there be both a tying and a tied product.[109] Both parties agreed, however, that 'Canadian jurisprudence [did] not provide much guidance on the test to be applied' in distinguishing between situations where 'there are two products involved, and thus at least the possibility of an illegal tie that should be prohibited, and those where there is a single product and no question of tying.'[110] The parties therefore relied on U.S. jurisprudence for guidance, in particular, the 1984 decision of the U.S. Supreme Court in *Jefferson Parish Hospital District No. 2 v. Hyde*,[111]

---

109 Tele-Direct went so far as to state that how it sold advertisements in its directories was a business decision the determination of which was within its exclusive domain and that, citing U.S. jurisprudence (*Jack Walters & Sons Corp. v. Morton Buildings, Inc.*, 1984–2 *Trade Cas.* (CCH) ¶ 66,080 at 66,024–5 (7th Cir. 1984)), the director's position was an attack on vertical integration. The tribunal did not agree. According to the tribunal, 'simply affixing the label of "vertical integration" does not conclusively decide anything.' *Tele-Direct, supra* (1997), 73 C.P.R. (3d) at 114–15. The tribunal noted that this conclusion was consistent with the *Jack Walters* case cited by Tele-Direct, in which Posner J. acknowledged that market power may affect how vertical integration is perceived for antitrust purposes. Ibid., at 115.
110 Ibid., at 118.
111 466 U.S. 2.

although they offered different interpretations of its application to the facts at hand. For its part, the tribunal adopted the test used by the majority in *Jefferson Parish*, which was that whether separate products existed depended on the existence of separate demand for the items rather than on their functional relationship.[112] To this end, the tribunal asked two questions: 'Do a significant number of advertisers want the items separated?; and, if yes, is it efficient to separate the products?'[113]

Applying this approach to the facts before it, the tribunal noted that '[w]hen advertisers have the choice, the vast majority choose an agent, rather than Tele-Direct, for services,' which suggested that '[t]here is clearly separate demand beyond what Tele-Direct considers a "national" account.'[114] The tribunal noted, however, that this demand appeared to be limited to larger advertisers. As for efficiency considerations, there was ample evidence that advertising space and services could be sold separately, and indeed had been sold separately in the past, which led the tribunal to conclude that efficiency did not justify Tele-Direct's tying of these products. Ultimately, therefore, the tribunal found that, for large advertisers (i.e., accounts of more than $10,000), advertising space and advertising services were separate products.

In the course of its separate products analysis, the tribunal also considered the applicability of an exception recognized by U.S. jurisprudence for tying where the seller of an alleged tying product does not receive an 'additional economic benefit' from the sale of the tied product. According to Tele-Direct, such an exception applied in this case since it charged a single fee for its services, with the result that it enjoyed no additional benefit from the sale of advertising services. However, given the evidence that Tele-Direct supplied advertising

---

112 *Tele-Direct, supra* (1997), 73 C.P.R. (3d) at 119.

113 Whether the tribunal should take efficiency considerations into account was disputed by the parties. The director noted that s. 77 of the Act does not include an efficiency defence and that, assuming the necessary elements of the section have been made out, he should not have to provide a plausible explanation of why or how a person benefits from a tie. While the tribunal agreed that it should not impose such a requirement on the director, it nonetheless stated that it regarded 'demand for separate products and efficiency of bundling' as 'flip sides' of the same question. In other words, '[a]ssuming demand for separate products, if efficiency is proven to be the reason for bundling, there is one product. If not, there are two products.' Ibid., at 115.

114 Ibid., at 136.

space and services on a commissionable and non-commissionable basis and that it regarded advertising agencies (as well as advertising consultants) as competitors, the tribunal reasoned that Tele-Direct could be presumed to be receiving compensation of some sort for its advertising services. Accordingly, the tribunal expressed no doubt that Tele-Direct received some additional economic benefit from the provision of advertising services.

Although the tribunal gave only short shrift to Tele-Direct's argument that it received no additional economic benefit from its advertising services, it proceeded to make three observations about the potential application of this exception to Canadian law. First, the tribunal posited that the exception 'is closely linked in American law to the *per se* nature of tying,' which made the tribunal reluctant to adopt the exception directly, given the different (rule of reason) section 77 standard of 'substantial lessening of competition.'[115] Second, the exception would appear to apply only where 'two separate [i.e., independent] corporate entities are involved in the tying and the tied products,' which was not the case under the facts before it.[116] And finally, in the U.S. cases cited by Tele-Direct, it was clear either that the party supplying the tying product was not a supplier of the tied product or that it received no 'hidden' or 'indirect' charge for the tied product. Tele-Direct, in contrast, supplied both advertising space and advertising services, and the compensation it received presumably applied to both. Accordingly, even if the tribunal had seen fit to import the exception to Canadian law, it would have been of no assistance to Tele-Direct.

The tribunal, in any event, went on to find that Tele-Direct had engaged in a practice of tied selling. The tribunal also found that this practice had lessened competition substantially, based on an assessment of the proportion of commissionable advertising services that were being excluded from Tele-Direct's competitors. The tribunal found that more than 50 per cent of accounts were tied, with the result that, '[b]oth in relative and absolute terms, the amount of revenue affected by the tie [was] undoubtedly sufficient to conclude that there [was] a substantial lessening of competition.'[117] In reaching this conclusion, the tribunal rejected a 'technical' argument raised by Tele-

---

115 Ibid., at 132.
116 Ibid.
117 Ibid., at 174.

Direct that the wording of section 77 required that the substantial lessening of competition be assessed in the market for the tying product, in this case, advertising space. In the tribunal's view, while one may quibble about the interpretation of a provision, it must be read in a way that 'makes sense.' To this end, '[s]ince tying generally, and certainly in this case, involves "leveraging" from the tying product to the tied product market, it is only sensible to assess the effects of the practice, or the lessening of competition, in the target or tied product market.'[118]

Finally, it is worth reflecting on the tribunal's approach to devising a remedy to address its finding that Tele-Direct had engaged in a practice of tied selling in a manner that lessened competition substantially. The tribunal noted that any prohibition order it might issue would have to involve 'unbundling' the tied products. Such unbundling, however, may take one of two forms: a requirement that Tele-Direct quote separate rates for advertising space and advertising services, or the imposition of an expanded definition of commissionable accounts. Of these, the tribunal favoured the latter because of the practical implications arising from Tele-Direct's predominance in the publishing market and the accreditation of agents that suggested that the marketplace in such an 'unbundled' environment would work largely the same as prior to its order.

D. Anticompetitive Acts under Abuse of Dominance

The discussion above demonstrates that there is considerable overlap in the adjudication of exclusionary and tied-selling type conduct between conduct adjudicated under section 77 and sections 78/79 of the Act. Having said that, there is a range of conduct that constitutes a vertical restraint on interbrand competition specific to abuse of dominance. Two cases that fall into this category are analysed below: *Laidlaw*[119] and *Interac*.[120]

---

118 Ibid., at 175

119 *Canada (Director of Investigation and Research) v. Laidlaw Waste System Ltd* (1992), 40 C.P.R. (3d) 289.

120 *Canada (Director of Investigation and Research) v. Bank of Montreal et al.* (1996), 68 C.P.R. (3d) 527 [hereinafter *Interac*]. Please refer to Chapter 8 for a complete discussion related to abuse of dominance.

1. *The Laidlaw Case*

In 1991, the director brought an application against Laidlaw Waste Systems Ltd. challenging certain of its business practices in the waste removal business on Vancouver Island. This was the second case heard by the tribunal under the abuse of dominance provisions, and it provided additional detail on how the tribunal would treat the issues of market power and exclusionary contractual provisions.

At the time of the proceedings, Laidlaw was the largest waste removal service provider in Canada and the third largest in North America. It was a latecomer to the Vancouver Island market but was able to expand quickly through the implementation of an aggressive acquisition policy that targeted smaller, local firms.

The director's application focused on Laidlaw's acquisition strategy, describing it as being designed to provide Laidlaw with control over the waste hauling business on Vancouver Island. In addition, Laidlaw was alleged to have entered into services agreements with customers that effectively precluded the customer from seeking the services of a competitor, and therefore allowed Laidlaw to maintain its dominant position. Finally, when the service contracts proved ineffective at ensuring a particular customer's loyalty, Laidlaw was alleged to have used threats of litigation in order to ensure compliance with the strict terms of the agreements.

On the preliminary issue of defining 'class or series of business' under section 79(1)(a), the tribunal adopted its earlier interpretation in *NutraSweet*, by treating the issue as one of product market definition. However, the tribunal did not elaborate on the issue, since the parties had agreed that the relevant product market in question was the provision of 'lift-on-board' waste removal services.[121] Lift-on-board service involves the collection and disposal of waste that has been placed in large bins that remain at all times on the premises of the customers.

The second requirement under section 79(1)(a) is that the class or species of business in question be controlled 'throughout Canada or any part thereof.' *Laidlaw* was no exception to the general rule in competition analysis that significant emphasis be placed on market definition. Laidlaw operated in several Vancouver Island communities in which its combined market share was approximately 87 per cent. However, Laidlaw argued that one of the director's geographic mar-

121 *Laidlaw, supra* (1992), 40 C.P.R. (3d) at 295.

kets was defined too narrowly and that if Laidlaw's market definition were adopted, the extent of its market share would be reduced to approximately 50 per cent in that market, or below the level required for a *prima facie* finding of dominance.[122]

The tribunal echoed the approach first adopted in *NutraSweet* by stating that the relevant geographic market is the area within which competitors must be based if they are to provide effective competition to Laidlaw. Effective competition exists where a competitor is able to provide a restraint on the allegedly dominant firm's ability to raise prices above a competitive level.[123] Laidlaw took the position that the analysis of the geographic market should make use of the *Merger Enforcement Guidelines'* hypothetical monopolist test.[124] It then provided the tribunal with cost and revenue figures that suggested that a significant and nontransitory price increase by Laidlaw was unsustainable, since other service providers would capitalize on those prices to claim some of Laidlaw's market share. However, the director, and ultimately the tribunal, rejected Laidlaw's argument.

Market definition in merger cases must be prospective, by virtue of its timing in a transaction. In abuse of dominance cases, on the other hand, the tribunal must consider the possibility that, if the director's allegations against the respondent are true, the dominant firm will already have exercised its market power by raising prices to supracompetitive levels.[125] What is required, therefore, is an approach that is retrospective, at least to the extent that it takes into account the effect the alleged anticompetitive behaviour may have had on present prices. Consistent with this observation, the tribunal cautiously accepted the evidence presented by the director on the historical and present con-

---

122 Ibid., at 317.

123 Ibid., at 316.

124 That is, a relevant market 'is defined in terms of the smallest group of products and the smallest geographic area in relation to which sellers, if acting as a single firm (a "hypothetical monopolist") that was the only seller of those products in that area, could profitably impose and sustain a significant nontransitory price increase above levels that would likely exist in the absence of the merger.' *Merger Enforcement Guidelines*, s. 3.1, reproduced in R.S. Nozick, ed., *The 1997 Annotated Competition Act* (Scarborough, Ont.: Carswell, 1997), at 288.

125 This is an example of the so-called cellophane fallacy, i.e., the use of prices as they exist in a non-competitive market to test the substitutability of alternative goods or services (for the product market definition) or suppliers from different locations (for geographic market definition).

duct of lift-on-board disposal operators in the areas in question. Most operated in such a way as to indicate that they viewed the geographic market as local. A similar view was expressed by Laidlaw itself in a statement made in the context of a separate matter. Each of the above factors led the tribunal to agree with the director in defining the geographic markets as local.

After the tribunal had made a determination on the relevant markets, it then turned to consider whether the respondent 'substantially or completely control[ed]' them.[126] The term 'control' as it is used in the Act was interpreted in *NutraSweet* to mean market power in an economic sense, or the ability to profitably maintain prices above competitive levels. A high enough market share will lead to a *prima facie* finding of market power. However, the tribunal in *Laidlaw* drew from the *NutraSweet* decision when issuing the following caution: 'While this [the ability to set prices above the competitive level] is a valid conceptual approach, it is not one that can be readily applied; one must ordinarily look to indicators of market power such as market share and entry barriers. The specific factors that need to be considered in evaluating control or market power will vary from case to case.'[127] To this list of additional analytical factors, the tribunal in *Laidlaw* added the number of competitors in the market, their respective market shares, and the extent of any excess capacity among firms in that market.

As noted above, the tribunal found that Laidlaw's market share was 87 per cent. In coming to this conclusion, the tribunal relied exclusively on a comparison of revenues of the lift-on-board service providers in the relevant market, but recognized that appropriate adjustments should be considered where gross revenue figures are provided for a service provider's total operations.[128] In addition, the tribunal warned that excess capacity among other firms in the relevant market may reduce the accuracy of market share as an indicator of market power, and that any surplus capacity could in theory be used to partially offset the dominant firm's market share. In considering these factors, the tribunal found that although there was evidence that some of Laidlaw's competitors were serving fewer customers than their capacity would

---

126 S. 79(1)(a).
127 Reproduced in *Laidlaw, supra* (1992), 40 C.P.R. (3d) at 325 (parentheses in original).
128 Ibid., at 326.

allow, this was tempered by the fact that, as discussed below, market entry for those firms was being adversely affected by Laidlaw's contracting practices. The tribunal was ultimately unable to make a decision on whether Laidlaw was in fact charging monopoly prices, but it did find that its pricing practices led more towards a conclusion that it was. Finally, on the issue of barriers to entry, the tribunal found that very few *natural* barriers existed, the most significant being the need to acquire a sufficient customer base in order to operate at a profit. The only significant barriers to entry were created by Laidlaw through the exclusionary nature of its contracts.

In assessing whether Laidlaw had engaged in anticompetitive acts, the tribunal considered the director's allegations relating to Laidlaw's pattern of acquisitions and to its contracting practices. In doing so, it indicated that it would be guided by 'an assessment of the nature and purpose of the acts which are alleged to be anti-competitive and the effect they have or may have on the relevant market,'[129] while taking into account the commercial interests of both parties and the extent of the resulting restraint.

The tribunal concluded that the purpose of Laidlaw's acquisition strategy was first to gain a dominant position in the market and then to eliminate any effective competition from that market. In reaching this finding, the tribunal considered a number of factors. First, the frequency and timing of Laidlaw's acquisitions were such that when it decided to enter a market, it would do so within a very short time frame, acquire the leading players in that market, and then attempt to acquire any new entrant. In one instance, for example, Laidlaw acquired the only two competitors in a market on the same day. Second, although the tribunal admitted that a finding of subjective intent was not a prerequisite to a finding of anticompetitive conduct, it was a factor to be considered in the analysis. It was found that Laidlaw had exhibited anticompetitive intent through the use of threats to put competitors out of business if they refused to sell. The tribunal rejected the argument that such tactics were undertaken without the knowledge or consent of Laidlaw itself, suggesting that it 'would rarely be the case' that an employer could successfully distance itself from the actions of its employees.[130] Third, the tribunal rejected Laidlaw's business pur-

---

129 Ibid., at 333.
130 Ibid., at 334.

pose arguments with respect to the acquisitions, which centred around its corporate policy of growth through acquisition. The tribunal noted the absence of any *pro forma* financial statements, the existence of which would have supported a conclusion that Laidlaw's interest in the acquisitions was for their potential gains. Finally, Laidlaw's contracting practices were taken by the tribunal as evidence of the firm's intention to monopolize the relevant markets.

A significant issue raised by counsel for Laidlaw was whether the acquisitions could be considered at all under section 79, since they are dealt with specifically under the section 91 merger provisions. Laidlaw argued that apart from not being enumerated as an anticompetitive act under section 78, the tribunal should be wary of interfering in, and labelling as anticompetitive, the actions of two willing corporate parties. The tribunal rejected both of Laidlaw's arguments. It stated that as a matter of statutory interpretation, the list of practices enumerated in section 78 was not exhaustive and that nowhere in the Act were mergers required to be governed solely by the provisions of section 91.[131]

Laidlaw's final argument against the anticompetitive nature of its business practices attempted to characterize the exclusivity provisions in its service contracts as motivated by efficiency concerns. Automatic price increase provisions, roll-over clauses, and liquidated damages were described as having the benefit of reducing or eliminating litigation and transaction costs.[132] The tribunal, however, found that in the circumstances, the combination of these and other exclusivity provisions amounted to an attempt on the part of Laidlaw to substantially raise switching costs. The provisions in the contracts themselves became more effective through Laidlaw's threats of litigation when customers expressed a desire to terminate the relationship. As the tribunal noted '[n]o one can read the evidence concerning the use Laidlaw made of litigation and the threat of litigation in this case without a sense of outrage.'[133]

The final criteria for a finding that a firm has abused its dominant position is that its anticompetitive acts have had 'the effect of preventing or lessening competition substantially in a market.'[134] Under this

---

131 Ibid., at 336–9.
132 Ibid., at 339–40.
133 Ibid., at 343.
134 S. 79(1)(c).

heading, the tribunal considered market concentration levels in the markets in which Laidlaw operated. It found that, although the evidence presented was inconclusive as to the effect Laidlaw's acquisition practices had on concentration levels, it was clear that as a result of its entrance, concentration at times reached monopoly levels, with Laidlaw controlling 100 per cent of the market. In coming to this conclusion, the tribunal looked to the concentration levels existing both before and after Laidlaw's entrance into the market. In addition, Laidlaw's contracting practices had erected significant barriers to entry for potential competitors. The tribunal considered substantial lessening of competition not simply from the perspective of overall concentration levels but also in terms of the ability of potential competitors to enter the relevant market, and the extent to which that ability was reduced by barriers erected by the dominant firm.

2. *The Interac Case*

Although *Interac*[135] was the second consent proceeding to be brought before the tribunal in an abuse of dominance case, it was the first in which substantive issues arose regarding the application of the consent proceedings under the Act. In the *CANYPS* case,[136] no evidentiary hearing was held by the tribunal and no leave for intervenor status was requested. As the tribunal in *Interac* itself noted, the *CANYPS* case 'generated little controversy,'[137] and not surprisingly, little guidance on standards according to which the tribunal should assess a consent order. The *Interac* consent order, on the other hand, produced significant public commentary; applications for intervenor status,[138] of which four were granted; and evidentiary proceedings before the tribunal.

The preliminary issue in *Interac* was the standard of review to be applied by the tribunal when assessing the merits of a draft consent order negotiated by the director and the respondent(s). Drawing on case law dealing with the review of draft consent orders in the merger

---

135 *Supra*, note 118.
136 *Director of Investigation and Research v. AGT Directory Limited* (18 November 1994), CT9402/19, Consent Order, [1994] C.C.T.D. No. 24 (QL).
137 *Supra* (1996), 68 C.P.R. (3d) at 530.
138 The intervenors were the Retail Council of Canada; the Canadian Life and Health Insurance Association of Canada; TelPay, a telephone bill payment operator; and a group consisting of Richardson Greeshields, Midland Walwyn, Mackenzie Financial, and Trimark Investment Management.

context,[139] the tribunal stated that the test in the abuse of dominance context is 'whether the consent order will in all likelihood eliminate the substantial lessening of competition which is presumed to result from the practice of anti-competitive acts identified in the application.'[140] The high standard apparently set by the words 'in all likelihood' is somewhat softened by the references made by the tribunal to the 'initial deference' it feels bound to show towards the commissioner's proposal. The tribunal is mandated to perform its duties in the public interest and there is the presumption on its part that the commissioner is bound by a similar obligation.

As for the role of the intervenors in the proceedings, the tribunal stated that it is open for them to challenge the director's formulation of any aspect of the abuse of dominance charge. Citing the 1994 consent order in the *Microsoft* case[141] in the United States, the director suggested that intervenors should be restricted from arguing the substantive merits of the regulatory authority's position. In rejecting this argument, the tribunal noted that American jurisprudence on quasi-judicial review is founded on constitutional principles that do not apply to the Canadian context. The tribunal ruled that intervenors should be permitted to challenge all aspects of the director's case, including his approach to any substantive issue, from market definition to the description of substantial lessening of competition itself. This role is tempered, however, by the deference shown to the judgment of the director. As the tribunal states, 'Of course, since the Tribunal begins with a presumption that the Director is acting in the public interest, compelling evidence will be required to overturn his judgment on this basis.'[142]

It is clear, therefore, that the onus is on the intervenors to show that the consent order presented by the parties does not meet the minimum test of correcting the substantial lessening of competition.

The Interac network had been formed between the late 1970s and the mid-1980s by Canada's leading financial institutions in order to provide their customers with electronic access to banking services. The

---

139 The tribunal quoted from *Canada (Director of Investigation and Research) v. Air Canada* (1989), 27 C.P.R. (3d) 476 at 513–14.
140 *Supra* (1996), 68 C.P.R. (3d) at 537.
141 *United States v. Microsoft Corp.*, 56 F. 3d 1448 (1995).
142 *Interac, supra* (1996), 68 C.P.R. (3d) at 540.

nine founding or 'charter' members[143] of the proprietary network subsequently expanded access to an additional eighteen members. However, only the founding members were entitled to maintain a 'switch' that allowed for direct access to the network. Sponsored members were restricted to accessing the network through the switch of one of the founding members.

The purpose of the network was originally to provide banking customers with access to their savings and chequing accounts through automatic banking machines (ABMs), enabling them to perform a number of banking transactions electronically from ABMs belonging to any Interac member. This service was supplemented in the mid-1990s with a feature that allowed for fund transfers at a point of sale using the same card issued by the Interac member as was used for ABM transactions. Any Interac member's cardholders could access the machines provided to the retailer by any other member.

Based on these facts, the parties agreed that there were two relevant markets in which the Interac network operated. The first market was an intermediate market for Shared Electronic Network Services (SENS), which were provided by the Interac Association to its members. The second market identified was the retail market for Shared Electronic Financial Services (SEFS), which were provided by members to their cardholding customers. The two markets were described as being 'inextricably linked'[144] since the reason why access to the SENS market is desirable to financial institutions is that it allows them to provide SEFS to their customers.

The tribunal's discussion of the *Interac* decision is significant in that it implicitly recognized the concept of 'joint dominance.' Specifically, the director alleged, and for the purposes of the application the respondents did not dispute, that through their control over Interac and the enactment of exclusionary by-laws governing membership in and operation of the network, the respondents engaged in a joint abuse of dominance, contrary to section 79 of the Act. From a theoretical perspective, therefore, *Interac* was an 'essential facilities' case. The main

---

143 The named respondents were the Bank of Montreal, the Bank of Nova Scotia, Canadian Imperial Bank of Commerce, Canada Trustco Mortgage Company, La Confédération des caisses populaires d'economie Desjardins du Québec, Credit Union Central of Canada, National Bank of Canada, Royal Bank of Canada, the Toronto-Dominion Bank, and Interac Inc.
144 *Interac, supra* (1996), 68 C.P.R. (3d) at 534.

thrust of the consent order, which was issued as proposed by the parties, involved opening up direct connection access to the network by revising the governance structure of Interac and by removing existing barriers to competition in respect of pricing and the offering of new services.

Canadian antitrust jurisprudence has yet to develop an essential facilities doctrine. However, the prospect that such a line of cases will arise grows greater as the importance of network and information-based industries continues to increase.[145] In this regard, Quinn and Leslie propose a thoughtful analytical framework for assessing abuse of dominance in essential facilities cases. It differs from the test under American jurisprudence on the subject and takes the form of a four-part test. According to this framework, the tribunal should be satisfied that the following four elements are in place before imposing an obligation to make a given facility available to competitors:

(1) control over the facility is exercised by a monopolist or shared by a group of competitors with a dominant market position,
(2) the foreclosed competitor is unable to reasonably duplicate the facility or its economic function,
(3) use of the facility is denied or there is the imposition of restrictive terms (i.e., raising rival's costs) on the use of the facility, with the consequence of substantial harm to competition in a relevant market, and
(4) there is an absence of a valid business reason.[146]

Although the above criteria do, at first blush, provide an effective means of identifying circumstances where intervention is desirable, they do not address the so-called free-rider problem.[147] If it is decided that a goal of competition policy should be to open proprietary networks to competitors once they become an essential facility, this will increase the incentive for firms to simply rely on the risks taken by others in attempting to innovate rather than undertaking the effort them-

---

145 J. Church and R. Ware, 'Abuse of Dominance under the 1986 Canadian *Competition Act*,' (1998) 13 *Review of Industrial Organization* 85 at 124.
146 J.J. Quinn and G.F. Leslie, 'Essential Facilities and the Duty to Facilitate Competition,' (1996) Mimeo, Blake, Cassels & Graydon (Toronto) 1 at 32.
147 Church and Ware, 'Abuse of Dominance under the 1986 Canadian *Competition Act*,' at 124.

selves. The test outlined above should, therefore, be subject to an understanding that, if remedies are to be imposed by the tribunal, they should appropriately compensate those involved in the initial risk-taking. This could be accomplished, at least in part, through a mechanism that would allow new entrants access, but only at a price that takes into account the initial investment provided by the founding parties.[148]

V. Conclusions

In no area of competition law is economic analysis more important than in the area of vertical restraints on interbrand competition, given the inherent ambiguity of the competitive impact associated with such conduct. Exclusionary conduct may be motivated by rational, procompetitive commercial initiatives. However, virtually identical conduct undertaken in a different market context may prevent or lessen competition substantially. In the absence of an economic framework within which to undertake such analyses, adjudicators risk either improperly denying a party from engaging in conduct that is commercially advantageous and does not harm competition or perpetuating conduct that is anticompetitive.

Fortunately, all the key pieces are in place to facilitate sophisticated legal and economic analyses. First, there is a rich and growing literature of economic analysis related to vertical restraints generally, and to their implications for interbrand competitors in particular. Second, the relevant legislative provisions and their interpretations provide wide latitude to the tribunal to conduct a thorough analysis grounded in economic theory. Third, the adjudicatory structure of a specialized tribunal, which includes layperson participation, establishes a decision-making framework that promotes the role of economic analysis. With this legal and economic framework in place, the onus rests with the tribunal to bring these elements together in a cohesive and productive way.

---

148 Ibid., at 125.

Abuse of Dominance

I. Introduction

The law of abuse of dominance has evolved considerably in Canada. A prohibition of monopolies was first introduced in the *Combines Investigation Act* of 1910[1] and remained largely unchanged until the *Competition Act* of 1986.[2] The law prior to 1986 criminalized monopoly. Section 33 of the *Combines Investigation Act of 1970*[3] provided that, '[e]very person who is a party or privy to or knowingly assists in, or in the formation of, a merger or monopoly is guilty of an indictable offense ...' Monopoly was defined in section 2 of the *Combines Investigation Act of 1970* as: '[A] situation where one or more persons either substantially or completely control throughout Canada or any area thereof the class or species of business in which they are engaged and have operated such business or are likely to operate it to the detriment or against the interest of the public '...

The pre-1986 law governing monopolies was largely ineffective, with only one contested proceeding, which concerned monopolization of the wooden match business, resulting in a conviction.[4] It was ineffective for two main reasons.[5] First, it was a criminal prohibition. This made con-

---

1 S.C. 1910, c. 9.
2 R.S.C. 1985, c. C-34.
3 R.S.C. 1970, c. C-23.
4 *R. v. Eddy Match Co. Ltd.* (1953), 20 C.P.R. 107 (Que. C.A.).
5 J. Church and R. Ware, 'Abuse of Dominance under the 1986 Canadian *Competition Act*,' (1998) 13 *Review of Industrial Organization* 85 at 87 suggest three reasons, adding the lack of a definition of 'control' to the list. In our view, it is not the absence of a

victions difficult because a successful prosecution required proof beyond reasonable doubt of each element of the offence and because courts may have been reluctant to characterize as criminal practices such as acquiring a competitor. Second, the provision required a showing of likely 'public detriment' without defining the term. Courts' interpretations of 'public detriment' significantly hampered prosecutions. For example, *R. v. K.C. Irving Ltd.*,[6] which involved Irving's acquisition of all the English-language newspapers in New Brunswick, held that there was no proof of public detriment even where there was proof of lessened competition. Relying on factors such as increased circulation post-merger and the fact that all profits were reinvested in New Brunswick, the court found that actual public detriment had not been proven. *R. v. Canadian General Electric et al.*,[7] also known as *'Large Lamps,'* found no proof of public detriment even in the face of frustration of public tenders and identical pricing among three manufacturers alleged to have a 'shared monopoly.'[8] In finding no proof of public detriment from the 'shared monopoly,' the court concluded that evidence of uniform prices did not necessarily imply unreasonable prices.[9]

As a response to the perceived failure of the monopoly provisions, the 1986 *Competition Act* changed the approach radically. The new law on monopolies, now commonly known as the law on abuse of dominance, addressed both the apparent flaws of the earlier law: the new provisions were civil, not criminal, and the standard changed from the amorphous 'public detriment' to the more concrete 'substantial lessening of competition.'

In this chapter we will describe the law of abuse of dominance as found in the *Competition Act* and in the case law, as well as some of the important economic theory underlying the section. As we will see, the abuse of dominance section both explicitly and implicitly embraces practices that other sections of the Act address. For example, sections

---

definition of control that proved problematic, but rather the lack of a definition of 'public detriment.' Since control was not sufficient to convict, the provision required the courts to determine whether the monopolist was a 'bad' or a 'good' monopolist, without setting out criteria for doing so.

6 [1978] 1 S.C.R. 408. Both monopoly and merger offences were alleged, and not proven, in this case.

7 (1976), 15 O.R. (2d) 360 (H.C.).

8 We will discuss 'shared monopoly' in more detail below.

9 *Large Lamps, supra* (1976), 15 O.R. (2d) at 414.

78(d) and 78(i) both concern practices that may also be encompassed by the specific predatory pricing provision, section 50.[10] Moreover, given that the list provided in section 78 is non-exhaustive, section 79 implicitly includes practices that other sections explicitly address. Thus, for example, the tribunal in *Canada (Director of Investigation and Research) v. NutraSweet*[11] indicated that while section 78 defines only particular types of predatory pricing,[12] predatory pricing more generally could be an anticompetitive act for the purposes of section 79. As a consequence of the overlap between section 79 and other provisions in the Act, many practices that may constitute abuse of dominance are dealt with elsewhere in this book. This chapter will not repeat the analysis of such practices in any detail. Rather, it will focus on two important issues likely to arise under section 79 which are not explicitly dealt with elsewhere: the essential facilities doctrine and the use of legal processes to impose costs on rivals.

II. General Considerations Under Section 79

Section 79(1) of the *Competition Act* sets out the consequences of an abuse of a dominant position, while section 78 helps to define what an abuse is by reference to a non-exhaustive list of practices. Section 79(1) provides:

> 79(1) Where, on application by the Commissioner, the Tribunal finds that
> (a) one or more persons substantially or completely control, throughout Canada or any area thereof, a class or species of business,
> (b) that person or those persons have engaged in or are engaging in a practice of anti-competitive acts, and
> (c) the practice has had, is having or is likely to have the effect of preventing or lessening competition substantially in a market,
> the Tribunal may make an order prohibiting all or any of those persons from engaging in that practice.

Section 79(2) gives the tribunal discretion to make orders where

---

10 Specifically, ss. 78(d) and 78(i) deal with fighting brands and the reselling of articles below their acquisition price.Note, however, that s. 50 is a criminal provision while s. 79 concerns civilly reviewable practices.

11 (1990), 32 C.P.R. (3d) 1 (Comp. Trib.).

12 That is, fighting brands and reselling below acquisition price.

merely prohibiting the practice is not likely to restore competition in the relevant market. The tribunal may 'make an order directing any or all persons against whom an order is sought to take such actions, including the divestiture of assets or shares, as are reasonable and as are necessary to overcome the effects of the practice in that market.'

It is clear on the face of section 79(1) that three requirements must be met before the tribunal may make an order pursuant to section 79(2): the person must be in control, the person must be engaged in an anticompetitive practice, *and* the practice must lessen or prevent competition substantially. While we will clarify the terms in the section below, it is apparent that these requirements imply that the mere existence of monopoly power will not give rise to grounds for an order; rather, that power must be used in a manner that lessens competition substantially. That is why the prohibition lies against 'abuse of dominance,' not simply 'dominance.' Indeed, the Competition Bureau's *Enforcement Guidelines on the Abuse of Dominance Provisions* provide that, 'The abuse provisions establish the bounds of competitive behaviour for dominant firms and provide for corrective action where such firms go beyond legitimate competitive behaviour in order to damage or eliminate competitors so as to maintain, entrench or enhance their market power.'[13] This is in keeping with U.S. antitrust law. Section 2 of the *Sherman Act* condemns monopolization, which has been interpreted to require: '(1) the possession of monopoly power in the relevant market and (2) the willful acquisition or maintenance of that power as distinguished from growth or development as a consequence of a superior business product, business acumen, or historic accident.'[14] Thus, under U.S. law, as under Canadian law, it is not monopoly power, but the willful acquisition or reinforcement of monopoly power, that is condemned. This implies that high prices themselves do not violate the law.[15]

It should be noted that U.S. law includes an offence not present in Canadian law: attempted monopolization. Such an offence implies that

---

13 Competitive Bureau, Enforcement Guidelines on the Abuse of Dominance Provisions [hereinafter Guidelines] at s. 1.3
14 *United States v. Grinnell Corp.*, 384 U.S. 563 at 570–1 (2000). See generally Herbert Hovenkamp, *Federal Antitrust Policy* (St Paul: West Publishing, 1994), chap. 6.
15 See guidelines at s.1.1. In contrast, European law specifically cites 'unfair' pricing as a potential abuse of dominance: see Article 82 (formerly Art. 86) of the *European Community Treaty.*

it may be possible to be guilty of unlawful monopolization in the United States even without any market power. However, it is established that in order to be guilty of an attempt, there must be a 'dangerous probability' of success in a particular antitrust market and there must be proof of this dangerous probability separate from proof of an intent to monopolize.[16]

Case law has clarified section 79 in various ways, as described below.

A. 'Substantially or completely control': Single-Firm Dominance

The phrase 'substantially or completely control', like others in the *Competition Act*, was found in the old *Combines Investigation Act*. In *Eddy Match*, the accused argued that 'control' must mean the power to exclude others from the relevant market.[17] The court rejected the suggestion, stating, 'Parliament has not attached any special or restrictive meaning to the term "control" and for this reason I am unable to see why it should be given any meaning other than that which it normally connotes.'[18]

The tribunal rejected the director's suggestion of adopting the dictionary meaning of 'control' in the *NutraSweet* case.[19] The tribunal stated:

> The respondent's view is that 'control' is most meaningfully treated as synonymous with 'market power'. Market power is generally accepted to mean an ability to set prices above competitive levels for a considerable period. While this is a valid conceptual approach, it is not one that can readily be applied; one must ordinarily look to indicators of market power such as market share and entry barriers. The specific factors that need to be considered in evaluating control or market power will vary from case to case.
>
> The tribunal is persuaded that the respondent's position is in keeping with the logic of the section and the Act.[20]

---

16 *Spectrum Sports, Inc. v. McQuillan*, 113 S. Ct. 884 (1993). See Hovenkamp, *Federal Antitrust Policy,* at chap. 6.5.

17 *Eddy Match, supra* (1953), 20 C.P.R. at 121–2.

18 Ibid., at 122.

19 *Supra*, note 16.

20 Ibid., at 28.

This approach was confirmed in *Laidlaw*[21] and *Nielsen*,[22] and is the approach taken in the guidelir.es.

As set out in *NutraSweet*, a variety of factors are relevant to an assessment of whether a party has market power, that is, as the tribunal stated, the ability to raise prices above competitive levels for a considerable period. As the case law demonstrates, and the guidelines observe, perhaps the two most important factors are market share and barriers to entry.

Market share in *NutraSweet* was very high; NutraSweet supplied 95 per cent of the aspartame market in Canada. Moreover, the barriers to entry into the aspartame market were high because of process patents associated with producing aspartame held by incumbents (the patent for aspartame itself had expired in Canada), significant economies of scale and sunk costs, and a long start-up time of around two years. The tribunal consequently found NutraSweet had substantial control of the Canadian aspartame market.

In *Laidlaw*, the focus remained on market share and barriers to entry. Laidlaw was found to have market shares between 87 per cent and 100 per cent in various commercial waste disposal markets. The tribunal observed in this case that a market share of less than 50 per cent would not give rise to a *prima facie* finding of dominance, perhaps implying that a market share above 50 per cent would give rise to a *prima facie* finding.[23] The tribunal in Laidlaw found that barriers to entry into the commercial waste disposal industry were generally not high, although it commented that various contracting practices of Laidlaw tended to raise barriers. In coming to the conclusion that Laidlaw had market power, the tribunal noted anecdotal evidence of high pricing and price increases.

Two recent cases confirm the tribunal's emphasis on market share and barriers to entry. In *Nielsen*,[24] the tribunal stated that, given Nielsen's 100 per cent market share of the market for scanner-based

---

21 *Canada (Director of Investigation and Research) v. Laidlaw Waste Systems Ltd.* (1992), 40 C.P.R. (3d) 289 (Comp. Trib.).

22 *Canada (Director of Investigation and Research) v. D&B Companies of Canada Ltd.* (1996), 64 C.P.R. (3d) 216 (Comp. Trib.) [hereinafter *Nielson*].

23 See Davies, Ward, and Beck, *Competition Law of Canada* (Yonkers, N.Y.: Juris Publishing [nd]) at para. 9.02[4].

24 *Supra*, note 22.

market tracking services, there was a *prima facie* finding of market power, or control, that required evidence of the absence of barriers to entry for rebuttal.[25] In *Tele-Direct*, the tribunal stated that it would require evidence of 'extenuating circumstances, in general, ease of entry' to overcome a *prima facie* determination of control based on market shares of 80 per cent and higher in local telephone directory advertising markets.[26] The tribunal also concluded in *Tele-Direct* that barriers to entry, aside from targeted 'niche' entry, to the telephone directory market were significant, given the requirement of significant sunk costs and the reputation of the incumbent, as well as the incumbent's affiliation with telephone companies. In finding market power, the tribunal noted Tele-Direct's high profits and its ability to price discriminate between buyers.

It is thus apparent from the case law that market share evidence, while not determinative in itself, is very important in determining the existence of substantial control, or market power. While the cases all involved market shares of 80 per cent and higher, lower market shares may also give rise to concern. The only guidance from the tribunal is that market shares below 50 per cent do not give rise to a *prima facie* finding of market power, but this does not imply that market power could never be found below 50 per cent. Consistent with the case law, the guidelines state that a market share of less than 35 per cent will generally not give rise to concerns of market power or dominance, while a market share over 35 per cent will generally prompt further examination.[27] The treatment of market share in this manner is also consistent with the approach in the *Merger Enforcement Guidelines*.[28]

The emphasis by the tribunal on barriers to entry in abuse of dominance cases also suggests the relevance of the MEGs, which provide a framework for analysing barriers to entry. We will not repeat here the

---

25 *Nielsen, supra* (1996), 64 C.P.R. (3d) at 255.
26 *Canada (Director of Investigation and Research) v. Tele-Direct (Publications) Inc.* (1997), 73 C.P.R. (3d) 1 at 83.
27 Guidelines, at s. 3.2.1(d).
28 Ottawa: Supply and Services Canada, 1991. A member of the bureau has outlined this approach: see G. Menard, Deputy Director of Investigation and Research (Civil Matters), 'Abuse of Dominance: Some Reflections on Recent Cases and Emerging Issues,' paper delivered to Canadian Institute Conference on Competition Law and Competitive Business Practices, 10 May 1996, at 24, cited in Davies, Ward, and Beck, *Competition Law of Canada*, at para. 9.02[4], n. 48.

bureau's approach,[29] but the following passage from the MEGs is a useful summary:

> The section 93(d) [barriers to entry] stage of the Bureau's assessment is directed toward determining whether entry by potential competitors would likely occur on a sufficient scale in response to a material price increase or other change in the relevant market brought about by the merger, to ensure that such a price increase could not be sustained for more than two years.
>
> In this assessment, consideration is given to any matter or combination of matters that would make entry on this scale within two years less likely or more difficult. This generally involves an examination of whether entry is likely to be delayed or hindered by the presence of absolute cost differences or the need to make investments that are not likely to be recovered if entry is unsuccessful. These investments are referred to ... as sunk costs.[30]

While proving low entry barriers may serve to rebut *prima facie* evidence of market power, parties have put forward other arguments seeking to rebut a presumption of market power. For example, in *NutraSweet*, NutraSweet argued that its two main customers, Coca-Cola and Pepsi, were sufficiently powerful to negate a finding that NutraSweet had any market power. The tribunal rejected this argument on the facts, finding that it was unlikely that either Coke or Pepsi would produce aspartame themselves or would switch products in response to a price increase by NutraSweet. The case demonstrates, however, that a variety of factors can conceivably suggest the existence or absence of market power.

B. 'One or more persons': Joint Dominance

While market dominance may be achieved by a single firm, section 79 contemplates that more than one person may enjoy substantial control over a class or species of business. The notion of 'shared monopoly' arose in earlier case law. In the *Large Lamps* case,[31] the court found that

---

29 See Chapter 4.
30 MEGs, at para. 4.6.
31 *Supra*, note 7.

three suppliers, with 95 per cent of the Canadian electric light bulb market between them, could together constitute a 'shared monopoly' pursuant to the monopoly provisions. A shared monopoly occurs where 'one or more persons, inclusive of independent corporations, through the coordination of their activities work together as a unit.'[32]

Joint dominance was central to the *Interac* case.[33] In *Interac*, the tribunal approved a consent order agreed to by the director and various parties that together formed the Interac association. Interac was the dominant entity in the electronic financial services market in Canada. Interac agreed to several undertakings, including easing access to membership in the association, in response to the director's investigation into possible abuses of dominance.

With respect to joint dominance cases, the *Interac* case is fairly straightforward. The parties involved were expressly acting collectively through Interac and thus Interac's dominance led in a straightforward way to a finding of joint dominance. Such an express agreement was also present in the only other joint dominance case, *CANYPS*. Support for finding joint dominance on the basis of an agreement is found in section 79(6), which provides that no application may be brought against a person under section 79 where proceedings have also been brought under the conspiracy provision, section 45.[34] This implies that section 79 may apply to agreements between firms.

It is an open question, however, whether joint dominance will be found in the absence of such an express agreement between firms. Church and Ware suggest that a small group of oligopolists who adopt a practice that facilitates their coordination in order to suppress competition, without expressly agreeing to do so, may be jointly held to be abusing dominance; the facilitating device constitutes an anticompetitive practice, as we will explain in more detail shortly.[35] Another commentator has noted that the abuse of dominance regime was adopted in the *Competition Act* in order to replace an ineffective regime hand-

---

32 Ibid., at 407.
33 *Canada (Director of Investigation and Research) v. Bank of Montreal et al.* (1996), 68 C.P.R. (3d) 527 (Comp. Trib.) [hereinafter *Interac*]. Joint dominance also arose in *Canada (Director of Investigation and Research) v. AGT Director Ltd. et al.*, [1994] C.C.T.D. No. 24 Trib. Dec. No. CT 9402/19 [hereinafter *CANYPS*].]
34 For a discussion of section 45, see Chapter 3.
35 Church and Ware, 'Abuse of Dominance,' at 94. A member of the bureau has made a similar suggestion in a speech: see Menard, 'Abuse of Dominance.'

cuffed by high standards of proof and undefinable standards of 'public detriment.'[36] Finding joint dominance even in the absence of an explicit agreement may be in keeping with the pragmatic approach to monopolization found in the modern *Competition Act*. This is especially so given the difficulty, both in fact and as a matter of theory, of proving an 'agreement' under the criminal conspiracy provisions when the firms in question have not explicitly agreed to set prices.[37]

To explain the concept of a facilitating device as an anticompetitive practice, it is first important to note that competition law prevents firms from explicitly agreeing to fix prices.[38] In order to realize supracompetitive profits, an oligopoly relying on an implicit agreement requires three elements: an agreement between the oligopolists; a means of detecting deviations from the agreement;[39] and a means of punishing such deviations.[40] Facilitating practices may assist with respect to all three elements. With respect to agreement, examples of facilitating practices may include pre-announcing price increases, using delivered pricing to increase transparency, or publicizing price lists, such that competitors become aware of the cartel price. In *R. v. Armco Canada Ltd.*,[41] metal pipe manufacturers adopted a policy of publicizing their price lists.[42] One of the firms, Robertsteel, became the price leader. An example of a facilitating practice that helps firms detect price deviations, as well as punish them, is a meet-or-release clause, pursuant to which a firm must either match an offer received by a customer or release the customer from any obligation to purchase from it. This clause would alert a firm to price-cutting by other firms, thereby facili-

---

36 Davies, Ward, and Beck, *Competition Law of Canada*, at para. 9.03.
37 See, e.g., *R. v. Atlantic Sugar Refineries Co. Ltd.* (1976), 26 C.P.R. (2d) 14. See, generally, Chapter 3.
38 See s. 45 of the *Competition Act*.
39 Since a successful cartel will raise price above marginal cost, there would be, in the absence of detection and punishment, an incentive to cheat by lowering price and selling a greater quantity. If all parties to the agreement cheat, the cartel will break down. See Chapter 3.
40 See J. Langenfeld and M. Sanderson, 'Practices that may Facilitate Collusion in an Oligopoly: The Canadian and U.S. Experiences' (unpublished); J. Howard and W. Stanbury, 'Oligopoly Power, Co-ordination and Conscious Parallelism,' in F. Mathewson, M. Trebilcock, and M. Walker, eds., *The Law and Economics of Competition Policy* (Vancouver: Fraser Institute, 1990), 219.
41 (1974), 6 O.R. (2d) 521 (H.C.J.).
42 See also, *Atlantic Sugar, supra*, note 37, where price lists were posted in a firm's lobby.

tating detection of deviations. It also allows punishment, in a sense, by allowing the firm to match the offer, thus preventing the price-cutter from making the sale. Similar practices incorporate stronger punishments, such as a promise by a firm to beat any rival's price by 10 per cent. Other facilitating practices related to punishment include most-favoured-nation (MFN) clauses, pursuant to which the seller commits to offer the buyer terms at least as favourable as those offered to any other customer. These effectively commit a firm to punishing itself for offering a selective price cut to a particular customer, since that price cut would have to be offered to all customers with MFN clauses. MFN clauses may deter selective price cuts and stabilize a cartel.[43]

It thus may be appropriate under section 79 to conclude that a group of firms acting in parallel fashion are jointly dominant and that the facilitating device used by the firms constitutes an anticompetitive act: the device substantially lessens competition. Of course, efficiency may explain many of the facilitating practices, depending on the circumstances. Publicizing price lists may be an innocuous way of informing customers; meet-or-release or most-favoured-nation clauses may be efficient in that they protect a customer from changes in the market price of a product for the duration of a long-term contract. Such efficiency explanations do not preclude the use of section 79 to address facilitating practices in a situation of joint dominance. As we will see, efficiency plays a role under section 79 in determining whether an act has the requisite anticompetitive purpose and also whether it lessens competition substantially. The abuse of dominance regime is thus equipped to deal sensibly with an oligopoly's use of facilitating practices.

Consistent with this analysis, the guidelines state that, 'the ability of a group of firms to coordinate actions without entering into an explicit agreement can be addressed under the abuse provisions.'[44] Moreover, section 4.4 of the guidelines explicitly contemplates facilitating practices as possible abuses of dominance. To infer joint control, the guidelines look to the market share of the firms in question, barriers to entry, evidence of attempts to stifle intragroup rivalry, evidence of countervailing market power by customers, and 'evidence that the alleged

43 For a more thorough examination of facilitating practices, see Langenfeld and Sanderson, 'Practices that may Facilitate Collusion,' and Howard and Stanbury, 'Oligopoly Power.'
44 Guidelines, at s. 3.2.1(e).

coordinated behaviour is intended to increase price or is for the purpose of engaging in some form of anti-competitive act.'[45] The guidelines state that a market share of a group that is 60 per cent or more will prompt further examination into joint dominance.[46]

C. 'Class or species of business': Product Market

The phrase 'class or species of business' originated in the earlier monopoly provisions of the *Combines Investigation Act* set out above. An important early monopoly case, *Eddy Match*,[47] offered a narrow interpretation. The accused, which produced wooden matches, argued that 'class or species of business' encompasses the product in question as well as its close substitutes, such as lighters and paper matches. The court rejected this approach, concluding that wooden matches were themselves a class or species of business, 'since this commodity can be distinguished from the other devices, such as mechanical lighters and the like ...'[48]

Jurisprudence under the *Competition Act* has rejected the narrow reading found in *Eddy Match*. In *NutraSweet*, the tribunal held that it would be in keeping with the structure of the Act to conclude that 'class or species of business' equates with the relevant product market. The tribunal stated that the critical question in defining the product market is whether competition from other sweeteners limits the ability of aspartame producers to raise prices.[49]

This approach was confirmed in *Laidlaw*, and later in *Nielsen*, where the tribunal set out the basic approach to product market definition:

> The standard test for establishing whether products that are differentiated in one or more ways are close substitutes and therefore in the same product market is to determine whether small changes in relative price would cause buyers to switch from one product to another. Direct evidence of switching behaviour in response to small changes in relative price would provide proof of substitutability. Where price and quantity changes are not in evidence, as was true in the instant case, it is necessary to answer the question less directly by examining the evidence of both buyers and

45 Ibid.
46 Guidelines, at s. 3.2.1(d).
47 *Supra*, note 4.
48 Ibid., at 119.
49 *NutraSweet, supra* (1990), 32 C.P.R. (3d) at 18.

516 The Law and Economics of Canadian Competition Policy

suppliers regarding the characteristics, the intended use and the price of various types of market tracking services [the product market in question in *Nielsen*].[50]

Thus, qualitative factors such as functional interchangeability will be important in defining the market, at least where cross-elasticity data are unavailable. The tribunal in *Nielsen* held that scanner-based market tracking services were distinct from other tracking services because of the speed of their production, their accuracy, and their detail.

The guidelines also equate 'class or species of business' with product market.' They look to many factors, such as the views of buyers, functional interchangeability, switching costs, and historical price movements, to determine the product market. The guidelines also take the hypothetical monopolist approach to defining the market, which is discussed more fully in the mergers chapter (Chapter 4).

This approach to 'class or species of business' is consistent with the tribunal's conclusion that 'control' equates with 'market power.' In both the determination of control and the class or species of business, it is important to consider the availability of substitutes for the product produced by the firm in question. The presence or absence of substitutes is clearly a key factor in determining whether market power, and the ability to abuse that power, exists for the purposes of section 79.

The tribunal in *Tele-Direct*[51] noted that the ability to price discriminate may affect the boundaries of the market. It stated:

A firm without the ability to price discriminate may be disciplined by the ready ability of at least some of its customers to switch if prices are increased and, when considering a price increase, must weigh what it will lose against what it will gain from that action.

However, where a firm has found a way to price discriminate, no weighing need be considered. The prices for customers who might switch will be left at a level where they will continue to purchase. However, for those customers who are so reliant on the firm that they cannot switch, the firm may extract higher prices and therefore higher profits on sales to them. The ability to price discriminate therefore tends to demonstrate that a

---

50 *Nielsen, supra* (1996), 64 C.P.R. (3d) at 241.
51 *Supra*, note 26.

firm is not, at least in respect to the customers who are subject to the discrimination, vulnerable to those customers substituting other products for that of the firm.[52]

While the approach to defining the product market in abuse of dominance cases theoretically resembles the approach taken in merger cases, it is important to note a practical difference between the two cases. Merger cases are largely concerned with the emergence or increased significance of market power, whereas abuse of dominance cases, as we have seen, treat the existence of significant market power as a prerequisite. The existence of significant market power may have an effect on the consideration of the availability of substitutes because of what is known as the 'cellophane fallacy.'

In a U.S. Supreme Court case, *United States v. E.I. Dupont de Nemours & Co.*[53] the court concluded that cellophane had close substitutes in part on the basis of evidence that small price changes in cellophane caused customers to switch to other types of flexible packaging. This conclusion was misguided. The court overlooked the fact that if the seller of cellophane had considerable market power, it would set prices at a high level; in economic terms, it would set price in the elastic portion of the firm's demand curve, or where a further increase in price would cause a decline in revenue. Evidence of customers switching products at the monopoly price does not imply that those substitutes are providing significant competitive discipline on the cellophane supplier. Rather, at competitive price levels, it may be that price could increase considerably before customers would switch products.

Given that product market definition is intended to determine sources of competitive discipline, sensitivity to the cellophane fallacy is important. In abuse of dominance cases, where significant market power is a prerequisite, it is particularly important that the fallacy be taken into account. This consideration has been noted explicitly by the tribunal in both the *Nielsen* and *Laidlaw* cases, as well as the guidelines, s. 3.2.1(c). It implies that when applying the hypothetical significant, nontransitory price increase, it may be appropriate to lower the base price relative to existing market prices.

---

52 Ibid., at 63.
53 351 U.S. 377 (1956).

D. 'Throughout Canada or any area thereof': Geographic Market

The case law has treated the phrase, 'throughout Canada or any area thereof,' to refer to the geographic market in which the allegedly dominant firm has market power. In determining the geographic market, the tribunal has stated that one must consider 'whether an area is sufficiently isolated from price pressures emanating from other areas so that its unique characteristics can result in prices differing significantly for any period of time from those in other areas.'[54] In *NutraSweet*, the tribunal concluded that Canada itself was a distinct geographic market, largely on the basis of evidence demonstrating that prices for aspartame in Canada were distinct from those in Europe and the rest of the world.

In *Laidlaw*, the tribunal adopted an approach to geographic market definition consistent with the hypothetical monopolist approach set out in the MEGs. Laidlaw argued that price increases in local regions could not take place independently; rather, competitors from other regions would enter and discipline these increases. Consequently, Laidlaw argued that the relevant geographic market should not be local. The tribunal noted that expansion of the geographic market would leave Laidlaw with market shares below 50 per cent. The director successfully countered Laidlaw's argument by raising the cellophane fallacy: the relevant question was not whether an increase in price from *existing* levels would cause customers to switch to waste disposal suppliers from other regions, but rather whether raising prices from *competitive* levels would cause such switching. The tribunal accepted this argument and on the facts concluded that the relevant geographic market was local. The tribunal reached this conclusion on evidence of transportation costs and the absence of historical competition between suppliers in different regions.

The approach in *Laidlaw* is thus consistent with the hypothetical monopolist approach in the MEGs that is now also found in the guidelines: suppliers are in the same geographic market if one exerts competitive pressure on the other. The process set out in the MEGs of asking whether a hypothetical monopolist could profitably impose a significant and nontransitory price increase is therefore relevant to abuse of dominance cases. The guidelines suggest an examination of

---

54 *NutraSweet, supra* (1990), 32 C.P.R. (3d) at 20–1.

factors such as customers' and suppliers' views, transportation costs, historical shipment patter.is and historical price movements across regions. As *Laidlaw* and the guidelines correctly point out, in abuse of dominance cases, where market power is a pre-requisite, it is particularly important to be alert to the cellophane fallacy.

E. 'Have engaged or are engaging in'

Section 79 refers not only to practices that a dominant firm or firms are presently engaged in, but also to practices they 'have engaged in.' It is apparent, therefore, that an order could be made on the basis of past practices as well as current practices. There are, however, two limitations on the application to discontinued practices.

First, section 79(6) provides, 'No application may be made under this section in respect of a practice of anti-competitive acts more than three years after the practice has ceased.' Thus, the section only encompasses practices that are ongoing or discontinued within the previous three years.

A second practical limitation on the retrospective application of section 79 is the availability of remedies. If a practice has already ceased, a cease and desist order is obviously of no use. If the practice has left a lasting impact, more drastic remedies, perhaps even structural remedies, may be required. It could be that the harm caused by structural remedies, perhaps to efficiency, exceeds the gains, thus implying that they are less likely to be ordered than cease and desist orders or other prospective orders.

F. 'Practice'

Pursuant to section 79(1), the dominant firm must have engaged in or must be engaging in a 'practice' of anticompetitive acts. Nowhere in the *Competition Act* or its predecessor legislation is 'practice' defined, although the term is found elsewhere in both. The resale price maintenance case of *R. v. William Coutts Co. Ltd.*[55] involved a question of whether a small chain of gift shops had engaged in a 'practice' of loss-leader selling that justified the accused's refusal to supply. The shop chain had a one-week sale at a new location and another sale at an

---

55 [1968] 1 O.R. 549.

older location. The court stated: 'I believe the word is used in the section in the sense that it denotes a distinction from an isolated act or acts ... [In examining the advertisements for the sales in this case,] there was uniformity and consistency for the term of each sale and for these periods of time the sales were extensive and in my opinion constituted a practice.'[56]

Price discrimination law also requires a 'practice of discriminating.'[57] In *Hurtig Publishers Ltd. v. W.H. Smith Ltd.*,[58] the court held that 'practice' meant 'habitual, customary, repeated, systematic,' and thus two sales of like quality and quantity at different prices did not constitute a practice of discrimination. The *Price Discrimination Enforcement Guidelines* provide that the director, in determining whether there is a 'practice' of discriminating, will consider factors such as the frequency and duration of discrimination and the consistency and purpose of the pricing behaviour.

A broad view of practice was also established under the abuse of dominance provisions in the *Competition Act* in the *NutraSweet* case. The tribunal held in that case: 'The interpretation of "practice" must be sufficiently broad so as to allow for a wide variety of anti-competitive acts. Accordingly, the tribunal is of the view that a practice may exist where there is more than an "isolated act or acts." For the same reasons, the tribunal is also of the view that different individual anti-competitive acts taken together may constitute a practice.'[59]

The guidelines take a similarly broad approach to 'practice,' stating that 'while a practice is normally more than an isolated act, it may also constitute one occurrence that is sustained and systemic or that has had a lasting impact on the state of competition.'[60]

G. *'The practice has had, is having or is likely to have the effect of preventing or lessening competition substantially in a market'*

The test of 'preventing or lessening competition substantially' replaced the amorphous 'public detriment' test of earlier competition statutes.

---

56 Ibid., at 555.
57 See s. 50(2) of the *Competition Act*.
58 (1989), 99 A.R. 70 at 79 (Alta. Q.B.).
59 *NutraSweet, supra* (1990), 32 C.P.R. (3d) at 35.
60 Guidelines, at s. 3.2.2(a).

While the modern test is not entirely clear without the benefit of case law, which we discuss shortly, it places the focus squarely on competition. This avoids the approach of earlier courts in looking at 'public detriment' to canvass factors unrelated to competition,[61] as well as the danger of looking solely at the effect of a practice on competitors, rather than competition. As the tribunal noted in *Tele-Direct*, 'seizing market share from a rival by offering a better product or lower prices is not, in general, exclusionary since consumers in the markets concerned are made better off.'[62] By setting the test as one based on a preventing or lessening of competition, section 79 better ensures that it is consumers, not competitors, that provide the focus of the abuse provisions.

It is clear from the wording of the statute that the negative effects on competition may be past, present, or future effects. The acts themselves, as noted above, may also be past or present, although there is a three-year limitation period.[63]

The case law has developed the meaning of 'substantially lessening competition.' The tribunal in *NutraSweet* stated: 'In essence, the question to be decided is whether the anti-competitive acts engaged in by NSC [NutraSweet] preserve or add to NSC's market power.'[64] The tribunal considered a variety of factors in concluding that the acts did preserve or add to NutraSweet's market power, and noted that many of the factors relevant to a determination of dominance, such as market shares and entry barriers, will also be relevant to this determination. The guidelines adopt this approach.

The tribunal held in *NutraSweet* that 'the exclusivity in NSC's contracts, which includes both the clauses reflecting agreement to deal only or primarily in NutraSweet brand aspartame and the financial inducements to do so, impedes "toe-hold entry" into the market and inhibits the expansion of other firms in the market.'[65] A logo display allowance, which involved significant discounts to buyers of aspartame that included NutraSweet's logo on the end-product's packaging, further impeded entry by increasing the cost to a customer of switching from NutraSweet to a different aspartame supplier. Any customer seeking to buy small quantities of aspartame from a party other than

---

61 See, e.g., *K.C. Irving, supra*, note 6.
62 *Tele-Direct, supra* (1997), 73 C.P.R. (3d) at 196.
63 S. 79(6).
64 *NutraSweet, supra* (1990), 32 C.P.R. (3d) at 47.
65 Ibid., at 48.

NutraSweet would face significant costs. These factors led the tribunal to conclude that NutraSweet's practice of anticompetitive acts lessened competition substantially.

Applying this test in the *Laidlaw* case, the tribunal concluded that Laidlaw's acquisition of 100 per cent of the market in some instances, along with exclusivity provisions and litigation threats to customers contemplating rival suppliers that raised barriers to entry, lessened competition substantially. In *Nielsen*, the tribunal rejected Nielsen's argument that competition was not lessened by Nielsen's exclusive control over the main input, scanner-based data for the market in scanner-based market tracking services. Nielsen argued that it was open to other rivals to attempt to bid for the exclusive contracts when they came up for renewal (competition 'for' the market rather than 'within' it), but the tribunal rejected the argument, noting that Nielsen's contracts came up for renewal on a staggered basis. An entrant could not obtain the access to a broad supply of data required for effective entry. The tribunal found that the practices lessened competition substantially.

In *Tele-Direct*, the director alleged as an abuse of dominance Tele-Direct's discriminatory tactics towards advertising consultants.[66] In finding a substantial lessening of competition, the tribunal set a variable standard for finding a 'substantial lessening' depending on how competitive the market is to begin with:

> Where a firm with a high degree of market power is found to have engaged in anti-competitive conduct, smaller impacts on competition resulting from that conduct will meet the test of being 'substantial' than where the market situation was less uncompetitive to begin with. In these circumstances, particularly Tele-Direct's overwhelming market power, even a small impact on the volume of consultants' business, of which there is some evidence, by the anti-competitive acts must be considered substantial. Of course, in the future, in the absence of any order by the tribunal, there would be no constraint on Tele-Direct intensifying discriminatory acts against consultants and exacerbating an already substantial effect on them. We have no difficulty concluding that Tele-Direct's proven practice of anti-competitive acts has had, is having or is likely to have the effect of lessening competition substantially in the market [for advertising services].[67]

---

66 We will outline these tactics below in discussing anticompetitive acts.
67 *Tele-Direct, supra* (1997), 73 C.P.R. (3d) at 247-8.

As we will see below, the efficiency motivation underlying a practice may be relevant to an assessment of whether an anticompetitive purpose exists. Efficiency considerations may also play a role in determining whether a practice is likely to lessen or prevent competition substantially. In *NutraSweet*, for example, the tribunal considered and rejected various efficiency explanations of the exclusive arrangements NutraSweet had with its customers. The tribunal concluded that exclusivity was not necessary to protect NutraSweet's investments in developing the aspartame market from free-riding by rivals in aspartame supply. It stated: 'The tribunal does not accept that NSC is entitled to any more protection against competition than it was able to obtain through patent grants that provided it with a considerable head start on potential competitors.'[68] Nevertheless, the approach by the tribunal indicates that efficiency considerations may play a role in determining whether a practice is likely to lessen or prevent competition substantially.

III. Anticompetitive Acts Pursuant to Sections 78 and 79

Section 78 provides a non-exhaustive list of anticompetitive acts may contribute to a finding of a practice of anticompetitive acts. It provides:

> 78 For the purposes of section 79, 'anti-competitive act,' without restricting the generality of the term, includes any of the following acts:
> (a) squeezing, by a vertically integrated supplier, of the margin available to an unintegrated customer who competes with the supplier, for the purpose of impeding or preventing the customer's entry into, or expansion in, a market;
> (b) acquisition by a supplier of a customer who would otherwise be available to a competitor of a supplier, or acquisition by a customer of a supplier who would otherwise be available to a competitor of the customer, for the purpose of impeding or preventing the competitor's entry into, or eliminating the competitor from, a market;
> (c) freight equalization on the plant of a competitor for the purpose of impeding or preventing the competitor's entry into, or eliminating the competitor from, a market;

---

68 *NutraSweet, supra* (1990), 32 C.P.R. (3d) at 52.

(d) use of fighting brands introduced selectively on a temporary basis to discipline or eliminate a competitor;

(e) pre-emption of scarce facilities or resources required by a competitor for the operation of a business, with the object of withholding the facilities or resources from a market;

(f) buying up of products to prevent the erosion of existing price levels;

(g) adoption of product specifications that are incompatible with products produced by any other person and are designed to prevent his entry into, or to eliminate him from, a market;

(h) requiring or inducing a supplier to sell only or primarily to certain customers, or to refrain from selling to a competitor, with the object of preventing a competitor's entry into, or expansion in, a market; and

(i) selling articles at a price lower than the acquisition cost for the purpose of disciplining or eliminating a competitor.

In keeping with the notion that it is not monopoly or dominance itself that is potentially subject to an order, but rather an abuse of that monopoly or dominance, it is noteworthy that section 78 does not describe the setting of high prices alone as an anticompetitive act. This is consistent with U.S. law, but contrasts with the approach taken in Europe. Article 82 (formerly Art. 86) of the *European Community Treaty* provides that it is an abuse of dominance for a dominant firm to impose 'unfair purchase or selling prices.'

Recently, the abuse of dominance provisions were amended to address the airline industry. As noted in Chapter 5, these amendments seem generally directed at predatory pricing in the airline industry, although other practices could also be defined to be abuses of dominance.[69] A regulation-making power, since exercised, has been granted to the governor-in-council (the federal Cabinet) to specify anticompetitive acts or conduct of a domestic air carrier on the recommendation of the ministers of industry and transport. Section 78 is enlarged to include such acts as are specified in the regulations. Moreover, the commissioner has the power (without consulting the tribunal) to make temporary orders prohibiting a person operating a domestic airline

---

69 See generally, M. Sanderson and M.J. Trebilcock, 'Bad Policy, Bad Law: Bill C-26 Amendments to the *Competition Act* on Airline Predation,' (2000) 20 *Competition Policy Record* 32.

from doing anything that could, in the commissioner's opinion, harm competition. Such a temporary order may be made if the commissioner has commenced an inquiry pursuant to section 79, and, absent the order, injury to competition or a competitor that cannot adequately be remedied by the tribunal would result. We leave discussion of these provisions to Chapter 5, but note here our conclusion that such a wide-reaching power to intervene in the face of *possibly* predatory prices could chill vigorous price competition in the airline sector.

The list in section 78, as noted, is non-exhaustive, which has been emphasized by the tribunal in several cases.[70] The difficulty then lies in determining whether an act not enumerated in section 78 is an 'anti-competitive act' pursuant to section 79. The case law has provided guidance on this question.

The tribunal in *NutraSweet* emphasized the unifying theme in the acts listed in section 78: they are all, except perhaps section 78(f), associated with an anticompetitive purpose.[71] More particularly, '[t]he purpose common to all acts, save that found in paragraph 78(f), is an intended negative effect on a competitor that is predatory, exclusionary or disciplinary.'[72] Such an intent, the tribunal reasoned, must therefore be found with respect to any act that is alleged to be an 'anti-competitive act' under section 79. This purpose test serves a valuable screening role with respect to finding an anticompetitive act. The acts enumerated in s. 78, and other acts that may be alleged to be anticompetitive, will often be at worst neutral with respect to competition while having significant efficiency properties. Vertical integration, found in section 78(b), for example, will frequently be a benign, efficient act. The case law implicitly recognizes this: only where its intended effect is predatory, exclusionary, or disciplinary will section 79 potentially be engaged. This suggests that most acts, even those by dominant firms, are unlikely to be anticompetitive acts under section 79.

While intent may serve a valuable role in distinguishing anticompetitive from benign conduct, it leaves open difficult questions of proving intent. *NutraSweet* helped resolve potential problems. The tribunal stated: 'The determination of an anti-competitive act, and particularly

---

70 See *NutraSweet, supra*, note 11; *Laidlaw, supra*, note 21; and *Tele-Direct, supra*, note 26.
71 *NutraSweet, supra* (1990), 32 C.P.R. (3d) at 34.
72 Ibid.

its purpose component, is a difficult task. The Director submits that evidence of subjective intent (through verbal or written statements of personnel of the respondent) or a consideration of the act itself (the premise that a corporation can be taken to intend the necessary and foreseeable consequences of its acts) can be used to establish purpose. The tribunal finds nothing objectionable in these submissions. In most situations, of course, the purpose of a particular act will have to be inferred from the circumstances surrounding it.'[73] Thus, proving intent does not require proof of the subjective intent of the party accused of anticompetitive acts, but rather may be inferred from the circumstances. This supports the view that the intent requirement helps distinguish benign acts from anticompetitive acts: if the circumstances are such that the act likely has procompetitive, or efficiency-enhancing, effects, it is unlikely that one could infer a predatory, exclusionary, or disciplinary intent from the circumstances.

Such a screening role for intent is also supported by *Nielsen* and *Tele-Direct*. In *Nielsen*, the parties submitted that various exclusive dealing contracts were justified in order to protect their investment in a new technology from free-riding by competitors. The tribunal rejected the argument on the facts, concluding that there was little evidence of investments that were appropriable by competitors. However, the fact that the tribunal entertained the argument suggests the screening role of the intent requirement.

Tele-Direct presents the best example of the role of intent in distinguishing efficient from anticompetitive acts. The tribunal reiterated in that case that subjective intent was not required to prove an anticompetitive act, but rather agreed with the director's submission that 'it might be more apt to speak of the overall character of the act in question.'[74] The tribunal went on to state that 'a case-by-case factual analysis will always be necessary to determine if, in the particular circumstances, an act is anti-competitive. All the relevant factors must be weighed in deciding whether a particular act is, in the circumstances, competition on the merits or an anti-competitive act. That question cannot be answered as a matter of law in a vacuum.'[75]

---

73 *NutraSweet, supra* (1990), 32 C.P.R. (3d) at 35–6.
74 *Tele-Direct, supra* (1997), 73 C.P.R. (3d) at 180.
75 Ibid., at 181.

Whether an act should be found to be an anticompetitive act will depend on whether an analysis of the particular circumstances suggests that it is indeed anticompetitive, as opposed to procompetitive or neutral. If circumstances suggest a pro-competitive, or an efficiency, motivation, the requisite predatory, exclusionary, or disciplinary intent will not be present and there is no anticompetitive act.

The tribunal's factual analysis in *Tele-Direct* confirms this approach. Tele-Direct, which produces Yellow Pages telephone directories, had refused to deal directly with advertising consultants and refused to act on either written or oral instructions from these consultants on behalf of their customers, the advertisers. The director alleged that the refusals to deal directly with consultants constituted anticompetitive acts in the market for advertising services. Stating that it was appropriate to weigh any anticompetitive effects with any business justifications, the tribunal rejected the allegation on the basis of scant evidence of harm to consultants combined with Tele-Direct's efficiency explanation of their practice. Tele-Direct submitted that dealing directly with consultants, who were not responsible for paying for advertising, would have required them to set up an additional interface. The tribunal stated, 'In the circumstances, we think that the additional costs that Tele-Direct would incur if it were forced to deal with consultants directly on behalf of advertisers is a valid justification for not doing so, given that no adverse cost effects on agents were proven and that any negative reputational effects that are attributable to the refusal to deal directly are, at best, weak. We conclude, therefore, that overall, Tele-Direct is not engaging in anti-competitive acts by refusing to deal directly with consultants on behalf of advertisers ...'[76]

To summarize, general principles governing the finding of an anti-competitive act include (a) each case is decided on its facts; (b) an anti-competitive act must involve a predatory, exclusionary, or disciplinary intent; and (c) subjective intent need not be proven; rather, intent may be inferred from the circumstances. Indeed, as the tribunal stated in *Tele-Direct*, it may be apt to speak of the overall character of the act in question rather than intent. Pro-competitive or efficiency explanations of an act, as opposed to predatory, exclusionary, or disciplinary expla-

---

76 Ibid., at 240.

nations, therefore, preclude a finding that the act is an anticompetitive act pursuant to section 79. The guidelines follow this approach.

Efficiency is also contemplated in section 79(4). Section 79(4) provides:

> In determining, for the purposes of subsection (1), whether a practice has had, is having or is likely to have the effect of preventing or lessening competition substantially in a market, the Tribunal shall consider whether the practice is a result of superior competitive performance.

Note that section 79(4) does not set out an efficiency defence; rather, efficiency is a factor to be considered by the tribunal. It is not clear from the wording, however, how efficiency is to be considered under section 79(4). A literal reading of the section requires the tribunal to consider whether the practice results from superior competitive performance. Most efficiency explanations of a practice are likely to run the other way around: superior competitive performance results from the practice. For example, vertical integration lowers distribution costs and therefore results in superior competitive performance. It is unclear what a literal reading of the Act would entail.

The tribunal has not explicitly considered section 79(4) to date. This by no means implies, however, that efficiency considerations, or superior competitive performance, are irrelevant. As noted above, efficiency considerations are crucial to deciding whether an act has the requisite anticompetitive purpose to be classified as an 'anti-competitive act' pursuant to section 79. If there is a procompetitive or competitively neutral efficiency explanation for the practice, it is unlikely to be found to have an 'exclusionary, predatory or disciplinary purpose.'

Moreover, efficiency may play a role in determining whether the practice lessens or prevents competition substantially. While the tribunal in *NutraSweet* rejected NutraSweet's proffered business explanations for its exclusive contracts, it was clear that it would entertain efficiency considerations in applying the substantial lessening of competition test. Thus, while section 79(4) has not been considered to date, perhaps because of its wording, efficiency considerations nevertheless play an important role in section 79 analysis.

Before embarking on specific explanations of various anticompetitive acts in the statute and case law, it is useful briefly to review a theory that may justify finding these acts anticompetitive: the theory of raising rivals' costs.

A. *Raising Rivals' Costs*

The basic idea of 'raising rivals costs' is that a dominant firm in a market may be able to gain an advantage over its rivals by raising their costs and thereby provide the dominant firm with supracompetitive profits. While, by definition, where a firm's actions raises its rivals' costs, there is a harm to competitors, it is harm to competition that should raise antitrust concerns. First, harm to competitors may not produce any social welfare costs. Second, there is little reason to expect firms to seek simply to harm competitors without the prospect of anti-competitive profits. Where a firm's actions harm its rivals but do not create anticompetitive effects, it is likely that socially benign motivations, such as efficiency, exist.

How can a firm's actions that increase its rivals' costs create anticompetitive effects and extra profits for the firm? In influential papers, Salop and Scheffman and Krattenmaker and Salop outline various possibilities.[77] Consider a market in which there is a dominant firm with a potential rival. The industry requires a scarce input. The dominant firm may be able to exclude its potential rival from the market by bidding up the price of the scarce input. It is clear that bidding up the price of the input will harm competitors, but it may also be profitable for the dominant firm. As a general proposition, the total profits realized in an industry decline in the face of entry: competitors do not account for the negative effect on others' profits when they make price and quantity decisions. There is an 'externality' that serves to dissipate industry profits. A monopolist's profits therefore exceed the sum of two duopolists' profits. Thus, an incumbent monopolist may be able to bid up the price of the scarce input to the point where entry is unprofitable, yet paying the high price for the input may be worth while to the monopolist, allowing it to avoid the dissipation of its profits that entry would bring.[78]

---

77 S. Salop and D. Scheffman, 'Raising Rivals' Costs,' (1983) 73 *Am. Econ. Rev.* 267. See also T. Krattenmaker and S. Salop, 'Anti-competitive Exclusion: Raising Rivals' Costs to Achieve Power over Price,' (1986) 96 *Yale L.J.* 209. For a review of the literature from a Canadian perspective, on which this review is based, see R. Ware, 'Understanding Raising Rivals' Costs: A Canadian Perspective,' March (1994) *Canadian Competition Record* 9.

78 This example, as with much of raising rivals' costs theory, is also relevant to the theory of exclusionary practices, such as exclusive dealing contracts, which are considered elsewhere in this book. A monopolist may be able to enter into an exclusive

Krattenmaker and Salop identify four types of raising rivals' costs strategies that a firm may pursue. They are grouped into two categories: in one, the rivals' access to the supply of an input is limited directly; in the other, the rivals' access to an input supply is limited indirectly, through the alteration of incentives facing suppliers as a result of a purchaser's actions. Following Krattenmaker and Salop, in describing these techniques, we will refer to the firm seeking to raise its rivals' costs as the 'purchaser,' since it will either be purchasing the input itself, or an exclusionary right associated with the supply of the input.

1. Bottleneck

Under this method, the purchaser obtains exclusionary rights from lower-cost input suppliers. This forces its rivals to purchase higher-cost inputs from other suppliers. The exclusionary rights may be in the form of agreements between suppliers and the purchaser to disadvantage rival purchasers, or they may result from the acquisition by the purchaser of a supplier. Krattenmaker and Salop point to the following example. In *St. Louis Railroad*,[79] a group of railroad operators purchased the only bridges across the Mississippi River into St Louis. The group made the bridges available to other, non-owner railroad operators only on disadvantageous terms. This example represents an overlap between the economic theory of 'raising rivals' costs' and the 'essential facility doctrine,' which we will discuss in greater detail below.

2. Real Foreclosure

Another method of raising rivals' costs through direct effects on supply involves a purchaser's obtaining exclusionary rights over a significant portion of the supply, thereby driving up the market price of the remainder of supply available to the purchaser's rivals.[80] The authors

---

dealing contract with the supplier of a scarce input, which hurts its rivals. The supplier may be willing to limit its options and enter into such a contract if the monopolist shares its profits with the supplier. The monopolist may be able to do so profitably relative to allowing entry because of the dissipation of the monopolist's profits that entry entails. (A monopolist's profits are greater that the sum of duopolist's profits.)

79 *United States v. Terminal Railroad Association of St. Louis*, 224 U.S. 383 (1912).
80 As Krattenmaker and Salop, 'Anti-compeition Exclusion,' point out at n. 84, bottleneck is a special case of real foreclosure in which all the lowest cost input is foreclosed from rivals.

refer to this as 'real foreclosure' because the purchaser gains actual and effective control over the input supply in order to drive its price higher.

The example of real foreclosure the authors provide is the *Alcoa* monopoly case.[81] It is factually uncontroversial that when Alcoa's patents on manufacturing aluminum expired at the turn of the century, it obtained promises from some electrical utilities not to supply power to any other aluminum manufacturer. As Krattenmaker and Salop point out, the price of electricity to Alcoa's potential rivals would increase as they bid for the remaining supply. It is also possible, although this is less clear factually,[82] that Alcoa overpurchased bauxite, a key ingredient in making aluminum. By buying more than it needed Alcoa may have raised its rivals' costs, as the price of the remaining bauxite supply would have been bid upward.

3. Cartel Ringmaster

Cartel Ringmaster is the first of the two theories involving behaviour by the purchaser that alters the incentives facing suppliers of an input to the detriment of the purchaser's rivals. The idea behind Cartel Ringmaster is that the purchaser orchestrates cartel-like behaviour on the part of suppliers of inputs to its rivals. For example, in *Interstate Circuit*,[83] a company that operated movie cinemas in Texas, Interstate Circuit, obtained from movie distributors the undertaking that they would not supply theatres with second-run movies unless these theatres charged a minimum price. This raised the costs of attracting customers to these rival theatres, as they were impeded in competing on price and would have had to resort, inefficiently, to other means such as advertising, comfortable seats and the like.[84]

---

81 *United States v. Aluminum Company of America*, 148 F. 2d 416 (2d Cir., 1945).
82 The trial court had found that Alcoa had not intended to overbuy. Judge Hand on appeal, however, found that Alcoa had illegally retained its monopoly by increasing its capacity continually. Krattenmaker and Salop 'Anti-competition Exclusion,' suggest that this reference to ever-increasing capacity may perhaps be interpreted to implicate overbuying. Otherwise, they ask, what was the competitive harm of increasing capacity to which Judge Hand was referring? One answer may be the largely discredited view that increases in capacity may deter entry (see Chapter 5 for more detail). In any event, the *Alcoa* case provides an example of how overbuying might work to raise rivals' costs.
83 *Interstate Circuit, Inc. v. United States*, 306 U.S. 208 (1939).
84 See Krattenmaker and Salop, 'Anti-competition Exclusion,' n. 97.

4. *Frankenstein Monster*

The Frankenstein Monster technique involves alteration of the market structure in the input supply market through vertical agreements between the purchaser and a subset of suppliers. An extreme example would be where the purchaser enters into exclusive dealing contracts with all input suppliers but one. The purchaser's rivals would then effectively face a monopoly supplier of the input and a higher price. Unlike the Cartel Ringmaster technique, it is the suppliers *outside* the vertical agreements that increase the costs to the purchaser's rivals.

These examples demonstrate how the purchaser may harm its rivals. As Krattenmaker and Salop point out, however, a firm that raises its rivals' costs 'has not necessarily gained anything. It may have harmed one or more of its competitors, but has it harmed competition? Competition is harmed only if the firm purchasing the exclusionary right can, as a result, raise its price above the competitive level.'[85] Two minimum conditions must hold for raising rivals' costs to be a profitable strategy for the purchaser. First, the increase in the input's price must be significant compared to the final cost of making the product. Second, the purchaser must be able to gain power over the final product's price. For this to hold, competitors must not be able to obtain sufficient supply through their own exclusionary arrangements such that they are able to compete effectively with the purchaser. Moreover, competition from unexcluded rivals or potential entrants may also threaten the purchaser's ability to raise price as well as its rivals' costs.

While this discussion conveys the basic ideas behind raising rivals' costs, there are many rich areas within the framework worthy of much greater exploration. Some of these are explored elsewhere in the book, particularly with respect to exclusionary practices like exclusive dealing and tying. There are specific legal provisions that deal with these matters outside the abuse of dominance catch-all sections that form the subject of the present chapter. For the remainder of this chapter, we will address briefly the anticompetitive acts listed in section 78, as well as others found in the case law. The list of acts we consider is, of course, incomplete, given that section 78 provides a non-exhaustive list and that the case law will no doubt present new allegations of anticompetitive behaviour in the future. The purpose of the review is to convey a sense of what is likely to be considered an anticompetitive act and

---

85 Ibid., at 242.

what is not. We will focus on two areas that fit squarely within the raising rivals' costs framework: the essential facility doctrine and the use of legal processes by a dominant firm to disadvantage its competitors.

B. Anticompetitive Acts Enumerated in Section 78

1. Section 78(a): Vertical Margin Squeezing

Section 78(a) involves the practice of vertical margin squeezing. It is premised on the ability of the dominant firm, operating at two levels of the distribution system, to raise the price of an input to a competitor operating only at the downstream level. This is known as a 'price squeeze.'[86] The dominant firm may also harm its downstream rival through a 'supply squeeze': limiting the supply available to its competitor in the downstream market.

These types of anticompetitive acts relate to the bottleneck and real foreclosure strategies of raising rivals' costs. The dominant firm may not only harm its competitor but may also reap supracompetitive profits by preserving monopoly profits that would otherwise be dissipated by competition at the downstream level.

Of course, as the guidelines acknowledge, vertically integrated firms may realize efficiencies in distribution, such as overcoming hold-up problems, that non-integrated firms do not.[87] It may therefore be difficult for an unintegrated firm to compete with an integrated firm in the downstream market for reasons that have little to do with squeezing. As with other potentially anticompetitive acts, each case has to be considered on its own merits.

2. Section 78(b): Vertical Integration

The second anticompetitive act enumerated in section 78 refers to vertical integration. A dominant firm may be able to harm its rivals by integrating with a firm at a different level of distribution. A downstream firm, for example, may harm rival downstream firms by purchasing an upstream firm. Such a purchase may leave the other upstream firms facing less competition, which in turn leads to higher input prices for rival downstream firms and higher profits for the

---

86 See D. Khosla, R. Anderson, P. Hughes, and J. Monteiro, 'Reference Document on Abuse of Dominance' (unpublished) at III-10.

87 Guidelines, at s. 4.2.

dominant integrated firm. This is the Frankenstein Monster technique of raising rivals' costs.

Of course, vertical integration may arise for reasons that have nothing to do with harming competitors or competition. Indeed, it may arise because of efficiencies in distribution, which implies potential procompetitive effects: the integrated firm will be in a better position to compete. This is recognized by the MEGs, which suggest that vertical mergers will rarely be considered anticompetitive. Caution is required in finding vertical integration to be an anticompetitive act.

3. Section 78(c): Freight Equalization

Freight equalization, listed in section 78(c), occurs where a firm quotes similar prices to customers located varying distances from the firm, even where transportation costs are significant. It may have anticompetitive effects in two ways.

First, it may act as a form of predatory pricing. The dominant firm may charge the same delivered price to a customer located near its own plant as that charged to a customer located nearer to a dominant firm's rival. The dominant firm thus effectively earns a lower margin, perhaps even negative profits, on the customer located nearer to its rival. This could amount to selective price cutting, that is, price cutting to customers most likely to deal with the dominant firm's rival, with predatory intent.

Freight equalization may also be anticompetitive in that it may facilitate collusion between firms. Freight equalization simplifies price lists and thus may make pricing more transparent to other firms. Moreover, it may stabilize a cartel by dividing the cartel's profits more evenly. In the absence of freight equalization, the firm located closest to the greatest source of demand would earn disproportionate profits, which could destabilize the cartel.[88]

This second way in which freight equalization can be anticompetitive may lend support to the conclusion that joint dominance contemplates conscious parallelism, or at least 'conscious parallelism-plus': conscious parallelism plus the use of a facilitating device. The role of freight equalization as a facilitating device is well known; thus its inclusion as an anticompetitive practice in section 78 may support a conclusion that firms may abuse joint dominance through the use of

---

88 See Khosla et al., 'Reference Document on Abuse of Dominance,' at III-19.

facilitating devices even where there is no explicit agreement between them.

4. Section 78(d): Fighting Brands

Section 78(d) suggests that the introduction of 'fighting brands' may be an anticompetitive act. 'Fighting brand' refers to a brand introduced by a firm to inflict harm on a rival, either in a predatory fashion (to limit or eliminate the rival's competitive significance) or in a disciplinary way (to seek to punish temporarily a rival for competing too vigorously). Fighting brands were central to the *Eddy Match* case, *supra*, where Eddy Match was found to have introduced new brands of matches intending to eliminate entry to the wooden match market.

Of course, there is also a procompetitive explanation for fighting brands. Responding to new rivals with new tactics is one of the essential attributes of competition. New brands may simply be legitimate, that is, procompetitive, responses to new competition.[89]

5. Section 78(e): Pre-emption of Scarce Facilities

Section 78(e) identifies as a potentially anticompetitive act the pre-emption of scarce facilities or resources. This refers to either the bottleneck or real foreclosure techniques of raising rivals' costs. A dominant firm, in order to ensure monopoly profits in the downstream market, would be able to outbid rivals for the upstream scarce resources and then limit rivals' access to the resources. In *Nielsen*, for example, Nielsen used various exclusivity terms to ensure that rivals could not obtain access to scanner-based data, which gave it a monopoly in the downstream market for selling scanner-based market tracking analysis.

This provision is also relevant to the essential facilities doctrine. We postpone discussion of this doctrine, which may entail more than section 78(e) provides, until our discussion of unenumerated anticompetitive acts below.

6. Section 78(f): Preventing Price Erosion

In order to prevent price erosion, a dominant firm may commit the anticompetitive act of buying up products. Unlike other provisions in

---

89 In *Tele-Direct, supra*, note 26, as we discuss below, the tribunal rejected the director's allegation that Tele-Direct's practice of aggressively competing with entry was anticompetitive. The tribunal held that responding to rivals is a fundamental aspect of competition.

section 78, this act does not on its face harm competitors. Indeed, if the dominant firm buys up final products in a manner comparable to a marketing board,[90] rival firms are benefited by higher prices for their output. On the other hand, if the dominant firm overbuys *inputs* in order to keep prices high, this could have harmful effects on competition by raising its rivals' costs. Of course, if the dominant firm is overbuying scarce inputs for the purpose of raising rivals' costs, this behaviour would likely come within the purview of section 78(e), which refers to the preemption of scarce resources as an anticompetitive act.

7. Section 78(g): Anticompetitive Product Standards

A dominant firm may commit an anticompetitive act u
78(g) if it manipulates product standards in order to harm competitors and competition. As Khosla et al. point out, product specifications could be used in a number of ways to raise rivals' costs and thereby diminish competition.[91] A dominant firm could petition standard setting bodies to set standards very close to its own products, but different from those of its rivals. A dominant firm in an upstream market could adopt specifications that give it an advantage over rivals in a downstream market. Finally, by adopting particular specifications, a firm could effectively impose a 'technological tie-in' that compels buyers of complementary goods to buy both goods from the dominant firm. However, there is the countervailing consideration that product specifications may be necessary for efficiency reasons, such as the optimal operation of a product.

8. Section 78(h): Boycotts

It may be an anticompetitive act pursuant to section 78(h) for a dominant firm to induce or require a supplier to sell only to certain customers or not to sell to other customers at all. Again, this is a type of the bottleneck or real foreclosure strategies of raising rivals' costs. A dominant firm in a downstream market, concerned about entry or the increased competitive significance of its rivals, may find it profitable to prevent the dissipation of its profits by inducing upstream suppliers not to sell, or to charge very high prices, to its downstream rivals. This

---

90 See Khosla et al., 'Reference Document on Abuse of Dominance,' at III-28.
91 Ibid., at III-29.

may harm competitors and competition by preserving market power downstream.

The director in the *Nielsen* case referred to section 78(h) in impugning the exclusive supply contracts entered into by Nielsen and the retail store suppliers of its input, scanner-based market tracking data. Nielsen was in a position to share its monopoly profits in the scanner-based market tracking services market with retailers through high prices in order to induce them to accept exclusive supply contracts. Such a strategy was more profitable than not entering exclusive supply deals and thereby allowing entry and the consequent dissipation of industry profits.

Exclusive supply contracts may, however, have efficiency-promoting effects depending on the circumstances. For example, they may be useful in protecting parties from opportunism by their contracting partners after they have made sunk, relationship-specific investments. As always, it requires a careful examination of the circumstances to conclude whether an act is anticompetitive.[92]

In *Tele-Direct*, the dominant supplier of business telephone directories, Tele-Direct, induced a supplier of a product called 'audiotext' to withhold supply from competing directories. Audiotext was a service providing information, such as the news and weather, which competing directories had linked to their products. The tribunal observed: '[T]he only perceptible effect on consumers and advertisers was a negative one. It would appear to us that the kind of conduct engaged in by Tele-Direct regarding audiotext in Sault Ste. Marie unequivocally falls within the class of anti-competitive acts against which s. 79 is meant to guard.'[93]

9. Section 78(i): Predatory Pricing in the Resale of Articles

Section 78(i) identifies as an anticompetitive act a dominant firm selling 'articles at a price lower than acquisition cost for the purpose of eliminating or disciplining a competitor.' This clearly refers to a dominant firm engaging in predatory pricing: that is, selling at a price below some measure of cost in order to harm a competitor.[94] It may

---

92 In *Nielsen, supra*, note 22, as noted above, the tribunal rejected Nielsen's claim that exclusive contracts were necessary to protect its investment in new technology from free-riding rivals.

93 *Tele-Direct, supra* (1997), 73 C.P.R. (3d) at 211.

94 See Chapter 5 on predatory pricing.

harm competition, and not simply competitors, if the low prices encourage rivals to exit, or not to enter, the market, or if it persuades rivals not to compete vigorously because of the threat of predation as punishment for doing so.

The provision is limited by its reference to 'articles' and 'acquisition cost.' In *NutraSweet*, the director attempted to apply section 78(i) to a manufacturer selling its product at a price below its manufacturing cost. The tribunal rejected this attempt, stating: 'There is no reason, however, for applying paragraph 78(i) to manufacturing situations where there is not a purchase and resale of articles.'[95]

There is also no reason, as *NutraSweet* acknowledged, why predatory pricing generally could not held to be an anticompetitive act not specifically enumerated in section 78, as we will examine below.[96]

C. Anticompetitive Acts not Enumerated in Section 78

As noted, the category of anticompetitive acts pursuant to section 79 is not limited to the list found in section 78. Indeed, the list of anticompetitive acts will never be defined exhaustively; as the Tribunal stated in *Tele-Direct*, each case will turn on its own facts. In what follows, we outline some of the anticompetitive acts that have been found in the case law. This should assist in deciding whether other acts could be considered anticompetitive pursuant to section 79.

1. Exclusivity

Exclusive contractual clauses were at the forefront of the *NutraSweet*, *Laidlaw*, and *Nielsen* cases. In *NutraSweet*, buyers of NutraSweet's aspartame agreed to exclusive supply and exclusive use clauses. These effectively required the customer to use NutraSweet aspartame as its primary or exclusive sweetener. The tribunal held that such exclusivity was not required for efficiency reasons, but rather was in place to exclude NutraSweet's prospective rivals from the market.

Along with condemnation of the exclusive supply contracts themselves as anticompetitive, the tribunal also impugned the use of various contractual terms that it asserted were 'inducements to exclusivity' and thus also anticompetitive. These included a trade mark display allow-

---

95 *NutraSweet, supra* (1990), 32 C.P.R. (3d) at 43.
96 Khosla et al., 'Reference Document on Abuse of Dominance,' at III-35.

ance, cooperative marketing allowances, meet-or-release clauses, and most-favoured-nation clauses.

The trade-mark display allowance provided a rebate of 40 per cent from the gross price of aspartame if the customer agreed to display the NutraSweet name and 'swirl' logo on the end product's packaging. Cooperative marketing allowances were given to customers who embarked on marketing campaigns that included the NutraSweet name and logo. Both these initiatives, the tribunal held, were designed to increase the cost to the buyer of switching to another sweetener supplier, and thus reinforced exclusivity and impeded NutraSweet's competition.

Meet-or-release and most-favoured-nation clauses were also held by the tribunal to induce exclusivity. Meet-or-release clauses ensured that agreeing to an exclusive contract would not disadvantage a customer who was later presented with a better offer and also discouraged entry by aspartame suppliers concerned that any bid for business would simply be used as a 'bargaining chip' with NutraSweet.[97] Most-favoured-nation clauses would serve to ensure that a customer in the downstream market was protected from relatively high input prices, since any better price offered to a downstream rival would have to be offered to it as well. Consequently, the clauses induced exclusivity and were also anticompetitive acts.[98]

Laidlaw also entered into exclusive contracts with customers that were found by the tribunal in *Laidlaw* to be anticompetitive. Three-year contracts for waste disposal with evergreen renewal clauses included a commitment by the customer to employ Laidlaw exclusively for all its garbage disposal requirements. The contracts gave Laidlaw a right of first refusal to meet an offer from competitors and included significant liquidated damages clauses if the customer breached the contract.

---

97 *NutraSweet, supra* (1990), 32 C.P.R. (3d) at 42.

98 The tribunal also noted that most-favoured-nation (MFN) clauses would limit a customer's incentives to negotiate a lower price since a lower price would benefit the customer's rivals as well. A related observation is that the MFN clause may give NutraSweet leverage in negotiating against price cuts: a cut to one customer requires a cut to all, thus NutraSweet will resist any price cut. This may lead to a prisoner's dilemma among customers, with each customer requesting a MFN clause in order to disadvantage their rivals in the end-product market, which leads to higher prices for aspartame: see E. Iacobucci, 'Most-Favoured Nation Clauses and Competition Policy,' (Autumn 1997) *Canadian Competition Record* 27.

In an important paper, Aghion and Bolton outline the potential anti-competitive effects of exclusivity and liquidated damages clauses.[99] Liquidated damages clauses increase the cost of entry by forcing an entrant to compensate potential customers for the damages they must pay to the incumbent if they switch suppliers. The incumbent is made better off either by deterring entry altogether, or by realizing more profit from the liquidated damages clauses than it would from operating the business. While such clauses oppose customers' collective interests, since they discourage entry, an individual customer may reason that its agreement to exclusivity and liquidated damages clauses alone is unlikely to affect the prospect of entry. Since the incumbent can compensate the customer with slightly lower prices, the customer individually may conclude she is better off with the clauses. Such individual reasoning by each customer may lead to widespread adoption of the clauses even if they are antithetical to the customers' collective interests.

It was argued that the exclusive arrangements were necessary to protect the specific investments Laidlaw would make in order to provide service to a customer. That is, exclusivity was an efficient term that assured Laidlaw of recovering its investment in the customer, which in turn encouraged the investment to take place. The tribunal rejected the argument on the facts, concluding that there was very little in the way of customer-specific investment that might otherwise have justified the contracts. It concluded that exclusivity was used simply to exclude Laidlaw's potential rivals and was therefore anticompetitive.

Exclusivity was at the centre of *Nielsen*. In that case, Nielsen was effectively the sole supplier of scanner-based market tracking services. It achieved exclusivity with the suppliers of the input, scanner-based data obtained from retailers, through a variety of means, such as exclusive contracts for supply of data, which were encouraged through offers of higher prices for the data. Nielsen staggered the expiry dates of its contracts with major grocery retailers, which made it difficult for would-be competitors to enter the market; effective entry requires a broad base of data. Furthermore, Nielsen required most-favoured-

---

99 P. Aghion and P. Bolton, 'Contracts as a Barrier to Entry,' (1987) 77 *Am. Econ. Rev.* 388. See also J. Brodley and C. Ma, 'Contract Penalties, Monopolizing Strategies and Antitrust Policy,' (1993) 45 *Stan. L. Rev.* 1161. For further discussion, see Chapter 7 on exclusionary vertical restraints (interbrand competition).

nation clauses in its supply contracts from retailers, which helped ensure exclusivity. The director's expert, Ralph Winter (one of the authors of this book), pointed out that adopting an MFN clause effectively commits the seller not to sell the input to a different buyer, given that the different buyer could not pay as much as the incumbent monopolist (since duopoly profits are lower than monopoly profits). The seller would not sell to the second buyer for a lower price since the MFN clause would force it to lower its price to the incumbent monopolist as well. The incumbent monopolist thus can exclude entry by setting a high price for the input and adopting an MFN clause. Finally, Nielsen was also found to be seeking to exclude rivals by entering into long-term contracts with its customers.

This behaviour by Nielsen was found by the tribunal to violate of section 79. Nielsen's exclusionary practices may have fitted the bottleneck or real foreclosure models of raising rivals' costs. Nielsen was able to obtain exclusive contracts with the input suppliers, retail stores, thus foreclosing competition in the scanner-based market tracking services market, because it was in a position to share its monopoly profits in the downstream market with the retailers. Since monopoly profits exceed the total profits in a duopoly, Nielsen could share its monopoly profits with retailer-suppliers in order to induce exclusivity, yet still make more than it would if entry occurred.

2. Acquisitions of Rivals

In *Laidlaw*, Laidlaw had frequently purchased competitors in various regional markets in the waste disposal business. Moreover, when it made the purchases, it often lumped the acquisitions together such that it would be the only disposal service left in the market. Laidlaw also imposed very broad restrictive covenants on the vendors that limited their ability to compete in the market in the future; the tribunal relied on these clauses as support for its finding of an anticompetitive intent behind the acquisitions. If rivals were reluctant to sell, Laidlaw would apparently threaten them with expensive litigation,[100] such as suits for inducing breach of contracts, or would threaten them with severe price competition.

While the acquisitions were found by the tribunal to have anticompetitive effects, the question of whether they could be classified as

---

100 See discussion below.

'anti-competitive' acts under section 79 remained. In the *NutraSweet* case, the tribunal held that an explicit contractual agreement between NutraSweet and Ajinomoto, a Japanese producer of aspartame, providing that Ajinomoto would not enter the Canadian aspartame market, was not an anticompetitive act under section 79. Section 78, the tribunal reasoned, was concerned generally with actions that harmed competitors, and thus the agreement was not an anticompetitive act for the purposes of section 79. The tribunal went on to say, however, that not all horizontal agreements would escape section 79 scrutiny.

While the acquisitions in Laidlaw did not harm competitors, the tribunal found them to be anticompetitive acts for the purposes of section 79. The tribunal stated:

> In the *NutraSweet* decision the tribunal refused to classify a voluntary agreement between competitors as an anti-competitive act. The agreement in question was a worldwide market sharing agreement by The NutraSweet Company with its suppliers. Reference was made in this regard to the fact that a feature of the enumerated acts listed in section 78 (except for that in paragraph (f)) is that the competitor of the dominant firm is a target, not a fellow actor. At the same time, the tribunal left open the question as to whether or not such horizontal arrangements might be classified as anti-competitive acts. It commented that it was reluctant to conclude that all horizontal arrangements were excluded from sections 78 and 79 and that, in any event, it was sufficient for the purposes of the *NutraSweet* decision to state that the tribunal had not been provided with adequate justification (insofar as effects in Canada were concerned) to allow the tribunal to categorize the market sharing agreement as an anti-competitive act.

> The tribunal in this case, insofar as the acquisition agreements are concerned, is dealing with horizontal arrangements between willing competitors. Extensive and detailed evidence and argument has been heard respecting the anti-competitive effects of the conduct in question. It is not seriously in dispute, as the tribunal noted in the NutraSweet decision, that the enumeration in section 78 is not controlling with respect to the scope of section 79. The tribunal in this case has no difficulty classifying the acquisitions as acts constituting an anti-competitive practice.[101]

---

101 *Laidlaw, supra* (1992), 40 C.P.R. (3d) at 336–7.

Such an approach is supported by section 79(7), which provides that no application may be made against a person against whom an order is also sought under section 92, the merger provision. While section 92 addresses vertical as well as horizontal mergers, since horizontal mergers are far more likely to raise competition concerns, the reference to section 92 in section 79(7) may support the conclusion that section 79 can apply to acquisitions of competitors.

3. Predatory Pricing

The director accused NutraSweet of selling aspartame at a price below acquisition cost, as set out in section 78(i). The tribunal held that section 78(i), because of its reference to 'acquisition cost,' does not apply to a manufacturer selling below cost. The tribunal made it clear, however, that predatory pricing generally could be an unenumerated anticompetitive act for the purpose of section 79. On the facts, it held that it could not conclude whether NutraSweet had engaged in predatory pricing, but gave some guidance by stating in *obiter dicta* that such a practice could be found where the seller operating below capacity was selling below average variable cost, a useful proxy for the economic notion of marginal cost; at capacity, the appropriate measure is average total cost.[102] Given that the director sought an order only with respect to selling below acquisition cost, the tribunal declined to make an order on the basis of predatory pricing.

The draft guidelines set out that predatory pricing may indeed be an anticompetitive act and essentially follow the approach to the practice set out in the *Predatory Pricing Enforcement Guidelines* discussed in Chapter 5.

4. Facilitating Practices

As noted in the discussion of joint dominance above, firms may adopt certain practices to facilitate coordination among the firms. Contractual clauses, such as MFN clauses or meet-or-release clauses, can assist firms (in ways described above) to coordinate their behaviour. Other practices, such as publicizing price lists, can also facilitate coordination. The draft guidelines state that the bureau may consider the use of facilitating devices as an anticompetitive act.

---

102 For the bureau's approach, see *Predatory Pricing Enforcement Guidelines* (Ottawa: Director of Investigation and Research, 1992).

5. *Essential Facility Doctrine*

It is first appropriate to outline the importance, or at least potential importance, of the essential facility doctrine in the Canadian competition law context. The doctrine has been developed in the United States but not Canada. Section 2 of the *Sherman Act* condemns monopolization, which has been interpreted to require: '(1) the possession of monopoly power in the relevant market and (2) the willful acquisition or maintenance of that power as distinguished from growth or development as a consequence of a superior business product, business acumen, or historic accident.'[103] The refusal by a firm to admit access on reasonable terms to its rivals to a facility that is essential for competing in a market has been held in the United States to infringe section 2. Clearly, as interpreted in *Grinnell*, the U.S. standard for illegal monopolization resonates with the Canadian abuse of dominance sections. In the United States it is not monopoly power that is illegal, but the 'willful acquisition of that power,' just as in Canada, it is not monopoly or a dominant position that is illegal, but abuse of that position. Thus, the law in the United States on the essential facility doctrine shares important foundations with Canadian law. Moreover, the analysis in a recent case before the Competition Tribunal in consent proceedings, *Interac*, is similar to the essential facility doctrine. We will first briefly[104] review U.S. law on essential facilities, because of its potential impact on the development of the doctrine in Canada. We will then review in greater detail the *Interac* case in Canada, canvassing some of the important economic considerations that lie behind the doctrine.

(a) U.S. Law

One of the cases of central importance in the development of the essential facility doctrine was *United States v. Terminal Railroad Association of St. Louis.*[105] Fourteen railroads serving St Louis formed an association that acquired all terminal facilities in St Louis and all bridges across the Mississippi into St Louis. The U.S. Supreme Court held that by excluding some companies from access to these facilities on equal terms, the

---

103 See *Grinnell, supra,* note 14.
104 For a more through review, see G. Werden, 'The Law and Economics of the Essential Facilities Doctrine,' (1987) 32 *St. Louis Univ. L.J.* 433.
105 *Supra,* note 79.

association violated sections 1 (which deals with unlawful agreements) and 2 (which deals with monopolization) of the *Sherman Act*. The court stated that when 'the inherent conditions are such as to prohibit any other reasonable means of entering the city, the control of less than all of the companies under compulsion to use them' violates sections 1 and 2. The court ordered 'the admission of any existing or future railroad to joint ownership and control of the combined terminal properties upon ... just and reasonable terms.'[106] Moreover, those railroads choosing not to join the association were not to be discriminated against: the facilities were to be made available to 'any other railroad not electing to become a joint owner, upon such just and reasonable terms and regulations as will ... place every such company upon as nearly an equal plane ... as that occupied by the proprietary companies.'[107]

While *Terminal Railroad* appears to depend in a straightforward way on the 'compulsion' of the non-association railroads to use the bridges and terminals into St Louis, other cases seem to rely less on such a 'compulsion,' or at least relax the requirement that the facilities be 'essential.' Some rely more on the intent of the firm seeking to exclude access to a facility.[108] For example, *Otter Tail Electric Power Co. v. United States*[109] involved an electric utility's refusal to allow municipalities access to its power transmission and distribution facilities. Some municipalities had decided to replace Otter Tail's retail power distribution franchises with municipal systems. Otter Tail thwarted such plans by refusing to sell wholesale power to the municipalities in question and by refusing to allow others who wished to sell power to the municipalities access to necessary transmission lines. The Supreme Court, rather than relying explicitly on an essential facility approach, upheld a finding of liability under section 2 because of an attempt to monopolize. Otter Tail's *intent* was to prevent the municipalities from competing in the distribution of electric power and the use 'of monopoly power "to destroy threatened competition" is a violation of the "attempt to monopolize" clause of section 2 of the Sherman Act.'[110]

Another case relying heavily on intent for a finding of an infringe-

---

106 Ibid., at 411.
107 Ibid.
108 See Werden, 'Law and Economics of the Essential Facilities Doctrine,' at 438–41.
109 410 U.S. 366 (1973).
110 Ibid., at 377.

ment of section 2 was *Aspen Skiing Co. v. Aspen Highlands Skiing Corp.*[111] In that case, Aspen Skiing, which owned three ski mountains in Aspen, and Aspen Highlands had for many years offered joint packages to skiers that allowed them to use any of the four ski facilities in Aspen. In the late seventies, Aspen Skiing offered to continue the joint marketing agreement, but only on terms that were disadvantageous to Aspen Highlands. Consequently, the joint agreement disintegrated and Aspen Highlands found it difficult to compete. Its share of the Aspen skiing market declined from 20.5 per cent in 1976–7 to 11 per cent in 1980–1.

In upholding the lower courts' finding of a violation of section 2, the Supreme Court placed particular emphasis on the apparent intent of Aspen Skiing to harm its rival.[112] It inferred this intent from the absence of a business justification for the discontinuance of the joint ticket, as well as the existence of joint tickets in other ski markets in which there was competition (including Aspen – the joint marketing arrangement began when there were three separately owned facilities). It also noted evidence that customers preferred the all-area tickets.

A final case in this brief sample is not from the Supreme Court, but provides one of the clearest statements of the essential facility doctrine. *MCI Communications v. American Telegram & Telegraph Co.*[113] involved MCI's challenge of many AT&T practices, including its refusal to grant MCI access to local Bell facilities. The Seventh Circuit upheld a jury's finding that AT&T violated section 2 of the *Sherman Act* on the basis of the essential facility doctrine. The court provided the following test, which has been influential in subsequent cases: 'The case law sets forth four elements necessary to establish liability under the essential facilities doctrine: (1) control of the essential facility by a monopolist; (2) a competitor's inability practically or reasonably to duplicate the essential facility; (3) the denial of the use of the facility to a competitor; and (4) the feasibility of providing the facility.'[114]

While *MCI* provides the clearest statement of the test, there is considerable confusion over the exact meaning of 'the essential facility doctrine,' as even this very small sample of cases indicates. While *Ter-*

---

111   472 U.S. 585 (1985).
112   For support, the court cited *Lorain Journal Co. v. United States*, 342 U.S. 143 (1951) (newspaper that refused to accept advertising from parties that advertised on a new radio station in the area violated 'attempt to monopolize' aspect of s. 2 by using its monopoly to destroy threatened competition).
113   708 F. 2d 1081 (7th Cir.), cert. denied, 464 U.S. 891 (1983).
114   Ibid., at 1132–3.

minal Railroad seems to progress from the necessity of the bridges and terminals for rival railroads to the order that access to the facilities by rivals be granted, without particularly canvassing intent, *Otter Tail* (at the Supreme Court; the Appeals Court adopted an alternative analysis that resembled that in *Terminal Railroad*) and *Aspen Skiing* appeared to treat the matter as an improper refusal to deal. While generally in the United States a party may deal with whom it pleases,[115] where a refusal to deal is motivated by an anticompetitive purpose, it may infringe the *Sherman Act*. There is significant debate over which cases fit within the 'essential facilities doctrine,' or even whether such an independent doctrine exists. Hovenkamp states, 'The so-called 'essential facility' doctrine is one of the most troublesome, incoherent and unmanageable of bases for Sherman s. 2 liability. The antitrust world would almost certainly be a better place if it were jettisoned, with a little fine tuning of the general doctrine of the monopolist's refusal to deal to fill in the remaining gaps.'[116]

(b) Canadian Law: *Interac*

In Canada, there has been no explicit adoption of the terminology, 'essential facility doctrine.' However, there are two provisions that may deal with similar matters. The first is the refusal to deal provision, section 75, which is dealt with elsewhere in this book. In the central essential-facility-like case in Canada, section 75 was not invoked. Rather, the abuse of dominance provisions, sections 78 and 79, were relied upon. Section 78 contains two provisions that lend themselves to essential facility analysis, which we reproduce here for convenience:

> 78 For the purposes of section 79, 'anti-competitive act', without restricting the generality of the term, includes the following acts,
> (a) squeezing, by a vertically integrated supplier, of the margin available to an unintegrated customer who competes with the supplier, for the purpose of impeding or preventing the customer's entry into, or expansion in, a market; ...
> (e) pre-emption of scarce facilities or resources required by a competitor for the operation of a business, with the object of withholding the facilities or resources from the market.

---

115 *U.S. v. Colgate*, 250 U.S. 300 (1919).
116 Hovenkamp, *Federal Antitrust Policy*, at 273.

Both these sections may be relevant to an essential facility analysis. If the supplier controls an essential facility, such as a railroad that also owns the only bridge into town, and charges potential railroad rivals a very high price to use the bridge, it may be found to have 'squeezed' under section 78(a). This is the bottleneck example of raising rival's costs. The practice captured by section 78(e) invokes the essential facility doctrine in a straightforward way. If a dominant firm controls an essential facility and refuses others access, it may be engaged in the practice of an anticompetitive act under section 78(e).

The abuse of dominance sections were relied upon by the director in the *Interac* case, which came before the tribunal in a consent order proceeding.[117] 'Interac' was a trade mark owned by an association of Canada's major financial institutions, the Canada Payments Association (CPA). There were two types of members in the Interac association, which was structured as a joint venture: charter members and sponsored members. Charter members controlled and connected directly to the relevant network; sponsored members negotiated contractually to connect to the network through a charter member. The Interac network allowed members to permit their customers to access cash from others' bank machines using any Interac card, and also allowed customers to make debit purchases at retail stores.

Two relevant antitrust markets (or 'class or species of business' under section 79) were cited in the consent order proceedings: the 'shared electronic network services' (SENS) market for services provided by Interac to its member institutions and the 'shared electronic financial services' (SEFS) market for services provided by Interac and its member institutions to their cardholder customers. Interac was dominant in both markets. Ninety per cent of automated cash dispensing transactions were made on Interac machines and 100 per cent of debit card purchases were made on the Interac network.

Following the review of this case by Church and Ware,[118] the numer-

---

117 *Supra*, note 33. We note that a merger case, *Canada (Director of Investigation and Research) v. Air Canada* (1989), 27 C.P.R. (3d) 476, also involved access to a network. Specifically, the case involved a merger of Air Canada and Canadian Airlines' reservation systems into one entity, Gemini. The director initially opposed the merger, but eventually successfully applied to the Tribunal for approval of a consent order that required Gemini to provide access to all computer reservation systems operating in Canada. See Chapter 4 for an extended discussion of this case.

118 Church and Ware, 'Abuse of Dominance.'

ous anticompetitive acts alleged by the director can be grouped into three categories: access, pricing, and governance.

(i) *Access*: In 1989 and 1990 Interac drastically changed its by-laws regarding the admission of new members. It refused to admit any new charter members, which were the only members with voting rights, and changed its fees for entry as a sponsored member. The original fee of $100,000 to join the network was altered to a fee of $100,000 or $10,000 plus $7.50 per card accessing the network, whichever was greater. To illustrate the impact of the change, American Express would have had to pay not $100,000, but more than $11 million to join.[119] All members of Interac were required to be members of the CPA and were prevented from using a sweep, pass-through, or zero balance account, which had the effect of preventing 'indirect' issuers, which issue cards to users while maintaining themselves an account at a bank on their cardholders' behalf.

(ii) *Pricing*: The cash dispensing services within Interac had been established on the basis of a seventy-five cent fee per transaction payable by the card issuer institution to the institution deploying the bank machine. An Interac by-law prevented the institution deploying the bank machine from charging a surcharge at the bank machine. The director contended in the application that these two factors together served to prevent profitable entry of new bank machines, either by existing members or 'acquirer only' members of Interac (i.e., bank machine providers, but not card issuers).

(iii) *Governance*: Only charter members had any voting rights over the association and a two-thirds majority was required for any changes in by-laws. This restriction was alleged to impede the introduction of new services. Moreover, any new shared services had to be universally adopted and all parties had to share in the development costs. This too was alleged to impede innovation. Finally, charter members shared any revenue from signing up a new sponsored member with other charter members, which dulled incentives to innovate on the terms of the sponsorship.

The director alleged that these anticompetitive acts substantially less-

---

119 Ibid., at 120.

ened competition in both the SENS and SEFS markets. The main remedial provisions in the consent order were the following. With respect to
access, membership was to be open to *any* entity satisfying minimum
security and viability requirements with the access fee set at the incremental cost of accommodating the new member. There would, however, be a switch fee levied per transaction so Interac could recover its
cost of developing the network software. Issuers could be restricted to
CPA members, but access to Interac generally could not be so restricted;
acquirers only could become members. The by-law preventing sweep,
pass-through and zero balance accounts was declared invalid, such that
indirect issuers would be able to compete. With respect to pricing, the
prohibition on surcharges at bank machines was removed. With respect
to governance, the board of Interac was expanded from nine to fourteen
members, of which five had to be from institutions other than directly
connecting financial institutions. The election of board members would
also give weight in proportion to a member's volume of transactions.
Finally, any groups of members wishing to provide new services could
license the relevant software at cost.

In its reasons approving the consent order, the tribunal took issue
with a variety of specific matters, such as the continued use of the CPA
as the clearing house for Interac and the restrictions on direct issue of
cards by non-financial institutions, but it ultimately approved the
order. It is noteworthy that at no time did the tribunal explicitly adopt
an essential facility doctrine.

It is clear that the Interac arrangement could have been used to raise
rivals' costs on the bottleneck theory. By setting very high access fees,
the member institutions would have been able to exclude competition.
Setting high, even prohibitive, usage fees in the SENS market (the
input market) to rival card issuers would clearly put these rivals at a
disadvantage in the retail SEFS market (the output market). Charging
American Express $11 million for access, rather than the previous
access fee, $100,000, clearly raises its costs and may even be sufficient
to deter it from entering the SEFS market.

An important question is whether it was in the self-interest of the
Interac network to exclude others from access. Before antitrust intervention is justified, there must, as Krattenmaker and Salop stress, be
some reason why harming competitors would give rise to anticompetitive profits such that competition is harmed. Indeed, if competition
were not harmed, it is not clear why the dominant firm would have
any reason to raise its rivals' costs. In the present case, it is apparent

that Interac was dominant in the relevant SENS and SEFS markets. It is not unreasonable to assume that its members jointly enjoyed some benefits as a result of this dominance. Allowing access to new members, who would then be better able to compete in issuing cards, for example, might have resulted in the erosion of some of the members' profits. It may have been rational for the members to deter access for newcomers in order to preserve supracompetitive profits. Consider again the *Terminal Railroad* case. By controlling the bridges, the railroads severely limited competition in railroad services into St Louis, thus giving the association's members an anticompetitive advantage. Hence, it may well have been a rational strategy in that case, as with the instant case, to prevent new access and the potential erosion of supracompetitive profits it might have brought.

In the *Interac* case, as in other essential facilities cases, it is possible that access was denied or limited in order to preserve supracompetitive profits. The difficulty, from a policy perspective, is what to do if such an anticompetitive motivation is found. Developing a network such as Interac is costly, given the actual costs of development and the risk of its failure. There may, for example, be competition among nascent networks at first such that one or more of the competing networks is at risk of failure. Indeed, the Bank of Montreal also controlled a network, Cirrus, which competed with Interac in the cash-dispensing service market. In many network industries, there is a value to a user of the network from an additional user; or 'network externality.' As a result, in a battle of networks, it may be that eventually only a single network will survive and dominate the industry. Once this dominance has emerged, it may be reasonable to conclude that that network has become an essential facility and that access to it by competitors should be mandated. The difficulty, however, is that mandating such access may create an incentive to free ride.[120] In the *Interac* context, for example, a financial institution, rather than joining Interac at its beginning and sharing in the cost of development and the risk of failure, can wait and seek to join the network once it has established itself as dominant. If denied access at this stage, it can complain to the competition authorities. The free rider avoids some of the costs of developing a successful network while reaping the benefits once its success is clear.

In *Interac*, the consent order acknowledged the potential for this

---

120 See ibid.

problem. New members would be compelled to pay a switch fee on every Interac transaction in order to defray the costs of the original investors. Church and Ware contend that 'Two concerns arise concerning this switch fee. First, if Interac members have already recovered their initial investment several times over, the "reward to innovation" argument is not all that compelling. Second, the switch fee is paid by Interac members, but it can be compounded by "double marginalization" to even higher fees levied onto cardholders at the terminal.'[121] The converse problem is also important. Recovering the initial investment, perhaps even multiples of the initial investment, may not account sufficiently for the risk of the initial investment. If there is a significant risk of failure, recouping the entire investment may not be sufficient compensation from an *ex ante* perspective. How, then, to set appropriate compensation for the original investors? This will be a tricky problem, compounded by the risk of 20/20 hindsight: there may be a tendency to underestimate the risk of failure given the success of the network. *Ex post*, it may be tempting to set a low access fee in order to encourage competition, but this may have a socially undesirable chilling effect on investments in networks such as Interac. In our view, as the essential facility doctrine develops further in Canada, striking an appropriate balance between competition and innovation incentives will prove to be the doctrine's most vexing problem.

6. *Abuse of Legal Process as Abuse of Dominance*

Unlike some of the techniques used by firms controlling an essential facility, the practice of employing the legal process to raise rivals' costs is theoretically easy to understand. A dominant firm imposes costs on its rivals, perhaps even deterring entry, by forcing the rivals into costly litigation or other forms of legal process. Such practices are widely perceived by competition policy commentators as having the potential for seriously undermining effective rivalry in many markets. In the United States it has been observed that powerful firms using lawsuits 'can tie up smaller businesses in uncertain and expensive proceedings, thereby increasing the cost of doing business and preventing or delaying new entries into a particular market.'[122] Combative litigation can

---

121 Ibid., at 125.
122 *MCI Communications v. American Telephone and Telegraph Co.*, 708 F. 2d 1081 at 1158 (7th Cir., 1983).

demotivate, block development or expansion, coerce compliance and, at the least, cause delay and raise the competitor's costs, even if unsuccessful.[123]

Even scholars such as Robert Bork, who takes a conservative view of the scope of competition law in general and price-based forms of predation in particular,[124] argue for the effective application of antitrust laws to anticompetitive forms of abuse of legal processes. In *The Antitrust Paradox*, Bork states:

> Predation by abuse of governmental procedures, including administrative and judicial processes, presents an increasingly dangerous threat to competition ...

> As a technique for predation, sham litigation is theoretically one of the most promising. Litigation, whether before an agency or a court, can often be framed so that the expenses to each party will be about the same. Indeed, if, as is usual, the party seeking to enter the market bears the burden of going forward with evidence, litigation expenses may be much heavier for him. Expenses in complex business litigation can be enormous, not merely in direct legal fees and costs but in the diversion of executive time and effort and in the disruption of the organization's regular activities. Thus, the firm resisting market entry through sham litigation can impose equal or greater costs upon the entrant and, if it has greater or even equal reserves, may be able to outlast the potential rival. This tactic is likely to find unqualified success only against smaller firms, since the costs of litigation must loom large relative to reserves if the firm is to be driven out. The tactic may be successful against larger firms if the costs are large relative to expected profits in a small market.

> The predator need not expect to defeat entry altogether. He may hope only to delay it. Sham litigation then becomes a useful tactic against any size firm, regardless of relative reserves, for it may be worth the price of litigation to purchase a delay of a year or several years in a rival's entry into a lucrative market. In such cases, successful predation does not require that the predator be able to impose larger costs on the victim, that

---

123 Sandra J. Welsman, 'Commercial Power and Competitor Litigation,' (1996) 24 *A.B.L.R.* 85 at 87.
124 See discussion in Chapter 5.

the predator have greater reserves than the victim, or that the predator have better access to capital than the victim. No other technique of predation is able to escape all of these requirements, and that fact indicates both the danger and the probability of predation by misuse of governmental processes ...

There is, of course, no way of estimating precisely how much competition is crippled or stifled each year through the abuse of governmental processes. However, the number of cases beginning to arise in this relatively new field of litigation (as well as some practical experience with local businessmen) leads one to believe that this form of predation may be common and that the aggregate annual loss to consumers may be very large. The antitrust laws can make a major contribution both to free competition and to the integrity of administrative and judicial processes by catching up with this means of monopolization.[125]

Bork provides an example of what he considers to be an anticompetitive form of abuse of legal process by an incumbent firm:

Suppose that a large chain of motion picture theatres decides to block the access of rivals to towns where it has the only theatre. To that end, the chain adopts the tactic of opposing the construction of any additional theatres before the local zoning boards and of pursuing such opposition through all state courts. The zoning boards, under state law, have no authority to consider the desirability of competition but may only consider effects upon surrounding residential property, the capacity of the streets to handle increased traffic flow, and like matters. The motion picture chain, though it has absolutely no interest in such issues and no legal right to raise them, nevertheless battles through the zoning boards and all state courts, striving for as much delay and expense at each stage as possible. Here no governmental agency is induced to take action that is outside its discretion, but the procedures of the zoning boards and the courts are invoked merely to create expense and delay in order to postpone or prevent the appearance of competition. If a would-be entrant could prove that it had been delayed by the invocation of the board procedures, that it had suffered heavy expense, that the opposition was sham and without merit and put up in bad faith for the sole purpose of monopolizing, then

---

125 R. Bork, *The Antitrust Paradox* (New York: Basic Books, 1978) at 347–9.

there can hardly be a doubt the entrant would have a valid claim under Section 2 of the *Sherman Act*.[126]

A similar view of the anticompetitive potential for abuse of legal processes is taken by more interventionist antitrust scholars such as Salop and Scheffman.[127]

The law in Canada is not yet clear on its approach to abuse of legal process as abuse of dominance. In what follows, we will review the American jurisprudence on the subject for two reasons: first, the cases illustrate the potential for abuse; second, as with essential facilities, the laws of monopolization in both countries are similar in approach and thus the American case law may have persuasive power in Canada. It is essential to note, however, that many of the U.S. cases are shaped by the First Amendment to the American Bill of Rights, which provides: 'Congress shall make no law respecting an establishment of religion or prohibiting the free exercise thereof; or abridging the freedom of speech, or of the press; or the right of the people peaceably to assemble, and to petition the government for a redress of grievances.' The Canadian constitution, on the other hand, does not contain an explicit provision recognizing and protecting the right to petition government, although it can be argued that as a matter of common law, and as a matter of the constitutional guarantee of freedom of expression contained in section 2 of the Charter of Rights and Freedoms, something close to a right to petition government has constitutional status.[128]

The right to petition the government has created difficult issues in the evolution of U.S. antitrust policy on abuse of legal process. We will briefly review the evolution of these issues below. As mentioned, in contrast to the U.S. experience, the issue of anticompetitive abuse of legal processes has attracted very little case law or commentary in Canada and in many respects the issue is one of first impression.

(a) U.S. Law
U.S. case law has recognized a substantial immunity for conduct that may otherwise violate antitrust laws where such conduct falls within

---

126 Ibid., at 362.
127 Salop and Scheffman, 'Raising Rivals' Costs.'
128 See Paul Michell, 'Litigation and the Competition Act: Procuring Anti-competitive Effects through Public Processes,' (1995) 26 *Canadian Business Law Journal* 244 at 289–96.

the protection of the First Amendment of the Bill of Rights. This immunity was first recognized by the U.S. Supreme Court in *Eastern Railroad Presidents Conference v. Noerr Motor Freight Inc.*[129] *Noerr* involved a dispute between the trucking industry and railroads over the market for long-distance transportation of heavy freight. In the course of the dispute, the railroads engaged in an advertising campaign to encourage the adoption and retention of laws and enforcement practices antithetical to the trucking industry. The campaign involved both propagandizing the general public and lobbying the Pennsylvania legislature. The complaint by the truckers alleged that the campaign entailed violations of sections 1 and 2 of the *Sherman Act*. A unanimous Supreme Court held that just as state action to create a monopoly or procure anticompetitive effects is not reviewable under the *Sherman Act*, neither are efforts by private citizens to persuade the government to undertake such action. However, the court also stated: 'There may be situations in which a publicity campaign ostensibly directed toward influencing government action is a mere sham to cover what is actually nothing more than an attempt to interfere directly with the business relationships of the competitor and the application of the *Sherman Act* would be justified.'[130]

In *United Mine Workers of America v. Pennington*,[131] the Supreme Court extended the *Noerr* doctrine to apply to lobbying efforts directed at the executive branch of government. This case involved the petitioning of the secretary of labour by coal mine operators and the United Mine Workers' Union to increase the minimum wage, which it was alleged would effectively preclude smaller mining companies from competing in the market.

The Supreme Court further extended the ambit of what has come to be called the *Noerr-Pennington* doctrine in *California Motor Transport Company v. Trucking Unlimited*[132] to include efforts to influence administrative agencies and adjudicative bodies. In this case the complaint alleged that the defendants, who were fifteen large trucking firms operating in the state of California, had banded together to create a joint trust fund to be used in opposing all applications for operating rights

129 365 U.S. 127 (1961).
130 Ibid., at 144.
131 381 U.S. 657 (1965).
132 404 U.S. 508 (1972).

by smaller trucking firms. Such opposition was to be pursued before all available courts as well as before the California Public Utilities Commission and the Interstate Commerce Commission. In this case the court held that the *Noerr-Pennington* doctrine governs the approach of citizens or groups of them to administrative agencies and to the courts. However, the right to petition to government was not viewed by the court as absolute. Justice Douglas stated that practices designed to harass and deter competitors, and in particular 'a pattern of baseless repetitive claims,' would not qualify for immunity under the First Amendment.[133] The court also noted that misrepresentations condoned in the political area are not immunized when used in the adjudicatory process, implying a somewhat narrower immunity than that applicable under *Noerr-Pennington* to representational activities directed at the legislative or executive arms of government.

In *Otter Tail Power Company v. United States*,[134] the sham exception to *Noerr-Pennington* immunity was invoked in the following circumstances. Otter Tail was an investor-owned electric utility that served small towns in Minnesota and the Dakotas. Some of the towns sought to replace Otter Tail with municipal systems, and Otter Tail responded with a variety of tactics, including, as noted above, refusing to allow access to its power transmission and distribution facilities, and sponsorship and financial support of litigation, in order to frustrate the sale of revenue bonds to finance the municipal system. The litigation failed on the merits. The District Court found that the delay occasioned by the litigation altered or appreciably slowed efforts at municipal ownership. On remand from the Supreme Court following its decision in *California Motor Transport Co.*, the District Court found that the repetitive use of litigation by Otter Tail was timed and designed principally to prevent the establishment of municipal electric systems and that it therefore came within the sham exception to the *Noerr* doctrine as defined in *California Motor Transport Co.* The Supreme Court summarily affirmed the judgment.

In *Columbia (City) v. Omni Outdoor Advertising Inc.*,[135] in attempting to delineate the scope of the First Amendment immunity and the so-called sham exception respectively, the court articulated an important

---

133 Ibid., at 513.
134 410 U.S. 366 (1973) and 417 U.S. 901 (1974).
135 111 S. Ct. 1344 (1991).

distinction in stating that the sham exception encompasses situations in which persons use the governmental process – as opposed to the outcome of the process – as an anticompetitive weapon, and that a sham situation involves a defendant whose activities are not generally aimed at procuring favourable government action at all, but rather as a means of imposing costs and delays on potential competitors. The facts involved a battle over the market for outdoor billboard advertising. The incumbent billboard firm induced municipal officials to enact zoning by-laws that resulted in the plaintiff's inability to erect new signs. The court held that the petitioning activity did not fall within the sham exception because the anticompetitive result depended upon the zoning ordinances being adopted by the City Council. This distinction has led many courts and commentators to conclude that competition policy cannot and should not attempt to regulate the substantive legal outcomes produced by the activities of firms in the political, administrative, or judicial systems. Yet it should ensure that dominant firms do not use the *processes* of courts and administrative agencies to impose costs upon their rivals. It is the imposition of 'process' costs and not those costs that may arise from the substantive resolution of disputes that is the appropriate focus of competition law. The essential distinction is between the abuse of judicial or regulatory *processes* to restrain competition (which should be subject to scrutiny under competition law) and initiating a lawsuit or regulatory proceedings which, if successful, will restrain competition (which should not be a concern of competition policy).[136]

This distinction between process and outcome, while compelling in principle, has proved very difficult to operationalize in practice. U.S. courts have taken widely divergent positions on the question of how to test for allegedly sham litigation, disagreeing as to whether the baselessness should be tested subjectively or objectively, and whether anticompetitive motivation must merely exist, must predominate, or must be the exclusive motivation.

In *Professional Real Estate Investors Inc. v. Columbia Pictures Industries Inc.,*[137] the U.S. Supreme Court attempted to resolve some of these uncertainties. *Professional Real Estate Investors* involved litigation relating to alleged copyright infringement. The defendant counterclaimed,

---

136 See Michell, 'Litigation and The Competition Act,' at 251–2.
137 113 S. Ct. 1920 (1993).

alleging that the plaintiff's suit was a sham cloaking its attempt to monopolize and restrain trade. The question presented by this case was whether litigation may be a sham merely because a subjective expectation of success does not motivate the litigant. The court answered this question in the negative and held that an objectively reasonable effort to litigate cannot be a sham regardless of subjective intent. The court held that anticompetitive litigation enjoys immunity from antitrust liability unless the litigation is 'objectively baseless.' The majority rejected the view that litigation is a sham where the litigant does not have a subjective expectation of success. Only where an attempt to litigate is not objectively reasonable – there is no probable cause to institute legal proceedings – will a litigant be denied immunity. Subjective intent does not affect the legality of otherwise objectively reasonable efforts to influence government policy.

The majority adopted a two-part definition of sham litigation. First, the court must determine whether the litigation is objectively baseless 'in the sense that no reasonable litigant could realistically expect success on the merits.'[138] Only if it is unreasonable will the court look at the litigant's subjective motivation. The court must determine whether a baseless lawsuit was an attempt to achieve anticompetitive effects through the result of the adjudicative process, or whether it merely sought to use the process itself to achieve anticompetitive effects. Only in the latter case would litigation be considered a sham. Thus, the legality of objectively reasonable petitioning directed towards obtaining governmental action is not affected by any anticompetitive purpose that the actor may have had.

However, not all the Supreme Court judges concurred with the majority's opinion. Justice Stevens, with whom Justice O'Connor concurred, held that while he agreed 'with the Court's disposition of this case and with its holding "that an objectively reasonable effort to litigate cannot be a sham regardless of subjective intent,"' he disagreed with the 'Court's equation of "objectively baseless" with the answer to the question whether any "reasonable litigant could realistically expect success on the merits."'[139] He stated, 'There might well be lawsuits that fit the latter definition but can be shown to be objectively *unreasonable*, and thus shams. It might not be objectively reasonable to bring a law-

---

138 Ibid., at 1928.
139 Ibid., at 1932.

suit just because some form of success on the merits – no matter how insignificant – could be expected.'[140]

According to the minority, the distinction between abusing the judicial process to restrain competition and prosecuting a lawsuit that, if successful, will restrain competition, must guide any court's decision whether a particular filing, or series of filings, is a sham. Justice Stevens wrote,

> The label 'sham' is appropriately applied to a case, or series of cases, in which the plaintiff is indifferent to the outcome of the litigation itself, but has nevertheless sought to impose a collateral harm on the defendant by, for example, impairing his credit, abusing the discovery process, or interfering with his access to governmental agencies. It might also apply to a plaintiff who had some reason to expect success on the merits but because of its tremendous cost would not bother to achieve that result without the benefit of collateral injuries imposed on its competitor by the legal process alone. Litigation filed or pursued for such collateral purposes is fundamentally different from a case in which the relief sought in the litigation itself would give the plaintiff a competitive advantage or, perhaps, exclude a potential competitor from entering a market with a product that either infringes the plaintiff's patent or copyright or violates an exclusive franchise granted by a governmental body.[141]

The minority opinion goes further and cites the *GripPak* case in which Judge Posner first introduced a cost-benefit test for sham litigation:

> But we are not prepared to rule that the difficulty of distinguishing lawful from unlawful purpose in litigation between competitors is so acute that such litigation can never be considered an actionable restraint of trade, provided it has some, though perhaps only threadbare, basis in law. Many claims not wholly groundless would never be sued on for their own sake; the stakes, discounted by the probability of winning, would be too low to repay the investment in litigation. Suppose a monopolist brought a tort action against its single, tiny competitor; the action had a colorable basis in law; but in fact the monopolist would never have brought the suit – its

---

140 Ibid.
141 Ibid.

chances of winning, or the damages it could hope to get if it did win, were too small compared to what it would have to spend on the litigation – except that it wanted to use pretrial discovery to discover its competitor's trade secrets; or hope that the competitor would be required to make public disclosure of its potential litigation in the suit and that this disclosure would increase the interest rate that the competitor had to pay for bank financing; or just wanted to impose heavy legal costs on the competitor in the hope of deterring entry by other firms. In these examples the plaintiff wants to hurt a competitor not by getting a judgment against him, which would be a proper objective, but just by the maintenance of the suit, regardless of its outcome. ... We think it is premature to hold that litigation, unless malicious in the tort sense, can never be actionable under the antitrust laws. The existence of a tort of abuse of process shows that it has long been thought that litigation could be used for improper purposes even when there is probable cause for the litigation; and if the improper purpose is to use litigation as a tool for suppressing competition in its antitrust sense, it becomes a matter of antitrust concern. This is not to say that litigation is actionable under the antitrust laws merely because the plaintiff is trying to get a monopoly. He is entitled to pursue such a goal through lawful means, including litigation against competitors. The line is crossed when his purpose is not to win a favorable judgment against a competitor but to harass him, and deter others, by the process itself – regardless of outcome – of litigating. The difficulty of determining the true purpose is great but no more so than in many other areas of antitrust law.[142]

The majority opinion's test of objective baselessness in *Professional Real Estate Investors* has been criticized by some American commentators. For example, Perrine argues,

If a lawsuit does not satisfy the objective prong of the PRE test, arguably there should be no danger of predation. However, this is where Justice Steven's criticism of the test is significantly relevant. In many cases, the litigation may only be a small part of a broader plan of predation, and though the predator may reasonably expect success on the merits, the potential recovery alone may not be great enough to justify the bringing of the action. In these situations, the Court's test does not prevent the

---

142 *GripPak Inc. v. Illinois Tool Works*, 694 F. 2d 466 at 472 (7th Cir., 1982).

predator from invoking the judicial process to obtain a market advantage as the predator's showing of an objective basis for its claim precludes an analysis of its economic motivation for filing the suit.[143]

The specific standard by which the *Professional Real Estate* court differentiated between sham activities and ones immunized from antitrust litigation has also been criticized for not balancing properly the different objectives that should be taken into account. As one commentator suggests: 'Although potentially eliminating some confusion in determining whether litigation is predatory, the Court's decision effectively rendered it impossible to prevent parties from using "meritorious litigation" for improper purposes. In limiting the judicial system's ability to control parties who initiate litigation for reasons other than success on the merits, the Supreme Court in *Columbia Pictures* potentially curtailed the market protections created by the *Sherman Act*.[144]

As another commentator argues, objective baselessness may be particularly difficult to demonstrate in the administrative context because agencies enjoy greater policy-making discretion than do the courts. Indeed, where the standards for approval of licences and applications make reference to undefined considerations of public interest, it may be impossible to show that a competitor's objections were objectively baseless.[145]

Even if the majority's objectively reasonable standard were to be adopted, it can be argued that its application as set forth by the minority opinion balances the competing interests in a more coherent and appropriate way. Where litigation is not meritless in the objective sense, but is nonetheless used to achieve an anticompetitive intent without regard to the outcome of the regulatory proceedings, such litigation should be found 'objectively baseless.' The minority's test fol-

---

143 James Perrine, 'Defining the Sham Litigation Exception to the *Noerr-Pennington* Antitrust Immunity Doctrine: An Analysis of the *Professional Real Estate Investors v. Columbia Pictures Industries* Decision,' (1995) 46 *Alabama L. Rev.* 815 at 839.

144 'Preventing Predatory Abuses in Litigation Between Business Competitors: Focusing on a Litigant's Reasons for Initiating the Litigation to Ensure a Balance Between the Constitutional Right to Petition and the *Sherman Act*'s Guarantee of Fair Competition in Business,' (1995) 36 *Wm. and Mary L. Rev.* 1135 at 1138.

145 Lars Noah, 'Sham Petitioning as a Threat to the Integrity of the Regulatory Process,' (1995) 74 *North Carolina L. Rev.* 1.

lows the Supreme Court decisions before *Professional Real Estate* (especially the *California Motors* and the *Omni* decisions)[146] which stated that even legal activity can be a sham where there is misuse of the process.

Reflecting these criticisms, the U.S. courts, after the *Professional Real Estate* decision, recognized an important exception to the 'objectively baseless' test in *USS-Posco Industries v. Contra Costa County Building & Construction.*[147] In this case, the Ninth Circuit held that the *Professional Real Estate* two-step inquiry does not apply in quite the same way to the situation identified in *California Motor Transport*, 'where the defendant is accused of bringing a whole series of legal proceedings ... without regard for the merits and for the purpose of injuring a market rival.'[148] Such activity would amount to a misuse of the administrative or judicial process. The court stated that the hallmark of a *California Motor Transport* sham claim is a pattern of baseless proceedings aimed at securing, through the very process of litigation, a benefit other than the prayed-for relief. Similarly, in *Hahn v. Codding* the Ninth Circuit found the exception applicable to a pattern of thirteen lawsuits when the very pendency of the lawsuits prevented the plaintiff from acquiring financing through the issuance of bonds.[149]

It should be pointed out that in its *Professional Real Estate* decision, the Supreme Court stated that in *California Motor Transport* 'we recognized that recourse to agencies and to courts should not be condemned as a sham until a reviewing court has "discerned and drawn" the "difficult line" separating objectively reasonable claims from "a pattern of baseless, repetitive claims ... which leads the factfinder to conclude that the administrative and judicial processes have been abused."'[150]

(b) Australian Case Law
Prior to reviewing the sparse Canadian case law on the subject, we will note two Australian cases on point. In *Woolworths v. Campbells Cash and Carry Pty Ltd.*,[151] Woolworths alleged that Campbells had breached its development consents at four sites by 'retailing' items in areas zoned

---

146 *Supra*, notes 132 and 135.
147 31 F. 3d 800 (9th Cir., 1994).
148 Ibid., at 810–11.
149 615 F. 2d 830 at 840–1 (9th Cir., 1980).
150 *Professional Real Estate Investors, supra* 113 S. Ct. 1920 at 1927.
151 (1993), 80 L.G.E.R.A. 104.

'industrial'. Bignold J. explained that he would have been unlikely to have exercised judicial discretion to grant an injunction, even if a limited breach had been proven, in part because the action was essentially brought and maintained by Woolworths as a trade competitor concerned about Campbells' marketing initiatives.

In *Fat-sel Pty Ltd. v. ACR Trading Pty Ltd.*,[152] the plaintiff mounted a challenge to the legality of land use by a trade competitor, the defendant, in accordance with the *Environmental Planning and Assessment Act*, which provides standing to 'any person' with objection to 'designated developments' via the process of public review. The plaintiff sought an injunction to stop receiving and processing waste activities on the defendant's land, arguing that the use was 'offensive and hazardous' and so prohibited in the zone. The land and environment court declared that the land was being misused, granting an injunction. Three years later, the New South Wales Court of Appeal disagreed. Kirby P. focused on the rationale for the plaintiff's actions: '[The plaintiff] is a trade competitor of the appellant's ... It may be inferred that its real concern was not anxiety about the amenity of the neighbourhood at Moorebank, nor a purist insistence upon compliance with the letter of the planning law. Clearly, it was invoking the Act to impede the operations of a competitor.[153] Kirby P. stressed that in granting an injunction, the court should also take into account the fact that 'the complaint when it came, was from a trade competitor who stood to gain commercial advantage from injunctive relief.' The matter was returned to the Land and Environment Court, the scope of the discretion having been made clear. However, on review, Bignold J. noted the remarks of Kirby P., but from additional evidence adduced that the appeal concluded that the breach did have adverse environmental effects and thus there should be an injunction.

(c) Canadian Law

Where anticompetitive abuse of legal processes is alleged of a single dominant firm, the legal avenue of redress would appear to be the abuse of dominance provision, section 79 of the *Competition Act*. As noted above, section 78 provides an illustrative list of anticompetitive acts. None of these examples is directly on point, but, as the tribunal

---

152 14 May 1985, Land and Environment Court (unreported).
153 *ACR Trading Pty Ltd. v. Fat-set Pty. Ltd.* (1987), 11 NSWLR 67 at 69.

has stressed, the list is non-exhaustive and other practices may constitute an abuse of dominant position.[154] Thus, if a dominant firm abuses the legal process in order to raise rivals' costs or otherwise gain or preserve market power, it may face an order pursuant to section 79.

The only relevant case is *Laidlaw*.[155] In that case, tribunal relied on a wide range of exclusionary practices in justifying its conclusion that Laidlaw had abused its dominant position in the commercial waste collection and disposal market on Vancouver Island and in the remedial orders that it issued. Laidlaw's litigation practices were found by the tribunal to constitute part of this broader set of anticompetitive practices. The tribunal found that Laidlaw had threatened in letters to its customers to sue for breach of contract those who contemplated switching to rival firms. The letters alleged that Laidlaw had brought many such actions against it customers in the past and that none of these actions had been unsuccessful. This was untrue: no such actions had actually been brought although several had been threatened. Laidlaw also wrote to rival firms threatening them with law suits for inducing breach of contract. With respect to these practices the tribunal stated: 'No one can read the evidence concerning the use Laidlaw made of litigation and the threat of litigation in this case without a sense of outrage. The respondent used its vastly larger size and economic resources together with the threat of litigation to prevent customers from switching to competitors. It commenced spurious litigation and threatened litigation against its competitors to drive or attempt to drive them out of business by raising their costs of doing business. This is certainly predatory behaviour.'[156]

The tribunal did not elaborate on how it defined 'spurious litigation,' nor did the remedial orders that it issued directly address this issue. However, a number of the contractual provisions Laidlaw employed with its customers to which the threats of litigation related, in particular the exclusivity and renewal provisions, were held by the tribunal to be unenforceable, thus effectively precluding future litigation by Laidlaw to enforce them and presumably discouraging threats of litigation to similar effect. Thus, it seems reasonable to conclude from the tribunal's decision in *Laidlaw* that in appropriate cases the tri-

---

154 See, e.g., *NutraSweet, supra*, note 11.
155 *Laidlaw, supra*, note 21.
156 Ibid., at 343–4.

bunal will view anticompetitive abuse of legal processes as an abuse of dominant position under section 79. However, this conclusion does not in itself resolve the question of what constitutes 'spurious' or abusive deployment of legal processes.

To answer this question, the American cases may be instructive, but they should not be treated as conclusive for two reasons. First, there is explicit constitutional protection for access to the legal process that does not exist in Canada.[157] Such a rule clearly creates a bias against finding abuse of legal process as infringing antitrust law. Second, there was a robust minority view in the leading U.S. Supreme Court case, as well as compelling commentary criticizing the majority opinion. Our view of an optimal approach for Canada is informed by the U.S. debate but not beholden to the U.S. outcome.

In our view, the 'objectively baseless' test set out in the United States should not be adopted without modification in Canada. There are two fundamental problems with the test. First, it will rarely, if ever, be the case that litigation has a zero chance of success. This implies excessive leeway for a dominant firm contemplating litigation as a strategy to raise its rivals' costs. Second, the probability of success in a regulatory or litigation context is only one of the factors that determine whether the strategy is rational on its own terms, as opposed to rational because of its harmful, anticompetitive effect on rivals. It is also relevant whether the expected gains of the action exceed the expected costs of the action. In *Grip-Pak*, Judge Posner pointed out that 'many claims not wholly groundless would never be sued on for their own sakes; the stakes discounted by the probability of winning, would be too low to repay the investment in litigation.'[158] Similarly in *Premier Electric Construction Company v. National Electrical Contractors Association Inc.*,[159] Judge Easterbrook, in adopting Judge Posner's reasoning from *Grip-Pak*, stated: 'If the expected value of a judgement is $10,000 (say a 10 percent chance of recovering $100,000), the case is not "groundless"; yet if it cost $30,000 to litigate no rational plaintiff will do so unless he anticipates some other source of benefit. If the other benefit is the costs litigation will impose on a rival, allowing an elevation of the market price, it may be treated as a sham.'[160]

---

157 But see Michell, 'Litigation and the Competition Act.'
158 *Supra*, 694 F. 2d at 472.
159 814 F. 2d 358 (8th Cir., 1987).
160 Ibid., at 372.

In other words, in this scenario, assuming rational behaviour by the litigant, the investment of $30,000 for an expected gain of $10,000 only becomes rational if the litigant has in mind some collateral purpose – in this case raising rival's costs or creating barriers to entry through the litigation process.

It should be noted that there is a difference in the cost rules in the two different countries:[161] unlike in the United States, successful litigants in Canada typically recover part of their legal fees from the unsuccessful opposition litigant. While different cost rules have some effect, they do not alter Posner and Easterbrook's conclusions. It remains true that, prior to launching the action, there is an expected cost and benefit to the action that will be affected by the cost rules, but not to the point that an action with a positive probability of success will always be rational to pursue on its own terms. Indeed, if the probability of success is less than 50 per cent and legal costs are symmetrical across parties, the Canadian cost rules make it even less likely that the action has a positive expected value than where costs are not awarded.[162] Returning to Judge Easterbrook's example, if the amount sought in a potential action is $100,000, the probability of success is 10 per cent, the cost of litigating is $30,000 for both sides, and the successful litigant is awarded the full $30,000 in costs on top of damages,[163] the expected value to the party deciding to launch the action is not –$20,000, as it would be under American cost rules, but rather –$44,000. (The litigant gets $100,000 if the action succeeds, which has a 10 per cent probability, but loses $60,000 if the action fails, which has a

---

161 For analyses on the effects of cost rules on incentives to litigate, see J.R.S. Prichard, 'A Systemic Approach to Comparative Law: The Effect of Cost, Fee and Financing Rules on the Development of the Substantive Law,' (1988) 17 *J. Leg. Stud.* 451; K. Roach and J.R.S. Prichard 'Comparative Common Law – The Consequences of Differing Incentives to Litigate,' in P. Newman, ed., *The New Palgrave Dictionary of Economics and the Law* (London: MacMillan, 1998).

162 To show this, let EV_C and EV_{US} be the expected values of the litigation under the Canadian and American rules respectively, let D be the damages awarded if successful, P be the probability of success, C be the costs of litigation for both parties and K be the award of costs payable by the loser to the winner. Under the U.S. rule, $EV_{US} = PD - C$. Under the Canadian rule, $EV_C = [P(D+K) - PC] - [(1-P)(C+K)] = PD - C + 2PK - K$. This implies, $EV_C = EV_{US} + (2P-1)K$, which implies $EV_C < EV_{US}$ if $P < 0.5$.

163 Ordinarily, the successful litigant does not recover its full costs, but the point of the example does not change if we consider a case of less than the full costs.

568   The Law and Economics of Canadian Competition Policy

90 per cent possibility). If such an action were launched by a dominant firm, it should surely be treated with suspicion.

Thus, in our view, the test should follow the cost-benefit analysis suggested by Judges Posner and Easterbrook. If litigation by a dominant firm appears irrational on its own terms, competition concerns arise. If there are anticompetitive gains to the dominant firm from pursuing such a litigation strategy, along the lines identified by Bork (such as delay of a rival's entry into the market), the abuse of process should be treated as an abuse of dominance.

It is important to note that Australian courts, in actions brought under the misuse of market power provisions of the *Trade Practices Act*,[164] have indeed adopted a cost-benefit rationale for much commercial conduct, including litigation. As Lockhart J. in *Dowling v. Dalgety Australia Pty. Ltd.* stated: 'If a corporation has market power which causes it to exercise rights which it would not exercise under competitive conditions then the exercise of these rights is the exercise of market power ... The central determinative question to ask is: has the corporation exercised a right that it would be highly unlikely to exercise or could not afford to exercise if the corporation was operating in a competitive market?'[165] Thus, our suggested approach for Canada is not only consistent with an economic approach, but is also consistent with the law of a similar jurisdiction.

7. Other Unenumerated Acts

As noted, there is no exhaustive list of acts that may, in the circumstances, be considered anticompetitive and thus subject to an order under section 79. To give a flavour of the potential variety of acts coming within the purview of section 79, we review here some of the idiosyncratic acts that have been found anticompetitive in the case law.

In *NutraSweet*, the director alleged that NutraSweet had engaged in a practice of anticompetitive acts by using its U.S. patent on aspartame to foreclose competition in Canada.[166] The tribunal found that NutraSweet had persuaded a Canadian customer of aspartame to switch from a rival, Tosoh, to NutraSweet by offering rebates to the customer on the basis of aspartame used in products manufactured in the United States

---

164 S. 46(1).
165 (1992), 34 F.C.R. 109 at 144.
166 *Supra*, note 11. The patent for aspartame in Canada had expired.

and imported into Canada. The rebate would depend on the difference between the U.S. and the Canadian prices. The tribunal held, among other things, that the fact that NutraSweet was willing to offer the rebate regardless of the size of the U.S.-Canada price differential indicated an intention to limit the expansion of its competitors. It held that the use of the monopoly position conferred by the U.S. patent for anticompetitive purposes was an anticompetitive act.

The tribunal rejected the director's allegation in *NutraSweet* that NutraSweet had committed an anticompetitive act by reporting losses on its Canadian income taxes. This, the director alleged, gave it an unfair competitive advantage. It also saved money by failing to complete accurately various import forms. The tribunal held that there was no demonstrated anticompetitive purpose to either of these practices, and thus no anticompetitive act.

The director in *Tele-Direct* alleged that Tele-Direct had abused its dominant position by aggressively targeting rivals in markets where entry into the telephone directory services market had occurred. The director contended that Tele-Direct used its significant profits in other markets to subsidize intense, 'near-predatory' competition in those markets involving entry. In rejecting this contention, the tribunal stated: 'Targeting cannot be distinguished as an anti-competitive act merely by the fact that there is a differentiated response. Targeting, in the sense of a differentiated response to competitors, is a decidedly normal competitive reaction. An incumbent can be expected to behave differently where it faces entry than where it does not.'[167]

The tribunal did find anticompetitive, however, Tele-Direct's policy of discriminatory tactics against consultants that advised advertisers on the content of their Yellow Pages advertisements. The tribunal outlined these tactics as follows: 'These include suspicious errors, last

---

167 *Tele-Direct, supra* (1997), 73 C.P.R. (3d) at 194. We note that courts in other jurisdictions have occasionally not appreciated the Tribunal's reasoning. In a European case, *AKZO Chemie BV v. EC Commission*, [1991] 5 C.M.L.R. 215, the European Court of Justice condemned AKZO for predatory pricing, even where price was above average variable cost, in part on the basis of the fact that prices quoted to customers of a rival were lower than prices quoted to those who were not customers of a rival. While the result may or may not have been correct (the price was below average total cost), the court neglected to note, as the tribunal did in *Tele-Direct*, that cutting price in the face of vigorous competition is entirely consistent with benign competitive behaviour.

minute contact resulting in confusion for the advertiser about what must be done to have the new advertising run or resulting in missed deadlines, identifying errors or problems in the advertising that would not otherwise be a problem and informing customers that their orders might not be processed.'[168]

A wide variety of anticompetitive acts was engaged by the consent order proceedings in *Interac*. While many of the anticompetitive acts related to limiting access to the Interac network by non-members, as noted above, some of them related to the effects of the governance rules of the association. For example, a two-thirds majority of voting (Charter) members was required to effect a change in Interac's by-laws, which potentially hindered the introduction of innovative new services that would require by-law amendments. Moreover, a change in service offered by one member had to be offered by all members; innovations by a member or a subset of members were thus discouraged. The consent order addressed these anticompetitive acts.

IV. Remedies

Section 79(1) provides that where a dominant person is, or persons are, engaging in a practice that lessens competition substantially, 'the Tribunal may make an order prohibiting all or any of those persons from engaging in that practice.' This section has been vital in all the litigated cases to date,[169] and indeed was the sole basis for the orders in *Tele-Direct*, which simply required Tele-Direct to cease certain practices.

Section 79(2) expands the scope of the tribunal's discretion, providing that 'the Tribunal may, in addition to or in lieu of making an order under subsection (1), make an order directing any or all the persons against whom an order is sought to take such actions, including the divestiture of assets or shares, as are reasonable and as are necessary to overcome the effects of the practice in the market.' The wide discretion in section 79(2) is limited somewhat by section 79(3), which provides that in making an order under section 79(2), 'the Tribunal shall make the order in such terms as will in its opinion interfere with the rights of any person to whom the order is directed or any other person affected by it only to

168 *Tele-Direct, supra* (1997), 73 C.P.R. (3d) at 241–2.
169 The Guidelines at 2. 5.1 emphasize that the bureau is open to alternative case resolutions that avoid litigation, although they express a preference for consent orders.

the extent necessary to achieve the purpose of the order.' The tribunal has emphasized this principle, stating in *Laidlaw* that 'it is not part of the tribunal's function to impose penalties or punitive measures.'[170]

The case law has involved a variety of orders by the tribunal. In *NutraSweet*, the tribunal made an order that NutraSweet must cease to enter contracts that resulted in exclusive supply with customers. This order contemplated not only the clauses that explicitly gave rise to exclusivity, but also clauses, such as the logo display allowance, that induced exclusivity. The order did not only concern future contracts, however. The tribunal held that NutraSweet could not enforce clauses related to exclusivity in its existing contracts with customers.

In *Laidlaw*, some of the central remedial aspects of the tribunal's decision were the following. Laidlaw was ordered not to purchase a rival in any of the relevant markets for a period of three years. Clauses relating to exclusivity, including the right of first refusal of Laidlaw over the renewal of the business and liquidated damages clauses, were to be deleted from service contracts and were not be entered into again. The tribunal refused the director's request that Laidlaw be forbidden from undercutting its rivals unless the price were made available to all customers on the grounds that not only had the director not proven the necessity of such an order, but such an order could have perverse effects on competition.

The tribunal in *Nielsen, supra*, ordered that Nielsen cease to require or induce exclusivity from its suppliers of scanner-based data. This included the use of MFN clauses, which could be used to exclude rivals from access to the data.[171] Following the minimal impairment requirement in section 79(3), however, the tribunal held that the ban on using MFN clauses would only extend for two years. Once competition appeared, the MFN clauses would no longer serve the exclusionary role they served prior to the order.

V. Conclusion

Actions under the abuse of dominance section are inevitably fact-specific. Practices that may be perfectly benign in some or perhaps most circumstances may have anticompetitive implications in others. The tri-

---

170 *Laidlaw, supra* (1992), 40 C.P.R. (3d) at 352.
171 See discussion above.

bunal's approach has sensibly accounted for these considerations. Efficiency motivations for a practice may preclude finding that the practice is anticompetitive because of the absence of a predatory, exclusionary, or disciplinary effect, or may preclude a finding of a substantial lessening of competition. Thus, while the tribunal may not have been clearly correct in all its orders under the section in the particular cases it has considered,[172] its case-by-case, efficiency-sensitive approach has a sound basis in economic theory.

172 See Church and Ware, 'Abuse of Dominance'; P. Collins, 'The Law and Economics of "Abuse of Dominant Position": An Analysis of NutraSweet,' (1991) 49 U. Tor. Fac. L. Rev. 276.

NINE

Competition Policy and Intellectual Property Rights

I. Introduction[1]

The legal and policy issues raised by intellectual property (IP) have attracted increasing attention from policy makers around the world. Modern advances in technology have created classes of products and processes that present new challenges for patent and competition authorities. Moreover, markets have changed. With the elimination of many barriers to trade, survival in highly competitive global markets depends on the development or adoption of state-of-the-art technologies. These changes have necessitated a re-evaluation of the laws that affect the development and diffusion of innovations, namely IP and competition laws.[2]

An inherent tension exists between competition and patent laws, as described by Louis Kaplow: 'A practice is typically deemed to violate the antitrust laws because it is anticompetitive. But the very purpose of the patent grant is to reward the patentee by limiting competition, in full recognition that the monopolistic evils are the price society will pay.'[3]

---

1 This chapter is drawn largely from M.J. Trebilcock and N.T. Gallini, 'Intellectual Property Rights and Competition Policy: A Framework for the Analysis of Economic and Legal Issues,' in N.T. Gallini and R. Anderson, eds., *Competition Policy and Intellectual Property Rights in the Knowledge-Based Economy* (Calgary: University of Calgary Press, 1998), 17.

2 The economic review conducted here focuses on IP in the form of patents. In section III, we briefly review other IP legislation, such as trade marks and copyright legislation.

3 L. Kaplow, 'Extension of Monopoly Power through Leverage,' (1985) 85 *Columbia Law Review* 515.

This tension can be traced to the familiar public goods problem. Intellectual property embodies information which is a public good. An inventor's consumption of the information does not preclude others from consuming it and so, in the absence of property rights, an innovation will be imitated. In recognition of the public goods nature of IP, patent law provides protection from direct imitation through intellectual property rights (IPRs) in innovations. Without IPRs, the incentive to invest in innovation would be diminished. The law also recognizes that the dynamic benefits from IPRs come at an allocative cost, in that the use of the innovation will be sub-optimal.[4] The IPR awarded under patent law attempts to strike the appropriate balance between these competing concerns by limiting the scope and duration of exclusive rights in an innovation.[5] Competition law affects the exercise of those rights, and therefore the innovator's reward, by restricting certain practices involving IPRs.

The dynamic-allocative efficiency trade-off that underlies patent law applies as well to competition law, and a tension has developed between the approaches to welfare maximization espoused by IP and competition laws.[6] Simply put, the IP grant seeks to protect property rights, and, in so doing, limits competition. In contrast, competition law generally has reflected the premise that consumer welfare is best served by removing impediments to competition. In recent years, this short-run view of competition authorities has gradually been replaced by a longer-term approach that acknowledges that technological progress contributes at least as much to social welfare as does the elimination of allocative inefficiencies from noncompetitive prices.[7] There is,

---

4 Since information is relatively costless to transmit, the efficient price of the information is zero. Exclusionary rights allow the patentee to set a positive price for the information, thus reducing output and the flow of that information.

5 For further analysis of the IP Competition interface, see W. Nordhaus, *Invention, Growth and Welfare: Theoretical Treatment of Technological Change* (Cambridge, Mass.: MIT Press, 1969). Also, W. Bowman, *Patent and Antitrust Law: A Legal and Economic Appraisal* (Chicago: University of Chicago Press, 1973); W. Baxter, 'Legal Restrictions on the Exploitation of the Patent Monopoly: An Economic Analysis,' (1966) 76 *Yale Law Journal* 267; Kaplow, 'Extension of Monopoly Power'; R. Merges and R. Nelson, 'On the Complex Economics of Patent Scope,' (1990) 90 *Columbia Law Review* 836; and G. Priest, 'Cartels and Patent License Arrangements,' (1977) 20 *Journal of Law and Economics* 309.

6 See Kaplow, 'Extension of Monopoly Power.'

7 See R. Barro, 'Economic Growth in Cross-Section of Countries,' (1991) 106(2) *Quarterly Journal of Economics* 407 and H. Demsetz, 'How Many Cheers for Antitrust after 100 Years?' (1992) *Journal of Economic Inquiry* 207.

therefore, a growing willingness to restrict competition today in order to protect increased efficiency and productivity arising from innovation in the future.[8] Viewed in this light, IPRs and competition policy can be seen as complementary ways of achieving efficiency in a market economy.[9]

The problem of coordinating patent and competition policy is subjected to economic analysis in the next section. A brief review of the economic literature regarding patent and licensing is provided, followed by alternative economic proposals for competition policy treatment of IPRs. The proposals are focused principally on licensing contracts,[10] which form the largest proportion of patent-competition cases. In section III, we analyse the interaction between IP and competition laws, again focusing on licensing arrangements for IPRs such as patents and trade marks. In this regard, both unilateral restrictions by a dominant firm (e.g., tying arrangements and exclusivity restrictions) and multilateral agreements among competitors (e.g., patent pooling and cross-licensing) are discussed.[11] The Competition Bureau's *Intellectual Property Enforcement Guidelines* are then reviewed and their potential effects considered.

II. Economics of the IP and Competition Interface

As discussed in the introduction, the challenge facing policy makers is to coordinate patent instruments (i.e., patent duration and scope) and competition instruments (i.e., contractual restrictions) so as to achieve an efficient allocation of resources among the development and use of

8 H. Demsetz recognizes this trade-off in 'Barriers to Entry,' (1982) 72 *American Economic Review* 47.

9 This view is stated clearly in an OECD report on *Competition Policy and Intellectual Property Rights* (Paris: OECD, 1989) and in *Atari Games Corp. v. Nintendo of America Inc.*, 897 F. 2d 1572 (1990).

10 IPRs can take several forms including the patents, copyright, trade secrets, or trade marks. Although the laws differ on the type of protection given, the economic issues (although not necessarily the legal issues) regarding competition and incentives are similar.

11 For other competition offences related to IPRs, for example, patent accumulation and violations concerning copyrights, see R. Merges, 'Antitrust Review of Patent Acquisitions: Property Rights, Firm Boundaries, and Organization' and J. Church and R. Ware, 'Network Industries, Intellectual Property Rights and Competition Policy,' in Gallini and Anderson, eds., *Competition Policy and Intellectual Property Rights*.

new products and processes. This section provides a brief review and analysis of the economic literature on this problem.

A. *Economic Literature on the IP-Competition Interface*

Starting with Nordhaus,[12] a line of economic literature has developed examining the appropriate relationship between patent and competition instruments. In this literature two patent instruments are considered: the length of the patent grant, and the scope (or breadth) of the patent.[13] While patent length establishes the extent to which firms have exclusive rights over their own inventions, patent scope establishes the extent to which an inventor has property rights over related inventions. That is, the scope of the patent will dictate how similar imitations can be to the original innovation without infringing the patent grant. The broader the patent, the more difficult it is for firms to 'invent around' the innovation and, therefore, the greater will be the return earned by the patentee. If patent scope is narrow, firms may develop a close substitute, for example, through small chemical changes in a drug's composition.

Tandon[14] and Gilbert and Shapiro[15] divide the question of optimal patent length and scope into two stages. In the first stage, the *level* of the reward to the innovator is determined. The second-stage problem is to design the *structure* of the patent policy (i.e., the combination of patent length and patent scope that provides the incentives to engage in the desired level of research).

The conclusion that flows from this model is that the most socially efficient way to provide the optimal reward to the innovator is through a patent policy that encourages patents of narrow scope[16] but unlimited duration, which combination effectively constrains the innova-

---

12 Nordhaus, *Invention, Growth and Welfare.*
13 For example, see P. Tandon, 'Optimal Patents with Compulsory Licensing,' (1982) 90 *JPE* 470, R. Gilbert and C. Shapiro, 'Optimal Patent Length and Breadth,' (1990) 21 *Rand Journal of Economics* 106; P. Klemperer, 'How Broad Should the Scope of Patent Be?,' (1990) 21 *Rand Journal of Economics* 113; N.T. Gallini, 'Patent Policy and Costly Imitation,' (1992) 23 *Rand Journal of Economics* 52; J. Green and S. Scotchmer, 'Novelty and Disclosure in Patent Law,' (1990) 21 *Rand Journal of Economics* 131.
14 Tandon, 'Optimal Patents with Compulsory Licensing.'
15 Gilbert and Shapiro, 'Optimal Patent Length and Breadth.'
16 Patent scope is defined here as the flow of profits that accrue to the innovator; more practically, it is the range of products that would be included under the patent.

tor's price. The model shows that a small reduction in the patentee's monopoly price, compensated by an extension in patent life to preserve the firm's incentive to innovate, enhances social welfare. That is, a reduction in scope contributes more to a reduction in dead-weight loss than to a reduction in the innovator's profits, thus yielding a case for long, narrow patents. These results are not responsive, however, to changes in the assumption of competition in the market. If the innovator faces competition from firms producing their own differentiated products or imitations of the patented product, as is typically the case, optimal policy may be reversed to one that provides for a large profit flow (i.e., a broad patent) over a short patent life.

Klemperer's model recognizes the circumstantial effects of competing products on optimal patent protection.[17] Klemperer defines scope with reference to the set of products on the market that are similar to the innovation protected by the patent. A wider patent allows the original innovator to set a higher price for the product, although the innovator may be accepting the risk that consumers will either purchase lower-priced varieties or switch consumption out of the product class entirely. According to the model, less-preferred varieties are costless to develop, but a transport cost is incurred when consumers purchase inferior products. Wider patents reduce the distortion of consumers' choices between the patented product and lower-priced imitations, but increase the dead-weight losses from consumers switching out of the product class. The results demonstrate that narrow patents of indefinite length may be optimal when substitution costs between varieties of the product are similar across consumers, since it will then be possible for the innovator to set a price that keeps inferior imitators out of the market. When consumers' valuations of the preferred variety relative to not buying the product at all are similar, however, a broad, short-lived patent may be desirable.

Gallini extends the analysis to allow for imitation responses by rivals in the market and, consequently, produces results that are in sharp contrast to previous results on the optimality of long, narrow patents.[18] As in earlier models, a monopoly over the patented product is granted for a specified length of time. Although *duplication* is prevented during the patent life, firms may *imitate* a product or process so long as it is differ-

---

17 Klemperer, 'How Broad Should the Scope of Patent Be?.'
18 Gallini, 'Patent Policy and Costly Imitation.'

entiated from the original patent in some way. For any patent length and scope, an imitator can either wait for the patent to expire to begin producing the identical product, or it can attempt to develop a similar product of its own. The longer the patent life, the greater is the incentive for the rival to 'invent around,' or imitate, the patented innovation. As patent life increases beyond its 'critical' point, further imitators will enter until profits are dissipated. Increasing patent life, then, encourages wasteful imitation. To prevent this, a broad scope patent with patent life adjusted to achieve the desired return to the innovator becomes the optimal policy.

In these models, competition policy is absent or, in some cases, redundant given the availability of patent scope. For example, Gilbert and Shapiro treat patent scope and competition policy as perfect substitutes for constraining the innovator's profits in each period. Patent scope is defined as the profit the innovator is allowed to earn (or, equivalently, the price it is allowed to set) in each period. Hence, the socially efficient profit level derived in the model can be achieved either through a narrow scope or a strict competition policy. In contrast, the substitutability between patent and competition policy is not perfect in the Klemperer and Gallini papers in that price can be controlled only indirectly by narrowing the scope of patent protection. An attempt to reduce price by narrowing the scope may result in inefficient imitation, however, suggesting that both policies are necessary to achieve an efficient allocation of resources towards development and use of innovations.[19]

In reality, patent and competition policy are complementary instruments for rewarding the innovator most efficiently: patent scope prevents imitation, while competition policy affects price through constraints on contracts for transferring technology. Green and Scotchmer[20] recognize this distinction. In their paper, the incentive to research depends not only on patent policy but also on the ability of firms to cooperate through licensing arrangements. Two types of cooperative arrangements are considered: *ex ante* licensing, or joint ventures

---

19 In the models, price is the equilibrium outcome of the innovator and imitators competing in the market, given patent scope. This contrasts to the framework in Gilbert and Shapiro, where price (or profit) is administered by the antitrust (or patent) authorities.

20 J. Green and S. Scotchmer, 'On the Division of Profits in Sequential Innovation,' (1995) 26 *Rand Journal of Economics* 20.

between the initial innovator and a subsequent innovator prior to making R&D investments in the second stage; and *ex post* licensing after the second-stage investment has been sunk. The breadth of patent claims establishes whether or not *ex post* licensing takes place. If claims are broad, the second-generation infringes and the firms enter into an *ex post* licensing agreement. If claims are narrow, then the two firms compete in the market. A subtle interaction is therefore identified between patent and competition policies insofar as patent scope fixes the bargaining strength of the innovator in its negotiations with the licensee. Patent scope and competition policy are, on this understanding, distinct instruments for affecting the incentives to research and to transfer technologies. While patent scope sets the 'threat points,' or the opportunity cost, of entering into the licensing agreement (e.g., whether or not a rival can introduce an imitation), competition policy establishes the feasible set of legal licensing contracts. Accordingly, Green and Scotchmer conclude that in a situation in which innovation is sequential (i.e., innovations build upon each other), a competition policy that allows joint ventures and *ex post* licensing and a patent policy that grants a broad scope to the initial innovator ensures the best allocation of resources.

Chang[21] follows Green and Scotchmer by examining the optimal policy towards price fixing between the innovator and potential entrants under different patent regimes. In particular, four cases in which patents are broad or narrow, and antitrust policy on price fixing is strict or lenient, are considered. Within these policy parameters, Chang shows that broad protection should be available under a patent regime to innovations that are either very valuable or have very little value relative to subsequent improvements, whereas price fixing between the innovator and entrants should be restricted through competition laws so as to reduce incentives for inefficient entry by imitators.

While this literature is illuminating, the results are not robust, nor do they go far enough in suggesting appropriate competition policy with respect to IP. For example, the papers by Green-Scotchmer and Chang focus almost exclusively on joint ventures and price fixing.[22] Perhaps

---

21 H. Chang, 'Patent Scope, Antitrust Policy and Cumulative Innovation,' (1995) 26 *Rand Journal of Economics* 34.

22 There is a large body of literature on strategic incentives for licensing. See, for example, N.T. Gallini, 'Deterrence through Market Sharing: A Strategic Incentive for

of greater concern, however, is the formidable task these authors assign to competition policy. In coordination with patent policy, it must determine the flow of patent profits that induces the firm to make the desirable R&D investment. In an environment of technological and market certainty and low transaction costs of coordination, such a task is not impossible to fulfil. In less ideal conditions, it would be difficult at best. A closer examination of the approaches competition policy might take towards IP reveals those that place less emphasis on R&D are more practical and socially efficient in a complex commercial environment.

B. Approaches for Competition Treatment of IPRs

We begin our quest for an efficient competition policy IP by identifying three effects that competition policy has on social surplus generated from innovation: (i) it affects *ex ante* incentives to innovate; (ii) it affects *ex post* incentives to transfer new technologies and products; and (iii) it promotes price competition in product markets that use the new products and processes. Hence, competition policy affects welfare through its effects on R&D, licensing, and prices. Competition policy typically concerns itself with anticompetitive effects on prices and output, although it should arguably focus equally on the procompetitive effects of diffusion. The role that competition policy should play in fostering R&D is more contentious, as discussed below.

C. A Framework for Competition Policy of IPRs

Given these initial observations, the following set of rules or principles should guide competition policy with respect to intellectual property:

P1 There should be no presumption that an IPR creates market power.
P2 Competition policy should acknowledge the basic rights granted under patent law.
P3 A licensing restriction should be permitted if it is not anticompeti-

---

Licensing,' (1994) 74 *American Economic Review* 931; K. Rockett, 'Choosing the Competition and Patent Policy,' (1990) 21 *Rand Journal of Economics* 161. In most of the papers, licensing contracts are assumed to include a royalty or fixed fee but no further restrictions that would be considered contentious under the antitrust laws.

tive relative to the outcome that would result if that license were proscribed; otherwise, an evaluation of potential efficiency effects of the restriction on the pricing and diffusion of the IPR should be made.

The first principle (P1) makes the important and well-known point that the scope of a patent is not commensurate with an antitrust market; that is, most products and processes, including those protected by a patent, face a large number of substitutes. For example, in a survey of businesses cited by the Organization for Economic Cooperation and Development (OECD), licensors faced no alternative suppliers in only 27 per cent of the cases in contrast to facing over ten competitors in 29 per cent of cases.[23] Such evidence leads to the conclusion that there should be no presumption of market power from a patent. Even where a patent does confer market power, this fact alone should not lead to a presumption that the patent infringes competition laws. This principle is consistent with that followed in the general enforcement of competition policy, where market power acquired through 'superior skill, foresight, and industry' is not condemned,[24] although the anticompetitive exercise of this power may be prevented.

The second basic principle (P2) is not as straightforward as it may seem. For patented innovations, patent law ensures the *existence* of property rights, while competition policy restricts the *exercise* of those rights. In Canada, section 79(5) of the *Competition Act*[25] recognizes the importance of IPRs by providing a qualified exemption from the abuse of dominant provisions to holders of IPRs. Essentially, it is important for competition law to recognize the value of the protection granted to IP holders and to allow the legitimate exercise of IPRs. Where the conduct in question goes beyond that which is inherent in the patent, however, and the efficiency of the market is threatened, the competition authorities may intervene to remedy the situation.

In the United States, the innovator's 'right to exclude others from making, using or selling the invention' under the *Patent Act* is respected by antitrust courts. However, beyond this right to 'refuse to licence,' not much more is explicitly guaranteed. For example, while the right to

---

23 OECD, *Competition Policy and Intellectual Property*.
24 *United States v. Aluminum Company of America*, 148 F. 2d 416 (2nd Cir. 1945).
25 R.S.C. 1985, c. C-34.

grant an exclusive licence of the entire bundle of rights is inherent in the patent, that right does not allow assignment to simply anyone. Nor does it allow partial restrictions to be attached to a licence, such as, for example, the right to make and use but not to sell, or the right to licence with price, quantity, or use restrictions. Moreover, where exclusion of others from using the property right extends market power beyond that intended by the patent right, antitrust policy may intervene, as in the case where patents are accumulated for the purpose of eliminating competition. That is, recognition of the existence of the right does not imply that the exercise of that right will escape antitrust scrutiny. The Competition Bureau's *Intellectual Property Enforcement Guidelines* endorse a similar approach.[26]

The third basic principle (P3) acknowledges the role that competition policy has to play in promoting the efficient diffusion of technology and in the pricing of goods that use the technology. Note that the principle evaluates the impact of a licensing restriction relative to a benchmark situation in which the restriction is prohibited. For example, if the licensor and licensee were horizontal competitors prior to licensing, an innovator might choose not to licence its competitor where restrictions in the contract are prohibited. In this case, the benchmark against which to compare the licence is the situation under no licensing. Where the transfer of technology generates social benefits relative to exclusive exploitation of the patent, this principle permits such restrictions, even when they have anticompetitive effects.

But licensing may not always be socially desirable. Firms may license 'sham agreements' that transfer technologies of little value for the purpose of dividing the market among competitors. Other contentious restrictions include those that foreclose the market to competing technologies (e.g., exclusive dealing), or that facilitate cartel patent pooling arrangements, unless there are offsetting efficiencies from diffusion and a less harmful arrangement is not feasible. Moreover, if the restriction in the licence were not necessary to encourage diffusion (e.g., in the case of vertically related firms), the analysis would be similar to that in non-IP cases. That is, anticompetitive effects would be

---

26 Competition Bureau, *Intellectual Property Enforcement Guidelines* (Ottawa: Competition Bureau, 2000). The guidelines are available from the Bureau's website (http://competition.ic.gc.ca). A more extensive discussion of the guidelines is contained in section III.F of this chapter.

weighed against possible efficiency benefits to determine the social merits of the restriction.

These rules or guidelines for competition policy explicitly acknowledge the rights provided by patents, the benefits to be gained from diffusion, the potential effects of particular licensing restrictions, and the possible adverse effects on prices. They are silent, however, on whether competition policy should evaluate the impact that the licensing restriction may have on incentives to innovate. The role that competition policy should take in promoting research and development is more contentious.[27] Three different views on the question of the importance to be attached to R&D considerations in competition cases are summarized below.

1 *Competition policy should intervene to correct perceived excesses or deficiencies of IP protection provided under patent policy.* This approach mirrors the one taken in the economic literature summarized above, whereby both competition and patent policies coordinate to provide the correct incentives for research and for the most efficient use of society's resources. Under this view, competition policy plays a direct role in ensuring that an innovator receives an adequate return on her R&D investment. For example, under this approach, if patent policy is perceived as providing inadequate incentives for research, competition policy should be more lenient. Where it is too generous, such that rival firms are discouraged from innovating, competition policy should intervene to prohibit or regulate certain licensing arrangements.

2 *Competition policy should determine whether a license reduces competition in innovation markets.* This approach echoes that proposed in the Department of Justice-Federal Trade Commission Intellectual Property Guidelines (the U.S. guidelines),[28] which state that restrictions that reduce innovation of future products and processes or, in the language of the U.S. Guidelines, competition in 'innovation mar-

27 See Gallini and Anderson, eds., *Competition Policy and Intellectual Property.*

28 U.S. Department of Justice and Federal Trade Commission, *Antitrust Guidelines for the Licensing of Intellectual Property* (Washington, D.C.: 1995). See also R. Gilbert and S. Sunshine, 'Incorporating Dynamic Efficiency Concerns in Merger Analysis: The Use of Innovation Markets,' (1995) 63 *Antitrust Law Journal* 569.

kets,' should be prohibited.[29] The innovation market is a forward-looking concept defined as 'the research and development directed to particular new or improved goods or processes, and the close substitutes for that research and development.'[30] The policy is similar to the first approach in that R&D considerations are taken into account; however, the focus is on the effect of contractual restrictions on future innovation, and not on the return to be expected on past innovation efforts. Several types of arrangements would be challenged under this approach, including: (i) mergers between firms capable of developing similar technologies; (ii) exclusive dealing restrictions that prevent a licensee from using technologies of the licensor's rival; and (iii) patent pooling arrangements perceived to suppress future innovation. In Canada, the Competition Bureau's *Intellectual Property Enforcement Guidelines* explicitly reject the approach of defining relevant markets around innovation.

3 *Competition policy should determine whether a licence reduces potential competition in product and/or technology markets.* In contrast to the previous two approaches, the third model advocates that the allocative effects from a contract on diffusion and pricing, and not on R&D, should be the paramount concerns of competition policy. In terms of the effects of competition policy identified above, this approach focuses on providing incentives for transferring technology and ensuring that product markets operate efficiently, while deferring the problem of providing incentives to innovate.[31] It should be noted that

29 More precisely, three relevant markets have been identified in the U.S. Guidelines: (a) product markets; (b) technology markets; and (c) innovation markets. The first two markets invoke conventional concepts that include, respectively, all substitute products and technologies that compete with each other.

30 The notion of an innovation market was used in a proposed acquisition of General Motors' Allison Transmission Division by the German firm, ZF of Friedrichshafen. The transaction was challenged by the DOJ on the grounds that it would have resulted in a concentration of R&D assets that might impact significantly on the future innovation in the market for heavy duty automatic transmissions. See 'GM sees North American Profit in '94; US to Block Sales of Allison Unit,' *Wall Street Journal (Eastern Edition)*, 17 Nov. 1993. Also, the U.S. Federal Trade Commission has employed innovation markets theory in a number of pharmaceutical industry mergers, including *Roche Holdings Ltd.*, 113 F.T.C. 1086 (1990) and *In the Matter of Ciba-Geigy Limited et al.*, FTC Docket No. C-3725 (24 March 1997).

31 For example, suppose the coordination of patent and competition policy results in a rule that allows firms to include price restrictions in licensing contracts when large R&D expenditures are required. Then, the task of the competition agencies would be

this approach, while avoiding innovation market analysis, relies on the more conventional *potential competition* doctrine. That is to say, if a licence restriction is perceived as reducing potential competition in product or technology markets, then it should be proscribed.[32]

Any of the three approaches might be appropriate, depending on the particular market or technological conditions. For example, the competition agency might decide that it will generally follow the second or third approach, while still allowing itself the flexibility to follow the first approach if there is strong evidence that IP protection is overbroad and unnecessarily stifling of competition.

Generally, however, competition policy should follow the third approach. This approach has the advantage of dividing the responsibilities according to the comparative advantages of the two legal institutions. The task of patent policy is to define those rights that encourage innovation (i.e., in terms of duration and protection from imitation), whereas the task of competition policy is to prevent the anticompetitive transfer and use of technology while respecting the basic exclusive rights as laid out by patent law. The third approach will affect the innovator's overall return, and therefore the initial incentive to innovate, but the decision to allow the licence will be based on the *ex post* incentives to license, not on the *ex ante* incentives to innovate.[33]

Even if R&D considerations are not explicitly taken into account, as recommended by the first approach, competition policy has a built-in mechanism for indirectly fine tuning patent policy. For example, if patent protection is weak, then imitation is easy, leaving the innovator with minimal market power. In contrast, where patents are strong and effective, restrictions (such as tying) would be more closely scrutinized. That is, to the extent that effectiveness of patent policy in pro-

---

to determine *ex post* whether or not the *ex ante* incentives to innovate justify price restrictions. Such a rule, besides requiring expertise beyond that possessed by competition agencies or courts, would encourage firms to argue for contract restrictions on behalf of research, regardless of the innovation.

32 *Anticipating the 21st Century: Competition Policy in the New High-Tech, Global Marketplace*, Special Supplement, A Report by the Federal Trade Commission Staff, chap. 7, vol. 70, no. 1765, 6 June 1996.

33 A policy based on encouraging research may look very much like one based on encouraging diffusion in that both may require leniency so as to increase the patentee's profits from engaging in those activities.

tecting property rights is correlated with the degree of market power acquired, a competition policy that is sensitive to market power may indirectly 'fine tune' the protection granted under a patent.

Similarly, conventional potential competition analysis appears to be adequate for addressing the concerns of the second approach. For example, if rival innovators who are affected by a licensing restriction are also potential competitors in the product market, the expected deleterious effect on prices in the product market from a reduction in potential competition may be sufficient to proscribe a particular restriction without appealing to innovation market analysis. If competitors in innovation are not competitors in the product market, potential competition analysis may continue to be adequate, in contrast to the recommendation made by the Federal Trade Commission.[34] In this case, the relevant market will be the technology, rather than the product, market. That is, a reduction in innovation competition implies a reduction in potential competition in technology markets, and conventional potential competition analysis can be applied to address concerns of contentious licensing restrictions.[35]

In summary, the above analysis suggests that competition authorities should give only limited attention to the effects of licensing restrictions on R&D. Extensive economic investigations have not uncovered an unambiguous causal link between innovation and competition, and to expect more success from competition authorities in predicting the social harm to innovative activity from certain arrangements is, at best, impractical. Indeed, failing to make the correct prediction could inhibit or deter innovation rather than further it.[36] Moreover, it may be that some restrictions, while potentially suppressing competition in future R&D, may be necessary to induce the patentee to transfer the innovation in the first place (e.g., in the case of grant-backs), thus rendering the concerns of future R&D less important.

---

34 Federal Trade Commission, *Anticipating the 21st Century.*

35 The difference between the second and third approaches may appear to be one of semantics in that even potential competition analysis must evaluate effects from reduced competition in innovation. In fact, there is a subtle difference between the approaches: under the potential competition doctrine, antitrust authorities need only consider the impact on prices in the technology and product markets owing to reduced competition, rather than nonprice effects (i.e., the level, speed, or diversity of R&D activity) evaluated under innovation market analysis.

36 See Federal Trade Commission, *Anticipating the 21st Century.*

Whether R&D considerations are explicitly taken into account by competition authorities or not, an important distinction exists between IP and other forms of property, as implied by the above framework. IP can be used by many individuals at the same time, unlike tangible property which, if transferred, merely changes hands. Since the social cost of transferring innovations is effectively zero, it is socially efficient for the innovation to be freely available. However, a patentee may be reluctant to license her competitors unless she can impose some restrictions on the use of the innovation. The issue of whether or not this distinction calls for a different application of competition law to IP remains contentious.

A second important distinction between IP and other property has important implications for the evaluation required under principle P3, and should be mentioned. In many licensing contracts, the relationship of the parties to the contract is both horizontal and vertical. The licensor and licensee are horizontally related if they would have been competitors in the product market without licensing; they are vertically related if the IP represents an input used in the production of the licensee's product.

We turn now to a review of IP and competition law and the jurisprudence related to intellectual property in Canada.

III. Competition Policy and Intellectual Property Rights

A. Overview

In Canada, both IP legislation and the *Competition Act* check the abusive exercise of IPRs and provide remedies for such practices.[37] The common law doctrine of restraint of trade has also been used in IP cases, albeit sparingly.[38] As in the United States, IPRs were viewed

---

37 For further analysis of the interface between patent and competition policy in Canada, see S. Globerman and R. Schwindt, 'Intellectual Property Rights: Anti-Competitive Abuses and Competition Policy Antidotes' and R.D. Anderson, S.D. Khosla, and M.F. Ronayne, 'Competition Policy Treatment of Intellectual Property Rights in Canada: Retrospect and Prospect,' in R.S. Khemani and W.T. Stanbury, eds., *Canadian Competition Law and Policy at the Centenary* (Halifax: Institute for Research on Public Policy, 1991).

38 Under this doctrine, a contract will not be challenged if it is reasonable as between the parties and reasonable with reference to the public interest, but may be challenged even if no anticompetitive abuse has been identified. The doctrine has been

with suspicion in Canada prior to the 1980s. In Canada, however, this suspicion was reflected more in legislative attempts to limit the exercise of patent rights than in jurisprudence.[39] The 1980s saw policy makers adopt a more positive view of IPRs, recognizing their importance to Canada's economic growth and ability to compete in world markets. The *Competition Act*, as well as recent patent policy, incorporates this new perspective. Given the paucity of Canadian case law in this area, it is particularly important to analyse the legislative provisions.

B. *Intellectual Property Law*

1. *The Patent Act*
The *Patent Act*[40] designates both the length and scope of a patent right, restricts the exercise of the patent, and provides for compulsory licensing and removal of patent rights. A potential abuse of IPRs can be challenged directly by a licensee under the provisions of the *Patent Act*, and jurisdiction to oversee these provisions is vested in the commissioner of patents and the attorney general. Under section 65(1) of the *Patent Act*, any person may, at any time after the expiration of three years from the date of the grant of a patent, apply to the commissioner of patents alleging an abuse. If the commissioner is satisfied that there has been an abuse, he may order that the patentee license the patent pursuant to section 66 of the *Patent Act*. Practices constituting abusive behaviour under the *Patent Act* are set out in section 65(2). These abuses include failing to meet the demand for the patented article in Canada to an adequate extent or on reasonable terms, refusing to license on reasonable terms when it is in public interest to do so, and unfairly prejudicing trade or industry in Canada through unfair conditions for licensing. The review of certain 'competition-related' restrictions such as tie-ins and field-of-use restrictions is included where they

---

held to be applicable to exclusive licensing arrangements, but they have usually survived scrutiny: see, for example, *Tank Lining Corp. v. Dunlop Industrial Ltd.* (1982), 140 D.L.R. (3d) 659 (Ont. C.A.); *Barsch v. Avtex Airservices Ltd* (1992), 107 A.L.R. 539, aff'd Fed. No. 5&9, unreported, 27 August 1993 (Fed. Ct.) For further discussion see M.J. Trebilcock, *The Common Law of Restraint of Trade: A Legal and Economic Analysis* (Toronto: Carswell, 1986).

39 For a more complete discussion, see Anderson, Khosla, and Ronayne, 'Competition Policy Treatment of Intellectual Property Rights in Canada: Retrospect and Prospect.'

40 R.S.C. 1985, c. P-4.

have been used to unfairly prejudice the manufacture, use, or sale of unpatented materials.

Section 66 of the *Patent Act* provides the commissioner with remedial powers in abuse cases, including compulsory licensing to the applicant on terms the commissioner considers appropriate. In cases where the invention is not being worked on a commercial scale in Canada and is such that it cannot be worked without the expenditure of capital that can be raised only by relying on the exclusive rights under the patent, the commissioner may, unless the patentee or those claiming under him will undertake to find that capital, order the grant of an exclusive licence on such terms as the commissioner thinks just to the applicant and/or any other person able and willing to provide that capital. If the commissioner is satisfied that the exclusive rights have been abused in the manner provided in section 65(2)(f) (i.e., that a patent for an invention relating to a process involving the use of materials not protected by the patent, or for an invention relating to a substance produced by an unprotected process, has been utilized by the patentee so as to unfairly prejudice the manufacture, use, or sale of any materials in Canada), then he may order the grant of licences to the applicant and to such of his customers on terms he thinks expedient. If the commissioner is satisfied that the objects of sections 65 and 66 cannot be attained by compulsory licensing, he may revoke the patent either forthwith or after a reasonable interval. If the commissioner is satisfied that the objects of sections 65 and 66 will be best attained by not making an order for a compulsory licence or a revocation, he may make an order refusing the application.

2. The Copyright Act

Copyright protection is given to original literary, musical, artistic, and dramatic works and covers books, films, choreographs, records, audio- and videotapes, songs, sculptures, lectures, paintings, photos, and computer programs. The *Copyright Act*[41] provides copyright protection during the lifetime of the creator and for fifty years thereafter. Like the *Patent Act*, the *Copyright Act* also provides for compulsory licensing, albeit to only a limited extent, in the event that material protected by copyright is withheld from the market. For example, section 15 of the *Copyright Act* provides that if, after the death of the author, the owner

---

41 R.S.C. 1985, c. C-30.

of the copyright refuses to allow re-exposure of a work that has been published or performed in public, the governor-in-council can impose compulsory licensing under terms and conditions at his discretion. It is also worth noting that section 19 of the *Copyright Act* provides for the cancellation of licences to print books if the licensees do not print and put on sale in Canada a number of copies of the book sufficient to supply the reasonable demands of the Canadian market.

3. The Trademarks Act
A trademark is a word, symbol, or picture, or a combination of these, used for the purpose of distinguishing the goods and services of a person or enterprise from those of another. A person or enterprise can be granted a mark if the mark is not already held and cannot be confused with a mark held by another person or enterprise. The life of a trade mark is indefinite because rights to the mark are granted for an initial fifteen years and can be renewed every fifteen years thereafter. Under section 45(3) of the *Trademarks Act*,[42] a mark can be expunged if it is not in use in Canada and if there are no special circumstances that excuse the absence of use. Otherwise, there are no abuse provisions in the *Trademarks Act*.

4. Trade Secrets and Confidential Information
The law of trade secrets and confidential information enforces obligations between two parties to maintain the confidentiality of information. Such an obligation may arise through a contractual relationship or may be imposed by the circumstances of the relationship between the parties. Trade secrets can be the result of original research or the result of a unique collection of information collected from public sources (for example, a customer list). Confidential information and trade secrets are usually communicated to another person to be used for a specific purpose. Thus, any use of that information for any other purposes constitutes misuse of the trade secret or confidential information.[43]

Although there is no legislation to protect trade secrets or confidential information, they are enforceable if the three prerequisites outlined

---

42 *Trademarks Act*, R.S.C. 1985, c. T-10.
43 In *R. v. Stewart*, [1988] 1 S.C.R. 963, the Supreme Court of Canada held that confidential information is not property that can be stolen because the copying of confidential information deprives its owner not of the information but of its confidentiality, and confidentiality is not 'anything' capable of being stolen.

in *LAC Minerals Ltd. v. International Corona Resources Ltd.*[44] are met: (i) the information conveyed is confidential rather than publicly available; (ii) the information was communicated by the owner to the recipient in confidence; and (iii) there is a misuse of the trade secret or confidential information by the party to whom it was communicated to the detriment of the party who communicated it.

5. Other IP Legislation

The *Industrial Design Act*[45] protects the physical appearance of a useful object. Thus, the ornamental design or the shape of the object itself is protected. Industrial design does not apply to functional or useful features. The term of protection accorded to an industrial design is five years, renewable for a further five years. There are no abuse provisions in the *Industrial Design Act*.

In addition, the topography of integrated circuits is protected under the *Integrated Circuit Topography Act*.[46] Under this Act, the owner of a registered topography has the exclusive right to reproduce, manufacture, import, and commercially exploit an integrated circuit product incorporating the registered topography or any substantial portion of it. These exclusive rights are available to both creators and manufacturers of a topography, regardless of whether it is incorporated into a manufactured integrated circuit or the integrated circuit is in a final or intermediate form. The *Integrated Circuit Topography Act* protects registered topographies for up to ten years. There are no abuse provisions under the Act.

The *Plant Breeders' Rights Act*[47] allows plant breeders to protect new varieties of sexually and asexually reproduced plants for a period of up to eighteen years, provided they are of a species prescribed by the regulations as eligible for protection. Under section 32 of the *Plant Breeders' Rights Act*, any person may apply to the commissioner of plant breeders' rights for a licence. The commissioner will confer a compulsory licence, whether or not another person already owns an exclusive licence, if the applicant can demonstrate that the holder of the right in respect of a particular variety has unreasonably refused to licence the

---

44 [1989] 2 S.C.R. 574.
45 *Industrial Design Act*, R.S.C. 1985, c. I-9.
46 *Integrated Circuit Topography Act*, R.S.C. 1985, c. I-14.6.
47 *Plant Breeders' Rights Act*, R.S.C. 1985, c. P-14.6.

variety. However, the compulsory licence ordered by the commissioner may not be an exclusive licence. In addition, under section 75(k)(i), an applicant may request an exemption from compulsory licensing under section 32 of the Act, although such an exemption is revocable by the commissioner. Section 35 of the Act provides for the revocation of a plant breeder's rights under certain conditions, including the revocation of a compulsory licence if the licensee has failed to meet the obligations under which the compulsory licence was conferred.

6. The GATT/WTO TRIPs Agreement
Under the GATT/WTO Agreement on Trade-Related Aspects of Intellectual Property Rights (TRIPs), negotiated during the Uruguay Round, member countries committed themselves to adopting domestic intellectual property regimes that conform to prescribed minimum substantive and procedural standards.[48] Under Article 8 of the TRIPs member countries may adopt appropriate measures to prevent the abuse of IPRs through resort to practices that unreasonably restrain trade or adversely affect the transfer of technology. With respect to patents, Article 31 permits compulsory licensing if the proposed user has attempted to obtain authorization for use from the patent holder on 'reasonable commercial terms' and been refused. However, compulsory licensing may only be required under certain conditions: it must be non-exclusive; production under licensing must be intended primarily for the internal market of the country to which the licence pertains; and 'adequate remuneration' must be paid to the patent holder, taking into account the 'economic value' of the patent.

C. Competition Policy

1. Competition Policy Pre-1986
The potential for anticompetitive abuse of IPRs was recognized early in the development of competition policy in Canada. For example, the *Combines Investigation Act* of 1910 included provisions that provided for the revocation of a patent if the owner used it 'so as ... unduly to prevent or lessen competition.'[49] The initial concerns regarding anticom-

---

48 See M. Trebilcock and R. Howse, *The Regulation of International Trade*, 2nd ed. (London and New York: Routledge, 1999), chap. 12.
49 9–10 Edward VII (1910), c. 9, s. 22.

petitive abuse of IPRs were due in large part to the operations of the United Shoe Machinery Company ('United Shoe'). In the early 1900s, United Shoe attained a dominant position in the North American shoe machinery market through mergers and acquisitions as well as through the accumulation of a 'killer patent portfolio' consisting of more than 2,000 shoe machinery patents 'covering every shadow of a shade in the parts of the many machines used in the manufacture of shoes.'[50] Instead of selling its machines, United Shoes employed exclusive leases that included provisions requiring lessees to use the machines to their full capacity, to use the company's machines exclusively and, which, in some cases, included a tying provision wherein lessees were required to lease other related machines under penalty of cancellation of existing leases. As a result of these practices, United Shoe was prosecuted in the United States in 1918, but the U.S. Supreme Court did not find a violation of antitrust laws.[51]

In Canada, United Shoe's restrictive leasing provisions were called into question in *United Shoe Machinery Company of Canada v. Brunet*.[52] Alleged to have breached the tying provisions in United Shoe's leases, the defendant claimed that such restrictive provisions in the leases violated the common law doctrine of restraint of trade.[53] The Judicial Committee of the Privy Council, adhering to a traditional reluctance to interfere with freely negotiated contractual agreements between

---

50 *U.S. v. United Shoe Machinery Co. of N.J.*, 223 U.S. Federal Antitrust Decisions 1917–1920 (U.S. Sup. Ct., 1918), 272. See also R. Merges, 'Antitrust Review of Patent Acquisitions: Property Rights, Firm Boundaries, and Organization,' in Gallini and Anderson, eds., *Competition Policy and Intellectual Property Rights*, 111.

51 *U.S. v. United Shoe Machinery Co. of N.J.*, United Shoe was prosecuted again under s. 2 of the *Sherman Act* in 1953: see *United States v. United Shoe Machinery Corp.* 110 F. Supp. 295 (D. Mass., 1953), aff'd *per curiam*, 347 U.S. 521 (1954). It was thought that by reason of United Shoe's possession of this huge patent portfolio, barriers to entry were impenetrable and thus no new entry into shoe manufacturing was feasible. Furthermore, United Shoe attempted to reinforce its dominant position through restrictive contracts including tying provisions and automatic renewal of long-term leases. The U.S. District Court (D. Massachusetts) found no violation of the *Sherman Act* flowing from United Shoe's patent portfolio as it was the result of 'superior skill, foresight and industry,' but the court did order that United Shoe modify its leasing practices to 'dissipate the effects of United's monopolization.'

52 (1909), A.C. 330 (P.C.).

53 See Anderson, Khosla, and Ronayne, 'The Competition Policy Treatment of Intellectual Property Rights in Canada,' for a detailed discussion on the development of Canadian competition policy since 1910.

knowledgeable parties, concluded that United Shoe was free to conduct its trade in the manner it deemed best for its own interests as long as that manner was not illegal. However, the Judicial Committee also noted that '[i]f the monopoly established by [United Shoe] and their mode of carrying on their business be as oppressive as is alleged , then the evil, if it exists, may be capable of cure by legislation.'[54]

In 1910, heeding the Judicial Committee's suggestion, Parliament included provisions relating to 'combinations of persons holding patents .who exercise their exclusive rights and privileges to restrict competition' in the new *Combines Investigation Act*.[55] Specifically, section 22 of the *Combines Investigation Act* provided for the revocation of the exclusive rights and privileges conferred under the *Patent Act* in cases where the owner of a patent made use of his rights 'so as unduly to limit the facilities for transporting, producing, manufacturing, supplying, storing or dealing in any article which may be a subject of trade or commerce, or so as to restrain or injure trade or commerce , or unduly to prevent, limit or lessen the manufacture or production of any article or unreasonably to enhance the price thereof, or unduly to prevent or lessen competition in the production, manufacture, purchase, barter, sale, transportation, storage or supply of any article.'[56] Under section 22, if the Board of Investigation (established pursuant to the *Combines Investigation Act*) reported that a patent had been used to unduly lessen competition, the minister of justice could apply to the Exchequer Court of Canada for a hearing to determine whether the patent in question should be revoked. However, despite the enactment of such remedies for abuse of patent power, there were no cases under which an IPR remedy was issued under section 22 of the *Combines Investigation Act* from its enactment in 1910 until its repeal in 1937.

In proposed amendments to the *Combines Investigation Act* in 1935 and 1937, recommendations were included for strengthening the application of the Act to IPR abuses. These recommendations arose in response to the *Report of the Royal Commission on Price Spreads* and concurrent allegations of abuse of IPRs in the markets for radios, electrical goods, and other products.[57] They would have replaced the competi-

---

54 *United Shoe Machinery Company of Canada v. Brunet*, (1909) A.C. 330 at 344 (P.C.).

55 (1910) *Debates of the House of Commons*, cols. 2060, 6854, 9918, and 8000–1.

56 *Supra*, note 49.

57 Anderson, Khosla, and Ronayne, 'The Competition Policy Treatment of Intellectual Property Rights in Canada,' 503.

tion and restraint of trade tests in the patent remedy provisions with a broad public interest requirement and arguably created the possibility that the mere exercise of IPRs would be subject to the monopolization provisions of the *Combines Investigation Act*. However, the proposed changes were met with strong opposition in both the House of Commons and the Senate, where it was argued that such amendments would undermine the incentive to innovate and thus vitiate the purpose of the patent system. Furthermore, it was asserted that the 1935 amendments to the *Patent Act* to include remedies for the failure to work patents in Canada or to meet Canadian demand for patented articles on reasonable terms rendered such proposed changes to the *Combines Investigation Act* unnecessary.[58]

Ultimately, to resolve the potential conflict between the proposed amendments and the intellectual property system, explicit recognition of exclusive rights relating to IP under the monopoly and combines provisions of the *Combines Investigation Act* was provided in section 2(4)(b), which stated that the provisions on combines and monopolies should not 'be construed or applied so as to limit or impair any right or interest derived under the *Patent Act, 1935*, or under any other statute of Canada.'[59] This provision thus ensured that the mere exercise of IPRs would not mean that IPR owners were guilty of illegal monopolization or combination.

In addition, the 1937 amendments to the *Combines Investigation Act* repealed the patent remedy provisions enacted in 1910. The repeal of the patent remedy provisions did not reflect a change in perception regarding the potential anticompetitive abuse of IPRs. Instead, their repeal can be attributed to the view that the expanded *Patent Act, 1935* was sufficient to deal with IPR abuse. Hence, the patent remedies in the *Combines Investigation Act* had become redundant.[60] As discussed below, the patent remedy provisions were subsequently reinstated and expanded in the 1946 amendments to the *Combines Investigation Act*.

Over the period 1937 to 1943, there were several decisions by the Supreme Court of Canada concerning alleged anticompetitive abuses as a defence in IPR infringement suits. The first of these cases was

---

58 See the (1937) *Debates of the House of Commons*, 2,410–21 for a discussion of the 1935 *Patent Act* amendments, 25–26 George V (1935), c. 150, ss. 65–66 and (1935) *Debates of the House of Commons*, 3,097–3,272.

59 *Combines Investigation Act*, 25–26 George V (1935), c. 54, s. 2.

60 (1937) *Debates of the House of Commons*, 2,555.

Massie & Renwick Ltd. v. Underwriters' Survey Bureau Ltd.,[61] an action for the infringement of copyright in fire insurance plans. In defence, the defendant pleaded that the plaintiffs combined and conspired together to prevent the defendant from obtaining copies of the plans in question. In its decision, the Supreme Court stated that the courts had the discretion, based on principles of equity, to consider the defence of illegal monopolization or combination if the defendant raised it in a suit involving the infringement of a proprietary right. That is, if the relief sought by the plaintiff related to the implementation of a conspiracy involving the plaintiff, the court could decline to grant relief. However, the Supreme Court narrowed the defence by stipulating that, for relief to be denied, the defendants had to establish that the plaintiffs had combined to 'further some illegal object injurious to the defendant.'[62]

Two years later, the Supreme Court again considered the scope of the defence of anticompetitive abuses of IPRs in infringement cases in a second appeal in the *Massie & Renwick* proceedings.[63] The Supreme Court further narrowed the scope of the defence by suggesting that, for a defence based on the anticompetitive abuse of IPRs to be successful, the defendants were required to prove that the plaintiffs had to rely on an agreement that constituted a criminal conspiracy to establish ownership of the copyrights.[64] However, the Supreme Court did not elaborate on this defence because it found that the defendants had failed to establish an anticompetitive abuse of copyright rights by the plaintiffs.

In *Philco Products Ltd. et al. v. Thermionics Ltd. et. al.*,[65] the Supreme Court revisited the issue of the scope of the defence of an illegal conspiracy involving the plaintiffs. The plaintiffs had alleged an infringement of vacuum tube patents, but the defendant claimed a violation of the *Combines Investigation Act* by the plaintiffs as a defence. In its first decision in the case, the Supreme Court acknowledged that the defendants could raise the defence where a plaintiff's title rested on an illegal conspiracy, but it found that the defendants had neither established nor properly pleaded such a defence in this case.[66] In subsequent proceedings, in an attempt to establish a violation of the *Combines Investi-*

---

61 [1937] S.C.R. 265 and [1939] S.C.R. 218.
62 *Massie & Renwick*, [1937] S.C.R. 265 at 268.
63 *Massie & Renwick*, [1939] S.C.R. 218.
64 Ibid., at 244.
65 *Philco Products Ltd. et al. v. Thermionics Ltd. et al.*, [1940] S.C.R. 501.
66 Ibid.

gation Act, the defendants adduced evidence to demonstrate that the relevant patents had been obtained through a conspiracy among the plaintiffs.[67] The alleged conspiracy involved the assignment of the relevant patents and other IPRs to Thermionics (a patent pool) by a number of competing manufacturers, with Thermionics in turn licensing the IPRs back to the assignors. On re-appeal of the case to the Supreme Court, the court held that even if the defendants had proven the alleged conspiracy, the defence would not be available in the circumstances of the case because the plaintiffs had a valid claim to the IPRs prior to the alleged conspiracy and were therefore entitled to enforce their patent rights.[68]

From these early cases, it can be observed that the Supreme Court supported the integrity of the intellectual property system by constraining the scope of anticompetitive abuses of IPRs as a defence in infringement cases. In particular, the Canadian courts required a defendant to prove that a plaintiff acquired the relevant IPRs through a conspiracy. The U.S. courts, on the other hand, allowed broad scope for invocation of antitrust violations as a defence in IPR infringement cases. In the United States, courts may refuse to grant relief in an infringement case if the defendant demonstrates that the plaintiff used the IPRs in question in violation of antitrust laws. A variety of market practices involving patents have been found to constitute grounds for denying enforcement of a patent, regardless of whether those practices were directly related to the particular infringement claim brought by the plaintiff. Examples of such practices includes requiring: (i) customers to purchase unpatented goods along with the patented product;[69] (ii) licensees to pay royalties on unpatented goods;[70] and (iii) licensees to accept unwanted licences together with desired licences.[71]

In 1946, in response to *Canada and International Cartels* (the *McGregor Report*),[72] which found that the *Patent Act* did not protect consumers' interests adequately with respect to anticompetitive abuses of patents,

---

67 *Philco Products Ltd. et al. v. Thermionics Ltd. et al.,* [1943] S.C.R. 396.

68 Ibid., at 406–7.

69 *Morton Salt Co. v. G.S. Suppiger Co.,* 314 U.S. 488 (1942).

70 *Zenith Radio Corp. v. Hazeltine Research, Inc.,* 395 U.S. 29 (1964).

71 *Zenith Radio Corp. v. Hazeltine Research, Inc.,* 395 U.S. 100 (1969).

72 *Canada and International Cartels: an imaging into the value & effects of international cartels & other trade bombinations,* Report of Commissioner, Combines Investigation Act, Ottawa, 10 October 1945.

the reinstatement and expansion of the IPR remedy provisions were included in amendments to the *Combines Investigation Act*. The IPR remedy provisions of 1946 were expanded from the original remedy provisions of 1910 to facilitate their application to IPR abuses. For example, the amendments addressed trade marks in addition to patents, recognizing that trade marks may also be used 'to enforce arrangements as to the division of markets.'[73] As well, the 1946 amendments provided the Exchequer Court with a broad range of remedies to deal with anticompetitive abuses that would be difficult to redress under the *Patent Act*,[74] including: (i) declaring void or restraining persons from carrying out offending terms in licences and other agreements; (ii) ordering the grant of licences on appropriate terms; and (iii) directing that other actions be undertaken to remedy an abuse. In addition, to avoid the problem of the IPR remedy provisions being applied to the mere exercise of IPRs, the 1946 amendments included a test of undueness with regard to the use of IPRs. That is, the IPRs had to be used so as 'unduly to restrain or injure trade or commerce'[75] in order to attract legal redress.

Another important new proviso included in the 1946 amendments to the IPR remedy provisions was a section to ensure that IPR remedies would not be applied in a manner contrary to Canada's obligations under any international treaty or agreement dealing with IP. This provision meant that international agreements on IPRs to which Canada was a signatory would take precedence over the application of competition policy to anticompetitive abuses of IPRs.

In the next three decades, spanning the period from 1950 to 1980, widespread scepticism emerged regarding the economic benefits of IPRs and concerns regarding the anticompetitive use of IPRs increased. The 1961 report by the director of investigation and research on competition in the pharmaceutical industry,[76] the 1963 *Report Concerning the Manufacture, Distribution and Sale of Drugs in Canada* by the Restric-

---

73 (1946) *Debates of the House of Commons*, 3051.

74 Ibid.

75 *Combines Investigation Act*, 10 George VI (1946), c. 44, s. 30.

76 D.H.W. Henry, *Material Collected for Submission to the Restrictive Trade Practices Commission in the Course of an Inquiry under Section 42 of the Combines Investigation Act, Relating to the Manufacture, Distribution and the Sale of Drugs, by the Director of Investigation and Research, Combines Investigation Act* (Ottawa: Department of Justice, 1961).

tive Trade Practices Commission (RTPC),[77] and the 1964 Royal Commission on Health Services (the Hall commission)[78] all found that patents in the pharmaceutical industry resulted in the restriction of competition and artificially high drug prices with insignificant compensating benefits to research activities in Canada.[79] These findings led to the 1969 enactment of legislation that strengthened the existing compulsory licensing provisions of the *Patent Act* applicable to drug patents. Although compulsory licences for the manufacture of drugs in Canada had been available under the *Patent Act* since 1923, the 1969 legislation expanded these provisions to permit the importation of drugs and their active ingredients under such licences. Providing for the importation of active ingredients was considered to be the key to increased competition from generic drug manufacturers, since these ingredients were not generally available from Canadian suppliers.

In the late 1960s the director of investigation and research initiated two proceedings against Union Carbide of Canada under section 32 (the IPR remedy provisions) of the *Combines Investigation Act*.[80] The two cases involved an alleged abuse of patents by Union Carbide, in which Union Carbide was accused of leveraging a patented product to lessen competition in the market for an unpatented product. In particular, Union Carbide required licensees of its patented machines to purchase non-patented resin (a substance used with the patented machines to produce polyethylene film) from a particular group of suppliers or face paying higher royalties.[81] However, neither of the cases proceeded to trial as they were settled through Union Carbide's undertaking to abandon certain restrictive clauses in its licences.

In addition, restrictive patent licensing practices were examined under the criminal monopoly provisions of the *Combines Investigation Act* in *R. v. Canadian General Electric and Union Carbide Canada Limited*,[82] but the case did not proceed to trial. In this case, the Crown alleged

---

77 Restrictive Trade Practices Commission, *Report Concerning the Manufacture, Distribution and Sale of Drugs* (Ottawa: Queen's Printer and Controller of Stationery, 1963).
78 *Royal Commission on Health Services* (Ottawa: Queen's Printer, 1964–5).
79 In the United States, the Senate Sub-committee on Antitrust and Monopoly found similar results with respect to the role of patents in the pharmaceutical industry.
80 See Director of Investigation and Research, *Annual Report for the Year ended March 31, 1968*, 42.
81 The Union Carbide cases will be discussed in greater detail in section III. D.1.
82 Provincial Court, Judicial District of York, Charles J., 9 March 1979 (unreported).

that a provision in a patent licence that Canadian General Electric provided to Union Carbide prevented Union Carbide from selling patented insulation to users that did not own a piece of equipment known
as a Banbury Mixer. However, a Banbury Mixer was not technologically necessary for the use or production of the patented insulation.
Thus, the Crown alleged that such a restriction was an act of shared
monopolization in violation of the *Combines Investigation Act*. The
alleged violation was dismissed on an interlocutory motion because
the Crown had failed to establish the high burden of proof of detriment
to the public required under the criminal monopoly provisions of the
Combines *Investigation Act*.

Finally, alleged anticompetitive abuses of IPRs were examined in
several inquiries by the director of investigation and research during
the 1960s and 1970s. These investigations involved the use of various
licensing and marketing practices, such as international price discrimination; exclusive licensing; tying; and refusal to supply in patents,
trade marks, and industrial designs. However, these investigations
were abandoned prior to the commencement of legal proceedings, primarily due to a lack of evidence establishing that the relevant IPRs had
been used to prevent or lessen competition within the meaning of the
Combines Investigation Act, or to operate a monopoly to the detriment of
the public.

The next phase of changes to the *Combines Investigation Act* in the
1970s contained important revisions regarding the treatment of IPRs
under competition policy. The Stage I amendments in 1975 included a
provision specifying that IPRs did not confer the right to maintain
prices. In particular, this provision stipulated that the general prohibition of resale price maintenance under section 38[83] of the *Combines
Investigation Act* applied specifically to persons enjoying the exclusive
rights and privileges of IPRs.[84] Other provisions in the Stage I amendments, while not dealing specifically with IPRs had important implications for the treatment of IPRs under the *Combines Investigation Act*. For
example, the amendments included provisions dealing with exclusive
dealing, tied selling, and market restriction and created new review

83 Now s. 61 of the *Competition Act*.
84 See R.D. Anderson and S.D. Khosla, 'Recent Developments in the Competition Policy
Treatment of Resale Price Maintenance,' (1995) 16(4) *Canadian Competition Policy
Record* 14.

mechanisms for dealing with these practices, which could be applicable to IPR licences. As well, the Stage I amendments provided certain exemptions for IPRs from the civil reviewable practices provisions. Section 77(5)(d) provided an exemption from the application of orders regarding exclusive selling, tied selling, and market restriction in respect of arrangements involving the grant of rights to use a trade mark or trade name where: (i) the grantee follows a marketing plan or system prescribed by the grantor for a 'multiplicity' of products from competing suppliers; and (ii) no single product dominates the industry. This has been called the 'Canadian Tire amendment,' as it is applicable to multiproduct franchise outlets such as Canadian Tire and Shoppers Drug Mart. In this way, franchisors would be exempt from the provisions of section 77. Similarly, section 77(6) provided an exemption from the application of the section in respect of a trade mark owner who supplies ingredients to be processed by another person into food or drink sold in association with the trade mark. These exemptions applied to franchise bottlers and franchise food outlets such as McDonald's.[85]

Another important provision included in the Stage I amendments was section 31.1 (now sectin 36), which provided for a civil cause of action for persons who have suffered loss or damage as a result of a violation of the criminal provisions of the *Combines Investigation Act* or a failure to comply with certain remedial orders.

The 1970s saw further attempts by defendants to invoke anticompetitive abuse of IPRs on the part of the plaintiff as a defence in infringement cases. In *RBM Equipment Ltd. v. Philips Electronics Industries*,[86] the owner of a registered industrial design brought an action alleging infringement of the design by a terminated licensee. The defendant asserted that the termination of its licence by the design owner was in furtherance of an illegal resale price maintenance scheme in violation of section 38 of the *Combines Investigation Act* (now section 61 of the *Competition Act*). In granting a motion to have the defence struck, the Federal Court referred to the Supreme Court's decision in *Philco Prod-*

85 See I. Nielsen-Jones, S.D. Khosla, and R.D. Anderson, *Product Distribution and the Competition Act: The Treatment of Reviewable Matters and Price Maintenance* (Notes for an Address to the Distribution Law Seminar, B.C. Continuing Legal Education Society, S-10172, 18 October 1988).
86 (1973), 9. C.P.R. (2d) 46 (F.C.T.D.); (1973), 9 C.P.R. (2d) 50 (F.C.A.); (1973), 10 C.P.R. (2d) 23 (F.C.T.D.).

ucts and stated that 'an allegation in a suit for infringement of an industrial right that the plaintiff is a party to an unlawful combine in restraint of trade does not constitute a valid defence in all cases where the owner of the right does not rely in any way on such illegal agreement or conspiracy to establish his cause of action.'[87] The court found that since the plaintiff's title to the industrial design did not rely in any way on any illegal agreement or conspiracy but was based on the rights to the design under the *Industrial Design and Union Label Act*, the defence should be struck out. The defendant appealed to the Federal Court of Appeal. After reviewing the Supreme Court's decisions in *Philco Products* and *Massie & Renwick*, the Federal Court of Appeal stated that 'it seems ... to be an open question whether the Court will ever decline relief in an infringement action to a party holding the title to industrial property save where what is being sought in the action is in substance the enforcement or furtherance of the illegal conspiracy or agreement.'[88] The court found that, in this case, the defendants' pleading did not amount to an allegation of a conspiracy among the plaintiffs to use their property rights to further an illegal resale price maintenance scheme. Thus, the defendants' attempt to invoke a violation of the *Combines Investigation Act* failed. Subsequently, the defendants sought to amend their pleadings to show a connection between the plaintiff's title and an illegal conspiracy.[89] The Federal Court interpreted the Federal Court of Appeal's decision to mean that 'if there is a connection between the plaintiff's title and an illegal conspiracy and the action taken is a step in this conspiracy, a Court may come to the conclusion that the action should fail even if the action is one to assert a proprietary right and not one to enforce an unlawful agreement,'[90] and allowed the amendment.

A similar interpretation of the Federal Court of Appeal's holding in *RBM Equipment* was adopted by the Federal Court – Trial Division in the 1975 patent infringement case of *Amoco Can. Petroleum Co. Ltd. v. Texaco Exploration Can. Ltd.*[91] In *Amoco*, the defendant brought a motion claiming that the patent at issue was an identical patent held by three

87 *RBM Equipment Ltd.* (1973), 9 C.P.R. (2d) 46 at 49 (F.C.T.D.).
88 *RBM Equipment Ltd.* (1973), 9 C.P.R. (2d) 50 at 59 (F.C.A.).
89 *RBM Equipment Ltd.* (1973), 10 C.P.R. (2d) 23 (F.C.T.D.).
90 Ibid., at 26.
91 [1976] 1 F.C. 258.

companies, one of which was the plaintiff. The defendant claimed that there was an agreement between the plaintiff and the two other patent holders to unreasonably restrain trade by requiring that the defendant pay a royalty fee to each of the three patent holders. Following *Philco Products* and *RBM Equipment*, the court found that there was no evidence that the plaintiff's patent had been acquired illegally or through a conspiracy, and that the proceedings were not steps by the plaintiff in furtherance of a conspiracy. Thus, the defendant's attempt to invoke a violation of the conspiracy provisions of the *Combines Investigation Act* on the part of the plaintiff failed.

In 1976, shortly after the inclusion of section 31.1 (now section 36) in the Stage I amendments to the *Combines Investigation Act*, the possibility of a defence based on anticompetitive abuse of allegedly infringed IPRs was again raised in *Eli Lilly and Co. v. Marzone Chemicals Ltd.*[92] The Federal Court – Trial Division refused to strike a statement of defence and part of a counterclaim in a patent infringement action in which the defendant claimed that the plaintiffs had conspired to limit the production of trifluralin and thus injure competition in the market for trifluralin. The court noted that, 'in view of the distinct possibility of section 31.1 now affording a defence at law which did not exist formerly, no useful purpose will be served in striking those allegations from the defence at this stage when the same allegations can legally be made in the counterclaim.'[93] This decision, which was later upheld by the Federal Court of Appeal,[94] suggests the possibility of a broader defence based on illegal use of IPRs than was allowed in the earlier cases.[95] As well, the court noted the possibility that a competition law violation could constitute grounds for denial of equitable relief, even where it did not provide a defence in law.[96] Such equitable relief (e.g., an injunction barring further use of patented technology) can be a key aspect of infringement cases.[97]

In the 1980s, with an increased understanding of the economic bene-

---

92 (1976), 29 C.P.R. (2d) 253 (F.C.T.D.); (1976), 29 C.P.R. (2d) 255 (F.C.A.).
93 *Eli Lilly and Co.* (1976), 29 C.P.R. (2d) 253 at 255 (F.C.T.D.).
94 *Eli Lilly and Co.* (1976), 29 C.P.R. (2d) 255 (F.C.A.).
95 Anderson, Khosla, and Ronayne, 'The Competition Policy Treatment of Intellectual Property Rights in Canada,' at 517.
96 *Eli Lilly and Co.* (1976), 29 C.P.R. (2d) 253 at 255 (F.C.T.D.).
97 See Anderson, Khosla, and Ronayne, 'The Competition Policy Treatment of Intellectual Property Rights in Canada,' at 517.

fits of IPRs, came a concomitant growing acceptance of the role of IPRs in competition policy. IPRs came to be viewed as serving useful, pro-competitive functions in a market economy, rather than as statutory monopolies conferred by the intellectual property system. As well, the interface between competition policy and IPRs began to receive more attention. The importance of IPRs to economic growth and welfare achieved particular prominence in the recent Uruguay Round negotiations of the WTO agreement on TRIPs.[98] Developed countries with a competitive advantage in innovation, in particular, the United States, sought to obtain a set of international rules that would ensure that their IPR rights would be as extensive and as effectively enforced abroad as they are by their respective domestic intellectual property systems at home. On the other hand, developing countries in which innovation is not a major source of economic activity and growth had much to gain, in terms of consumer welfare, from countenancing cheap domestic imitations of innovations made elsewhere (i.e., their comparative advantage lies in imitation rather than innovation) and thus were concerned that an agreement on TRIPs that raised intellectual property protection to developed country levels would result in a reduction of their welfare. Despite these basic differences of perspective between some developed countries and most of the developing world, the Uruguay Round negotiations were successful in producing a comprehensive agreement on TRIPs. The WTO TRIPs agreement and other international agreements[99] that exist with respect to other forms of IPRs reflect the important role IPRs play in economic growth and the difficulty in balancing the protection of IPRs with other social interests (such as ensuring healthy competition). In the following sections, we review the provisions of the *Competition Act* that relate to IPRs and the jurisprudence on the competition-IPR interface.

2. *The Competition Act*

The *Competition Act* covers IPR holders by either exempting them from provisions in the Act or ensuring that they are covered. Two sections

---

98 See Trebilcock and Howse, *The Regulation of International Trade*, chap. 12.
99 Other such international agreements with respect to IPRs include, for example, the Rome Convention (Performers' Rights), the International Convention for the protection of New Varieties of Plants (UPON) (Plant Breeders' Rights), and the Washington Treaty (Integrated Circuits).

enacted in 1986 provide specific exemptions from provisions in the *Competition Act*. First, section 79(5) creates an exemption from the abuse of dominance provisions in sections 78 and 79. This exemption is limited to acts engaged in only pursuant to the exercise of any right or enjoyment of any interest derived under IP statutes. It should not be read as a blanket exemption – if the exercise of the IPR goes beyond the purposes contemplated in the statutes, violations of sections 78 and 79 may be found to exist.[100] Second, section 86(4), dealing with specialization agreements, provides for a specific exemption from scrutiny under section 45 (conspiracies) and section 77 (exclusive dealing) for agreements which, for example, ration output so that firms may meet international competition more effectively, or that involve cross-licensing or pooling of patents. The latter agreements must receive the approval of the tribunal, which may require widespread licensing of the patents throughout the industry as a condition for the registration of a specialization agreement.

Many of the provisions relevant to IPRs had existed in the *Combines Investigation Act*. The 1986 amendments, which renamed the statute the *Competition Act*, contained few direct IPR provisions outside of sections 79(5) and 86. It is important to note, however, that the *Competition Act* replaced the criminal monopoly provisions of the *Combines Investigation Act* with reviewable practices provisions: the standard of proof under the previous criminal monopoly provisions had required evidence of control over a market and detriment to the public interest that made it difficult for a violation to be established. Two sections of the *Competition Act* specifically ensure that conduct that goes beyond the exercise of inherent IP rights falls within the ambit of the Act. First, section 32 allows the attorney general to apply to the Federal Court of Canada for various remedial orders to address the abuse of IPRs.[101] The remedial powers of the Federal Court are broad and include the power to revoke a patent, to declare a contractual arrangement void, or

---

100 See, for example, *Canada (Director of Investigation and Research) v. NutraSweet Co.* (1990), 32 C.P.R. (3d) 1 (Comp. Trib.), discussed below.

101 As discussed above, a somewhat differently worded precursor to the current s. 32 was introduced into anticombines legislation in 1910. For more information on the specific forms of abuse see s. 32, *Competition Act*; see also, Globerman and Schwindt, 'Intellectual Property Rights: Anti-competitive Abuses and Competition Policy Antidotes,' in Khemani and Stanbury, eds., *Canadian Competition Law and Policy at the Centenary*, at 463.

to impose compulsory licensing.[102] Specifically, section 32 provides that where the exclusive rights and privileges conferred by patents, trademarks, or copyright have been used so as to (a) limit unduly the facilities for transporting, producing, manufacturing, supplying, storing, or dealing in any article or commodity that may be a subject of trade or commerce; (b) restrain or injure unduly trade or commerce in relation to any such article or commodity; (c) prevent, limit, or lessen unduly the manufacture or production of any such article or commodity or unreasonably enhance the price thereof; or (d) prevent or lessen unduly competition in the production, manufacture, purchase, barter, sale, transportation, or supply of any such article or commodity, then the Federal Court may (i) declare void, in whole or in part, any agreement, arrangement, or licence relating to the use of the IPR in question; (ii) restrain any person from carrying out or exercising any or all of the terms or provisions of the agreement, arrangement, or licence; (iii) direct the grant of licences under the IPR to persons on terms and conditions as the court may deem proper, or if such a grant and other remedies would appear insufficient to prevent such anticompetitive use, revoke the patent; (iv) direct that the registration of a trade mark in the register of trademarks be expunged or amended; and (v) direct that such other acts be done or omitted as the court may deem necessary to prevent any anticompetitive use. As well, section 32 retains the proviso enacted in 1946 providing that no remedial order shall be made that would be at variance with any treaty or arrangement respecting IPRs to which Canada is a party.

It is worth noting, however, that although section 32 specifically addresses IPRs, it has rarely been invoked.[103] As noted above, such provisions for remedial orders have existed in competition legislation since the enactment of the *Combines Investigation Act 1910*, but there have been no cases in which a remedy was granted. There appear to be several reasons for this lack of use. First, it has proven difficult for competition authorities to establish jurisdiction over the exercise of IPRs.

---

102 Compulsory licensing may be invoked under both the *Patent Act* and the *Competition Act*.

103 In fact, it was not until 1967 that a case proceeded under the precursor to this section. For a discussion of this case, see *Union Carbide*, discussed in the next section of this paper. Other than the *Union Carbide* cases which did not go to trial, no other proceedings have occurred under s. 32. See Anderson, Khosla, and Ronayne, 'The Competition Policy Treatment of Intellectual Property Rights in Canada,' at 497.

Even if jurisdiction is established, the attorney general must show that the practices in question have led to an *undue* lessening of competition, which is a relatively high standard. Finally, section 61, which prohibits resale price maintenance, contains a specific 'no exemption' clause for IPR holders, so that if they attempt to influence prices in the downstream market they may be held criminally liable.

In addition to the explicit reference to IPRs in these four sections, several other sections contain provisions that may affect the exercise of these rights. Section 77 (reviewable vertical restrictions) includes licensing practices of IPRs such as tied selling, exclusive dealing, and territorial market restrictions. Although section 75 covers refusals to deal, the provision does not appear to be applicable to refusals to license IP, in light of the Competition Tribunal's decision in *Warner Music*.[104] Section 45 renders conspiracies subject to criminal sanctions. As well, as can be observed by past efforts of defendants in patent infringement suits, section 45 can be used as a defence if a criminal conspiracy among the plaintiffs can be demonstrated.[105] One example of such a defence is found in the patent infringement case of *Procter & Gamble v. Kimberly-Clark of Canada Ltd.*,[106] in which the defendant alleged that the plaintiffs had engaged in predatory pricing contrary to the criminal provisions of the *Competition Act* with respect to the diaper products that embodied the patent in question. The Federal Court of Appeal, in reversing the motions judge, held that the allegation of predatory pricing could not have any bearing on the defence to the plaintiffs' action for patent infringement. Instead, according to Hugessen J.A., '[f]or past conduct to be relevant to a refusal of equitable relief under the "clean hands" doctrine, relief to which the party would otherwise be entitled, such conduct must relate directly to the subject-matter of the plaintiffs' claim, in this case, their patent.'[107] This decision appears to follow the earlier Supreme Court decisions as it implies that, even if the plaintiffs had engaged in predatory pricing, they were

---

104 *Canada (Director of Investigation and Research) v. Warner Music Canada Ltd.*, [1997] C.C.T.D. No. 53 Trib. Dec. No. CT9703/22 (Q.L.). See the section below entitled 'Refusal to Deal' for a discussion of the *Warner Music* case.
105 See section III.C.1. above, for a review of the decisions of the Supreme Court of Canada regarding the use of anticompetitive abuses of IPRs as a defence in IPR infringement suits.
106 (1990), 29 C.P.R. (3d) 545 (F.C.A.).
107 Ibid., at 546.

still entitled to enforce their patent rights because the alleged illegality did not relate directly to the existence of the rights. That is, the plaintiffs did not need to rely on an illegality to establish their patent rights. When the case proceeded to trial,[108] the defendants argued that the plaintiffs were estopped from claiming relief from patent infringement because they had violated the civil provisions relating to abuse of dominant position. The defendants asserted that at the time the plaintiffs acquired an exclusive licence to the patent, they substantially controlled the relevant product market. Thus, the acquisition of the exclusive rights constituted an anticompetitive act. The Federal Court rejected this argument, holding instead that the *ex dolo* defence did not extend to alleged violations of the civil provisions of the *Competition Act*. In addressing the applicability of this defence, Teitelbaum J. stated:

> With respect to the defence of *ex dolo* it is narrow in scope and limited to situations where a party relies on a criminal act to make its claim (*Philco Products Ltd. v. Thermionics Ltd.*[109]). In the case before me, abuse of dominant position in the *Competition Act* is not a criminal or even a civil illegality. It is a reviewable practice under Part VIII of the Competition Act and any proceedings relating to the practice are conducted before a civil administrative tribunal. There is no improper conduct until such time as the Competition Tribunal so finds. Furthermore, no proceedings have taken place before the Tribunal. Therefore, *ex dolo* has no application in this case.[110]

Subsequently, in *Eli Lilly and Co. v. Novopharm Ltd.*,[111] the Federal Court referred to its decision in the *Procter & Gamble* case in rejecting the defendant's argument that the plaintiff was not entitled to relief because it had engaged in the use of 'fighting brands' in violation of Part VIII of the *Competition Act*. Thus, it appears that even under the *Competition Act*, alleging that the plaintiffs had engaged in anticompetitive abuses of IPRs will not constitute a successful defence unless the

108 *Procter & Gamble Co. v. Kimberly-Clark of Canada Ltd.* (1991), 40 C.P.R. (3d) 1 (F.C.T.D.).
109 [1943] S.C.R. 396. See section III.C.1. for a brief review of the *Philco Products* case.
110 *Procter & Gamble Co., supra* (1991), 40 C.P.R. (3d) 1 at 55.
111 (1996), 68 C.P.R. (3d) 254 (F.C.T.D.).

defendants can establish that the IPRs in question were acquired in connection with a criminal conspiracy.

Complaints under the *Competition Act* must in most cases be made to the Commissioner of Competition, although section 36 provides for a private right of action for violations of the criminal provisions of the Act or for failure to comply with an order of the tribunal or another court under the Act (and recent amendments to the Act will provide private party access to the tribunal for some reviewable practices). Section 36 has been included in competition legislation since its enactment as section 31.1 in 1975 in the Stage I amendments to the *Combines Investigation Act*, and the section has been invoked by defendants as the basis of counterclaims in IPR infringement suits. For example, in *Procter & Gamble Co. v. Kimberly-Clark of Canada Ltd.*,[112] a patent infringement action, the Federal Court refused to strike a counterclaim for damages under section 36 alleging that the plaintiffs had conspired to enforce a patent they knew to be invalid.

In the following sections, we examine the exercise of IPRs with regard to specific aspects of competition policy. We consider both the unilateral exercise of IPRs by a dominant firm and the use of such rights in conjunction with other parties through patent pools and cross-licensing.

D. Unilateral Licensing Practices by a Dominant Firm

1. Tied Sales and Extension of IPRs
A tie is the supply of one product (the tying product) either on the condition that the buyer also take a second product (the tied product) or on terms that induce the buyer to take the second product in addition to the first. Tying restrictions are of two types: bundling (for example, the bundling of patents in licensing contracts), and requirements tying, in which the buyer's right to buy one product is tied to the obligation to buy all requirements of a second product exclusively from the same seller. Licensing a bundle of products or setting royalties on the total sales of the licensee, as opposed to the use of the licensed input, are alternative forms of tying. A notable example of such a form of tying can be observed in the consent decree negotiated between Microsoft and the U.S. Department of Justice in 1995 regarding the prohibition of

---

112   (1986), 12 C.P.R. (3d) 430 (F.C.T.D.).

Microsoft's use of central processing unit (CPU) licences.[113] The majority of computers are sold with an operating system loaded on the CPU. Although Microsoft did not hold a patent on CPUs used by original equipment manufacturers, it had required that all original equipment manufacturers pay a royalty for MS-DOS (Microsoft's operating system) for every CPU shipped. Since each machine contained a CPU, manufacturers were required to pay for a copy of MS-DOS regardless of whether the operating system was preloaded onto the computer.[114] Microsoft would sell MS-DOS licenses to manufacturers who refused the CPU licence, but only at significantly higher prices. Under the CPU licence, a manufacturer also had to commit to a minimum requirement that approximated its annual shipments. If a manufacturer shipped a computer preloaded with a competing operating system, it would not receive a reduction in its payment to Microsoft. Therefore, a manufacturer who accepted a CPU licence faced a zero marginal price for units of MS-DOS up to the minimum requirement. The CPU licence thus drove manufacturers to use only Microsoft's operating system because they faced 'paying double' if they used another operating system.

Another practice that can be interpreted as a form of 'tying' in licensing contracts is the inclusion of grantbacks, a restriction in which the licensor requires that the licensee transfer the patent, or grant a licence to the licensor, on any improvement that it may develop on the original innovation. Such arrangements may be prohibited by the tribunal under section 77 of the *Competition Act* if they meet all the other requirements of that section; that is, if the tying is a practice engaged in by a major supplier and results in a substantial lessening of competition. The principal concern is that firms that have market power through IPRs in one market will leverage that market power to attempt to monopolize, or at least attain an advantage in, markets in which products are not subject to IPRs. One prominent example is the recent

---

113 *Microsoft Corp. v. Bingamen*, DC SNY, Misc. No MB-85. 7/3/95. 7/13/95. The Department of Justice had negotiated a consent decree with Microsoft regarding some of its market practices.
114 For a discussion of the 1995 proposed consent decree, see K.C. Baseman, F.R. Warren-Boulton, and G.A. Woroch, 'Microsoft Plays Hardball: The Use of Exclusionary Pricing and Technical Incompatibility to Maintain Monopoly Power in Markets for Operating System Software,' (1995) 40 *Antitrust Bulletin* 265, and J.E. Lopatka and W.H. Page, 'Microsoft, Monopolization, and Network Externalities: Some Uses and Abuses of Economic Theory in Antitrust Decision Making,' (1995) 40 *Antitrust Bulletin* 265.

suit brought by the U.S. Department of Justice and the attorneys-general of various states regarding Microsoft's attempts to extend its dominant position in the operating systems market into markets for computer applications. Among the anticompetitive practices alleged is the tying of licences for operating systems with the sale of Microsoft's applications software. As discussed above, the 1995 consent decree with the U.S. Department of Justice had attempted to address such concerns by prohibiting Microsoft from tying licences of operating systems to the sale of other Microsoft products. However, the *amicus curiae* submitted a brief expressing concern that the consent decree would not be sufficient to address anticompetitive tying by Microsoft. Such fears were realized: in the recent suit, the U.S. Department of Justice alleged that Microsoft entered into agreements with PC original equipment manufacturers, Internet service providers, and Internet content vendors requiring them to favour its Internet browser over that of its chief rival, Netscape. The Department of Justice alleged that Microsoft's inclusion of its Internet browser with its Windows 95 operating system constitutes an improper leveraging of its monopoly position in operating systems to create a competitive advantage in the market for Internet access. Microsoft responded by contending that it was entitled to continue innovating to improve its operating system, and the inclusion of its Internet browser (which it asserted was inseparable from the Windows operating system) was merely an improvement of its operating system, not a tying arrangement.

Judge Thomas Penfield Jackson, of the U.S. District Court for the District of Columbia, however, found merit in the Department of Justice's allegations of anticompetitive tying.[115] Judge Jackson found that no competitors existed for Microsoft's Windows operating system in the relevant marketplace[116] and that Microsoft's market share was persistently dominant.[117] Microsoft had perceived the rise of Netscape's Navigator internet browser as a significant threat to its dominance in

---

115 *United States of America v. Microsoft Corporation; State of New York ex rel. Eliot Spitzer, et al. v. Microsoft Corporation*, 65 F. Supp. 2d 1 (D.D.C., 1999) (findings of fact); *U.S. v. Microsoft Corp.; State of New York ex rel. Eliot Spitzer et al. v. Microsoft Corp.*, 87 F. Supp. 2d 30 (D.D.C., 2000) (conclusions of law).

116 The relevant market was Intel-based PC operating systems. 65 F. Supp. 2d at 6.

117 Judge Jackson found that Microsoft's market share ranged from 90 to 95 per cent depending on the year. Ibid., at 10.

the operating systems market.[118] Microsoft's concern was that consumers would eventually be able to access and use applications remotely through the use of Netscape. The tendency of developers to work primarily with the Microsoft operating system, Windows, could then significantly diminish, as the costs of using alternative platforms were removed from end consumers and centralized in companies with the expertise and ability to make use of such platforms effectively. Microsoft therefore tied its own internet browser, Internet Explorer, to Windows, not only for the purpose of dominating the nascent market for browsers, but to preserve the very monopoly position in operating systems it was exploiting in the tying arrangement.

Microsoft's tying strategy primarily targeted PC manufacturers.[119] Microsoft both contractually and technologically tied Internet Explorer to Windows by, in the first place, refusing to license Windows to manufacturers unless they agreed in the licence agreement not to alter the operating system or its interaction with the browser. In the second place, Microsoft removed Internet Explorer from the list of programs that could be added or removed from a PC running Windows. Microsoft thereby ensured that all PCs sold with Windows preinstalled featured Internet Explorer permanently affixed to the desktop. Judge Jackson applied a four-part test gleaned from U.S. Supreme Court jurisprudence, as follows: 'Liability for tying .exists where (1) two separate "products" are involved; (2) the defendant affords its consumers no choice but to take the tied product in order to obtain the tying product; (3) the arrangement affects a substantial volume of interstate commerce; and (4) the defendant has "market power" in the tying product market.'[120]

Judge Jackson found Microsoft liable on the grounds that, first, internet browsers and operating systems were regarded by consumers as different products, satisfying the first requirement. The fact that the defendant viewed the products as unified was irrelevant; objective market perception that Windows and Internet Explorer were discrete products established their separateness. Second, Microsoft's insistence

---

118 Microsoft was just as concerned with Sun Microsystems' Java product, which already gave users the capacity to remotely program and remotely access applications based on different platforms than the Windows platform. Ibid., at 20–1.

119 Microsoft also targeted Internet Access Providers by distributing Internet Explorer to them free of charge, for inclusion in the software the providers themselves distributed to users. Ibid., at 61–84.

120 87 F. Supp. 2d 30 at 47.

that manufacturers refrain from deleting or hiding Internet Explorer if they were to receive licences to distribute Windows resulted in consumers having no choice but to take the browser if they wished to obtain the operating system. The presence of significant interstate commerce was clear from Microsoft's nationwide, and indeed, global operation. Finally, the market power requirement was easily satisfied given Windows' dominance in the operating system marketplace.

Based on this anticompetitive tying, and on several other grounds, Judge Jackson ordered a breakup of Microsoft into an operating systems company and an applications company.[121] Microsoft appealed the District Court's conclusions of law and divestiture order. In a *per curiam* unanimous decision, the D.C. Circuit Court of Appeals allowed Microsoft's appeal in part and remanded certain issues to a new District Court judge.[122] The Circuit Court upheld Judge Jackson's finding that Microsoft had used predatory conduct to maintain its Intel-compatible operating systems monopoly,[123] but otherwise found largely in Microsoft's favour. It reversed the finding that Microsoft had attempted to monopolize the browser market on the basis that the District Court had failed to define the browser market. Since this oversight flowed from the plaintiffs' failure to 'articulate and identify evidence' necessary for a court to define such a market, the Circuit Court also refused to remand the issue for reconsideration. Finally, the Circuit Court abandoned the *per se* standard for cases of technological tying and remanded the issue of whether Microsoft had illegally tied its Internet Explorer browser to Windows for redetermination using a rule of reason standard.[124] However, given the Circuit Court's previous findings

---

121 *U.S. v. Microsoft*, Memorandum and Order, 7 June 2000, Civil Action Nos. 98–1232, 98–1233 (TPJ) (D.D.C. 2000).
122 *U.S. v. Microsoft Corporation*, No. 00-5212 (D.C. Cir., 28 June 2001).
123 In upholding this finding, the Circuit Court rejected Microsoft's defence that it was 'exercising its rights as a holder of valid copyrights' by imposing restrictions as conditions of its Internet Explorer licenses. The Circuit Court said that this claim 'bordered upon the frivolous' since it implied that intellectual property rights place conduct beyond antitrust laws. However, the Circuit Court conceded that copyright laws allow for the imposition of a licence restriction that prohibits 'drastic alternation' of a copyrighted work if the benefits of the prohibition to the copyright owner outweigh the competitive effect of the prohibition. Ibid., at 33–4.
124 Ibid., at 77. The court noted that, while certain tying arrangements 'pose an unacceptable risk to competition and are unreasonable "per se" ... there are strong reasons to doubt that the integration of additional software functionality into an [operating system] falls among these arrangements.' On the contrary, it concluded that applying a *per se* rule 'might stunt valuable innovation.' Ibid.

on Judge Jackson's failure to define the browser market, it would appear that this remand will be of little, if any, consequence. The Circuit Court's remand, therefore, likely will be limited essentially to determining an appropriate remedy to address the illegal maintenance of Microsoft's Intel-compatible operating systems monopoly. In November 2001, Microsoft, the Department of Justice, and nine states agreed on a conduct-oriented proposed consent decree, which had not been finalized as of this writing. Moreover, nine states and the District of Columbia continued to seek stronger sanctions than contained in the settlement. Resolution of these outstanding issues is not expected to occur until spring 2002 at the earliest.

Tying arrangements need not always be anticompetitive – that is, aimed at foreclosing the market for the tied product and thus resulting in dead-weight loss. In some cases, tying can be welfare enhancing. For instance, tying can achieve economies of scope and protection of good will.[125] If the tying product has uncertain value to customers, as in the case of an innovation, then charging less for the innovation and tying it to a good whose demand is correlated with the revealed value of the innovation can insure customers against the possibility of an imprudent purchase.[126] It may be difficult to ascertain whether a tying arrangement is aimed at gaining an anticompetitive advantage or whether it results in an increase in welfare. For example, in 1992, the Competition Bureau examined the practices of the Digital Equipment of Canada (DEC) under the tied selling provisions.[127] DEC tied the sale of updates for its copyrighted operating system software to hardware servicing of its equipment. The director alleged that DEC's practices were an attempt to leverage or extend market power derived from IPRs on software into the servicing market, as a result of impeding entry and expansion of third-party service providers into the servicing market.

125 See W.F. Baxter and D.P. Kessler, 'The Law and Economics of Tying Arrangements: Lessons for the Competition Policy Treatment of Intellectual Property,' in Gallini and Anderson, eds., *Competition Policy and Intellectual Property Rights*, 137; M. Whinston, 'Tying, Foreclosure, and Exclusion,' (1990) 80 *American Economic Review* 837, and W. Baxter and D. Kessler, 'Toward a Consistent Theory of the Welfare Analysis of Agreements,' (1995) 47 *Stanford Law Review* 615.
126 See J. Lunn, 'Tie-in Sales and the Diffusion of New Technology,' (1990) 146 *Journal of Institutional and Theoretical Economics* 249, for a review and example.
127 Director of Investigation and Research, *Annual Report for the Year Ended March 31, 1993*, 14. This example is drawn from P. Rey and R.A. Winter, 'Exclusivity Restrictions and Intellectual Property,' in Gallini and Anderson, eds., *Competition Policy and Intellectual Property Rights*, at 159.

This matter was resolved by an undertaking in which DEC agreed to drop the tying restriction. However, there are two more plausible explanations for such tying. First, the ability of buyers to distinguish between software and hardware faults would give rise to an externality that would distort the incentives to provide high-quality servicing, since increased quality would benefit the reputations of both DEC and the service provider. Such an externality can be internalized through tying. Second, there could be a correlation among buyers between (a) the value that they place on the software, and (b) the intensity with which the system was used and, therefore, the quantity of servicing required. Under this condition, tying, together with marking up the price of servicing over cost, allows price discrimination, since a greater share of the surplus can be extracted from high-value users. This is a standard price discrimination explanation of tying. Neither of these explanations supports prohibiting the practice on the basis of efficiency.

We next examine Canadian cases on tying, although it should be noted that the paucity of case law makes a detailed analysis extremely difficult. To date, there have been only four tying cases in the IP area in which proceedings were commenced.

As noted above, complaints under the IPR remedy provisions of the *Combines Investigation Act* (now section 32 of the *Competition Act*) were filed in two cases against Union Carbide, both of which were resolved through settlements. In the first of these, the licensee used patented machines that extracted polyethylene film from resin and was required to purchase resin from the licensor and a particular group of suppliers.[128] Licensees were forced to pay higher royalties if they imported polyethylene resin from other suppliers. The Crown alleged that this practice caused an undue lessening of competition in the market for resin. In the settlement, Union Carbide agreed to abandon this practice. In the second case, several of Union Carbide's practices involving process and machinery patents for polyethylene film were alleged to be anticompetitive. These practices included sliding scale royalties believed to be discriminatory against small suppliers, royalty payments beyond the patent life, restraints on patent challenges, and field-of-use restrictions. Union Carbide agreed to cease all of these practices and the complaint was dropped.

The first IP tying case to proceed to trial was *Culzean Inventions Ltd.*

128 *R. v. Union Carbide Canada Limited*, minutes of settlement in the Exchequer Court of Canada, 9 Dec. 1969 and 19 June 1971, respectively. See also, *Annual Reports* of the Director of Investigation and Research for years ending 31 March 1970 and 1972.

616 The Law and Economics of Canadian Competition Policy

v. Midwestern Broom Company Ltd. et. al.,[129] a patent extension decision heard under the common law of restraint of trade. In this case, the patentee attempted to obtain royalties from the licensee after patent expiration. The licensee argued that this was an illegal attempt to extend the patent life. However, since the agreement was freely made between the parties and the respondent had failed to demonstrate 'unreasonableness,' the court concluded that the royalties were not in violation of the doctrine.

The second case regarding an allegation of tying in the IP area to proceed to trial was the 1990 case of *NutraSweet*.[130] At the time of the proceedings before the Competition Tribunal, NutraSweet held use patents on the production of aspartame (an artificial sweetener) in the United States and in Canada. Its Canadian patents had expired, but its U.S. patent would not expire until 1992. In anticipation of the expiration of its patents and the accompanying end to its monopoly in the market for aspartame, NutraSweet had pursued a 'branded ingredient' strategy. That is, NutraSweet 'branded' its aspartame and created a distinctive trade mark (the 'Swirl' logo), which had been registered worldwide for its aspartame. Such a strategy was considered to be highly innovative as commodity ingredients are generally not branded.[131] NutraSweet devised a means of inducing customers to purchase their aspartame requirements exclusively from it: if customers displayed the NutraSweet logo on their products, they would be entitled to trademark display allowances, which could amount to as much as 40 per cent of the price.[132] However, to be entitled to display the NutraSweet logo, customers would have to purchase all their aspartame requirements from NutraSweet. The director commenced a proceeding against NutraSweet under section 77(1) of the *Competition Act*, in which NutraSweet was accused of requiring its customers to refrain from using the aspartame of any other producer as a condition of supplying its trade mark. In effect, the director alleged that NutraSweet tied the use of its logo and trade mark to its aspartame. Under section 77(2), tying is prohibited when it is engaged in by 'a major supplier of a product in a market and is likely to (a) impede entry into or expansion of a firm in the market, (b) impede introduction of a product into or expansion of sales of a

---

129 [1984] 3 W.W.R. 11.
130 *Supra*, note 100.
131 Ibid., at 39.
132 Ibid., at 41.

product in the market, or (c) have any other exclusionary effect in the market,' with the result that competition is or is likely to be lessened substantially. Thus section 77(2) structures the assessment of tying as a rule-of-reason inquiry, unlike the *per se* treatment tying receives under U.S. antitrust law.[133] In *NutraSweet*, the tribunal held that in appropriate circumstances, a trade mark could be the subject of a tying arrangement, but in this case, the tribunal was not convinced by the director's arguments regarding the tying of the trade mark to the aspartame, finding that they had 'not been consistent.'[134] The tribunal stated that in his notice of application, the director had alleged that the tying product was NutraSweet-brand aspartame, but in his written argument, the trade mark itself was alleged to be the tying product. Furthermore, since the director did not appear to seek a remedy with regard to NutraSweet's alleged tying in addition to the remedies sought with regard to the company's exclusivity practices, the tribunal did not make any finding with respect to the tied selling of NutraSweet's trade mark and its aspartame.[135]

2. Refusal to License

Under the *Patent Act*, compulsory licensing is an instrument that can be and has been used if the innovation is not being worked to an adequate degree, especially when licensing (on reasonable terms) would be in the public interest.[136] As noted above, the *Copyright Act* also provides for compulsory licensing in circumstances where, after the death of the author, the copyright holder refuses to allow the re-exposure of the work in question and there are no special reasons to account for such refusal.

The courts have found royalties to be 'unreasonable' under patent law if they were so high that the patent could not be worked where the patent was not being worked by the patent holder. In some cases, this has been seen as a 'refusal to license' and compulsory licences have been issued.[137] This diverges sharply from practice in the United States,

---

133 See Baxter and Kessler, 'The Law and Economics of Tying Arrangement,' 137, for a discussion of the treatment of tying under U.S. law.

134 *NutraSweet, supra* (1990), 32 C.P.R. (3d) at 57.

135 Ibid.

136 The public interest may refer to prospective consumers.

137 See, for example, *International Cone Co. Ltd. v. Consolidated Wafer Co.* (1926), 2 D.L.R. 1015 (Exch. Ct.).

where courts have held that an innovator does not have to offer a royalty that is acceptable to a licensee.[138] A showing of anticompetitive effects is not necessary to establish this 'abuse' under the *Patent Act*.

With regard to the *Competition Act*, the Competition Tribunal's decisions in *Chrysler*,[139] *Tele-Direct*,[140] and *Warner Music*[141] indicate that section 75 (refusal to supply under the *Competition Act*) does not apply to IPRs. Although not directly an IP case, *Chrysler*, the first refusal-to-supply case reviewed by the Competition Tribunal, had some IP features that indicated how future cases might be resolved. In this case, Chrysler stopped supplying branded auto parts to a Canadian distributor on terms more favourable than those for distributors in the United States. After considering the entire circumstances of the case, including the long relationship that had subsisted between Chrysler and the distributor, the tribunal exercised its discretion in favour of the grant of an order under section 75 to require Chrysler to supply the distributor with parts on former trade terms. However, in its decision, the tribunal suggested that the existence of a trade mark, in particular, and an IPR, in general, will not necessarily imply the existence of a separate market.

In *Tele-Direct*, the Competition Tribunal considered the application of the abuse of dominance provisions to a situation involving a refusal to license a trade mark. The director alleged that Tele-Direct, which dominated the market for Yellow Pages telephone directories, had engaged in an anticompetitive practice by selectively licensing its Yellow Pages trade mark. In particular, the director alleged that Tele-Direct refused to license its trade mark to competitors for the purpose of restraining competition. The director also argued that section 79(5) of the *Competition Act* did not preclude a finding that 'abuses' of intellectual property rights are anticompetitive acts. The tribunal agreed with the director that there may be instances in which a trade mark may be misused. However, in the tribunal's view, 'something more' than the mere exercise of statutory rights, even if exclusionary in effect, must be present before there can be a finding of misuse of a trade mark, and section

---

138 *Bement v. National Harrow Co.*, 186 U.S. 70 (1982).
139 *Canada (Director of Investigation and Research) v. Chrysler Canada Ltd.* (1989), 27 C.P.R. (3d) 1, aff'd (1991), 38 C.P.R. (3d) 25 (C.A.).
140 *Canada (Director of Investigation and Research) v. Tele-Direct (Publications) Inc.* (1997), 73 C.P.R. (3d) 1 (Comp. Trib.).
141 *Canada (Director of Investigation and Research) v. Warner Music Canada Ltd., supra*, note 104.

79(5) of the *Competition Act* explicitly recognizes that the mere exercise of IPRs does not constitute an anticompetitive act. In finding no violation of the abuse of dominance provisions in Tele-Direct's refusal to license its Yellow Pages trade mark to competitors, the tribunal stated: 'The respondents' refusal to license their trademark falls squarely within their rights. Inherent in the very nature of the right to license a trademark is the right for the owner of the trademark to determine whether or not, and to whom, to grant a licence; selectivity in licensing is fundamental to the rationale behind protecting trademark. The respondents' trademarks are valuable assets and represent considerable goodwill in the market place. The decision to license a trademark – essentially, to share the goodwill vesting in the asset – is a right which rests entirely with the owner of the mark.'[142]

In *Warner Music*, the director sought an order that Warner issue licences to BMG Direct Ltd, a mail order record club, under usual trade terms so that BMG could make compact discs from Warner master recordings. The director alleged that BMG needed such licences in order to compete in the mail order record club business in Canada. At that time, the only other participant in the Canadian market was Columbia House, an equal partnership of Warner and Sony Music, to which Warner had granted licences to manufacture, distribute, and sell in Canada sound recordings made from Warner master recordings. Columbia House had enjoyed a monopoly in the Canadian record club market until the entry of BMG. In *Warner*, the central issue before the tribunal was whether a copyright licence was a 'product' for the purposes of section 75. The tribunal found that the word 'product' cannot be read to include copyright licences in the context of section 75. The tribunal held that although the word 'product' as used throughout the *Competition Act*[143] is broad enough to include a copyright licence, 'the requirements in section 75 that there be an "ample supply" of a "product" and usual trade terms for a product show that the exclusive legal rights over intellectual property cannot be a "product" because there cannot be an "ample supply" of legal rights over intellectual property which are exclusive by their very nature and there cannot be usual trade terms when licences may be withheld.'[144]

---

142 *Supra*, note 141, at para. 66.
143 The term 'product' as used in the *Competition Act* is defined in s. 2 of that Act.
144 *Supra*, note 104, at 27–8.

Thus, as a matter of copyright law, which grants rights to exclude others, Warner had the right to refuse to license if it so chose. The tribunal further noted that there was nothing in the legislative history of section 75 of the *Competition Act* that indicated an intention to have it operate as a compulsory licensing provision for intellectual property. Instead, the tribunal accepted Warner's argument that the language of the *Competition Act* does not give the power to override the simple exercise of IPRs to the tribunal. In order for such power to be granted, the statute would have to contain clear and unequivocal language to that effect. As well, the tribunal accepted Warner's argument that since section 32 of the *Competition Act* employs clear and unequivocal language to provide the Federal Court with powers to revoke or compel licensing, and since section 79(5) of the *Competition Act* expressly exempts acts engaged in merely pursuant to the exercise of IPRs from being anticompetitive, section 75 could not reasonably be interpreted to override the simple exercise of IPRs. The tribunal noted that copyright rights and trade-mark rights are very similar and thus referred to its own decision in *Tele-Direct*[145] where it stated that the refusal to license trade marks falls squarely within the prerogative of the intellectual property right holder and, moreover, is inherent in the very nature of the right to license a trade mark. Therefore, it appears very likely that unless the practice engaged in were a part of a conspiracy reviewable under section 45 of the *Competition Act* or constituted an undue restraining of competition and is thus reviewable under section 32, refusals to license IPRs would not be reviewed under section 75 of the Act.

3. Resale Price Restrictions
There have been no cases regarding price restrictions on the resale of licensed products, but section 61 of the *Competition Act* clearly states that IP will be treated no differently from other forms of property. In particular, the provision specifies that IPRs cannot be used directly or indirectly to attempt to influence upward or to discourage a reduction in price of the product. Further, refusal to supply a product to a particular person or class of persons because of their low pricing policy is prohibited.

---

145 *Supra*, note 141.

4. *Exclusivity Restrictions*[146]

As noted above in section II, the effects of exclusive restrictions can be classified as either horizontal or vertical in nature. Contracts that coordinate activities among horizontal competitors in a market, resulting in reduced competition among them, are horizontal, while contracts that coordinate the incentives of a downstream licensee with the interests of an upstream producer or licensor are vertical. Horizontal effects can be measured across three markets: (i) the product market in which a product embodying an IPR is sold; (ii) the market for the rights to the use of a technological innovation (i.e., technology diffusion); and (iii) the innovation market – that is, innovation or R&D that leads to the discovery of new technologies and products.[147]

In general, restrictions motivated by horizontal effects tend to be inefficient because of substitution effects, while contracts with vertical effects tend to be efficient because of complementary effects. Agreements that reduce competition in a product market will lead to prices that are higher than marginal costs, thus representing a loss of consumer surplus. Horizontal effects in diffusion and in product markets include higher costs and prices in the final product market and perhaps inferior products. Contracts with horizontal effects in the diffusion of technology will primarily be those that exclude some firms from using patented technology, such as an exclusive licence. However, the impact of increased competition on innovation is more ambiguous, for there is no definitive evidence that competition enhances innovation.[148] The effects of a decrease in competition are potentially more severe in diffusion and innovation than in product markets. Less competition in product markets leads to higher prices, but high prices, although resulting in dead-weight loss, are mainly a transfer of surplus from buyers to sellers. Higher costs or inferior products as a result of reduced competition in diffusion or innovation are not a transfer of surplus, but rather a loss of efficiency on every unit sold. In industries where patent licensing is very important, the pace of innovation is a much more important indicator of social welfare than are prices.

---

146 This section is derived in part from Rey and Winter, 'Exclusivity Restrictions and Intellectual Property.'
147 The 1995 *Antitrust Guidelines for the Licensing and Acquisition of Intellectual Property* issued by the U.S. Department of Justice assess the level of competition in these three markets in enforcing antitrust law on IP.
148 See section I of this chapter for a discussion of the effect of competition on innovation.

On the other hand, the effect of prohibiting restrictions in licensing contracts driven purely by vertical or efficiency considerations is a loss in surplus. The costs of diffusing the technology through licensing are greater, and firms respond by licensing less. The lower returns from licensing in turn reduce the incentive to patent. Instead of patenting, firms will tend to keep new discoveries secret and reduce R&D expenditures.

In this section, we examine three main types of restrictions – (i) territorial restrictions, (ii) exclusive licensing, and (iii) exclusive dealings – and discuss the cases concerned with the anticompetitive use of such restrictions.

(a) Territorial Restrictions

Territorial restrictions, a vertical restraint, restrict the territory in which the licensee can produce and sell. An exclusive territory typically entails a restriction on both the licensor, who is constrained from licensing others in the specified territory, and the licensee, who is restricted from operating outside the designated area. Exclusive territory restrictions in licensing agreements take two forms. Open-territory restrictions guarantee that the licensee will be the only licensed firm in a specified territory but do not protect against competition from licensees outside the territory, while full, or closed-territory restrictions provide licensees with the complete, exclusive right to customers within a territory.

Exclusive territory restrictions can give rise to grey markets. In a typical grey market case in Canada, a foreign manufacturer is the original owner of the IP in question, such as a trade mark. The foreign IP owner distributes its products, which embody the IP, through distributors in Canada and in other countries. The Canadian distributor may be assigned an exclusive territory or user/ownership rights with regard to the IP, or both user/ownership rights and exclusive territory status; typically, the distributor has the exclusive right to use the IP in a particular territory.[149] Grey marketing occurs when a price differential exists between two areas. For example, the price for the same good may be higher in Canada than in another country because the value of the Canadian dollar has appreciated vis-à-vis the currency of the other

---

149 N.T. Gallini and A. Hollis, 'A Contractual Approach to the Gray Market,' (1999) 19 *International Review of Law and Economics* 1.

country. The existence of a price differential creates the opportunity for arbitrage. Grey marketers will be able to purchase the product in the low-price country and sell it in the high-price country.

One government policy or legal principle that allows open-territory exclusivity but prohibits closed-territory exclusivity is the principle of exhaustion.[150] Exhaustion is the removal of the rights of IPR owners to control parallel imports of legitimately manufactured foreign versions of their products. This doctrine does not apply in Canada, but it does apply within the European Community and to internal trade in the United States.[151]

It is important to note that grey marketers are not selling counterfeit goods. Rather, they import genuine goods sold in another country which have a lower price than that in Canada. Such goods, imported without the authorization of the Canadian IPR holder, are known as grey goods or parallel imports. Although grey marketers argue that they import genuine goods and that consumers benefit from the additional intrabrand competition, distributors who have been assigned an exclusive territory complain that these sales infringe upon their exclusive rights. Since grey goods are usually sold in direct competition with the authorized distributor's goods through a discount store without warranties or other services,[152] authorized distributors have sought to use various mechanisms for restricting parallel imports, such as claiming infringement using IP legislation. Before reviewing the actions under which distributors can undertake (or have undertaken) to prevent the parallel importation of goods, we examine a manufacturer's motivations for establishing exclusive territories.

There are several incentives for closed territories. First, closed territorial restrictions may be the result of a desire to protect against 'hold-up.' Manufacturers often impose territorial restrictions to encourage

---

150 See N.K. Dahl, 'Grey Market Imports: Stemming the Tide,' (1986) 65 *Oregon Law Review* 123 and R.D. Anderson, P.J. Hughes, S.D. Khosla, and M.F. Ronayne, 'Working Paper on Intellectual Property Rights and International Market Segmentation: Implications of the Exhaustion Principle,' (October 1990) Economics and International Affairs Branch, Bureau of Competition Policy.

151 For a detailed analysis, see R.D. Anderson, P.M. Feur, B.A. Rivard, and M.F. Ronayne, 'Intellectual Property Rights and International Market Segmentation in the North American Free Trade Area,' in Gallini and Anderson, eds., *Competition Policy and Intellectual Property Rights*, 397.

152 Gallini and Hollis, 'A Contractual Approach to the Grey Market.'

the exclusive distributor to invest substantially in specific assets,[153] such as goodwill. This goodwill includes developing a reputation for delivering a prescribed quality of products and services, advertising to cultivate brand awareness, providing pre-sale information and post-sale services (such as warranties), and is created by investing in marketing, customer service, quality control, and protection from counterfeits.[154] When a licensee must invest substantially in specific assets such as goodwill, an exclusive territory may be necessary to ensure that the licensee appropriates the entire return on this investment, or the threat of free-riding by or positive externality to a future licensee within the territory may deter the original licensee from undertaking the initial investment. Usually, because grey marketers need not incur the expense of specific investments, they are able to price above marginal cost but below the price set by the authorized distributor while at the same time enjoying the benefits of the goodwill developed by that distributor. Thus, grey marketers can frustrate the protection against free-riding that the manufacturer hopes to achieve through establishing exclusive territories.

Second, closed territorial restrictions may be needed to eliminate distortions among licensees in setting product quality, price, product service, and product differentiation that arise from competition among the licensees. For example, licensees choose among different mixes of instruments (such as price and product quality) to find those most effective for promoting product competition and for promoting competition among licensees selling the same product. These different strategies may distort downstream decision making. Territorial restrictions resolve such distortions by simply assigning the entire ownership of a market territory to each licensee.

Third, manufacturers may establish closed territorial restrictions in order to price discriminate. This motivation may be more important for field-of-use restrictions in licensing contracts, which restrict the field in which a licensee may use an innovation and typically give the licensee exclusive rights to that field in a given territory. In order to price discriminate, three conditions must exist: (i) the firm must possess some market power; (ii) the firm must be able to sort customers

153 This refers to investment in assets that have value only in connection with the use of a specific innovation.
154 Gallini and Hollis, 'A Contractual Approach to the Grey Market.'

according to different demand elasticities; and (iii) the firm must be able to prevent resale from one region to another. Therefore, if the two regions are established as separate fields and the three conditions are satisfied, a higher price can be charged in the region with the more inelastic demand and the overall profits from licensing are maximized. Typically, goods protected by IP legislation, such as trade-marked goods, give the firm some market power, and the price elasticity of demand generally varies across countries in relation to income per capita. Thus, the first two conditions for price discrimination are satisfied.[155] However, grey goods disrupt a manufacturer's price discrimination strategy, since the third condition of preventing resale from the low-price country to the high-price country will not be satisfied.

There are also horizontal incentives for closed territorial restrictions. The simplest horizontal incentive for exclusive territorial restrictions in a licensing contract is the 'sham' agreement used for dividing the market. A division of the market can also facilitate collusion on prices between manufacturers of differentiated products, because agreements to set prices are more easily monitored if licensees each sell in only one territory rather than compete across territories. Parallel imports create more competition and can attenuate the tacit collusion between manufacturers.[156] In the European Community, in which market integration is the paramount purpose of the *Treaty of Rome* (which governs the licensing of patent and know-how) closed territorial restrictions are prohibited.[157]

The ability of a patentee to segment international markets extends to the domestic market. For both international and domestic market segmentation, territorial restrictions used by major suppliers that have the effect of lessening competition are subject to a case-by-case review under section 77 of the *Competition Act*.[158] In international territorial

---

155 Ibid.
156 N.T. Gallini, 'An Economic Analysis of Grey Market Imports in Canada,' paper prepared for the Policy Directorate Bureau of Competition Policy, November 1992.
157 For a comprehensive review of competition treatment of IP in the European Community, in its member countries, and in other jurisdictions, see OECD, *Competition Policy and Intellectual Property;* and see Richard Whish, *Competition Law,* 3rd ed. (London: Butterworths, 1993), chap. 19.
158 For an offence, it must be shown that the firm is (a) a major supplier of the product and (b) competition has been lessened substantially. There have been no exclusive territory cases regarding intellectual property.

division, restrictions on a foreign licensee's territory of production/ sale are dealt with under both the *Competition Act* and intellectual property legislation such as the *Patent Act* and the *Trademark Act*. The *Patent Act* allows the patent holder to claim infringement against the parallel importation of goods embodying the IP, whereas the *Competition Act* is the vehicle by which territorial arrangements are challenged. There have been few cases on parallel importation of patented goods in Canada to test whether exclusive territories will be challenged, although cases on trade-marked goods abound.[159] Proponents of the free flow of grey goods argue that these goods should be encouraged so that Canadians can enjoy lower prices through increased intrabrand competition. On the other hand, the exclusion of grey goods is one method of preserving territorial segmentation, which may be anticompetitive. Opponents of grey goods argue that permitting parallel importation could frustrate the objectives of trademark protection, namely preventing consumer confusion and protecting a firm's goodwill. Furthermore, as discussed above, if the firm is unable to appropriate the full benefits of specific investment, it would not have the incentive make the investment in the first place. Although grey goods are typically of identical quality to the trademark owner's goods (therefore not creating consumer confusion or threatening the trade-mark owner's goodwill in providing a consistent quality), some of the return on the trademark owner's investment in creating goodwill has been appropriated by grey marketers. Hence, the incentive to continue to expend resources to provide that level of quality may be reduced. In the extreme case of free-riding, trade-mark owners may stop making specific investments at all. This recalls our earlier observation that without IPRs *ex ante* investments would not be undertaken.

In Canada, trade-mark owners have sought relief from grey goods through infringement actions against the grey marketer under the

---

159 Owners of trade-mark goods appear to have the same protection against 'grey goods' or parallel imports that bear a legitimate trade-mark but that have not been authorized for importation by the trade-mark owner in Canada. See, for example, *Remington Rand Ltd. v. Transworld Metal Co. Ltd.* (1960), 32 C.P.R. 99; *Mattel Canada Inc. v. GTS Acquisitions and Nintendo of America Inc.* (1989), 27 C.P.R. (3d) 358 (F.C.T.D.); *H.J. Heinz of Canada Ltd. v. Edan Food Sales* (1991), 35 C.P.R. (3d) 213 (F.C.T.D.). See also Anderson et al., 'Intellectual Property Rights and International Market Segmentation in the North American Free Trade Area,' 397.

Trademarks Act[160] and through the common law tort of 'passing off.'[161] Three potential actions are available: first, the foreign trade-mark owner can bring a case on behalf of the exclusive distributor under the *Trademarks Act*; second, the distributor can bring a case against another authorized distributor that has entered its exclusive territory under contract law if the contract specified exclusive rights to sell the product in a particular territory; third, the exclusive distributor can bring a case against the grey marketer under the common law tort of passing off.[162] While the *Competition Act* is clearly relevant to grey goods cases because of the effect of exclusivity contracts on intrabrand competition, there have been no cases on the application of the Act in grey goods cases.

(b) Exclusive Licensing
An exclusive licence is the assignment of exclusive rights to the use of an IPR to a single party for a specified period of time. The exclusive transfer of IP rights is not necessarily an offence under either intellectual property or competition law. For example, in the *Warner Music* case discussed above, a licensor's refusal to license was not found to be anticompetitive: the tribunal held that Warner's exclusive licence to Columbia House did not constitute a violation of the refusal to supply

160 Infringement actions brought under the *Trademarks Act* include *Remington Rand Ltd.*, *supra*, note 159; *Wilkinson Sword (Canada) Ltd. v. Juda* (1966), 51 C.P.R. 55 (Exch. Ct); *Ulay (Canada) Ltd. v. Calstock Traders Ltd. et al.* (1969), 59 C.P.R. 223 (Exch. Ct); *Breck's Sporting Goods v. Magder* (1975), 17 C.P.R. (2d) 201 (S.C.C.); *Mattel Canada Inc.*, *supra*, note 159; *H.J. Heinz of Canada Ltd.*, *supra*, note 159. See Gallini, 'An Economic Analysis of Grey Market Imports in Canada,' and P.A. Dubois, 'I.P. Rights v. Grey: Who Wins in Canada?,' (1992) 9 *C.I.P.R.* 244 for a detailed discussion of these cases. See also Joseph F. Caruso and Christopher Aide, 'Claiming Trademark Infringement as a Means to Stop Grey Marketing: *H.J. Heinz Co. of Canada Ltd. v. Edan Foods Sales Inc.*,' (1992) 5 *C.U.B.L.R.* 183.
161 Recent cases on passing off include *Seiko Time Canada Ltd. v. Consumers Distributing Co. Ltd.* (1984), 1 C.P.R. (3d) 1 (S.C.C.); *Commodore Business Machines v. 116772 Canada Inc.* (1983), C.S. (Que.) 1186; and *Sharp Electronics of Canada Ltd. v. Continental Electronic Info* (1989), 23 C.P.R. (3d) 330 (B.C.S.C.). See also George S. Takach, 'Case Comment: *Seiko Time Canada Ltd. v. Consumers Distributing Co. Ltd.*,' (1985) 63 *Can. Bar. Rev.* 645 and Howard P. Knopf, '*Seiko v. Consumers Distributing:* More Shades of Grey Marketing Law,' (1984) 1 *I.P.J.* 337 for a discussion of the *Seiko* case.
162 Gallini, 'An Economic Analysis of Grey Market Imports in Canada.'

provisions of the *Competition Act* (s. 75) because Warner's copyright rights gave it the prerogative to exclude other potential licensees. However, since the *Patent Act* prohibits the suppression of innovations, an exclusive licence will be viewed with suspicion if the licensee is a potential competitor of the licensor and does not work the invention. Such an arrangement might imply cartelization.

The principal vertical incentive for the preference of exclusive contracts over non-exclusive contracts is that exclusivity may be necessary to protect the returns on specific investment by the licensee against the 'hold-up' problem, wherein a second licensee, through a subsequent licensing contract, or the IPR holder itself, enters the market after the specific investment has been sunk by the original licensee. Unless the original licensee's return on its investment is protected by exclusivity, its incentive to invest is dampened or eliminated. The investment is distorted because of the nonappropriability, or positive externality, on the subsequent entrant's profits that an additional dollar of investment involves. The investment in a distribution system, advertising, and services to build loyalty to the brand name will be compromised if the licensee-investor who incurs the expense captures only a share of the benefits. Therefore, exclusive contracts can represent an efficient contractual guarantee against the hold-up problem. Where protection against hold-up accounts for exclusivity, efficiency is enhanced because without exclusivity the product might not be developed at all and, at the very least, the investment in product-specific assets such as a distribution system and product brand name would be reduced.

Exclusive licences may also arise as part of an inefficient horizontal scheme. In the simplest case, the licensor and the licensee compete in the same product market. The sale of an exclusive licence for a product that is a close substitute for the licensee's product may represent simply the sale of the rights to a monopoly in a product market. Duopolists can always strike a mutually profitable contract in which one sells to the other the exclusive rights to a market. This follows from the fact that monopoly profits exceed the sum of duopoly profits when products are close substitutes. Similarly, duopolists or oligopolists may assign exclusive licensing rights to exploit the market to a third party, with the result that the market is monopolized. Where the gains from transfer of exclusive rights to an IPR can be identified as the sale of the rights to monopolize a market, the restriction is inefficient.

(c) Exclusive Dealing

Under an exclusive dealing contract, the licensee is required not to engage in the use or sale of the technology or products of other licensors' work. The vertical incentives in exclusive dealing include ensuring that other manufacturers do not free-ride on the investment by a producer in its product. For example, exclusive agency may be efficient in the life insurance market or in the automobile market because without the restriction, customers attracted to an agent by the advertising of one seller may end up purchasing the product offered by another seller at the same agency. Any expenditure by the seller in improving the product offered by the licensee is subject to free-riding in the case of a common agent. Such free-riding, which would lead to underinvestment in the promotion of products, disappears when each agent represents only a single seller. A second vertical incentive for exclusive dealing is that it can encourage further development of relationship-specific technology by both the licensor and the licensee. The licensee is encouraged to invest in more specific capital because it is contractually constrained against exploiting general capital during the term of the contract. The licensor is motivated to invest more in specific capital, knowing that the absence of alternative suppliers to the licensee in the future reduces the licensee's threat of leaving the relationship, thereby reducing the likelihood that the return on the investment in specific capital will be held up. Thus, commitment by one party (the licensee) to a bilateral contract renders more secure the specific investment by the other party to the contract.

The horizontal incentive for inefficient exclusive dealing restrictions is contentious. The argument is that a producer (or licensor) with a monopoly in a product market can prevent entry by a competitor through the exclusive dealing restrictions placed on each buyer. One response to this argument is that a buyer (or licensee) will not accept a contractual restriction such as an exclusive dealing restriction unless the price of the transaction is reduced to compensate the buyer for the costs imposed by the restriction. It pays the buyer and the seller in any transaction to strike a contract that maximizes their combined net benefit.[163] However, a counter response to this argument is that such an analysis assumes that the benefits from exclusive contracting are internalized by the contractual parties when, in fact, two kinds of externali-

---

163 R. Bork, *The Antitrust Paradox: A Policy at War with Itself* (New York: Basic Books, 1978).

ties are involved.[164] First, a potential entrant into the market is harmed by an exclusive dealing restriction, since it reduces its likelihood of entry or reduces its profit if it does enter successfully, since the entrant will be forced to offer a lower price in order to induce buyers to drop the incumbent's product entirely. Second, and more importantly, in a market with many buyers, the decision by each buyer to enter into an exclusive dealing contract imposes a cost on other buyers by reducing the chance of successful entry by another firm, since the probability of successful entry by another firm increases with the number of buyers free from any exclusive dealing contracts with the incumbent. The result of these externalities is that a seller can bribe a buyer into entering an exclusive contract with only a small reduction in price. The total cost to the buyers' side of the market can be much larger than the total bribe that must be paid to buyers to accept the restriction. As a result, the choice of exclusivity can be inefficient. It should be noted that the necessary condition for this theory is that the licensor have a large share of the product market, or at least that it have a significant advantage over other differentiated licensors in the competition for a significant number of buyers.

The only Canadian exclusive dealing case involving IPRs is *NutraSweet*,[165] an abuse of dominance decision. The director applied to the tribunal for remedial orders on the grounds that NutraSweet was foreclosing the market from its principal competitor through rebates to customers for using the NutraSweet trade-marked logo, reinforced by most-favoured-customer and meet-or-release clauses in NutraSweet's agreements with its customers.[166] The tribunal concurred with the director in holding that NutraSweet was not 'entitled to any more protection against competition than it was able to obtain through patent grants that provided it with a considerable head start on potential competitors,'[167] and prohibited use of exclusivity, most-favoured-customer, and meet-or-release provisions, including logo rebates.

---

164 P. Aghion and P. Boulton, 'Contracts as a Barrier to Entry,' (1987) 77 *American Economic Review* 388.

165 *Supra,* note 100.

166 The director alleged that NutraSweet had engaged in several other practices, including customer meet-or-release and most-favoured-nation clauses.

167 This practice of removing a rebate from licensees who turn to other suppliers bears a resemblance to the practice of imposing a cost on licensees who used other suppliers contested in the Microsoft case.

E. *Multilateral Agreements: Pooling and Cross-Licensing*

Patent pools that do not enhance efficiency and have the effect of eliminating competition between members of the pool, or of fixing or restricting prices, will be treated like any other collusive agreement to eliminate competition.[168] The only Canadian case dealing with patent pools is *Philco Products*,[169] which dealt with an unsuccessful attempt by an alleged infringer to plead 'patent misuse' through conspiracy. As noted previously, this defence is rare in Canada because of the courts' view that even if patent misuse is found, the patent will not be revoked if it had been acquired legally prior to the anticompetitive offence.[170] In the United States, the 1995 IP guidelines take the view that while cross-licensing and pooling arrangements are not intrinsically anticompetitive, attendant restrictions may raise antitrust concerns. The guidelines caution against agreements with horizontal competitors, especially where they comprise exclusive pools involving a large proportion of market participants, involve joint coordination of substitute innovations,[171] or appear to suppress innovation,[172] unless there are offsetting efficiencies.[173]

---

168 The *Report of the Commissioner of Canada and International Cartels* had strong words for collusive arrangements involving IPRs: 'If the members of a patent pool have agreed to eliminate competition between themselves, as by restricting production or fixing prices, the agreement is in no basic way different from any other agreement to eliminate competition, and is punishable as such when against public interest' (Commissioner, *Combines Investigation Act*, 1945, 52). It is important to note that an agreement that rationalizes output with efficiency results would benefit from the exemption for specialization agreements under s. 86.

169 *Supra*, note 67.

170 See, for example, ibid., at 403–4. See section III.C for a discussion of the case law on allegations of anticompetitive abuses as a defence in infringement cases; see also Anderson, Khosla, and Ronayne, 'The Competition Policy Treatment of Intellectual Property Rights in Canada.'

171 See example 8 in the guidelines.

172 For example, in *United States v. Automobile Manufacturers Association*, 307 F. Suppl, 617 (C.D. Cal., 1969), modified *sub nom. United States v. Motor Vehicle Manufacturers Association*, 1982–83 *Trade Cases* (CCH) 65,088 (C.D. Cal., 1982), suppression of innovations was especially of concern since the agreement involved a large proportion of the market participants.

173 For example, a pooling arrangement that would be acceptable to the U.S. Department of Justice is an arrangement such as that in *Broadcast Music, Inc. v. Columbia Broadcasting System, Inc.*, 441 U.S.1 (1979), in which a blanket licence of copyrighted musical compositions reduced transaction costs.

F. *The Intellectual Property Enforcement Guidelines*

In September 2000 the Competition Bureau released its long-awaited *Intellectual Property Enforcement Guidelines* (the IPEGs).[174] The September 2000 release was preceded by two earlier drafts and public consultations.

The IPEGs explain the bureau's views on the interface between IPRs and competition law, as well as the analytical framework used by the bureau to assess conduct involving IP. According to the bureau, the IPEGs are, in part, at least, a response to an increasing number of requests made to it for information on the application of the *Competition Act* to IP. This section provides a brief overview and assessment of the IPEGs.

The approach introduced in the IPEGs is premised on the principle that the *Competition Act* generally applies to conduct involving IP in the same manner as it applies to conduct involving other forms of property. Under the bureau's analysis, the economic incentives underlying ownership are fundamentally the same for all types of private property. That is, individuals derive a benefit from property ownership through exchange, which can only be effective where owners are granted the right to control access to the property by excluding others from its use. At the same time, the bureau recognizes that IP has unique characteristics – in particular its intangible nature, which makes it difficult for owners to exercise rights over it – that have made it necessary to develop laws that confer rights in IP comparable to other kinds of private property.

Rejecting the classic 'monopoly – anti-monopoly' dichotomy, the bureau regards IP and competition laws as complementary instruments with a similar objective: the promotion of efficiency, innovation, and diffusion of technology. The role of IP laws is to ensure that innovators can, in fact, restrict access to their IP, which in turn protects the economic benefit to be derived from innovation. In other words, IP laws guarantee that the basic property rights of innovators will be recognized and respected. Competition law, on the other hand, intervenes in particular circumstances where those rights are exercised in such a way as to restrict the competition necessary to ensure the efficient allocation of resources.

---

174 (Ottawa: Competition Bureau, 2000).

The bureau summarizes its overall approach to the application of the *Competition Act* to IP as comprising the following basic principles:

- The circumstances in which the Bureau may apply the *Competition Act* to conduct involving IP or IP rights fall into two broad categories: those involving something more than the mere exercise of the IP right, and those involving the mere exercise of the IP right and nothing else. The Bureau will use the general provisions of the *Competition Act* to address the former circumstances and section 32 (special remedies) to address the latter.
- In either case, the Bureau does not presume that the conduct is itself anti-competitive, violates the general provisions of the *Competition Act* or should be remedied under section 32.
- The analytical framework the Bureau uses to determine the presence of anti-competitive effects stemming from the exercise of rights to other forms of property is sufficiently flexible to apply to conduct involving IP, even though IP has important characteristics that distinguish it from other forms of property.
- When conduct involving an IP right warrants a special remedy under section 32, the Bureau will act only in the very rare circumstances described in the Guidelines and when the conduct cannot be remedied by the relevant IP statute.[175]

Given the centrality of the dichotomy between section 32 of the *Competition Act* and its so-called general provisions to the bureau's enforcement approach, whether conduct constitutes the 'mere exercise' of an IPR becomes critical. In this regard, the IPEGs define the mere exercise of an IPR as 'the exercise of the owner's right to unilaterally exclude others from using the IP.' More particularly, the Bureau states expressly that '[t]he unilateral exercise of the IP right to exclude does not violate the general provisions of the *Competition Act* no matter to what degree competition is affected.' The bureau, therefore, will not use the *Competition Act*'s general provisions to compel compulsory licensing of IP.

The bureau's approach is a reasonable one. As it points out, '[a]pplying the *Competition Act* in this way may limit to whom and how the IP owner may license, transfer or sell the IP, but it does not challenge the fundamental right of the IP holder to do so.' In other words, an IP

---

175 IPEGs, at 1.

owner is free to use (or not use) IP without subjecting such conduct to scrutiny under the general provisions of the Act. According to this view, '[w]hen joint conduct of two or more firms lessens or prevents competition, the competitive harm clearly flows from something more than the mere exercise of the IP right to refuse.'[176]

As for section 32, the bureau acknowledges that it will rely on it only in 'very rare' circumstances, where all of the factors described in the IPEGs are present and the conduct in question cannot be remedied by the relevant IP statute. The bureau will seek a remedy under section 32 only if the alleged competitive harm (such as a refusal to license IP) adversely affects competition such that it would be considered substantial in a relevant market that is different or significantly larger than the subject of the IP. This first step is satisfied if the IP owner possesses dominance in the relevant market and the 'refusal to allow others to use the IP prevents other firms from effectively competing in the relevant market.' Second, a section 32 remedy would not be invoked if it would 'adversely alter the incentives to invest in research and development in the economy.' Even without such assurance, however, section 32 would likely prove of little practical concern to holders of IPRs. As noted earlier in the chapter, while the provision has been part of the *Competition Act*'s framework for decades, it has almost never been used. The IPEGs do not suggest a change in enforcement policy on the part of the bureau in this regard, although they do indicate that it could include industries that exhibit 'network effects' (i.e., industries in which the value or benefit derived from using a product increases with the number of users, as in the case of fax machines). In any event, it is the application of the general provisions of the Act to IPRs which is likely to be the focus of enforcement activity.

The bureau's methodological approach to applying the *Competition Act* consists of the following steps:

- identifying the transaction or conduct;
- defining the relevant market(s);
- determining if the firm(s) under scrutiny possess market power by examining the level of concentration and entry conditions in the relevant market(s), as well as other factors;

---

176 Ibid., at 8.

- determining if the transaction or conduct would unduly or substantially lessen or prevent competition in the relevant market(s); and
- considering, when appropriate, any relevant efficiency rationales.[177]

With respect to the types of conduct that might involve IP, the bureau notes that they include mergers, pooling of licences, setting standards for products, and exclusive dealing.

The IPEGs state that 'there may be instances in which restrictions on competition can lead to more efficient use of resources.'[178] While cognizant of the fact that the *Competition Act* contains a full statutory efficiency defence only for mergers, the bureau imports a similar defence into other provisions, in particular sections 77 (exclusive dealing, tied selling, and market restriction) and 79 (abuse of dominant position), on the basis that, as suggested by the Competition Tribunal in the *Tele-Direct* case, 'efficiency rationales and business justifications may be relevant to determining whether conduct is, on balance, anti-competitive.'[179]

The IPEGs indicate that the bureau intends to focus, in IP-related cases, on markets for: (i) intangible knowledge or know-how that constitutes the IP; (ii) processes that are based on the rights, and (iii) final or intermediate goods resulting from or incorporating the IP. In contrast to the U.S. guidelines, the bureau will not focus on 'innovation markets' (i.e., an approach whereby innovation in a product is defined as a relevant product distinct from the product itself). In addition, the bureau will not define the relevant market in terms of IP licences, but rather on the IP rights underlying such licences, so as to avoid a recurrence of the situation in the *Warner* case.[180] Finally, the IPEGs indicate that horizontal effects must be present before the bureau will consider a transaction or type of conduct to be anticompetitive. Essentially, there must be a substantial lessening of competition between horizontal competitors in order for the conduct or transaction to fall within the ambit of the *Competition Act's* general provisions.

The IPEGs reflect to a certain degree recent developments in the

---

177 IPEGs, at 6 (footnote excluded).
178 Ibid., at 13.
179 Ibid., at 14.
180 See section III.D.2 for a discussion of the *Warner* case.

United States, including the release of the *Antitrust Guidelines for the Licensing of Intellectual Property*[181] and the even more recent Microsoft litigation.[182] The IPEGs, however, are said to reflect a uniquely Canadian approach. In contrast to the U.S. guidelines, which focus exclusively on the licensing of IP, the draft IPEGs address a broader range of conduct and transactions, including mergers and refusals to deal involving IP.[183]

While the initiative of the bureau in drafting guidelines has generally been endorsed, response to early drafts of the IPEGs was mixed. The final IPEGs are widely regarded as a substantial improvement.

The bureau defines the mere exercise of an IP right as the exercise of the owner's right to unilaterally exclude others from using the IP. In earlier drafts of the guidelines, there were a number of troubling exceptions to this principle. For example, the bureau stated that 'a firm terminating its IP licenses with other firms that rely on the licensed IP as an essential input would be cause for concern under the general provisions of the *Competition Act* when the licensor led the licensees to believe that they would have an ongoing license for the IP and the termination of the licenses resulted in competitive harm.' Such use of the *Competition Act* was ill-conceived, since such a refusal, which exists in the context of a contractual relationship between licensor and licensees, is better resolved on the basis of the law of contract.

The bureau also indicated that 'if a firm acquires a controlling collection of IP rights' and then 'refuses to license the rights to others,' it would regard 'the acquisition and the refusal to licence' as anticompetitive and therefore susceptible to challenge under the general provisions of the *Competition Act*. The bureau has now recognized that it would be inconsistent with its definition of the mere exercise of an IP right to regard both the acquisition and the refusal as anticompetitive. Instead, if such an acquisition were to have an adverse effect on competition, the bureau would consider challenging only the acquisition of

---

181 U.S. Department of Justice and Federal Trade Commission, *Antitrust Guidelines for the Licensing of Intellectual Property* (Washington D.C., 1995). See also U.S. Department of Justice, Antitrust Division, *Antitrust Enforcement Guidelines for International Operations* (10 Nov. 1988).

182 Discussed at length in section III.D.1.

183 See Stikeman Elliott, *The Competitor* ('Competition Bureau releases revised IP enforcement guidelines'), June 2000.

rights pursuant to either section 92 (mergers) or section 79 (abuse of dominant position) of the *Competition Act.*

Finally, the bureau had indicated in earlier drafts that an IP licence could be anticompetitive if it reduces competition below the level that would have existed in the absence of the licence. The bureau now recognizes that a licence is only objectionable under the *Competition Act* if it lessens or prevents competition either unduly or substantially (depending on the precise provision under which the licence is objectionable) or is likely to do so.

Part 7 of the IPEGs sets out ten hypothetical situations involving conduct in relation to IP and how the bureau would apply the general provisions and section 32 of the *Competition Act* to such conduct. The hypotheticals address a wide variety of issues, including alleged infringement of IP rights, price fixing, exclusive licensing and exclusive contracts, output royalties, patent pools, refusal and termination of licences, and foreclosure of competitors' access to IP rights. While a detailed examination of these hypotheticals is beyond the scope of this chapter, they are generally consistent with the principles set out elsewhere in the IPEGs.

IV. Conclusions

Competition policy should be based not on whether licensing generates too much or too little reward for the innovator's research efforts, but rather on the efficiency merits of the practice. The basic exclusive rights provided by the patent grant should be respected at all points of the analysis, however.

It is important to recognize that intellectual property differs from other property in its public goods nature, which may imply a different application of competition law in some cases. For example, a price-fixing agreement between horizontal competitors may be close to *per se* illegal. In the case of IP licensing, while a price restriction between firms may dampen competition between the licensor and licensee, efficiency features of vertical restrictions (e.g., eliminating free-riding) may mean that the restriction is not as deleterious as it would be in strictly horizontal contracts. Moreover, the benefits of diffusion may be sufficient to offset the negative effects. Considerations of both diffusion and the allocative effects of a mixed, vertical-horizontal contract imply that competition policy should be more lenient towards restrictions between horizontal competitors where the agreements deal with IPRs.

That is, such considerations may alter the evaluation of a practice, for example, from near *per se* illegality (in the case of a horizontal arrangement among competitors) to a rule of reason standard if the transfer of the technology is deemed sufficiently important.

In many cases, the application of the law may be the same as in non-patent cases (for example, for purely vertical arrangements), but certain criteria characteristic of innovations (such as uncertainty and specific investments) may justify the use of restrictive practices. Therefore, while the law may be the same, the percentage of cases involving IP that receives more lenient treatment will likely exceed that for non-IP cases. The usual efficiency arguments for vertical restrictions in contracts on unpatented products apply to IP,[184] as do the arguments against vertical restrictions that foreclose firms with competing technologies from downstream markets (e.g., exclusive dealing) or that facilitate a cartel among competing patents.

Just as competition law should not attempt to take on the mandate of patent policy in encouraging innovation, patent law should not attempt to rule on anticompetitive practices. In many of the cases on patent misuse in the United States,[185] contractual provisions were found illegal although an analysis of neither market power nor of the effect on competition was undertaken.

The division of tasks discussed in this chapter – in particular, Approach 3 of the framework presented in section II – may seem reminiscent of the historical conflict between patent and competition policy. In fact, the division of tasks we propose differs in an important way. Based on the fact that the two policies (should) strive to strike the efficient balance between dynamic and allocative considerations, this framework recognizes that patent rights promote, rather than hinder, competition. Consequently, unlike the old approach, which under-

---

184 For example, see G.F. Mathewson and R.A. Winter, 'The Economics of Vertical Restraints in Distribution,' in G.F. Mathewson and J. Stiglitz, eds., *New Developments in the Analysis of Market Structure* (Cambridge, Mass.: MIT Press, 1986); and J. Tirole, *The Theory of Industrial Organization* (Cambridge, Mass.: MIT Press, 1990).

185 For example, in *Morton Salt, supra*, note 69, the court held that it was 'unnecessary to decide whether [the patent owner] has violated the Clayton Act.' In *B.I.C. Leisure v. Windsurfing Int'l Inc.*, 761 F. Supp. 1032 (1991), the court noted that while the misuse defence must show that competition in the relevant market is restrained, it also notes that 'less evidence of anticompetitive effect .than in antitrust cases' may be needed.

mined patent rights by placing constraints on contractual arrangements, this framework recommends that competition policy work with patent policy to provide adequate incentives for innovators to share their discoveries with others when this is efficient. In this sense, the division of tasks proposed here should not create tension between the two laws. Rather, it allocates complementary roles to patent and competition policy for striking the right balance between dynamic and allocative efficiencies.

TEN

Competition Policy and Trade Policy

I. Introduction[1]

The United States and Canada have had domestic competition laws for more than a century. For many other industrialized countries, and for the European Union, competition laws are a much more recent phenomenon (adopted largely after the Second World War). Almost half the members of the General Agreement on Tariffs and Trade / World Trade Organization (GATT/WTO), including many developing countries, have no competition laws at all and may, in many cases, lack the institutional capacity to implement and administer an effective domestic competition law regime.[2] Among member countries with such laws, there are significant substantive, institutional, and procedural differences.[3] These differences or divergences in domestic antitrust or com-

---

1 This chapter is derived from M. Trebilcock, 'Competition Policy and Trade Policy: Mediating the Interface,' (1996) 30 *Journal of World Trade* 71; 'Antidumping Laws,' and 'Competition Policy and Trade Policy,' in M. Trebilcock and R. Howse, *The Regulation of International Trade*, 2nd ed. (London and New York: Routledge, 1999); M. Trebilcock, 'Competition Policy, Trade Policy, and the Problem of Second-Best,' in R.S. Khemani and W.T. Stanbury, eds., *Competition Policy at the Centenary* (Halifax: Institute of Research on Public Policy, 1991).

2 See William Kovacic, 'Creating New Competition Policy Institutions in Transition Economies,' (1997) *Brooklyn Journal of International Law* 403.

3 See American Bar Association Antitrust Section, *Report of the Special Committee on International Antitrust* (1991); *Report of the OECD Committee on Competition Law and Policy*, 'Interim Report on Convergence of Competition Policies' (1994); Barry Hawk, *Antitrust and Market Access* (Paris: OECD, 1996); Alan Ballard and Kerrin Vautier, 'The Convergence of Competition Law within APEC,' in Rong-I Wu and Yun-Peng Chu,

petition regimes have led to increasing calls for harmonization or integration, much like the impetus for harmonizing domestic intellectual property regimes that led to the Uruguay Round Trade-Related Intellectual Property Rights (TRIPS) agreement.[4] Dr Sylvia Ostry argues in a recent book[5] that, as tariffs and other border measures have been eliminated or reduced, the new arena for international policy cooperation is moving beyond the border to domestic policies. The basic reason for this shift lies in changes in the extent and nature of the international linkages among countries, which have produced a new type of friction that she calls 'system friction.' Ostry argues that a globalizing world has a low tolerance for system divergence. In particular, different traditions of government involvement in domestic economies and different industrial organization traditions have rendered increasingly contentious public-private distinctions in international trade law where trade regimes have traditionally focused on governmentally induced impediments to trade but not private restrictions on competition (including foreign competition). This view often argues for broad international commitments to ensuring effective market access or contestability, whatever the source of existing constraints thereon.[6]

Tensions between the objectives and application of domestic competition laws and international trade policy have a long genesis. Competition laws were enacted in Canada and the United States late in the nineteenth century at the same time as governments in these countries were adopting high tariff policies (Senator Sherman in the United States and the Canadian Conservative Party under John A. Macdonald energetically championed both), attracting tenable claims of 'political fraud.'[7] Thus, for a good part of the twentieth century, competition

---

eds., *Business Markets and Government in the Asia Pacific* (London: Routledge, 1998); *Final Report of International Competition Policy Advisory Committee to U.S. Attorney General and Assistant Attorney General for Antitrust*, 28 February 2000 ('the ICPAC Report').

4 See symposium on international competition policy in (1999) 2 *J. of International Economic Law* 399.

5 *The Post-Cold War Trading System: Who's On First?* (Chicago: University of Chicago Press, 1997).

6 See Paul Crampton and Milos Barutiuski, 'Trade Distorting Private Restraints: A Practical Agenda for Future Action,' (1999) 6 *Southwestern Journal of Law and Trade in the Americas* 3.

7 See Trebilcock, 'Competition Policy, Trade Policy, and the Problem of Second Best,' chap. 4.

laws in these two countries were interpreted and applied in a deep 'second-best' world, where domestic competition was sought to be promoted in contexts where foreign competition was often severely restrained by self-imposed protectionist trade policies. It is noteworthy how many of the major Canadian monopoly, merger, and collusion cases that have been the subject of prosecution or special inquiry, have involved domestic industries protected from foreign competition by substantial tariffs or other barriers to trade. For example, in two well-known merger cases, *R. v. Canadian Breweries Ltd.*[8] and *R. v. B.C. Sugar Refinery Ltd.*[9] and three well-known conspiracy cases, *Atlantic Sugar Refineries Co. Ltd. v. A.-G. Canada,*[10] *Container Materials v. R.,*[11] and *R. v. Canadian General Electric Ltd.,*[12] the trial records reveal evidence of substantial tariff and non-tariff barriers to trade. It is also difficult to imagine how the alleged monopolies or conspiracies could have been sustained without significant impediments to foreign entry in *Eddy Match Co. Ltd. v. R.*[13] (wooden matches), *Howard Smith Paper Mills v. R.*[14] (fine paper), *R. v. Armco Canada Ltd.*[15] (metal piping), and *R. v. Anthes Business Forms Ltd.*[16] A systematic analysis of the contexts of all the major Canadian merger, monopoly and conspiracy cases to test the significance of artificial barriers to foreign or extra provincial competition would be a very instructive research exercise.

The history of competition law in Europe and Japan is much more recent and dates primarily from the early post–Second World War years. The United States, as the hegemonic power that played the central role in the reconstruction of the European and Japanese economies, was able to impose a competition law on Germany and Japan, for political as well as economic reasons. Dispersion of economic and political power was intended as a check against the resurgence of authoritarian states, bearing in mind the political ends sought to be promoted by the fascist states through international cartels in the inter-

---

8 (1960), 126 C.C.C. 133 (Ont. H.C).

9 (1960), 129 C.C.C. 7 (Man. Q.B.).

10 [1980] 2 S.C.R. 644.

11 [1942] S.C.R. 147.

12 (1976), 15 O.R. (2d) 360 (H.C.).

13 (1953), 20 C.P.R. 107 (Que. C.A.).

14 (1957), S.C.R. 403.

15 (1974), 6 O.R. (2d) 521 (H.C.); (1976), 13 O.R. (2d) 32 (C.A.).

16 (1976), 26 C.C.C. (2d) 349 (Ont. C.A.).

war years. With the emergence of the European Economic Community in the late 1950s, competition policy was seen as an integral element of the process of economic integration, designed to prevent private economic actors from perpetuating or recreating market division arrangements that the *Treaty of Rome* sought to dismantle on a state-to-state basis.[17] In assessing the relevance of the European experience with economic integration to other geo-political contexts, it is important to remember that the process was driven as much by political as economic considerations. It reflected the premise that substantially greater economic interdependence would promote a peace that had eluded Europe for most of the first half of the twentieth century, thus providing the inducement to member states to cede substantial political sovereignty to pan-European institutions with extensive law-making, enforcement, and adjudicative powers.

While the trade liberalization that has occurred in the post-war period under GATT and various regional trading arrangements, such as the European Union (EU), the Free Trade Agreement (FTA), and now the North American Free Trade Agreement (NAFTA), has mitigated somewhat the older tensions between competition policy and trade policy, many trade restrictions still remain. These now are less in the form of tariffs than quantitative restrictions, other non-tariff barriers to trade (NTBs), and the increasing utilization of trade remedy laws, in particular antidumping laws. Many countries adopted antidumping regimes for the first time during the 1980s and utilization rates worldwide grew dramatically during the 1990s, to the point that they have now become the protectionist remedy of choice.

While some have argued that completely unrestricted international trade largely obviates the need for domestic competition laws, there are reasons for reservations about this claim. In the traded goods sector, depreciated exchange rates and transportation costs may often attenuate the impact of import competition; in the non-traded goods sector, especially the service sector, which is an increasingly important element in many domestic economies, import competition will often not be an effective competitive threat, and restrictions on foreign investment (i.e., effective market presence rather than effective market

---

17 See the masterful historical survey by Eleanor Fox, 'Anti-Trust, Trade and the 21st Century -- Rounding the Circle,' the Handler Lecture, *The Record of the Association of the Bar of the City of New York* (June 1993).

access) may constitute major impediments to foreign competition. But even if it is accepted that an unqualifiedly liberal international trade policy is not a complete substitute for effective domestic competition law, the question remains to be resolved of what form effective domestic competition laws should take in a liberal international trade policy environment. Here the concern increasingly voiced is that while liberal international trade policies will remove *public* (state-imposed) impediments to foreign competition, such policies will leave unaddressed *private* restrictions on competition, including foreign competition, and indeed may increase reliance on such restrictions by uncompetitive domestic producers as a substitute for directly imposed state restrictions. In this respect, inadequately framed or enforced domestic competition laws are seen as an impediment to foreign competition and international trade and investment, to the extent that they permit private market restrictions that preclude effective market access or an effective market presence by foreign competitors. Thus, reflecting the converse of the tensions between competition policy and trade policy manifested a century ago, at the time of the initial enactment of competition laws in Canada and the United States, inadequate domestic competition laws are seen as an increasingly important non-tariff barrier to trade.

In this chapter we ask how protectionist trade policies constrain the efficacy of domestic competition policies, and conversely, how domestic competition policies (or their absence or ineffective or selective enforcement of them) may constrain the efficacy of a liberal international trade and investment order.[18] We review in section II, especially in a North American context, the major remaining constraints that trade policies impose on effective domestic competition policies, in particular the largely unreformed international and domestic trade remedy law regimes. In this section, we use the example of antidumping laws to demonstrate the inconsistencies that arise when a trade remedy that restricts foreign competition is applied in conjunction with a domestic competition policy that seeks to promote competition. In section III of this chapter, we reverse the perspective and ask what constraints divergent domestic competition policies impose on a lib-

---

18 For more detailed reviews of the range of situations where these concerns arise, see WTO *Annual Report* (1997), section IV; *Report* (1998) of WTO Working Group on the Interaction Between Trade and Competition Policy to the General Council.

eral international trading order, leading to impediments to effective international competition. Section III begins by providing a brief historical review of international efforts at reconciliation of competition and trade policy. We then review outstanding issues with respect to the interface between domestic competition policy and international trade policy and evaluate some of the institutional implications countries are likely to face in the future if progress is to be made in the international coordination of the relationship between competition policy and trade policy. Here we distinguish between two separate classes of problems that are sometimes elided but that raise rather different issues: (a) domestic competition policies that are explicitly or implicitly discriminatory as between domestic and foreign interests and (b) conflict of laws or jurisdictional overlaps that may arise even in the absence of discrimination.

II. Protectionist Trade Policies and Domestic Competition Policy

Among the trilogy of trade remedy regimes – countervailing duty, safeguard, and antidumping actions – antidumping actions are by far the remedy of choice. By the end of 1989, twenty-eight countries had adopted antidumping laws.[19] Nearly 1,200 actions were initiated between July 1980 and June 1988.[20] Four jurisdictions' actions accounted for 97.5 per cent of all actions brought: 30 per cent were brought by producers in the United States, 27 per cent were brought in Australia, 22 per cent were brought in Canada, and 19 per cent were brought in the European Union. The targets of these actions are more diverse. The European Union was the largest single target, defending 27 per cent of the actions, while Canada, the United States, and Australia in total were targeted in fewer than 14 per cent of the actions. The second most targeted group of countries were the newly industrialized

---

19 Sylvia Ostry, 'Antidumping: The Tip of the Iceberg,' in M.J. Trebilcock and R.C. York, eds., *Fair Exchange: Reforming Trade Remedy Laws* (Toronto: C.D. Howe Institute, 1990), 3 at 17.

20 GATT, *Basic Instruments and Selected Documents, Thirty-sixth through Forty-fourth Session* (Geneva: GATT, March 1981 – June 1989), Appendix Tables; Summary of Antidumping Actions and Countervailing Duty Actions; reported in A. Anderson and A. Rugman, 'Country Factor Bias in the Administration of Anti-Dumping and Countervailing Duty Cases,' in Trebilcock and York, *Fair Exchange*, at 152.

countries (NICs), representing 18 per cent of the defenders. The actions against the NICs were most often initiated by the United States and Australia, who, along with the European Union, also initiated 106 actions against Japan. The European Union's main targets were the socialist countries of Eastern Europe, who defended 15 per cent of the world's actions. Overall, Western industrialized countries accounted for 58 per cent of the targets and developing countries (other than NICs) only 9 per cent. Finally, of the actions initiated by the major users, the success rate ranged from 44 per cent for Australia to 71 per cent for the European Union. Recent GATT data suggest some important new trends, with Brazil and Mexico joining the list of major users of anti-dumping laws.[21]

A. *The GATT/WTO Provisions on Antidumping*

Article VI of the GATT contains general rules governing the application of antidumping and countervailing duties. The first paragraph of the article condemns export sales below normal value when they cause or threaten material injury to an established industry in the territory of the contracting party or materially retard the establishment of a domestic industry. In addition, the article describes the basis for determining when sales are below normal value: when the export price is less than 'the comparable price, in the ordinary course of trade, for the product when destined for consumption in the exporting country.'[22] When these criteria are satisfied, the importing country is entitled to levy an antidumping duty equal to the difference between the normal value and the export price. However, the wording of the article is vague in important respects, leading to inconsistent interpretations and applications of the provision. Moreover, two of the biggest users of antidumping duties – Canada and the United States – did not consider themselves bound by its terms because their domestic antidumping laws pre-dated the GATT and to the extent of any inconsistencies were arguably 'grandfathered' under the Protocol of Provisional Applica-

---

21 See Jorge Mirandes, Raul Torres, and Mario Ruiz, 'The International Use of Anti-dumping 1987–1997,' (1998) 32 *J. of World Trade* 5.

22 In the alternative, according to Article VI, the normal value can be based on either the highest comparable price for the like product for export to any third country in the course of trade or the cost of production of the product in the country of origin plus a reasonable addition for the selling cost and profit.

tion.[23] In the Kennedy, Tokyo, and Uruguay Rounds, detailed anti-dumping codes were negotiated.

Canada amended its *Customs Tariff* in 1904 to provide for antidumping duties and in so doing became the first country in the world to establish an antidumping regime. The current legislation is set out in the *Special Import Measures Act*, 1985 (the SIMA).[24] The first specific American antidumping statute, which is still in force, is known as the *Antidumping Act* of 1916.[25] Because of the onerous predatory intent requirement, there has never been either a successful prosecution or a civil judgment under this Act. This parallels experience under predatory pricing provisions in domestic antitrust laws where convictions or successful civil suits are rare. The U.S. Congress enacted the *Antidumping Act* of 1921[26] to provide complainants with a greater scope for relief than the 1916 Act. The current American legislation is embodied in Title VII of the *Tariff Act* of 1930.

In Canada and the United States, the institutional responsibilities for determining 'dumping' and 'material injury' are separated. 'Dumping' determinations are made by the deputy minister of national revenue (DMNR) in Canada[27] and by the International Trade Administration of the Department of Commerce (DC) in the United States. 'Material injury' determinations in Canada and the United States are made by the Canadian International Trade Tribunal (CITT) and by the U.S. International Trade Commission (the ITC), respectively.

B. *Economic Rationales for Antidumping Laws*

Dumping can be characterized as international price discrimination, as predatory pricing, or as intermittent dumping. These characterizations, if well-founded, each give rise to possible economic justifications for the existence of antidumping laws.

---

23 Both countries used the grandfather clause, contained in the Provisional Protocol of Application governing accessions of countries to membership of the GATT, to retain their own legislation with respect to these duties. For more details on this and other aspects of the development of the GATT antidumping regime, see J.F. Beseler and A.N. Williams, *Antidumping and Antisubsidy Law: The European Communities* (London: Sweet and Maxwell, 1986), 3.
24 R.S.C. 1985, c. S-15.
25 15 U.S.C. ss. 71–72 (1988).
26 19 U.S.C. s. 1673 *et seq.* (1988).
27 SIMA, ss. 38–41.

1. International Price Discrimination

According to Jacob Viner, Canada's first antidumping legislation was a response to the US Steel Corporation's practice of selling its exports at prices substantially below its domestic prices.[28] U.S. antidumping laws are also often characterized as a means of responding to international price discrimination.[29]

Traditional arguments for prohibiting domestic price discrimination are inconclusive. Among antitrust scholars, there is no consensus on whether domestic price discrimination should be prohibited. First, whether output will increase or decrease under price discrimination is an empirical question.[30] In a wide range of (perhaps most) circumstances, a monopolist is likely to maximize profits by price discriminating in a way that increases output over that obtaining with a single monopoly price – indeed, a perfectly discriminating monopolist will charge each consumer his or her reservation price and produce the competitive output (appropriating all consumer surplus in the process). However, perfect price discrimination is rarely feasible because it entails a monopolist acquiring information on every potential customer's elasticity of demand and preventing arbitrage between low-priced and high-priced consumers. Second, while the costs the monopolist incurs in acquiring and segregating its market may be wasteful, if the monopolist produces more output under price discrimination those costs may be outweighed by the benefits of the increased output. Third, since some monopolies are efficient, expenditures to secure such monopolies are not necessarily wasteful.

---

28 J. Viner, *Dumping: A Problem in International Trade* (Chicago: University of Chicago Press, 1933), 86.

29 A U.S. Congressional subcommittee remarked: '[Antidumping laws are] designed to free U.S. imports from unfair price discrimination practices [by foreign exporters].' S. Rep. No. 93D1298, 93rd Cong., 2d Sess. 179, cited in W. Caine, 'A Case for Repealing the Antidumping Provisions of the Tariff Act of 1930,' (1981) 13 *Law & Pol'y Int'l Bus.* 681 at 682.

30 Joan Robinson showed that the output effects of price discrimination depend on the shape of consumer demand curves. See *The Economics of Imperfect Competition* (London: Macmillan, 1933), 188–93. R. Schmalensee, in 'Output and Welfare Implications of Monopolistic Third-degree Price Discrimination,' (1981) 71 *Amer. Econ. Rev.* 242, and H. Varian, 'Price Discrimination and Social Welfare,' (1985) 75 *Amer. Econ. Rev.* 870, find that welfare effects also depend on the shape of consumer demand curves. Hence, generalizations about the output and welfare effects of price discrimination are impossible.

Even if one assumes the validity of the arguments for prohibiting domestic price discrimination (although they are often contested), the case for prohibiting dumping is not analogous. Domestic price discriminators and dumpers have different effects on the importing country. A seller only 'dumps' if it charges a lower price to the importing market customers than it charges to its home market customers.[31] Therefore, while domestic price discriminators create both a higher-priced market and a lower-priced market within the same country, dumpers create only a lower priced market in the country to which they are exporting.

The importing country benefits from low import prices. The consumers in the importing country enjoy more consumer surplus, since they receive more output at a lower price per unit. When the importing country imposes antidumping duties on low-priced imports, its consumers lose these benefits. By increasing the price of dumped goods to the exporter's supracompetitive home market price, antidumping duties impose supracompetitive prices on consumers in the importing market and force them to settle for an inefficiently low level of output. Those consumers who remain in the market pay higher prices and enjoy less consumer surplus, and some consumers are priced out of the market, generating a dead-weight social cost.

In addition, when dumping occurs, the higher-priced market is by definition located in the dumper's home country. The dumper's home country thus bears most of the dumper's costs of identifying and segregating its markets, and the social costs associated with the dumper's monopoly profits. The efficiency losses associated with domestic price discrimination, which drive the arguments for prohibiting price discrimination, are borne primarily by the dumper's home market. Hence, the arguments for prohibiting domestic price discrimination do not justify a corresponding prohibition against dumping; dumping gives the importing country the benefit of the price discriminator's low-priced market without the social costs of its high-priced market. Even if the importing country were concerned about the dumper's home market abuses through some altruistic motive, forcing domestic

---

31 It is not 'dumping' for the seller to charge lower prices in its home market than in its export market and this practice is not prohibited by current legislation. See Alan Deardorff, 'Economic Perspectives on Antidumping Law,' in J.H. Jackson and E.A. Vermulst, *Antidumping Law and Practice: A Comparative Study* (Ann Arbor: University of Michigan Press, 1989), at 26.

consumers to pay the dumper's home market monopoly price seems a wholly ineffective response.

Finally, while the potential reduction in output is an argument against price discrimination, and whether total world output will rise or fall under international price discrimination is an empirical question, in the case of dumping prices are by definition lower in the export market, so the output available to the importing country is unambiguously higher with dumping, rendering highly problematic the appropriateness of providing any remedy to producers in the latter country on this account. The losses to consumers will almost always outweigh any gain to producers who are thereby protected. This is borne out by the empirical evidence.[32]

However, recent 'revisionist' literature by WTO officials[33] attempts to provide a rationalization for antidumping laws by drawing on the persistent and pervasive influence of concepts of reciprocity in international trade relations. This literature argues that international price discrimination is symptomatic of asymmetric market access and economic distortions in exporters' home markets that antidumping duties should properly seek to redress. An illustrative case is the antidumping complaint brought in Canada by General Motors and Ford against Hyundai for allegedly selling cars in Canada in the mid-1980s at 36 per cent less than it sold them for in South Korea.[34] One might argue that it is unfair for domestic automobile manufacturers to have to face competition in the Canadian market from Korean imports when these manufacturers lack equivalent access to the Korean market. (The price differential presumably reflected some form of protection of the

---

32 See U.S. International Trade Commission, 'The Economic Effects of Antidumping and Countervailing Duty Orders and Suspension Agreements,' Investigation No. 332–344, June 1995 estimating that the removal of ADD and CVD orders in 1991 would have created a welfare gain of U.S. $1.59 billion in that year; Keith B. Anderson, 'Antidumping Laws in the United States: Use and Welfare Consequences,' (1993) 27 *J. of World Trade* 99, analysing eight antidumping measures and estimating the average consumer cost per dollar of increased profit to be US$8.00: Brink Lindsey, 'The U.S. Antidumpting Law – Rhetoric Versus Reality,' (2000) 34(1) *J. of World Trade* 1.

33 See Jorge Miranda, 'Should Antidumping Laws Be Dumped?' (1996) 28 *Law & Policy in International Business* 255; Clarisse Morgan, 'Competition Policy and Anti-Dumping: Is it Time for a Reality Check,' (1998) 30 *J. of World Trade* 61.

34 See *Cars Produced By or on Behalf of Hyundai Motor Co.*, Canadian Import Tribunal, 1987; Matthew Kronby, 'Kicking the Tires: Assessing the Hyundai Anti-Dumping Decision from a Consumer Welfare Perspective,' (1991) 18 *Canadian Business L.J.* 95.

South Korean market from import competition.) Moreover, to the extent that the imposition of antidumping duties might induce Hyundai to reduce its home market prices, this would remove the economic distortion in the allocation of resources reflected in overproduction for export markets and underproduction for the home market.

There are a number of responses to this line of argument: First, it is far from clear that the imposition of antidumping duties will, in fact, in many cases remove the distortion in the exporter's home market – the exporter will have to weigh the loss of sales (and profits) in export markets from the imposition of duties against the loss of profits entailed in abandoning supracompetitive pricing in the home market. Second, it is far from clear in most antidumping cases that the gravamen of domestic producers' concerns about dumped imports is denial of equivalent access to the exporter's home markets; hence this seems a curiously coincidental or indirect means of addressing market access problems in these markets. Third, to the extent that differences in prices between home and export markets are explained by export subsidies from the home country's government, these are properly not the domain of antidumping laws but of countervailing duty laws. Fourth, to the extent that the price differences between the two markets are explained by trade restrictions (e.g., tariffs or quotas) in the home country's market, their legality should be addressed directly. If the home country has high unbound or bound tariffs, it is entitled to maintain these under the GATT/WTO pending mutual negotiations to reduce them. If it is utilizing quotas, these may be objectionable under Article XI of the GATT (quantitative restrictions). If it has conferred a state-protected monopoly on the exporter, it is entitled to do so provided that it satisfies the non-discrimination conditions of Article XVII of the GATT (state trading enterprises). If it is a developing country and is seeking to protect and promote an infant industry, it is entitled to do so provided it meets the conditions of Article XVIII. If the home country's domestic competition laws are being applied to the exporter in a preferential way, this is likely to be challengeable under the national treatment principle (Article III). Fifth, operationalizing this focus on market access conditions in exporters' home markets in antidumping proceedings seems intractable. If a precondition to imposing antidumping duties is a judgment by competition authorities in importing countries that conditions in exporting countries' markets would violate importing countries' domestic competition laws, this would seem a clearly unacceptable extraterritorial application of an importing country's domestic laws. If, on the other hand, this judgment is remitted to competition authorities in exporting countries (many of which, however, do not have such authorities) under a theory of positive comity, their judgments will often be viewed as non-credible and self-serving in importing countries.[35]

In short, it is not and never has been a precondition to international trade that the domestic policy environment in exporting and importing countries be in all respects the same – an extreme version of level playing field or reciprocity concepts – subject to the important explicit constraints on discrimination embodied in the above articles of the GATT.

2. Predatory Pricing

Predatory pricing is the second characterization of dumping that gives rise to an economic rationale for antidumping laws. It consists of 'systematically pricing below cost with a view to intimidating and/or eliminating rivals in an effort to bring about a market price higher than would otherwise prevail.[36] U.S. antidumping laws were initially enacted out of a concern for predatory pricing by foreign competitors.[37] Canadian, U.S., and EU antidumping laws penalize predatory pricing in addition to international price discrimination by authorizing the constructed-cost method of calculating the normal value when there are insufficient home market sales to use as a reference point.

As we saw in Chapter 5, the conditions under which predatory pricing is likely to prove a profitable strategy are stringent, and convictions or civil liability for such conduct are quite rare. The gains from predatory pricing are even more uncertain in the international arena. For a predator to achieve a monopoly in its export market it must not only drive out domestic competitors from the export market but other foreign competitors as well. Foreign producers compete with each other just as vigorously as they compete with domestic competitors in their export markets.[38] Thus, the likelihood of one seller achieving a worldwide monopoly is slim, and vigorous competition among foreign com-

---

35 For proposals along these lines, see Bernard Hoekman and Petros Mavroidis, 'Dumping, Antidumping and Antitrust', (1996) 30 *J. of World Trade* 27.

36 Dunlop, McQueen, and Trebilcock 208; see more generally, Chapter 5

37 The original U.S. antidumping law, the *Antidumping Act* of 1916, 19 U.S.C. 1673, made evidence of predatory intent an element of the dumping offence.

38 Deardorff, 'Economic Perspectives on Antidumping Law,' at 36.

petitors implies a small likelihood, in most markets, of successful oligopoly formation.[39]

Although true international predatory pricing (predatory dumping) may be expected to occur infrequently, where it does occur it harms competition in the importing country. Indeed, predatory dumping is more harmful than wholly domestic predatory pricing because resulting monopoly profits are captured by the foreign exporter. On efficiency grounds, antidumping laws are justifiable insofar as they prevent predatory dumping. However, the current antidumping regimes of Canada, the United States, and the European Union penalize behaviour that may be neither predatory nor prohibited by antitrust legislation. Indeed, Hutton and Trebilcock conclude that of the thirty cases between 1984 and 1989 in which Canada imposed antidumping duties, none could be supported on predatory pricing grounds.[40] An unpublished study for the OECD of a much larger sample of cases reaches similar conclusions.[41] Currently, antidumping duties are imposed when 'fully-allocated costs' exceed export market prices. As argued in Chapter 5 on predatory pricing, below-total-cost pricing need not be predatory. Hence, antidumping laws penalize non-predatory conduct by foreigners that is not penalized when engaged in by domestic firms.

Moreover, even below-marginal-cost pricing by the exporter need not reflect an underlying predatory intention. When the exporter makes its production decisions, it estimates the price its output will eventually realize in the export market. As long as the estimated export market price exceeds its marginal cost, it will produce output for sale in the export market. If, owing for example to fluctuating exchange rates or changed market conditions, the actual export market price turns out to be lower than estimated, the exporter will have no choice but to sell its output at the best available price. This price may be lower than the *ex ante* marginal costs the exporter faced when it

---

39 For further support for this view, see J. Barcelo, 'Antidumping Laws as Barriers to Trade – The United States and the International Antidumping Code,' (1972) *Cornell L. Rev.* 491 at 501–3.

40 S. Hutton and M.J. Trebilcock, 'An Empirical Study of the Application of Canadian Antidumping Laws: A Search for Normative Rationales,' (1990) 24 *J. of World Trade* 123 at 128.

41 See 'Attack on Antidumping Law Sparks OECD Row,' *Financial Times*, 21 September 1995, 16, referring to a study by a team led by Robert Willig.

made its production decision. However, the exporter will continue to sell in the export market because the output has already been produced and it can recoup a portion of its sunk costs by selling its output.[42] Although the exporter is engaging in below-marginal-cost pricing, there is no predatory intention. The exporter is doing what it can to minimize its losses in the face of its inaccurate *ex ante* estimate of the market price. Hutton and Trebilcock find that frustrated *ex ante* market price estimates accounted for below-marginal-cost pricing in four antidumping actions initiated in Canada against U.S. exporters.[43]

Finally, in some cases below-marginal-cost pricing may actually promote competition. Depending on the product, sellers may engage in below-marginal-cost pricing to compete for market share. Deardorff[44] identifies two product characteristics, 'experience' and 'learning by doing,' that make below-marginal-cost pricing likely for some goods. Consumers may pay more for 'experience' goods after their first and subsequent purchases than before their first purchase: the quality of 'experience' goods is only discernible after their first use. To induce consumers to sample their goods for the first time, as a marketing strategy, sellers may initially price their goods below their marginal cost. Sellers will recoup their initial losses once consumers pay more for the goods on their subsequent purchases. Sellers produce 'learning by doing' goods when they experiment with new technology or new products. When they first enter the market with new goods, sellers may be inefficient and suffer losses. At this point, marginal costs may exceed the sale price. Sellers gradually reduce their costs as they 'learn' more about efficient production methods. In the meantime, they gain a valuable toehold in the market.[45]

---

42 For a mathematical proof of this result see S.W. Davies and A.J. McGuiness, 'Dumping at Less than Marginal Cost,' (1982) 12 *J. Int'l Econ.* 169 at 171–6; see also P. Nicolaides, 'The Competition Effects of Dumping,' (1990) 24 *J. of World Trade* 115 at 119, 120.

43 Antidumping duties were imposed in each case. Hutton and Trebilcock, 'Empirical Study of the Application of Canadian Antidumping Laws,' 128.

44 Deardorff, 'Economic Perspectives on Antidumping Law.'

45 It may be objected that dumped goods cannot be characterized as 'learning by doing' goods because any technological learning would have the same effect on both the home market and the export market. However, if home market sales were 'insufficient' within the meaning of antidumping legislation, antidumping investigations would examine only the 'fully-allocated costs' of the exporter. If those costs exceeded the export market price, there would be a positive finding of dumping even if the exporter were merely pricing below cost (in both markets) to gain technological know-how.

Below-marginal-cost pricing for 'experience' or 'learning by doing' goods is typical for sellers expanding into new markets and cannot be viewed as predatory. In fact, it increases consumer demand, competition, and productive efficiency, and sellers can recoup their costs without acquiring significant market power. Many sellers, regardless of their degree of market power, may increase their market share by selective below-marginal-cost pricing. These legitimate roles for below-marginal-cost pricing suggest that antidumping laws should not categorically penalize below-marginal-cost pricing. Significantly, domestic antitrust laws do not prohibit these kinds of activities in the case of domestic firms.[46]

Again, the recent 'revisionist' literature that seeks to provide an economic rationalization for antidumping laws contests this analysis of the constructed cost aspect of antidumping laws as inconsistent with notions of predation.[47] It is argued that European Commission decisions in domestic predation cases under EU competition laws have rejected pricing above average variable cost as presumptively non-predatory and have in fact adopted an average total cost test, which is close to the constructed cost test employed in antidumping law. It is also argued that U.S. courts have adopted divergent cost tests in domestic predation cases under U.S. antitrust law, some of which are consistent with the constructed cost test. It is then argued that pricing below average total cost is irrational unless a firm plans to exit a market or is doing so only on a temporary basis (e.g., because of depressed demand), or is engaged in predatory behaviour towards its rivals.

Several responses are in order. First, while it is true that courts have taken different positions on appropriate cost tests in domestic predation cases, they all nevertheless require proof of some kind that the alleged predator's behaviour is in fact predatory – that is to say that the intent or effect of its behaviour is likely to entrench or reinforce a dominant market position, permitting it then to behave monopolistically. The constructed cost inquiry in antidumping cases never views as relevant any of the evidence that in domestic predation cases might

---

46 In the United States, the legality of aggressive pricing policies to increase market share has been upheld: *Telex Corp. v. IBM*, 510 F. 2d 894 (10th Cir. 1975), cert. dismissed, 423 U.S. 802 (1975); *Berkey Photo v. Eastman Kodak Co.*, 603 F.2d 263 (2d Cir., 1979). Canadian courts have also recognized the legitimacy of promotional sales: *R. v. Hoffman-La Roche Ltd.* (1981), 28 O.R. (2d) 164 at 196 (C.A.).

47 See Morgan, 'Competition Policy and Anti-Dumping.'

be viewed as demonstrating predatory (monopolizing) intent or effect. For example, is it seriously arguable that Hyundai was using supra-competitive profits garnered in its protected South Korean market to finance below-cost exports to the North American market with a view to predating (monopolizing) the latter market? Thus, the argument that the constructed cost test is a close surrogate for predation tests in domestic competition or antitrust cases is wholly unpersuasive. It bears repeating that in the OECD and Canadian empirical studies of antidumping cases referred to above, few or no cases were found that satisfied conventional economic conceptions of predation. Second, even acknowledging room for debate about the appropriate tests to be applied under competition or antitrust law in domestic predation cases, surely the national treatment principle requires that whatever tests are applied to domestic producers should also be applied to foreign producers. Manifestly, antidumping laws violate this precept by according domestic producers much greater pricing latitude than that accorded to foreign producers. Domestic firms are rarely found guilty of predation under domestic antitrust or competition law regimes; foreign firms are frequently found guilty of dumping, suggesting the extent of the discrepancy between the two regimes.

More transparently baseless economic rationalizations for anti-dumping laws are also advanced in this literature.[48] One is that export-ers facing recessions in their home markets may export these recessions to export markets by below full-cost pricing and thus anti-dumping duties are a useful anticyclical policy. Given that it is at the same time claimed that antidumping duties often affect only about 1 per cent of imports (let alone GNP), it is difficult to think of a more futile anticyclical policy. It is also argued that where importing coun-tries devalue their currency for balance of payment reasons, this objec-tive may be defeated by exporters into their markets adjusting their export prices downwards (below home market prices) to offset the effect of the devaluation and thus to retain market share. Again, given the very small percentage of imports said to be affected by antidump-ing duties and the large and complex set of forces that determine exchange rates, it is difficult to believe that such a strategy could have any discernible impact on the balance of payments. Moreover, domes-tic producers who use imported inputs may be required to adopt the

---

48 See Miranda 'Should Antidumping Laws Be Dumped?'.

same strategy in order to remain competitive, yet would not be penalized on that account.

3. Intermittent Dumping

The final characterization of dumping that gives rise to an economic rationale for antidumping laws is intermittent dumping. Jacob Viner defined intermittent dumping as systematic dumping that lasts for several months or years at a time.[49] Viner viewed this form of dumping as objectionable because it lasts long enough to injure domestic producers without providing consumers with a constant long-run supply of goods.[50] A situation in which intermittent dumping might occur is in the context of the oversupply of perishables. Agricultural producers often make planting decisions long before selling their produce. Because of the cyclical nature of supply in agricultural markets, producers often find they have excess produce and rather than allowing it to rot they sell at low prices. For these agricultural producers, the relevant cost at the time of selling is the cost of packaging and marketing. Hutton and Trebilcock[51] find that the only Canadian antidumping cases that exhibited any indication of intermittent dumping were agricultural cases. They argue that the case of perishables is not a dumping problem and that agricultural price instability should be addressed, if at all, through income stabilization programs rather than antidumping laws.[52]

Non-predatory intermittent dumping cannot occur unless certain structural conditions are present.[53] First, exporters must be unable to compete with domestic producers under normal market conditions. Otherwise, exporters would provide a permanent source of supply instead of an intermittent one. Second, intermittent dumping must be so extensive that it substantially disrupts domestic production. The losses incurred by selling below-cost products into export markets

---

49 Viner, *Dumping*, at 30–1.
50 For a fuller discussion of intermittent dumping see F. Lazar, 'Antidumping Rules Following the Canada-U.S. Free Trade Agreement,' (1989) 23 *J. of World Trade* 45.
51 Four of the thirty cases studied exhibited indications of intermittent dumping: Hutton and Trebilcock, 'Empirical Study of the Application of Canadian Antidumping Laws,' at 61.
52 Ibid.
53 See M. Trebilcock and J. Quinn, 'The Canadian Antidumping Act,' (1979) 2 *Canada-U.S. L.J.* 101 at 108–11.

makes it unlikely that the dumping will last long enough to disrupt domestic production. As well, disruption will only occur if domestic purchasers substitute foreign goods for domestic goods. By substituting foreign goods for domestic goods during the intermittent dumping period, domestic purchasers will disrupt domestic production. As a result, when the intermittent dumping period is over, domestic producers will charge higher prices than before to recoup their post-intermittent-dumping readjustment costs. Domestic purchasers can avoid the higher price by not substituting away from domestic goods in the first place, although collective action problems may inhibit this response.

The conditions necessary for non-predatory intermittent dumping to occur are unlikely to arise. Moreover, the effect of non-predatory intermittent dumping on welfare is ambiguous. When foreign exporters dump, domestic producers in the export market must adjust to meet lower import prices. Some domestic producers may be forced out of the market and if the dumping is only temporary, domestic producers will then have to readjust to fill the vacuum left by the departing dumper. The adjustment and readjustment costs incurred by domestic producers unquestionably harm *producer* welfare.[54] Corporate resources that would go to skills training, expansion, or research and development are diverted to maintaining the producer's market share in the more competitive market. Losses incurred during the dumping period may force some producers into bankruptcy. Since domestic capital markets may be imperfect, the producers forced into bankruptcy may not be the least efficient.[55]

Adjustment and readjustment costs associated with intermittent dumping may also be passed on to consumers. Intermittent dumping harms consumers if they end up paying a higher long-run average price for goods than they would pay if there were no dumping. If intermittent dumping occurs with sufficient frequency that the domestic

---

54 Ibid.

55 Several studies have shown that the cost of capital in markets with strong import competition and demand fluctuation exceeds its cost in markets with constant demand and weak import competition: see W. Wares, *The Theory of Dumping and American Commercial Policy* (Lexington, Mass: Lexington, 1977), 67D73; Agnar Sandmo, 'On the Theory of the Competitive Firm under Price Uncertainty,' (1971) 61 *Amer. Econ. Rev.* 65; and Albert Zucker, 'On the Desirability of Price Instability: An Extension of the Discussion,' (1965) 33 *Econometrica* 437.

producer's cost of capital is higher over the long run (reflecting higher risk) than it would be in the absence of intermittent dumping, this cost will be passed on to consumers. However, the dumping margin may so depress prices during the period of dumping that, notwithstanding the producers' increased cost of capital, the consumer ends up paying lower long-run average prices. The net effect of intermittent dumping on consumer welfare is thus uncertain.

Given both the uncertain effect of intermittent dumping on consumer welfare and the low probability of the structural conditions for intermittent dumping being satisfied, it is questionable whether antidumping laws should seek to prevent intermittent dumping. In any event, the present antidumping laws of Canada and the United States are ill-adapted to addressing problems of intermittent dumping. Antidumping investigations assess dumping margins and material injury without regard to whether the dumping is temporary or permanent. This conclusion is borne out by Hutton and Trebilcock's finding that the *possibility* of intermittent dumping concerns was present in only four of the thirty Canadian cases they examined in which antidumping duties were imposed.[56]

(a) Reforming Antidumping Laws

While current antidumping regimes might seek to prevent international price discrimination, international predatory pricing, and intermittent dumping, only predatory pricing gives rise to a legitimate economic rationale for prohibiting dumping: when dumping is merely international price discrimination, the importing country market benefits. Intermittent dumping can be expected to occur only rarely and its net welfare effects are ambiguous.[57] Yet antidumping laws are ill-designed to identify and penalize true international predatory pricing. Instead, they result in duties being levied upon goods priced at non-predatory levels, thereby imposing costs on consumers in importing countries through supracompetitive prices and subjecting foreign firms to burdens that domestic competitors do not bear. At present, the only avenue in Canada for weighing the effect on consumer welfare of

56 Hutton and Trebilcock, 'Empirical Study of the Application of Canadian Antidumping Laws,' 130.
57 See Nicolaides, 'Competition Effects of Dumping,' B.M. Hoekman and M.P. Leidy, 'Dumping, Antidumping and Emergency Protection,' (1989) 23 *J. of World Trade* 27.

antidumping duties is a 'public interest' hearing by the CITT under section 45 of the *Special Import Measures Act*, which since 1984 has vested in the CITT discretion to hold a 'public interest' hearing following findings of dumping by the Department of National Revenue and material injury by the CITT and recommending to the minister of finance elimination or reduction of the duties otherwise payable. While section 45 has been sparingly invoked, in a recent case (1998) involving prepared baby food,[58] the Department of National Revenue found margins of dumping of 60 per cent of normal value by the sole importer into Canada (Gerber, a U.S.-based manufacturer) and the CITT found material injury to the sole Canadian producer (Heinz, a U.S.-based company with a plant in Canada) in the form of price erosion and suppression and loss of market share and reduced profitability. Following these determinations (which led Gerber to exit from the Canadian market) and the public controversy that they provoked, the CITT held a public interest hearing in which the commissioner of competition and various other parties intervened, and recommended to the minister of finance the reduction of duties by approximately two-thirds, reflecting concerns over the impact of price increases on low-income families, lack of consumer choice, security of supply, rates of innovation, and quality of service with only one supplier to the Canadian market. These recommendations were accepted by the minister of finance. The duty reduction would be implemented through setting specific indexed minimum domestic resale prices for each category of prepared baby food imported from the United States, with penalties imposed in the event that import prices fall below these minima – a form of detailed regulation of imports.

However, the discretionary and exceptional nature of this form of relief from antidumping duties is a highly inadequate response to the fundamentally protectionist and anticompetitive character of most antidumping actions. We favour instead much more radical reforms. In our view, antidumping laws should be replaced by either supranational or harmonized domestic antitrust regimes that penalize international predatory pricing without penalizing non-predatory international price

---

58 'Report to the Minister of Finance: Public Interest Investigation into Certain Prepared Baby Food Originating in or Exported from the United States of America,' *Report of the Canadian International Trade Tribunal*, 30 November 1998; see also Inquiry No. NQ-97-002, statement of reasons, 14 May 1998 (CITT).

discrimination. Price discrimination laws should play no role in regulating cross-border trade. Among member states of the European Union, this solution has largely been adopted. Antidumping duties with respect to intermember trade have been abolished and replaced with Union competition laws that bind member states and their citizens. However, EU competition laws constrain not only predatory pricing but also price discrimination, including cross-border price discrimination.[59] The European model is thus more expansive than our analysis suggests is warranted.

The more modest goal of harmonizing domestic antitrust laws, ideally under the aegis of the WTO, with respect to international predatory pricing seems a more appropriate goal. In this respect, the 1988 Protocol between Australia and New Zealand, pursuant to the Australian–New Zealand Closer Economic Relations Trade Agreement (ANZCERTA) is much more apposite. Both countries agreed that as of July 1990, all antidumping actions between the two should cease and that any antidumping duties then in place should be terminated. Harmonized provisions have been substituted in both countries' competition law pertaining to abuse of dominant position. These provisions permit a complainant located in one country to complain of abusive behaviour by a firm or firms located in the other country. The courts in the first country are then authorized to hold hearings in the second country and to use the second country's courts to enforce subpoenas and other orders. The provisions on abuse of dominant position clearly focus on cross-border predatory pricing rather than cross-border price discrimination. Warner has proposed a similar harmonized antitrust regime for bilateral Canada-U.S. trade.[60] In principle, such a regime could also be implemented multilaterally, through a GATT cross-border predatory pricing code that would require signatories to harmonize their domestic antitrust laws in line with the code, in much the same way that, at present, domestic antidumping laws must conform with the GATT/WTO antidumping agreement or that domestic intellectual property regimes must conform to the WTO TRIPS agreement. A variant on this approach would be to preserve antidumping regimes at a formal level

---

59 See *United Brands v. E.C. Commission*, [1978] E.C.R. 207, 1 C.M.L.R. 429 (C. Ct. of Justice).

60 Presley Warner, 'The Canada-U.S. Free Trade Agreement: The Case for Replacing Antidumping with Antitrust,' (1992) 23 *Law and Policy in International Business* 791.

but seek to agree on harmonization requirements that would incorporate predation concepts explicitly into these regimes (including tests for predation or abuse of dominant position in export markets; definition of relevant (not 'like') product (and geographic) markets; and protection of competition, not competitors). The initial U.S. *Antidumping Act* of 1916 in part exemplifies this approach. This would, in effect, turn antidumping actions into private actions for cross-border predation, with duties rather than damages as the available remedy. In moving in this direction, one of the major forms of the 'New Protectionism' would be radically constrained, while legitimate concerns about domestic impacts of surges in low-priced imports, whether dumped or not, would be dealt with through a well-conceived multilateral safeguards regime[61] and domestic adjustment assistance programs.[62]

We have used antidumping laws as an illustration of the tensions between the objectives and application of domestic competition laws and protectionist international trade policies; in particular we have used them as an example of 'unfair trade' laws to demonstrate the constraints that a protectionist trade policy can impose on the efficacy of domestic competition laws. In the next section, we reverse the perspective and ask how domestic competition policies (or their absence or the ineffective or selective enforcement of them) may inefficiently constrain international trade and investment.

III. Divergent Domestic Competition Polices and Liberal Trade Policies

It is now widely argued that as firms attempt to improve or maintain their competitive position in an increasingly more open economic environment, they may take actions aimed at effectively freezing competing imports or foreign investors out of their domestic market. A dominant firm or a colluding group may engage in predatory behaviour to fend off the efforts of a foreign rival attempting to gain access to its market. Some forms of price discrimination, such as loyalty bonuses, rebates and discounts accorded to local purchasers may deter them from dealing with foreign firms. A group of firms may engage in horizontal

---

61 See Hoekman and Leidy, 'Dumping, Antidumping and Emergency Protection.'
62 See more generally, Thomas Boddez and Michael Trebilcock, *Unfinished Business: Reforming Trade Remedy Laws in North America* (Toronto: C.D. Howe Institute, 1993).

exclusionary behaviour by collectively practising predatory pricing or by collectively boycotting distributors or suppliers who deal with foreign firms seeking to gain access. Import cartels may seek to exercise monopsony power against foreign suppliers. The operation of trade associations may also be anticompetitive if they provide a forum to organize industry cartels with exclusionary effects on foreign competitors, or if they are used to discriminate against foreign-controlled domestic companies by limiting their rights to participate in association activities, including access to product or service certification regimes, thus impairing their competitiveness. Vertical restraints may also be a vehicle to impede market access and presence. If incumbent manufacturers have tied up all distributors or retailers through exclusive dealing arrangements or through full vertical integration, a foreign entrant will have to overcome barriers created by the larger amount of capital required and the risks entailed in setting up its own distribution network. Alternatively, a producer that controls all distribution outlets may charge foreign rivals a higher price for access to the market, thus limiting their competitiveness. Global rationalization through mergers and acquisitions can promote monopoly, oligopoly, or oligopsony in domestic markets. Strategic alliances, which are becoming increasingly common in high technology sectors where R&D costs are often substantial, may be efficiency enhancing but they may also provide a vehicle to segment markets or to achieve a dominant position.[63] State-owned or protected monopolies may foreclose competitive foreign entry and distort competitive conditions in upstream or downstream competitive markets in which these domestic entities are also active. Firms given protected home market positions may be able to use their supracompetitive profits to engage in 'strategic' (predatory) dumping in export markets. Alternatively, monopolies or mergers leading to dominant positions may be permitted by domestic antitrust authorities if most of their output is sold in foreign markets where rents can be realized by supracompetitive prices at the expense of reductions in foreign consumer welfare. Similarly, export cartels or domestic cartels that sell most of their output in foreign markets may be tolerated.

---

63 See Americo Zampetti and Pierre Sauvé, 'New Dimensions of Market Access: An Overview,' in OECD, *New Dimensions of Market Access in a Globalizing World Economy* (Paris: OECD, 1995), at 19–20; see also Eleanor Fox and Janusz Ordover, 'The Harmonization of Competition and Trade Law,' (1995) 19 *World Competition* 5.

A. Past Efforts at International Coordination of Domestic Competition Policies

As noted in the introduction to this chapter, it is often argued that globalization yields a lower tolerance for divergent domestic competition polices. This has led to initiatives for the international coordination of domestic competition policies. This section provides a brief historical review of efforts at international co-ordination of domestic competition policies.

1. Multilateral Fora

In the 1940s the precursor to the GATT – the Havana Charter and the International Trade Organization (ITO) that it contemplated – envisaged multilateral regulation and review of restrictive business practices (Chapter 5). These provisions would have obliged the members of the proposed ITO to take appropriate measures to prevent private commercial enterprises that had effective control of trade from restraining competition, limiting access to markets, or fostering monopolistic control in international trade. Member nations would have been entitled to complain about prohibited restraints to the ITO. The ITO would have been authorized to investigate and to demand information in the course of its investigation, and to recommend remedial action to the governments of member nations. Upon finding a complaint valid, the ITO would have been required to publish its findings and request full reports from the offending member state about the progress of its remedial measures. However, the Charter could not withstand opposition in the U.S. Congress motivated by concerns over international incursions into U.S. domestic political sovereignty.[64]

In 1953 the United States, Canada, and others, through the Economic and Social Council of the United Nations, prepared a draft agreement envisaging the formation of an international coordinating agency that would receive, investigate, and recommend remedial action relating to complaints about restrictive business practices in

---

64 See Olivier Long, *Law and Its Limits in the GATT Multilateral Trade System* (London: Graham and Trotman-Martinus Nijohff, 1987), at 1–2; Kenneth Dam, *The GATT* (Chicago: University of Chicago Press, 1970), chap. 2; Frank Stone, *Canada, GATT, and the International Trade System* (Montreal: Institute for Research on Public Policy, 1987), at 52–3; and John Jackson, *The World Trading System* (Cambridge, Mass.: MIT Press, 1989), chap. 2; Eleanor Fox, *Competition Law and the Next Agenda for the WTO*, in OECD, *New Dimensions of Market Access*, at 169.

international trade. Five years later, at the instance of Norway, the GATT struck a committee to study the extent to which, and how, the GATT should undertake to deal with such practices. These early attempts to reach international agreements yielded no practical results: differences in national policies at the time were too great to permit more than general recommendations.[65]

In 1980 the United States Conference on Trade and Development (UNCTAD) adopted a Code on Restrictive Business Practices.[66] However, the code takes the form of recommendations that lack binding legal force, and it has had negligible impact. Similarly, the U.N. Commission on Transnational Corporations has encountered severe difficulties in attracting legal endorsement by industrialized countries of a proposed code of conduct for transnational corporations, which would include provisions on restrictive business practices similar to those contained in the UNCTAD Code.[67] In both cases, developing countries promoted provisions designed to control and regulate the conduct of transnational enterprises that were widely perceived in less-developed countries as abusive and rapacious, while developed countries sought to apply competition principles to state-owned as well as private enterprises. These differences in perspective resulted in often vague and largely exhortatory provisions.[68] The OECD Agreement on Restrictive Practices Affecting International Trade of 1986 (which has a lineage dating back to more modest OECD initiatives beginning in 1959) is endorsed by all OECD Members but imposes only modest obligations, that is, member states commit themselves to notifying other member states where enforcement action is contemplated that may affect important interests of the latter and to providing an opportunity for consultations.[69] Conciliation provisions, including use of the good

---

65 See George N. Addy, 'International Co-ordination of Competition Policies,' in E. Kantzenbach, H. Scharrer, and L. Waverman, eds., *Competition Policy in an Interdependent World Economy* (Baden-Baden: Nomos Verlagsgesellschaft, 1993), at 292.

66 *The Set of Multilaterally Agreed Principles and Rules for the Control of Restrictive Business Practices*, 5 December 1980, UNCTAD Doc. TD/RBP/Conf. 10/Rev. 1.

67 See P. Ebow Bondzai Simpson, *Legal Relationships between Transnational Corporations and Host States* (New York: Quorum Books, 1990), chap. 5.

68 Fox, in OECD, *New Dimensions of market Access*, at 170.

69 See Edward Glynn, 'International Agreements to Allocate Jurisdiction Over Mergers,' in Barry Hawk, ed., *International Mergers and Joint Ventures* (New York: Fordham Corporate Law Institute, 1991), at 38–43; Addy, 'International Co-ordination of Competition Policies,' at 292–4.

offices of the OECD Committee on Competition Law and Policy, in the event of members being unable to resolve conflicts, have rarely – if ever – been invoked.

An important recent development has been the incorporation of competition-related provisions in various GATT/WTO Agreements.[70] These provisions include:

- The Agreement on Technical Barriers to Trade contains detailed rules regulating the adoption of technical regulations and conformity assessment procedures by non-governmental bodies to ensure that they are not more trade restrictive than necessary.
- The Understanding on the Interpretation of Article XVII of the GATT provides for increased surveillance of state trading enterprises.
- The Agreement on Safeguards requires member states not to encourage or support the adoption or maintenance by public and private enterprises of equivalent non-governmental measures to voluntary export restraints.
- The General Agreement on Trade in Services (GATS) includes rules designed to ensure that monopolies and exclusive service suppliers do not nullify or impair obligations and commitments under the GATS, particularly where monopolies are also active in related competitive market segments. The 1997 Plurilateral Agreement on Basic Telecommunications Service incorporates regulatory principles aimed at preventing anticompetitive practices by major suppliers (such as anticompetitive cross-subsidization, use of information obtained from competitors, and withholding technical and commercial information) and ensuring that the interconnection practices of such suppliers do not impede market access and that they meet non-discrimination requirements.
- The Trade-Related Intellectual Property Rights Agreement (TRIPS) permits the application of competition policy to abuse of intellectual property rights, including compulsory licensing.
- The Agreement on Government Procurement regulates tendering procedures so as to ensure optimum effective international competition and addresses certain competition problems such as collusive tendering.
- The Trade-Related Investment Measures Agreement (TRIMS)

---

70 See E.U. Petersmann, 'International Competition Rules for Governments and Private Business,' (1996) 30 *J. of World Trade* 5.

requires the WTO Council on Trade in Goods to consider whether the agreement should be complemented with provisions on investment policy and competition policy.

- The Draft Multilateral Agreement on Investment, formerly subject to negotiations under the auspices of the OECD (now suspended), also contemplates the possibility of including commitments to prevent abuses of dominant position by public or private monopolies.
- At the first WTO Ministerial in December 1996 in Singapore, members agreed to constitute a WTO Working Group to study more broadly the interaction between trade policy and competition policy.
- The Doha Ministerial Declaration in November 2001 contemplates multilateral negotiations on aspects of competition policy in the new WTO Round.

2. Bilateral Agreements[71]

The United States has negotiated formal, bilateral, competition law enforcement protocols with Canada (recently renegotiated and expanded),[72] Australia,[73] Germany,[74] and the European Union.[75] While important variations exist among these protocols, all are roughly pat-

---

71 For an overview of these agreements, see draft report by the International Chamber of Commerce, *Competition and Trade in the Global Arena* (February 1998), 17–25.

72 'Memorandum of Understanding Between the Government of Canada and the Government of the United States of America as to Notification, Consultation and Co-operation with Respect to the Application of National Antitrust Laws,' (1984) 23 I.L.M. 275, see also the 'Treaty Between the Government of Canada and the Government of the United States of America on Mutual Legal Assistance in Criminal Matters,' (18 March 1985) 24 I.L.M. 1092; see generally Lawson Hunter and Susan Hutton, 'Where There Is a Will There Is a Way: Co-operation in Canada-U.S. Antitrust Relations,' paper presented in the American Conference Institute on Multinational Antitrust Enforcement, New York, 7 March 1994; Neil Campbell, Jeffrey Roode, and William Rowley, 'The Proper Framework for Co-operation Among National Antitrust Agencies,' paper presented at Roundtable on Competition Policy Reform, University of Toronto, 8 December 1995.

73 Agreement Between the Government of the United States of America and the Government of Australia Relating to Co-operation on Antitrust Matters, (1982) 20 I.L.M. 702 (renegotiated in 1995).

74 Agreement Between the Government of the United States of America and the Government of the Federal Republic of Germany Relating to Mutual Co-operation Regarding Restrictive Business Practices, 1976.

75 Agreement Between the Commission of the European Communities and the Government of the United States of America Regarding the Application of their Competition Laws, Washington, D.C, 23 September 1991. This agreement was held invalid by the European Court of Justice as *ultra vires* the commission's powers, but was subsequently approved by the council.

terned on a model of cooperation recommended by the OECD and now promoted by the U.S. *International Antitrust Enforcement Assistance Act* of 1994.[76] They do not extend, for the most part, beyond requiring the parties to notify each other of pending enforcement actions that may have an impact on important interests of the other party, and to take account of the views of the latter in deciding whether to proceed.[77] The Canada-U.S. Mutual Legal Assistance Treaty goes somewhat further in requiring assistance from the parties in criminal matters (including criminal aspects of competition policy), extending to the use of formal investigative powers where suspected criminal conduct has occurred in one country but the parties involved in the conduct reside in the other country.[78] The recent U.S.-E.U. Protocol, the renegotiated Canada-U.S. Agreement, and the recent Canada-EU Agreement go somewhat further again in identifying a set of both negative and positive comity principles by which the parties will be guided in deciding whether to forgo or exercise jurisdiction. Positive comity principles require a country to give sympathetic consideration to taking enforcement action against conduct on its territory that is allegedly causing harm to interests in another country. Negative comity principles, in contrast, require a country not to take enforcement action that may affect another country's nationals before consulting the latter country's government.

3. Regional Trading Blocs

Under Articles 85 and 86 of the *Treaty of Rome*, the European Union has been successful in adopting a unified competition policy for all member states with respect to transactions that have a community dimension. Moreover, with respect to transactions covered by the treaty, enforcement is unified in the European Commission, and ultimate adjudicative authority resides with the European Court of Justice.[79]

---

76 See OECD, *Revised Recommendation of the Council Concerning Co-operation between Member Countries on Restrictive Business Practices Affecting International Trade,* [C(86)44(Final)] 1986, and predecessor versions referenced therein.

77 See Glynn, 'International Agreements to Allocate Jurisdiction Over Mergers,' at 39–43.

78 See Chapter 12.

79 See Valentine Korah, *An Introductory Guide to EC Competition Law and Practice,* 6th ed. (London: Sweet & Maxwell, 1997); Richard Whish and Brenda Sufrin, *Competition Law,* 3rd ed. (London: Butterworths, 1993); Vivien Rose, ed., *Bellamy and Child: Common Market Law of Competition,* 4th ed. (London: Sweet & Maxwell, 1993); Ivo Van Bael and Jean-Francois Bellis, *Competition Law of the EEC,* 2nd ed. (Bicester: CCH Editions, 1990).

NAFTA contains a short chapter (Chapter 15) on competition policy, monopolies and state enterprises. Under this chapter, each party commits itself to adopting and maintaining measures to proscribe anticompetitive business conduct and to take appropriate action with respect thereto. Pursuant to this commitment, Mexico has recently enacted a comprehensive competition law. The parties also commit themselves to cooperating on issues of competition law enforcement policy, including mutual legal assistance, notification, consultation, and exchange of information relating to the enforcement of competition laws in the free trade area. However, no party may have recourse to dispute settlement under the agreement in the foregoing matters. In the case of monopolies and state enterprises, each party commits itself to ensuring that state-sanctioned monopolies will minimize or eliminate any nullification or impairment of benefits anticipated under the agreement. Moreover, in the case of both privately owned and government owned monopolies, they must act solely in accordance with commercial considerations in the purchase or sale of goods or services in the relevant market, and provide non-discriminatory treatment to investments of investors, and to goods and services providers, of another party.[80]

With respect to services generally, Article 1201 contains several obligations aimed at ensuring that licensing and certification measures of parties do not 'constitute an unnecessary barrier to trade.' The telecommunications chapter (Chapter 13) provides that where a monopolist competes in a segment of the market that is open to competition, a party must ensure 'that the monopoly does not use its monopoly to engage in anti-competitive conduct,' including discriminatory network access requirements. Under the intellectual property chapter (Chapter 17), parties may limit the intellectual property rights they are otherwise obligated to recognize where licensing practices or conditions 'constitute abuses of intellectual property rights having an adverse effect on competition in the relevant market.' In the case of patents, compulsory licensing is explicitly contemplated as a potential remedy.

This brief historical sketch of efforts to date, either to harmonize domestic competition laws or to create some form of supranational

---

80 These provisions are similar to the state-trading provisions in Article XVII of the GATT.

review process for anticompetitive or restrictive business practices, suggests very modest progress over the past four decades (with the notable exception of the European Union).

B. A Framework for Evaluating Future International Initiatives

In considering future reform strategies, the 'system frictions' thesis advanced by Ostry is not especially helpful as an analytical guide. If the whole world spoke the same language, there would be fewer system frictions (e.g., in facilitating foreign investment). If everyone in the world drove on the same side of the road, there would again be fewer system frictions (e.g., in exporting automobiles). If preferences and priorities regarding education and credentialing policies, labour policies, environmental policies, culture, health care, law and order and the rule of law, property rights, and almost every other area of domestic policy making were the same the world over, there would be fewer system frictions. In a world of nation states, however, system frictions are unavoidable. Yet in her otherwise magisterial Handler Lecture on the evolution of competition policy, Professor Eleanor Fox speaks repeatedly of her vision of 'one world' and the inspiration afforded to the rest of the world in this context by the evolution of the European Union.[81]

Reflecting this perspective, the Draft International Antitrust Code[82] (the Munich Code) published by the International Antitrust Working Group (primarily a group of German competition scholars), proposes a complete mandatory World Competition Code. This code sets out minimum standards to be incorporated into the GATT, and enforceable in domestic jurisdictions by an International Antitrust Authority operating under the auspices of the WTO, with disputes being adjudicated by a permanent International Antitrust Panel operating as part of the new GATT dispute resolution regime.[83] In some respects, this proposal is a more ambitious form of the GATT/WTO Agreement on Intellectual

---

81 Fox, 'Antitrust Trade and the Twenty-First Century.'

82 See Special Supplement, 64 BNA Antitrust and Trade Reg. Rep., 19 August 1993 (Special Supplement, No. 1628). For a review of the code, see W.F. Kentscher, 'Competition Rules for Private Agents in the GATT/WTO System,' (1994) 49 *Aussenwirtschaft* 281 (code annexed).

83 It should be noted that several members of the working group (including Professor Fox) dissented, favouring a more modest set of common minimum standards.

Property, which provides for common minimum substantive and procedural standards to be applied by domestic administrative and judicial authorities, subject to international dispute resolution mechanisms. The difficulties and controversies engendered in negotiating this more modest multilateral harmonization regime during the Uruguay Round should be salutary.[84]

The general captivation with the EU model seems to be seriously misguided in the present context. In few, if any, other parts of the world do the special geo-political circumstances that led to the evolution of the European Union exist, and the prospects for creating the supranational institutions that have been central to the integration project of the European Union are close to non-existent. In a multilateral context such as the GATT/WTO, agreement among the more than 160 member states on both the substance and enforcement of domestic competition laws would seem remote.

In our view, it is difficult to approach the case for harmonizing domestic competition laws in a substantially different way from that of harmonizing any number of other domestic laws or policies that may create 'system frictions.' In thinking about harmonization issues generally, and competition policy issues specifically, in either a regional or multilateral context, it is useful to bear in mind the distinction often drawn in the economic integration literature between negative and positive integration.[85] Negative integration essentially tells countries what policies they may *not* adopt, while positive integration tells them which policies they *must* adopt. It is obviously true that harmonized domestic laws and policies are likely to reduce the administrative (compliance) costs of firms operating across a wide range of jurisdictions, which would have to undertake compliance with only one set of rules. In this respect, harmonization can facilitate freer movement of goods, services, and capital. Second, differential or distinctive regulatory requirements can constitute a barrier to entry to a foreign market, where a foreign producer is required to adapt its products to distinctive requirements of the importing jurisdiction. Third, common regulatory standards across a range of jurisdictions may enable economies of

---

84 See Chapter 9.
85 See, e.g., J. Pelkmans, 'The Institutional Economics of European Integration,' in M. Cappelletti, M. Seccombe, and J. Weiler, eds., *Integration Through Law* (Florence: European University Institute, 1986); J. Pinder, 'Positive Integration and Negative Integration – Some Problems of Economic Union in the EEC,' (1968) 24 *World Today* 88.

scale in production and distribution to be realized. However, as David Leebron suggests, 'if the optimal policies for national populations do differ, then harmonization requires that some measure of local welfare be sacrificed.'[86] These welfare losses are unlikely to be completely captured in measured income estimates. It is true that in many contexts, domestic policies may not reflect the true preferences of a majority of the population, perhaps because the government is undemocratic or even predatory. In other cases, policy differences may largely reflect the contingencies of history and no longer reflect current social objectives or at least the most appropriate means of realizing them (but rather simply policy inertia). In these cases, policy harmonization carries few, if any, costs, and potentially significant benefits. But in a wide range of other cases, Leebron's observation presumably holds true. Indeed, many pro–free trade economists, who have generally supported harmonization efforts within the European Union and elsewhere, have at least implicitly recognized this in their rejection of fair trade and related harmonization claims in the labour and environmental areas.[87]

Professor Fox herself, in a recent paper with Professor Ordover, recognizes the fact of policy differences among nations in identifying as 'the aspiration and guiding light world welfare, appropriate sovereignty, and national autonomy,' or 'the one-world-with-appropriate-autonomy vision.'[88] But rather like Ostry's 'system friction' thesis, the 'guiding light' provides very little illumination, in itself (like the elusive concept of 'subsidiarity' in the EU), on how to strike the appropriate balance. In other recent papers,[89] Fox spells out in more detail this more cautious vision – what she describes as 'a targeted constitutional approach,' in contrast to a 'comprehensive' approach, on the one hand, or a 'minimalist' approach, on the other. A somewhat similar

---

86 David W. Leebron, 'Lying Down with Procrustes: An Analysis of Harmonization Claims,' in Jagdish Bhagwati and Robert E. Hudec, eds., *Fair Trade and Harmonization* (Cambridge, Mass.: MIT Press, 1996), 1:41, and 'Claims for Harmonization: A Theoretical Framework,' (1996) 27 *Canadian Business L.J.* 63.
87 See R. Howse and M. Trebilcock, 'The Fair Trade-Free Trade Debate: Trade, Labour and the Environment,' (1996) 16 *International Review of Law and Economics* 61.
88 Fox and Ordover, 'Harmonization of Competition and Trade Law.'
89 Eleanor Fox, 'Competition Law and the Next Agenda for the WTO,' in OECD, *New Dimensions of Market Access*, at 181–3; 'Jurisdiction and Conflicts in the Global Economy: Crafting a Systems Interface,' mimeo, N.Y.U. Law School, 3 March 1995.

approach has recently been proposed by an E.C. Expert Group[90] in the form of a plurilateral agreement containing (a) procedural rules relating to notification, cooperation, and negative and positive comity obligations; (b) minimum substantive rules for cross-border cases to be embodied in domestic competition laws of signatories; and (c) an international institutional structure to perform monitoring and dispute resolution functions.

The Canadian Competition Bureau, in a discussion paper of May 1999, entitled 'Options for the Internationalization of Competition Policy,' outlines the possible elements of a multilateral agreement on Trade-Related Aspects of Anti-competitive Measures (TRAMS) that might be negotiated during the next WTO Round. These elements could include:

> an obligation to establish a competition law, with appropriate scope and independence in investigation and adjudication; commitment to the principles of transparency, national treatment, non-discrimination and procedural fairness; common substantive approaches to cartels, abuse of dominance and mergers; mechanisms to facilitate and foster cooperation between competition authorities. Disputes about whether domestic competition law conforms to the obligations in a TRAMS could be accommodated under existing WTO dispute procedures. However, the application of WTO dispute procedures to a review of individual decisions by a national competition authority is complex as it would touch directly upon the independence of competition agencies, and enforcement decision-making processes, thereby raising fears of WTO second guessing of individual decisions of competition authorities.

> The establishment of support mechanisms would be a key prerequisite to the successful implementation of a WTO agreement on competition policy. A peer review process similar to the existing Trade Policy Review Mechanism – a Competition Review Mechanism (CPRM) – could provide countries with an objective review both of the substantive provisions of the law to determine if they are in compliance with the TRAMS provisions and the competition agency's enforcement record. A peer review

---

90 EC Expert Group, *Competition Policy in the New Trade Order: Strengthening International Co-operation and Rules* (Brussels: EC Commission, 1995); see Petersmann, 'International Competition Rules.'

would also have the added benefit of fostering transparency. A council of experts could provide a forum for consultations and for discussions on the establishment of arrangements for cooperation. Additionally, a TRAMS Council could offer members a forum to consult and seek mutually satisfactory resolution of problems related to market access. Technical assistance will be essential for those countries without a competition policy or who are in the first stages of implementing one to help them get up to speed with the requirements set out under the TRAMS.

We believe that a cautious approach is warranted to proposals for radical harmonization of domestic laws and policies, including competition policies.[91] In adopting this more cautious approach, we return to the negative and positive integration distinction noted above. International trade treaties such as the GATT have traditionally emphasized negative integration, that is, what kinds of policies countries may not adopt. In particular, they have prohibited the adoption of domestic policies that either explicitly or implicitly discriminate between foreign trading powers (the most-favoured-nation principle) or between domestic producers and foreign producers (the national treatment principle), at least beyond certain clearly identified exceptions, such as bound tariffs and health and safety and related exceptions set out under Article XX of the GATT, and national security exceptions set out in Article XXI. In a competition policy context, Bacchetta, Horn, and Mavroidis[92] usefully distinguish between 'spillovers' and 'distortions' from domestic competition policy. A negative spillover may occur where a competition policy decision taken in one country has adverse effects on parties in another. For example, an efficiency-enhancing merger permitted in Country A may disadvantage competitors in Country B, or a price fixing-prosecution in Country A may disadvantage conspirators located in Country B but trading onto Country A's market, but in neither case is there necessarily a distortion from a global perspective. This would entail evaluating whether the decision reduces global welfare. Only when a domestic competition policy deci-

---

91 A similarly cautious approach is advocated in the Global Competition Initiative proposed in the recent U.S. International Competition Policy Advisory Committee (ICPAC) Report (2000) and seems contemplated in the recent Doha WTO Ministerial Declaration (November 2001).

92 M. Bacchetta, H. Horn, and P. Mavroidis, 'Do Negative Spillovers from Nationally Pursued Competition Policies Provide a Case for Multilateral Competition Rules?' Working Paper, 14 August 1997.

sion, while perhaps maximizing domestic welfare, reduces global welfare is there presumptively the kind of distortion that causes a tension in the interface between competition policy and trade policy. In a recent paper, Guzman[93] argues that, with respect to imperfectly competitive goods and services markets, net exporters will seek to maximize producer surplus and underregulate anticompetitive activities while net importers will seek to maximize consumer surplus and overregulate potentially anticompetitive activities. A global welfare perspective would require that the sum of global producer and consumer surplus be maximized.

C. Application of Framework to Specific Aspects of Competition Policy

In developing a tractable agenda for reconciling domestic competition policies and international trade policies, a negative integration (or non-discrimination) approach enables us to develop a useful perspective on a number of problems.[94] First, exemption from, or non-enforcement of, competition laws for export or import cartels are clearly discriminatory, in that they explicitly treat domestic producers or consumers differently from foreign producers or consumers.[95] While dispensations for export or import cartels may enhance national income (at least in the case of export cartels) in the short run, they are myopic in that they encourage a downward spiral or beggar-thy-neighbour dynamic through reciprocal measures that in the long-run reduce both national and global welfare (much as do reciprocal tariffs).[96] These are easy cases. These dispensations should be removed and appropriate procedural mechanisms adopted for ensuring non-discriminatory enforcement of anticollusion laws. Professor Fox has developed some useful proposals with respect to complaints by exporters of anticompetitive private restrictions on access to foreign markets. She suggests that the

---

93 Andrew Guzman, 'Is International Antitrust Possible?' (1998) 73 N.Y.U. L.R. 150.
94 See Edward Iacobucci, 'The Interdependence of Trade and Competition Policies,' (1997) 21 World Competition 5.
95 For a useful comparative review of the evolution and effects of these exemptions, see American Bar Association Antitrust Section, Report of the Special Committee on International Antitrust, 1 September 1991, chaps. 3 and 4.
96 See Fox and Ordover, 'Harmonization of Competition and Trade Laws,' at 15; Alan Wolff, 'The Problems of Market Access in the Global Economy: Trade and Competition Policy,' in OECD, New Dimensions in Market Access, chap. 19.

home nation in which the internal market conduct has occurred should have the primary right to take enforcement measures. A harmed nation may request a home nation to take enforcement action against an apparent violation, and the home nation should be obliged to give sympathetic regard to this request. If recourse cannot be had through action by home-nation authorities or otherwise in home-nation courts, the harmed nation should be entitled to assert enforcement jurisdiction over the subject matter of the controversy, but at the option of the defendant the court should apply the substantive principles of the defendant nation's law.[97] Assertion of jurisdiction by the harmed nation will, of course, be of little value if the injurers maintain no presence in the form of personnel or assets in the harmed country's territory. Thus, an additional step would be to build on the Chapter 19 binational panel experience under the FTA and NAFTA, relating to the application of domestic trade remedy laws,[98] by providing a WTO or NAFTA panel procedure whereby aggrieved foreign parties (states or firms) could complain to a supranational panel in cases where it is alleged that member states are not faithfully interpreting or enforcing *their own* domestic competition laws in a non-discriminatory manner.

Within our suggested framework, there are other easy cases. Foreign producers trading into the U.S. market who collude to fix prices in that market should not be permitted to complain of the relatively stringent U.S. price-fixing laws, on the grounds that in their home jurisdiction price fixing laws are lax or non-existent. Thus, we see no objection to the United States asserting jurisdiction in such cases, as the majority of the U.S. Supreme Court held in *Hartford Fire Insurance Co. v. California*.[99] In *Hartford*, where U.S. insurers were alleged to have conspired with U.K. reinsurers to curtail the availability of certain forms of liabil-

---

97 See Eleanor Fox, 'Jurisdiction and Conflicts in the Global Economy: Crafting a Systems Interface,' mimeo, NYU Law School, 3 March 1995, at 34; Fox, 'Competition Law and the Next Agenda for the WTO,' at 182.

98 See John Mercury, 'Chapter 19 of the United States-Canada Free Trade Agreement 1989–95: A Check on Administered Protection?' (1995) 15 *Northwestern J. of International Law and Business* 525.

99 (1993), 1621 A.T.R.R. 30; for extensive discussions of this case, see Fox, 'Jurisdiction and Conflicts in the Global Economy,' Kenneth Dam, 'Extraterritoriality in an Age of Globalization: The Hartford Case,' [1993] *Supreme Court Review* 289; Alan Swan, 'The Hartford Insurance Company Case: Antitrust in the Global Economy – Welfare Effects and Sovereignty,' in J. Bhandari and A. Sykes, eds., *Economic Dimensions in International Law* (Cambridge: Cambridge University Press, 1997).

ity insurance coverage in the U.S. market, to have treated local insurers as subject to domestic price-fixing laws while exempting foreign reinsurers on grounds of extraterritoriality would have entailed discrimination in favour of foreign firms. On the other hand, to the extent that domestic insurers were able to claim the insurance exemption under the *McCarran-Ferguson Act* from U.S. antitrust laws, to hold the foreign reinsurers liable would have entailed discrimination against them relative to domestic insurers.

Conversely, U.S. producers trading into or investing in jurisdictions with lax or non-existent anticollusion laws (that, e.g., may affect the price or supply of inputs) equally have no basis for complaint, provided that these policies are applied in a non-discriminatory manner. This observation would extend to permissive provisions on joint research and production ventures, research consortia, and other forms of strategic alliances, provided again that the provisions are not framed or applied in a discriminatory manner. We are thus sceptical of the case for the United States asserting jurisdiction against *Pilkington Glass*,[100] alleging restrictive distribution arrangements impeding effective market access by U.S. competitors to other markets around the world.[101] Equally, U.S. or other producers trading into or operating in the European market have no basis for complaint because the abuse of dominant position provisions of Article 86 of the *Treaty of Rome* are applied somewhat more stringently than the monopolization provisions in section 2 of the Sherman Act. Similarly, if the European Union should choose to take account of industrial policy considerations, and not only consumer welfare considerations, in the administration of its merger law, or if, conversely, some other country should apply its merger law in a more populist fashion designed to prevent concentrations of economic power, foreign firms operating in these markets, notwithstanding sharp differences from competition laws obtaining in their home market, should accept the local rules of the game (whether perceived to be well-conceived or not), *provided* that these rules are applied in a non-discriminatory fashion to both domestic and foreign firms. Again,

---

100 *United States v. Pilkington plc, and Pilkington Holdings Inc.,* IV No. 94-345 JVC CD Ariz. 1994.

101 Both the United States *Foreign Trade Antitrust Improvements Act* of 1982 and the *Antitrust Enforcement Guidelines for International Operations* of the United States Department of Justice and Federal Trade Commission (April 1995) contemplate substantial U.S. extraterritorial jurisdiction over foreign restrictions on outbound U.S. trade.

if one country chooses to create or maintain state-owned or sanctioned monopolies in some sectors, foreign producers should have no right of complaint about being excluded from these markets, given that other domestic producers face similar exclusion, although discrimination by such monopolies in sales or purchasing decisions against foreign firms would be objectionable (as both the GATT/WTO and NAFTA presently provide).[102]

Other cases are admittedly more difficult. One controversial case relates to the relatively quiescent state of Japanese competition law as it applies to both vertical and horizontal keiretsu. Vertical production and distribution keiretsu and other exclusive dealing arrangements are often alleged to prevent foreign firms from gaining ready access to Japanese manufacturing, retail, and distribution networks. Horizontal keiretsu, because of the prominent role played by lead banks and because of cross-shareholdings, are also alleged to have anticompetitive effects in preventing foreign investors from readily acquiring Japanese firms as a means of lower-cost and more efficient entry into the Japanese market than greenfield entry. Data indicate a dramatically lower level of foreign investment stock in Japan than in most other industrialized economies, and notwithstanding the major growth in foreign direct investment flows in the 1980s, dramatically lower levels of inflows into Japan.[103]

Some of these issues figured prominently in an important recent (1998) GATT/WTO panel proceeding[104] involving a complaint by the United States on behalf of Eastman Kodak that Fuji, with government support, enjoyed access to an exclusive wholesale and retail distribution system in Japan for consumer film to which Kodak (and other foreign film producers) could not gain access. The United States alleged under Article XXXII (1)(b) of the GATT that various Japanese government measures constituted non-violation nullification and impairment of benefits reasonably anticipated by the United States under tariff concessions on consumer film made by Japan during the Kennedy,

---

102 See Neil Campbell, William Rowley, and Michael Trebilcock, 'The Role of Monopoly Law in the International Trading System,' (1995) 1 *International Trade Law and Regulation* 167.
103 See Sylvia Ostry, 'Challenges for the Trading System,' in OECD, *New Dimensions of Market Access*, 25 at 31.
104 *Japan – Measures Affecting Photographic Film and Paper*, Report of the Panel, 31 March 1998.

Tokyo, and Uruguay Rounds. These measures covered (a) distribution measures that allegedly encouraged and facilitated the creation of a market structure in consumer film in which imports are excluded from traditional distribution channels; (b) restrictions on large retail stores, which allegedly restrict the growth of an alternative distribution channel for imported film, and (c) promotion restrictions that allegedly disadvantage imports by restricting the use of sales promotion techniques that foreign suppliers might wish to deploy in expanding their presence in the Japanese market. In the alternative, the United States argued that many of these practices were a violation of the national treatment principle contained in Article III (4) of the GATT.

The WTO panel rejected all of the U.S. allegations. As to non-violation nullification and impairment, the panel held that the United States bore the burden of adducing 'a detailed justification' for its allegations, recognizing the exceptional nature of this ground of complaint. This justification would need to address three issues: (a) whether the practices in question were government 'measures'; (b) if so, whether the measure in question related to a benefit reasonably anticipated to accrue from prior tariff concessions by upsetting the competitive relationship between imports and domestic products; and (c) whether the benefit accruing to the complainant state had in fact been nullified or impaired by the measure in question (causality).

The panel affirmed that purely private rather than governmental measures were not reviewable under the GATT, and that purely advisory reports or recommendations to government by specialist committees and task forces were not government measures, unless clearly adopted or acted on by government. However, the panel was prepared to accept that many traditional forms of 'administrative guidance' engaged in by the Japanese government constituted government measures, even though informal and lacking explicit sanctions, provided that such guidance entailed implicit incentives to comply.

With respect to the requirement that a challenged measure relate to a reasonably anticipated benefit from prior tariff concessions, the panel held that many of the disputed measures were in force prior to the concessions in question, and imputed knowledge of them to the U.S. government, rejecting the latter's claim of opaqueness or unpredictability in administration.

With respect to the requirement that the measures in question cause the nullification or impairment of a benefit reasonably anticipated from the prior tariff concessions, the panel found that none of the measures were *de jure* or *de facto* discriminatory and applied equally to domestic and foreign suppliers. For similar reasons, the panel rejected U.S. claims of violation of the national treatment principle.

In the wake of this decision, the U.S. government announced an interagency monitoring committee whereby Japanese government assurances to the WTO panel on non-discriminatory access to Japan's distribution channels, on large retail stores, and on non-restrictive application of promotions laws, so as to permit free competition with respect to pricing and quality, are viewed as 'commitments' potentially attracting section 301 trade sanctions if not adhered to.

While Japanese competition laws on vertical and horizontal organizational arrangements are facially neutral as between the ability of domestic and foreign firms to challenge these arrangements, the analysis should not be terminated there. If, as in the case of import cartels, the evidence disclosed discrimination in the application and enforcement of these laws depending on whether the complainant was a domestic firm or a foreign firm, this would constitute a form of discrimination for our purposes. Moreover, even if the laws were both framed and enforced in a neutral fashion, one would still want to ask (as many GATT decisions under Article III [National treatment] and Article XX [exceptions to GATT obligations] have done), whether these laws are a form of disguised protectionism or discrimination. This question is not always easily answered. It may be the case that Japanese competition laws do have a disparate impact on foreign exporters or investors relative to domestic producers. However, this is equally true (as argued above) of different language laws, driving laws, and so forth. Mere demonstration of disparate impact is not sufficient; that impact must also be indicative of a disguised attempt at discrimination. In the case of the Japanese keiretsu, given the central role that they have traditionally played in corporate governance and organizational structures in Japan,[105] it is difficult to believe that the primary purpose for their adoption has been to differentially disadvantage foreign producers, even though that may be a consequence. An ironic feature of current United States concerns over Japanese vertical

---

105 See Michael Gerlach, *The Keiretsu: A Primer* (New York: Japan Society, 1992) and *Alliance Capitalism: The Social Organization of Japanese Business* (Berkeley: University of California Press, 1992); Ronald Gilson and Mark Roe, 'Understanding the Japanese Keiretsu: Overlaps Between Corporate Governance and Industrial Organization,' Columbia University Law School, Working Paper No. 83, 14 September 1992.

arrangements and lack of antitrust scrutiny of them is that (as discussed in Chapter 6) much recent thinking among U.S antitrust scholars (reflected increasingly in U.S. case law) has rejected sinister (anticompetitive) explanations of vertical restraints and views many such restraints as benign (efficiency-enhancing).[106]

Even if domestic competition policy is not applied in a discriminatory fashion to private restrictions, more fundamental objections to such restrictions, and indeed other domestic policies of foreign countries, such as the maintenance of state-owned or sanctioned monopolies in given sectors, invoke instead a notion of *reciprocity.* It could be argued, for example, that if the United States has adopted much more assertive antitrust policies on vertical restraints and has privatized and/or deregulated state-owned or sanctioned monopolies while Japan has adopted much more permissive policies on vertical restraints and allows much greater scope for state-owned or sanctioned monopolies, Japanese firms have much more favourable access to U.S. markets, both as exporters and investors, than U.S. exporters and investors have with respect to Japanese markets. This claim may well be true. It is also true that the notion of reciprocity has long played a central role in international trade policy, for example, in tariff negotiations under the GATT and various regional trading arrangements. However, if this broad notion of reciprocity, or functional *equality of access,* rather than the national treatment principle, were to become the normative touchstone in addressing divergences in domestic competition and related policies, the ability of countries to maintain any diversity or distinctiveness in a whole range of domestic policies would be largely forfeited, with serious implications for notions of political sovereignty. Countries which have chosen unilaterally to adopt more assertive domestic antitrust policies, for example with respect to vertical restrictions, or which have chosen to privatize and/or deregulate state-owned or sanctioned monopolies, have presumably done so for what were conceived to be good domestic reasons, taking fully into account the implications for foreign trade and investment, *inter alia.* That other countries have chosen to pursue different policies in this respect, provided that they are non-discriminatory, should provide no basis for complaint by the first

---

106 See N. Campbell and M. Trebilcock, 'Interjurisdictional Conflict and Merger Review,' in E. Kantzenback, H. Scharrer, and L. Wavermane, eds., *Competition Policy in an Interdependent World Economy* (Baden-Baden: Nomos Verlagsgesellschaft, 1993).

country. Otherwise the latter would be in a position to 'export' its domestic policies to every foreign market in which it has present or prospective trading or investment interests, dramatically expanding notions of extraterritoriality beyond any scope hitherto considered defensible. This is not, of course, to foreclose the possibility of international negotiations over such policies (by way of analogy with tariff negotiations), but it is to argue for a highly restrained role for *unilateral* action by one country with respect to another country's domestic policies, or indeed agreements on modifications to these policies extracted under threat of unilateral action.

Another problematic case is transnational mergers. Some cases are easier than others. If two firms which are based in Country A but sell most of their output in Country B merge and acquire a dominant position in Country B's market, monopoly rents will be realized in Country A but consumer welfare losses will be sustained primarily in Country B. This may induce the competition authorities in Country A to approve the merger. In our view, this is a form of disguised discrimination against consumers in Country B if the competition authorities in Country A would have reached a different and adverse conclusion if all the affected producers and consumers had been located within their own jurisdiction. In other words, this is to discriminate against consumers in Country B – and, as with export cartels or tariffs, is myopic in the longer run.[107] Thus, in our view, competition authorities in Country B – are entitled to object to this merger, as the Federal Trade Commission did in the *Institut Merieux/Connaught* case,[108] despite being widely criticized for doing so. This kind of case is not conceptually different from the export cartel case, except that the discrimination is implicit.

Other cases are not so straightforward. One such example is the widely discussed decision of the European Commission[109] prohibiting the acquisition of de Havilland, a Canadian-based commuter aircraft producer (owned by an American firm, Boeing) by a European joint venture, ATR (owned, respectively, by French and Italian interests), on

---

107 See Fox and Ordover, 'Harmonization of Competition and Trade Laws,' 39.
108 (1990) No. 891–0098 Fed. Reg.1614; and commentary by Deborah Owen and John Parisi, 'International Mergers and Joint Ventures: A Federal Trade Commission Perspective,' in Barry Hawk, ed., *International Mergers and Joint Ventures* (N.Y.: Fordham Corporate Law Institute, 1991), at 11.
109 Aerospatiale-Alenia/de Havilland, Commission Decision 91/619 of 5 December 1991, 1 CEC at 2,034 (1992).

the grounds that the merger would give the merged entity excessive market power in the European and global market (ATR was the leading producer of commuter aircraft in the EU and global markets), despite the fact that the merger was not opposed by the Canadian competition authorities. On a charitable view of the facts, we assume that the Canadian competition authorities had approved the merger pursuant to the efficiencies defence under section 96 of the Canadian *Competition Act* (a provision unique to Canadian competition law), despite some enhanced ability of the merged entity to raise prices in its output markets (primarily outside of Canada), and not simply because of a desire to save Canadian jobs or to appropriate monopoly rents from foreigners. In this case, we may have a genuine problem of interjurisdictional conflict. That is to say, assuming the Canadian authorities would have made the same decision if all of the merged entities' output had been sold in the Canadian market, it would no longer be possible to impute discrimination against foreign customers. Rather, the source of the conflicting determinations would genuinely reside in differences in the domestic competition law regimes applied to the transaction. Conversely, of course, one would want to be reassured that the EU competition authorities would have reached the same decision had the acquired firm been located not in Canada but in the European Union, and the claimed efficiency gains from the merger would have been fully realized within the European Union and not Canada.[110] Given any reasonable understanding of the 'effects' test for asserting extraterritorial jurisdiction, which is now well-established at least in U.S. and EU case law and which holds that jurisdiction extends to parties located outside the jurisdiction if the effects of their conduct occur within the jurisdiction, both jurisdictions could legitimately lay claim to jurisdiction in this case, and on the facts assumed neither could be shown to have discriminated against either foreign producers or foreign consumers. The European Union could claim that the consumer welfare test it applied enjoys wide currency in other countries' competition law regimes (in particular that of the United States) and in academic literature. On the other hand, the Canadian authorities could reasonably claim that the total welfare test they applied, while perhaps less justiciable and more speculative, actually accords better with pure

---

110 See Fox and Ordover, 'Harmonization of Competition and Trade Laws,' for a similar approach.

economic theory. Short of a meta-choice, presumably through international agreement, by affected jurisdictions between the two welfare tests, such cases of interjurisdictional conflict are not easily resolved.

A situation in which two firms merge and the relevant geographic market is either the global market or at least a regional market (e.g., North America) also presents difficulties. The merger between Boeing and McDonnell Douglas presented this scenario in the global large passenger aircraft manufacturing market, leading to conflicts between U.S. and EU competition authorities that were finally resolved via an undertaking by Boeing to restrict its use of long-term exclusive supply contracts with major airlines. Even applying a consumer and not a total welfare test, in the first case every competition authority in the world could legitimately assert jurisdiction, invoking a reasonable interpretation of the 'effects' test, while in the second case every competition authority within the regional market could properly assert jurisdiction. In some cases, the merger may be addressed by requiring divestiture of subsidiaries or assets in particular sub-markets within the regional market; in other cases the entire market may be served by single companies. It may be possible to negotiate an international agreement by which a lead jurisdiction is designated by reference to a 'primary effects' test, perhaps operationalized by identifying the market in which the largest percentage of the merged entity's output is likely to be sold.[111] In a regional context, this will usually be the United States, and this will also often be the case in global markets, given the size of the U.S. economy. In addition, the creation of a supranational authority in which jurisdiction is vested to determine the lead jurisdiction in the event of disputes over whether the relevant market is supranational or where the largest proportion of the merged entity's output is likely to be sold might also be contemplated.[112] It should be emphasized that in these last two examples the problem is not necessarily one of discrimination but rather a problem of conflict of laws, where a choice of law (and forum) rule is required in order to resolve the potential for interjurisdictional conflict. It should also be acknowledged that these problems of interjurisdictional conflict would obviously be reduced or eliminated if all countries could agree on a common set of competition laws and credibly commit to a consistent enforcement policy. For rea-

---

111 See Campbell and Trebilcock, 'Interjurisdictional Conflict in Merger Review.'
112 Ibid.

sons noted above, such an agreement would forfeit the value of policy diversity for both purely domestic and supranational transactions. Agreement on a choice of law and forum rule would target much more narrowly the area of required agreement on supranational cases.

Beyond these difficult substantive issues, a range of procedural harmonization measures are much more likely to be resolved in that they appear to represent positive-sum strategies for most countries and their constituents. In this respect, the American Bar Association's NAFTA Task Force and the ICPAC Report offer a number of useful suggestions for enhancing cooperation between domestic competition authorities, and thus minimizing duplicate investigative efforts (public transaction costs), and for minimizing the direct transaction costs faced by private parties in meeting divergent information requirements and decision timetables under existing domestic competition law regimes.[113] Bilateral agreements between the United States and the European Union, the United States and Canada, the United States and Australia, and New Zealand and Australia already go some distance towards providing for interagency cooperation in competition law enforcement but could reasonably be expanded in scope to permit exchange of confidential information under certain conditions.[114]

IV. Policy Implications

In contrast to 'one world' (or 'flat earth') visions of competition as a global organizing economic principle, 'system frictions' theories, or inappropriate EU analogies applied to the multilateral or trilateral context, analogies which are politically unrealistic and indeed normatively uncongenial in their implications for political sovereignty and democratic accountability (concerns that are increasingly manifest even in Europe over more ambitious integration proposals), a series of more modest multilateral or trilateral initiatives might usefully be contemplated. These initiatives would focus on several distinct problems: (a) minimizing the scope for explicit or implicit discrimination in the formulation or enforcement of domestic competition laws; (b) mini-

---

113 See ABA NAFTA Task Force Report, chaps. 4 and 5, ICPAC Report, chap. 2; see also J. William Rowley, Omar K. Wakil, and A. Neil Campbell, 'Streamlining International Merger-Control,' Canadian Bar Association Annual Conference on Competition Law, Ottawa, 21 September 2000.
114 See Chapter 12.

mizing the potential for interjurisdictional conflict and hence risk and uncertainty in transactions affecting supranational geographic markets, through international agreements on choice of law and forum rules and supranational mechanisms to oversee their application; (c) minimizing public and private transaction costs in the administration of competition laws through harmonized information requirements, decision timetables, and exchange of information and cooperation among enforcement authorities; and (d) maximizing transparency in the administration of domestic competition law regimes and hence minimizing the arbitrary and non-accountable exercise of administrative discretion (and unpredictability).

To advance these objectives, member states of the WTO (or NAFTA) should agree to ensure that their domestic competition laws adopt prohibitions against both export and import cartels and complementary procedural mechanisms to ensure effective enforcement. With respect to merger law as it might affect international mergers, various forms of procedural harmonization might be contemplated pertaining to information requirements, decision timetables, and information sharing among competition authorities. In addition, member states with merger laws might commit themselves, in the interests of transparency, to publishing a set of non-binding merger enforcement guidelines that indicate how these laws are likely to be enforced with respect to a common checklist of issues the guidelines would be required to address (but without a commitment to a common position on these issues). In the case of transnational mergers affecting supranational geographic markets, international negotiations need to be contemplated over choice of law and forum rules such as a 'primary effects' test designed to identify a lead jurisdiction for evaluating such mergers, with a possible role for a supranational authority to resolve disputed issues of jurisdiction. With respect to the contentious issue of vertical foreclosure of effective access to foreign markets, controversy here is likely to be particularly intense, given widely differing industrial organization and antitrust traditions in different countries and substantial theoretical controversy as to the appropriate form laws should take with respect to vertical restrictions.[115] In this area, it is dif-

---

115 See the *Report of the OECD Committee on Competition Law and Policy,* 'Interim Report on Convergence of Competition Policies' (1994), for a useful review of major commonalities and differences in OECD member countries' competition laws.

ficult to contemplate ready multilateral consensus on an appropriate set of legal norms. Perhaps the most that might be hoped for is that member countries would agree that, as a baseline, vertical restrictions should be included in domestic competition laws as discrete reviewable practices or as reviewable practices within a more general abuse of dominant position provision, without sectoral or similar exemptions, but without any common commitment to the legal norms governing the review process. Again, as with merger review, it may be possible to reach agreement on a commitment for each member state to publish a set of non-binding vertical restraint enforcement guidelines that address a common checklist of issues. By way of analogy with the Chapter 19 binational dispute resolution panels provided for under NAFTA in domestic antidumping or countervailing duty determinations, a WTO or NAFTA panel procedure would provide aggrieved foreign parties (states or firms) the ability to complain to a supranational panel in cases where it is alleged that member states are not faithfully interpreting or enforcing *their own* domestic competition laws in a non-discriminatory manner. Providing a broader mandate for multilateral or supranational adjudication of competition law issues is likely to raise a host of difficult institutional and procedural issues relating to standing, information-gathering, expertise, and remedies.[116] It may also be useful for the OECD Competition Law and Policy Committee to convene a group of internationally recognized apolitical competition law experts to work on a non-binding model competition code[117] that, over time, may exert an exemplary or exhortatory influence over the evolution of domestic competition law regimes (rather like the United States *Restatements*).[118] This might use-

---

116 See Petros Mavroidis and Sally Van Siclen, 'The Application of the GATT/WTO Dispute Resolution System to Competition Issues,' (1997) 31 *J. of World Trade* 5.

117 See Bernard J. Phillips, 'Comments on the Draft International Antitrust Code,' and annexed Report of OECD Committee on Competition Law and Policy, 'Interim Report on Convergence of Competition Policies,' (1994) 49 *Aussenwirtschaft* 327, for an initial statement of consensus views.

118 Ibid. This evolutionary approach to international harmonization of competition is also advocated by E.U. Petersmann, 'Proposals for Negotiating International Competition Rules in the GATT-WTO World Trade and Legal System,' (1994) 49 *Aussenwirtschaft* 231 at 276, 277. A more sceptical view of whether there is any problem of significance is taken by David Palmeter, 'Competition Policy and "Unfair Trade": First Do No Harm,' (1994) 49 *Aussenwirtschaft* 417. Palmeter notes that, according to

fully build on the Report of the OECD Committee on Competition Law and Policy, 'Interim Report on Convergence of Competition Policies.'[119]

Beyond these competition policy innovations, we should return to the historical origins of the tension between competition law and international trade policy in North America that consigned the former to a deep second-best policy role and attend to the remaining protectionist elements in international trade policy, particularly trade remedy regimes such as antidumping and countervailing duty regimes, and set seriously about the task of exorcising these elements of mercantilism that constrain the operation of international competitive forces far more than do any aspect of current domestic competition policy regimes.[120] Because trade remedy laws apply pricing constraints to foreign firms that do not apply to domestic firms, they are inherently discriminatory (and inconsistent with the national treatment principle). In this respect, the outlines of a political deal may be discernible: in return for LDCs and NICs adopting basic competition law measures of the kind outlined above, industrialized countries would agree to substantial curtailment of their trade remedy laws and some supranational oversight in their application – a deal that Mexico in effect accepted under NAFTA by agreeing to enact an effective domestic competition law regime. As outlined in our discussion of antidumping laws, more radical proposals, which we favour, would entail the complete repeal

research by Finger and Fung, in only one of the eighty-two section 301 cases concluded in the United States between 1975 and 1992 was an affirmative determination based on anticompetitive provisions in a foreign country's laws and in only two other cases were competition issues even raised: see J.M. Finger and K.C. Fung, 'Can Competition Policy Control S.301?' (1994) 49 *Aussenwirtschaft* 379. Palmeter concludes that 'whatever might be limiting import competition in various national markets, the record suggests it is not likely to be lack of competition policy' (at. 421).

119 See Phillips, 'Comments on the Draft International Antitrust Code.'
120 See Michael Trebilcock and Thomas Boddez, 'The Case for Liberalizing North American Trade Remedy Laws,' (1995) 4 *Minnesota J. of Global Trade* 1; see Palmeter, 'Competition Policy,' at 422 for a similar view, although he regards this 'highly meritorious' proposal as 'highly utopian' for the present and foreseeable future (at 418). See also the *Report of the Antitrust Section of the American Bar Association on the Competition Dimension of the North American Free Trade Agreement*, 20 July 1994, chap. 6; and Fox and Ordover, Harmonization of Competition and Trade Laws,' at 32, for similarly circumspect positions.

of antidumping laws and their replacement with non-discriminatory harmonized cross-border predatory pricing laws, along the lines of the regime adopted by Australia and New Zealand in 1990 under ANZCERTA. This distinctive role for harmonized competition laws surely warrants a high priority.

ELEVEN

Competition Policy and Regulated Industries

I. The Regulated Industry Defence

Under the Canadian federal system, the power to legislate and regulate is granted to either the provinces or the federal government under sections 91 and 92 of the constitution.[1] However, the delineation of powers provided within the *Constitution Act* does not prevent overlap between provincial and federal jurisdictions and as such does not prevent citizens and firms from facing conflicting provincial and federal statutes, which cannot both be followed. Since it is unreasonable to leave in place two sets of regulations where one prescribes what the other prohibits, it was necessary to develop a method for dealing with situations where two laws are both *intra vires* but cannot both be operational. Hence the doctrine of paramountcy developed. The doctrine of paramountcy is a working rule that states that when there are two valid laws that conflict, one federal and one provincial, the federal law will be paramount and the provincial law will be of no force or effect.[2]

According to this rule, whenever a conflict exists between provincial and federal legislation, either specifically or because the federal government has covered the field[3] and created a regulatory scheme so complete that there is no room for provincial legislation, the federal legislation will be operative and the provincial legislation inoperative.

---

1 *Constitution Act, 1867* (UK), 30 & 31 Vict., c. 3.
2 See *Ross v. Registrar of Motor Vehicles*, [1975] S.C.R. 207; *Multiple Access Ltd. v. McCutcheon*, [1982] S.C.R. 211; and *Bank of Montreal v. Hall*, [1990] S.C.R. 216.
3 See *Bank of Montreal v. Hall, supra*, note 2.

However, in the case of competition law and policy, jurisprudence has developed that is at variance with the rationale behind the paramountcy rule. Rather than applying the doctrine of paramountcy, courts have held that even when there is an express conflict between provincial regulation and federal competition legislation, the regulatory scheme will be operative and provide a defence to a breach of the *Competition Act*.[4] In the case of a federal regulatory scheme that appears to conflict with the *Competition Act*, the issue posed is not one of federalism but one of statutory interpretation, to which a 'presumption of legislative coherence' applies whereby the courts will attempt to interpret the statutes so as to eliminate any apparent operational conflict. If an operational conflict is indeed unavoidable such that it is impossible for a party to fulfil simultaneously its legal obligations under two regulatory regimes, the courts will determine which of the regimes Parliament would have intended to take precedence in the event of a conflict.[5] In some cases, the empowering legislation may specify the order of precedence. For example, section 94 of the *Competition Act* provides that the minister of finance may approve a bank merger in the public interest, in which case the Competition Bureau and Tribunal's jurisdiction in the matter is terminated.

The first case to deal with conflict between competition legislation and provincial regulatory schemes, *R. v. Chung Chuck*,[6] was decided by the British Columbia Court of Appeal in 1929. Chung Chuck argued that the British Columbia *Produce Marketing Act*[7] was *ultra vires* the province's powers as it infringed on the federal government's exclusive jurisdiction over trade and commerce. Chung Chuck had previously been convicted of marketing potatoes without permission of the Mainland Potato Committee of Direction, contrary to the provisions of the *Produce Marketing Act*. The court held that the provincial statute did not infringe on the federal domain sufficiently to be found *ultra vires*.[8] 'Regulation of particular trades or callings by a provincial legislation is permitted if it falls short of such infringement and the question of

---

4 R.S.C. 1985, c. C-34.
5 *British Columbia Telephone Co. v. Shaw Cable Systems (B.C.) Ltd.* (1995), 125 D.L.R. (4th) 443 (S.C.C.).
6 [1929] 1 D.L.R. 756 (B.C.C.A.).
7 1926–27 (B.C.), c. 54.
8 For an explanation of what would be considered sufficient infringement see *Citizens Ins. Co. v. Parsons* (1881), 7 App. Cas. 96.

whether it does or does not is, I think, a question of fact, being the question whether or not it unduly trenches upon the powers of the Dominion Parliament to regulate trade and commerce in the sense referred to above.'[9] The regulatory scheme was seen as dealing primarily with property and civil rights within provincial jurisdiction and as such was *intra vires*.[10]

Given that the regulatory scheme was *intra vires*, a question then arose whether Chung Chuck could be convicted of violating the provincial scheme in light of the fact that that scheme could be seen as forcing Chung Chuck to do that which was illegal according to the federal *Combines Investigation Act*[11] and sections 496 and 498 of the Criminal Code, which dealt with unlawful restraints on trade. If it were true that the provincial Act could not be followed without violating the federal Act, then it was argued that the provincial law would be of no force or effect. The court ruled that the provincial statute did not conflict with the federal statute as the federal statute dealt with voluntary restraints on trade while the provincial statute created an involuntary restraint on trade.

The next case that addressed the applicability of regulatory schemes in light of the *Combines Investigation Act* was *R. v. Simoneau*,[12] heard by the Montreal Court of the Sessions of the Peace. In this case Simoneau had been accused of selling milk at a price lower than that fixed by the Quebec Dairy Board. Simoneau asserted that the Quebec legislation creating a dairy board was *ultra vires* the provincial legislature as it related to the general regulation of trade and commerce granted to the federal government under the Constitution of Canada.[13] It was also argued that the regulation was *ultra vires* the province's power as 'the Provincial Legislature can neither order nor permit what the federal law prohibits.'[14] In addition, it was argued that since section 498 of the Criminal Code and the *Combines Investigation Act* are valid,[15] and that when there is a conflict between a federal and provincial Act, the fed-

---

9 *Chung Chuck, supra* [1929] 1 D.L.R. at 756.
10 Ibid., at 758.
11 *Combines Investigation Act*, 1923, S.C. 1923, c. 9.
12 [1936] 1 D.L.R. 143.
13 Ibid., at 143.
14 Ibid., at 144.
15 See *Proprietary Article Trade Association v. A.-G. Canada*, [1931] 2 D.L.R. 1, 55 C. C.C. 241.

eral Act prevails, the provincial Act was of no force or effect.[16] While both the presiding judge and the attorney general of Quebec accepted that the *Combines Investigation Act* was 'valid' and that federal legislation was usually paramount, the presiding judge nonetheless found that the Quebec *Dairy Products Act*[17] was operative. The judge ruled that 'since the act does not unduly restrict trade or competition and the fixing of prices by the commission does not operate to the detriment of or against the interest of the public and is not the result of an agreement, there is no conflict between it and s. 498 of the Criminal Code or with the Combines Investigation Act.'[18] The fact that the restrictive practices were the result of provincial legislation was sufficient to show that the provincial Act did not unduly lessen competition, as would have been necessary for a violation of the *Combines Investigation Act*.[19] Without an undue lessening of competition or without detriment to the public, there would be no violation of the *Combines Investigation Act*: 'The fixing of prices by the commission does not operate to the detriment of or against the interest of the public and is not the result of an agreement. What is prohibited by the *Combines Investigation Act* is not to sell at the same price, but to do so to the detriment of the public.'[20]

In *Cherry v. The King ex rel. Wood*,[21] a case heard by the Saskatchewan Court of Appeal, the relationship between the federal government's power to regulate trade and commerce and the provincial government's power over property and civil rights within the province was once again in issue. The accused, Cherry, appealed from a conviction for violating the Saskatchewan *Milk Control Act*[22] by selling milk without a licence. Cherry argued that the Saskatchewan regulatory scheme that controlled the distribution and sale of milk in the province of Saskatchewan violated the *Combines Investigation Act*. However, as in *Simoneau* and *Chung Chuck*, the judge ruled that the legislation was not in conflict with the *Combines Investigation Act*:[23] 'It is clear that the purpose of the legislation is to improve conditions in the production, pro-

---

16 *R. v. Simoneau*, [1936] 1 D.L.R. at 144.
17 1933 (Que.), c. 24 and as amended 1934 (Que.), c. 27.
18 *Simoneau, supra* [1936] 1 D.L.R. at 143.
19 Ibid., at 149.
20 Ibid., at 153.
21 [1938] 1 D.L.R. 156.
22 S.S. 1934–35, c. 58.
23 *Cherry, supra* [1938] 1 D.L.R. at 158.

cessing and distribution of milk, having due regard to the interests of the producer, the distributor and the consumer public.'[24] 'The object of the *Milk Control Act* is not to augment the revenue [of the provincial government] but to regulate the production, distribution and sale of milk, an important commodity produced in the Province, in order to protect the public health, to ensure an adequate supply and to protect the interest alike of the producer, processor and consumers.'[25]

The *Cherry* decision expanded the scope of the developing regulated industry defence. The court found that acts of a regulatory board which are not specifically legislated but which are ancillary powers to the regulatory scheme are also by definition in the public interest and thus do not fall under the scrutiny of the *Combines Investigation Act*.[26] In order to violate the *Combines Investigation Act* it was necessary to conspire with another person; the board created under the Saskatchewan regulatory scheme was not a person and as such could not conspire.[27] The very fact that a board was operating under a power granted to it by the province within its legislative powers meant that the board could not violate the *Combines Investigation Act*. 'It surely cannot be successfully argued that a board, in exercising the powers conferred upon it by the Legislation ... renders itself liable to a prosecution under s. 498; if this were so the Province could not exercise the powers conferred upon it with respect to property and civil rights over which it has exclusive power.'[28]

In *Cherry*, the regulated conduct defence as it exists today was first elaborated. While the decision ultimately rested on the fact that there was no conflict between the provincial and federal legislation, the case went further and took a step towards exempting regulatory schemes because if such schemes validly implemented by the provinces were not exempted, provincial power over property and civil rights within the province would be negated. If all regulatory schemes were to fall under the scrutiny of the *Combines Investigation Act*, any regulatory scheme that was a restraint on trade would be illegal as a conspiracy to restrain trade. Thus in *Cherry*, the Saskatchewan Court of Appeal provided the rationale for allowing regulatory schemes to operate even if

---

24 Ibid., at 159.
25 Ibid., at 161.
26 Ibid., at 162.
27 Ibid., at 163.
28 Ibid., at 162.

it was found that they were in conflict with the federal *Combines Investigation Act*. In order to preserve some domain for a province in which it could exercise its exclusive jurisdiction over property and civil rights, provincial regulatory schemes must be exempted from the scrutiny of the *Combines Investigation Act*.[29]

In 1960 the Ontario High Court decided the *Canadian Breweries* case.[30] Canadian Breweries was charged with entering into mergers in the beer industry 'to the detriment of the public.'[31] The Crown argued that by acquiring breweries simply for the purpose of shutting them down, Canadian Breweries was acting to the detriment of the public and was able to adversely influence the price of beer.[32] In all the provinces in which Canadian Breweries held a significant market share and had significant production capacities, the production and distribution of beer was subject to provincial regulation.[33] Given the degree of regulation to which brewers are subject in every province, the defence argued 'that the merger did not prevent or lessen competition unduly having regard to the restrictions on competition validly imposed by Government authorities ...'[34] McRuer J. held: 'when I apply the *Combines Act* as an Act designed to protect the public interest in free competition, I am compelled to examine the legislation of the Provinces to see how far they have exercised their respective jurisdictions to remove the sale of beer from the competitive field and to see what areas of competition in the market are still open. Having made this examination I must then decide whether the formation or operation of the merger lessened or is likely to lessen competition to an unlawful degree in the areas were competition is permitted.'[35] So long as the mergers only affected areas of the brewing industry covered by a valid provincial regulatory scheme, they could not be viewed as a violation of the *Combines Investigation Act*.

In *Canadian Breweries* the Crown claimed that the mergers had an adverse influence on the price at which beer was being sold, especially in the province of Ontario. Under section 46 of the Ontario *Liquor Con-*

29 Ibid., 160–4.
30 *R. v. Canadian Breweries Ltd.* (1960), 126 C.C.C. 133.
31 Ibid.
32 Ibid., at 134.
33 Ibid., at 146.
34 Ibid., at 145.
35 Ibid., at 146.

trol Act[36] a government agency licensed the sale of beer and controlled the price at which it could be sold.[37] Given this, the court ruled, 'the evidence establishes to my entire satisfaction that the Liquor Control Board fixed the price at which beer was sold in Ontario on all levels throughout the entire period of the indictment.'[38] 'The references to price-cutting in the evidence must be read in the light of the fact that the prices were fixed by the Liquor Control Board.'[39]

The *Canadian Breweries* case found that with respect to violations of the *Combines Act* in industries which are regulated, the conduct in question must either create a public detriment in an area of the industry not regulated or prevent the proper operation of a regulatory board. 'When a Provincial Legislature has conferred on a Commission or Board the power to regulate an industry and fix prices, and the power has been exercised, the Court must assume that the power is exercised in the public interest. In such cases, in order to succeed in a prosecution laid under the *Combines Act* with respect to the operation of a combine, I think it must be shown that the combine has operated, or is likely to operate, so as to hinder or prevent the provincial body from effectively exercising powers given to it to protect the public interest.'[40]

In 1982 the relationship between legislation to establish regulatory schemes and the federal *Combines Investigation Act* was reviewed by the Supreme Court of Canada in the *Jabour* case[41] relating to the Law Society of British Columbia's decision to ban most forms of advertising of lawyers' services. The Law Society of British Columbia had taken steps to discipline Jabour for advertising his practice contrary to the society's rules for 'conduct unbecoming a member.' Jabour argued that this application of the rule violated the *Combines Investigation Act*. The Law Society argued that the *Combines Investigation Act* did not apply to the Law Society, which was established under the *Legal Professions Act*.[42] However, there was no specific provision in the legislation that

---

36   R.S.O. 1937, c. 294.
37   *Canadian Breweries, supra* (1960), 126 C.C.C. at 149.
38   Ibid., at 150
39   Ibid., at 157.
40   Ibid., at 167.
41   *Attorney-General of Canada et al. v. Law Society of British Columbia et al., Jabour v. Law Society of British Columbia et al.,* [1982] 2 S.C.R. 307.
42   R.S.B.C. 1960, c. 214, now the *Barrister and Solicitors Act,* R.S.B.C. 1979, c. 26.

required or authorized an advertising ban. Under the *Legal Professions Act* the Law Society was given wide-ranging powers to determine what constituted 'conduct unbecoming' of a lawyer.

The central question in issue in *Jabour* was whether the *Combines Investigation Act*[43] applied to the Law Society of British Columbia, its governing bodies, and its members.[44] It was argued that as the provincial statute does not expressly allow for a ban on advertising, while the federal statute arguably prohibits such a ban, the *Combines Investigation Act* would indeed apply to the advertising ban. As such, the actions of the benchers could be viewed as a violation of the *Combines Investigation Act*.[45] However, the court ruled that 'the courts in these cases have said in various ways that compliance with the edicts of a validly enacted provincial measure can hardly amount to something contrary to the public interest.'[46] 'So long as the CIA [Combines Investigation Act] ... is styled as a criminal prohibition, proceedings in its implementation and enforcement will require a demonstration of some conduct contrary to public interest.'[47] So long as the Law Society was acting under the authority granted it under provincial legislation there could be no violation of the *Combines Investigation Act*. Therefore, given the broad-ranging powers granted to the Law Society to determine what constituted conduct unbecoming a lawyer, the advertising ban the society instituted under this power was not subject to the scrutiny of the *Combines Investigation Act*.

In *R. v. Independent Order of Foresters*[48] the Ontario Court of Appeal further clarified the regulated conduct defence. The Independent Order of Foresters were charged with fifteen offences of misleading advertising contrary to the *Combines Investigation Act*. The trial judge ruled that the Independent Order of Foresters could not be found guilty of violating the *Combines Investigation Act* as the industry of which they were members, the insurance industry, was regulated. However, the Court of Appeal found that simply because an industry is regulated does not mean that all conduct of firms or individuals within the industry is immune from prosecution under the *Competition*

---

43 R.S.C. 1970, c. C-23.
44 *Jabour, supra* [1982] 2 S.C.R. at 331.
45 Ibid., at 347.
46 Ibid., at 354.
47 *Jabour, supra* [1982] 2 S.C.R. at 354.
48 (1989), 26 C.P.R. (3d) 229 (Ont. C.A.).

Act. 'The doctrine simply means that a person obeying a valid provincial statute may, in certain circumstances, be exempted from the provisions of a valid federal statute. But there can be no exemption unless there is a direction or at least an authorization to perform the prohibited act.'[49] While the lower court decision that the regulated conduct defence applied was overturned, the appeal was nonetheless dismissed and the accused found not guilty. The evidence did not support a finding that the advertising was misleading.

In *Industrial Milk Producers et al. v. Milk Board et al.*[50] a provincial regulatory scheme and a federal quota system relating to the sale and distribution of dairy products were challenged under the *Competition Act.* The case was heard in the Federal Court – Trial Division. The Industrial Milk Producers Association brought an action against the British Columbia Milk Board, claiming that the board's method of allocating industrial milk quotas was an unreasonable restraint on trade. The Industrial Milk Producers Association also argued that the regulated industry defence only applied when the regulators were operating in the public interest.[51] The federal court ruled that the Milk Board was entitled to rely on the fact that its conduct was authorized by provincial and federal regulation to avoid being found in breach of the *Competition Act.*[52] This case affirmed that the regulated industry defence which had developed under the *Combines Investigation Act* remained in effect under the *Competition Act* 1986. Earlier cases had decided that 'provincial marketing boards, when exercising authority conferred on them by provincial or federal legislation, cannot be said to be committing an offence under ... the *Combines Investigation Act.*'[53] Following these cases the court decided that it did not have a mandate to review whether as a matter of fact a regulatory scheme is operating in the public interest.[54] 'Rather, the jurisprudence ... indicates that when such a board is acting within its statutory mandate it is *deemed* to be acting in the public interest.'[55] While the established case law held that provincial regulatory schemes should not be scrutinized for their effective-

---

49 Ibid., at 232.
50 (1988), 47 D.L.R. (4th) 710.
51 Ibid., at 711.
52 Ibid., at 711.
53 Ibid., at 718.
54 Ibid., at 719.
55 Ibid.

ness by the court, there was still a question as to whether the preambular clause (s. 1) of the *Competition Act*, which states that the purpose of the *Competition Act* is *inter alia* to promote efficiency, means that certain regulatory schemes would fall under the scrutiny of the Competition Tribunal or the courts. Despite the court's finding in *Industrial Milk Producers* that the general purpose of the *Competition Act* differed from the general purpose of the *Combines Investigation Act*, it was held that the changed purpose 'cannot be interpreted as signaling a departure from the pre-existing jurisprudence which established the "regulated industries defence".'[56]

In 1996 the issue of the status of the regulated industry defence under the *Competition Act* 1986 was considered by the Ontario Court (General Division) in a reference case.[57] The case concerned whether the director could initiate an investigation into the mandatory insurance program for lawyers instituted by the Law Society of Upper Canada. The ruling of the Ontario Court (General Division) concurred with the decision in *Industrial Milk Producers* that the regulated industries defence still applies under the *Competition Act* 1986. It held that 'the Law Society has a regulated conduct defence from the *Competition Act*, because the *Law Society Act*, R.S.C. 1990, c. L.8, s. 61 authorizes it to implement its own ... scheme.'[58] It held 'that provinces may, in the exercise of their exclusive jurisdiction, regulate industries notwithstanding the provisions of federal competition laws.'[59] So long as the Law Society is acting within powers granted to it under a valid provincial scheme, even if the power is not specifically delineated, but is instead residual to another power, the actions of the Society are not subject to the *Competition Act*.[60] Since the regulated conduct exemption applied, the director did not have the jurisdiction to investigate whether conduct authorized under the regulatory scheme violates the *Competition Act*.[61] Therefore, the regulated industry defence not only prevents prosecution under the *Competition Act*, it can also be used to prevent an investigation from proceeding. Following this decision, the director

---

56 Ibid., at 725.
57 *Re Law Society of Upper Canada and Attorney General of Canada et al.* (1996), 134 D.L.R. (4th) 300.
58 Ibid., at 301.
59 Ibid., at 306.
60 Ibid., at 312.
61 Ibid., at 313.

acknowledged that with respect to industries which are heavily regulated his power to police the activities of firms within such industries is limited.[62]

The *Law Society* reference case also helped clarify whether the regulated conduct defence applies to the entire *Competition Act* or only to its criminal provisions. Under the *Combines Investigation Act* most competition offences were criminal matters. The defence originally developed because criminal offences were required to be 'undue' restrictions on competition or contrary to the public interest and, by definition, government regulatory schemes were not 'undue' or contrary to the public interest. However, in the *Law Society* case it was found that the director could not even begin an investigation into conduct that is regulated. Regardless of whether the alleged violation is criminally or civilly reviewable, the Competition Bureau cannot investigate regulated conduct.

The extent to which regulated industries are exempt from competition law was once again examined in *2903113 Canada Inc. v. Quebec (Regie des marches agricoles et alimentaires).*[63] This case, heard by the Quebec Court of Appeal, concerned the marketing of pork under a provincial regulatory scheme. While the lower court found that the actions of the Quebec Pork Marketing Board violated the *Competition Act,* the Court of Appeal held that the presiding judge in the lower court failed properly to consider the regulated conduct defence.[64] The Quebec Court of Appeal found that the acts of the Pork Marketing Board, despite being wide-ranging, and often not specifically required or authorized in the legislation, were indeed within the regulatory authority of the board.[65] Given the role of the Pork Marketing Board under a provincial regulatory scheme the *Competition Act* could not have been violated. Violation of the Act requires proof of public harm and the Pork Marketing Board's actions were, by definition, deemed to be in the public interest.[66] This case provided confirmation by an appellate court that the *Jabour* decision still applies despite the enactment of the *Competition Act.*

---

62 See *Canada (Director of Investigation and Research) v. Bank of Montreal et al.* (1996), 68 C.P.R. (3d) 527 [hereinafter *Interac*].

63 [1997] A.Q. no 2125.

64 Ibid., at 3.

65 Ibid., at 14.

66 Ibid., at 16.

While the regulated conduct defence limits the application of the *Competition Act* to regulated industries and thus prevents the nature of the regulatory schemes themselves from being subject to the scrutiny of the court under the that Act, the common law of restraint of trade could arguably allow the courts to review the actions of regulatory bodies for arbitrarily depriving people of their livelihood.[67] British cases suggest that legal monopolies (such as those created through provincial and federal regulation) must exercise their power so as not unreasonably to restrain the freedom of trade[68] of members or aspiring members. In *Dickson v. Pharmaceutical Society of Great Britain*[69] the court found that the restraints placed on members by self-governing professions needed to be reasonable. In this case, the plaintiff, Dickson, was a member of the society that exercised a legal monopoly over certain aspects of the pharmaceutical profession in Great Britain. No one could practise as a registered pharmacist in Great Britain without being a member of the society, and no one could become a member without agreeing to be bound by the rules of the society. The society passed a rule limiting the range of products that could be sold in a pharmacy to traditional pharmaceutical goods, apparently with a view to restricting the growth of large drugstore chains. In the Court of Appeal, Lord Denning set out two criteria for evaluating involuntary restraints of trade. The first was whether the rule was in the interest of the pharmaceutical profession and the second was whether it was in the interest of the public. Lord Denning found that the rule was not in the interest of the profession and probably not in the interest of the public and thus was 'arbitrary and capricious' and void. The House of Lords unanimously affirmed the decision of the Court of Appeal, although expressing some cautions about overly stringent application of the doctrine to traditional professions not engaged in retail trading of goods.

In *Nagle v. Feilden*,[70] the rules of a self-governing body were also challenged and overturned in an English court. Nagle, the plaintiff, was denied a licence as a trainer by the Jockey Club, an organization

---

67 Michael Trebilcock, *The Common Law Restraint of Trade: A Legal and Economic Analysis* (Toronto: Carswell, 1986), chap. 4.
68 Ibid.
69 [1967] 1 Ch. 708 (C.A.); [1970] A.C. 403 (H.L.).
70 [1966] 2 Q.B. 633 (C.A.).

with the exclusive legal right to issue such licences, although she was fully qualified for such a licence. It appeared that she had been denied the licence because of an unwritten and informal policy of the club not to issue such licences to women. Nagle sought a declaration that the club's policy of refusing to issue licences to women to train horses was an unreasonable restraint of trade and an injunction requiring the club to issue her such a licence. In the Court of Appeal, Lord Denning M.R., in deciding that the refusal to grant a licence was unreasonable, stated '[w]e live in days when many professional associations are "closed shops." No person can work his trade or profession except by their permission ... When a man is wrongly rejected or ousted by one of these associations, has he no remedy? I think he has ... Just as the courts will intervene to protect his right of property, they will also intervene to protect his right to work.'[71]

These cases suggest that the common law doctrine of restraint of trade (in addition to administrative law doctrines relating to judicial review) can prevent regulatory bodies from arbitrarily exercising the discretion granted to them. Individuals who have had their freedom to trade restricted through the arbitrary or unreasonable exercise of regulatory powers can seek relief through the courts. Thus, some of the regulatory schemes exempted from scrutiny under the *Competition Act* may nevertheless be vulnerable to attack under the common law.

In addition, some forms of professional or industry regulation may be vulnerable to constitutional challenge on various grounds. For example, professional regulations restricting entry into the legal profession to Canadian citizens have been held to violate the equality provisions of the Charter of Rights and Freedoms;[72] regulations restricting the formation of interprovincial law firms have been held to violate the personal mobility and trade and commerce provisions of the constitution;[73] regulations banning advertising by dentists have been held to violate the freedom of expression guarantees in the Charter;[74] and regulations restricting the issuance of Medicare billing entitlements to physicians practising in particular geographic locations have been held

---

71 Ibid., at 441.
72 *Andrews v. Law Society of British Columbia* (1989), 56 D.L.R. (4th) 1 (S.C.C.).
73 *Black v. Law Society of Alberta* (1989), 58 D.L.R. (4th) 317 (S.C.C.).
74 *Rocket v. Royal College of Dental Surgeons of Ontario* (1990), 71 D.L.R. (4th) 68 (S.C.C.).

to violate the personal mobility guarantees and equality provisions of the Charter.[75]

The U.S. courts have also found it necessary to address conflicts between antitrust and other federal or state regulatory schemes. Just as the federal government has paramountcy in Canada, under the supremacy clause of the U.S. constitution[76] the federal government has the power to pre-empt state regulation. However, as in Canada, the courts have found that there was no intent to lessen the states' powers to regulate through the implementation of antitrust law.[77] The mere fact that there is a conflict between state law and federal antitrust law is not enough to pre-empt the state law.[78] In the United States, federal antitrust laws are primarily concerned with private conduct, and, as such, under the state action doctrine, many restraints that would violate the *Sherman Act* are tolerated if they are implemented as part of a state regulatory scheme, so long as the state possesses the power to implement such schemes.[79] Courts have found that when Congress passed the *Sherman Act* it never intended to undermine the regulatory powers of state and local governments.[80] However, in order for an action to qualify for the state action exemption, the challenged activity must be authorized by a state and clearly articulated in laws or regulations. In addition, the authorized private conduct must be actively supervised by the state.[81] Thus, unlike in Canada, vague and unspecified powers are not exempted from scrutiny under the *Sherman Act*. If the state has authorized conduct but is not actively regulating this conduct, antitrust authorities would still have the power to prevent anticompetitive practices. Thus, the U.S. state action doctrine is more limited in its scope than its Canadian counterpart. In our view, there would be considerable merit to limiting the scope of the Canadian regulated industries defence to cases where the allegedly anticompetitive conduct or activities in question are *inherent* in the regulatory scheme

---

75 *Waldman v. British Columbia (Medical Services Commission)* (1997), 150 D.L.R. (4th) 405 (B.C.S.C.).

76 U.S. Const. Art. VI.

77 Herbert Hovenkamp, *Federal Antitrust Policy: The Law of Competition and Its Practice* (St Paul: West Publishing Company, 1994), at 670.

78 See *Exxon Corp. v. Governor of Maryland*, 437 U.S. 117 (1978).

79 Hovenkamp, *Federal Antitrust Policy*, at 671.

80 Ibid., at 673.

81 Ibid., at 676.

(e.g., production quotas under agricultural marketing board regimes) or have been *specifically* directed or authorized by statute. In cases where regulatory bodies arc vested with broad discretion there should be a presumption that this discretion should not be exercised so as to direct or authorize conduct that would violate the *Competition Act*. This presumption should be stronger in the case of self-regulatory professional, trade, or industrial bodies, where protectionist biases are always a concern, than in the case of independent public regulatory agencies.

II. Competition Policy and Regulation in Network Industries[82]

A. *Introduction*

In recent years there has been a worldwide trend towards the deregulation and deintegration of network industries. Most first world countries arc shifting towards regulatory systems[83] organized, to the extent possible, around competition.[84] This transformation, propelled by technological changes that have undermined economies of scale in some industry segments and supported by the current teachings of economics, has been characterized by a move from command-based regulation and natural monopoly models towards increased market governance and deintegrated market structures.

Over the past fifteen years major changes have occurred in the telecommunications, electricity, natural gas, and transportation sectors of the Canadian economy. Industries which were once directly regulated

---

82 Part II of this chapter is closely derived from Michal S. Gal and Michael Trebilcock, 'Natural Monopolies in Transition,' in J. Musgrove, ed., *Competition Law for the 21st Century* (Yonkers, N.Y.: Juris Publishing, 1998).

83 The term 'regulation' is used in its generic sense, to cover all methods of regulation, including competition (antitrust) laws and sector-specific regulatory regimes.

84 This regulatory trend has been extensively discussed in the literature. See, for example, C.D. Foster, *Privatization, Public Ownership and the Regulation of Natural Monopoly* (Oxford: Blackwell, 1992); W. Kip Viscusi, John M. Vernon, and Joseph E. Harrington, Jr, *Economics of Regulation and Anti-Trust* (Toronto: D.C. Heath 1992); Mark Armstrong, Simon Cowan, and John Vickers, *Regulatory Reform: Economic Analysis and British Experience* (Cambridge, Mass.: MIT Press, 1994); and Joseph Kearney and Thomas Merrill, 'The Great Transformation of Regulated Industries Law,' (1998) 98 *Columbia L. Rev.* 1323.

by industry-specific regulators are being deregulated and subjected to market forces. In telecommunications all sectors of the industry, including local service, are being deregulated. In October 1993 the *Telecommunications Act*[85] came into force and changed the way in which the Canadian Radio-television and Telecommunications Commission (CRTC) regulates telecommunications in Canada. While the Act allows the CRTC to continue regulating in many of the areas in which it had previously regulated, explicit provisions for regulatory forbearance were also included. The CRTC is given the authority to forbear when it determines that forbearance is consistent with the goals of the *Telecommunications Act*. As well, the CRTC is required to forbear when it determines that there is sufficient competition in sectors of the industry to protect the interests of the public.[86] In transportation, rail, air transportation, trucking, and intercity buses have been deregulated and entry and competition has been encouraged. In energy, natural gas production and retailing has been deregulated, and competition in electricity generation and retailing is being implemented in provinces such as Ontario and Alberta. U.S. studies have consistently found that deregulation has been accompanied by large price reductions to consumers and substantial improvements in quality and service.[87] The balance of this chapter focuses on the relationship between industry-specific regulation and framework competition laws in so-called network industries in transition to competition in at least some of their segments. Such industries typically involve network externalities. Demand-side networks externalities can occur when there are substantial benefits to being a member of a network or standard. As the network or standard (e.g., the telephone system) is embraced by more people or organizations, its value to existing members rises. Supply-side efficiencies can arise when the costs of providing services to additional consumers reduces the overall cost of the network (e.g., telephone systems, natu-

---

85 S.C 1993, c. 38, s. 34.
86 Lawson Hunter et al., 'All We are Saying is Give Competition a Chance – The Role of Competition Policy in Industries in Transition from Regulation to Competition,' *The Competition Act Ten Years On: A Stock Taking*, University of Toronto Law School, Competition Policy Round-table, 1995, at 15.
87 See R. Grandall and C.J. Ellig, *Economic Deregulation and Customer Choice* (Washington, D.C.: George Mason University, Center for Market-Processes, 1997), C. Winston, 'U.S. Industry Adjustment to Economic Deregulation,' (1993) 31 *J. of Economic Perspectives* 1263.

ral gas pipelines, electricity transmission, and distribution systems).[88] As an increasing number of hitherto regulated network industries are deregulated (at least in some segments), the question of when the sector-specific regulator cedes effective jurisdiction to the federal competition authorities poses important issues. Problems of concurrent jurisdiction may arise. However, just as seriously, problems of absence of effective regulatory oversight may arise if the regulator decides to forbear from regulating aspects of the industry in the transition from regulation to competition and the competition authorities are prevented by the regulated conduct defence from monitoring the transition in the light of residual or contingent regulatory authority vested in the industry-specific regulator. We now turn to these issues.

The network industries' dual nature – combining non-competitive and potentially competitive activities which are vertically integrated – complicates deregulation. In most network industries, such as electricity and natural gas, transmission and distribution segments are characterized as natural monopolies, the most concentrated of all market structures. In contrast, in the potentially competitive segments of the industry market forces can usually provide the necessary discipline. The fact that these two 'polar cases' are often vertically linked together creates a policy dilemma, since the benefits of vertical coordination among these segments have to be balanced against the benefits of competition. Financial integration of industry segments can seriously weaken competition in the potentially competitive segments.[89] It is widely believed that in many cases it is more efficient to deintegrate, at least partially, the potentially competitive from the non-competitive activities.[90] Deintegration may entail complete divestiture of competitive facilities from monopoly facilities, or organizational separation through separately incorporated commercial affiliates. While full structural separation of competitive from non-competitive facilities ('full divestiture') largely resolves the problem, it also entails non-

---

88 See Paul Crampton and Brian Facey, 'Revisiting Regulation and Deregulation through the Lens of Competition: Getting the Balance Right,' paper presented at the APEC Regulatory Reform Symposium, Malaysia, 5 and 6 September 1998.
89 John Vickers and George Yarrow, *Privatization: An Economic Analysis* (Cambridge, Mass.: MIT Press, 1988), 291.
90 For an overview of this issue in the context of the electricity supply industry see Michael S. Gal, 'Traditional Natural Monopolies in Transition: The Case of the Electricity Supply Industry' (LL.M. thesis, Faculty of Law, University of Toronto, 1996).

trivial costs that have discouraged the adoption of this option in many jurisdictions. Given that *vertical economies of scope* exist in interconnection between competitive and non-competitive segments,[91] the benefits of greater competition have to be traded off against the benefits of vertical and horizontal economies of scale and scope. Thus, the current challenge for public policy in network industries is to deregulate the potentially competitive segments while maintaining adequate regulatory safeguards over remaining non-competitive activities in which competition cannot provide adequate discipline. *Inter alia*, the non-competitive segments have to be prevented from leveraging their monopoly power into the potentially competitive segments.

The difficulty lies in identifying the regulatory instruments best suited to meet this challenge. A complex relationship exists between regulatory regimes and industry structure, conduct, and performance. The introduction of competition does not necessarily imply competition law. The challenge is to identify contexts in which competition law or other methods of regulation, or some combination of these regulatory mechanisms, are appropriate. The main policy options for regulating the industry in its new structure are regulation by general framework competition laws or economic regulation by industry-specific rules. Of course, these options may be deployed as complements rather than substitutes. The relationship among the options has yet to be rationalized in an economically coherent and consistent way in Canada and other jurisdictions and poses challenging policy issues. This regulatory task is clearly much more important under a vertically integrated market structure than under a fully deintegrated structure. Where full vertical deintegration of non-competitive and competitive activities is implemented, the non-competitive segments have weaker incentives and opportunities to leverage their monopoly power than where only partial vertical deintegration is implemented. Nonetheless, under both structures conduct regulation is necessary. We focus primarily on conduct regulation by either a specialized regulatory agency using industry-specific rules or by general or framework competition laws. Some commentators favour 'light-handed regulation,' where

---

91 One study estimated that arm's-length contracting between electricity generators and distributors raises costs by 11.95 per cent relative to vertically integrated production. David L. Kaserman and John W. Mayo, 'The Measurement of Vertical Economies and the Efficient Structure of the Electricity Utility Business,' (1991) 39 (5) *J. of Industrial Economies* 483.

competition laws are primarily relied on to deal with such concerns.[92] In contrast, we argue below for greater reliance on direct regulation.

Vertical integration enables many strategies to bias the conditions of competitive markets in favour of the integrated firm. This is especially so where the non-competitive segments controlled by a competitor are 'bottleneck' or 'essential' facilities required by competitors in order to gain access to the market. The bottleneck operator has economic incentives to exploit opportunities resulting from its market power in the non-competitive segments of the industry to extend this power into the competitive segments of the industry. The economic outcome of such leveraging of monopoly power involves creating an 'artificial' competitive advantage for the competitive arm of the integrated firm.

The vertically integrated firm might leverage its monopoly power either by giving its competitive arm(s) *interconnection benefits* over potential rivals (discrimination) or by *cross-subsidizing* its competitive arm(s). The first practice involves offering competitors of a monopolist lower-quality or higher-priced interconnection services than those offered to its competitive arm. *Cross-subsidization* involves the use of profits earned from monopoly markets where these are not effectively constrained by regulation to fund a policy of predatory pricing in the competitive markets. By setting low prices the firm can impose losses on its competitors and perhaps induce them to exit the industry. The same can be achieved by *tying* – refusing to sell interconnection services to downstream consumers unless they also buy products or services from its affiliated competitive arm(s) or *exclusive dealing*, where as a condition of supplying a product/service to a customer, the supplier requires that the customer use only its products/services.

The economic incentives for such actions may involve driving out a competitor, with a view to recouping lost revenues by charging high prices after the rival's exit from the market (predatory actions in a broad sense). Although predatory conduct is a contested notion in economics, most economists agree that predation can be profitable if the monopolist is prevented in some way from extracting monopoly profits from its monopoly facilities, for example, if the monopoly facilities are placed

---

92 See Hunter et al., 'Give Competition a Chance,' Henry Ergas, 'Telecommunications Across the Tasman,' in Megan Richardson, ed., *Deregulation of Public Utilities: Current Issues and Perspectives* (Melbourne: Centre for Corporate Law and Securities Regulation, University of Melbourne Law School, 1996); and David Goddard, 'Comments,' in ibid.

under conduct regulation that prevents it from charging supracompetitive rates for its services. It may extract supracompetitive profits by creating an advantage for its competitive facilities and driving its rivals out of the market.[93] Such conduct might also be profitable where the competitive arm of the monopolist has a dominant position in the competitive segment and there are high barriers to entry into this segment.

A rate-regulated integrated firm also has strong economic incentives to behave strategically with respect to cost allocation. Where the monopoly activity is regulated, the integrated firm may *misallocate its costs* by attributing some of the costs of its competitive arm(s) to its rate-regulated activities, passing the misallocated cost along to its captive rate payers. By transferring costs that are in fact incurred to underwrite commercial activities into the rate base of its regulated non-competitive activity, an integrated firm has the ability to distort the price of both its regulated and its competitive activities.[94] This may permit circumvention of the regulation of the monopoly by the collection of rents through an unregulated affiliate. Experience suggests that, due to information asymmetries, such cost manipulations are both costly and difficult (perhaps impossible) for any external regulatory authority to monitor and control with complete accuracy.

B. *The Role of Competition Policy in Network Industries*

The choice of regulatory methods must be based on their comparative capabilities[95] as well as on the specific characteristics of the industry and the goals of regulation. To determine when the Competition Bureau and Competition Tribunal and when the industry-specific regulator is the appropriate industry overseer, it is necessary to outline the differences between competition law and economic regulation.

Competition laws seek to foster the conditions necessary for a competitive market-place by supplementing or defining the rules of the game by which competition takes place to protect the competitive process and to ensure that market forces can achieve economic efficiency.[96]

---

93 For an overview, see Viscusi et al., *Economics of Regulation and Anti-Trust*, chap. 8.
94 Ibid., at 220.
95 Ronald Coase, 'The Regulated Industries Discussion,' (1964) 54 *American Economic Review* 195.
96 Philip Areeda and Louis Kaplow, *Antitrust Analysis: Problems, Texts, Cases*, 4th ed. (Boston: Little, Brown, 1988), 13.

Several basic conditions must be present to guarantee that the long-run market equilibrium that results from rivalry will be efficient. Competition is effective when there is strong mutual pressure among comparable rivals and where no firm dominates the market. Accordingly, the domain of competition is intrinsically limited. It is not capable of affecting competition in markets where competition cannot remedy market failure. In particular, market forces are an ineffective and undesirable means of controlling natural monopolies. By assumption, creating competition entails loss of the scale or scope of operation of the dominant firm, which in turn implies, where natural monopolies are concerned, higher costs per unit of output which are greater than the dead-weight loss from monopoly.

The proper task of economic regulation is to intervene where competitive forces alone are too weak to defend the public interest. Its aim is to restrict or prevent behaviour, inadvertent or deliberate, that threatens to damage the public interest. Thus goal is usually accomplished by setting the regulated factors at an economically efficient level. Economic regulation may also be used to achieve non-economic goals.

The problem of regulatory policy is one of incentive mechanism design: how can the regulator induce the firm to act in accordance with the public interest when it is not always able to observe directly the firm's behaviour? Two main options are available to the direct regulator: rate-of-return regulation and performance-based regulation.[97] However, the role of the regulator remains, initially, negative: setting maximum prices, specifying minimum service, in short, contravening the decisions of regulated firms only in specific cases that do not conform to various performance variables set by the regulator.

While economic regulation has the potential to raise welfare and achieve other regulatory goals, it has inherent limitations as an institution of effective social control. The main difficulties involve asymmetric information, which leads to an inability to regulate effectively the firm's decisions; principal-agent problems, which lead to difficulties in achieving the formal objectives of regulation; and incentive-incompatible regulatory instruments, which prevent or diminish the introduction of change and innovation. In addition, economic regulation

---

97 W.J. Baumol and J.G. Sidak, *Toward Competition in Local Telephony* (Cambridge, Mass.: MIT Press and American Enterprise Institute, 1994).

imposes direct administrative costs upon the government, the regulator and the regulated parties. The principal institutional deficiency of regulation is dynamic: the absence of a spur to progressive performance comparable to and as reliable as that of competition.[98]

Competition law and economic regulation differ in their institutional characteristics and in their enforcement. These differences are summarized in Table 11.1.

Taking into consideration the comparative characteristics of competition laws and alternative regulatory tools, this section evaluates the best regulatory method to meet the regulatory tasks of preventing the leveraging of monopoly power in network industries.

To be effective, the regulatory framework must accomplish at least the following goals. First, it should establish the parameters, and ensure the existence, of acceptable business practices in order to maximize social welfare and achieve non-economic regulatory goals. Second, it must ensure that the transition to competitive markets is not unduly delayed. Third, it must afford the industry the flexibility to operate and adjust to changing market conditions. Finally, it must be clear and workable and it must provide an exclusive division of regulatory functions. Any overlap or potential overlap of regulatory responsibility is likely to result in confusion and uncertainty among both regulators and regulated firms, which in turn is likely to lead to unjustified costs and delays, waste of resources, and unfairness to the regulated firms. The proposed allocation of regulatory responsibilities should not only be theoretically clear but also should afford an administratively workable solution. It should be realistic in the regulatory burdens that it imposes on the regulatory process.

In this section we argue that competition laws may provide an appropriate tool for regulating the monopoly leveraging problem if and only if they are used in conjunction with other methods of regulation. Competition laws can, in most cases, regulate efficiently the potentially competitive segments of the industry – for example, collusion, mergers (except mergers between monopoly and potentially competitive segments of the industry, which should be reviewed for leveraging concerns by the industry-specific regulator), and restrictive or exclusionary practices that do not depend directly on the network

---

98 Richard A. Posner, 'Natural Monopoly and Its Regulation,' (1969) 21 *Stanford Law Review* 563.

TABLE 11.1
Competition Law and Direct Regulation

	Competition authorities	Direct regulator
Institutional characteristics application	Applies to all areas of the economy except those excluded by law.	Pertains to a specific industry or a specific sector in an industry, as specified in its regulatory mandate.
Regulatory methods	Creating and maintaining market conditions necessary to allow the market to operate efficiently.	Placing limits on the performance of firms so as to limit the losses to society that might result from market failures. The direct regulator intervenes directly in the conduct of the regulated firms by regulating levels of service, quality, prices, and/or profits.
Responsibility for economic outcomes	Outcomes are determined by the influence of competitive market forces.	Responsibility for efficient economic outcomes lies with the direct regulator.
Area of expertise	Defining the conditions and rules that enable competition to take place, distinguishing market activities that are likely to undermine the competitive market process from socially beneficial competitive activities, and eliminating market power that is not a result of technological barriers.	Expertise in the economic characteristics of the industry or industry segment regulated.
Expertise of members	The Competition Bureau has economic expertise in competition-related issues. The Competition Tribunal is a specialized body made up of judges and economic and business experts. But appeals go to courts, which are unaided by expert adjudication. Also, alleged violations of criminal provisions are adjudicated by regular courts.	Depends on the individuals chosen by government to serve as regulators. In most cases, some members of the regulatory body have economic expertise in the specific industry which is regulated.

TABLE 11.1 *(Continued)*

	Competition authorities	Direct regulator
Timing of regulation	Usually *ex post facto* review of behaviour. Designed to achieve objectives in the medium to long run.	*Ex ante* review. Regulation usually involves prior approval of a course of business conduct. Has the potential to achieve objectives in the short run.
Scope of review	Independent review of business behaviour against a more or less predetermined set of rules.	Standards of economic regulation tend to be more 'public interest'-based. Greater discretion to take non-economic issues into account in deciding which policies to adopt.
Initiation of regulatory proceedings	To effect change, the authorities (or, in some jurisdictions, private parties) must initiate the proceedings and go to courts, the tribunal, or regulatory bodies.	Initiation by regulator either on its own initiative or as a result of a complaint by a market player.
Regulatory process	Competition authorities must bring alleged offenders to court or the tribunal in order to prevent them from engaging in anticompetitive conduct. Tribunal and first-instance court decisions can be reviewed and overruled by appellate courts.	Regulators must follow a specified set of administrative procedures in reaching their decision. Regulation must be consistent with the legislative mandate, or else it runs the risk of being overturned by courts on judicial review.
Nature of proceedings	Legal proceedings, based on alleged economic offences, either criminal or civil, which include evidentiary and procedural matters.	Regulatory proceeding necessary in order to create an effective regulatory regime. Do not require an activity to come within the scope of a predetermined offence in order to regulate it.
Right of participation	Only granted to parties directly affected by proceedings. Procedural fairness does not require the court or tribunal to allow the participation of competitors or other groups indirectly affected by the decision, although it may choose to do so.	The direct regulator needs to afford all the parties substantially affected by its decisions, directly or indirectly, considerably more opportunity to participate in the regulatory process than do the competition authorities.

TABLE 11.1   (*Concluded*)

	Competition authorities	Direct regulator
Length of proceedings	Varies depending on complexity of issue, number of parties, and number of appeals.	Varies depending on complexity of the issues and number of parties.
Proof necessary to regulate conduct	Offence requires proof of anti-competitive conduct.	Regulator's decision must be reasonable under the circumstances.
Outcome of proceedings	Win/lose situation. Conduct labelled as 'anti-competitive' and in criminal cases as 'criminal.'	Regulatory measures necessary in order to regulate the market. No criminal/anticompetitive label.
Remedies	Remedies are prescribed in accordance with the provision which has been breached. Where the provision is criminal in nature, remedies include fines and imprisonment. Where the provision is civil in nature, they usually are structure or conduct related.	'Micro-management' model, enables the regulator to set conduct factors in a potentially efficient form.
Option of second review of the same conduct	If the plaintiff fails to prove the case against the firm the first time, it cannot issue proceedings against the firm for the same conduct (double jeopardy doctrine).	Regulators may review regulatory measures as many times as they deem necessary. Limited by reasonableness and fairness.
Effect of outcome	Affects only direct parties to the proceedings.	Affects all parties that the regulator enumerates in its decision.
Continuity of monitoring	Few tools for ongoing monitoring	Enables ongoing monitoring.

operator's ability to leverage off its monopoly power as network operator into the competitive segments of the industry. However, most of the monopoly leveraging problems should be regulated by direct regulation. Some 'checks and balances' can be achieved through an extensive use of the intervention power by the competition authorities before industry-specific regulatory agencies.

1. *Preventing the Leveraging of Monopoly Power into Competitive Segments by Cross-Subsidization*

The most relevant provision of the *Competition Act* is the predatory pricing provision (s. 50(1)(c)), discussed in Chapter 5.[99] Cross-subsidization might fall within the scope of the provision. However, proof remains difficult. There is a strong case for requiring transparent information on an historic and current-cost basis from a vertically integrated monopoly, which should reveal short- and long-run marginal costs. Even then it will be a demanding task to allocate the costs of the firm to its natural monopoly and competitive activities, due to the existence of vertical economies of scope. Where separating joint costs is difficult, the monopoly might try to prove that it priced its output at or above average total cost. The competition authorities do not have the tools or the expertise to allocate such costs.

2. *Preventing the Leveraging of Monopoly Power into Competitive Segments by Cost Misallocation*

As in the case of cross-subsidization, predation is the most relevant provision for the prevention of cost misallocation problems. In addition to those surveyed above, several difficulties may arise in applying the predatory pricing provision in order to prevent cost misallocation problems. Although the outcome of both the usual predatory pricing scenario and cost misallocations by the network operator may be similar – driving out of the market competitors which have competitive advantages over the predating firm by producing false economic signals and reducing economic welfare in the long run – it is achieved in different ways. 'Ordinary' predatory pricing usually involves conduct of one firm or one operational division of a firm, whereas cost misallocation requires coordination between the network and competitive

---

99 The abuse of dominance provisions of the *Competition Act* might also be used to address cross-subsidization.

divisions of the firm; 'ordinary' predatory pricing involves temporary pricing below cost whereas the network operator might engage in cost misallocation for unlimited periods, since it does not entail a loss to the overall profitability of the firm. Unlike 'ordinary' predatory pricing, cost misallocation could be profitable to the monopolist even if it does not possess market power in the competitive market or if barriers to entry into the competitive segment are low. Assume for example, that the 'real' costs of electricity generation are 100, but the monopolist succeeds in covering 50 per cent of such costs by 'smuggling' them into the cost structure of its regulated activities. It would be profitable for the monopolist to sell its generated electricity at any price above 50, whether or not there are barriers to entry into the predated market or whether or not it possesses market power in the generating segment.

In such a situation it will be difficult, if not impossible, to establish some of the elements of the offence, especially that the competitive arm of the network operator sets its prices 'unreasonably low.' By 'smuggling' some of the costs of its competitive arm or affiliate into its regulated rates the operator can price its competitive services at a price which, although below its 'real' costs, does not generate any loss for the firm as a whole. The crucial question then becomes whether a court will apply the economic criteria for 'unreasonably low' prices to the costs of competitive services alone, or whether it will adopt a broader test that takes into account all the costs of the firm. It seems that the interpretation adopted so far in the case law, which takes into account all circumstances surrounding the alleged predatory action, might be broad enough to allow the firm to justify its actions on economic grounds: it covers all its costs and does not suffer any losses. Nonetheless, such justification will expose the firm to the scrutiny of the direct regulator, whose failure to regulate the natural monopolist and to prevent it from 'smuggling' costs incurred by its competitive arm into its cost structure has enabled cost misallocation to take place in the first place.

3. Preventing the Leveraging of Monopoly Power into Competitive Segments by Tying

Section 77(2) of the Act prohibits tied selling where 'it is engaged in by a major supplier of a product in a market or because it is widespread in a market, [and] is likely to have exclusionary effect in the market, with the result that competition is or is likely to be lessened substantially ...'[100] The first element of the reviewable practice is tied selling. Section 77(1) defines tied selling as (a) any practice whereby a supplier of a product, as a condition of supplying the product (the 'tying' product) to a customer, requires that customer to acquire any other product (the 'tied' product) from the supplier or the supplier's nominee or (b) any practice whereby a supplier of a product induces a customer to meet a condition set out in (a) by offering to supply the tying product to the customer on more favourable terms if the customer agrees to meet the condition. In the case of the network operator, this element is present when the operator attaches conditions to the supply of interconnection services, or offers better terms for such services, when a customer acquires other products or services from the operator's affiliated facilities. The second element requires that the tied selling be engaged in by a major supplier of a product. The network operator is the sole supplier of interconnection services. The third element involves the exclusionary effect that the tied selling has in the market. The commissioner of competition should have no problem establishing that the tie impedes entry or expansion of firms not affiliated with the network operator. The fourth element requires proof of 'substantial lessening of competition.' The result of tied selling is the elimination of competitive options to consumers, since independent suppliers cannot supply services if they are tied to interconnection services provided by the network operator.

4. Preventing the Leveraging of Monopoly Power into Competitive Segments by Setting Discriminatory Interconnection Terms

(a) Refusal to Deal

Canada has a stand-alone refusal-to-deal provision that represents a potential limitation on the right of suppliers to exercise independent discretion in selecting the persons with whom they will transact and on which terms.[101] Section 75 of the *Competition Act* grants the tribunal power to order a supplier to accept a person as a customer according to 'usual trade terms' where that person is substantially affected in his business or precluded from carrying on business because he is unable to obtain adequate supplies of a product anywhere in a market on

---

100 See Chapter 7.
101 See Chapter 6.

usual trade terms owing to insufficient supplies of the product, due in turn to insufficient competition among suppliers of the product in the market.

Determinations of the relevant product and the relevant market are critical in assessing the potential application of section 75. With respect to the definition of the relevant product, the tribunal has focused on 'the presence or absence of acceptable substitutes to customers,' and it has been prepared to define a relevant market with respect to articles of a particular manufacturer.[102] In a case against a network operator, given the fact that its network facilities are unique and cannot be economically duplicated, the relevant product market will likely be defined as the interconnection facilities. Can the network operator then raise a technical argument to the effect that the reference in section 75(1)(b) to insufficient competition among suppliers in the market implies that the relevant market must be defined to include more than one supplier? This argument was raised in *Xerox* by Xerox Canada. The tribunal held that section 75(1)(b) could apply to a situation in which there is only one supplier and commented that 'it would import a logical inconsistency into the section to hold that a supplier of the relevant product in, for example, a market with three or four suppliers, could be subject to review by the Tribunal for refusing to supply while a supplier with a monopoly position could not be.'[103]

Once the relevant market is defined as proposed above, it becomes clear that the network operator occupies a strong market position. It has monopoly power over its interconnection facilities. Although market power is not a necessary element of the offence, it is an important element in most cases of refusal to deal. Market power is relevant in the causation requirement – the inability to obtain supply must arise 'because of insufficient competition among suppliers' – and at the stage of the tribunal exercising its discretion to grant or withhold a remedy.[104]

The tribunal may make an order under section 75 only if the com-

---

102 *Canada (Director of Investigation and Research)* v. *Chrysler Canada Ltd.* (1989), 27 C.P.R. (3d) 1, aff'd (1991), 38 C.P.R. (3d) 25 (F.C.A.), *Canada (Director of Investigation and Research)* v. *Xerox Canada Inc.* (1990), 33 C.P.R. (3d) 83.

103 *Xerox, supra,* note 102 at 17.

104 William Rowley and Neil Campbell, 'Refusal to Deal (with Economics),' paper prepared for symposium on Recent Developments in Canadian Competition Law, University of Toronto, 15 December 1992), 10–11.

plainant is substantially affected in, or is precluded from carrying on, its business as a result of its inability to obtain adequate supplies. In our context, the refusal to supply may have dramatic effects on potential competitors in potentially competitive segments of the market: it may prevent them from entering this market by depriving them of an essential input. Section 75(1)(b) requires that the person refused supply be unable to obtain adequate supplies of the product 'because of insufficient competition among suppliers of the product in the market.' Where there is only one supplier in the relevant market, it is relatively easy to determine that the competitor's inability to obtain adequate supplies of the product was a result of insufficient competition.

The main difficulty of applying section 75 against a network operator involves interpretation of the phrase 'usual trade terms.' 'Trade terms' are defined to mean 'terms in respect of payment, units of purchase and reasonable and technical servicing requirements' (s. 75(3)). Thus, they are broad enough to include most types of discriminatory interconnection terms. However, the tribunal's decisions do not indicate what is 'usual' in a monopolized market. Is 'usual' determined in accordance with a competitive benchmark or with respect to the past practice of the sole supplier with other customers? In the first interpretation, 'usual' is difficult to establish. The complexity of setting the trade terms for a specific service may be beyond the tribunal's expertise. There is no simple economic formula for competitive trade terms and the fact that in the past only one firm has operated in the market makes it impossible to rely on ready examples.[105]

The second interpretation, however, might not eliminate discriminatory behaviour. The language of the Act refers to usual trade terms rather than to reasonable,[106] competitive, non-discriminatory, or efficient trade terms. Can the operator argue that since most competitors receive the same access terms these terms are the 'usual' ones, even

---

105 Chen et al. note that 'it is not clear how the trade terms can be enforced without turning the antitrust authority into a regulator of prices.' Zhiqi Chen, Thomas W. Ross, and W.T. Stanbury, 'Refusals to Deal and Aftermarkets,' (1998) 13 *Review of Industrial Organization* 131.

106 While s. 75(3) requires technical and servicing requirements to be 'reasonable,' it does not apply these requirements to terms of payment or units of purchase. It would therefore appear to be sufficient that such terms are 'usual' and they need not be justified as 'reasonable.'

though its own affiliate may receive better terms? It can be argued that the network operator should set the same terms for all users of its services in order to facilitate competition in the potentially competitive segments of the market. Although section 75 does not expressly require a finding that the conduct in question has had any particular impact on competition,[107] the refusal-to-deal provision forms part of a larger statutory scheme of economic regulation to promote competition in the market-place.[108]

(b) Abuse of Dominance

Sections 78 and 79 of the Act deal with abuse of dominant market position.[109] They address a situation in which a dominant firm engages in a practice of anticompetitive acts which has had, is having, or is likely to have the effect of preventing or lessening competition substantially in a market, and which is not a result of superior competitive performance.

The Act contains no definition of the term 'anti-competitive acts' but enumerates in section 78 nine non-exclusive examples. In a case against the network operator, the most relevant provision will probably be section 78(e): '[p]re-emption of scarce facilities or resources required by a competitor for the operation of a business, with the object of withholding the facilities or resources from the market.' Section 78(e) addresses the practice of cutting off the source of supply to potential entrants. A scarce facility will likely be defined as a facility that cannot be economically or physically duplicated by competitors wishing to enter the market. The test should focus on the magnitude of the sunk costs associated with by-passing the facility, which permits the foreclosure of effective competition in the upstream or downstream market. Network facilities meet this definition. Nonetheless, a number of obstacles to its application in our context can be identified. First, it is

---

107 Chen et al. note that unlike almost all the other provisions of the Act, the commissioner is not required to prove a substantial (or undue) lessening of competition. Therefore, they argue that while most provisions of the Act are oriented towards promoting competition and efficiency in general, s. 75 appears to be designed to protect competitors said to be disadvantaged by the actions of a supplier. They propose that s. 75 be eliminated from the Act, and refusals to supply be reviewed as an abuse of dominance under s. 79. Chen et al., 'Refusals to Deal and Aftermarkets.' See Chapter 6 supra.

108 Xerox, supra (1990), 33 C.P.R. (3d) at 126.

109 See Chapter 8.

unclear whether, in order for the section to apply, the supplier should withhold the facilities from the entire market or only from certain competitors. One could argue that since the section relates to pre-emption of scarce facilities 'from the market,' once it allows access to these facilities to at least one competitor, the elements of the offence are not met. However, such interpretation will limit the scope of the section in such a manner that it will rarely, if ever, apply. A monopolist would always have incentives to sell its output in the market since it would gain nothing by withholding the use of its scarce facilities and resources from the entire market. Second, it is not clear whether the network operator's acts amount to 'pre-emption.' Nonetheless, since fostering competition is the main goal of the Act, charging high interconnection rates or refusing to interconnect some potential competitors probably amounts to 'pre-emption.'

Section 78(a) may also apply in a case against the network operator. The section defines as anticompetitive 'squeezing, by a vertically integrated supplier, of the margin available to an unintegrated customer who competes with the supplier, for the purpose of impeding or preventing the customer's entry into, or expansion in, a market.' If setting discriminatory access terms for rivals raises the costs of participation in the potentially competitive segment of the industry in such a way as to impede the expansion of existing rivals or prevent the entry of potential rivals in the market, this provision may be breached.

Even if sections 78(e) and (a) do not apply directly, the network operator's acts can still fall within the general anticompetitive clause of section 79. An anticompetitive act is one involving an intentional negative effect on a competitor that is predatory, exclusionary, or disciplinary in nature.[110] In all cases, the focus will be on the issue of which access terms are to be considered anticompetitive and which are founded on sound economic principles. Since there has been no decision by the tribunal concerning reasonable fees and charges by a dominant firm operating an essential facility, it is not clear which approach the tribunal would adopt.[111] The tribunal may follow the U.S. example and require a cost-based pricing approach for access fees paid by different

---

110 *Canada (Director of Investigation and Research) v. Nutrasweet Co.* (1990), 32 C.P.R. (3d) 1 (Comp. Trib.) at 34; *Canada (Director of Investigation and Research) v. Tele-Direct (Publications) Inc.* (1997), 73 C.P.R. (3d) 1 (Comp. Trib.).

111 Although the tribunal's decision in the consent order proceedings in *Interac, supra*, note 62, involved similar issues.

competitors. However, there is an ongoing controversy with regard to how cost-based fees and charges imposed by the owner of a bottleneck facility should be determined – whether the cost should be based solely on marginal or incremental costs of granting access to competitors or on fully allocated costs of the facility, plus a fair rate of return on the owner's investment.[112] Thus, parties in future competitive access disputes will be able to marshal strong arguments in favour of and against various access pricing strategies. Also, it is unclear whether absolute equality of terms will be required.

Section 79(1)(c) requires a finding that the practice of anticompetitive acts has or is likely to have 'the effect of preventing or lessening competition substantially in a market.' Once the tribunal finds that the monopolist has discriminated among competitors, it should not be difficult to establish this element of the provision.

Where the tribunal finds that all the elements of the provision have been proven, it may 'make an order prohibiting all or any of those persons [accused of abuse of dominance] from engaging in such practice' (s. 79(1)). In *Laidlaw*, the tribunal noted that 'simple clear-cut remedies targeted at the fundamental issues are preferable to more complex and interventionist ones that will have a perpetual life and may not cover adequately all situations present and future,'[113] raising serious questions as to the ability and inclination of the tribunal to act as ongoing overseer of interconnection terms.

(c) Price Discrimination
Although some practices of the network operator can be viewed as welfare-reducing forms of price discrimination, they are not covered

---

112 The correct basis for interconnection charges is controversial. For a review of the controversy, see, for example, William J. Baumol, Janusz A. Ordover, and Robert D. Willig, 'Parity Pricing and Its Critics: A Necessary Condition for Efficiency in the Provision of Bottleneck Services to Competitors,' (1997) 14 *Yale Journal of Regulation* 145. See also *Telecom Corporation of New Zealand Ltd. v. Clear Communications Ltd.*, [1995] 1 NZLR 385; Mark Armstrong et al., 'The Access Pricing Problem: A Synthesis,' (1996) 44 *J. Indus. Reg* 131; Nicholas Economides and Lawrence J. White, 'Access and Interconnection Pricing: How Efficient is the "Efficient Component Pricing Rule"?' (1995) *Antitrust Bulletin* 557; and Baumol and Sidak, *Toward Competition in Local Telephony*.
113 *Canada (Director of Investigation and Research) v. Laidlaw Waste Systems Ltd.* (1992), 40 C.PR. (3d) 289 at 355 (Comp. Trib.).

by the discriminatory pricing provision in the Canadian *Competition Act*. Section 50(1)(a) of the Act prohibits 'any sale that discriminates, directly or indirectly, against competitors of a purchaser of articles ... of like quality or quantity.' The section does not prohibit price discrimination between buyers who do not require 'articles of like quality and quantity,' even if such discrimination is not based on cost-economies. Thus, the section is only applicable to purchasers of a like quality and quantity of goods, who are rarely found in practice.[114] In addition, the section does not apply to sale of services.[115] Also, according to the commissioner's enforcement guidelines, the provision applies only to price-related advantages. Non-price-related advantages such as superior technical assistance are not covered by the provision.[116]

(d) The 'Essential Facilities' Doctrine[117]
The United States has often dealt with the problem of discriminatory interconnection terms through the 'essential facilities doctrine,'[118] which imposes liability under sections 1 and 2 of the *Sherman Act* if a firm that controls an essential facility denies a second firm reasonable access to a product or a service the second firm must obtain in order to compete. The wrong perpetrated by the misuse of the facility is that a monopolist 'can extend monopoly power from one market into another.'[119]

A facility has been found to be essential if competitors cannot effectively compete in a market without access to it. It is highly unlikely, even impossible, to find a facility to be 'essential' if it can, in fact, be technically and economically duplicated. Turning to the key issue of what constitutes a denial of access, the case law implies that essential facilities must be made available on 'fair and reasonable' or 'nondiscriminatory' terms. The cases provide no clear guidance as to when terms of access are unreasonable. In *AT&T*, for example, the District

---

114 See Chapter 5.
115 S. 2 of the *Competition Act*.
116 Director of Investigation and Research, *Price Discrimination Enforcement Guidelines* (Ottawa: Consumer and Corporate Affairs 1992).
117 See Chapter 8.
118 As Areeda points out, '[i]t is less a doctrine than an epithet, indicating some exceptions to the right to keep one's creations to oneself'; Phillip Areeda, 'Essential Facilities: An Epithet in Need of Limiting Principles,' (1990) 58 *Antitrust L. J.* 841.
119 *MCI Communications Corp.* v. *AT&T*, 708 F. 2d 1081 (7th Cir., 1983).

Court for the District of Columbia relied on *Terminal Railroad*[120] in ruling that 'access must be offered upon such just and reasonable terms and regulations as will, in respect of use, character, and cost of service, place every company upon as nearly as equal a plane as may be.'[121] Just a few years later, however, in a civil suit against AT&T, the D.C. Circuit ruled that 'absolute equality of access to essential facilities ... is not mandated by the antitrust laws.'[122] This latter dictum reflects the general tenor of the cases, but exactly how equal the terms of access should be remains unclear.[123]

The doctrine has been applied expansively to permit competition policy to displace economic regulation as the regime for governing the behaviour of networks, including access to electric power transmission facilities.[124] The first antitrust case that dealt with access to transmission facilities was *Otter Tail Power*.[125] In that case, a public utility's refusal to 'wheel' or distribute power for municipal utility companies that wished to supply their own electricity by purchasing it elsewhere was condemned as anticompetitive. Otter Tail's apparent purpose was to force the municipalities to become its own customers. The court applied the doctrine as an alternative basis for Otter Tail's liability. Since Otter Tail was partially regulated, a major issue in *Otter Tail* concerned whether the natural monopoly characteristics of the industry and its pervasive regulation impliedly excluded the antitrust laws. The majority held that 'there is nothing in the legislative history that reveals a purpose to insulate electric power companies from the operation of the antitrust laws.'[126]

---

120 *United States v. Terminal R.R. Association of St. Louis*, 224 U.S. 383 (1912).
121 *United States v. American Telephone and Telegraph Company*, 524 F. Supp. 1336 at 1353 (1981).
122 *Southern Pac. Communications Co. v. American Telephone and Telegraph Co.*, 740 F. 2d 980, 1009 (D.C. Cir., 1984).
123 Greg Werden, 'The Law and Economics of the Essential Facility Doctrine,' (1987) 32 *St. Louis U.L.J.* 433 at 456–7.
124 William E. Kovacic, 'The Antitrust Law and Economics of Essential Facilities in Public Utility Regulation,' in Michael A. Crew, ed., *Economic Innovations in Public Utility Regulation* (Boston: Kluwer Academic Publishers 1992). See also W. Collins, 'Electric Utility Rate Regulation: Curing Economic Shortcomings Through Competition,' (1983) 19 *Tulsa Law Review* 141.
125 *Otter Tail Power Co. v. United States*, 410 U.S. 366 (1973), 93 S. Ct. 1022, rehearing denied, 411 U.S. 910.
126 Ibid., at 374–5. Three members of the court dissented on this issue.

Following *Otter Tail*, a significant number of antitrust cases have been decided in which an outright or qualified refusal to wheel power figured prominently in the plaintiff's theory of liability.[127] To date, few law suits have succeeded, but the potentially broad reach of the doctrine ensures that antitrust litigation remains an important device for electric power suppliers, local distribution companies, and individual consumers in demanding transmission or distribution access.[128] Where antitrust is the tool for facilitating competition, the essential facilities doctrine typically provides the principal legal justification for mandating transmission access.

In applying the essentiality screen to claims involving network industries, U.S. courts have tended to proceed from a rebuttable presumption that assets such as pipelines and transmission lines are essential facilities. However, courts have upheld sound business justifications to support decisions to deny access or to set access conditions that the plaintiff subsequently has challenged as unreasonable. In *Town of Massena*, for example, the District Court concluded that Niagara Mohawk properly had refused access to 'essential' transmission lines when the municipal power company failed to resolve legitimate engineering concerns.[129] In *City of Groton v. Connecticut Light & Power Co.* a refusal to consent to general requests to wheel that failed to specify the timing of the transaction or the quantity of power to be wheeled was sustained.[130] The *Massena and Groton* courts also emphasized that the defendant utilities had not categorically refused to deal but had raised efficiency concerns in the course of good faith efforts to negotiate wheeling agreements with the plaintiffs.

In recent case law the courts have also upheld business justifications rooted in public policy concerns other than efficiency, such as equity concerns: the protection of captive consumers from the redistributional

---

127 See, for example, *City of Cleveland v. Cleveland Elec. Illuminating Co.*, 734 F. 2d 1157 (6th Cir.), cert. denied, 469 U.S. 884 (1984); *City of Chanute* v. *Kansas Gas & Elec. Co.*, 564 F. Supp. 1416 (D. Kan., 1983) rev'd in part, aff'd in part, 754 F. 2d 310 (10th Cir., 1985); *Town of Massena v. Niagara Mohawk Power Corp.*, 1980–2 Trade Cas. (CCH) ¶ 63, 526 (N.D. N.Y., 1980); *City of Newark v. Delmarva Power & Light Co.*, 467 F. Supp. 763 (D. Del., 1979).
128 'Antitrust Law and Economics, Essential Facilities,' at 2.
129 *Town of Massena, supra,* note 127, at 822–4.
130 662 F. 2d 921 at 932 (U.S.C.A.) 1981.

aims of a rent-seeking plaintiff.[131] In *City of Abenheim v. California Edison Co.*[132] and *City of Vernon v. California Edison Co.*[133] the courts recognized the validity of a refusal to deal where wheeling access would ignore collateral regulatory requirements such as equity concerns. Courts have adopted the view that an integrated electric utility has no duty to devote transmission capacity to serve a municipally owned distribution company's wheeling requirements where the principal effect of complying with the plaintiff's demand would be to shift costs from one subset of the utility's consumers to another. Thus, where regulatory requirements reflect concern for wealth distribution effects or other concerns that do not directly implicate efficiency considerations, the defendant utility can invoke the fulfilment of regulatory requirements to justify a refusal to grant transmission access.[134] Courts have also recognized a business justification based on a filed rate doctrine: no anticompetitive act is found if interconnection rates were filed and approved by the regulator.[135]

The antitrust scrutiny of transmission access has been strongly criticized, and commentators have questioned the desirability of efforts to supplant regulation with competition policy in the electric utility industry.[136] Criticisms focus on two concerns. First, since competitive conditions cannot, by themselves, remedy the anticompetitive incentives of the market players, ongoing regulation of the firms' activities is necessary. Such regulation, however, is most effectively undertaken in industry-wide regulatory proceedings rather than through antitrust enforcement.[137] Some commentators suggest that the doctrine 'should not be invoked unless there is a pre-existing regulatory agency capable

---

131 See, for example, J. Pace and J. Landon, 'Introducing Competition into the Electric Utility Industry: An Economic Appraisal,' (1982) 3 *Energy Law Journal* 1.

132 955 F. 2d 1373 (9th Cir., 1992).

133 955 F. 2d 1361 (9th Cir., 1992).

134 Kovacic, 'Antitrust Law and Economics of Essential Facilities,' at 11. See also Werden, 'Law and Economics, the Essential Facility Doctrine,' at 458.

135 Michael O. Wise, 'Overview: Deregulation and Antitrust in the Electric Power Industry,' (1996) 64 *Antitrust L.J.* 267. This implies that the U.S. FERC has more power of change over transmission issues than the competition courts.

136 P.L. Joskow and R.M. Schmalensee, *Markets for Power: An Analysis of Electric Utility Deregulation* (Cambridge, Mass.: MIT Press, 1983).

137 K. Watson and T. Brunner, 'Monopolization by Regulated "Monopolies": The Search for Substantive Standards,' (1977) 22 *Antitrust Bulletin* 559.

of adequately supervising relief.'[138] Second, concerns have been voiced about the likely efficiency and equity consequences of competition-oriented policies that entail compulsory wheeling.[139]

As discussed more fully in Chapter 8, the U.S. 'essential facilities' doctrine has, to date, no direct or explicit counterpart in Canadian competition legislation or case law. There is, however, a broad hint of recognition of some such doctrine in both the consent order proceedings under the merger review provisions of the *Competition Act* before the Competition Tribunal in *Gemini I*,[140] involving terms of access to the dominant airline reservation system created as a result of a joint venture between the two major Canadian carriers, and the consent order proceedings under the abuse of dominance provisions of the *Competition Act* before the tribunal in the *Interac* case,[141] involving terms of access to the dominant automated banking network in Canada.

(c) The Available Legal Remedies

The desirability of applying competition laws to prevent discriminatory access to network facilities is directly related to the adequacy of remedial tools at the tribunal's disposal to establish the terms for such access. Even if competition tribunal's or agencies can effectively determine what constitutes anticompetitive access conditions, the remedial tools should also be appropriate. Due to the basic conditions of the market, the tribunal cannot use structural remedies to prevent the anticompetitive conduct: economies of scale of interconnection facilities prevent any structural change from being effective. The only remedy possible relates to the *conduct* of the economic actors: setting access terms and conditions that prevent discrimination.

If the tribunal is to require the defendant to grant access, it must be prepared to prescribe to the defendant – or to have another entity prescribe to the defendant – terms on which the defendant must give the plaintiff access to its interconnection facilities. Such interconnection

---

138 Werden 'Law and Economics of the Essential Facility Doctrine,' at 479–80. For a different view see Mary L. Azcuenaga, 'Essential Facilities and Regulation: Court or Agency Jurisdiction?' (1990) 58 *Antitrust Law Journal* 879, 880.

139 J. Pace, 'Wheeling and the Obligation to Serve,' (1978) 8 *Antitrust L. J.* 265.

140 *Canada (Director & Investigation and Research) v. Air Canada* (1993), 49 C.P.R. (3d) 417 (F.C.A.), reversing (1993), 49 C.P.R. (3d) 7 (Comp. Trib.), leave to appeal to S.C.C. refused (1993), 49 C.P.R. (3d) ix (note).

141 *Supra*, note 62.

terms, on the one hand, should not prevent competitors from entering into the market, nor, on the other hand, should they deprive the monopolist of its legal rights to enjoy profits obtained from its interconnection facilities more than to the extent necessary.[142] Since pricing is not the only factor to be supervised, the tribunal must also be prepared to arbitrate highly technical interconnection disputes.

The application of such remedies raises great difficulties. First, the tribunal is ill-suited to perform regulatory functions such as rate making or price setting that require industry-specific expertise.[143] The setting of fair and competitive access terms is an economically demanding task, and involves a multifactual analysis. The unique technical features of the industry, as well as distortions in prices aimed at achieving non-efficiency objectives, make the resolution of access issues technically complex and politically controversial. For example, should new network users pay only the incremental cost imposed by the new user, or should they bear a portion of the sunk costs in order to preserve incentives to create new essential facilities and to prevent free-riding?[144]

Second, the newly established interconnection terms necessitate careful, ongoing scrutiny. Such a remedy would put the tribunal in the position of controlling the operator's contractual provisions and would necessitate constant adjustments to reflect changes in the costs of the operator. Consequently, the tribunal would be cast in the role of a permanent price regulator. As Areeda and Turner observe, 'requiring a vertically integrated monopolist to deal with outsiders requires some mechanism for supervising and adjusting the price and other terms of dealing. No such mechanism is available to the antitrust court.'[145] The tribunal has eschewed such a role in similar contexts in the past.[146]

Third, litigation costs alone may make any relief inefficient when

---

142 *Clear Communications, supra,* note 112.
143 See *Town of Concord v. Boston Edison Co.,* F. 2d 17, 25–9 (1st Cir., 1990), which emphasizes the effectiveness of economic regulatory systems in curbing an integrated utility's ability to execute an anticompetitive price squeeze against a municipally owned distribution company; cert. denied, 111 S. Ct. 1337 (1991).
144 See Chapter 8.
145 Phillip Areeda and Donald F. Turner, *Antitrust Principles* (New York: Little, Brown and Company, 1978), 241. See also Kovacic, 'Antitrust Law and Economics of Essential Facilities.'
146 See, for example, *Canada (Director of Investigation and Research) v. Palm Dairies* (1986), 12 C.P.R. (3d) 540.

sought by large numbers of small competitors. Since competition remedies apply only to the specific parties to a specific dispute, eliminating anticompetitive access terms would require all the competitors to have their day in court. This entails high costs, given the large number of suits that might be needed to remedy an industry-wide problem. Although the commissioner may initiate proceedings on behalf of all aggrieved parties, he will still have to prove that each party was afforded discriminatory interconnection terms. In Canada, a competitor's inability to sue the monopolist in private litigation complicates matters even further.[147]

Fourth, regulatory oversight may be more timely than competition litigation. Since competition law usually applies *ex post*, the monopolist's distortions might seriously impair competitive conditions in the industry before the matter is finally resolved. In contrast, *ex ante* economic regulation may avoid these consequences.

Fifth, direct regulation avoids some of the procedural and proof-related problems inherent in litigation, especially in the criminal context (such as predation), which may not be relevant to the economic impact of the conduct. For example, no proof of anticompetitive intent is necessary in order to remedy an anticompetitive interconnection regime where economic regulation is applied.

Sixth, the remedies issued by a court or the tribunal might leave room for the network operator to manoeuvre in order to create an anticompetitive advantage for its competitive affiliate. Competition laws do not require a monopolist to aid its rivals to enter, survive, or expand in the market,[148] although the right of a monopolist not to help its rivals is not absolute. Assume, for example, a scenario where the capacity constraints of existing interconnection facilities allow only the monopolist's affiliates to transport power through them. U.S. courts have not required an essential facility to expand its facilities even if such expansion is needed in order to allow a competitor to enter the market.[149]

---

147 See Kent Roach and Michael J. Trebilcock, 'Private Enforcement of Competition Laws,' (1996) 34 *Osgoode Hall L.J.* 461.
148 Areeda and Turner, *Antitrust Principles*, at 286; John Quinn and Glenn Leslie, 'Essential Facilities and the Duty to Facilitate Competition,' (Symposium on Competition Law and Deregulation in Network Industries, University of Toronto Law School, 14 June 1996), at 16–22.
149 See *Oahu Gas Serv., Inc. v. Pacific Resources, Inc.*, 838 F. 2d 360 (9th Cir.), cert. denied, 488 U.S. 870 (1988).

Moreover, antitrust laws do not require an essential facility to be shared if such sharing would be impractical or if it would inhibit the defendant's ability to serve its own customers adequately, nor does it impose a common carrier obligation with a concomitant requirement of proportioning when operating at full capacity.[150] Rather, the courts have considered that the provision of access to the competitor in such circumstances is not feasible and the monopolist's refusal is a sound business justification.[151] Thus, a network operator might use the power not to expand its facilities in order to drive out its competitors. While the Canadian abuse of dominance provision might be interpreted as imposing certain affirmative duties to provide access to interconnection facilities,[152] the tribunal might be reluctant to mandate a monopolist to invest capital in additional facilities.[153]

Finally, specialized regulatory bodies are likely to be more competent than competition authorities in reconciling efficiency and equity considerations in interconnection disputes. A mandate that permitted a direct regulator to account for efficiency and distributional consequences would facilitate more explicit consideration of these factors than adjudication under the traditional competition law standards.[154]

Given the difficulties described above, the argument that the competition authorities have sufficient tools to fashion appropriate remedies in network bottleneck cases is highly problematic. Economic regulation is better equipped to formulate a comprehensive set of rules and processes to determine all the material terms and conditions of access necessary in order to achieve economic efficiency.

These difficulties have led U.S. courts to adopt a solution whereby courts decide liability disputes with regard to interconnection terms and charges and delegate the remedial authority to direct regulatory

---

150 Werden, 'Law and Economics of the Essential Facility Doctrine,' 457.
151 See, for example, *City of Anaheim v. Southern California Edison Co.*, 955 F. 2d 1373 (9th Cir., 1992).
152 Quinn and Leslie, 'Essential Facilities,' at 26, citing *R. v. Allied Chemicals* (1975), 69 D.L.R. (3d) 506 (B.C.S.C.). See also *Canada (Director of Investigation and Research) v. D&B Companies of Canada Ltd.* (1996), 64 C.P.R. (3d) 216 (Comp. Trib.) [hereinafter *Nielsen*].
153 It is noteworthy that all the above issues are present also in setting interconnection rates so as to prevent the monopolist from charging supracompetitive rates.
154 Kovacic, 'Antitrust Law and Economics of Essential Facilities.'

bodies. As Kovacic observes,[155] this solution responded to oversight deficiencies of traditional public utility regulation and reflected robust confidence in the curative powers of antitrust law, which manifested itself in transpositions of antitrust principles to highly idiosyncratic regulated industry environments. Nonetheless, courts have come to appreciate the shortcomings of antitrust litigation as an oversight and monitoring tool and they have realized the comparative institutional advantage of a direct regulator: '[i]n Otter Tail the willingness of the district court and the Supreme Court to find liability depended heavily upon the availability of the Federal Power Commission to set and supervise the terms of access.'[156]

Such bifurcation of powers raises several fundamental problems. It may not only result in duplication of resources but could also jeopardize the regulatory task. There are several grounds for unifying access jurisdiction within a direct regulatory body:[157] Industry expertise suggests that regulatory bodies are better suited to decide whether an obligation to provide access based on competitive considerations should be recognized in the first place. Unification within a single body will serve to eliminate inconsistencies that may arise from the possible application of different criteria in the liability and remedial phases of the litigation, or from divergent assessments of the merits of arguments raised in the liability phase of the proceedings. Where a direct regulator sets the natural monopoly rates of the network operator in order to prevent it from exacting supracompetitive rents, there is a strong case for unifying authority for deciding interconnection issues in the same regulatory body. Terms of access are so inextricably linked to price that they are best handled in the context of rate proceedings rather than in a liability trial.[158] Duplication of scrutiny might raise concerns regarding the fairness to a regulated entity of being subject to two independent proceedings in respect of the same matter.

In Britain, the transmission and distribution charges for electricity are subject to regulation by the direct regulator (the Director General of

---

155 Ibid.
156 Ibid., 11.
157 The first two grounds are noted by Kovacic, 'Antitrust Law and Economics of Essential Facilities.'
158 Werden, 'Law and Economics of the Essential Facilities Doctrine,' at 479.

Electricity Supply and the Office of Electricity Regulation (OFFER).[159] Where a licence condition is to be changed or where there is a fair-trading offence, there is a right of appeal to the Monopolies and Mergers Commission (MMC). Given that the MMC is not a court and is comparatively informal in its procedures, excessive legalism problems do not arise.[160] Nonetheless, this arrangement has several disadvantages. First and foremost, the MMC does not have any comparative advantage in issues regarding the efficient setting of interconnection terms. Second, as in the U.S. solution, the scope of review by the MMC of the specialized regulator creates a duplication of resources, and the process may create uncertainty due to the fact that the two regimes may differ in their economic approaches and thus may apply different sets of rules. In any case, however, the initial power to regulate interconnection terms is in the hands of the direct regulator while the competition authorities regulate the regulator.

In Australia, recent amendments to the *Trade Practices Act* create a regulatory regime vested in the competition authorities to ensure third-party access to essential facilities which a competitor cannot practically or reasonably duplicate in circumstances where such access would significantly increase competition.[161] This provision resembles the U.S. essential facilities doctrine. However, one of the conditions for mandating access is that access to the service is not already the subject of an effective access regime. The natural monopoly segments of the network industries are still regulated by a direct regulator.

The New Zealand experience in regulating interconnection terms in the telecommunications industry may also shed light on the suitability or lack thereof of competition laws to regulate such terms. New Zealand is the only country which has moved directly from government monopoly to private competition without putting in place an industry-specific regulator. In the 'light-handed' regulatory approach adopted, the industry was to be treated like any other and made fully subject to the provisions of the *Commerce Act 1986* (the framework

---

159 Vickers and Yarrow, *Privatization*, at 243; Armstrong et al., *Deregulation of Public Utilities*, at 279.
160 Foster, *Privatization*, at 281–7.
161 1974, no. 51, s. 44G. See also Frances Hanks, 'The Competition Law Framework for Deregulation of Public Utilities in Australia,' in Richardson, ed., *Deregulation of Public Utilities*, at 2.

competition statute), although some special constraints were put in place.[162] While the New Zealand telecommunications industry differs in some important aspects from the electricity industry (technological innovations have eroded the natural monopoly segments of the telecommunications industry further than in the electricity industry), it is nonetheless illuminating. First, the New Zealand experience stresses the importance of special provisions for preventing the setting of discriminatory access terms. Part IV of the *Commerce Act* enables goods or services to be placed under *direct price control* by the Commerce Commission where the minister determines that there is limited competition in the market and it is necessary or desirable for prices to be controlled in the interests of users, consumers, or suppliers. Although the provision has not been used to date, it can be viewed as a threat which may constrain the pricing behaviour of dominant firms. No parallel provision exists in the competition laws of most industrial nations. Second, as the New Zealand regulatory regime suggests, the provisions of the *Commerce Act* are not, in themselves, sufficient to regulate the industry. Thus, the New Zealand government has limited the scope of action of the deregulated firm by numerous sector-specific regulatory methods, including, *inter alia*, disclosure regulation and the power to impose more direct controls. Third, in the *Clear* case,[163] in which the courts dealt with setting interconnection prices in the telecommunications industry, the expertise and ability of the Privy Council in setting interconnection rates engendered vigorous debate.[164] The New Zealand experience reveals the problems involved in using competition laws alone to prevent discriminatory access terms.[165] As Janisch rightly observes, 'the issue is not so much whether there is industry-specific regulation, but whether effective institutional means have been adopted to implement it.'[166]

---

162 1986, no. 5. See Ergas, 'Telecommunications Across the Tasman.'

163 *Clear Communications, supra*, note 112.

164 S.M. Lojkine, 'Competition Litigation in the High Court,' *Materials for Third Annual Workshop, Competition Law and Policy Institute of New Zealand* (August 1992), 10.

165 For a sceptical view regarding the efficacy of industry-specific regulatory solutions, see Ergas, 'Telecommunications Across the Tasman,' and Goddard, 'Comment.'

166 Hudson Janisch, 'From Monopoly Towards Competition in Telecommunications: What Role for Competition Law?', (1994) 23 *Canadian Business Law Journal* 239 at 264–5.

III. Conclusions

The introduction of competition into network industries creates new regulatory challenges that require rethinking the institutional division of responsibilities of industry-specific regulators and general competition authorities. For the residual natural monopoly functions in these industries, presumably some form of industry-specific pricing regulation remains necessary to protect customers (rather than competitors) from monopoly pricing. Within the actually or potentially competitive segments of these industries, certain kinds of practices or transactions seem equally naturally to fall within the purview of framework competition laws: for example, collusion, mergers, and exclusionary practices. In these respects, it is important that the regulated industries defence discussed in Part I of this chapter not be interpreted so expansively as to preclude jurisdiction on the part of the competition authorities or to discourage industry-specific regulators from partial or conditional regulatory forbearance for fear of creating a regulatory void. Indeed, moving quickly to regulatory forbearance in potentially competitive segments of networks industries and yielding jurisdiction to competition authorities within these segments seems highly desirable in facilitating a rapid transition from regulation to competition. Announcing *ex ante* targets or milestones as to when specific regulatory constraints, including specific pricing constraints, in these segments will be removed – for example, reduction of the incumbent operator's market share below some threshold – and rigorous attention to removing or reducing regulatory barriers to entry are likely to facilitate such a transition. However, in vertically integrated network industries, preventing the leveraging of monopoly power from the non-competitive to the potentially competitive segments of the industry, first by prejudicing competitors and ultimately by harming consumers, is of paramount ongoing importance in order for effective competition to be both achieved and sustained. This task includes several sub-tasks, including the prevention of cross-subsidization, cost misallocations, tying, and setting discriminatory access terms, which are, for the most part, best dealt with by industry-specific regulation. Nonetheless, checks and balances can be achieved through extensive use of the commissioner's intervention powers before industry-specific federal regulatory agencies under section 125 of the *Competition Act* and provincial regulatory bodies (with consent) under section 126, through appropriate interagency agreements on information sharing, and through prior notification and consultation on investigative and enforcement/regulatory initiatives. The confusion of institutional roles in the U.S. energy sector between state regulators, the Federal Energy Regulatory Commission, the Department of Justice, and the Federal Trade Commission exemplifies the problems that result from a failure to address coherently the issue of the institutional division of labour in network industries.

The complexity of new market structures has not made regulatory tasks any easier. New challenges should be met with suitable regulatory instruments. Although many have advocated the elimination of the direct regulator's role, it is likely to continue. The idea that direct regulation of network facilities would wither away as competitive forces emerged has turned out to be something of an illusion.

TWELVE

Enforcement

I. Introduction

The *Competition Act* (the 'Act')[1] may be enforced in many ways, public and private, voluntary and involuntary. This range of possibilities is necessary given the broad scope of conduct that may be impugned. Under the Act there are five primary competition law enforcement actors: the commissioner of competition; the attorney general of Canada; the Competition Tribunal; private litigants; and the courts. The minister of industry, whose ministry is ultimately responsible for the Act, has only a marginal role in the process.[2]

The role of each of these enforcement actors will be addressed throughout this chapter, which is structured as follows. Part II discusses the economics of competition law enforcement. Part III addresses voluntary compliance with the Act, including a discussion related to various educational activities of the commissioner as well as advisory opinions, compliance programs and various informational sources made available by the Competition Bureau. Part IV reviews involuntary compliance with the Act and, in particular, the investigation process of the commissioner, the issue of confidentiality of information, the criminal process under the Act, the current and proposed scope for private enforcement, and multi-jurisdictional cooperation. Finally, Part V sets outs our conclusions.

---

1 R.S.C. 1985, c. C-34.
2 Pursuant to s. 10(c) of the Act, the minister may direct the commissioner to commence an inquiry in respect of any criminal offence or reviewable practice. However, the minister has no authority to require the discontinuance of an inquiry.

II. The Economics of Competition Law Enforcement

There has been a historical tendency to assume that laws designed to produce public benefits should be enforced by public authorities while laws designed to regulate the interactions of private actors should be enforced by private actors. Economic theory has contributed significantly to the debate between proponents of public and private enforcement and is particularly relevant in the context of the enforcement of competition law.

On the side of private enforcement, following his pioneering work stressing the need for high penalties to compensate for low probabilities of detection,[3] Gary Becker and George Stigler argue that deterrence could be as effectively achieved if private individuals enforced the law by competing for the high damages that would follow from demonstrating that a defendant was liable.[4] In essence, Becker and Stigler justify private enforcement as a response to governmental failure, given the possibility of malfeasance or inaction among public regulators. In this regard, they argue that it is preferable to reward private enforcers 'by a "piece-rate" or a "bounty"' than to pay fixed salaries to public enforcers. They conclude: 'Society is more likely to use fines equal to damages divided by the probability of conviction to punish offenders if it must pay this amount to successful enforcers. Although private enforcement of rules need not change the rules, we predict that they would gain more currency and relevance because enforcement would then be much more efficient and transparent.'[5]

Despite their preference for private enforcement, Becker and Stigler acknowledge possible shortcomings. In particular, they recommend that both public and private enforcers who bring unsuccessful actions should be required to compensate the innocent defendant and that 'the concept of double jeopardy' needs elaboration,[6] given anticipated competition among private enforcers.

William Landes and Richard Posner challenge the conclusion that

---

3 G. Becker, 'Crime and Punishment: An Economic Approach,' (1968) 76 *J. Pol. Econ.* 169.

4 G. Becker and G. Stigler, 'Law Enforcement, Malfeasance and Compensation of Enforcers,' (1974) 3 *J. Legal Stud.* 1.

5 Ibid., at 14.

6 Ibid., at 16.

private enforcement could be as efficient as public enforcement.[7] They argue that if fines or damages higher than the social costs of the illegal activity are required to deter defendants, this would attract higher than optimal numbers of individuals seeking to collect such fines or damages by being private enforcers of the law and devoting their own private resources to detection and prosecution. Simply stated, Landes and Posner are concerned about overenforcement and deterrence above socially optimal levels. They further argue that public enforcers, who are not driven by profit maximization, may make better decisions about what resources to devote to prosecution than private individuals competing for high fines or damages.

While concern about the potential for overdeterrence and private enforcement is valid, it does not justify taking the extreme position of abandoning private enforcement. Rather, it suggests a need for careful control of the rewards offered for private enforcers to ensure that private actors do not divert more private resources than are socially optimal to the enforcement of public standards.

The Landes and Posner thesis of overdeterrence was challenged by Mitchell Polinsky, who argues that rational private enforcers would only act in cases where the reward available was greater than the costs of enforcement.[8] Private enforcers would not engage in enforcement activity where the enforcement costs were high and/or the net worth of the defendant was low. 'Under private enforcement, firms are willing to invest in enforcement only if they at least break even – their fine revenue must be at least as large as their enforcement costs. Under public enforcement, however, the optimal solution may result in fine revenue which is less than enforcement costs.'[9]

Again, however, Polinsky's theory does not justify the abandonment of private enforcement of the law. In fact, it implicitly recognizes the complementary roles that private and public enforcement can play, depending on the facts. Private enforcement is valuable in those

---

7 W.M. Landes and R.A. Posner, 'The Private Enforcement of Law,' (1975) 4 *J. Legal. Stud.* 1 at 15. See also W.F. Schwartz, *Private Enforcement of the Antitrust Laws: An Economic Critique* (Washington, D.C.: American Enterprise Institute for Public Policy Research, 1981) at 9 and R.A. Posner, *Economic Analysis of Law*, 4th ed. (Boston: Little Brown, 1992) at 596 for similar conclusions.
8 A.M. Polinksy, 'Private versus Public Enforcement of Fines,' (1980) 9 *J. Legal Stud.* 105 at 107.
9 Ibid.

instances where the rewards available are greater than their enforcement costs (although excessive rewards may result in overenforcement).[10] Public enforcement is most needed in those cases where the fine or damages that can be extracted from a wrong-doer are significantly less than the costs of enforcement.

In the first systematic treatment of the policy implications of alternative antitrust penalties, Kenneth Elzinga and William Breit pose the question of the optimal enforcement of antitrust laws.[11] They argue that the marginal social benefits of enforcement decline as more cases are brought with respect to less serious or more debatable practices, while the marginal social costs of enforcement rise with increasing levels of enforcement. Thus, in an ideal world, public and private resources would be invested in enforcement activity up to the point where the marginal cost of enforcement is equated with the marginal benefit of enforcement – not less and not more. However, Elzinga and Breit acknowledge that it would be impossible to determine whether existing levels of enforcement are at, below, or above, this level. Such a determination would require detailed information of the underlying incidence of antitrust violations, and not merely those that have attracted formal enforcement activity. This information is unknown, and almost by definition, unknowable. Elzinga and Breit argue that while the four principal sanctions available for antitrust violations (i.e., fines, incarceration, treble damages, and structural remedies) all present their own problems, appropriately structured fines are a more effective deterrent than any other type of sanction.[12]

---

10 Polinksy recognizes that private enforcement may, in different circumstances, result in both over- and underenforcement. See A.M. Polinksy, 'Detrebling versus Decoupling Antitrust Damages: Lessons from the Theory of Enforcement,' (1986) 74 *Geo. L.J.* 1231 at 1234: 'If the same fine is used as under optimal public enforcement, the resulting probability of detection (generated by the self-interested choices of private enforcers) may be too high or too low. In other words, if the enforcing is done privately, there may be too much enforcement or too little enforcement.'

11 *The Antitrust Penalties: A Study in Law and Economics* (New Haven: Yale University Press, 1976).

12 With respect to incarceration, Elzinga and Breit point to the traditional reluctance to jail antitrust violators, in part because in large corporations it is often difficult to identify with confidence the individuals and senior management ultimately responsible for initiating the offending practice. With respect to structural remedies, such as divestiture, which have also been infrequently used, there are problems in fashioning remedies that do not forfeit economies of scale and scope; administrative problems in

Along the spectrum of public and private enforcement, the enforcement of the Act is weighed far more heavily in favour of public enforcement. This contrasts sharply with the American experience where a large role is assigned to private, treble damages actions for enforcement of U.S. antitrust laws. As discussed below, the debate between private and public enforcement has become highly germane in Canada in light of proposed amendments to the Act.

III. Voluntary Compliance with the *Competition Act*

A. *Overview of Educational Activities*

The bureau has long taken the view that voluntary compliance is critical to a well-functioning Act. As former Commissioner George Addy stated, '(v)oluntary compliance with the *Competition Act* remains paramount for us ... (and this) can best be achieved when the business community has a sound understanding of the *Act*.'[13] The bureau has thus established a series of programs and policies to actively encourage voluntary compliance through, among other things, educational efforts, the issuance of advisory opinions, information contacts, and the encouragement of internal company compliance programs.[14] Voluntary compliance initiatives are based on the premise that the large

---

unscrambling assets once combined; and problems of determining to whom divestitures should occur in order to promote a more procompetitive outcome. With regard to treble damages, Elzinga and Breit argue that such damages engender three sets of social costs. First, perverse incentive costs arise where plaintiffs have an incentive not to adopt precautions to avoid or minimize the impact of antitrust violations on them, given the windfall that treble damages often represent; second, misinformation effects arise where plaintiffs have a strong incentive to misrepresent procompetitive or competitively neutral behaviour as anticompetitive in order to realize the gains from a treble damages award; and third, reparation (transaction) costs are entailed both in determining liability and in fixing quantum.

13 George N. Addy, 'Luncheon Address to the National Competition Law Section' Canadian Bar Association (1 October 1993).

14 The commissioner has published a bulletin (*Conformity Continuum Information Bulletin* [Industry Canada, 16 June 2000]) related to the general approach of the commissioner and the bureau toward the administration and enforcement of the Act. The bulletin refers to the collection of instruments used by the commissioner to create a balanced approach to enforcement within the context of the five guiding principles for the administration of the Act: transparency, fairness, timeliness, predictability, and confidentiality.

majority of businesses do not intend to violate the provisions of the Act, but are instead willing to ensure that their business, sales, marketing and distribution programs, and strategies are in compliance with the law. That is, it is recognized that violations often occur, not out of a wilful flouting of the Act, but due to an unawareness or unfamiliarity with its provisions and their application to a particular business practice or transaction. Even business people familiar with the Act do not always have a sound enough understanding of its provisions to ensure that their business is in compliance.[15] With this knowledge, the commissioner seeks to educate and inform the business community about the Act.

For example, the commissioner and the bureau staff often address businesses and trade associations on competition-related topics. The bureau also publishes a series of Information Bulletins and Enforcement Guidelines on topics ranging from product labelling to misleading advertising, and predatory pricing to price discrimination. The *Misleading Advertising Bulletin* is published quarterly and provides commentary of general application to advertisers as well as information on recent convictions. The Annual Report to the minister describes bureau activity and enforcement action in the previous year. The commissioner and the bureau also run more active programs which, like the education and communication programs, seek to facilitate and encourage voluntary compliance with the Act.

The advisory opinion program and the program of compliance allow businesses and individuals to seek the input of the commissioner when developing and implementing new business strategies, programs, and initiatives. The advisory opinion program allows businesses, for a relatively modest fee, to have the bureau opine as to the competitive implications of a particular program or initiative. Under the compliance program, the bureau has developed guidelines of general application, which help to assist businesses in developing an in-house program aimed at creating internal procedures to ensure that the

---

15 One of the principal reasons that parties will inadvertently contravene provisions of the Act is that conduct which, from the perspective of the business person, is viewed as being advantageous to the business and within the clear purview of its operations, is nevertheless, offensive under the Act. For example, many parties believe that they should be able to exercise control over the price at which their dealers or distributors resell their goods. They are often surprised to learn that this is a *per se* criminal offence under s. 61 of the Act.

business and its employees know the scope of the Act and how violations may be avoided.

To summarize, the collection of voluntary programs established by the bureau is aimed at encouraging and facilitating compliance with the law; it is the bureau's form of 'preventive medicine.' The balance of Part III of this chapter will provide a detailed assessment of these efforts. However, it is clear that not all businesses and individuals will make use of these bureau initiatives. Some will, whether consciously or inadvertently, contravene the Act. Where this occurs, Canadian competition law provides the commissioner (and to a far lesser extent, private parties) with the means to enforce compliance with the law through contested proceedings and a range of possible penalties. In the context of reviewable matters, the commissioner may seek an order from the tribunal prohibiting anticompetitive conduct prospectively. In criminal matters, the attorney general has carriage of the prosecution in the courts following an investigation by the commissioner. Fines or imprisonment may result from successful criminal prosecution. The scope for involuntary compliance under the Act is discussed in Part IV, below.

B. Advisory Opinions

1. Overview
The advisory opinion program facilitates voluntary compliance with the Act by inviting businesses to submit business plans to the bureau before they are implemented. Upon application, an advisory opinion is issued by the bureau once it has assessed the competitive effects and legality of a proposed business plan or initiative. The applicant may use the opinion to tailor, modify, or amend its plan so that it is in compliance with the Act before the program is actually put in place, or it can simply choose to ignore the opinion (albeit at its peril). The program therefore facilitates and encourages compliance with the law by providing businesses with the opportunity to 'test the waters' before fully implementing a new initiative.

An advisory opinion is based on the written submission of the applicant as well as existing jurisprudence, previous opinions, bureau knowledge, and the stated policies of the commissioner.[16] In providing

---

16 These may include, for example, the *Misleading Advertising Guidelines* (Ottawa: Industry Canada, 1991) or the *Merger Enforcement Guidelines* (Ottawa: Supply and Services Canada, 1991).

its opinion, the bureau does not undertake third-party contacts or verification unless the applicant consents. The opinion process is not an investigation. Rather, it is simply an assessment by the bureau of a certain set of facts presented to it by an applicant. The advice rendered is not binding upon the commissioner, the bureau, or the applicant. The applicant is free to disregard the opinion on the understanding that the matter may ultimately be tested before the tribunal or in the courts. The applicant may also modify its proposed plan or program in accordance with the opinion or in any other way it so chooses. Of course, where the plan presented to the commissioner is varied, or where the conditions external to the plan change, the reliability of the opinion may diminish. For an additional fee, an applicant may submit revised proposals for another opinion.

An advisory opinion is, like all opinions, grounded upon a certain set of facts. Altering an underlying fact may alter the opinion; applicants should therefore provide full and complete disclosure of all material facts. An opinion based on generalities, misstatements of fact, or failure to state a material fact will not be useful to the applicant. For example, while the overestimation of the market share of a competitor may provide for a favourable advisory opinion, it would not change the fact that the applicant may have a dominant market share. Because it lacks any binding force, the opinion will not shield the applicant from subsequent enforcement action. In other words, little can be gained by the applicant who presents the facts in less than a complete form. Similarly, an advisory opinion based on general information will likely be burdened with qualifications and subject to revision upon a clearer understanding of the facts. The level of comfort and assurance an applicant takes from receiving an advisory opinion will always be directly proportional to the accuracy and depth of information provided by the applicant to the bureau.

2. *Information Required in an Advisory Opinion Application*
The extent of information required to be submitted when seeking an advisory opinion will vary significantly based on the specific business initiative contemplated and the provision of the Act pursuant to which the opinion is sought. As a general proposition, however, the more information provided to the bureau, the more accurate and reliable the advisory opinion will be. Yet, the greater the quantum of information and complexity surrounding the business initiative, the greater the time and expense involved with obtaining the advisory opinion. Keep-

ing in mind that the advisory opinion program is meant to facilitate compliance with the Act, the bureau seeks to balance the competing interests of accuracy and cost. That is, the bureau must remain cognizant that the program would not encourage compliance with the Act if it became so costly so as to have a 'chilling effect' on businesses.[17]

The bureau's *Fee and Service Standards Handbook Pursuant to the Competition Act* ('Fee Handbook')[18] sets out the fees payable for a variety of bureau services, including advisory opinions. The handbook also describes the information required in an advisory opinion application. The scope of what must be provided to facilitate a thorough analysis by the bureau will vary depending on, among other things, the provision of the Act pursuant to which the opinion is sought. For example, the information required where the proposed initiative relates to a new distribution policy, and the applicant is concerned that the initiative may violate the refusal-to-deal provision (s. 75) of the Act, will differ from an advisory opinion being sought in respect of a new advertising campaign. An applicant should always consult the Fee Handbook for a detailed listing of the information to be included in its submission, or, preferably, should discuss the possible contents of its application with the bureau before the application is filed. This will reduce the risk that the bureau will ask for more information and both increase the reliability of the advisory opinion received.

There are four different categories of advisory opinion applications. The information required depends on whether the opinion is in respect of the Act's (1) civil provisions (other than mergers), (2) merger provisions (both complex and non-complex), (3) misleading advertising and deceptive marketing practices provisions, or (4) criminal provisions (other than misleading advertising and deceptive marketing practices). For most opinions, except those sought in relation to misleading advertising or deceptive marketing practices, however, the core of the analysis of a proposed plan will relate to determining the relevant geographic and product market. While each application will be fact specific, information related to the relevant product market should include:

---

17 The early indication would suggest that a 'chilling effect' has occurred. That is, as described in *Competition Bureau Fee and Service Standards (Performance Report – 1998)* (Ottawa: Competition Bureau 1998), since the implementation of the filing fees and a more formal definition of what constitutes an advisory opinion, there has been an 80 per cent decrease in advisory opinion requests.

18 (Ottawa: Competition Bureau, Industry Canada, 1998).

- a physical description of the product[19] and its uses;
- any regulations affecting its distribution, production, or sale;
- a list of complementary or substitutable products and customers' willingness to purchase those products; and
- the availability of the product and the level of choice with respect to quality, size, and selection of the product.

To assist in determining the relevant geographic market, the applicant should include information relating to:

- sources of supply for all customers in Canada of the product and its substitutes;
- transportation costs associated with distributing the product;
- the willingness of customers to accept transportation costs as part of the price and what distance they will tolerate;
- tariff and non-tariff barriers;
- regulatory restrictions relating to transporting, exporting, and importing the product; and
- the effect of a rise in price on purchasers' tendencies to source product from distant markets and suppliers' tendencies to sell in the market.

The second portion of an advisory opinion application will include initiative-specific information. For example, a company concerned about breaching section 75 (refusal to deal) would be required to include information regarding its customers, including their purchases and the types of businesses they operate; a list of names of companies to whom they sell the same products; and a description of the usual trade terms on which the product is sold as well as trade terms proposed under the new distribution system. The Fee Handbook details the type of plan-specific information required for different provisions under the Act.

3. The Advisory Opinion Process
Since November 1997 the bureau has instituted fees for many of its services, including the issuance of advisory opinions. An advisory opin-

---

19 'A product' refers to both services and articles, and includes (among other things) real and personal property.

ion sought in respect of sections 52 to 60 (misleading advertising and deceptive marketing practices) has a fee of $500. Advisory opinions for all other provisions of the Act are levied a fee of $4,000.[20] In recognition of these fees, the bureau has established maximum 'turn-around times' for the issuance of advisory opinions. Specifically, advisory opinions sought in respect of 'non-complex' misleading advertising or deceptive marketing practices provisions are to be issued within eight days, while the bureau will provide its opinion within thirty days for 'complex' matters in the context of these provisions. For all other provisions of the Act, an applicant can expect an advisory opinion within four weeks, except where the matter is designated as 'complex' by the bureau.[21] In such instances, the applicant can expect to wait up to eight weeks for an advisory opinion.

Following an initial assessment of the proposed plan and depending on the complexity of the issues raised, the bureau may request other information in order to analyse manufacturing, distribution, sales, pricing, promotional, or other situations contemplated by the applicant. This obviously tends to slow the process down. The bureau therefore invites applicants to contact it, in advance of filing, in order to discuss the information which should be submitted with the application. In fact, the bureau may defer the complexity designation of an advisory opinion until it has what in its view is sufficient information. This deferral may have the practical effect of extending the 'maximum' review period.

C. Compliance Programs

An important part of the process of facilitating voluntary compliance with the Act is the fostering of in-house compliance programs. Given that most businesses have every intention of operating in compliance

---

20 Requests for advisory opinions by non-profit groups are subject to a fee of only $50.

21 Appendix C to the Fee Handbook defines complex and non-complex advisory opinions. To qualify as a non-complex advisory opinion, all related and pertinent information must be supplied by the applicant. As well, there must exist related jurisprudence and an established bureau policy to formulate an opinion. An opinion will be complex where it deals with a novel issue, where there is a paucity of jurisprudence, where there is no previous bureau interpretation of the subject, or where the amount of time needed to review the material submitted substantially exceeds the turn-around time for a non-complex opinion.

with the law, internal compliance programs can provide an effective means of reducing the enforcement burden on the bureau by shifting the detection and remedial functions to the entity where the anticompetitive activity occurs. In 1997, the bureau published *Corporate Compliance Programs* (CCP), an Information Bulletin, with the objective of assisting companies in developing in-house compliance programs.[22] This bulletin is not law, is not binding, and is not mandatory. The implementation of a compliance program, as well as its contents and processes, are ultimately at the implementing entity's discretion. In publishing the CCP, the bureau's aim was to outline, in a generic manner, what a credible and effective compliance program would entail. To be credible, the program must demonstrate the entity's commitment to conducting business in conformity with the Act. To be effective, it must inform employees, officers, and directors about the contents of the Act as it affects the entity's business.

A compliance program may also serve as an effective business strategy. By identifying the bounds of permissible conduct for both criminal offences and reviewable practices, and assisting employees, officers, and directors in operating within those boundaries, a company may be able to save money, goodwill, and time, avoiding protracted (and costly) investigations and litigation, or large fines and possibly jail sentences for those associated with the commission of a criminal violation. While no compliance program can ever completely assure a company that violations of the Act will never occur, an effective program will minimize those risks. Moreover, where a company and its employees have a sound understanding of the Act, they will be well-positioned to compete aggressively within its parameters.

In the CCP, the bureau identified the elements it considers necessary in any effective compliance program. There are clearly tangible benefits to a company basing its program on the bureau's recommendations, even though they are not binding. The commissioner may use these criteria in considering alternative case resolution or whether immunity should be granted in a particular case. One of the factors the commissioner considers in determining whether to recommend 'favourable treatment' under his immunity program is the conduct of the person seeking immunity (including the speed with which the person came forward to report a violation). A compliance program will make that

---

22 (Ottawa: Competition Bureau, Industry Canada, 1997).

person's commitment to lawful business conduct more credible, and it will likely increase the speed with which violations are detected. The existence of a compliance program will also be a mitigating factor in sentencing after a conviction under the criminal provisions of the Act.[23] The bureau views the following five elements as fundamental to the success of any compliance program, regardless of what specific model is adopted or the complexity of the program:

- the involvement and support of senior management;
- the development of relevant policies and procedures;
- the ongoing education of management and employees;
- effective monitoring, auditing, and reporting mechanisms; and
- disciplinary procedures.

Each of these elements is addressed, in turn, below.

1. Senior Management
It is only with the unequivocal support and commitment of senior management to a compliance program that such a program can be effectively organized, promoted, and implemented. Senior management's commitment sends the message that violations of the Act will not be tolerated and thereby establishes a climate within the particular organization conducive to the conduct of business within the bounds of the Act.

2. Policies and Procedure
In order to be effective, the substantive content of a compliance program must be made available in written form. There is clearly no one form applicable to all businesses, as there is no simple set of procedures and policies. Rather, each entity must tailor its policies to its business, paying particular attention to those areas where anticompetitive conduct is most likely to arise. Nevertheless, the bureau does suggest some typical items for inclusion in written materials. These include:

- a statement by the chief executive officer stressing the entity's commitment to the policies and procedures of the program;

---

23 Particularly in respect of criminal matters, it is common for the bureau to seek the mandated implementation of a compliance program.

- a general description of the Act and its enforcement, penalty, and remedial provisions;
- clear examples to illustrate the specific practices that are prohibited;
- a practical code of conduct that identifies activities that are illegal or open to question;
- a statement outlining the consequences of breaching corporate policies;
- procedures that detail exactly what an employee should do when concerns arise out of certain situations; and
- an acknowledgment, signed by each employee, indicating that they have read, understood, and will adhere to the policy program.

3. Training and Education

Effective compliance requires a training program that targets personnel at all levels of the company who are in a position to engage in or who may be exposed to anticompetitive conduct. All members of an organization should have an understanding of the limits of acceptable behaviour. The bureau's communication and education programs can be of some assistance to companies in helping them organize and present training sessions.

4. Monitoring, Auditing, and Reporting

Once a compliance program is in place and has the support of senior management, it can only be fully effective where it is periodically reviewed. While there is no one set procedure for monitoring, auditing, and reporting, the chosen procedure should be able to detect, address, and deter anticompetitive conduct.

Monitoring seeks to prevent systematic violations of the program. If a program is not monitored, the entity's commitment to it will not be credible in the eyes of its employees or management, nor will it be able to identify flaws in its procedures and processes. Effective monitoring is necessary to prevent violations before they occur.

Audits aim to determine whether violations of the Act have occurred and to ensure that any such violations are dealt with appropriately. The bureau does not endorse any particular form of audit – periodic, *ad hoc*, or event-triggered – but rather looks to see whether the audit process of the company ensures that violations are identified and resolved. The choice of audit approach will likely depend on what activities the firm considers to be at greatest risk for violation of the Act. Periodic auditing may be more suitable for a business with a large sales force engaged in many transactions on a daily basis, while event-triggered auditing may be more suitable to an entity with larger but relatively fewer transactions.

Internal reporting procedures complete the process and encourage employees to provide timely, reliable information that can be the basis of further investigation by the entity. Reporting must carry no fear of reprisal. Were an employee to fear for his or her employment for reporting actual or suspected anticompetitive activity on the part of the entity or another employee, the effectiveness of the program would be compromised.

5. Disciplinary Procedures

A disciplinary policy serves to deter anticompetitive behaviour while reinforcing the commitment of the entity to the compliance program. This ultimately improves the credibility of the program. The program must make employees aware of the consequences of their behaviour and provide that disciplinary measures such as suspensions, fines, or dismissal may be applied in such circumstances.

6. Critique

While it is prudent for many businesses to have some type of compliance program in place, the bureau's framework is arguably impractical for many smaller and medium-sized enterprises (SMEs). Larger, public companies have the money, time, and human resources necessary to study their business, to develop a compliance program, to consult with the bureau, to prepare training and education programs, and to monitor the effectiveness and implementation of their program on a regular basis. There are clearly economies of scale to implementing compliance programs. Unfortunately, the CCP does not address the reality that businesses are not homogeneous, and by failing to do so, the CCP may be deterring the creation of compliance programs by SMEs. That is, after undertaking a cost-benefit analysis of implementing a compliance program, an SME may rationally conclude not to pursue such an initiative. The bureau would be well advised to down-scale its expectations in connection with SMEs' compliance programs to further its objective of promoting compliance.

D. Voluntary Information Contacts

Voluntary information contacts are typically undertaken by the bureau when an issue is brought to its attention that merits further consideration. An issue may come to the attention of the bureau in any number of ways. Most often this will occur as a result of a complaint being lodged by a third party. The bureau will then typically attempt to test the veracity of the complaint by contacting the target of the complaint as well as other market participants who possess information that may advance the bureau's understanding of the relevant facts. The contacted person need not justify his or her conduct or discuss the matter with the bureau. Having said that, it is often advisable for the contacted persons to cooperate with the bureau, depending on the circumstances. However, in every instance, it is advisable for the contacted person to seek legal counsel before cooperating with the bureau.

A possible benefit of being contacted by the bureau is that such contact may serve as a warning to a business that certain activities in which it is engaged may not be in compliance with the Act or that the bureau is particularly interested in the ongoing activities in a particular industry. While an information contact from the bureau is not a truly voluntary means of facilitating compliance with the Act, it heightens the sensitivity of the contacted person to the application of the Act in the context of its day-to-day operations.

IV. Involuntary Compliance with the *Competition Act*

A. *Overview*

While the commissioner and the bureau encourage and facilitate voluntary compliance with the Act, where compliance needs to be enforced, the Act turns primarily to public enforcement via the commissioner and the bureau. However, a private right of action may also be commenced to enforce certain of the Act's provisions. The scope for private action appears likely to broaden if proposed amendments to the Act are implemented. Each of the public and private methods of enforcement of the Act will be addressed below.

B. *The Investigation/Inquiry Process*

The first formal step in the public enforcement of the Act is the commencement of an inquiry by the commissioner. Section 10 governs the commencement of both criminal and civil inquiries under the Act. Under section 10, the commissioner *must* commence an inquiry when either (i) six adult residents of Canada make an application to the commissioner, pursuant to section 9 of the Act, for an inquiry, based on their opinion that a violation of the Act has or is about to be commit-

752 The Law and Economics of Canadian Competition Policy

ted; or (ii) the commissioner is so directed by the minister of industry. However, the commissioner has complete discretion to discontinue an ongoing inquiry at any time.

The commissioner is also empowered to conduct an inquiry when he believes, on reasonable grounds, that:

(i)   a person has contravened or failed to comply with an order made pursuant to section 32, 33 or 34, or Part VII.1 or VIII,

(ii) grounds exist for the making of an order under Part VII.1 or VIII, or

(iii) an offence under Part VI or VII has been or is about to be committed ...[24]

Most investigations are commenced when the commissioner believes an inquiry is warranted, and often this belief is prompted by an informant or other person who comes forward with information. The purpose of an inquiry, as set out in section 10, is to determine the facts, and the Act provides the commissioner with a formidable array of powers that can be used once a formal section 10 inquiry is undertaken.

Under section 11, the commissioner can make an *ex parte* application to the Federal Court or to a provincial superior court for an order requiring a person to attend under oath, to produce records or other things, or to provide a written return under oath.[25] Section 11 is available only if the commissioner has commenced an inquiry under section 10 of the Act. Section 15 of the Act permits the commissioner to apply to a judge of a provincial superior court or the Federal Court for a search warrant. Where exigent circumstances exist, the commissioner may conduct a warrantless search.[26] Section 16 deals specifically with searches of computer systems and allows the warrant holder to access the data contained therein. The formal powers under sections 15 and 16 of the Act apply in connection with inquiries related to either criminal offences or reviewable practices.

---

24 S. 10(1).

25 The commissioner's ability to compel information from the targets of criminal inquiries was upheld by the Federal Court of Canada in *Samson v. Canada*, [1994] 3 F.C. 113.

26 Exigent circumstances exist where the requirement of obtaining a warrant would likely result in the loss or destruction of evidence.

In recent years, the propensity of the commissioner to make section 11 applications has increased significantly. Moreover, to date, courts have shown substantial deference to the commissioner's decision to seek information by way of section 11.[27]

The foregoing powers are all, of course, subject to the *Canadian Charter of Rights and Freedoms*, and bureau officers typically will work closely with the attorney general to ensure that the inquiry is conducted fairly, impartially, and objectively with respect to the accused, and with a view to ensuring that the evidence collected will stand the test of scrutiny in the criminal court system, particular under section 24 of the Charter.[28]

As noted above, under section 22 of the Act, the commissioner may discontinue an inquiry at any stage. However, where an inquiry is discontinued, a written report outlining the reasons for the discontinuance must be given to the minister of industry. Where the inquiry was commenced as a result of a six-resident application, the commissioner must give reasons to the residents.

C. *Confidentiality*

Once commenced, an inquiry must be conducted in accordance with the confidentiality requirements of section 29 of the Act. Section 29 protects certain information collected pursuant to the Act from being disclosed. It states as follows:

> 29. (1) No person who performs or has performed duties or functions in the administration or enforcement of this Act shall communicate or allow to be communicated to any other person except to a Canadian law enforcement agency or for the purposes of the administration or enforcement of this Act

---

27 In particular, a number of decisions related to s. 11 arose out of the acquisition of Cast North America Inc. by Canadian Pacific Ltd between 1995 and 1997. See also P. Collins, '*British Columbia Securities Commission v. Branch*: Implications for Section 11 of the *Competition Act*,' (Spring 1995) *Canadian Competition Record* at 6.

28 S. 24 of the Charter provides that where evidence is collected in violation of the Charter, a court may refuse to admit the evidence where such an admission would bring the administration of justice into disrepute.

(a) the identity of any person from who information was obtained pursuant to this Act;

(b) any information obtained pursuant to section 11, 15, 16 or 114;

(c) whether notice has been given or information supplied in respect of a particular proposed transaction under section 114; or

(d) any information obtained from a person requesting a certificate under section 102.

Supplementing this legislatively enforced confidentiality protection is the commissioner's May 1995 policy entitled Communication of Confidential Information Under the Competition Act (the confidentiality policy).

Technically speaking, the Act only protects from disclosure information that falls into one of the four categories set out in section 29. The problem that frequently arises, however, is that information collected by the commissioner is often voluntarily provided and not gathered under the commissioner's formal information gathering powers. As a result, the information is not specifically covered by section 29(1)(b) and, but for any policy to the contrary, would be subject to disclosure. However, as set out in the confidentiality policy, it is the bureau's stated intention to treat such information as though it were covered by section 29. The bureau will therefore avoid communicating the information it has gathered during the course of its investigations, despite the fact that there is no statutory prohibition from doing so. This respect for confidentiality helps facilitate voluntary compliance by businesses who can be assured that their information will be treated in a confidential manner. Without such protection, corporations may be less inclined to volunteer information. Lack of voluntary disclosure would, in turn, make the enforcement of the Act more time consuming and costly, as the commissioner would have to resort to his formal powers to compel the production of documents and testimony with even greater frequency than is currently the case.[29]

---

29 The premise underlying the confidentiality policy is expected to become law assuming Bill C-23, An Act to Amend the Competition Act and the Competition Tribunal Act, is enacted in 2002. Specifically, Bill C-23 would amend section 29 of the Act by adding a new paragraph 29(1)(e), which would supplement the current language by including 'any information voluntarily provided pursuant to the Act.' Bill C-23 also proposes to amend section 29(2).

Section 29 does, however, contain three important exceptions. The first is that the commissioner may communicate confidential information to a 'Canadian law enforcement agency.' In its confidentiality policy, the bureau attempts to limit disclosure only to the extent required for the Canadian law enforcement agency to provide the commissioner with the assistance sought. However, the bureau also maintains that the release of confidential information under this exception need not 'necessarily occur to advance any particular matter under the Act and may be done for the express purpose of assisting the Canadian law enforcement agency in carrying out its duties.'[30]

The second exception permits the commissioner to release confidential information for the purpose of the 'enforcement or administration' of the Act. In the commissioner's view, this exception is broad enough to permit the communication of information in order to advance a specific investigation and to allow the divulging of confidential information to a foreign law enforcement agency for the purpose of advancing a Canadian investigation. In the area of international mutual legal assistance, discussed in greater detail below, the commissioner takes the position that information will be provided where formal requests under the *Treaty between Canada and the United States on Mutual Legal Assistance in Criminal Matters* are received, so long as the bureau and the foreign agency are working on the same matter and the communication of the information would assist the commissioner in advancing his investigation. It is unclear whether such disclosure is truly permitted or contemplated by section 29. Nevertheless, a recent practical development in the context of multijurisdictional mergers is for the bureau to request, on a voluntary basis, all filings made in respect of the proposed transaction with all foreign competition law authorities.

Finally, information which has been made public may be released under section 29(2). Typically, this occurs where the media seeks confirmation of an ongoing investigation.

D. Criminal Penalties

1. Overview
Part VI of the Act sets out criminal competition law offences. The

---

30 *Communication of Confidential Information unde the Competition Act* (Statement of the Bureau of Competition Policy, 1 May 1995).

enforcement of these provisions proceeds much differently from reviewable matters (discussed below) as the commissioner must work much more closely with the attorney general of Canada, whose office actually carries the prosecution before the courts.[31] The prosecution of criminal offences under the Act is affected, like all criminal offences, by Charter considerations as well as by the much higher burden of proof pursuant to which the Crown must prove each and every element of the offence beyond a reasonable doubt. In a reviewable matter the anti-competitive conduct need only be proved on a balance of probabilities.

Criminal prosecution under the *Competition Act* is meant to achieve compliance with its aims in much the same manner as any other criminal prosecution. First, a successful prosecution is meant to deter the actual offender (specific deterrence). Second, the imposition of a penalty, in the form of a fine or imprisonment, is meant to serve the aim of general deterrence of other potential violators. The stigma associated with a criminal conviction may also deter conduct that violates the Act. Often the name of the perpetrator, whether it is a company, its directors or officers, or an individual, will appear in the media. The spectre of such penalties frequently leads parties to plead guilty rather than take the matter to trial.

Upon referral, and where recommended by the commissioner, the accused and the attorney general may ask a court to issue a prohibition order under section 34(2). As a result of recent amendments to the Act, these orders are mandated to last for ten years, unless a court orders a shorter period, and may include any terms the court determines necessary to prevent the commission, continuation or repetition of the offence. Prohibition orders avoid the costs associated with litigation and do not result in a conviction or a guilty plea for the accused. Where enforcement objectives are better served by a conviction and fine, the matter proceeds under section 34(1). The end result may be imprisonment.[32]

---

31 S. 23(3) provides that it is the attorney general who institutes and prosecutes criminal violators of the Act.

32 Fines levied in connection with the violation of criminal provisions of the Act have grown exponentially in recent years. See, for example, William T. Stanbury, 'Expanding Responsibilities and Declining Resources: The Strategic Responses of the Competition Bureau, 1986–1996,' (1998) 13 *Review of Industrial Organization* 205. For example, in September 1999, the Federal Court of Canada levied fines in a series of pharmaceutical industry conspiracies that totalled $88.4 million, shattering the previous record.

2. The Criminal Process

While it is the attorney general who is formally charged with prosecuting violations of the criminal provisions of the Act, and while there is no legal impediment to the attorney general's office separately conducting an investigation into alleged infractions of the Act, in practice, it is the commissioner who typically investigates a violation before carriage of the matter is turned over to the attorney general for formal prosecution.

Typically, once the commissioner is satisfied, usually as a result of the findings of a section 10 inquiry, that an offence has been or is about to be committed, he will refer the matter to the attorney general under section 23. At this point, the commissioner would turn over all records and evidence collected as part of his investigation. As a practical matter, such a referral is rarely the first indication that the attorney general receives of the investigation. Department of Justice lawyers tend to be involved in a criminal investigation well before the matter is formally referred, and correspondingly, the commissioner and bureau officers remain involved after such referral. In this way, the expertise of the Department of Justice as it relates to the constitutional collection of evidence and the tactics and strategies of a successful criminal prosecution can be brought to bear beforehand, while the bureau can lend its expertise in interpreting evidence that is often voluminous and technical.

The problem that the commissioner faces with criminal enforcement,

---

Specifically, F. Hoffman-La Roche of Switzerland was fined $50.9 million ($48 million of which related to bulk vitamins with the balance related to citric acid) (*R. v. Hoffman La Roche* (unreported), 22 September 1999, Toronto T-1665-99, F.C.T.D.). BASF AG of Germany was fined $18 million for its participation in the bulk vitamins conspiracy and an additional $1 million for its criminal activity related to choline chloride (*R. v. BASF AG* (unreported), 22 September 1999, Toronto T-1664-99, F.C.T.D.) Rhone-Poulenc S.A. of France was fined $14 million related to its criminal activity in the context of Vitamin A and E (*R. v. Rhone-Poulenc S.A.* (unreported), 22 September 1999, Toronto T-1666-99, F.C.T.D.). Eisai Co. Ltd and Daiichi Pharmaceutical Co., Ltd., both of Japan, were fined $2 million and $2.5 million, respectively, for their role in these vitamin conspiracies (*R. v. E. Esai Co. Ltd.* (unreported), 22 September 1999, Toronto T-1667-99, F.C.T.D.; *R. v. Daiichi Pharmaceutical Co. Ltd.* (unreported), 22 September 1999, Toronto T-1668-99, F.C.T.D). The offences ranged from price fixing to allocating markets. The previous record fine had been levied in May 1998 against Archer Daniels Midland ($16 million) in connection with its role in an international lysine and citric acid conspiracy. Also in 1999, Russell Cosburn, a former vice-president of Chinook Group Limited, was given a nine-month prison sentence for his role in an international conspiracy related to the fixing of prices and allocation of markets for choline chloride.

as with the enforcement of reviewable matters, is obtaining the requisite evidence to prove the contravention of the Act. Often criminal matters may be very difficult to detect.[33] As a result, the commissioner has instituted a number of programs aimed at encouraging parties to approach the bureau with information regarding potential offences. Consider for example, a price-fixing conspiracy where numerous participants have entered into an oral agreement to set a fixed price. It may go undetected unless one of the parties to the conspiracy, or perhaps an employee thereof, is willing to come forward to provide evidence of the conspiracy, or simply to alert the commissioner to its existence. An employee or company in this situation may avail itself of certain protections provided by the commissioner, as discussed below.

3. 'Whistleblowing'
'Whistleblowing' has gathered an increasing amount of attention in recent years, both within Canada and elsewhere. Whistleblowing has been defined in numerous ways but is typically conceived of as an act of a person who, not being in a position to affect events within an organization, and who believes the public interest overrides the private interest of the organization he or she serves, alerts authorities to the existence of corrupt, illegal, or harmful activity.[34] This type of whistleblowing, where a member of an organization involved in the activity comes forward, is typically conceived of as internal whistleblowing. It is distinguishable from external whistleblowing, where the whistleblower is a third party not involved in the illegal activity, a customer of a firm who is the victim of a price-fixing conspiracy, for example, or a member of the public who learns of the illegal activity.

The problem for the internal whistleblower, as opposed to the external whistleblower, is that the person is faced with competing loyalties. On the one hand, there is a duty of loyalty and confidentiality owed to his or her employer. On the other hand, there is the public interest in

---

33 An important amendment to the evidence gathering powers of the commissioner involved the amendment to s. 183 of the *Criminal Code* adding ss. 45, 47, and 52.1 of the Act to the list of offences under the Code for which the attorney general may seek a 'wiretap.'

34 Ralph Nader may have been the first to coin this definition. See M. Myers and V.J. Mattews Lemiux, 'Whistleblowing Employee Loyalty and the Right to Criticize – the Employee's Perspective,' in W. Kaplan, J. Sack, and M. Gunderson, eds., *Labour Arbitration Yearbook* (Toronto: Butterworths, 1991), 211 at 212.

ensuring that unlawful acts are prevented and prosecuted where they occur. The internal whistleblower, as a reward for his or her meritorious deed, may expect to be dismissed from his or her employment. While Canada has no broad, antiretaliatory whistleblowing statute, certain antiretaliatory provisions have been included in environmental, occupational health and safety, and other legislation.[35]

In the competition law context, informal protections have been provided for whistleblowers in a number of ways. Since 1991 the commissioner's immunity program has offered an incentive to internal whistleblowers who decide to come forward with evidence of competition law violations in which they were involved (see below). However, this program offers no incentive to the innocent whistleblower who wishes to come forward with information about the misconduct of his or her employer or another employee. Protection from employment retaliation, which is what the whistleblower really needs, is not available under the immunity program.

Retaliation may be mitigated through the use of a 1–800 number which allows people to communicate concerns or complaints anonymously. However, resort to this method of disclosure is not foolproof. An employer may be able, for example, to guess the identity of an informant on the basis of the employee's knowledge, position, or experience.

The existing provisions of the *Competition Act* also offer limited protection to whistleblowers. While section 29 prohibits the communication of the names of informants and section 10 requires investigations to be conducted in private, should a matter proceed to trial, the employee's identity as a witness will likely have to be disclosed. Certain protections are available under the law of employment but a discussion of those protections is beyond the scope of this chapter.[36]

---

35 In the field of environmental protection, Ontario's *Environmental Protection Act*, R.S.O. 1990, c. E.19, s. 174(2) provides that no employer shall dismiss, discipline, penalize, intimidate or coerce an employee for complying with the Act or for complying with a number of other environmental statutes including the *Pesticides Act*, R.S.O. 1990, c. P.11 and the *Environmental Assessment Act*, R.S.O. 1990, c. E.18. Under Part VI of Ontario's *Occupation Health and Safety Act*, R.S.O. 1990, c. O.19, employers are barred from making reprisals against employees for complying with or seeking enforcement of the occupational health and safety legislation.

36 For a review of employment law protections against unjust dismissal, see the report on whistleblowing prepared by Charles I. Dubin, available on the Competition Bureau's internet website.

As a result, the Act was recently amended to include a whistleblowing provision, which states as follows.

> 66.1 (1) Any person who has reasonable grounds to believe that a person has committed or intends to commit an offence under the Act, or that grounds exist for the making of an order under Part VII.1 or VIII, may notify the Commissioner of the particulars of the matter and may request that his or her identity be kept confidential with respect to the notification.
>
> (2) The Commissioner shall keep confidential the identity of a person who has notified the Commissioner under subsection (1) and to whom an assurance of confidentiality has been provided by any person who performs duties or functions in the administration or enforcement of this Act.

Under section 66.2(1), employers are prohibited from dismissing, suspending, demoting, disciplining, harassing, or otherwise disadvantaging an employee who has, in good faith, come forth to 'blow the whistle' under section 66.1, or who the employer suspects will imminently do so. Section 66.2(2) confirms that this section does not impair any right of an employee at law or under an employment contract or collective agreement. Finally, section 66.2(3) defines an employee to extend to an independent contractor.

4. Immunity

Another approach for facilitating the detection of criminal violations of the Act involves the use of the commissioner's immunity program. The immunity program was created originally as an incentive for corporations to voluntarily report their participation in conspiracy or bid-rigging activities before that activity became known to the bureau. The rationale for the program was simply that these activities are often difficult to detect, and even more difficult to prosecute, absent some assistance from those involved. However, since it was first introduced in 1991,[37] the program has been expanded to include individuals as well as corporations. That is, an individual or company may receive the

---

37 The program was first outlined in a speech given by the former commissioner, Howard Wetston, to the Canadian Corporate Counsel Association in Calgary, Alberta, on 19 August 1991.

benefits of the program where they come forward, voluntarily, and are able to offer valuable information and cooperation to the bureau regarding a criminal violation of the Act.

There are a number of key points to note about the immunity program. First, the program is not a replacement for traditional investigations conducted under the Act. Undoubtedly, evidence will come to the attention of the bureau upon the grant of immunity. However, the bureau does not 'offer immunity' in return for information. The program is, instead, voluntary. The commissioner requests that those seeking immunity voluntarily approach the bureau.

Second, the granting of immunity from criminal prosecution is ultimately at the behest of the attorney general. The commissioner makes a recommendation to the attorney general that a certain individual and/or entity be granted immunity or receive other favourable treatment but cannot himself guarantee favourable treatment. In practice, however, the attorney general will in almost all cases accept the recommendation of the commissioner for favourable treatment.

'Favourable treatment' is the third feature of the program. The immunity program is not an 'all-or-nothing' affair. Immunity is simply one form of favourable treatment – the ultimate form – that the commissioner may recommend be granted by the attorney general. What is meant by 'favourable treatment' has been described by Harry Chandler, then deputy commissioner in a speech in 1994: 'Favourable treatment means any penalty or obligation that is less severe than one which would be sought in the absence of disclosure and co-operation by the party who may have contravened the criminal provisions of the Act.' In situations where full immunity is not recommended, the acceptance of a guilty plea or a joint submission on sentencing would likely result in a lesser fine or period of incarceration being recommended to the presiding judge.

In deciding whether to recommend immunity or other favourable treatment, the commissioner considers a number of factors.[38]

1. The person (or company) must be the first to approach the bureau

---

38 See the unpublished speech given by Harry Chandler, Deputy Director of Investigation and Research (Criminal Matters) Competition Bureau, 10 March 1994, 'Getting Down to Business: The Strategic Direction of Criminal Competition Law Enforcement in Canada,' Appx III.

with evidence of the offence in question before an investigation is launched.
2. The person must provide full and frank disclosure of the facts and there must be no misrepresentation of material facts.
3. The person must cooperate fully with the bureau's investigation and with any ensuing prosecution.
4. The evidence provided by the person must be important and valuable in the context of any prosecution.
5. The person must be prepared to make restitution commensurate with the facts and its responsibility in the matter.
6. The person must have taken immediate steps to terminate the activity and to report it to the commissioner as soon as it was discovered.
7. The conduct of the person coming forward will be questioned and favourable treatment will be considered in the context of prior violations of the Act. As well, favourable treatment will be less likely to be recommended where the person was the instigator of the offence.
8. The person should be prepared to consent to the issuance of a prohibition order of fixed duration in relation to the offence admitted.

In making its decision, the bureau will focus upon who is coming forward and the circumstances surrounding the request for immunity. The failure to fully state the facts, or the discovery of further offences known to the offender but not disclosed to the bureau, will not likely lead to a recommendation of favourable treatment. The bureau must always consider the effect on the administration of justice of a recommendation of immunity, as well as whether such favourable treatment would be consistent with responsible enforcement of the Act. Where the bureau has already commenced an investigation, the same considerations apply, although the first criteria is obviously dropped.[39]

---

39 In post-investigation considerations regarding the potential granting of favourable treatment the process is slightly different. Typically, counsel and the person seeking immunity meet on a 'without prejudice' basis to discuss how the information may be used. This is followed by a 'proffer' of information in which the immunity request is couched in terms of the information that could be provided. Where it is decided that the proffered information can form the basis for considering immunity, an agreement setting out the conditions upon which immunity would be granted is entered into. The person is then interviewed under oath and their evidence is compared to evidence already collected. Based on this assessment of the criteria for favourable treatment, the bureau decides what form of favourable treatment to recommend to the attorney general.

The immunity program is a valuable tool in the enforcement of the Act. It encourages compliance without the expenditure of significant resources by the bureau. The program was confirmed when Abbott Laboratories agreed to a prohibition order in 1992, and has been important in securing convictions and fines in some of Canada's largest conspiracy and bid-rigging cases.[40]

E. Private Enforcement

1. The Debate for and Against
The debate over what role private enforcement should play in the context of competition law has been long-standing and vigorous in many jurisdictions including Canada. The catalyst for the latest iteration of this debate in Canada was a 1995 Discussion Paper[41] that proposed a number of amendments to the Act, including the establishment of a right of direct access to the tribunal by private litigants with respect to certain reviewable practices. Following the release of the Discussion Paper, a consultative panel was formed by the commissioner to advise him in connection with the proposals therein. During this process, the bureau also commissioned a study by Professors Trebilcock and Roach related to the issue of private enforcement of the Act.[42] However, the ultimate amending legislation – Bill C-20[43] – did not include any changes regarding private party access.

The next key development in the context of private enforcement was Bill C-472[44] – a private member's bill – that had proposed to amend the Act by, among other things, allowing for private access to the tribunal

---

40 In July 1998 two Japanese entities offered guilty pleas and agreed to fines of $3.5 million and $70,000 in an international conspiracy to fix prices for lysine (a feed additive) and citric acid. A third co-conspirator had been the first to approach the bureau with valuable and extensive cooperation and was granted immunity. The case was part of a larger conspiracy in which the American agri-food giant, Archer Daniels Midland Company, agreed to pay a fine of $16 million, at that time, the largest fine ever levied under the Act.

41 Commissioner of Competition , Competition Bureau, Discussion Paper on Competition Law, 28 June 1995 (unpublished).

42 K. Roach and M. Trebilcock, 'Private Enforcement of Competition Laws,' (1996) 4 (3) Osgoode Hall Law Journal at 462 was derived from this study.

43 Bill C-20 was not implemented until 18 March 1999.

44 An act to amend the Competition Act, the Competition Tribunal Act and the Criminal Code as a consequence.

for refusal to deal, exclusive dealing, tied selling, and market restrictions. This Bill died on the Order Paper with the dissolution of Parliament in October 2000. However, as discussed below in this chapter, the current amendments initiative – Bill C-23[45] – resurrects much of what was proposed related to private access in Bill C-472.

Trebilcock and Roach provide a compelling case for allowing private party access to the tribunal. They view such access as being consistent with the pursuit of corrective justice while supplementing the constrained resources of the commissioner. In addition, they view private access as promoting accountability for the commissioner's decisions not to challenge certain reviewable matters. Trebilcock and Roach survey the experiences in other jurisdictions and readily concede that there are weaknesses inherent in private enforcement – most notably, potential disruption to the commissioner's enforcement policy and the imposition of strategic costs on others participating in a given market. In response to such concerns, they identify certain 'design issues' that merit attention rather than engaging in an 'all or nothing' debate over private enforcement. These issues include: standing, intervention, preventing frivolous and improper private actions, cost rules, discovery, limitation periods, and so forth.

On an objective basis, the efficacy of private access to the tribunal appears undeniable for the reasons described by Professors Trebilcock and Roach. Moreover, their concern with design issues is well placed in that the appropriate scope for private enforcement must be determined. For example, one of the principal shortcomings of Bill C-472, and now Bill C-23, is that it appears destined to be caught on the 'slippery slope' of reviewable practices. That is, while Bill C-23 does not propose to permit private access in the context of abuse of dominance, most of the recent cases that have dealt with section 77 were, or could easily have been, argued under the abuse of dominance provision. Therefore, a private party would not likely find it difficult to argue indirectly what it cannot do under Bill C-23 directly. Issues such as this make it evident that structuring an appropriate regime of private

---

45 An act to amend the *Competition Act* and the *Competition Tribunal Act*. This Bill received first reading on 4 April 2001. Interestingly, Bill C-23 did not contain amendments related to private enforcement at the stage of First Reading. These specific provisions were added at the committee stage by The Standing Committee on Industry, Science and Technology.

access to the tribunal represents one of the greatest challenges facing Canadian competition law in the foreseeable future.

An important recent contribution to the debate between private and public enforcement is Professor Roberts' study, 'International Comparative Analysis of Private Rights of Access,'[46] which compares international practices and experiences in the private enforcement of competition legislation in five selected jurisdictions: Australia, New Zealand, the United Kingdom, Ireland, and the United States. Roberts provides important insight into the following areas in each of these jurisdictions: the enforcement philosophy; the extent of cooperative enforcement; the distribution of enforcement power between the public and private sectors; the areas of competition law most suitable to private enforcement; the focus of public enforcement activity; the various attempts at cost reduction and private enforcement; the role of governmental oversight of private actions; the prevention of strategic use of private actions for any competitive, unmeritorious, or frivolous purposes; and the guidance to be derived for the design of an effective private enforcement regime in Canada.

2. Overview of section 36

Currently, enforcement of the Act is not left solely to public officials. In addition to enforcement by the commissioner, the Act creates a private right of action under section 36. This right was introduced with a package of legislative changes in 1976; until that time, public enforcement was the only vehicle for enforcing the Act, save for common law rights of action.[47] The constitutional validity of section 36 was in some doubt until the Supreme Court of Canada upheld the provision as a valid exercise of the federal government's legislative power over trade and commerce in *City National Leasing Ltd. v. General Motors of Canada Ltd.*[48] Section 36 is a useful tool in competition law enforcement, particularly

---

46 A study commissioned by Industry Canada – Competition Bureau (18 April 2000). This study is available on the Competition Bureau website at *www.strategis.ic.gc.ca \ SSG \ ct01713e.html*.

47 A full discussion of common law rights of action is beyond the scope of this chapter. However, it should be noted that common law claims are often made in conjunction with a s. 36 action, when that action is commenced in a court of competent jurisdiction. The most often pleaded common law causes of action are civil conspiracy, unlawful interference with economic relations and in misleading advertising cases, claims of injurious falsehood and defamation.

48 [1989] 1 S.C.R. 641.

in an era of declining resources for public enforcement, despite the fact that relatively few private actions have been brought.[49]

Section 36 does not provide for an unlimited private right of action. Rather, it is fairly circumscribed. The provision reads as follows:

> 36. (1) Any person who has suffered loss or damage as a result of
> - (a) conduct that is contrary to any provision of Part VI, or
> - (b) the failure of any person to comply with an order of the Tribunal or another court under this Act,
>
> may, in any court of competent jurisdiction, sue for and recover from the person who engaged in the conduct or failed to comply with the order an amount equal to the loss or damage proved to have been suffered by him, together with any additional amount that the court may allow not exceeding the full cost to him of any investigation in connection with the matter and of proceedings under this section.

Part VI of the Act consists of the criminal offences, of which the most important are conspiracy, bid-rigging, price discrimination, predatory pricing, price maintenance, and misleading advertising and deceptive marketing practices. An action can be launched under section 36 in respect of an alleged breach of any of these provisions. However, reviewable matters are not actionable under section 36 unless the tribunal or another court has entered an order prohibiting that conduct. In that context, the offence, which is actionable under section 36 is the breaching of the order related to a reviewable practice and not the committing of the specific reviewable practice. This is the first of three significant legal limitations in commencing a section 36 action: reviewable practices are not themselves actionable. In addition, actions under section 36 are difficult to prove and the relief that can be claimed is limited. These limitations are discussed below.

3. Reviewable Practices

Only an alleged violation of the criminal provisions of the Act is itself actionable under section 36. Reviewable matters are not on their face actionable. However, it may be possible given a certain set of circum-

---

49 For a review and discussion of the few s. 36 cases that have been advanced, see G. Leslie and S. Bodley, 'The Record of Private Actions Under Section 36 of the *Competition Act*,' (1993) *Can. Comp. Record* 50.

stances to characterize reviewable conduct as falling within the criminal provisions of the Act. A merger, for example, is an agreement. If the commissioner declined to bring an application before the tribunal in respect of a particular merger, there is nothing in law to prevent a private party from suing the parties to the merger in a section 36 action on the basis that the merger agreement amounts to a conspiracy under section 45 of the Act. The Act specifically contemplates that proceedings based on the same facts could be brought under sections 45, 79 (abuse of dominance), or 92 (mergers). Nevertheless, the extent to which *prima facie* reviewable matters could be recharacterized as criminal offences is extremely limited.

4. Burden of Proof in Section 36 Cases

Section 36 cases are difficult to prove, particularly where the action is based on a breach of a Part VI offence. To establish liability, the plaintiff must prove all of the elements of the criminal offence. However, unlike in a criminal prosecution, an action based on section 36 need only be proved on a balance of probabilities, and not beyond a reasonable doubt.[50] The use of the lower standard in section 36 actions raises the possibility that a violator may be liable under section 36 for damages but found not guilty in the criminal matter. Nevertheless, the task of proving the offence may be daunting, time consuming, and expensive for the prospective plaintiff, and, in practice, a court may insist on a burden of proof somewhere between the civil and the criminal standard.[51] The very few section 36 cases that have been brought to date are a testament to the fact that these allegations are not easily proved.

One element that makes the private plaintiff's task of proving a criminal violation more difficult is that the plaintiff must commence the action without the benefit of the commissioner's investigative powers. However, the Act does assist the prospective plaintiff in proving his or her case where a criminal conviction has been entered against the defendant for a Part VI violation.

Section 36(2) of the Act provides that the record of proceedings where a conviction was entered, in the absence of evidence to the contrary, is proof that the person engaged in the conduct that violated Part VI of the Act. Furthermore, the section provides that evidence in those

---

50 *Continental Insurance v. Dalton Cartage Co.*, [1982] 1 S.C.R. 164.
51 Ibid.

other proceedings can be admitted as evidence in the private action under section 36. However, this benefit to the plaintiff only applies where there is an actual conviction. The laying of charges and a subsequent acquittal will not entitle the section 36 plaintiff to use the record and evidence from those proceedings in the private action. An order on consent under section 34(2) is also not a conviction for the purposes of section 36. Also, the entering of a guilty plea in criminal proceedings, while constituting a conviction, may be of little use to the private plaintiff where little evidence is placed on the record.

Where a private action plaintiff can get the benefit of section 36(2), its proof concerns are greatly reduced. As a result, a private plaintiff may want to consider attempting to invoke the investigative powers of the commissioner, in the hope of securing a conviction. If a private party can convince the commissioner to investigate the matter and have it turned into a successful criminal prosecution by the attorney general, the only major issue remaining would be proof of damages and their quantum. The discussion immediately below considers certain factors a plaintiff's counsel should consider in deciding whether to make a complaint to the bureau.

First, it should be noted, a complaint to the bureau and a subsequent investigation or prosecution (successful or not) is not a precondition to launching a section 36 action. Second, counsel will have to consider the cost of making a complaint to the bureau versus the expected result. Executive time and lost opportunity costs must be added to the legal and administrative costs involved in contacting the bureau. Plaintiff's counsel should consider whether there is any reasonable chance the bureau will investigate the case. Some guidance may be derived here from the case selection criteria used by the bureau. The bureau's case selection criteria assist it in organizing its financial and human resources in a manner consistent with its enforcement goals. The bureau will make an assessment of the economic welfare aspects of the case, an assessment of the extent to which the enforcement policy interests of the bureau would be met through an investigation, and finally, an assessment of the expected costs to the bureau in financial and human resources. Counsel should be aware of the bureau's general criminal enforcement policy, which tends to focus more resources on conspiracy and bid-rigging as opposed to other Part VI offences. Even where the bureau declines to investigate further, the potential plaintiff may have gained valuable insight from having 'tested the waters' of the bureau. Also, bureau commentary may assist a proposed plaintiff in determining the reasonableness of its proposed section 36 action.

Finally, in deciding whether to make a complaint to the bureau, the complainant may want to consider any long-run benefits to making the complaint. Is there sufficient evidence to establish the criminal violation absent a bureau investigation? If there is, the cost of complaining to the bureau may not justify the expense. The plaintiff may also want to consider the implications of the Act's two-year limitation period under section 36(4)(a)(ii). The general limitation period applicable to a section 36 action is two years from the day the conduct was engaged in or from the 'day on which any criminal proceedings relating thereto were finally disposed of.' As a result of the oddly worded limitation period, a criminal proceeding may actually 'revive' a civil cause of action that had expired.

Where a section 36 plaintiff does not have a prior conviction to assist in proving its case, and where the commissioner has not investigated, the evidentiary hurdles are usually insurmountable. However, where the commissioner has investigated but not turned the matter over to the attorney general for prosecution, or has terminated the inquiry under section 22, the commissioner's files may be a potential 'gold mine' of information for the plaintiff. Accessing that information may, however, prove difficult.

As discussed above, section 10(3) requires that inquiries be conducted in private, and the confidentiality provisions of section 29 make accessing the investigative record difficult. The commissioner will not voluntarily disclose information to parties contemplating a section 36 action. In the commissioner's view, the civil discovery and subpoena mechanisms available to plaintiffs are the appropriate mechanisms to be used in collecting such information. The commissioner will therefore comply with court-ordered disclosure, subject to claims of solicitor-client or public interest privilege.

Ultimately, proving section 36 cases is difficult in the absence of a prior conviction. Moreover, where a plaintiff is capable of proving the offence, the damages available to it are limited and may render the pursuit of a section 36 action ill-advised.

5. Damages and Injunctive Relief
Under section 36, the only damages a section 36 plaintiff is entitled to are those damages 'actually suffered by him,' along with the costs of the investigation. This provision has been interpreted as limiting dam-

ages to special damages and costs.[52] While the cost provision is generous, given that in general civil litigation party-and-party costs rarely, if ever, cover the actual costs of litigation,[53] limitation of damages to actual or special damages may unduly limit the just recovery of plaintiffs and act as an impediment to private actions. Consider a section 45 conspiracy that was never actually implemented. A conviction under section 45 could result, at least theoretically, even where the agreement, arrangement, combination, or conspiracy entered into was not actually carried out. Where this was the case, consider the plaintiff's *actual* damages. They would in all likelihood be zero. As a result, a situation can occur where Part VI of the Act may be violated and a conviction entered, yet the potential private plaintiff would have no special damages that could be proved.

On its face, section 36 of the Act does not provide for injunctive relief and, until recently, it appeared that injunctive relief was not available under this provision unless the impugned conduct gave rise to an independent action.[54] There are, however, clear signs that this state will not prevail as a result of the decision in *Mead Johnson Canada v. Ross Pediatrics*.[55] In *Mead Johnson*, the plaintiff sought an interlocutory injunction to restrain the defendant from making certain representations in the promotion of its new brand of infant formula. In addition, Mead Johnson alleged that the representations being made were false and misleading and sued Ross Pediatrics (i) under sections 36 and 52 of the Act; (ii) for injurious falsehood; and (iii) for unlawful interference with economic relations.

Justice Brennan held that he possessed the jurisdiction to grant an

---

52 *Westfair Foods v. Lippens* (1989), 64 D.L.R. (4th) 335 (Man. C.A.).

53 Consider also what is meant by costs of any 'investigation in connection with the matter.' This seemingly broad phrase presumably covers expensive economic analysis or market studies that may be necessary for proving a s. 36 claim.

54 See, for example, *ACA Joe International v. 147255 Canada Inc.* (1986), 10 C.P.R. (3d) 301 (F.C.T.D.), and *947101 Ontario Ltd. v. Barrhaven Town Centre Inc.* (1995), 121 D.L.R. (4th) 748 (Ont. Gen. Div.). See also, D.B. Houston, R.M. Bell, S. Bhattacharjee and J. Chan, 'Private Remedies for Anticompetitive Conduct,' in *Annual Fall Conference on Competition Law (1998)* Canadian Bar Association – Competition Law Section, (Ottawa: Juris Publishing, 1999); N. Finkelstein and R. Kwinter, 'Section 36 and Claims for Injunctive Relief,' (1990) 69 *Can. Bar Rev.* 298; and P. Collins, 'Injunctive Relief under Section 36 of the *Competition Act*,' (Spring 1995) *Canadian Competition Record* at 18.

55 (1997), 31 O.R. (3d) 237 (Gen. Div.).

interlocutory injunction, relying on the Supreme Court of Canada's decision in *Brotherhood of Maintenance of Way Employees v. Canadian Pacific Ltd.*[56] In that case, it was held that the power to grant an interlocutory injunction was a matter of inherent jurisdiction of the court. Justice Brennan then applied the well-established test for granting interlocutory relief set out in *RJR-MacDonald Inc. v. Canada (Attorney General).*[57] Specifically, the court held that (i) there was a serious issue to be tried; (ii) Mead Johnson would suffer irreparable harm from Ross Pediatrics' representations; and (ii) the balance of convenience favoured Mead Johnson.

Houston et al. make an important observation regarding the decision in *Mead Johnson.*[58] They point out a critical distinction between the Act (s. 36) and the legislative framework applicable in *Canadian Pacific.* Specifically, Justice Brennan relied on the inherent jurisdiction of the court to grant an interlocutory injunction in the context of legislation – the *Canada Labour Code* – which contained no provision for interlocutory injunctions. Justice Brennan applied this reasoning to the Act, in taking the view that an interlocutory injunction could be granted despite the Act's silence on the issue. However, Houston et al. point out that section 36 specifically provides for damages but is silent on any other kind of relief, which would leave defendants with the ability to argue that it was the intention of Parliament to exclude injunctive relief from section 36.

6. Use of the Private Action Right

Private actions are rarely commenced in Canada.[59] Some authors have commented that this may be due to the difficulty the Crown has had in securing criminal convictions under Part VI, or perhaps to the limited scope of section 36, or it may simply be that the costs of bringing such a suit are large compared to the damages that may be recovered.[60] There

---

56 (1996), 136 D.L.R. (4th) 289 (S.C.C.).

57 [1994] 1 S.C.R. 311. The court in *RJR MacDonald* adopted the test for the granting of an interlocutory injunction from *American Cyanamid Co. v. Ethicon Ltd.*, [1975] 1 All E.R. 504.

58 'Private Remedies for Anticompetitive Conduct' at 209–10.

59 See Trebilcock and Roach, 'Private Enforcement of Competition Laws,' at 464–6 for a discussion regarding the statistics of private antitrust actions.

60 See Robert Nozick's commentary on s. 36 in the *Annotated Competition Act 1999* (Scarborough, Ont.: Carswell, 1999).

is still much uncertainty in the law relating to issues such as who has standing and when damages are too remote.

American antitrust enforcement relies to a significantly greater extent on the private law suit. Under both the *Sherman Act* and the *Clayton Act*, any private person 'injured in his business or property by reason of anything forbidden in the antitrust laws ... shall recover threefold the damages by him sustained, and the cost of suit, including a reasonable attorney's fee.'[61] It is this treble damages rule, more than any other provision in American antitrust law, which promotes the large volumes of private litigation in the United States.[62]

The treble damages rule is based on the rationale of compensation but also on the fact that, without it, there would be little incentive for private parties to detect and prosecute antitrust violations, and hence deterrence objectives would be compromised. If all that could be recovered were the actual damages sustained, fewer parties would go to court. Antitrust violators may also be encouraged to continue violating the law if all they stand to lose is their ill-gotten gain. The worst that could happen to the violator would be a return to the status quo. On the other hand, the lure of the 'windfall' of treble damages has led to a bonanza of both legitimate and trivial antitrust suits. Plaintiffs struggle to turn ordinary tort and contract claims into antitrust violations, and undoubtedly many actions are commenced solely as a business tool to punish or harass competitors.[63]

The American experience has not led to discussions of whether section 36 is too restrictive or whether it should be changed to encourage more private actions in Canada. While a full debate on this issue is beyond the scope of this chapter, there has never been much of an impetus from the private sector to move the legislation in that direction.[64]

---

61 *Clayton Act*, 38 Stat. 730 (1914), §4.
62 The spectre of treble damages has also been a factor in considering the disclosure of information to U.S. antitrust authorities by the bureau, which should not want to expose Canadian companies to such high damage claims.
63 Quare, however, how many of these frivolous law suits are generated by the 'parties pay' rule of costs in American litigation, whereby each side pays its own costs regardless of the outcome of the litigation. Presumably, contingency fees also play a significant role.
64 On private actions generally see James Musgrove, 'Civil Actions in the *Competition Act*,' (1994) 16 *Advocates' Quarterly* 94.

7. Class Actions

An important recent development in the realm of private actions which has significant implications under the Act is the rise in prominence of class actions. In a province where class actions are permitted,[65] a legal proceeding may be commenced by a private party on his or her own behalf and on behalf of all other persons who have suffered similar loss or damage as a result of the defendant's breach of the Act's criminal provisions or failure to comply with an order of the tribunal or a court. For the reasons discussed below, prospective plaintiffs are increasingly considering the benefits of pursuing a private action through a class action forum.

The objectives of the *Class Proceedings Act, 1992*[66] in Ontario are, according to the Ontario Divisional Court, (i) judicial economy; (ii) improved access to the court for those whose actions might not otherwise be asserted; and (iii) modification of behaviour of actual or potential wrongdoers who might otherwise be tempted to ignore public obligations.[67] Plaintiffs alleging that they have sustained damages as a result of anticompetitive behaviour can point to these objectives in support of their application for certification of a class action. In cases such as these, damages on an individual basis tend to be small and claims would not generally otherwise be litigated. Furthermore, the common issues tend to be significant, such that judicial economy could be said to be achieved by certification of the action. In this regard, the types of damages that can arise under a price-fixing scenario are highly conducive to being litigated through a class action proceeding.

Generally, in order to obtain certification of a class proceeding in Ontario the representative plaintiff must establish that:

1. the statement of claim discloses a cause of action;
2. there is an identifiable class of two or more persons;
3. the claims of the class members raise common issues;
4. a class proceeding would be the preferable procedure for the determination of those common issues; and
5. the proposed class representative:
   (a) can fairly and adequately represent the interests of a class in accordance with a workable plan; and

---

65 To date, these provinces are Quebec, Ontario, and British Columbia.
66 S.D. 1992, c. 6.
67 *Abdool v. Anaheim Management Ltd.* (1995), 21 O.R. (3d) 453.

(b) does not have a conflict of interest with other class members on
    the common issues to be raised.

If the foregoing key criteria are not met, certification will not be
granted by the court.

A typical certification order will specify the manner in which class
members may opt out of the class proceeding and a deadline for doing
so. Class members who opt out are at liberty to pursue separate proceedings; however, such individual litigants are neither bound by nor
can they take the benefit of the adjudication of the common issues in the
class action. If class members do not opt out by the deadline they will be
bound by the determination in the action, which provides some finality
to the proceedings for the defendant. A recent important case brought as
a class action in Ontario arising under behaviour related to the Act is
Chadha v. Bayer Inc.[68] The decision is important for two reasons: (1) it is
the first case to consider the so-called indirect purchaser rule established by the U.S. Supreme Court in *Illinois Brick v. Illinois;*[69] and (2) from
an enforcement perspective, the court favoured the Bureau and the Act
over a class action, for achieving the goal of behaviour modification.
The plaintiffs have appealed to the Ontario Court of Appeal.

A host of issues arise where there are numerous class actions commenced with overlapping plaintiffs in multiple jurisdictions. As has
been reported with some vigour by the press, the attorney general has
successfully prosecuted a number of defendants in respect of conspiracies related to various vitamins. Quickly following a series of guilty
pleas and convictions, at least nine class actions have been commenced
in Ontario, Quebec, and British Columbia in respect of the so-called
vitamins conspiracies. The classes of plaintiffs overlap substantially,
and most of the actions purport to be brought on behalf of both direct
and indirect purchasers. There is a great deal of work to be done in trying to sort out the various issues that arise in these cases.

In Ontario, for example, although now more difficult with the decision in *Chadha v. Bayer Inc.,* indirect purchasers may sue for damages,
notwithstanding what is alleged to be an inability to prove that the costs
of the anticompetitive conduct have been passed down to the indirect
purchasers. This raises a multitude of issues regarding damages calcu-

---

68   (2001), 54 O.R. (3d) 520.
69   431 US 720 (1977).

lations and quantification for plaintiffs. If plaintiff A, a direct purchaser of a product manufactured by defendant B, sues B, can B successfully argue that plaintiff A has sustained no damages, insofar as any increase in price (for example) has been passed down the chain to the ultimate purchaser? Would this line of argument, however, not be an invitation to even more plaintiffs? What does that mean for third party claims and crossclaims? The quantification of these damages will be difficult. This situation (unfortunately for some) translates to considerably more work for lawyers, expert economists and others.

It also bears noting that U.S. class action litigation arising from anti-competitive behaviour provides an active and easily accessible frame of reference for Canadian plaintiffs and their counsel, and many of these cases make their way north in one fashion or another. Issues also arise regarding damages sustained and whether those damages have been compensated by reason of a settlement or other payment made in the United States. As is well known, products are often manufactured in the United States and elsewhere and imported into Canada, such that the damages agreed to and paid in the United States arguably compensate Canadians as well.

8. Bill C-23

As noted above, Bill C-23, at the stage of First Reading, did not create a private right of access. However, as one commentator noted, it did at that stage 'lay the groundwork' for a private access regime.[70] Specifically, granting the tribunal powers related to references, summary dispositions, and cost awards would provide it with a greater ability to stop frivolous proceedings in their early stages. As Kieley observed, it would be curious to provide the tribunal with these powers if it were contemplated that the commissioner would be the only person who would ever have the power to bring applications to the tribunal. Rather, the inclusion of these provisions appeared to have been the first step towards the creation of a right of private access to the tribunal. In largely replicating the private access proposal contained in the now expired Bill C-472, following the consideration of Bill C-23 by the Standing Committee on Industry, Science and Technology, Bill C-23 ultimately included private access provisions related to exclusive dealing, tied selling, market restrictions and refusal to deal.

---

70 G. Kieley, Parliamentary Research Branch Report (LS-406E) 10 September 2001 at 6.

In addition, Bill C-23 provides the tribunal with the powers to issue an interim order in connection with the key Part VIII reviewable practices. In this regard, Bill C-23 represents a major improvement to Bill C-472, which had proposed to have the granting of interim orders reside exclusively with the commissioner. That proposal had met with almost universal opposition. Under Bill C-23, the tribunal would be authorized to issue interim orders upon an *ex parte* application being brought by the commissioner. The preconditions for the tribunal issuing an interim order would be as follows:

- the commissioner certifies that an inquiry is being made under section 10; and
- the tribunal finds that in the absence of an interim order:
  - injury to competition that cannot adequately be remedied by the tribunal is likely to occur;
  - a person is likely to be eliminated as a competitor; or
  - a person is likely to suffer significant loss of market share, significant loss of revenue, or other harm that cannot adequately be remedied by the tribunal.

The National Competition Law Section of the Canadian Bar Association (the 'NCLS') is critical of the proposed amendments to the Act related to interim orders from several key perspectives.[71] First, the NCLS finds it unacceptable that Bill C-23 would allow the tribunal to issue an interim order where the commissioner did not necessarily hold a reasonable belief that grounds existed for the tribunal to make an order under Part VIII. Second, the NCLS observes that the tribunal could issue an interim order prohibiting a person from engaging in conduct that could injure competition, in the absence of market power and a substantial lessening of competition. The NCLS concludes that these and related concerns could be addressed by amending section 100 to include anti-competitive acts and other reviewable matters.

F. Multijurisdictional Cooperation

1. Overview
The globalization of business and the increasing reduction of barriers

71 Submission on Bill C-23: Competition Act Amendments, National Competition Law Section – Canadian Bar Association (October 2001) at 28–37.

to market access via the auspices of the World Trade Organization and the North American Free Trade Agreement are creating a host of enforcement issues for the commissioner and the bureau. The commissioner is increasingly being asked to investigate potential offences involving transnational firms and transnational conduct where the connections to Canada may be tenuous and access to information difficult to obtain. In addition, there are difficulties associated with overlapping jurisdictions and the ever-present possibility of multiple investigations into the same set of facts in several jurisdictions at the same time. International business means multiple antitrust authorities may be interested in any one transaction or set of facts.

In the context of a liberalized North American and even global market-place, it is not difficult to imagine any number of scenarios that would create enforcement difficulties for the commissioner. For example, an American company with a dominant market position may refuse to supply a Canadian distributor in favour of supplying the Canadian branch of an American distributor. One could also imagine a conspiracy among Mexican and American farmers to fix the price at which they supply fruits and vegetables to the Canadian market. In the absence of specific inter-jurisdictional arrangements, the commissioner's powers to have records provided or testimony compelled are potentially useless where the records or persons sought are in another jurisdiction. Leaving aside issues of substantive law and whether these actions would even be caught by the Act, the bureau can rely on an increasing number of international cooperative arrangements to assist it in finding, investigating, and prosecuting these types of multijurisdictional competition questions.

2 *Treaty Between the Government of Canada and the Government of the United States of America on Mutual Legal Assistance in Criminal Matters* (MLAT)

The MLAT was signed in 1985 and is directly enforceable in the United States and was implemented into Canadian law by the *Mutual Legal Assistance in Criminal Matters Act.*[72] Given that many offences in the Act are criminal,[73] the treaty can be a valuable tool in securing the assistance of U.S. antitrust authorities in Canadian competition investigations.

---

72 S.C. 1985, c. 30 (4th Suppl.).
73 The MLAT has a much wider application than merely competition law enforcement.

Under Article II of the MLAT, the parties are to provide assistance in all 'matters relating to the investigation, prosecution and suppression of offences.' The assistance to be given ranges from the serving of documents and the execution of search warrants to the collection of records and the taking of evidence. The treaty is quite clear, however, that it does not give rise to any rights to private parties to obtain information pursuant to its provisions. It simply assists in the public enforcement of domestic competition laws.

3. Agreement Between the United States and Canada Regarding the Application of their Competition and Deceptive Marketing Practices Laws (Competition Law Treaty)

A tool specific to competition law enforcement is the Competition Law Treaty, which entered into force in August 1995. This treaty has been followed recently by a similar agreement with the European Union.[74]

The purpose of the Competition Law Treaty is to promote and facilitate co-ordination between the respective competition law enforcement agencies. To that end, the agreement places a number of obligations on each party. Under the notification provisions of Article II, each party must notify the other when its enforcement activities may affect the 'important interests' of the other party. Important interests are undefined but certain examples are given which include enforcement activities carried out in the territory of the other party, enforcement activities directed at conduct in the territory of another party, and enforcement activities that involve seeking information located in the territory of another party. For example, should the commissioner ask a person located in the United States to provide information under the commissioner's investigatory powers, the U.S. Justice Department and the Federal Trade Commission would have to be notified.

Under Article III, the United States and Canada agree to assist each other in enforcement (to the extent such assistance is compatible with their domestic laws relating to such matters as confidentiality). Each party must assist in locating and securing evidence and in securing voluntary compliance with requests for information, and each must

---

74 *Agreement Between the Government of Canada and the European Community Regarding the Application of their Competition Laws* (17 June 1999). This treaty is designed to enhance economic and trade relations between Canada and the European Union by increasing cooperation and coordination in the enforcement of competition laws in their respective jurisdictions.

provide information upon request which is relevant to the other competition authority's investigations. Each party must also inform the other party when conduct that occurs in their territory may also have an adverse effect on competition in the other's territory. For example, a price-fixing conspiracy in Quebec, New Brunswick, and Maine would have to be reported to U.S. antitrust authorities once it was discovered in Canada and vice versa. Such a fact situation would raise the issue of separate but independent investigations into the same set of facts. That situation is also addressed in the Competition Law Treaty.

Under Article IV, the commissioner and the Antitrust Division of the U.S. Department of Justice are to 'consider' coordination of enforcement activities. In doing so they must take account of the following factors:

1. The effect of such coordination on the ability of both parties to achieve their respective enforcement objectives.
2. The relative abilities of the parties' competition authorities to obtain information necessary to conduct the enforcement activities.
3. The extent to which either party's competition authorities can secure effective relief against the anticompetitive activities involved.
4. The possible reduction of cost to the parties and to the person subject to enforcement activities.
5. The potential advantages of coordinated remedies to the parties and to the person subject to the enforcement activities.

Through such coordination efforts, duplication of efforts can be saved, and enforcement resources used more efficiently on both sides of the border.

Another important provision of the treaty relates to 'positive comity' or the idea that one jurisdiction would defer its own enforcement activity and allow the other to deal with the violation. Under Article V, where one party believes that anticompetitive activity being carried out in the other's territory is adversely affecting its important interests, it may request the other jurisdiction to take enforcement action. The requested party is obligated to 'carefully consider' whether to initiate or expand enforcement activities. In the hypothetical case of the Quebec, New Brunswick, and Maine price-fixing conspiracy, and assuming that activity originated in Maine, the commissioner would request the U.S. Department of Justice to take the appropriate action and defer to that investigation. This would save resources and avoid much of the extraterritorial conflict which has been evident in the enforcement of

U.S. and Canadian competition laws. Commissioner Konrad von Finckenstein, in an address to the International Competition Policy Advisory Committee, expressed himself as in favour of extending positive comity further by setting rules for when it would be invoked by another party, and not merely considered.[75]

Another important aspect of the treaty deals with confidentiality. Article X explicitly provides that each party need not provide information if communication of that information is prohibited under the laws of the party possessing the information. Thus, the commissioner would be prohibited under section 29 from disclosing information collected in an investigation subject to the stated exceptions.

4. Bill C-23: Mutual Legal Assistance with Foreign States

Arguably, the most significant amendment proposed for the Act under Bill C-23 is that related to mutual legal assistance with foreign states. There is little controversy over the need for such a provision, as it is widely recognized that '[t]he globalization of markets and the significant increase in international trade and transactions has created an environment where co-operation between the Bureau and its foreign counterparts is necessary for the effective enforcement of the Act.[76] It is also clear that the current legal infrastructure is insufficient for achieving this objective. That is, the MLAT, discussed earlier in this chapter, governs, among other things, cooperation between the bureau and foreign enforcement agencies in the context of criminal competition law offences. However, as many jurisdictions do not criminalize much anticompetitive activity, the scope for the MLAT's application is limited in the realm of competition law. From a Canadian perspective, for example, the MLAT does not encompass the broad scope of reviewable practices set out under Part VIII of the Act.

The proposal under Bill C-23 for mutual legal assistance with foreign states operates as follows. First, the process is triggered with the mak-

---

75 See the Speaking Notes of Konrad von Finckenstein, Q.C., Director of Investigation and Research to the International Competition Policy Advisory Committee (to the U.S. Attorney General and the U.S. Assistant Attorney General for Antitrust) given in Washington, D.C., on 2 November 1998, and available on the Competition Bureau's website.

76 Submission on Bill C-23: Competition Act Amendments, National Competition Law Section – Canadian Bar Association (October 2001) at 5.

ing of a 'request' by a foreign state for the gathering of information pursuant to an 'agreement' (i.e., a treaty, a convention or other international agreement to which Canada is a party). Second, the Bill outlines a three-step process for dealing with requests from foreign states:

- a court order related to one of the forms for information gathering contemplated by Bill C-23 must be issued;[77]
- once the requested information is obtained, the Minister of Justice and the court each determine whether such information should be provided to the foreign state; and
- once the determination is made to share the information with the foreign state, a separate process is contemplated by the Bill for the parameters of such sharing.

Bill C-23 has made substantial improvements to Bill C-471[78] through its implementation of safeguards regarding issues such as (i) when Canada would share information; (ii) the scope for the use of such information by the foreign state; and (iii) notice being provided to interested parties. Moreover, following its consideration by The Standing Committee on Industry, Science and Technology, Bill C-23 was amended to address certain concerns raised by the NCLS.[79]

V. Conclusions

Facilitating compliance with the Act in the most efficient and expeditious manner is the goal of all means of enforcement of the Act. To achieve this end, Canada's public antitrust enforcers, the commissioner and the bureau, have created numerous programs to encourage voluntary compliance with the Act, as well as showing a willingness

---

77 The various orders contemplated by Bill C-23 include a search and seizure order, an order to permit evidence gathering for use in the foreign state, an order to permit the 'virtual presence' (i.e., video-conferencing) of a person; and an order permitting the lending to a foreign state of an exhibit admitted previously as evidence in another proceeding.

78 An act to amend the *Competition Act* and the *Competition Tribunal Act*. This Bill died on the Order Paper with the dissolution of Parliament on 22 October 2000.

79 See, for example, the proposed language in section 30.291 of Bill C-23.

to agree to orders on consent and 'favourable treatment' where the overall enforcement objectives are better served by such means. Contested proceedings are often the last resort in enforcement. Rather, entities are given many opportunities to bring their practices in line with the Act. Where they do not, they will face investigation and potential prosecution by the commissioner or the attorney general of Canada, as well as the possibility, however small, of a private claim for damages.

Subject Index

Abuse of dominant position
anticompetitive acts under,
    enumerated acts: anticompeti-
    tive product standards, 536;
    boycotts, 536–7; *Competition
    Act* provisions. *See Competi-
    tion Act*, 1986; freight equal-
    ization, 534–5; pre-emption of
    scarce facilities, 535; prevent-
    ing price erosion, 535–6; verti-
    cal integration, 533–4; vertical
    margin squeezing, 533
    raising rivals costs: bottleneck,
    530; cartel ringmaster, 531;
    explained, 529; Frankenstein
    Monster technique, 532–3;
    real foreclosure, 530–1
    remedies, 570–1
    unenumerated acts: abuse of
    legal process. *See* abuse of
    legal process; acquisition of
    rivals, 541–3; essential facili-
    ties doctrine. *See* essential
    facilities doctrine; exclusivity,
    538–41; facilitating practices,
    543; other unenumerated acts,
    568–70; predatory pricing, 543

barriers to entry and. *See* Barriers
    to entry
Draft Enforcement Guidelines on
    Abuse of Dominance,
    evidence of joint control, 514–15
    treatment of market share, 510
    treatment of product market,
    516–17
efficiency considerations, 528
geographic market and, 518–19
intent and, 525–26
joint dominance, 122, 501–2, 511–1!
monopoly
    definition under *Combines Inves-
    tigation Act*, 1970, 504
    natural, 40
    welfare loss and, 50–4
network industries and. *See* Net-
    work industries
'practice' explained, 519–20
predatory pricing and, 295
price discrimination and, 344–6,
    352–68
retrospective application, 519
single firm dominance, 508–11
'substantially lessening competi-
    tion' defined, 520–3

tying explanations and, 475–6
Abuse of legal process
  as abuse of dominance
    explained, 552–3
    Australian case law, 563–4
    Canadian case law, 564–8
    U.S. case law, 555–63
Alliances Bulletin, 123–5
American Bar Association, 685
ANZCERTA, 661, 689
Attempted monopolization, 507–8

Barriers to entry
  abuse of dominance and, 509–10
  Competition Act, 1986, and, 183,
    255–6, 259
  contestable markets and. *See* Contestable markets
  economies of scale as, 137, 139, 260
  exclusive contracts and, 472–3
  high capital costs as, 261
  likelihood of entry, 261–2
  Merger Enforcement Guidelines and,
    258, 511
  merger review and, 137, 162, 180,
    255–62
  predatory pricing and, 291, 327–8,
    330–1
  sunk costs and, 260, 262
Bilateral trade agreements, 667–8
Bill C-256, 19
Board of Commerce Act, 13–14
British Statute of Monopolies, 3–4

Canada-United States Free Trade
    Agreement, 263, 643
Cartels
  basis for condemnation, 90–1
  collusion and,
    tacit, 88–90, 140–1

explicit, 87–8
conditions for stability, 67–8, 91–6,
    178
facilitating devices, 96–7, 178–9
merger review and, 177–9
monopsony power and. *See*
    monopsony power
natural price leader, 178
oligopoly. *See* oligopoly
price discrimination and. *See* price
    discrimination
Canadian Charter of Rights and Freedoms, 753
'Chicago school' of industrial organization
  exclusivity contracts and, 471–2
  'Harvard school,' compared. *See*
    'Harvard School' of industrial organization
  influence of, 34–5
  introduced, 33
  predatory pricing and, 301
Clayton Act, 459
Combines and Fair Practices Act, 13–14
Combines Investigation Act, 1910
  monopoly provisions, 452, 504
  origin, 11
  patent revocation provisions, 592,
    594
  repeal of, 12–13
Combines Investigation Act, 1923, 13
  Economic Council of Canada
    changes proposed by. *See* Economic Council of Canada
  effect of 1960s–1970s jurisprudence, 16–17
  intellectual property rights provisions, 595, 598–600
  resale price maintenance provisions, 399–401

Stage I amendments, 1975
  'Canadian Tire' amendment, 601
  intellectual property rights pro-
    visions, 600–1, 603, 615
  origin, 19–20
  retail price maintenance provi-
    sions, 400
Stage II amendments, 21–2
Combines Investigation Act, 1976
  abuse of dominance provisions, 504
Comity principles, 668
Competition Act, 1986
  abuse of dominance provisions,
    evolution of, 452–3, 505
    exception to intellectual prop-
      erty right holders, 581
    overview, 506–7
    provisions, 453–4, 523–4
    relation to other provisions,
      505–6
  barriers to entry and. *See* Barriers
    to entry
  confidentiality provisions,
    exceptions to, 755
    introduced, 753–4
  economic theory, influence of, 31
  ex parte application proceeding
    provisions, 198–9, 752
  exclusive dealing and tied selling
    provisions, 440–55
  exclusive territories and, 373, 414–
    20
  horizontal arrangements and:
    agreements between federal
    financial institutions, 108–10;
    bid-rigging, 104–8; partial
    rule-of-reason standard, 111–
    20; rule-of-reason analysis,
    120–2; *per se* legal arrange-
    ments, 122

intellectual property right provisions, 604–9, 615–17, 619–20
interbrand competition and, 439–
  40, 477
investigation under
  conditions forcing an inquiry,
    751–3
  criminal prosecution under:
    aims of, 755–6; attorney gen-
    eral and, 756, 757; criminal
    provisions, 29–31, 102, 120–1,
    392; immunity, 760–2; prohibi-
    tion orders, 756; whistleblow-
    ing provisions, 759–60
merger provisions
  efficiency exception, 184–5, 215,
    221, 270–8, 683
  evaluation of anticompetitive
    effects, 251–2, 262–9
  exemptions from, 227–8
  foreign competition and, 262–3
  merger defined, 226
  total surplus criteria, 146–7, 271
origin, 18, 21–2
predatory pricing provisions
  abuse of dominant position pro-
    visions. *See* abuse of domi-
    nant position
  airline amendments, 316–17,
    338, 524–5
  criminal provisions, 316
  critical observations, 337–9
  'fighting brands' provision, 316,
    535
  'policy of selling' defined, 325
price discrimination provisions,
  352–3
private enforcement provisions
  burden of proof and, 767–9
  class action and, 773–5

damages and, 769–71
scope of, 765–6
purpose clause, 38–9
reform proposals
Bill C-23, 764, 775
Bill C-471, 781
Bill C-472, 127–9, 775
hybrid proposal, 129–30
Kennish and Ross, 126–7
Warner and Trebilcock, 125–6
refusal to deal provisions, 421,
424–5
retail price maintenance provisions, 401, 620
voluntary compliance with
advisory opinions and: categories, 744; fees, 746
educational activities, 740–2
internal compliance programs,
747–51
Common law of restraint of trade
introduced, 4
intellectual property and, 587
legal monopolies and, 701
Competition Tribunal
introduced, 22–4
appeal from, 222–6
approach to market definition. See
market definition, Hillsdown
approach
compliance-oriented approach,
188–96
composition of, 23
economic evidence, increasing use
of, 37
enabling legislation. See Competition Tribunal Act, 1986
lay members, 285
options for redesign, 281–7
power to issue orders, 197–201,
280, 435

proceedings of
1994 amendments to, 213–14
consent order proceedings, 201–
6, 499–500
contested proceedings, 215–22
intervenors and, 209–15, 283
variation proceedings, 206–9
Competition Tribunal Act, 1986, 22,
210–1, 215, 222–4
Competitive markets
conditions for, 46–7
departure from, 49–50
equilibrium, 47–9
'first theorem' of welfare economics, 40
Consignment selling, 28
Constitution Act, 690
Contestable markets
characteristics of, 138–9
single firm equilibrium and, 180–1
Coordination of domestic competition policies
GATT/WTO, relationship with,
661
overview, 662–3
framework for evaluating future
initiatives
applied, 675–85
described, 670–4
past efforts, 664–70
Corn laws, 4
Creative destruction, 5–6
Criminal Code, 10, 16
Customs Tariff Act, 11

Diversion ratio, 134
Doctrine of paramountcy, 691
Dominion Trade and Industry Act,
1935, 15
Draft International Antitrust Code,
670

Economic Council of Canada
 1969 report, 18–19, 400, 420–1
Economic integration
 negative and positive explained,
  671
Economic profits
 explained, 56
Effects test for extraterritorial jurisdiction, 684
Elzina-Hogarty test. *See* Market
  definition, geographic
  market
Enforcement
 multijurisdictional cooperation
  competition law treaties; with
   European Union, 778; with
   U.S., 778–80
  mutual legal assistance in criminal matters, 777–8
 private enforcement
  debate over, 763–5
  economics of, 737–40
  provisions. *See Competition Act*,
   1986
 public enforcement. *See Competition Act*, 1986, Investigation
  under
Essential facilities doctrine
 Interac case and, 501–3, 547–52
 network industries and. *See* Network industries
 U.S. case law, 544–7
Estimation of residual demands. *See*
  market definition
European Union
 antitrust convergence and, 643,
  670
 Directorate General IV
  Competition Tribunal compared, 280–1
 Treaty of Rome, 625, 643, 668

Exclusive dealing
 case law, 478–85
 common clauses, 456–7
 Competition Act, 1986, and. *See*
   Competition Act, 1986
 exclusive supply, 456
 exemptions, 449–50
 explained, 442, 455–6

GATT/WTO
 Agreement on Trade-Related
  Aspects of Anti-competitive
  measures (TRAMS), 673
 Agreement on Trade-Related
  Aspects of Intellectual Property Rights (TRIPS), 592, 641,
  661
 antidumping provisions
  intermittent dumping, 657–62
  international price discrimination, 648–52
  predatory pricing, 652–7
 Competition Review Mechanism
  (CPRM), 673
 General Agreement on Trade in
  Services (GATS), 666
 domestic antitrust laws, and. *See*
  Coordination of domestic
  competition policies
Grey marketing, 622–4

Hall commission, 599
'Harvard School' of industrial orga-
  nization, 33–4
Havana Charter, 664

Intellectual Property Rights
 competition policy interface,
  economics of, 575–87
 DOJ-FTC Intellectual Property
  Guidelines, 583–4

exclusivity restrictions
  territorial, 622–7
  exclusive dealing, 629–30
  exclusive licensing, 627–8
explained, 574
grey marketing and. *See* Grey mar-
    keting
*Intellectual Property Enforcement
    Guidelines*
  enforcement approach, 632–7
  innovation market definition,
    583–4
  Patent Act compared, 581
licensing
  *Antitrust Guidelines for the
    Licensing of Intellectual Prop-
    erty,* 636
  competition policy and, 580,
    582–3, 584–5
patents
  optimal structure of, 576–80
  scope of, 576
public goods problem and, 574
research & development, 580, 583,
    586
refusal to license, 617–20
statutes
  Copyright Act, 589–90
  Industrial Design Act, 591
  Integrated Circuit Topography Act,
    591
  Patent Act, 588–9, 598
  Patent Act, U.S., 581–2
  Plant Breeders' Rights Act, 591–2
  Trademarks Act, 590, 626–7
trade secrets, case law on, 590–1
TRIPs. *See* GATT/WTO
Interbrand competition
  Competition Act, 1986, and. *See
    Competition Act,* 1986

efficiency explanations, 458–69
entry deterrence strategies, 458
exclusive dealing and. *See* Exclu-
    sive dealing
intrabrand compared, 439
monopsony power and, 473
reverse free-riding argument, 471
    3
tied selling and. *See* Tied selling
International Trade Organization. *Se*
    Havana Charter
Intrabrand competition
  exclusive territories
    Competition Act, 1986, and. *See
      Competition Act,* 1986
    explained, 373
    exemptions, 420
    legal definition, 414
    resale price maintenance com-
      pared, 395–7
  resale price maintenance. *See*
    Resale price maintenance

Keiretsu, 678–82

Laissez-faire era, 4

MacQuarrie Committee, 15–16, 399
Market definition
  'cellophane fallacy' and, 75, 165,
    248, 495, 519
  cross-elasticity of demand and,
    72–3, 164
  geographic, 74–5, 168–72, 243–8
  Hillsdown approach, 231–5
  hypothetical monopolist test, 164
    166, 230–5, 239, 248, 495, 518
  refusal to deal and. *See* Refusal to
    deal
  strategy documents, and, 167

switching costs and, 168
Market power
    abuse of dominance and, 509–10
    cartels and, 92
    input markets and, 84–5
    Landes-Posner expression for, 81,
        92, 135, 171
    Lerner index, 73, 78, 133, 153, 158
    merger reviewand, 249–51, 255
    predatory pricing and, 327–8
    price discrimination and, 339–40
McCarran-Ferguson Act, 677
McGregor Report, 597
Measured concentration
    four-firm concentration index
        (C4), 78, 174, 253 .
    Herfindahl-Hirschman index
        (HHI), 79, 174, 253
    safe harbour benchmarks, 16, 78,
        173–4, 227, 510
Merger
    cartel theories and, 141–2
    conglomerate, 270
    innovation, effect on, 143–4
    market definition and. See Market
        definition
    non-price competition, effect on,
        142–3
    predation, alternative to, 290, 293–
        4, 299–300
    review of
        comparison to similar mergers,
            162–3
        Competition Act, 1986, and. See
            Competition Act, 1986
        compliance-oriented approach
            to, 188–97
        critique of review process, 278–
            87
        failing-firm defence, 176, 264–5

    guidelines. See Merger Enforce-
        ment Guidelines
    impact review, 162–80
    Williamson analysis, 151–5
    transnational, 682–4

Merger Enforcement Guidelines
    bank mergers and, 227–8
    compared to Court of Appeal
        jurisprudence, 239
    econometric evidence and, 163
    foreign competition and, 263–4
    hypothetical monopolist test. See
        Market definition
    justification for total surplus crite-
        ria. See Competition Act, 1986
    market definition, 489–90
    safe harbour concentration. See
        Measured concentration
    seller identification and, 172–3
    tariff constraints in markets, 263
Microsoft, 476, 609–14
Monopolistically competitive mar-
        kets
    Described, 32–3, 60–2
    Excess capacity theorem, 393–4
Monopoly. See Abuse of dominant
        position
Monopsony
    cartels and, 99–100
    described, 69–70
Munich Code. See Draft International
        Antitrust Code

NAFTA
    American Bar Association and. See
        American Bar Association
    competition policy and, 669, 678
Nash equilibrium, 136
Network externalities, 307, 705–6

Network industries
  abuse of dominance in, 720–2
  cost misallocation, 715–16
  cross-subsidization, 708, 715
  essential facilities doctrine and,
    723–7
  remedial approaches
    Australian approach, 732
    U.K. approach, 731–2
    U.S. bifurcated approach, 730–1
    New Zealand Approach, 732–3
  interconnection benefits, 708
  price discrimination in, 722–3
  refusal to deal in, 717–20
  tying and, 716–17
Noerr-Pennington doctrine. *See*
    Abuse of legal process, U.S.
    case law

OECD Agreement on Restrictive
    Practices Affecting Trade,
    665–6

Predatory pricing
  abuse of dominance and, 315
  anticompetitive excess pricing,
    305–6
  asymmetric information and,
    between firm and lenders, 294–5
    and limit pricing theory. *See*
    limit pricing theory
  case law on, 317–26
  Competition Act, 1986, and. *See*
    Competition Act, 1986
  definitions of
    Joskow and Klevorick, 288
    Posner, 306
  economic theories of
    capital markets imperfections
      and long-purse version, 294–5

  limit pricing and signalling ver-
    sion, 298–300
  reputational theory, 295–8
  exit barriers and, 291
  freight equalization, 534
  intent and, 320–1, 323, 333
  learning by doing and, 332, 397,
    654, 655
  per se legality approach to, 301–2
  Predatory Pricing Enforcement
    Guidelines,
    case law compared, 332–4
    evaluated on policy grounds,
      334–7
    reasonableness approach, 327–9
  tests for
    other tests, 310–15
    price-cost comparisons, 303–7,
      330
    problems with price-cost com-
      parisons, 336–7
    recoupment, 300–1, 313
    two-stage tests, 307–10
Price discrimination
  arbitrage
    services and, 371–2
    techniques to minimize, 341–2
    types of, 341
  buyer discrimination, 348–51
  cartels and, 339–40, 349–50
  Competition Act, 1986, and. *See*
    Competition Act, 1986
  competition and
    lines of injury, 347–51
    small business, protection of,
      347
  cost-justification defence, 351
  customer sorting, 340–1
  defined, 339
  enabling conditions, 339–40

market power and, 340, 346, 369–70

network industries and. *See* Network industries

Price Discrimination Guidelines
  competitors of purchaser, 363–4
  conditional discounts, treatment of, 359–61
  cooperative exception, 367–8
  discriminatory sale, 357–61
  'like,' defined, 365–6
  parties to an offence, 355
  'purchaser' defined, 361–3
  rationale for offence, 354-5
  relevant time, 364–5
  scope of, 355–6
types of, 342–4
welfare aspects
  ambiguity of, 371
  imperfect price discrimination, 345–6, 348
  perfect price discrimination, 344–5

Refusal to deal
  case law on, 425-38
  Competition Act, 1986, and. *See Competition Act, 1986*
  economic theories of,
    customer myopia, 423
    efficiency explanations, 424
    opportunism, 422–3
    price discrimination, 423–4
  market definition and, 426–32
  network industries and. *See* Network industries
  origins, law of, 420
  other restraints, relation to, 373
Regional trading blocs, 668–70

Regulated industries defence, 16, 690–704
Regulatory policy
  competition policy compared, 712–14
  performance-based regulation, 710
  rate-of-return regulation, 710
Resale price maintenance
  anticompetitive explanations
    manufacturers' cartel hypothesis, 377–8
    retailer cartel hypothesis, 378–80
  attempts to influence price upwards, 402–4
  defences
    bait and switch, 405
    inadequate services defence, 406–8
    loss-leading, 405–6, 410–11
    misleading advertising, 405
  efficiency explanations
    free-riding, 386–7
    inventory arguments, 391
    monitoring costs, 384, 389–91
    price floors and single manufacturer, 380–6
  historical basis for condemnation, 375
  Macquarrie Committee recommendations on. *See* Macquarrie Committee
  price ceilings, 391–5
Report Concerning the Manufacture, Distribution and Sale of Drugs in Canada, 598–9
Restricted Trade Practices Committee, 16, 23
Robinson-Patman Act, 326
Royal Commission on Price Spreads, 14–15, 594–5

Sham litigation, 556–9
Sherman Act
  essential facilities doctrine and. *See*
    essential facilities doctrine
  introduced, 6–7
  predatory pricing and, 326
  section I, 395
  section II, 507
  Treaty of Rome compared, 677
Skeoch-McDonald report, 20–1
Special Import Measures Act, 647, 660
Strategic dumping, 663
Structuralist school of industrial
    organization. *See* 'Harvard
    school'
Supremacy clause, U.S. Constitution,
    703

Tied selling
  defined, 450–1
  efficiency explanations, 463–8
  horizontal explanations of related
    instruments, 475–7

leverage theory of tying, 474–5
tying restrictions
  efficiency explanations, 614–15
  Microsoft and. *See* Microsoft
  network industries and. *See* Net-
    work industries
  types of: bundling, 609–10;
    grantbacks in licensing con-
    tracts, 610–11; requirements
    tying, 609–10
Trade Practices Act (Australia), 568

United Nations
  Commission on Transnational
    Corporations, 665
  Economic and Social Council of
    the United Nations, 664
  UNCTAD
    Code on Restrictive Business
      Practices, 665

Wallace Act, 9–10, 87

Table of Cases

2903113 Canada Inc. v. Quebec (Regie des marches agricole et alimentaires), [1997] A.Q. no 2125 700

947101 Ontario Ltd. v. Barrhaven Town Centre Inc. (1995), 121 D.I..R. (4th) 748 (Ont. Gen. Div.) 770

Abdool v. Anaheim Management Ltd. (1995), 21 O.R. (3d) 453 773

ACA Joe International v. 147255 Canada Inc. (1986), 10 C.P.R. (3d) 301 (F.C.T.D.) 102, 770

ACF Chmiefarma v. Commission (Quinidine) Case 41/69, [1969] ECR 661 95

Acier D'Armature Ro Inc. v. Stelco Inc. (1996), 69 C.P.R. (3d) 204 (Que. C.A.) 358

ACR Trading Pty Ltd. v. Fat-sel Pty. Ltd. (1987), 11 NSWLR 67 564

Aerospatiale-Alenia/de Havilland, Commission Decision 91/619 of 5 December 1991, 1 CEC (1992) 682

Aetna Insurance Co. v. R. (1977), [1978] 1 S.C.R. 731 .... 17, 114

Air Canada v. American Airlines, Inc., [1989] 1 S.C.R. 236 211

AKZO Chemie BV v. EC Commisssion, [1991] 5 C.M.L.R. 215 569

American Airlines, Inc. v. Competition Trib., [1989] 2 F.C. 88; *Canada (Director of Investigation and Research) v. Air Canada* (1988), 33 Admin. L. R. 229 210–11

American Cyanamid Co. v. Ethicon Ltd., [1975] 1 All E.R. 504 771

Amoco Can. Petroleum Co. Ltd. v. Texaco Exploration Can. Ltd., [1976] 1 F.C. 58 602

Andrews v. Law Society of British Columbia (1989), 56 D.I..R. (4th) 1 (S.C.C.) 702

Applewood Stoves v. Vermont Castings, Inc. CCH Trade Regulation Reports, 58, 344 12 386

Arizona v. Maricopa County Medical Society, 457 U.S. 332 (1982) 394

Asea Brown Boveri Inc. (6 September 1989) CT-89/1, #101(a)............................ 259
Aspen Skiing Co. v. Aspen Highlands Skiing Corp., 472 U.S. 585 (1985) 546
Atari Games v. Nintendo of America Inc., 897 F. 2d 1572 (1990) 575
Atlantic Refining Co. v. FTC, 381 U.S. 357 (1965) 468
Atlantic Sugar Refineries Co. Ltd. v. A.G. Canada, [1980] 2 S.C.R. 644
.... 17, 112–13, 642
*Attorney-General of Canada et al. v. Law Society of British Columbia et al.; Jabour v.
Law Society of British Columbia*, [1982] 2 S.C.R. 307 .... 16, 696–7
Bank of Montreal v. Hall, [1990] S.C.R. 216 690
Barsch v. Avtex Airservices Ltd. (1992), 107 A.L.R. 539, aff'd Fed. No. 5&9,
    unreported, 27 August 1993 (Fed. Ct.) 588
Bekey Photo v. Eastman Kodak Co., 603 F. 2d 263 (2d Cir., 1979) 655
Bement v. National Harrow Co., 186 U.S. 70 (1982)...................................... 618
Black v. Law Society of Alberta (1989), 58 D.L.R. (4th) 317 (S.C.C.) 702
Breck's Sporting Goods v. Magder (1975), 17 C.P.R. (2d) 201 (S.C.C.) 627
British Columbia Telephone Co. v. Shaw Cable Systems, (B.C.) Ltd. (1995), 125
    D.L.R. (4th) 443 (S.C.C.).. 691
Broadcast Music, Inc. v. Columbia Broadcasting System, Inc., 441 U.S. 1 (1979)
.... 631
Brooke Group Ltd. v. Brown and Williamson Tobacco Corp., 509 U.S. 209 (1993)
.... 325–7, 332
Brotherhood of Maintenance of Way Employees v. Canadian Pacific Ltd. (1996), 136
    D.L.R. (4th) 289 (S.C.C.).. 771
Brunswick Corp. v. Pueblo Bowl-O-Mat, Inc., 429 U.S. 477 (1977).................. 40, 82
Business Electronics Corp. v. Sharp Electronics Corp., 485 U.S. 717 (1988)......... 387
California Motor Transport Company v. Trucking Unlimited, 404 U.S. 508 (1972)
.... 556–7, 563
Canada (Commissioner of Competition) v. British American Tobacco No.3 Trib.,
    [1999] C.C.T.D. No. 12 Trib. Dec. No CT9901/017 (consent order)............ 205
Canada (Commissioner of Competition) v. Superior Propane Inc. (2000), 7 C.P.R.
    (4th) 385 (Comp. Trib.)..................... 27, 38, 40, 73, 147, 148, 198–9, 215, 220–1,
    229, 248, 257, 267, 268, 271, 273, 278, 279, 315
*Canada (Competition Act, Director of Investigation and Research) v. Canadian Waste
    Services Inc.* (Reasons for Consent Order), [1997] C.C.T.D. No.22 Trib. Dec.
    NO. CT9701/12.. 205
Canada (Director of Investigation and Research) v. ADM Agri-Industries, Ltd.,
    [1997] C.C.T.D. No. 25 Trib. Dec. No. CT9702/13 (Q.L.) 195
Canada (Director of Investigation & Research) v. Air Canada (Requests for Leave
    to Intervene) (1988), 23 C.P.R. (3d) 160 (Comp. Trib.) 209, 211
Canada (Director of Investigation and Research) v. Air Canada (March 3, 1988)
    CT-88/1, #1.. 269

Canada (Director of Investigation and Research) v. Air Canada (12 January 1989),
CT-88/1 (Comp. Trib.) 212
Canada (Director of Investigation and Research) v. Air Canada (Reasons for Consent
Order) (1989), 27 C.P.R. (3d) 476 (Comp. Trib.) 212
Canada (Director of Investigation and Research) v. Air Canada (1989), 27 C.P.R. (3d)
476 .... 201, 203, 204, 210, 212, 217, 219, 229, 255, 500, 548
Canada (Director of Investigation and Research) v. Air Canada (1993), 49 C.P.R. (3d)
7 (Comp. Trib.) 206–7, 266
Canada (Director of Investigation and Research) v. Air Canada (1993), 49 C.P.R. (3d)
417 (F.C.A.) 208, 727
Canada (Director of Investigation and Research) v. Air Canada (1993), 51 C.P.R. (3d)
143 209
Canada (Director of Investigation and Research) v. Asea Brown Boveri Inc. (1989),
(Reasons for Consent Order) (CT-89/1, #1019a) (15 September 1989), [1989]
(Q.L.) C.C.T.D. No. 35 Trib. Dec. No. CT8901/101 202
Canada (Director of Investigation and Research) v. Asea Brown Boveri Inc. (1989), 27
C.P.R. (3d) 65 (Comp. Trib.) 202–3
Canada (Director of Investigation and Research) v. Asea Brown Boveri Inc. (1989),
(Reasons for Consent Order) CT-89/(6 September 1989) varied on reconsid-
eration CT-89/1 (1 March 1990) (Comp. Trib.) 263
Canada (Director of Investigation and Research) v. Bank of Montreal et al. (1996), 68
C.P.R. (3d) 527 .... 493, 499, 500, 501, 512, 548, 551–2, 570, 700, 721, 727
Canada (Director of Investigation and Research) v. Bombardier Ltd. (1980), 53 C.P.R.
(2d) 4728 .... 28, 417, 446, 448, 477–9
Canada (Director of Investigation and Research) v. Chrysler Canada (1989), 27 C.P.R.
(3d) 1 (Comp. Trib.), aff'd (1991), 38 C.P.R. (3d) 25 (F.C.A.)
.... 421, 425–7, 432–8, 618, 718
Canada (Director of Investigation and Research) v. Chrysler Canada (1992), 44 C.P.R.
(3d) 430 (Comp. Trib.) 28
Canada (Director of Investigation and Research) v. D & B Companies of Canada Ltd.
(1996), 64 C.P.R. (3d) 216 (Comp. Trib.)
.... 25, 76, 454, 475, 484–5, 509–10, 516, 517, 526, 535, 537, 540–1, 571, 730
Canada (Director of Investigation and Research) v. Hillsdown Holdings (Canada) Ltd.
(1992), 41 C.P.R. (3d) 289 (Comp. Trib.) 26, 146, 149, 215, 216, 220, 230,
231, 233, 234, 244–6, 249–50, 253–9, 261–2, 266, 269, 273, 274–5, 276–7, 287, 447
Canada (Director of Investigation and Research) v. Imperial Oil Ltd. (1989), 45 B.L.R.
1 (Comp. Trib.) 257
Canada (Director of Investigation and Research) v. Imperial Oil Ltd., 26 January
1990, Doc. no. CT-89/3 (Comp. Trib.) (unreported)
.... 194, 204–6, 209–10, 213–15, 219, 229, 233, 246–7, 251, 261–2, 273, 284
Canada (Director of Investigation and Research) v. Laidlaw Waste Systems (1992), 40

C.P.R. (3d) 289 (Comp. Trib.)............................ 25, 493–9, 509, 517, 518–19, 525, 539, 542, 565–6, 571, 722

Canada (Director of Investigation and Research) v. NutraSweet Co. (1990), 32 C.P.R. (3d) 1 (Comp. Trib.).......... 24, 29, 83, 97, 324, 333, 415, 417, 440, 443, 444, 445, 446–7, 448, 450, 454, 478, 479–84, 487, 506, 508, 511, 515, 518, 520, 521, 523, 525, 526, 538, 539, 565, 568, 605, 616, 617, 630, 721

Canada (Director of Investigation and Research) v. Palm Dairies Ltd. (1986), 12 C.P.R. (3d) 540 .... 200–1, 202–3, 210, 728

Canada (Director of Investigation and Research) v. Southam Inc. (Order of August 9, 1991 Denying Request for Leave to Intervene) (1991), 37 C.P.R. (3d) 478 (Comp. Trib.) 217

Canada (Director of Investigation and Research) v. Southam Inc. (1992), 43 C.P.R. (3d) 61 (Comp. Trib.).............. 26–7, 215, 216, 235, 236–8, 250, 258, 260–1, 282

Canada (Director of Investigation and Research) v. Southam Inc. (1992), 47 C.P.R. (3d) 224 (Comp. Trib.).. 217, 226–7

Canada (Director of Investigation and Research) v. Southam Inc. (1992), 47 C.P.R. (3d) 240 (Comp. Trib.).. 217–8, 238

Canada (Director of Investigation and Research) v. Southam Inc. (1995), 63 C.P.R. (3d) 1 (F.C.A.)... 218, 222, 223–4, 230, 239

Canada (Director of Investigation and Research) v. Southam Inc. (1995), 127 D.L.R. (4th) 263 .... 27, 119

Canada (Director of Investigation and Research) v. Southam Inc., [1997] 1 S.C.R. 748 .... 27, 218, 224–5, 240–1

Canada (Director of Investigation and Research) v. Southam Inc., [1998] C.C.T.D. No.1 (QL) (Comp. Trib.) 220

Canada (Director of Investigation and Research) v. Tele-Direct (Publications) Inc. (1997), 73 C.P.R. (3d) 1 (Comp. Trib.). 25, 447, 451, 452, 487–93, 510, 516–17, 521, 522, 526, 527, 535, 537, 569–70, 618, 635, 721

Canada (Director of Investigation and Research) v. Warner Music Canada Ltd., [1997] C.C.T.C. No. 53 Trib. Dec. No. CT9703/22 (Q.L.) 607, 618, 619–20, 635

Canada (Director of Investigation and Research) v. Washington (Reasons for Consent Order Dated January 29, 1997), [1997] C.C.T.D. No. 4 Trib. Dec. No. CT9601/224 205

Canada (Director of Investigation and Research) v. Xerox Canada Inc. (1990), 33 C.P.R. (3d) 83 (Comp. Trib.).................. 28, 421, 426, 428–9, 430, 431, 434, 435, 436, 438, 718, 720

Chadha v. Bayer Inc. (2001), 54 O.R. (3d) 520...................................... 774

Cherry v. The King ex rel. Wood, [1938] 1 D.L.R. 156 693–5

Citizens Ins. Co. v. Parsons (1881), 7 App. Cas. 96 691

City of Abenheim v. California Edison Co., 955 F. 2d 1373 (9th Cir., 1992) 726

City of Anaheim v. Southern California Edison Co., 955 F. 2d 1373 (9th Cir., 1992) 730

City of Chanute v. Kansas Gas & Elec. Co., 564 F. Supp. 1416 (D. Kan., 1983) rev'd in part, aff'd in part, 754 F. 2d 310 (10th Cir., 1985) 725

City of Cleveland v. Cleveland Elec. Illuminating Co., 734 F. 2d 1157 (6th Cir.) cert. denied, 469 U.S. 884 (1984) 725

City of Groton v. Connecticut Light & Power Co., 662 F. 2d 921 (U.S.C.A., 1981) 725

City of Newark v. Delmarva Power & Light Co., 467 F. Supp. 763 (D.Del., 1979) 725

City of Vernon v. California Edison Co., 955 F. 2d 1361 (9th Cir., 1992) 726

City National Leasing Ltd. v. General Motors of Canada Ltd., [1989] 1 S.C.R. 641 765

Columbia (City) v. Omni Outdoor Advertising Inc., 111 S. Ct. 1344 (1991) 557–8, 563

Commissioner of Competition v. Canadian Waste Services Holdings Inc., [2001] C.C.T.D. No.3 Trib. Dec. No. 2000002/59a 205, 215, 247

Commissioner of Competition v. Ultramar Ltd., CT-2000-2001 229

Commodore Business Machines Ltd. v. Canada (Director of Investigation and Research) (1988), 27 O.A.C. 310, 63 O.R. (2d) 737, 50 D.L.R. (4th) 559, 41 C.C.C. 232, 21 C.P.R. (3d) 396, 36 C.R.R. 147 353

Commodore Business Machines v. 116772 Canada Inc. (1983), C.S. (Que.) 1186 627

Container Materials Ltd. v. The King, [1942] S.C.R. 147 .... 114, 642

Continental Insurance v. Dalton Cartage Co., [1982] 1 S.C.R. 164 .... 164, 767

Culzean Inventions Ltd. v. Midwestern Broom Company Ltd. et al., [1984] 3 W.W.R. 11 615–16

Dickson v. Pharmaceutical Society of Great Britain., [1967] 1 Ch. 708 (C.A.); [1970] A.C. 403 (H.L.) 701

DIR, RTPC v. BBM Bureau of Management (1981), 60 C.P.R. (2d) 26 (R.T.P.C.), aff'd (1985), 82 C.P.R. (2d) 60 .... 463, 486

Director of Investigation and Research v. AGT Directory Limited (18 November 1994), CT9402/19, Consent Order, [1994] C.C.T.D. No. 24 (QL) 499, 512

Dowling v. Dalgety Australia Pty. Ltd. (1992), 34 F.C.R. 109 568

Eastern Railroad Presidents Conference v. Noerr Motor Freight Inc., 365 U.S. 127 (1961) 556

Eastman Kodak Co. v. Image Technical Services, 504 U.S. 451 (1992) 464

Eli Lilly and Co. v. Novopharm Ltd. (1996), 68 C.P.R. (3d) 254 (F.C.T.D.) 608

Eli Lilly v. Marzone Chemicals Ltd. (1976), 29 C.P.R. (2d) 253 (F.C.T.D.) 603

Eli Lilly v. Marzone Chemicals Ltd. (1976), 29 C.P.R. (2d) 255 (F.C.A.) 603

Exxon Corp. v. Governor of Maryland, 437 U.S. 117 (1978) 703

Fat-sel Pty Ltd. v. ACR Trading Pty. Ltd., 14 May 1985, Land and Environment
  Court (unreported) 564

FTC v. Corning Glass Works, 509 F. 2d 293 (7th Cir., 1975) 398

FTC v. Texaco Inc., 393 U.S. 223 (1968) 468

General Motors of Canada v. City National Leasing et al. (1989), 58 D.L.R. (4th) 255
  20

GripPak Inc. v. Illinois Tool Works, 694 F.2d 466 (7th Cir., 1982) 560–1, 566

H.J. Heinz of Canada Ltd. v. Edan Food Sales (1991), 35 C.P.R. (3d) 213 (F.C.T.D.)
  .... 626, 627

Hahn v. Codding, 615 F. 2d 830 (9th Cir., 1980) 563

Hartford Fire Insurance Co. v. California (1993), 1621 A.T.R.R. 30 676–7

Howard Smith Paper Mills v. The Queen, [1957] S.C.R. 40 .... 114, 642

Hugin Kassaregister AB v. Commission of the European Communities, [1979]
  C.M.L.R. 7439 (E.C.J.) 429

Hurtig Publishers Ltd. v. W.H. Smith Ltd. (1989), 99 A.R. 70 (Alta. Q.B.)
  .... 365, 367, 520

Illinois Brick v. Illinois, 431 U.S. 720 (1977) 774

Illinois Corporate Travel v. American Airlines Inc. (CCH Trade Regulation Reports,
  61,921) 390, 396

Image Technical Services v. Eastman Kodak Co., 903 F.2d 612 (1990, 9th Cir.), aff'd
  112 S. Ct. 2072 (1992) 429

In the Matter of Ciba-Geigy Limited et al., FTC Docket No. C-3725 (24 March 1997)
  584

Industrial Milk Producers et al. v. Milk Board et al. (1988), 47 D.L.R. (4th) 710
  698–699

Institut Merieux/Connaught, (1990) No. 891-0098 Fed. Reg. 1614 682

International Cone Co. Ltd. v. Consolidated Wafer Co. (1926), 2 D.L.R. 1015 (Exch.
  Ct.) 617

International Salt Co. v. U.S., 332 U.S. 392 (1947) 463, 465

Interstate Circuit, Inc. v. United States, 306 U.S. 208 (1939) 531

Jack Walters & Sons Corp. v. Morton Buildings, Inc., 1984-2 Trade Cas. (CCH)
  66,080 (7th Cir., 1984) 490

Jefferson Parish Hospital District No. 2 v. Hyde, 466 U.S. 2 (1984)
  .... 451, 452, 463, 491, 613

Kartell v. Blue Shield of Massachusetts Inc., 749 F. 3d 922 (1984) 395

LAC Minerals Ltd. v. International Corona Resources Ltd., [1989] 2 S.C.R. 574
  591

Lorain Journal Co. v. U.S., 342 U.S. 143 (1951) 463, 546

Massie & Renwick Ltd. v. Underwriters' Survey Bureau Ltd., [1937] S.C.R. 265
  596

Massie & Renwick Ltd. v. Underwriters' Survey Bureau Ltd., [1939] S.C.R. 218
.... 596
Mattel Canada Inc. v. GTS Acquisitions and Nintendo of America Inc. (1989), 27
C.P.R. (3d) 358 (F.C.T.D.).. 626, 627
MCI Communications v. American Telegram & Telegraph Co., 708 F. 2d 1081 (7th
Cir.), cert. denied, 464 U.S. 891 (1983)................................... 546, 552, 723–4
Mead Johnson Canada v. Ross Pediatrics (1997), 31 O.R. (3d) 237 (Gen. Div.)
.... 102, 770–1
Microsoft Corp. v. Bingamen, DC SNY, Misc. No MB-85f. 7/3/95.7/13/95
.... 610
Morton Salt Co. v. G.S. Suppiger Co., 314 U.S. 488 (1942)....................... 597, 638
Motion Picture Patents Co. v. Universal Film Manufacturing Co., 2453 U.S. 502
(1917) 473
Mozart Co. v. Mercedes-Benz of North America Inc., 833 F.2d 1324 (9th Cir., 1987)
.... 465
Multiple Access Ltd. v. McCutcheon, [1982] S.C.R. 211.............................. 690
Nagle v. Feilden, [1966] 2 Q.B. 633 (C.A.)... 701
Nova Scotia (Attorney General) v. Ultramar Canada Inc. (1995), 127 D.L.R. (4th)
517.. 194-195
Oahu Gas Serv., Inc. v. Pacific Resources, Inc., 838 F. 2d 360 (9th Cir.), cert. denied
488 U.S. 870 (1988) 729
Otter Tail Electric Power Co. v. United States, 410 U.S. 366 (1973)
.... 545, 547, 557, 724
Pezim v. British Columbia Superintendent of Brokers, [1994] 2 S.C.R. 557
.... 223
Philco Products Ltd. et. al. v. Thermionomics Ltd.et. al., [1940] S.C.R. 501
.... 596–7, 602, 603, 608, 631
Pick Mfg. Co. v. General Motors Corp., 80 F.2d 641 (7th Cir., 1935) 465
Premier Electric Company v. National Electrical Contractors Association Inc., 814
F.2d 358 (8th Cir., 1987) 566
Procter & Gamble v. Kimberley-Clark of Canada Ltd. (1990), 29 C.P.R. (3d) 54
(F.C.A.) 607–9
Procter & Gamble/VO Schickedanz (II), [1995] 1 CEC 2, 466 (Decision 94/893)
.... 280
Professional Real Estate Investors Inc. v. Columbia Pictures Industries Inc., 113 S. Ct.
1920 (1993) 558–63
Quebec Ready to Mix Inc. v. Rocois Construction (1989), 60 D.L.R. (4th) 124
.... 20
R. v. Abitibi Power and Paper Co. Ltd. et al. (1960), 131 C.C.C. 201........ 92, 99, 115
R. v. Allied Chemicals (1975), 69 D.L.R. (3d) 506 (B.C.S.C.) 730
R. v. Aluminum Co. of Can. (1977), 29 C.P.R. (2d) 183 113

R. v. Anthes Business Forms Ltd. (1976), 26 C.C.C. (2) 349 (Ont. C.A.)
.... 118–19, 642
R. v. Armco Canada Ltd. (1974), 6 O.R. (2d) 521 .... 513–14, 642
R. v. Armco Can. Ltd. (1977), 13 O.R. (2d) 32 (Ont. C.A.) 109, 113
R. v. Atlantic Sugar Refineries Ltd. (1976), 26 C.P.R. (2d) 14 .... 98, 513
R. v. British Columbia Sugar Refining Co. (1960), 129 C.C.C. 7 (Man. Q.B.)
.... 16, 20, 642
R. v. Canada Safeway Ltd. (1973), 14 C.C.C. (2d) 14 (Alta. T.D.) 317
R. v. Canadian Breweries Ltd. (1960), 126 C.C.C. 133 (Ont. H.C.)
.... 16, 20, 642, 695–6
R. v. Canadian Gen. Elec. Co. (1976), 15 O.R. (2d) 360 (H.C.)...... 112, 505, 511, 642
R. v. Canadian General Electric and Union Carbide Canada Limited, Provincial
Court, Judicial District of York, Charles J., 9 March 1979 (unreported)
.... 599–600
R. v. Chung Chuck, [1929] 1 D.L.R. 756 (B.C.C.A.) 691–2
R. v. Clarke Transport Canada Inc. et al., 64 C.P.R. (3d) 289 117–19
R. v. Cluett, Peabody (1982), 64 C.P.R. (2d) 30 (Ont. Co. Ct.) 402
R. v. Consumers Glass Co. Ltd. (1981), 33 O.R. (2d) 288 (H.C.J.) 322–3
R. v. Daiichi Pharmaceutical Co. Ltd., (unreported), 22 September 1999, Toronto
T-1668-99, (F.C.T.D.) 757
R. v. Dave Spear Ltd. (1986), 11 C.P.R. (3d) 63 112
R. v. Deschenes Construction Co. (1967), 51 C.P.R. 255 (Que Q.B., Crown Side)
.... 88
R. v. E. Esai Co. Ltd. (unreported), 22 September 1999, Toronto T-1667-99,
(F.C.T.D.) 757
R. v. Eddy Match Co. Ltd. (1951), 17 C.P.R. 17 (Que. K.B.), aff'd (1953) 20 C.P.R.
107 (Que. C.A.)........................ 317–18, 453, 504, 508–9, 515, 535, 642
R. v. Epson (Canada) Ltd. (1987), 19 C.P.R. (3d) 195 (Ont. Dist. Ct.) 388
R. v. Gage, [1908] 18 Man. R. 175.. 112
R. v. Griffith Saddlery & Leather Ltd. (1986), 14 C.P.R. (3d) 389 (Ont. Prov. Ct.
(Crim. Div.)).. 404
R. v. H.D. Lee of Canada (1980), 57 C.P.R. 186 (Que. Ct. Sessions of the Peace
(Montreal District).. 407–9
R. v. Hoffman-La Roche Ltd. (1981), 30 O.R. (2d) 461 (H.C.J.), aff'd (1981), 33 O.R.
(2d) 694 (C.A.).. 318–20
R. v. Hoffman La Roche (unreported), 22 September 1999, Toronto T-1665-99,
F.C.T.D. 756
R. v. Independent Order of Foresters (1989), 26 C.P.R. (3d) 229 (Ont. C.A.)... 697–8
R. v. J.W. Mills & Son Ltd., [1968] Ex. C.R. 275 115
R. v. K.C. Irving, [1978] S.C.R. 408........................ 17, 20, 453, 505, 521

R. v. Kilo Canada Ltd. (1975), 22 C.P.R. (2d) 275 (Man. Q.B.) 404

R. v. Kralinator Filters Ltd. (1962), 41 C.P.R. 201 409

R. v. Levi Strauss of Canada (1979), 45 C.P.R. 215 408

R. v. Miss Mary Maxim Ltd. Ex. Ct., 16 May 1968 (unreported) 354

R. v. Moffat (1980), 30 O.R. (2d) 129 (C.A.) 401

R. v. Moffats, [1957] O.R. 93 (C.A.) 404, 409

R. v. Neptune Meters Ltd. Ont. Dist Ct., 2 June 1986, Borins D.C.J. (unreported),
reasons for committal are found in R. v. Neptune Meters Ltd., Ont. Prov. Ct.
(Criminal Division), 23 June 1983, Hashborn P.C.J. (unreported) 354

R. v. Nova Scotia Pharmaceutical Society, [1992] 2 S.C.R. 606
....111, 114–16, 120, 392–3

R. v. Nova Scotia Pharmaceutical Society (1993), 49 C.P.R. (3d) 289
.... 29, 100, 413

R. v. Phillips Appliances Ltd., [1969] 1 O.R. 386 (C.A.) 405–6

R. v. Phillips Electronics (1980), 30 C.P.R. (2d) 129 403–4

R. v. Producers Dairy Ltd. (1966), 50 C.P.R. (2d) (Ont. C.A.) 325, 328–9

R. v. Rhone-Poulenc S.A. (unreported), 22 September 1999, Toronto T-1666-99,
(F.C.T.D.) 756

R. v. Royal Lepage Real Estate Services Ltd., 24 October 1994 (unpublished),
cited in Davies, Ward, and Beck, Competition Law of Canada, para.
4.06(4) 405

R. v. Shell Canada Products Ltd. (1989), 24 C.P.R. (3d) 501 (Man. Q.B.)
.... 404, 412

R. v. Simmons Ltd., Ont. Prov. Ct. (Criminal Division), 15 October 1984,
Richards P.C.J. (unreported) 354, 360–1

R. v. Simoneau, [1936] 1 D.L.R. 143 692–3

R. v. St. Lawrence Corporation (1966), 51 C.P.R. 170 98

R. v. Station Mont-Tremblant Lodge, F.C.T.D., 6 April 1989 (unreported) 354

R. v. Stewart, [1988] 1 S.C.R. 963 590

R. v. Sunoco (1986), 11 C.P.R. (3d) 557 (Ont. Dist. Ct.) 411–12

R. v. Thompson Newspaper (28 October 1983) (unreported) 20

R. v. William Coutts Co. Ltd., [1968] 1 O.R. 549 (C.A.) 406, 410, 442, 519

R. v. York-Hanover Hotels Ltd. (1986), 9 C.P.R. (3d) 440 (Ont. Prov. Ct.) 106

RBM Equipment Ltd. v. Phillips Electronics Industries (1973), 9 C.P.R. (2d) 46
(F.C.T.D.) 601–2

Re: Board of Commerce Act and Combines and Fair Practices Act of 1919 (1920), 60
S.C.R. 456 13

Re: The Concentration between Aerospatiale and Alenia and de Havilland, [1992] 4
C.M.L.R. 2 280

Re: The Concentration between Nestle SA and Source Perrier SA (Case IV/M190),

[1993] 4 C.M.L.R. M17... 280

Re Law Society of Upper Canada and Attorney General of Canada et al. (1996), 134
D.L.R. (4th) 300 699

Reference re Dominion Trade and Industry Commission Act, 1935, [1936] S.C.R. 379
.... 15

Remington Rand Ltd. v. Transworld Metal Co. Ltd. (1960), 32 C.P.R. 99
.... 626, 627

RJR-MacDonald Inc. v. Canada (Attorney General), [1994] 1 S.C.R. 311 771

Robert's Waikiki U-Drive, Inc. v. Budget-Rent-A-Car Systems Inc., 491 F. Supp.
1199 (D. Hawaii, 1980), aff'd 732 F. 2d 1403 (9th Cir., 1984)...................... 390

Roche Holdings Ltd., 113 FTC 1086 (1990) 584

Rocket v. Royal College of Dental Surgeons of Ontario (1990), 71 D.L.R. (4th) 68
(S.C.C.) 702

Ross v. Registrar of Motor Vehicles, [1975] S.C.R. 207.. 690

Samson v. Canada, [1994] 3 F.C. 113.. 752

Seiko Time Canada Ltd. v. Consumers Distributing Co. Ltd. (1984), 1 C.P.R. (3d) 1
(S.C.C.) 627

Sharp Electronics of Canada Ltd. v. Continental Electronic Info (1989), 23 C.P.R. (3d)
330 (B.C.S.C.)... 627

Southern Pac. Communications Co. v. American Telephone and Telegraph Co., 740 F.
2d 980, 1009 (D.C. Cir., 1984) 724

Spectrum Sports, Inc. v. McQuillan, 113 S.Ct. 884 (1993)..................................... 508

Standard Fashion v. Magrane-Houston Co., 258 U.S. 346 (1922) 82, 461–2

Standard Oil Co. v. United States, 337 U.S. 293 (1949) 459, 468

Staples, Inc. v. Federal Trade Commission, 970 F.S. 1066 (D.D.C., 1997)........... 163

State Oil v. Khan, 118 S.Ct. 275 (1997) 395

Tampa Electric Co. v. Nashville Coal Co. et al., 365 U.S. 320 (1960)................. 458–9

Tank Lining Corp. v. Dunlop Industrial Ltd. (1982), 140 D.L.R. (3d) 659 (Ont.
C.A.)... 588

Telecom Corporation of New Zealand Ltd. v. Clear Communications Ltd., [1995] 1
NZLR 385... 722, 728, 733

Telex Corp. v. IBM, 510 F. 2d 894 (10th Cir., 1975), cert. dismissed, 423 U.S.
802.. 655

Town of Concord v. Boston Edison Co., F. 2d 17, 25-9 (1st Cir., 1990) 728

Town of Massena v. Niagara Mohawk Power Corp., 1980-2 Trade Cas. (CCH) 63,
526 (N.D. N.Y., 1980) 725

Ulay (Canada) Ltd. v. Calstock Traders Ltd. et al. (1969), 59 C.P.R. 223 (Exch.
Ct.) 627

United Brands v. E.C. Commission, [1978] E.C.R. 207; 1 C.M.L.R. 429 (C.Ct. of
Justice)... 661

United Mine Workers of America v. Pennington, 381 U.S. 657 (1965) 556

United Shoe Machinery Company of Canada v. Brunet (1909), A.C. 330 (P.C.)
.... 593–4

United States v. Aluminum Company of America, 148 F.2d 416 (2d Cir., 1945)
.... 531, 581

United States v. American Telephone and Telegraph Company, 524 F. Supp. 1336
(1981) 724

United States v. Automobile Manufacturers Association, 307 F. Suppl, 617 (C.D.
Cal., 1969), modified sub nom. United States v. Motor Vehicle Manufacturers
Association, 1982–83 Trade Cases (CCH) 65,088 (C.D. Cal., 1982)............. 631

United States v. E.I. du Pont de Nemours & Co., 351 U.S. 377 (1956) 75, 517

United States v. Grinnell Corp., 384 U.S. 563 (2000) 507, 544

United States v. Microsoft Corp., 56 F. 3d 1448 (1995) 500

United States v. New York Great Atlantic & Pacific Tea Co. Inc. Et al., 67 F. Suppl.
626 (Ill. Dist. Ct., 1946), aff'd 173 F.2d 79 (7th Cir., 1949).......................... 348

United States v. Pilkington plc, and Pilkingtion Holdings Inc., IV No. 94-345 JVC
CD Ariz. 1994 677

United States v. Terminal Railroad Association of St. Louis, 224 U.S. 383 (1912)
.... 530, 544–5, 551, 724

United States v. United Shoe Machinery Corporation, 110 F. Supp. 295 (D.Mass.,
1953), off'd per curiam, 347 U.S. 521 (1954)...................................... 471, 593

*United States of America v. Microsoft Corporation; State of New York ex. rel. Eliot
Spitzer, et al. v. Microsoft United States of America v. Microsoft Corporation; State
of New York ex. rel. Eliot Spitzer, et al. v. Microsoft Corporation Corporation*, 65 F.
Supp. 2d 1 (D.D.C., 1999) (findings of fact) 611

*United States of America v. Microsoft Corporation; State of New York ex. rel. Eliot
Spitzer, et al. v. Microsoft United States of America v. Microsoft Corporation; State
of New York ex. rel. Eliot Spitzer, et al. v. Microsoft Corporation Corporation*, 87 F.
Supp. 2d 30 (D.D.C., 2000) (conclusions of law)............................. 611

U.S. v. Colgate, 250 U.S. 300 (1919).. 547

U.S. v. Microsoft, Memorandum and Order, 7 June 2000, Civil Action Nos.
98-1232 613

U.S. v. Microsoft, Memorandum and Order, No. 00-5212 (D.C. Cir., 28 June
2001) 613

U.S. v. United Shoe Machinery Co. of N.J., 223 U.S. Federal Antitrust Decisions
1917–1920 (U.S. Sup. Ct., 1918)... 593

Waldman v. British Columbia (Medical Services Commission) (1997), 150 D.L.R.
(4th) 405 (B.C.S.C.).. 703

Weidman v. Shargge (1912), 46 S.C.R. 1 114

Westfair Foods v. Lippens (1989), 64 D.L.R. (4th) 335 (Man. C.A.) 770

Wilkinson Sword (Canada) Ltd. v. Juda (1966), 51 C.P.R. 55 (Exch. Ct.).............. 627
Woolworths v. Campbells Cash and Carry Pty Ltd. (1993), 80 L.G.E.R.A.
.... 104, 563
Zenith Radio Corp. v. Hazeltine Research, Inc., 395 U.S. 29 (1964)...................... 597
Zenith Radio Corp. v. Hazeltine Research, Inc., 395 U.S. 100 (1969).................... 597